A HISTORICAL INTRODUCTION TO PHILOSOPHY

A HISTORICAL INTRODUCTION TO
PHILOSOPHY

Texts and Interactive Guides

James Fieser
*University of Tennessee
at Martin*

Norman Lillegard
*University of Tennessee
at Martin*

New York • Oxford
OXFORD UNIVERSITY PRESS
2002

Oxford University Press

Athens   Auckland   Bangkok   Bogotá   Buenos Aires   Cape Town
Chennai   Dar es Salaam   Delhi   Florence   Hong Kong   Istanbul   Karachi
Kolkala   Kuala Lumpur   Madrid   Melbourne   Mexico City   Mumbai   Nairobi
Paris   São Paulo   Singapore   Taipei   Tokyo   Toronto   Warsaw

and associated companies in
Berlin   Ibadan

Published by Oxford University Press, Inc.
198 Madison Avenue, New York, New York, 10016
http://www.oup-usa.org

Oxford is a registered trademark of Oxford University Press

Library of Congress Cataloging-in-Publication Data

A historical introduction to philosphy: texts and interactive guides/
[compiled by] James Fieser, Norman Lillegard.
    p. cm.
   ISBN 0-19-513984-4 (alk. paper)
    1. Philosophy—Introductions. I. Fieser, James. II. Lillegard, Norman, 1938-

BD21 .H57 2001
100-dc21
                                                                2001036226

Printing number: 9 8 7 6 5 4 3 2 1

Printed in the United States of America
on acid-free paper

CONTENTS

8   BRITISH EMPIRICISM   403

9   LATE MODERN AND 19TH-CENTURY PHILOSOPHY   509

PREFACE

This historical introduction is a flexible tool for introductory philosophy courses and for history of philosophy sequences. A wide selection of primary source materials allows a diversity of approaches to major figures and themes. The texts are selected from the most influential works in Western philosophy, including the major works from Plato to Kant usually covered by historical anthologies. Additionally, the Hellenistic and Renaissance periods, which are often barely mentioned in anthologies but which have considerable intrinsic interest, get fairly extensive treatment, as do nineteenth- and twentieth-century philosophy. But the major distinction of this text resides in its attention to pedagogical issues.

Most philosophy instructors find that introductory courses with primary texts as the main required reading pose multiple pedagogical problems. Many students will not read the material at all, and even students who do attempt to read the material typically do not understand it very well. Consequently, few students come to class with the kind of focused questions that can facilitate good discussions. This text attempts to address these problems by combining primary text, commentary, and study questions.

All the selections are presented in short and manageable sections set off with vertical lines; organizational headings and subheadings have been added. Some of the Greek texts are newly translated or have newly revised translations that appear here for the first time. Other translated material is corrected and adapted for clarity. The writings of Hobbes, Locke, Berkeley, Hume, Reid, and Mill present a special problem because of their dated English. In these texts, spelling and punctuation are modernized, parentheses are introduced when appropriate, longer sentences are divided when possible, and bracketed words are added for clarification. The commentaries provide a gloss on difficult passages, explain archaic or technical terminology, and expand upon allusions to unfamiliar literature and arguments.

The study questions vary with respect to format and level of difficulty. They variously require students to reconstruct arguments in their own words, summarize passages, fill in blanks in statements and arguments, evaluate the success or viability of an author's point, and draw contemporary parallels and applications. Questions are framed so as to avoid commitment to any particular side in interpretive controversies. To answer many of these questions, students must learn to identify arguments, determine what premises and conclusions, note missing elements, and reflect on logical relations. Students are sometimes required to relate parts of a given text to earlier discussions, so that a continuous review of material already covered is facilitated. This format for the presentation of classic texts has been found helpful by the majority of student users; in fact, a majority claim that the questions are indispensable for reading comprehension and good class preparation.

It is not intended that students write their answers in the book itself; rather, they can record their answers on a separate piece of paper or in an essay booklet that can then be evaluated by teachers or student assistants. This is of particular benefit for classes with large enrollments since it adds a systematic written component to a course's requirements. Answers to the questions could also be submitted electronically.

The study questions were designed with several possibilities in mind. (1) All questions in any assigned section can be assigned; or, alternatively, selected questions can be assigned. (2) The study guides can be used primarily to determine that the students have read the material. Some of the questions are designed to determine simply that the material has indeed been read, with at least minimal comprehension. (3) Some of the questions require more than minimal comprehension, and some are intended to provide an impetus to independent philosophical rumination. Some instructors will want to stress these questions and omit others. These questions can also help students to focus in a way that enlivens class discussion. (4) Questions can be assigned with the specific intention of provoking class discussion. Students can be advised ahead of time that they will be asked to comment on certain questions in class. (5) Instructors often have difficulty knowing which parts of a text are most challenging. Students can be encouraged to bring up difficulties they are having with any question. As a result, instructors will often find that further explanation is needed for topics they may have thought obvious or to have been sufficiently covered. Individual instructors will doubtless find other ways of using the guides that fit their particular pedagogical/philosophical aims.

Also included is a comprehensive time line, which relates the philosophers studied (and some only mentioned) to contemporary events and cultural movements. This feature facilitates a more fully historical approach. Finally, a list of further readings in both primary and secondary sources concludes each chapter. The secondary sources have been selected partly on the basis of accessibility, partly on the basis of dating (more recent scholarship is given some priority), and partly on the basis of pertinence to the selections in the text, although the recommendations also include some readings related to other parts or aspects of an author's work not included here.

This text can also be used for more topical approaches to works by major historical figures. The following is a sample course outline for a topically oriented course:

1. *Epistemology*. Readings might include those by Protagoras, Plato, Augustine, Descartes, Locke, Berkeley, Hume, Reid, Kant, Hegel, Nietzsche, Russell, Wittgenstein, and Quine. Central issues might include skepticism, Rationalism, Empiricism, perspectivalism, and twentieth-century critiques of epistemology.

2. *Metaphysics.* Readings might include those by various Presocratic philosophers, Plato, Aristotle, Leibniz, Kant, and Hegel. Central issues might include change and constancy, the one and the many, Atomism, the categories, and the nature of time and space.

3. *Philosophy of Mind.* Readings might include those by Plato, Aristotle, Epictetus, Descartes, Conway, Locke, Berkeley, Hume, Kant, Wittgenstein, and Sartre. Central issues might include dualistic, monistic, and idealistic solutions to the mind/body problem; free will and determinism; features of human mentality; and private languages.

4. *Philosophy of Religion.* Readings might include those by Xenophanes, Plato, Epicurus, Augustine, Anselm, Averroës, Maimonides, Aquinas, Calvin, Pascal, Galileo, Descartes, Spinoza, Hume, Kant, Hegel, Kierkegaard, Nietzsche, and Sartre. Central issues might include theistic proofs, the nature of religious language and interpretation, the relation of religion to civil society, the suspicion of religion, and current conflicts between religion and science.

5. *Ethics.* Readings might include those by the Presocratics, Plato, Aristotle, Epicurus, Augustine, Aquinas, Hume, Kant, Kierkegaard, Nietzsche, Wollstonecraft, Mill, Sartre, and Anscombe. Central issues might include moral relativism, virtue theory, natural law, the relation between religion and ethics, reason versus feeling, duty theory, utilitarianism, and emotivism.

An **Instructor's Manual** is available for this text, which provides test questions and other teaching aids. Instructors may contact the publisher to obtain the manual.

TIME LINE

THE ANCIENT PERIOD

Philosophers	Dates (Some Are Approximate)	Corresponding Political/ Cultural Events (Many Approximate Dates)
		Homer composes the *Iliad* and *Odysey*, 750 BCE
		Hesiod composes Birth of the Gods and Works and Days, 700 BCE
Thales	623–545 BCE	Thales predicts solar eclipse, 585 BCE
Anaximander	610–545 BCE	Lao-tzu, 575 BCE (China) Exile of Israelites to Babylon (587) Works of Isaiah II, Ezekiel, and so forth
Anaximenes	580–500 BCE	Buddha (India), 563–483 BCE
Pythagoras	570–495 BCE	Confucius (China), 551–479 BCE
Xenophanes	570–478 BCE	
Heraclitus	540–480 BCE	Republic of Rome established, 508 BCE
Parmenides	515–450 BCE	Sophocles, 495–406 BCE

THE ANCIENT PERIOD *Continued*

Philosophers	Dates (Some Are Approximate)	Corresponding Political/ Cultural Events (Many Approximate Dates)
Anaxagoras	500–428 BCE	Battle of Marathon, 490 BCE Greek civilization preserved from Persian invasions
Empedocles	495–435 BCE	
Zeno the Eleatic	490–430 BCE	Parthenon built in Athens, 438 BCE
Protagoras	490–420 BCE	
Gorgias	483–375 BCE	Peloponnesian War between Athens and Sparta, 431–404 BCE
Socrates	470–399 BCE	Trial and death of Socrates, 399 BCE
Democritus	460–360 BCE	
Plato	428–348 BCE	Plato founds the Academy, 388 BCE
Aristotle	384–322 BCE	Aristotle founds the Lyceum, 334 BCE
Pyrrho the Skeptic	360–270 BCE	Death of Alexander the Great, 323 BCE
Epicurus	341–270 BCE	Epicurus opens school in Athens, 306 BCE
Zeno the Stoic	336–264 BCE	Zeno opens his school at the Stoa, 301 BCE
		Rome conquers the Greek world, 200–128 BCE
		Caesar is dictator of Rome, 49–44 BCE
		Battle of Actium, 31 BCE
		Octavius (Augustus) extends Roman power over entire Mediterranean area

		Life of Jesus Christ, 4 CE–30 CE
Epictetus	50–138 CE	Later Stoicism
Marcus Aurelius	121–180 CE	Emperor Aurelius governs an empire beset by invasions of barbarian tribes and composes one of the classics of Stoicism (the *Meditations*)
Plotinus	205–270 CE	
Sextus Empiricus	250 CE	Skepticism of Pyrrho further developed

THE MEDIEVAL PERIOD

Philosophers	Dates (Some Are Approximate)	Corresponding Political/ Cultural Events (Many Approximate Dates)
		Constantine grants tolerance to Christianity (the "Edict of Milan"), 313 CE
Saint Augustine	354–430 CE	Theodosius I makes Christianity the state religion of Rome, 392 CE
Boethius	480–524 CE	Fall of the Roman Empire in the West, 476 CE Muhammad, ca. 570–632 CE
John Scotus Erigena	810–877 CE	Charlemagne crowned emperor of "Holy Roman Empire" by the Pope, Christmas day, 800 CE
		Carolingian Renaissance
		Spread of Islam throughout the Mediterranean area, as far west as Spain
		Arab scholars translate and comment on Aristotle

THE MEDIEVAL PERIOD *Continued*

Philosophers	Dates (Some Are Approximate)	Corresponding Political/ Cultural Events (Many Approximate Dates)
Anselm	1033–1109	William the Conqueror invades England, 1066
		Start of the Crusades, 1096
Al-Ghazali	1058–1111	
Peter Abelard	1079–1142	
Averroës	1126–1198	University of Paris founded, 1160
Moses Maimonides	1135–1204	Oxford University founded, 1167
		Cambridge University founded, 1209
Saint Thomas Aquinas	1225–1274	Aristotelianism in philosophy, theology, science, literature
		Dante Alighieri, 1265–1321
John Duns Scotus	1266–1308	
William of Ockham	1280–1349	The Black Death ravages Europe, 1347–1351

THE RENAISSANCE AND THE MODERN PERIOD

Philosophers	Dates (Some Are Approximate)	Corresponding Political/ Cultural Events (Many Approximate Dates)
		Johannes Gutenberg invents the printing press, 1445
		Leonardo Da Vinci, 1452–1517
Pico della Mirandola	1463–1494	Rise of Renaissance Humanism

Nicholas Copernicus	1473–1543	Rise of a new astronomy
Thomas More	1478–1535	
Martin Luther	1483–1543	Protestant Reformation
		Luther protests certain Church practices, 1517
		Anti-Aristotelianism in theology
John Calvin	1509–1564	
Michel de Montaigne	1533–1592	
Francis Bacon	1561–1626	Empiricism, aspects of scientific method developed
Galileo Galilei	1564–1642	Mechanistic science, rejection of Aristotelianism in science
		Science and religion in conflict
René Descartes	1596–1650	Reign of Louis XIV in France, 1643–1715
		Pilgrims land at Plymouth Rock, 1620
Blaise Pascal	1623–1662	Fideism, Skepticism become widespread
Benedict (Baruch) Spinoza	1632–1677	
Anne Conway	1631–1678	
John Locke	1632–1704	Two Treatises on Government, 1689
Nicholas de Malebranche	1638–1715	
Pierre Bayle	1647–1706	
Sir Issaac Newton	1642–1727	Publication of the *Principia*, 1687, stating the principle of gravitation
		Mechanistic science triumphant
Gottfried Leibniz	1646–1716	

THE RENAISSANCE AND THE MODERN PERIOD *Continued*

Philosophers	Dates (Some Are Approximate)	Corresponding Political/ Cultural Events (Many Approximate Dates)
George Berkeley	1685–1753	
Thomas Reid	1710–1796	
David Hume	1711–1776	Wolfgang Amadeus Mozart, 1756–1791
		Enlightenment era (1700–1800)—reaction against religion, monarchy; radical versions particularly in France
		Voltaire writes *Candide*, 1759
Jean Jacques Rousseau	1712–1778	American Revolution, 1775–1783
Immanuel Kant	1724–1804	Critique of Pure Reason, 1781
		French Revolution, 1789–1792, incited partly by Enlightenment ideals
		Ludwig von Beethoven, 1770–1827
Jeremy Bentham	1748–1832	Industrial revolution in England, ca. 1790
		Napoleon crowns himself Emperor of France, 1804
		Development of Romanticism: Wordsworth 1770–1850; Goethe, 1749–1832; Schubert, 1797–1828
Mary Wollstonecraft	1759–1797	
George W. F. Hegel	1770–1831	Leo Tolstoy, 1828–1910
		Fyodor Dostoyevsky, 1821–1881

John Stuart Mill	1806–1873	*On Liberty*, 1859
		Darwin's *Origin of the Species*, 1859
Søren Kierkegaard	1813–1855	
Karl Marx	1818–1883	*The Communist Manifesto*, 1848
		American Civil War, 1861–1865
Friedrich Nietzsche	1844–1900	Rise of modernism in the arts and culture: Stravinsky, 1882–1971; Pablo Picasso, 1881–1973; James Joyce, 1882–1941

THE CONTEMPORARY PERIOD

Philosophers	Dates (Some Are Approximate)	Corresponding Political/ Cultural Events (Many Approximate Dates)
Gottlob Frege	1848–1925	Albert Einstein presents theory of relativity, 1905
		Sigmund Freud, 1856–1939
		World War I, 1914–1918
		Russian Communist Revolution, 1917
		Gandhi begins his crusade for Indian independence, 1919
Alfred North Whitehead	1861–1947	Joseph Stalin becomes General Secretary of the Communist Party, 1922
Bertrand Russell	1872–1970	The Great Depression, 1929
Ludwig Wittgenstein	1889–1951	World War II, 1939–1945

THE CONTEMPORARY PERIOD *Continued*

Philosophers	Dates (Some Are Approximate)	Corresponding Political/ Cultural Events (Many Approximate Dates)
Martin Heidegger	1889–1976	Dropping of the Atomic Bomb on Hiroshima, August 6, 1945
		India gains independence, 1949
		Israel becomes a nation, 1949
		The People's Republic of China under Mao Tse-tung established, 1949
		Korean War, 1950–1952
		Crick and Watson identify the structure of DNA, 1953
Jean-Paul Sartre	1905–1980	Cuban Missile Crisis, 1962
		Assassination of John F. Kennedy, 1963
Willard V. O. Quine	1908–2000	War in Vietnam, 1963–1972
		Assassination of Martin Luther King, 1968
G. E. M. Anscombe	1919–2001	
John Rawls	1921–	*A Theory of Justice*, 1971
Thomas Kuhn	1922–1996	The fall of the Soviet Union, 1991
		Apartheid ends in South Africa, 1994

A HISTORICAL INTRODUCTION TO

PHILOSOPHY

CHAPTER 1

EARLY GREEK PHILOSOPHY

here did the world come from? What explains the constant changes taking place in it? If there are Gods or a God, what are they, or he or she, like? Philosophy in Western civilization began when philosophers attempted to answer these probing questions in a systematic fashion. The place was Greece and the time was about 600 BCE (that is, Before the Common Era, or "BC"). These early Greek philosophers set an agenda that inspired later Greek figures—particularly Socrates, Plato, and Aristotle—who in turn defined a conception of philosophy that is prevalent still today.

INTRODUCTION

Homer and Hesiod

Greek civilization was deeply influenced by the great poetic epics of Homer, who probably lived about 750 BCE. It is possible that Homer could neither read nor write. His works constituted an oral tradition carried on for centuries by *rhapsodes*, people skilled in remembering long poems by heart. The poems were recited in public gatherings, so many people were familiar with them. These long poems contain information on sailing, farming, warfare, the workings of nature, what constitutes courage and justice, the nature of the Gods, and much else. The Greeks considered Homer to be their teacher in all of these topics, so before launching into a study of ancient Greek philosophy, it is worth considering a few features of Homer's picture of the world.

Homer supposes that there are many Gods and that those Gods participate in human affairs. He portrays the Gods as arguing among themselves, lying to each other, and as subject to fits of jealousy and anger. Natural events were often the result of the Gods' actions. For instance, a bolt of lightning may indicate that Zeus is angry, or a disease may be a divine punishment. Thus what goes on in nature is unpredictable, since so much of it depends upon the capricious moods and constant squabbling of the Gods.

Both Gods and humans are concerned with the dangers of excess of any kind. The anger of Achilles, the main hero of Homer's *Iliad*, is excessive, and the Gods punish Achilles for this excess. Moderation or temperance, the opposite of excess, is central to a good life. Homer sees justice as giving each his or her due, whether God or human. Conventional conceptions of honor determine what is due each being. Injustice is often punished by the Gods. For example, the God Apollo infests the Greek forces with a disease when he is offended by the Greek leader Agammemnon, who failed to honor him properly.

Another poet who deeply influenced Greek culture was Hesiod (ca. 700 BCE). His account of the origins of the Gods and the cosmos contains elements from ancient Near Eastern mythologies. Hesiod writes that in the beginning there was just chaos, out of which emerged heaven, earth, and the underworld. He does not suppose that any God created the chaos. Rather, the Gods are themselves products of, or identical with, parts of nature or natural forces. Thus the earth is itself a deity, called Gaia. An important feature of Hesiod's poems is the idea that there are principles of order that explain the emergence of an orderly cosmos from chaos. For example, opposites produce opposites. Darkness produces light, and the earth brought forth the starry heavens. Although he often pictures the Gods as capricious and unpredictable, just as Homer did, Hesiod also proposes a universe with built-in ordering principles.

It is important to note that both Hesiod and Homer base many of their claims about the world and the Gods on the testimony of the Muses, who were themselves divine beings. Thus only someone who believes that there are Muses, and that they communicate truthfully with humans, would be able to regard Homer and Hesiod as completely reliable authorities on the many subjects treated in their works.

 ASK YOURSELF

1.1. Briefly state the main characteristics of the Homeric view of the world. Include definitions of temperance and justice; then mention one idea found in Hesiod that is not prominent in Homer.

Principals Concerns of the Presocratics

The early Greek philosophers are often called *Presocratics* because they lived before or during the life of the great philosopher Socrates (470–399 BCE), who stands apart from them in various ways (how much, and in what ways, is controversial). The Presocratics challenged the Homeric worldview in significant ways. For example, instead of trying to explain nature in terms of arbitrary divine interventions from the outside, many early philosophers looked for principles that could be discovered in nature itself. As the brief discussion of Hesiod indicates, these ideas were not entirely new. However, the Presocratics tried to discover those principles primarily through observation and reasoning, rather than by consulting popular myths or relying on the Gods or the testimony of the Muses (see, however, the discussions of Parmenides and Heraclitus later in this chapter). This tendency to rely on reason and observation in attempting to understand very general features of the world marks the beginning of something new, something that can be called *science*. These thinkers were in fact interested in biology, mathematics, and studies of nature and the heavens that were in some respects like contemporary physics and astronomy. Scholars believe that many Presocratic scientific notions were inspired by Babylonian and Egyptian ideas that circulated at the time.

From the beginning science and reasoned views of the world generally tended to conflict with popular religious beliefs, and that conflict between reason and religion has continued in one form or another throughout history to the present day. Presocratic thinkers are also rightly considered philosophers, for the emphasis on reason and experience as the main source of knowledge is typically philosophical. They were also often reflective about their own methods and the status of their own theories, and some of their discussions show a regard for logical and semantic issues, which is typical of philosophy. The Presocratics wrestled with several issues that still play a central role in philosophy, science, literature, and the arts.

One of these was a puzzle about "the one and the many," which is as follows: without some kind of unity within diversity, we could have no thought or language, and thus nothing would be intelligible. Even the simplest concept—for example, the concept of "dog"—brings many individual things, such as my dog Fido and your dog Rover, under a single concept. It thereby brings order into the bewildering variety of the world. But how, or in what sense, can all these many things be one? The nature philosophers among the Presocratics, the Milesians (discussed in the next section) in particular, were seeking some unifying principle in nature, such as an underlying substance, which would be the "one" that would explain the "many" different kinds of things and events. Their way of trying to make sense of the physical world, make it intelligible, was in some ways like modern chemical and physical theories about the fundamental constituents of matter.

A second related puzzle involved the relations between what is unchanging, stable, and eternal, on the one hand, and what changes or is in flux, on the other. Continual and unpredictable change would also make our world unintelligible. It seems that there must be something permanent that underlies change and explains it; there must be some source of unity and coherence. It is easy to see how this concern might dovetail or overlap with religious concerns. The emotional and spiritual need for permanence, for an eternal home, is a prominent source of much religious imagery and devotion.

A third puzzle becomes the focus of attention late in this period and in the time of Socrates himself. The Greeks became familiar with various cultures and learned that beliefs about important matters vary from culture to culture. Thus they discovered that the Ethiopians viewed God in a very different way than did the Persians. There were also differences in how oligarchs or dictators of various sorts, and believers in democracy, viewed justice. Do such differences show that there are no right answers to questions about the nature of the Gods or of justice? Are beliefs about such matters merely "relative to" particular ways of life? Or is there in fact an absolute truth about these matters, the knowledge of which would show that some people are right about them, while others are simply wrong? This puzzle, known as the *problem of relativism*, provoked continued discussion throughout this period and has been a centerpiece of discussion throughout the history of philosophy.

 ASK YOURSELF

1.2. Name one outstanding trait of philosophy mentioned in the preceding discussion.

1.3. Sum up the three principal concerns of the Presocratics.

Only fragments of the original writings of the Presocratics survive, in some cases merely a single sentence. The knowledge we have of them derives from accounts of early philosophers, such as Plato, Aristotle, Aristotle's pupil Theophrastus—particularly his book *The Opinions of the Physicists*—and from early writers during the Hellenistic period that followed Aristotle. The fragments and testimonials quoted in the following sections vary with respect to accuracy. Some, particularly those taken from Aristotle, are largely summaries of the views of the philosopher in question rather than quotations from his works. Others may be close to being, or may actually be, verbatim quotes. In this text each fragment or testimonial is set apart from the regular text as an extract.

All of the selections from the Presocratics that are included in this chapter are from Diels and Kranz, *Die Fragmente der Vorsokratiker*, translated by N. Lillegard. The collection by Diels and Kranz is considered the standard source for these works. It includes passages from writers such as Aristotle who discuss PreSocratic views in the course of presenting their own views. The numbers assigned to the fragments and testimonies by Diels and Krantz have been omitted. The early Greek philosophers treated here are the Milesians, other Ionians, the Eleatics, pluralist alternatives to Parmenides, and the Sophists.

THE MILESIANS

Three of the earliest philosophers were from Miletus, a Greek city-state on the coast of Asia Minor, across the Aegean Sea from Greece itself. At this period there was no nation called Greece, but simply a number of city-states scattered about the Mediterranean Sea. They were united only by a more or less common language and by Homeric culture.

Thales

Thales (fl. ca. 585 BCE) was the first of the Milesians. Aristotle refers to him as the founder of philosophy. He was alive and already famous about the year 600 BCE. One of the better-attested reports about Thales is that he successfully predicted an eclipse of the Sun, perhaps by using Babylonian data. According to modern calculations an eclipse that would have been visible in Asia Minor occurred in 586 or 585 BCE, which gives us further evidence for the dates of Thales's career. He may have used geometrical knowledge to determine the distance of ships at sea and to perform other scientific feats. But it remains unclear how much Thales relied on external sources rather than on original thinking and experimenting.

Water Is the Basic Stuff. Aristotle attributes to Thales and to some other nature philosophers the following view:

> It is necessary that there be a certain nature (substance), either one or more than one, from which other things originate while it is preserved. . . . Thales, the originator of this sort of philosophy, says that the nature in question is water.

According to Aristotle, Thales held that water is the source or fundamental nature of everything else (dirt, rocks, air, and so forth). It is as though Thales has a chemical table of elements with only one item on it (although he thinks of water simply as "the moist"). Perhaps one reason for thinking water to be so fundamental is that it takes many observable forms (e.g., ice, mist, clouds), so it is not implausible to think that other things (e.g., kittens, rocks) might be still further transformations of this one stuff.

Another reason mentioned by Aristotle is that many things come into being only where there is moisture (think up your own examples). But it is not certain what reasons Thales had for this view.

 ASK YOURSELF

1.4. Can you think of another reason why water might be a good candidate for the fundamental "stuff" of the world?

1.5. In Thales's view, what is the "one" and what is the "many"?

1.6. Thales is also credited by Aristotle with this saying: "All things are full of Gods." Does this contradict the claim made in the Introduction that the early philosophers challenged popular religious conceptions? Explain your answer.

Anaximander

Anaximander (ca. 610–546 BCE) was a younger contemporary and perhaps pupil of Thales. Although we have little accurate information about his life, he is credited with predicting an earthquake in Sparta and with making the first map of the celestial globe.

The Boundless. If everything comes from or is based in water, where does water come from? It is just one more thing in the universe, needing as much explanation as the other things. Some such thought may have occurred to Anaximander.

> Anaximander of Miletus, son of Praxiades, a successor and pupil of Thales, said that the first principle and element of things was the "boundless" (infinite), he being the first to introduce this name of the first principle. He says it is neither water nor any of the other so-called elements, but a nature different from them which is boundless, from which are generated all the heavens and the worlds within them.
>
> He says that this is " everlasting and undying," and that it "encompasses all the worlds."

Here we see a conception of the source of everything that sounds quite theological, for "everlasting" and "encompasses all the world" are terms that might be used of God in theistic religions. But the "boundless" appears to be a physical substance, not a spiritual being.

 ASK YOURSELF

1.7. Explain why someone might think it does not make sense to wonder where the "boundless" comes from, whereas it does makes sense to wonder where water comes from. (Hint: If something, x, comes from something else, y, then x must be distinct from y in some respect, and thus must be "bounded" by y. What about the "boundless" itself, then?)

> And into that from which things rise they decay once more, as is needful; for they make reparation to one another for their injustice according to the ordering of time, as [Anaximander] says in such poetical terms.

Perhaps what Anaximander had in mind was something like this: There must be a kind of balance in the world, something like the balance noted by biologists in ecosystems, in which the various elements keep each other in check. For example, insect populations are kept in check by birds, whose population is in turn kept in check by various predators. Balance among such opposites as hot and cold or wet and dry amounts to a kind of "temperance" in nature. Any violation of that balance such as a too hot summer, or for that matter a normally hot summer, will have to be compensated for elsewhere, perhaps by a very cold winter, or a normally cold one. The result is a kind of justice, where each element, hot and cold, "gets its due." If you remember what Homer said about rendering each their due, you can see that Anaximander is not entirely free of the Homeric way of thinking. That is, he does not distinguish between justice as a human institution and the natural balances exhibited in nature. But he clearly supposes that the principles that determine the course of natural events are built into nature itself, rather than coming from the outside as the result of decisions made by gods.

 From ARISTOTLE: *Physics*

Further, there cannot be a single, simple body which is boundless, either, as some say, one distinct from the elements, which they then derive from it, or not distinct. For there are some who make this [something distinct from the elements] the boundless, and not air or water,—in order that the other things may not be destroyed by their infinity. For they are in opposition to one another—air is cold, water moist, and fire hot. So if one of them were unbounded, it would have destroyed the rest by this time. Accordingly they say that it is other than the elements, and from it the elements arise.

 ASK YOURSELF

1.8. Anaximander opposes the view of Thales, for example, who in effect makes one of the elements, water, the infinite. Why, according to Aristotle in the previous quote, does Anaximander do this? (Ask yourself: What would the universe be like if water were boundless?)

Anaximenes

Anaximines (fl. sixth century BCE), an associate and pupil of Anaximander, wrestled with the same problems that Anaximander and Thales did.

Condensed and Rarefied Air. Anaximenes seems to hold a view that to some extent synthesizes the ideas of Thales and Anaximander. He makes the basic stuff definite or particular (determinate) as Thales did, but since it is "air" it also seems to have some of the features of the infinite or boundless (he in fact refers to it as "boundless" or infinite).

Anaximenes of Miletus, son of Eurystratos, who had been a companion of Anaximander, said, like him, that the underlying substance was one and boundless. He did not, however, say it was indeterminate, like Anaximander, but determinate; for he said it was Air.

From it, he said, originated the things that are, and have been, and will be, the Gods and things divine, while other things come from its descendants.

 ASK YOURSELF

1.9. Compare what Anaximines has just stated about the Gods to Hesiod's view.

"Just as," he said, "our soul, being air, holds us together, so do breath and air embrace the whole world."

And the form of air is as follows. Where it is most even, it is unknown to sight; but cold and heat, moisture and motion, make it evident. It is always in motion. If it did not move . . . it would not change as it does.

It differs in different substances in virtue of its thinning out [rarefaction] and condensation.

When it is thinned out so as to be more expanded, it becomes fire; while winds, on the other hand, are condensed Air. Cloud is formed from Air by compression; and this, still further condensed, becomes water. Water, condensed still more, turns to earth; and when condensed as much as it can be, to stones.

 ASK YOURSELF

1.10. When you burn a piece of paper some of the paper turns into smoke. When cold air hits a warm cloud you get water drops. In Anaximenes' terminology, these would be examples of _____ and _____, respectively.

1.11. A fundamental idea in the science of our own era is the idea that qualitative variety can be understood in terms of quantitative changes. Using the examples from the last extract, show how Anaximenes is accounting for qualitative diversity in terms of quantitative change.

OTHER IONIANS

Miletus, the home of the Milesians, was a principal city in an area of the coast of Asia Minor known as Ionia. The entire area produced a rich crop of philosophers, including Xenophanes, Pythagoras, and Heraclitus.

Xenophanes

Xenophanes was originally from Colophon, about forty miles north of Miletus. He reportedly fled from Colophon at the time of the Persian invasion in 546 BCE and went to live in Sicily. At that time Greek civilization extended both to the coast of Asia Minor and westward to Italy and to various islands.

Satires on Anthropomorphic Theology. In the following remarks we see that Xenophanes attacks the Homeric view of the Gods and the account of nature that goes with Homer's view.

> For from the beginning all have learnt according to Homer. . . .
>
> Homer and Hesiod have ascribed to the gods all sorts of things that are a shame and a disgrace among men, such as stealing and adultery and deception.
>
> But mortals think the gods are begotten as they are, and have clothes and voice and form like theirs.

The unjustified attribution of human traits to something that is not human is called *anthropomorphism*. Anthropomorphism is common in children's books. For example, in the story of Goldilocks bears live in houses and eat soup from bowls with spoons. Children may sometimes believe that such things really happen. When adults try to understand the world around them, or the Gods, they should presumably avoid such childish anthropomorphisms. Xenophanes thinks it ridiculous that the kinds of human traits mentioned in the second and third fragments should be attributed to the Gods. We will run into a very similar criticism of popular ways of conceiving the Gods in a later writer. (Be on the lookout.)

> But if oxen and horses or lions had hands, and could draw with their hands, and execute works of art as people do, horses would draw the forms of the gods like horses, and oxen like oxen, and make the gods' bodies in the image of their various kinds.
>
> The Ethiopians make their gods black and snub-nosed; the Thracians say theirs have blue eyes and red hair.

Here we have a further claim, namely, that the Gods will be conceived differently within different cultures. That in turn suggests (although it does not prove) that there may be *no correct* conception of the Gods. Here we run into one of the "principal concerns" mentioned earlier, the problem of relativism. Suppose we manage to avoid anthropomorphism and relativism. What conception of God will we have? Or can we never be sure about the Gods?

> The gods have not revealed all things to people from the beginning, but by seeking they eventually find what is better.
>
> One god, the greatest among gods and humans, neither in form nor in thought like mortals . . .
>
> He sees all over, thinks all over, and hears all over.
>
> But without toil he sways all things by the thought of his mind.

And he abides always in the same place, entirely motionless; nor does it seem appropriate for him to go about now here, now there.

Here we see Xenophanes' positive conception of God. He supposes that there is *one* God over all the others.

 ASK YOURSELF

1.12. Does Xenophanes succeed in conceiving of God in a way that is entirely nonanthropomorphic? Justify your answer.

Xenophanes' physics is typical of Ionian nature philosophy. He looks for certain primary elements and concludes that earth and water are primary.

... all things come from the earth, and all things end in earth.

All things are earth and water that come into being and grow.

The sea is the source of water and of wind. . . . The mighty sea is father of clouds and of winds and of rivers.

She they call "Iris" is a cloud, observed as purple, scarlet and green.

A popular Greek belief was that the rainbow was a minor Goddess, a kind of messenger for other Gods. Iris is mentioned fulfilling this role in Homer. Xenophanes is claiming that this Goddess is really just a natural phenomenon, a particular kind of cloud. Here we see how nature philosophy joins up with a critique of Homeric religion. Even today naturalistic explanations of phenomena are sometimes combined with attacks on traditional religion.

 ASK YOURSELF

1.13. Today some people think that some nontheistic explanations of certain theories about nature are in conflict with religious belief. Mention one example.

Xenophanes shows an unusual interest in the status of knowledge claims. What can we really know for certain? The following fragments, quite possibly the conclusion of his book, show unusual caution for thinkers of this period. He is not prepared to claim that his views can be known with certainty. Some scholars call Xenophanes the "father of epistemology" on the basis of these fragments.

There never was nor will be a person who has certain knowledge about the gods and about all the things of which I speak. Even if he should by chance say the complete truth, yet he does not himself know that it is true. But each person fashions his own belief.

Let these things be regarded as resemblances of the truth.

ASK YOURSELF

1.14. Xenophanes' opinion is somewhat agnostic and skeptical. Given the difficulty of knowing anything about God, doesn't his position seem to be the most sensible one? Explain your answer.

Pythagoras and the Pythagoreans

We know few details about Pythagoras's life. It is widely accepted that he was born about 570 BCE on Samos, an island off the coast of Ionia, not far from Melitus, and that he left Samos about the age of forty and eventually settled in Croton, a city in southern Italy. He and his followers formed an association that became politically powerful. The Pythagorean brotherhood was religious in character and imposed dietary restrictions on its members as a result of the belief that the souls of people "transmigrate" to other animals after their deaths. What if the hamburger you had for lunch was made from a cow containing the soul of good old uncle Charley? Therefore, one should not eat meat. Beans were also prohibited, although the reason is a matter of speculation.

Pythagoras did not write any books. The views of his followers may have been sometimes treated as though they were his, so when we refer to Pythagorean ideas or ascribe a view to Pythagoras we do not imply that we know for certain that Pythagoras himself held that view. Pythagoreanism as a religious and political movement died out by the end of the fourth century BCE, but the influence of Pythagorean ideas is very evident in Plato. Since Plato himself influenced so much of the history of philosophy, Pythagoras's direct and indirect influence has also been great.

The Immortality of the Soul. Pythagoras taught that the soul is immortal. This idea became quite crucial later on in Plato's thought.

> First he declares that the soul is immortal, then that it changes into other kinds of animals. He also claims that events recur at certain intervals, and nothing is absolutely new, and that all things that come to life must be thought to be related.
>
> Pythagoras seems to have been the first to introduce these opinions into Greece.

Mathematics and Reality. Pythagorean speculation about the world centers around mathematical notions, yet music appears to have been the starting point. The ancient Greek lyre had seven strings, four of which were tuned to the intervals of the octave, the fourth and the fifth. You will get these intervals on a piano if you play middle C, the F above it (the fourth), the G above it (the fifth), and the C above it (the octave). The Pythagoreans discovered that these intervals could be expressed numerically. If you pluck a taut string it will emit a tone. If you shorten the string by one half you will get a tone exactly one octave higher. Thus the musical interval of the octave can be expressed as the numerical ratio 1:2. Similar considerations apply for the other intervals, which can be expressed as 2:3 and 3:4. It does not matter what the string is made of or how tightly it is stretched, these relations will always apply. This is worth emphasizing. It is not the *material* that matters but the mathematical ratio. This idea represents a clear departure from the thinking of such cosmologists as Thales, who looked for the source of order in the world in some sort of material or "stuff."

 ASK YOURSELF

1.15. When a violinist or guitarist plays, he or she presses on the strings to vary their lengths. If you were to press on the D string of a violin halfway up, thus making it half as long, and then pluck it, what note would you hear?

These sorts of facts suggested to the Pythagoreans that something numerical might be at the root of all that is. The following statement from Sextus Empiricus, *Against the Mathematicians* 7.94–95 summarizes their view and mentions some crucial concepts:

> The tetractys, a certain number composed of the four first numbers produces the most perfect number, ten. For one and two and three and four come to ten. This number is the first tetractys, and is called the source of ever flowing nature since according to them [the Pythagoreans] the entire *kosmos* is organized according to *harmonia*, and *harmonia* is a system of three concords— the fourth, the fifth, and the octave—and the proportions of these three are found in the four numbers just mentioned.

This is the tetractys:

.

. .

. . .

. . . .

Scan this figure from top to bottom, and think to yourself, "the ratio of 1 (the top dot) to 2 (the next row) is the octave, 2 to 3 the fifth, and 3 to 4 is the fourth." Then add up the dots. The intervals of the octave, fourth, and fifth seem particularly consonant or harmonious to many people, and in fact have been basic in thinking about what harmony is for a very long time. Even the twelve-bar blues, which is the basis for much jazz and popular music, is structured around chords built on a "tonic" root (for example, C) and on the fourth and fifth above the tonic (F and G).

This tetractys had mystical significance for the Pythagoreans; they swore oaths by it and associated it with the oracle at Delphi. According to the account given here, it is the source of the natural world, which is considered a "kosmos" (or "cosmos"). This Greek word suggests beauty and order (it is present in the English word "cosmetic"). "Harmony" also suggests beauty and order. When music is harmonious, as it is when it contains such intervals as the octave—as opposed to such intervals as a minor second (play C and C sharp to get a minor second)—it also seems orderly. Dissonant music, containing minor seconds, augmented fourths (play C and F sharp to get an augmented fourth), and other dissonant intervals, can seem chaotic. So there is an association between numbers, harmony, order, and beauty. The tetractys itself has a systematic and orderly appearance.

These ancient ideas continue to affect us today. Someone who studies *cosmology* is trying to discover what the ordering principles are behind the universe or cosmos. And modern cosmologists are likely to use a lot of math in trying to figure that out! The laws of nature, as in Newtonian mechanics, are expressed in mathematical formulae. And those formulae enable us to understand how many different things go together in a harmonious way. For example, the motion of a bullet and the orbits of the planets fall under the same formula. Moreover, it is not unusual to hear scientists and mathematicians speak of the "beauty" of various mathematically elegant theories and formulas. But of course the way in which the Pythagoreans associated numbers with physical reality is quite obscure, as the following passage no doubt suggests. (We might well wonder how opportunity, for instance, is expressible in numbers.)

> . . . the so-called Pythagoreans, who were the first to take up mathematics, not only advanced this study, but, having been brought up in it, they thought its principles were the basis of all things. Since numbers are by nature the first of these principles, and in numbers they seemed to see many similarities to the things that exist and come into being—more so than in fire and earth—a certain modification of numbers being justice, another being soul and reason, another being opportunity—and similarly almost all other things being numerically expressible, and since they saw that the modifications and ratios of the musical scales were expressible in numbers and since, then, all other things seemed in their entire nature to be modelled on numbers, and numbers seemed to be the first things in the whole of nature, they supposed the elements of numbers to be the elements of all things, and the whole heaven to be a musical scale and a number.

The idea that "the whole heaven" is a musical scale hung on for a long time, as we shall see in subsequent study. In the passage just cited we see that the Pythagoreans were trying to do what the Ionian nature philosophers did when they explained everything in terms of water or air, but they thought numbers would do the job better. Yet it is unclear how numbers could be the elements of anything. As we shall see, Aristotle thinks the Pythagorean position is full of inconsistencies.

There is one problem, however, that the Pythagoreans attempt to deal with that should be mentioned. The Ionians, as we have seen, were looking for one or a few basic principles or underlying stuffs to explain everything. They were seeking to reduce the many to the one. But there are infinitely many numbers, so what happens to the "one" or unity when reality is reduced to numbers, as it is in the Pythagorean view? The Pythagoreans had to find some basic principles governing all numbers in order to preserve the idea of seeking some kind of unity in the world.

> Evidently, then, they also consider that number is the principle both as matter for things and as forming both their modifications and their permanent states, and maintain that the elements of number are the even and the odd, and of

these the latter is bounded (limited), and the former unbounded. The One proceeds from both of these (for it is both even and odd), and number from the One . . .

 ASK YOURSELF

1.16. What are the elements of numbers?

1.17. Which of the elements is associated with the "limited" or "bounded"?

The Pythagoreans may have had something like the following in mind: Individual things require limitation in order to be individual. We can think of things being differentiated by their limits. For example, one thing that differentiates me from my oldest brother is height. There is a different limit on my height than on his. So if we can find a principle of limitation in numbers, we will have a clue to the varieties of things in the world. The association of the odd with the limited is based in a certain theory about numbers, which will not be discussed here.

Whatever its shortcomings, Pythagoreanism is a very suggestive set of teachings, as our discussion here hopefully indicates. The notion that nature is expressible in numbers, if not actually composed of or identical with them, is certainly an idea that most modern physicists would find at all bizarre.

 ASK YOURSELF

1.18. Define: cosmos; harmony expressed by numbers; tetractys.

1.19. In what way does Pythagorean theory resemble modern scientific theory, and in what way does it differ?

Heraclitus

Heraclitus, who was active about the year 500 BCE, was a native of Ephesus, which is also an Ionian city. He wrote a book of which about 130 fragments have survived.

Change and the Logos. Some of Heraclitus's ancient readers found his sayings so difficult to understand that he became known as Heraclitus the obscure, or "the dark." It is not difficult, however, to see in the following remarks how he is struggling with the problem of the one and the many and the problem of the changing versus the eternal or unchanging. His solution to these problems depends primarily upon his use of the concept of the *logos*. This Greek term can be translated in various contexts as "word," "account," "order," "reason," "structure," "pattern," and related terms. The term is rich with connotations; much of the subsequent history of philosophy, and religion too, can be seen as a series of reflections on this concept. For example, in the Gospel of John in the Christian New Testament Jesus is identified with the *logos*.

Although the *logos* is a principle of order, Heraclitus stresses the notion that what is ordered is a process of constant change. Moreover, that process is eternal. It has no beginning, and no origin in a God. The following fragments express these ideas through various images.

> It is not possible to step into the same river twice. . . .
>
> We step and do not step into the same rivers; we are and are not.
>
> This *cosmos*, which is the same for all, was made neither by any of the gods or by humans, but it always was, and is, and will be an ever-living Fire, kindling by measure and quenched by measure.

At first glance it may seem that Heraclitus has given up the hope of finding something permanent amid change, or one amid the many. Flowing water and especially fire may seem to be instances of pure change or process without any continuing "stuff" or substance to give identity. But there is also reference to "measure" here, implying that the process has an order to it, which imparts sameness amid difference. There *is* a sense in which we can step into the same river twice. If I step into the Ohio River twice have I not done just that? But what makes it "the same" river is not the water, which is constantly changing.

 ASK YOURSELF

1.20. What then *does* make it the same river the second time I step into it?

There is, after all, *some* kind of order or unity in the world. In fact, "all things are one." But learning to discern that order is not easy.

> Widsom is to listen, not to me, but to the Word (*logos*), and to confess that all things are one.
>
> The Word (*logos*) is as explained, yet people are as uncomprehending when they hear it for the first time as before they have heard it at all. For, though all things come to pass in accordance with this *logos*, people seem to have had no experience of it, when they encounter theories and actions such as I expound, when I distinguish each thing according to its kind and show how it really is made. But the rest of the human race are unaware of what they are doing after they awake, even as they forget what they do in sleep.

Notice how Heraclitus insists that there is a definite truth to be known, the truth of the *logos*, which explains everything. Yet he also is sure that very few people know this truth. Heraclitus did not think highly of most people, including many of the philosophers who preceded him. He thought ignorance was the rule rather than the exception.

If there is, for Heraclitus as for the Milesians, a single element that pervades the world, it would seem to be fire. But fire may be the focus partly because of its value as an image of ordered change.

> The transformations of Fire are, first of all, sea; half of the sea is earth, half fiery waterspout. . . . [E]arth becomes liquid sea, and is measured by the same *logos* as before it became earth.

> There is an exchange of all things for Fire, and Fire for all things, even as goods for gold and gold for goods.

> Fire is want and excess.

> Fire lives the death of air, and air lives the death of fire; water lives the death of earth, earth that of water.

 ASK YOURSELF

1.21. Do you think of fire as being made of some "stuff," or do you tend to think of it simply as a process, with no underlying and constant stuff?

Even though a quietly burning candle emits a flame that seems to stay the same, we know that the flame itself is a process of constant change. For this reason fire is a particularly good manifestation or sign (or symbol?) of the *logos*, which is the unifying principle amid constant change. Heraclitus thinks his explanatory principle (the *logos*) extends to all domains of existence. Thus he has striking views on the soul, religion, politics, and morals. The following are a few examples:

> Souls of those slain in war are purer than those that perish from diseases.

> You would not discover the limits of the soul although you traveled the whole way: it has so deep a *logos*.

> Time is a child playing checkers; the kingdom belongs to a child.

> The people should fight for the law (*nomos*) as they fight for the city wall.

> It is not better for humans to obtain all they want.

It is worth mentioning that the remark about *nomos* is probably best interpreted in the following way: The *nomos* of any community is worth fighting for just to the extent that it is a reflection of the *logos*, the true principle that orders everything. It would be very untypical of Heraclitus to suppose that every city's laws are worthwhile. Some are foolish. But some reflect a deeper, even divine, principle. We will find this important idea appearing in later thinking on the status of human law.

 ASK YOURSELF

1.22. Do you think of any of the laws under which you live as being rooted in something divine (perhaps, as commanded by God)? Mention a law that some people might regard in that way.

THE ELEATICS

The city of Elea in southern Italy hosted two philosophers of great importance: Parmenides and his follower Zeno. Being from the same city, their views are often referred to as "Eleatic." Even Melissus, another early Greek not from Elea, is thought of as an "Eleatic" because his views are so close to those of Parmenides. The Eleatics have this much in common with Heraclitus; unlike some of the Ionians, they are less likely to be thought of as natural scientists than as early philosophers, for they are more interested in grasping concepts and drawing out the logical implications of common beliefs than in proposing physical theories. There is, however, a strong contrast between Eleatic philosophy and the views of Heraclitus. Where the latter sees reality as a flowing stream or a flame that embodies permanence amid change, Parmenides and his followers *deny* that change is real in any respect whatsoever.

Parmenides

Parmenides was born about 515 BCE; as with most of the Presocratics, the details of his life are sketchy. He wrote a single work—a long philosophical poem—the third part of which is presented in this section. This part has two divisions: (1) The Way of Truth and (2) The Way of Belief.

The Unchanging One. In his poem, we see Parmenides reflecting in a striking way on the concepts of being, change, nonbeing, and knowledge. His conclusions seem bizarre at first, but he has the courage to follow out fully the implications of his own thoughts.

> Come now, I will tell you—and do you listen to my saying and accept it—the only two ways of inquiry that can be thought of. The one that *it is*, and that it is impossible for it not to be, is the way of belief, for it follows truth. The other, namely, that *it is not*, and that it is bound not to be,—that, I tell you, is a path that none can learn of at all. For you cannot know what is not nor express it.
>
> For it is the same thing that can be thought and that can be.

  ASK YOURSELF

1.23. Fill in the blank:
    There is an obvious reason for claiming that it is not possible to know what is not, for knowledge must have an object. And what is not, nothing, is not an object! Similar reasoning applies to learning. You cannot learn what is _____.

The claim that "it is the same thing that can be thought and that can be" is very characteristic of *rationalism*, a basic option in philosophy that will be discussed in connection with later thinkers.

> It must be that what can be spoken and thought is; for it is possible for it to be, and it is not possible for what is nothing to be. This is what I command

you to consider. I hold you back from that first way of inquiry, and from this other also, upon which ignorant mortals wander, of two minds; for perplexity in their hearts steers their thoughts astray, so that they are carried along stupefied like people deaf and blind. . . .

For this will never be proved, that That Which is Not, exists. Restrain your thought from this way of inquiry.

One way only is left for us to describe, namely, that *It Is*. In this path are very many indications that What Is has no coming into being or destruction, for it is complete, without motion, and without end. And it never Was, nor Will it Be, for It Is now, all at once, a continuous one. What kind of origin for it might you see? How, and whence, could it have come? . . . I will not let you say nor think that it came from Not Being. For it can neither be thought nor expressed that What is Not is. And, if it came from nothing, what necessity could have made it arise later rather than sooner? Therefore it must either be altogether or not be at all. Nor will the force of truth permit anything to arise besides itself from that which is not. For this reason, justice does not loose her fetters and let anything come into being or pass away, but holds fast. Our decision depends on this: "Is it or is it not?" Surely it is decided, as it must be, that we are to set aside the one (latter) way as unthinkable and inexpressible (for it is no true way), and that the other path is real and true. How, then, can Being perish, or come to Be? If it came into being, it is not; nor is it if it is going to be in the future. Thus is becoming destroyed and passing away not to be heard of.

The fundamental idea here is that it is impossible to express or think what is nothing. That seems obviously true, doesn't it? But notice the consequences that are drawn from this obvious truth. One is as follows (fill the blanks):

a. If what is (exists now) came into existence then there would have to be a time when it (what is) was not.

b. But what is not is _____.

c. Therefore it is not thinkable that what is or exists now came into existence.

d. Only what is thinkable can be.

e. Therefore what is did not come into _____.

The same reasoning shows that what is could not cease to be. Therefore what is must be eternal.

 ASK YOURSELF

1.24. Why must what is be eternal?

Nor is it divisible, since it is homogeneous, and there is no more of it in one place than in another, to keep it from holding together, nor less of it, but everything is full of Being. For this reason it is altogether continuous. . . .

Moreover, it is motionless in the bonds of mighty chains, immovable, without beginning or end; since coming into being and passing away have been driven away, and true belief has rejected them. It is the same, and it rests in the self-same place, abiding in itself. Thus it remains constant in its place, for mighty necessity keeps it in the bonds of the limit that holds it fast on every side. For this reason it is not permitted for "what is" to be interminable; for it is in need of nothing, but if it were (spatially) interminable, it would be lacking everything.

The thing that can be thought and that for which the thought exists is the same; for you cannot find thought without something that is, as to which it is expressed. And there is not, and never will be, anything besides What Is, since fate has chained it so as to be whole and motionless. For this reason all these things mortals believe in are just names—coming into being and passing away, being and not being, change of place and alteration of bright color.

Coming into being, or any other kind of change, such as a change from being yellow to being blue, are mere illusions, names invented by mortals as a result of false belief. Think what is being claimed here. If you think your hand is in a different place now than it was two minutes ago, you must be mistaken! For that would be a change, a change of place.

Since, then, there is a limit, it is complete on every side, like the mass of a rounded sphere, equally balanced from the center in every direction; for it cannot be greater or smaller in one place than in another. For there is no nothing that could keep it from reaching out equally, nor can Being be more here and less there than Being, since it is all inviolable. For from the point from which it is equal in every direction it reaches its limit uniformly.

Zeno

Parmenides' extraordinarily counterintuitive views were reinforced by some clever paradoxes devised by his disciple Zeno. Plato tells us that the two of them came to Athens together once and that Zeno was about twenty-five years younger than Parmenides. So Zeno must have been born about 490 BCE.

Paradoxes of Motion and Plurality. Zeno constructs arguments that begin with obvious truths and end in the denial of plurality and the denial of motion or change of any other kind.

If what is had no magnitude, it would not even be. . . . [But if what is has a magnitude] the same may be said of that part of it which is in front; for it, too, will have magnitude, and it [the front] will have a front. And so on ad infinitum. So if things are a many, they must be both small and great, so small as not to have any magnitude at all, and so great as to be infinite.

We ordinarily think of the world as composed of many three-dimensional objects. Take any such object, say, a brick. We can think of it as having parts. For example, it has a front half and a back half. Consider the front half. We can think of it as also having a front. And the front of the front as having a front. And so on and so on. Therefore if there were such objects they would have to be infinite. But you obviously cannot have more than one infinite object. So reality must be one.

 ASK YOURSELF

1.25. Why could there not be more than one infinite object?

Suppose then that the world is not composed of three-dimensional objects, but rather of things that have no magnitude (size) at all. Then those things would be infinitely small. So, on the assumption that there are many things, they would have to be both small and great. But that of course is absurd. Zeno's argument here is an example of a *reduction to absurdity*. He takes a seemingly innocent assumption and shows that it leads to absurd results. Therefore it must be rejected. The assumption that must be rejected is that there are many things (the assumption of plurality).

> You cannot cross a race-course. You cannot traverse an infinite number of points in a finite time. You must traverse half of any distance before you traverse the whole, and half of that again before you can traverse it. This goes on ad infinitum, so that there are an infinite number of points in any given space, and you cannot touch an infinite number one by one in a finite time.
>
> Achilles will never overtake the tortoise. He must first reach the place from which the tortoise started. By that time the tortoise will be a little bit ahead. Achilles must then make up that distance, and again the tortoise will be ahead. He is always coming nearer, but he never catches up.
>
> The arrow in flight is at rest. For, if everything is at rest when it occupies a space equal to itself, and what is in flight at any given moment always occupies a space equal to itself, it cannot move.

The structure of each of these arguments is the same. They work by showing that a seemingly true assumption leads to absurd results.

 ASK YOURSELF

1.26. What is the seemingly true assumption in the case of Achilles (a Greek hero noted for his swiftness) and the tortoise?

Parmenides and Zeno seem to have proved, simply by logical argument, that most of our ordinary beliefs—such as that there are many things in the world and that they change, come into being, and go out of existence—are all false. They have proved that reality is *one*. That view is one kind, an extreme kind, of *monism*. In their case, *ration-*

alism led to *monism*. We will discover that some later philosophers with rationalist tendencies also tended toward monism. It is worth adding that there is also a mystical or quasireligious dimension to these ideas. Mystics from various religions regularly refer to God or Reality as "One" and claim to experience the dissolution of all individuality, including their own, and thus the relegation of plurality to the status of mere illusion.

 ASK YOURSELF

1.27. Define: eleatic; reduction to absurdity; rationalism; monism.

PLURALIST ALTERNATIVES TO PARMENIDES

As we've seen, Parmenides is a kind of monist, one who argues that reality is one. We've also seen that Parmenides used reason to arrive at a view of reality that strongly conflicts with common sense. In particular, it conflicts with what sense perceptions (seeing, hearing, tasting) reveal. Several philosophers after Parmenides were inspired by much of what he said, but they resisted his monism, no doubt at least in part because it conflicted too much with common sense. These philosophers were *pluralists* since they believed there is a plurality of things or basic elements in nature.

Empedocles

Empedocles was a poet, prophet, natural philosopher, and physician from the Sicilian city of Acragas who lived about 450 BCE. He considered himself to be a God and dressed in flamboyant clothing. One ancient writer claims that he "proved" his divinity by leaping into the crater of Mount Aetna. But he didn't survive that event!

Love, Strife, and the Four Roots. Like Parmenides, Empedocles accepts the permanency of "what is" and that reality is uncreated and indestructible. Unlike Parmenides, however, he holds that there are four "roots" or primary elements of reality, each of which is eternal: earth, air, fire, and water. Everything we see around us, then, results from a combination of these elements. Many earlier thinkers also viewed earth, air, fire, and water as primary substances. However, we can credit Empedocles with the view that the elements combine together to make differing conglomerates. His view dominated Western cosmology and medical thought until the Renaissance. Empedocles poetically describes how individual things come into and go out of existence. Change results from the combination, separation, and regrouping of indestructible entities.

> I will tell you a twofold tale. At one time it grew to be one only out of many; at another, it divided up to be many instead of one. There is a double becoming of perishable things and a double passing away. The coming together of all things brings one generation into being and destroys it; the other grows up and is scattered as things become divided.

Ultimately, all change amounts to mixing and separation of the four elements. What makes things change in this way? According to Empedocles, there are two primary forces that mix and separate the elements: love and strife. Love is a force that attracts elements to each other, and strife makes them repel each other.

> And these things never cease continually changing places, at one time all uniting in one through Love, at another each carried in different directions by the repulsion of Strife. Thus, as far as it is their nature to grow into one out of many, and to become many once more when the one is parted asunder, so far they come into being and their life abides not. But, inasmuch as they never cease changing their places continually, so far they are ever immovable as they go round the circle of existence.
>
> But come, listen to my words, for it is learning that increases wisdom. As I said before, when I declared the heads of my discussion, I will tell you a twofold tale. At one time it grew together to be one only out of many, at another it parted to pieces so as to be many instead of one; Fire and Water and Earth and the mighty height of Air; dread Strife, too, apart from these, of equal weight to each, and Love in their midst, equal in length and breadth.

 ASK YOURSELF

1.28. What is pluralistic about Empedocles' theory?

The right combination of love and strife is needed to produce the composite objects that we see around us. Think of the universe as though it were one huge mixing pot, filled with clumps of earth, air, fire, and water. If we only tossed love into the mix, then everything would congeal into one amorphous mass. On the other hand, if only strife was tossed into the mix, then none of the four elements would mix together and would remain distinct clumps. Empedocles describes this mixing pot as the great swirling vortex of the universe. More precisely, the vortex for Empedocles is the Parmenidean sphere composed of the four elements. With strife on the outside of the swirling sphere and love on the inside, the four elements congeal into a single mass. However, as strife enters into the sphere, love is forced to the center and the four elements separate. As love and strife move around in the vortex, the four elements combine in different shapes.

> When Strife was fallen to the lowest depth of the vortex, and Love had reached to the center of the whirl, in it do all things come together so as to be one only; not all at once, but coming together at their will each from different quarters; and, as they mingled, strife began to pass out to the furthest limit. Yet many things remained unmixed, alternating with the things that were being mixed, namely, all that Strife not fallen yet retained; for it had not yet altogether retired perfectly from them to the outermost boundaries of the circle. Some of it still remained within, and some had passed out from the limbs of the All. But in proportion as it kept rushing out, a soft, immortal stream of blameless Love kept running in, and immediately those things became mortal which had been immortal before, those things were mixed that

had before been unmixed, each changing its path. And, as they mingled, countless tribes of mortal creatures were scattered abroad endowed with all manner of forms, a wonder to observe.

 ASK YOURSELF

1.29. What are some of the results of the mixing process when love is blended into the vortex?

The best combination of the two forces is more strife than love, as this produces the proper combinations of things around us. If too much love pours in, then we get grotesque combinations, such as people with heads growing directly out of their torsos without any necks.

Many creatures with faces and breasts looking in different directions were born; some, offspring of oxen with faces of people, while others, again, arose as offspring of people with the heads of oxen, and creatures in whom the nature of women and men was mingled, furnished with sterile parts.

 ASK YOURSELF

1.30. Why would too much love produce grotesque things, such as "people with the heads of oxen"?

Anaxagoras

We find a second pluralistic response to Parmenides in the written fragments of Anaxagoras, a contemporary of Empedocles from the city of Clazomenae in Asia Minor. He lived for a long time in Athens and was a friend of the great politician Pericles. Eventually he was tried on a charge of impiety and exiled from Athens. He was not the last philosopher to be treated so badly by that city, as we shall see.

Mind and the Infinitely Divisible Seeds. Like Empedocles, Anaxagoras believed that the cosmos was composed of several different elements and that the arrangement of these elements constituted the things that we see around us. He called these elements "seeds." In speculating about the nature of the elements, however, Anaxagoras faced a problem. Suppose, for example, that we take a rock and break it in half. We then break one of those halves in half and continue breaking each piece into smaller and smaller parts. How far can we go in breaking up the pieces? Logically, there are two possibilities: (1) We keep breaking it until we arrive at its tiniest pieces that can't be broken any further, or (2) we keep breaking the pieces into smaller and smaller ones, to infinity. Anaxagoras went with this second option and maintained that matter is an infinitely divisible continuum.

> Nor is there a least of what is small, but there is always a smaller; for it cannot be that what is should cease to be by being cut. But there is also always something, greater than what is great, and it is equal to the small in amount, and, compared with itself, each thing is both great and small.

Unlike Empedocles, who reduced the number of elements to four, Anaxagoras was convinced that the world contains "a multitude of innumerable seeds in no way like each other." They are infinite in number, eternal, divisible, and differ in shape, color, and taste. Not only are the seeds infinitely divisible and infinite in number, he also believed that they blended together in such a way that every substance contains every element, but in differing degrees. For example, a piece of gold contains a lot of gold, but it also contains elements of fire, water, and everything else as well.

> And since the portions of the great and of the small are equal in amount, for this reason, too, all things will be in everything. Nor is it possible for them to be apart, but all things have a portion of everything. Since it is impossible for there to be a least thing, they cannot be separated, nor come to be by themselves; but they must be now, just as they were in the beginning, all together. And in all things many things are contained, and an equal number both in the greater and in the smaller of the things that are separated off.

 ASK YOURSELF

1.31. Why, according to Anaxagoras, can't the elements be separated?

Imagine, then, that the universe is like a huge chocolate swirl cake that has been inconsistently mixed. Each part will have all the ingredients, but some parts will have more chocolate than others. Anaxagoras's reasoning on this point is clear in the following fragment:

> How can hair come from what is not hair, or flesh from what is not flesh?

For Anaxagoras, it makes no sense to say that a piece of hair is made of a combination of other elements such as earth, air, fire, and water. Instead, a piece of hair is made primarily of the element *hair*, although it will contain every other element in lesser degrees. Thus, for each distinct kind of thing that we find in the world, there is a specific infinitely divisible element that makes up the primary portion of that thing.

As we've seen, Empedocles felt compelled to explain the origin of change by means of the forces of love and strife. Anaxagoras also felt compelled to explain the origin of change within the swirling universe of inconsistently mixed elements. For Anaxagoras, the origin of this change was something he called *Mind*, the Greek word for which is *Nous*. Nous is not itself an element, but a force that acts on elements. In place of Empedocles' forces of love and strife, Mind, for Anaxagoras, is the external cause that accounts for all motion, growth, and change. It initiates a rotation in the small parts of the vortex, which is slowly passed on to larger parts.

All other things partake in a portion of everything, while Nous is infinite and self-ruled, and is mixed with nothing, but is alone, itself by itself. For if it were not by itself, but were mixed with anything else, it would partake in all things if it were mixed with any; for in everything there is a portion of everything, as has been said by me in what goes before, and the things mixed with it would hinder it, so that it would have power over nothing in the same way that it has now being alone by itself. For it is the thinnest of all things and the purest, and it has all knowledge about everything and the greatest strength; and Nous has power over all things, both greater and smaller, that have life. And Nous had power over the whole revolution, so that it began to revolve in the beginning. And it began to revolve first from a small beginning; but the revolution now extends over a larger space, and will extend over a larger still. And all the things that are mingled together and separated off and distinguished are all known by Nous. And Nous set in order all things that were to be, and all things that were and are not now and that are, and this revolution in which now revolve the stars and the sun and the moon, and the air and the aether that are separated off. And this revolution caused the separating off, and the rare is separated off from the dense, the warm from the cold, the light from the dark, and the dry from the moist. And there are many portions in many things. But no thing is altogether separated off nor distinguished from anything else except Nous. And all Nous is alike, both the greater and the smaller; while nothing else is like anything else, but each single thing is and was most manifestly those things of which it has most in it.

 ASK YOURSELF

1.32. Describe some of the features of Mind (*Nous*) as presented in the preceding selection.

It is tempting to see Mind as a conscious divine force that is actively involved in the operations of the universe. It would seem, then, that Anaxagoras is regressing to an earlier Homeric conception in which the Gods run the universe. However, even if we see *Nous* as a divine force, it is a force that is elevated to a degree far beyond the power and function of the Homeric Gods. Anaxagoras is perhaps the first to introduce what some call the *God of the philosophers*, as distinguished from the God of religious practice and tradition. This God is not described anthropomorphically, and in particular is not driven by passions like jealousy or lust.

The Atomists: Parmenides as Pluralist

Parmenides, as we have seen, used reason to arrive at a view of the real that strongly conflicts with common sense. In particular, it conflicts with sense perceptions such as seeing and hearing, which most people trust as a guide to what is real. A particularly ingenious attempt to reconcile Parmenidean reason with commonsense reliance on perception is found in the Atomists, Leucippus and Democritus. Little information has survived about Leucippus, so our discussion will focus on Democritus, about whom we know a bit more. Democritus lived around 450 BCE in Abdera, northern Greece, and numerous fragments of his writings have survived.

Atoms and the Void. Remember that Parmenides argues that reality is one. It follows that there can be no empty space, since we could only think of it apart from the one, and that would require thinking of what is not real, or what is nothing, and nothing cannot be thought. Moreover, only what is thinkable can be real. Thus Parmenides is a kind of monist. A pluralist holds the more commonsense view that there is more than one thing, and usually, many things. Democritus thinks there is much to be said for Parmenides' reasoning, but he wants to reject the latter's monism.

> No-thing exists just as much as thing.

Democritus also calls "no-thing" the "void." It is not a bodily object, but it still exists. This remark suggests that he is on to something askew in Parmenides's reasoning. To deny reality to "nothing" could be to deny that there is any other reality than bodily things, rather than to assert the truism that nothing is indeed nothing. Think about this point and try to answer the following question:

 ASK YOURSELF

1.33. Does Democritus contradict himself when he says no-thing exists? Why or why not?

In addition to the void (no-thing) Democritus postulates the existence of "atoms," indivisible objects so small they cannot be seen, but which are eternal and unchanging, except with respect to position within the void. They are thus like the Parmenidean "one" except that there are many of them. That is of course an *important* difference.

> He [Democritus] held that the number of shapes of the atoms was infinite since there was no reason why any one of them should be of one shape rather than another.

> He thinks [that atoms] have all kinds of shapes and differences in size. So he is able to build up from them objects that are perceptible to sight and other senses.

Ordinary objects, a table for instance, are built up from indestructible and invisible atoms that combine in various ways, depending on their various "shapes" and sizes. One could imagine that some might "hook onto" others because of their particular shapes, somewhat like pieces in a jigsaw puzzle. This view is remarkably modern in certain respects.

ASK YOURSELF

1.34. Just a very little knowledge of modern chemistry should enable you to give an example of a visible object, for example a fluid, that is built up from "atoms" in somewhat the way Democritus supposes. Give such an example here.

> All things happen according to necessity, for the cause of the coming into being of all things is the vortex, which he calls necessity.

This remark is clearly opposed to the popular view of the world as being subject to the unpredictable will of the Gods or even the will of humans. This sort of view is said to be *deterministic*, and many contemporary scientists are determinists in this sense. Everything that happens is the causal result of previous states or concurrent states of affairs. But there must be some initial source of motion in the atoms that would explain their interactions and the resulting changes in the perceptible world. This initial source Democritus calls "the vortex"(or "swirl") and *it* he does not explain, except to say that it comes from "chance." That of course is no explanation.

Democritus's view also clearly implies that there is no purpose or meaning in the universe. Everything that takes place is determined by previous states of the universe, and the whole process is just the result of an accident. It is not going anywhere; there is no goal or ultimate destiny for the world or anything in it, including human beings.

 ASK YOURSELF

1.35. If Democritus is right, could there be such a thing as individual responsibility? Explain.

If everything is just atoms in motion, one might wonder how Democritus could explain mental phenomena, including perception itself. His account is once again striking in the way it anticipates some modern views.

> Sweet and bitter, hot and cold, and color, are so only by convention (*nomos*). But only atoms and the void exist in reality. We apprehend nothing precisely, but only in relation to the condition of our own bodies. . . .

 ASK YOURSELF

1.36. Is the sourness of a lemon actually objectively in the lemon, or is it just a function of the interaction between the lemon and our body, and in that sense something that exists only "subjectively" rather than as part of objective reality?

Democritus's notion of certain things being what they are only by "convention" (the Greek word is *nomos*, which can also be translated as "law" or "custom") antici- pates a theme that will be discussed later. There is a strong suggestion in the last frag- ment that what is so "by convention" is not really real, not genuinely true, because not somehow objective or independent of human thought and activity.

 ## ASK YOURSELF

1.37. Do you think of heat and cold or colors as "real"? Does the old conundrum about a tree falling in a forest where no one is present come into the discussion? (The question is whether there would be any *sound*.)

1.38. A number of standard philosophical terms or concepts will be found somewhat useful in thinking about the philosophers studied so far: rationalism; monism; pluralism; determinism. Explain each of these terms and then show how they apply to the following figures: Thales; Anaximines; Anaxagoras; Pythagoras; Parmenides; Democritus.

THE SOPHISTS: RHETORIC AND VIRTUE FOR A PRICE

In the fifth century BCE Athens became wealthy and powerful partly as a result of its leadership in the Persian wars. It also became a democracy, in which the power of hereditary elites was replaced by a ruling assembly. That assembly could often be ma- nipulated by powerful speech makers. One of the most famous leaders of Athenian democracy was Pericles, who was just such a charismatic personality and skilled speaker. Athenians, somewhat like Americans in recent years, also spent a lot of time conducting lawsuits against one another. Since there were no attorneys or public pros- ecutors the key to success in the courts was the ability of those involved in a suit to skillfully and persuasively present a case. So skill in the arts of persuasive speech mak- ing was worth having, and if someone could teach those skills they could command an impressive fee for doing so.

The sophists were itinerant teachers who filled this need. They claimed knowledge of many matters and taught a variety of subjects, but their most valuable asset was a knowledge of rhetoric, that is, the arts of persuasive speech. Unfortunately, there is no necessary connection between being persuasive and speaking the truth. Most of us have believed lies at some time or another simply because they were presented so persuasively. We may be persuaded by various tricks and by certain forms of falla- cious reasoning. So it is not surprising that the name "sophist" gradually became as- sociated with trickery, dishonesty, and persuasive but fallacious reasoning. In like man- ner the English word "rhetoric" has negative associations since it implies a kind of speech that is tricky and persuasive but does not necessarily convey the truth.

Protagoras and Gorgias

Protagoras of Abdera (Democritus's hometown) and Gorgias of Leontini (southern Italy), both born toward the beginning of the fifth century BCE, were two of the best- known representatives of the sophist movement. Much of what we know of their ideas comes from Plato and Aristotle, both of whom were hostile toward the sophists. The picture we have of them may thus be biased and unfair to some degree.

Deceptive Speech. Gorgias is credited with the following remarks:

> It can be shown that persuasion, when added to speech, can make whatever impression it wishes on the soul [by considering] the arguments of the meteorologists . . . and legal contests, in which a speech can move and persuade a crowd not by truth but by the skill of its composition, and to contests of philosophers' speeches, in which is revealed how easily the quickness of thought makes our confidence in our opinion change.
>
> The power of speech has the same relation to the constitution of the soul as drugs have to bodily states: For as various drugs . . . put an end to sickness and others put an end to life, so some speeches cause grief, pleasure or fear . . . and still others drug and bewitch the soul through an evil persuasion.

 ## ASK YOURSELF

1.39. Gorgias mentions three contexts in which rhetorical skill is important. What is the third one?

1.40. Name a drug that can "bewitch the soul" and explain how certain speeches might be compared to such a drug.

Gorgias argues that even in philosophy one cannot have confidence in one's own opinions. There is too much to be said for both sides in any controversy. It is quite understandable then that the sophists taught their pupils the art of *antilogic,* or making as strong an argument as possible for both sides on any issue. In his play *The Clouds,* Aristophanes, a contemporary of the sophists, stages a mock sophistical debate between the stronger, and just, argument, and the weaker and unjust argument. The weaker argument wins, of course! Aristophanes's reaction to the practice of antilogic was not untypical. Aristotle tells us how the practice of antilogic affected the reputation of Protagoras:

> This is making the weaker argument the stronger. And people were legitimately annoyed at Protagoras' promise.

The Sophists could command impressive fees for their work as teachers of speech and argument. Plato expresses resentment against Protagoras and other sophists for profiting from their teaching and in particular from the teaching of "excellence" or virtue. In the dialogue *Protagoras* Plato portrays Protagoras as advertising his wares to a prospective pupil:

> My boy, if you associate with me, the result will be that the very day you begin you will return home a better person, and likewise the next day also. Each day you will make constant progress towards being better.

The content of the improvement Protagoras promises is described in the same dialogue and includes the ability to manage the affairs of the city:

> . . . so that as far as the city's affairs go he [Protagoras' pupil] may be most powerful in acting and in speaking.

So far we have seen the sophists portrayed as skeptical and indifferent to truth, as teachers of manipulative techniques for achieving success and acquiring power in the city-state. And they received substantial fees for their tutoring. It seems that people like the sophists are very popular and influential in the twenty-first century, at least if the number of best-selling books on "how to succeed" is any indication of popularity and influence. Those books usually stress techniques for manipulating or influencing other people and usually have little or nothing to say about *truth* or about moral constraints on behavior.

 ASK YOURSELF

1.41. List the characteristics of the sophists mentioned so far.

1.42. Think of some contemporary parallels to the sophists; list and describe them.

Protagorean Relativism. Protagoras is perhaps best known for the following remark:

> A human being is the measure of all things; of the things that are, that they are, and of the things that are not, that they are not.

This is generally taken to be an expression of *relativism*. The concept of relativism will be explained in stages in what follows, and we will be returning to this concept at many points in the history of philosophy. It is an idea that will not go away. To say that a human being is the measure of all things could be to say that each individual person is the measure or standard for what is true. Thus if something is sweet to me, then it *is* sweet (to me), and if the same thing is sour to you then it *is* sour (to you). There does not seem to be any truth of the matter existing independently of the experience of individuals. On the basis of such a fact someone might insist that the only truth there is is truth "relative to" each individual. Thus we get the term "relativism."

We might also interpret Protagoras as saying that humans in general, or human societies, are the measure of all things. Someone who argued that incest, for example, might be morally right in one society and morally wrong in another would be taking this interpretation. His or her claim would be that truth is "relative to" a given society, culture, group, or historical epoch. Since it cannot be true, in the usual sense of "true," that incest is both wrong and not-wrong, relative truth is clearly not "truth" in the usual sense.

 ASK YOURSELF

1.43. What are the two kinds of relativism mentioned in the preceding discussion?

It is unclear exactly what Protagoras meant, but there is some evidence that he had the first interpretation in mind. It does make sense to say that if something tastes sweet to me then it *is* sweet to me, and if it tastes sour to you it *is* sour to you. Sense perceptions often seem to be "relative to" particular perceivers for the kinds of reasons discussed by the Atomists. (Go back and review the discussion of perception in the section on Democritus.)

Some people think that ethical judgments in particular are relative to individuals or groups. One reason for this view is that it does seem difficult to find standards of moral right and wrong that are "objective" in the sense that all people, or even all reasonable people, can come to agreement on what they are. Ethical relativism was not uncommon in fifth-century Athens, and various versions of it are extremely common in twenty-first-century America.

 ASK YOURSELF

1.44. What are some ways people today express a belief in relativism?

If Protagoras thinks that each individual is the standard for what is the case, for what is true, then it is not clear how anyone could persuade anyone else to change their mind about what the truth is. Yet the sophists were in the business of teaching the art of persuading people, and that means, often, persuading them to change their minds. So Protagorean relativism seems to be in conflict with Protagorean instruction in rhetoric. Is Protagoras inconsistent, then? In Plato's dialogue *Theatetus*, Theatetus's Protagorean views are presented and defended against this charge of inconsistency in the following way:

> . . . each of us is the measure of the things which are and the things which are not. Nonetheless there is a difference between one person and another in just this respect: the things which both are and appear to one person are different from the things which are and appear to another. I do not mean to say that there is no such thing as wisdom or a wise man, but I call a

man wise who can make what is and appears evil to any of us, appear and be good. . . . Not that any one ever made another think truly, who previously thought falsely. For it is not possible to think what is not, or think anything different from that which he experiences; and this is always true . . . [what] the inexperienced call true, I maintain to be only better, and not truer than others . . . and the wise and good rhetoricians make the good instead of the evil to seem just to states; for whatever appears to a state to be just and fair, so long as it is regarded as such, is just and fair to it; but the wise one makes what seems and is beneficial replace the evil [which seemed beneficial to the state]. And in like manner the sophist who is able to train his pupils in this spirit is a wise man, and deserves to be well paid by them. And so one man is wiser than another; and no one thinks falsely, and you, whether you will or not, must put up with being a measure.

 ASK YOURSELF

1.45. Theatetus is credited with the view that the sophist or wise man is not someone who can turn people from believing what is false to believing what is true, since *whatever* anyone believes is true (for them). What the sophist can do is to get people to turn from believing what is _____ to believing what is _____.

Relativism in any form runs into many difficulties. If individual relativism is true then if I believe that what Protagoras says is false, then it is false (for me, at any rate). So relativism seems to be self-defeating. If I think $1 + 2 = 4$, then it does. If I think it is true that I can play basketball better than Michael Jordan, then it is true. It is not clear that Theatetus has shown any way out of these difficulties. He appeals to a distinction between what is better or beneficial and what is not. But does that distinction really help? On the relativist's view, if, for instance, I think evil laws are beneficial, then they *are* beneficial (for, or to, me). It is not clear how a wise man could get me to see the opposite, unless of course the opposite is *objectively* true, is in fact the case, even though no one may believe it to be so. Thus it appears that Theatetus's argument implicitly appeals to an objective standard for what is beneficial.

Nomos *(Custom) versus* Physis *(Nature)*. Throughout the entire ancient period philosophers, poets, politicians, and historians debated such questions as these: Is morality simply a matter of custom (*nomos*), or is it rooted in nature (*physis*)? Do the Gods exist just as a matter of custom, or by nature? Are political arrangements simply a matter of custom, or rather of nature? These and related questions constitute the *physis–nomos* debate.

ASK YOURSELF

1.46. Would someone who thought morality was just a matter of custom probably be an ethical relativist? Explain.

1.47. Review the fragments about the Gods in the discussion of Xenophanes. Does he think common religious beliefs are just a matter of custom or not?

Nomos (law, custom) is something invented by humans that can be changed or done away with by humans. In fact, laws were changed regularly in the Athenian assembly, just as they are in our legislatures. *Physis*, on the other hand, is permanent. When the Milesians, for example, wrote about the essential unchanging reality or realities that underlie all things, they were writing *peri physeos* (about nature). But the sophists usually focused on *human* nature. Some sophists argued that humans are "by nature" selfish and that one should follow one's nature and ignore man-made "law" as far as possible. The idea that it is right for the strong man to get whatever he can, unconstrained by considerations of "man-made" justice, has its roots in this ancient view. This view is expressed in the saying "might makes right." Socrates, Plato, and Aristotle argued against the sophists. We will encounter some of those arguments in the next chapter.

 ASK YOURSELF

1.48. Define: Sophist; rhetoric; antilogic; relativism; *nomos*; *physis*.

SUGGESTIONS FOR FURTHER READING

Primary Sources

Barnes, J. *Early Greek Philosophy* (Harmondsworth: Penguin, 1987). A translation of all of the surviving fragments and doxographies.

Freeman, Kathleen. *Ancilla to the Presocratic Philosophers: A Complete Translation of the Fragments in Diels' Fragmente der Vorsokratiker* (Oxford: Basil Blackwell, 1956). Diels produced the definitive collection of Presocratic writings in Greek. Freeman provides a good english translation.

McKirahan, Richard D., Jr. *Philosophy before Socrates* (Indianapolis: Hackett Publishing Company, 1994). New translations by the author of almost all of the fragments plus an interesting introduction and detailed discussion of each of the major Presocratic figures.

Critical Analyses and Discussions

Frankfurt, H., et al. *Before Philosophy* (Harmondsworth: Penguin Books, 1949). A study of the myths and Egyptian and Mesopotamian cosmological speculations that prevailed in the world of the Presocratics.

Guthrie, W. K. C., *The Greek Philosophers: From Thales to Aristotle* (New York: Harper and row, 1960; reprint of 1950 Methuen and Co. edition). Tried and useful discussion for the classical Greek period.

Long, A. A. *The Cambridge Companion to Early Greek Philosophy* (Cambridge: Cambridge University Press, 1995). Recent scholarship dealing with some of the most philosophically interesting aspects of the Presocratics.

Mourelatos, A. P. D., ed. *The Presocratics* (Princeton, NJ: Princeton University Press, 1993). A collection of critical essays. Includes an extensive bibliography.

CHAPTER 2

SOCRATES AND PLATO

I n the fifth century BCE (i.e., from 500 to 400 BCE) Greek civilization came to be more and more centered in Athens. The reasons in part are political. Athens took a leading role in defending the Greek states against the attacks of the Persians in the early part of the century, and since that defense was successful (even though the Greeks were greatly outnumbered) Athens acquired much prestige in the process. But the extraordinary flowering of culture in that city from 450 to 350 BCE is difficult to explain without the assumption of a good deal of individual genius. In politics the Athenians were perhaps the first community to produce a democracy. In the arts (architecture, sculpture, drama) works were produced that have commanded the admiration of people to the present. And certainly the philosophers who appeared at this time, Socrates, Plato, and Aristotle, have been of unparalleled importance in the history of thought. One recent philosopher went so far as to claim that the entire history of philosophy is nothing but a series of footnotes to Plato.

We have already seen how the sophists appeared on the Greek scene and reflected changes in culture that were taking place. Socrates and Plato both react against sophistic relativism and what they perceive as a lack of regard for truth and the misuse of learning for profit.

SOCRATES

Although ethical or moral issues were not absent in the thinkers considered so far, none of them focus so exclusively on questions about how to live as does Socrates (469–399 BCE). He was and remains the archetype of philosophy as the search for personal wisdom, or of philosophy as what the Greeks called *psychagogia*, that is, training of the soul for life.

Socrates himself left no written record of his thoughts, but various accounts of him are available, including the remarks cited here from Aristotle. The Greek playwright Aristophanes satirized Socrates, classifying him with the sophists and nature philosophers and thus encouraging the public perception of Socrates as himself a sophist. It is quite certain that Aristophanes had a distorted conception of who Socrates was and what he was about. The Greek historian Xenophon recalls Socrates in a more favorable light in his *Memorabilia* and other works, but again, the accuracy of some of the details is in doubt. Xenophon does, however, provide an interesting account of a "beauty contest" in which Socrates participated. No one has ever seriously claimed that Socrates was good-looking, but according to Xenophon, Socrates argued that his bulging eyes were better for seeing than were those of the handsome young Critobulus, his flat snub nose better for smelling, and his thick lips better for kissing—therefore all of these were more beautiful, too, since the most functional things are the most beautiful! It was, however, the remarkable character of Socrates, his courage, honesty, and fairness, that attracted many people.

We are almost entirely dependent upon Plato for our knowledge of Socrates' thought. Most of Plato's writings are in the form of philosophical dialogues. Plato was a devoted student of Socrates and showed that devotion by making Socrates the leading character in many of his dialogues. Sometimes the character of Socrates is only a mouthpiece for Plato's own views, but it is highly probable that Plato's earlier dialogues present the teaching and character of Socrates himself. Just exactly what in Plato's work reflects the views of the historical Socrates and what does not continues to be a matter of controversy. The selections that follow reflect a fairly common view on what is genuinely "Socratic."

One distinguishing feature of Socrates' teaching or method is his dialectic, or teacher-student dialogue. The teacher poses a question, such as "What is justice?" and thereby draws out the student's intuition on the subject. A second typical feature is that the search for answers to such "What is?" questions is treated as the search for precise definitions or essences. Aristotle comments on this feature:

> Socrates occupied himself with the excellences of character, and in connection with them became the first to raise the problem of universal definition. . . . It was natural that Socrates should be seeking the essence, for he was seeking to syllogize, and "what a thing is" is the starting-point of syllogisms. . . . Two things may be fairly ascribed to Socrates, inductive arguments and universal definition, both of which are concerned with the starting point of science; but Socrates did not make the universal or the definitions exist apart. (*Metaphysics* 13 1078b)

We will discuss the notion of making the definition "exist apart" shortly. A third characteristic of Socrates' method is the use of *elenchus*, a way of refuting an opponent by showing that his own premises or beliefs lead to absurd results. Younger students did not always mind the humiliation of the elenchus process. However, Socrates would often use this technique on older and well-respected members of the community who didn't always appreciate having their views undermined.

Fourth, Socrates is also famous for the use of irony. Typically he will approach his conversational partners by praising them for their superior wisdom or expressing amazement at how much they must know. As the conversation proceeds, however, it becomes all too evident that they are considerably more ignorant than Socrates himself, and that the praise was thus insincere. Socrates' irony goes even deeper, for he tends not to commit himself to answers to the questions he raises, but maintains an ironic distance from "answers" or the dogmatic views prevalent among his fellow citizens. A fifth characteristic of Socrates' approach to inquiry is his profession of ignorance. He seldom offers a positive view on matters, but instead shows how shaky the views of those who *claim* to know really are.

In the excerpt from the *Euthyphro* that follows, make a note of uses of irony as you go along. The use of dialectic, the search for definition, the reduction of the opponent's position to absurdity (elenchus), Socratic ignorance, and the applications of all of this to matters of conduct are all also very obvious.

The *Euthyphro*

At the beginning of this dialogue by Plato Socrates encounters a fellow Athenian, Euthyphro, outside the courts. Socrates expresses amazement at the superior wisdom of Euthyphro, who has dared to challenge conventional piety by prosecuting his own father for killing a servant caught committing a crime. He asks Euthyphro to explain his reasons for doing so. Euthyphro replies that it is the pious or holy thing to do. Socrates then asks for a definition or account of the essence or nature of piety. We can rightly think of this dialogue as an enquiry into the basis for moral claims in general, as well as those based in religious ideas.

Euthyphro's First Definition

 From PLATO: *Euthyphro*

[SOCRATES] I adjure you Euthyphro to tell me the nature of piety and impiety, which you said that you knew so well, and of murder, and of other offences against the gods. What are they? Is not piety in every action always the same? and impiety, again—is it not always the opposite of piety, and always self-identical, having, as impiety, one notion which includes whatever is impious?

[EUTHYPHRO] To be sure, Socrates.

[SOCRATES] And what is piety, and what is impiety?

[EUTHYPHRO] Piety is doing as I am doing; that is to say, prosecuting any one who is guilty of murder, sacrilege, or of any similar crime—whether he be your father or mother, or whoever he may be—that makes no difference; and not to prosecute them is impiety. And please to consider, Socrates, what a notable proof I will give you of the truth of my words, a proof which I have already given to others:—of the principle, I mean, that the impious, whoever he may be, ought not to go unpunished. For do not men regard Zeus as the best and most righteous of the gods?—and yet they admit that he bound his father (Cronos) because he wickedly devoured his sons, and that he too had punished his own father (Uranus) for a similar reason, in a nameless manner. And yet when I proceed against my father, they are angry with me. So inconsistent are they in their way of talking when they are concerned, and when I am concerned.

 ASK YOURSELF

2.1. Euthyphro begins his definition by giving specific applications of the term in question ("piety," or, we might say, the "right" or "godly"). How does he defend his definition?

2.2. Prepare to answer this question as you read what follows. Mention one thing that Socrates' skepticism about popular religious notions has in common with Xenophanes's critique of popular religion.

[SOCRATES]   May not this be the reason, Euthyphro, why I am charged with impiety—that whenever anyone tells such stories about the Gods I get annoyed? Therefore I suppose that people think I err terribly. But, as you who are so well informed about them approve of them, I cannot do better than assent to your superior wisdom. What else can I say, confessing as I do, that I know nothing about them? Tell me, for the love of Zeus, whether you really believe that they are true.

[EUTHYPHRO]   Yes, Socrates; and things more wonderful still, of which the world is in ignorance.

[SOCRATES]   And do you really believe that the gods fought with one another, and had dire quarrels, battles, and the like, as the poets say, and as you may see represented in the works of great artists? The temples are full of them; and notably the robe of Athene, which is carried up to the Acropolis at the great Panathenaea, is embroidered with them. Are all these tales of the gods true, Euthyphro?

[EUTHYPHRO]   Yes, Socrates; and, as I was saying, I can tell you, if you would like to hear them, many other things about the gods which would quite amaze you.

[SOCRATES]   I dare say; and you shall tell me them at some other time when I have leisure. But just at present I would rather hear from you a more precise answer, which you have not as yet given, my friend, to the question, What is "piety"? When asked, you only replied, Doing as you do, charging your father with murder.

[EUTHYPHRO]   And what I said was true, Socrates.

Socrates' Critique of Euthyphro's First Definition

[SOCRATES]   No doubt, Euthyphro; but you would admit that there are many other pious acts?

[EUTHYPHRO]   There are.

[SOCRATES]   Remember that I did not ask you to give me two or three examples of piety, but to explain the essential form that makes all pious things to be pious. Do you not recollect that there was one idea which made the impious impious, and the pious pious?

[EUTHYPHRO]   I remember.

[SOCRATES]   Tell me what is the nature of this idea, and then I shall have a paradigm to which I may look, and by which I may measure actions, whether yours or those of any one else, and then I shall be able to say that such and such an action is pious, and another impious.

Socrates' remarks here are of particular importance. The term translated as "form" is *eidos*, the term Plato uses to refer to that "something which exists apart," as Aristotle put it. Here Socrates thinks of the form or idea of holiness as a kind of paradigm or standard. A paradigm is a particularly clear example of something (e.g., Michael Jordan might be a paradigm of a basketball player), and a standard is something that is used to measure something (Jordan might be a standard also, since he may be thought of as setting the standard for being a basketball player; you are a basketball player just to the extent that you have, even just a little bit, some of the characteristics he has). The interesting thing to note here is that paradigms are often particular concrete things, whereas definitions are general and abstract. So it looks as though Socrates wants a general definition that is at the same time anchored somehow to a particular. The development of these ideas by Plato is fundamental to his thought, as we shall see.

Euthyphro's Second Definition and Socrates' Critique.   Clearly the "sort of answer which [Socrates] wants" is a general definition rather than a list of examples. Euthyphro produces one, but it has a deadly defect.

[EUTHYPHRO]   Piety, then, is that which is dear to the gods, and impiety is that which is not dear to them.

[SOCRATES]   Very good, Euthyphro; you have now given me the sort of answer which I wanted. But whether what you say is true or not I cannot as yet tell, although I make no doubt that you will prove the truth of your words.

[EUTHYPHRO]   Of course.

[SOCRATES]   Come, then, and let us examine what we are saying. That thing or person which is dear to the gods is pious, and that thing or person which is hateful to the gods is impious, these two being the extreme opposites of one another. Was not that said?

[EUTHYPHRO]   It was.

[SOCRATES]   And well said?

[EUTHYPHRO]   Yes, Socrates, I thought so; it was certainly said.

[SOCRATES]   And further, Euthyphro, the gods were admitted to have enmities and hatreds and differences?

[EUTHYPHRO]   Yes, that was also said.

[SOCRATES]   And what sort of difference creates enmity and anger? Suppose for example that you and I, my good friend, differ about a number; do differences of this sort make us enemies and set us at variance with one another? Do we not go at once to arithmetic, and put an end to them by a calculating?

[EUTHYPHRO]   True.

[SOCRATES]   Or suppose that we differ about magnitudes, do we not quickly end the differences by measuring?

[EUTHYPHRO]   Very true.

[SOCRATES]   And we end a controversy about heavy and light by resorting to a weighing machine?

[EUTHYPHRO]   To be sure.

[SOCRATES]   But what differences are there which cannot be thus decided, and which therefore make us angry and set us at enmity with one another? I dare say the answer does not occur to you at the moment, and therefore I will suggest that these enmities arise when the matters of difference are the just and unjust, good and evil, honorable and dishonorable. Are not these the points about which men differ, and about which when we are unable satisfactorily to decide our differences, you and I and all of us quarrel, when we do quarrel?

[EUTHYPHRO]   Yes, Socrates, the nature of the differences about which we quarrel is such as you describe.

Socrates is here pointing out a feature of what we would call moral disagreement, namely, that there seems to be no generally agreed-upon way of settling such disagreement. On the other hand on many factual matters there are such agreed-upon ways.

 ASK YOURSELF

2.3. Give an example of a moral disagreement.

2.4. Give an example of a factual disagreement, and show how it could be resolved to everyone's satisfaction. If you cannot think how to answer this, look at Socrates' examples just given.

This feature of moral disagreements, namely, that there seems to be no agreement on methods for resolving them, has troubled philosophers for millennia. It has led some to claim that moral opinions do not bear on any facts at all, but are mere expressions of personal taste.

 ASK YOURSELF

2.5. Try to think of an example of a moral disagreement, and say why it could *not* be just a matter of taste.

[SOCRATES]   And the quarrels of the gods, noble Euthyphro, when they occur, are of a like nature?

[EUTHYPHRO]   Certainly they are.

[SOCRATES]   They have differences of opinion, as you say, about good and evil, just and unjust, honorable and dishonorable: there would have been no quarrels among them, if there had been no such differences—would there now?

[EUTHYPHRO]   You are quite right.

[SOCRATES]   Does not every man love that which he deems noble and just and good, and hate the opposite of them?

[EUTHYPHRO]   Very true.

[SOCRATES]   But, as you say, people regard the same things, some as just and others as unjust,—about these they dispute; and so there arise wars and fightings among them.

[EUTHYPHRO]   Very true.

[SOCRATES]   Then the same things are hated by the gods and loved by the gods, and are both hateful and dear to them?

[EUTHYPHRO]   True.

[SOCRATES]   And upon this view the same things, Euthyphro, will be pious and also impious? . . . Then, my friend, I remark with surprise that you have not answered the question which I asked. For I certainly did not ask you to tell me what action is both pious and impious: but now it would seem that what is loved by the gods is also hated by them.

And therefore, Euthyphro, in thus chastising your father you may very likely be doing what is agreeable to Zeus but disagreeable to Cronos or Uranus, and what is acceptable to Hephaestus but unacceptable to Hera, and there may be other gods who have similar differences of opinion.

 ASK YOURSELF

2.6. Socrates has now reduced to absurdity Euthyphro's second definition. Restate the definition, and show how an absurd consequence follows.

Euthyphro tries to defend his definition by simply asserting that all of the Gods would surely agree that a murderer should be punished. But he is unable to give a reason for believing this. Look for examples of irony in the following remarks by Socrates.

[SOCRATES]   Well then, my dear friend Euthyphro, do tell me, for my better instruction and information, what proof have you that in the opinion of all the gods a servant who is guilty of murder, and is put in chains by the master of the dead man, and dies because he is put in chains before he who bound him can learn from the interpreters of the gods what he ought to do with him, dies unjustly [this is a description of the details of the "killing" committed by Euthyphro's father]; and that on behalf of such a one a son ought to proceed against his father and accuse him of murder? How would you show that all the gods absolutely agree in approving of his act? Prove to me that they do, and I will applaud your wisdom as long as I live.

[EUTHYPHRO]   It will be a difficult task; but I could make the matter very clear to you.

[SOCRATES]   I understand; you mean to say that I am not so quick of apprehension as the judges: for to them you will be sure to prove that the act is unjust, and hateful to the gods.

Socrates Offers a Third Definition and Criticizes It.   Socrates' own suggestion gives rise to a famous dilemma.

[SOCRATES]   But they will be sure to listen if they find that you are a good speaker. There was a notion that came into my mind while you were speaking; I said to myself: "Well, and what if Euthyphro does prove to me that all the gods regarded the death of the serf as unjust, how do I know anything more of the nature of piety and impiety? For granting that this action may be hateful to the gods, still piety and impiety are not adequately defined by these distinctions, for that which is hateful to the gods has been shown to be also pleasing and dear to them." And therefore, Euthyphro, I do not ask you to prove this; I will suppose, if you like, that all the gods condemn and abominate such an action. But I will amend the definition so far as to say that what all the gods hate is impious, and what they love pious or holy; and what some of them love and others hate is both or neither. Shall this be our definition of piety and impiety?

[EUTHYPHRO]   Why not, Socrates?

[SOCRATES]   Why not! Certainly, as far as I am concerned, Euthyphro, there is no reason why not. But whether this admission will greatly assist you in the task of instructing me as you promised, is a matter for you to consider.

[EUTHYPHRO]   Yes, I should say that what all the gods love is pious and holy, and the opposite which they all hate, impious.

[SOCRATES]   Ought we to enquire into the truth of this, Euthyphro, or simply to accept the mere statement on our own authority and that of others? What do you say?

[EUTHYPHRO]   We should enquire; and I believe that the statement will stand the test of enquiry.

[SOCRATES]   We shall know better, my good friend, in a little while. The point which I should first wish to understand is this: Is the pious or holy beloved by the gods because it is holy, or, Is it holy because it is beloved of the gods?

The dilemma that Socrates states here has been much discussed throughout the history of philosophy. Since it is first stated clearly in this dialogue, it is often referred to as "The Euthyphro dilemma." The dilemma could be restated in this way: Either (1) God loves or commands what is right (holy, etc.) because it is right, or (2) What is right (holy) is right because God commands (loves) it.

Suppose that (1) is correct, that is, that God wills what is right because it is right. That would imply that there is a standard of rightness that even God must observe, and that is thus above God in a sense. But how could anything be above God? On the other hand, suppose that (2) is correct, that is, that what is right (holy, etc.) is right because God loves it or proclaims it right. Then, it seems, *anything* that God loves or proclaims as right would be right. It seems to follow that if God loved the torture of innocent children, or proclaimed it to be right on some occasion to murder one's child (see the story Abraham and Isaac in the Hebrew scriptures) then such torture or murder would be right. But how could torturing innocent people be right? But either (1) is correct or (2) is. This dilemma poses a difficulty for anyone who supposes that morality is grounded in the will of God, which is just what many people do believe. It also poses a problem for the belief in a personal God.

 ASK YOURSELF

2.7. Would this dilemma be useful to someone who wanted to prove that ethics does not depend upon belief in God? Explain your answer.

Socrates goes on to argue that even if it is true that all the Gods should approve of a certain action and call it holy (right), that still does not tell us what the essence or nature of holiness is. Here is a parallel to think about: Even if it is true (it is in fact) that any triangle is easier to imagine than any chiliagon (a thousand-sided figure), that fact does not tell us *what* a triangle is, what its essence (definition) is, but only that it has a certain attribute (namely, the attribute of being relatively easy to imagine). Or to take a more Greek example: Even if it is true that all the Gods love ambrosia, that fact does not tell us *what* ambrosia is. Likewise, if all the Gods love what is holy, that does not tell us what holiness is.

[SOCRATES]   Thus you appear to me, Euthyphro, when I ask you what is the essence of holiness, to offer an attribute only, and not the essence—the attribute of being loved by all the gods. But you still refuse to explain to me the nature of holiness. And therefore, if you please, I will ask you not to hide your treasure, but to tell me once more what holiness or piety really is, whether dear to the gods or not (for that is a matter about which we will not quarrel) and what is impiety?

[EUTHYPHRO]   I really do not know, Socrates, how to express what I mean. For somehow or other our arguments, on whatever ground we rest them, seem to turn round and walk away from us.

[SOCRATES]   Your words, Euthyphro, are like the handiwork of my ancestor Daedalus [Daedalus was a sculptor who made such realistic looking sculptures that people said they could get up and walk away.]; and if I were the sayer or propounder of them, you might say that my arguments walk away and will not remain fixed where they are placed because I am a descendant of his. But now, since these notions are your own, you must find some other gibe, for they certainly, as you yourself allow, show an inclination to be on the move.

[EUTHYPHRO]   Nay, Socrates, I shall still say that you are the Daedalus who sets arguments in motion; not I, certainly, but you make them move or go round, for they would never have stirred, as far as I am concerned.

[SOCRATES]   Then I must be a greater than Daedalus: for whereas he only made his own inventions to move, I move those of other people as well. And the beauty of it is, that I would rather not. For I would give the wisdom of Daedalus, and the wealth of Tantalus, to be able to detain them and keep them fixed. But enough of this. As I perceive that you are lazy, I will myself endeavor to show you how you might instruct me in the nature of piety; and I hope that you will not grudge your labor.

Euthyphro here expresses how frustrating a conversation with Socrates could be, for by this time Euthryphro is completely confused and no longer knows what he means or believes. At first he was confident that he could instruct Socrates. Now he has become the pupil. But the most he can learn is the extent of his own ignorance, for the dialogue ends with no satisfactory answer to the question about the definition of holiness anywhere in sight. Socrates has destroyed Euthryphro's pretensions to wisdom, but he has not shown that he himself knows what holiness is. But at least Socrates never claimed to know. So he is wiser than Euthyphro in that respect.

 ASK YOURSELF

2.8. Review the preceding selection, find one example of each of the five characteristics of Socrates' method and style mentioned earlier, and list them.

Meno

Although Socrates is famous for his profession of ignorance, there are certain things that he eventually claims to know, such as these three: virtue is knowledge and vice is ignorance; a good man cannot be harmed; the unexamined life is not worth living. The first of these is a topic for discussion in the following selection from Plato's dialogue *Meno*.

 From PLATO: *Meno*

[SOCRATES]   Now, if there be any sort of good which is distinct from knowledge, virtue may be that good; but if knowledge embraces all good, then we shall be right in thinking that virtue is knowledge?

[MENO]   True.

[SOCRATES]   And virtue makes us good?

[MENO]   Yes.

[SOCRATES]   And if we are good, then we are profitable; for all good things are profitable?

[MENO]   Yes.

[SOCRATES]   Then virtue is profitable?

[MENO]   That is the only inference.

[SOCRATES]   Then now let us see what are the things which severally profit us. Health and strength, and beauty and wealth—these, and the like of these, we call profitable?

[MENO]   True.

[SOCRATES]   And yet these things may also sometimes do us harm: would you not think so?

[MENO]   Yes.

[SOCRATES]   And what is the guiding principle which makes them profitable or the reverse? Are they not profitable when they are rightly used, and hurtful when they are not rightly used?

[MENO]   Certainly.

[SOCRATES]   Next, let us consider the goods of the soul: they are temperance, justice, courage, quickness of apprehension, memory, magnanimity, and the like?

[MENO]   Surely.

[SOCRATES]   And such of these as are not knowledge, but of another sort, are sometimes profitable and sometimes hurtful; as, for example, courage wanting prudence, which is only a sort of confidence? When a man has no sense he is harmed by courage, but when he has sense he is profited?

[MENO]   True.

[SOCRATES]   And the same may be said of temperance and quickness of apprehension; whatever things are learned or done with sense are profitable, but when done without sense they are hurtful?

[MENO]   Very true.

[SOCRATES]   And in general, all that a person attempts or endures, when under the guidance of wisdom, ends in happiness; but when he is under the guidance of folly, in the opposite?

[MENO]   That appears to be true.

[SOCRATES]   If then virtue is a quality of the soul, and is admitted to be profitable, it must be wisdom or prudence, since none of the things of the soul are either profitable or hurtful in themselves, but they are all made profitable or hurtful by the addition of wisdom or of folly; and therefore if virtue is profitable, virtue must be a sort of wisdom or prudence?

[MENO]   I quite agree.

[SOCRATES]   And the other goods, such as wealth and the like, of which we were just now saying that they are sometimes good and sometimes evil, do not they also become profitable or hurtful, accordingly as the soul guides and uses them rightly or wrongly; just as the things of the soul herself are benefited when under the guidance of wisdom and harmed by folly?

[MENO]   True.

[SOCRATES]   And the wise soul guides them rightly, and the foolish soul wrongly.

[MENO]   Yes.

[SOCRATES]   And is not this universally true of human nature? All other things hang upon the soul, and the things of the soul herself hang upon wisdom, if they are to be good; and so wisdom is inferred to be that which profits—and virtue, as we say, is profitable?

[MENO]   Certainly.

[SOCRATES]   And thus wisdom, if they are to be good; and so wisdom is inferred to be that which profits—and virtue, as we say, is profitable?

[MENO]   Certainly.

[SOCRATES]   And thus we arrive at the conclusion that virtue is either wholly or partly wisdom?

 ASK YOURSELF

2.9. How might wealth do a person harm?

2.10. Fill in the blanks in this reconstruction of Socrates' argument:

    a. Virtue is profitable.

    b. Anything that is profitable must be included in or fall under _____.

    c. Therefore, virtue is included in or falls under _____.

2.11. Give one of Socrates' reasons for thinking that premise (b) is true.

The *Apology*

At the age of seventy, Socrates was condemned to death before an Athenian jury. The *Apology* is an account of Socrates' trial that led to his execution. The term "apology" as used here means "defense," rather than an expression of regret. The charges against him were those of atheism and corrupting the youth. At least one of the "youth" his accusers had in mind was a young student and associate of Socrates named Alcibiades. Alcibiades, a general in the Athenian army during the Second Peleponesian War, had a less than favorable reputation. On one occasion he defaced statues of the gods. In the eyes of the Athenians, Socrates was blamed for misguiding Alcibiades.

For political reasons that require explanation, the proceedings at the trial were awkward. Athens ultimately lost the war with Sparta, and for the next few years Athens went through a period of political turmoil. A government of thirty commissioners was set up by Sparta, in cooperation with oligarchic elements in Athens. The Athenians overthrew the thirty after it had executed and banished literally thousands of people. Several of the tyrants were related to Socrates. The Athenian democracy was restored and a general amnesty was granted to all past political activists. Socrates was tried during this period of general amnesty, and, thus, no direct reference could be made to Socrates' association with Alcibiades or to his relatives who were among the Thirty Tyrants.

The official charges brought against Socrates were therefore more general: atheism and corrupting the youth. In Athens criminal trials were initiated by individuals. Socrates' official accuser was a local religious fanatic named Meletus. But Meletus was simply the tool. The real initiator was an admired leader of the restored democracy named Anytus; everyone, including Socrates, was aware of this. Motives of religious fanaticism probably had nothing to do with Anytus's action since in the same year Anytus was helping in the defense of another Athenian on the very same charge of "irreligion." Anytus's main complaint against Socrates was his corrupting the youth and threatening the stability of the democracy. The charge of "irreligion" was added since this was Meletus's area of expertise. In short, Socrates' trial was a charade with unspoken evidence and an invisible accuser. To show his contempt for the proceedings, Socrates conducted the first half of his defense in a flippant manner.

As you read this dialogue by Plato, pay particular attention to the following ideas that are very characteristic of Socrates. First is the idea that honest self-examination is central to a good life. Second is the idea that a good man cannot be harmed. Also keep notes on further examples of the five characteristics mentioned earlier (irony, ignorance, etc.) that show up in this selection from the *Apology*.

 From PLATO: the *Apology*

Socrates I cannot tell how you have felt, O men of Athens, at hearing the speeches of my accusers; but I know that their persuasive words almost made me forget who I was—such was the effect of them; and yet they have hardly spoken a word of truth. But many as their falsehoods were, there was one of them which quite amazed me;—I mean when they told you to be upon your guard, and not to let yourselves be deceived by the force of my eloquence. They ought to have been ashamed of saying this, because they were sure to be detected as soon as I opened my lips and displayed my deficiency. They certainly did appear to be most shameless in saying this, unless by the force of eloquence they mean the force of truth; for then I do indeed admit that I am eloquent. But in how different a way from them!

Well, as I was saying, they have hardly uttered a word, or not more than a word, of truth; but you shall hear from me the whole truth: not, however, delivered after their manner, in a set oration duly ornamented with words and phrases.

 ASK YOURSELF

2.12. Socrates is here distancing himself from certain individuals studied in the last chapter who emphasized oratorical technique rather than truth. Those individuals are known as the _____.

No indeed! but I shall use the words and arguments which occur to me at the moment; for I am certain that this is right, and that at my time of life I ought not to be appearing before you, O men of Athens, in the character of a juvenile orator—let no one expect this of me. And I must beg of you to grant me one favor, which is this— If you hear me using the same words in my defense which I have been in the habit of using, and which most of you may have heard in the agora [marketplace], and at the tables of the money-changers, or anywhere else, I would ask you not to be surprised at this, and not to interrupt me. For I am more than seventy years of age, and this is the first time that I have ever appeared in a court of law, and I am quite a stranger to the ways of the place. Therefore I would have you regard me as if I were really a stranger, whom you would excuse if he spoke in his native tongue, and after the fashion of his country;—that I think is not an unfair request. Never mind the manner, which may or may not be good; but think only of the justice of my cause, and give heed to that: let the judge decide justly and the speaker speak truly.

Two Groups of Accusers

And first, I have to reply to the older charges and to my first accusers, and then I will go to the later ones. For I have had many accusers, who accused me of old, and their false charges have continued during many years; and I am more afraid of them than of Anytus and his associates, who are dangerous, too, in their own way. But far more dangerous are these, who began when you were children, and took possession of your minds with their falsehoods, telling of one Socrates, a wise man, who speculated about the heaven above, and searched into the earth beneath, and made the worse appear the better cause. These are the accusers whom I dread; for they are the circulators of this rumor, and their hearers are too apt to fancy that speculators of this sort do not believe in the gods. And they are many, and their charges against me are of ancient date. They made them in days when you were impressionable—in childhood, or perhaps in youth—and the cause when heard went by default, for there was none to answer. And, hardest of all, their names I do not know and cannot tell; unless in the chance of a comic poet [namely, Aristophanes, who portrayed Socrates as a sophist and speculator on nature in his play *The Clouds*]. But the main body of these slanderers who from envy and malice have wrought upon you—and there are some of them who are convinced themselves, and impart their convictions to others—all these, I say, are most difficult to deal with. For I cannot have them up here, and examine them, and therefore I must simply fight with shadows in my own defense, and examine when there is no one who answers.

I will ask you then to assume with me, as I was saying, that my opponents are of two kinds—one recent, the other ancient; and I hope that you will see the propriety of my answering the latter first, for these accusations you heard long before the others, and much oftener.

 ASK YOURSELF

2.13. The newer accusers include Anytus and Meletus, whose charges we come to later. Briefly describe the accusations of the older type of accusers.

Well, then, I will make my defense, and I will endeavor in the short time which is allowed to do away with this evil opinion of me which you have held for such a long time; and I hope I may succeed, if this be well for you and me, and that my words may find favor with you. But I know that to accomplish this is not easy—I quite see the nature of the task. Let the event be as God wills: in obedience to the law I make my defense.

I will begin at the beginning, and ask what the accusation is which has given rise to this slander of me, and which has encouraged Meletus to proceed against me. What do the slanderers say? They shall be my prosecutors, and I will sum up their words in an affidavit. "Socrates is an evil-doer, and a curious person, who searches into things under the earth and in heaven, and he makes the worse appear the better cause; and he teaches the aforesaid doctrines to others." That is the nature of the accusation, and that is what you have seen yourselves in the comedy of Aristophanes; who has introduced a man whom he calls Socrates, going about and saying that he can walk in the air, and talking a deal of nonsense concerning matters of which I do not pretend to know either much or little—not that I mean to say anything disparaging of anyone who is a student of natural philosophy. I should be very sorry if Meletus could lay that to my charge. But the simple truth is, O Athenians, that I have nothing to do with these studies. Very many of those here present are witnesses to the truth of this, and to them I appeal. Speak then, you who have heard me, and tell your neighbors whether any of you have ever known me to hold forth in few words or in many upon matters of this sort. . . . You hear their answer. And from what they say of this you will be able to judge of the truth of the rest.

 ASK YOURSELF

2.14. The playwright Aristophanes is included among the older accusers. How does Aristophanes misrepresent Socrates?

As little foundation is there for the report that I am a teacher, and take money; that is no more true than the other. Although, if a man is able to teach, I honor him for being paid. There is Gorgias of Leontium, and Prodicus of Ceos, and Hippias of Elis, who go the round of the cities, and are able to persuade the young men to leave their own citizens, by whom they might be taught for nothing, and come to them, whom they not only pay, but are thankful if they may be allowed to pay them. There is actually a Parian philosopher residing in Athens, of whom I have heard; and I came to hear of him in this way:—I met a man who has spent a world of money on the sophists, Callias the son of Hipponicus, and knowing that he had sons, I asked him: "Callias," I said, "if your two sons were foals or calves, there would be no difficulty in finding someone to put over them; we should hire a trainer of horses or a farmer probably who would improve and perfect them in their own proper virtue and excellence; but as they are human beings, whom are you thinking of placing over them? Is there anyone who understands human and political virtue? You must have thought about this as you have sons; is there anyone?" "There is," he said. "Who is he?" said I, "and of what country? and what does he charge?" "Evenus the Parian," he replied; "he is the man, and his charge is five minae." Happy is Evenus, I said to myself, if he really has this wisdom, and teaches at such a modest charge. Had I the same, I should have been very proud and conceited; but the truth is that I have no knowledge of the kind.

 ASK YOURSELF

2.15. Others among the older accusers maintain that Socrates teaches things that corrupt the youth, specifically that weaker arguments can be made to appear the strongest. In short, Socrates is thought to be an undesirable sophist. How does Socrates defend himself against this charge?

In ancient Greece people believed that the gods made themselves known by many means. Poets such as Homer and Hesiod were considered divinely inspired. Alternatively, the gods could make their wishes known at temples through a medium that was called an oracle. At the temple of Apollo near Delphi, the oracle or medium was a prophetess.

The Inspiration for Socrates' Career as a "Gadfly"

I dare say, Athenians, that someone among you will reply, "Why is this, Socrates, and what is the origin of these accusations of you: for there must have been something strange which you have been doing? All this great fame and talk about you would never have arisen if you had been like other men: tell us, then, why this is, as we should be sorry to judge hastily of you." Now I regard this as a fair challenge, and I will endeavor to explain to you the origin of this name of "wise," and of this evil fame. Please to attend then. And although some of you may think I am joking, I declare that I will tell you the entire truth. Men of Athens, this reputation of mine has come of a certain sort of wisdom that I possess. If you ask me what kind of wisdom, I reply, such wisdom as is attainable by man, for to that extent I am inclined to believe that I am wise; whereas the persons of whom I was speaking have a superhuman wisdom, which I may fail to describe, because I have it not myself; and he who says that I have, speaks falsely, and is taking away my character. And here, O men of Athens, I must beg you not to interrupt me, even if I seem to say something extravagant. For the word which I will speak is not mine. I will refer you to a witness who is worthy of credit, and will tell you about my wisdom—whether I have any, and of what sort—and that witness shall be the god of Delphi. You must have known Chaerephon; he was early a friend of mine, and also a friend of yours, for he shared in the exile of the people, and returned with you. Well, Chaerephon, as you know, was very impetuous in all his doings, and he went to Delphi and boldly asked the oracle to tell him whether—as I was saying, I must beg you not to interrupt—he asked the oracle to tell him whether there was anyone wiser than I was, and the Pythian prophetess answered that there was no man wiser. Chaerephon is dead himself, but his brother, who is in court, will confirm the truth of this story.

Why do I mention this? Because I am going to explain to you why I have such an evil name. When I heard the answer, I said to myself, What can the god mean? and what is the interpretation of this riddle? for I know that I have no wisdom, small or great. What can he mean when he says that I am the wisest of men? And yet he is a god and cannot lie; that would be against his nature. After a long consideration, I at last thought of a method of trying the question. I reflected that if I could only find a man wiser than myself, then I might go to the god with a refutation in my hand. I should say to him, "Here is a man who is wiser than I am; but you said that I was the wisest."

 ASK YOURSELF

2.16. Socrates believes that the real reason he is unpopular among his older accusers is because he doesn't think his accusers are as smart as they claim—and he lets them know it. Socrates feels compelled to do this because of something Apollo revealed to his friend Chaerephon at Delphi. What was that?

2.17. What did Socrates do to try to prove that Apollo was wrong?

How Socrates Was Received by the Athenians

Accordingly I went to one who had the reputation of wisdom, and observed to him—his name I need not mention; he was a politician whom I selected for examination—and the result was as follows: When I began to talk with him, I could not help thinking that he was not really wise, although he was thought wise by many, and wiser still by himself; and I went and tried to explain to him that he thought himself wise, but was not really wise; and the consequence was that he hated me, and his enmity was shared by several who were present and heard me. So I left him, saying to myself, as I went away: Well, although I do not suppose that either of us knows anything really beautiful and good, I am better off than he is—for he knows nothing, and thinks that he knows. I neither know nor think that I know. In this latter particular, then, I seem to have slightly the advantage of him. Then I went to another, who had still higher philosophical pretensions, and my conclusion was exactly the same. I made another enemy of him, and of many others besides him.

ASK YOURSELF

2.18. What problem did Socrates find with the wisdom of the politicians?

After this I went to one man after another, being not unconscious of the enmity which I provoked, and I lamented and feared this: but necessity was laid upon me—the word of God, I thought, ought to be considered first. And I said to myself, Go I must to all who appear to know, and find out the meaning of the oracle. And I swear to you, Athenians, by the dog I swear!—for I must tell you the truth—the result of my mission was just this: I found that the men most in repute were all but the most foolish; and that some inferior men were really wiser and better. I will tell you the tale of my wanderings and of the "Herculean" labors, as I may call them, which I endured only to find at last the oracle irrefutable. When I left the politicians, I went to the poets; tragic, dithyrambic, and all sorts. And there, I said to myself, you will be detected; now you will find out that you are more ignorant than they are. Accordingly, I took them some of the most elaborate passages in their own writings, and asked what was the meaning of them—thinking that they would teach me something. Will you believe me? I am almost ashamed to speak of this, but still I must say that there is hardly a person present who would not have talked better about their poetry than they did themselves. That showed me in an instant that not by wisdom do poets write poetry, but by a sort of genius and inspiration; they are like diviners or soothsayers who also say many fine things, but do not understand the meaning of them. And the poets appeared to me to be much in the same case; and I further observed that upon the strength of their poetry they believed themselves to be the wisest of men in other things in which they were not wise. So I departed, conceiving myself to be superior to them for the same reason that I was superior to the politicians.

ASK YOURSELF

2.19. Why were the poets not as wise as people believed?

At last I went to the artisans, for I was conscious that I knew nothing at all, as I may say, and I was sure that they knew many fine things; and in this I was not mistaken, for they did know many things of which I was ignorant, and in this they certainly were wiser than I was. But I observed that even the good artisans fell into the same error as the poets; because they were good workmen they thought that they also knew all sorts of high matters, and this defect in them overshadowed their wisdom—therefore I asked myself on behalf of the oracle, whether I would like to be as I was, neither having their knowledge nor their ignorance, or like them in both; and I made answer to myself and the oracle that I was better off as I was.

ASK YOURSELF

2.20. What fault did Socrates find with the wisdom of the craftsmen?

This investigation has led to my having many enemies of the worst and most dangerous kind, and has given occasion also to many calumnies, and I am called wise, for my hearers always imagine that I myself possess the wisdom which I find wanting in others: but the truth is, O men of Athens, that God only is wise; and in this oracle he means to say that the wisdom of men is little or nothing; he is not speaking of Socrates, he is only using my name as an illustration, as if he said, He, O men, is the wisest, who, like Socrates, knows that his wisdom is in truth worth nothing. And so I go my way, obedient to the god, and make inquisition into the wisdom of anyone, whether citizen or stranger, who appears to be wise; and if he is not wise, then in vindication of the oracle I show him that he is not wise; and this occupation quite absorbs me, and I have no time to give either to any public matter of interest or to any concern of my own, but I am in utter poverty by reason of my devotion to the god.

 ASK YOURSELF

2.21. In what way is Socrates the wisest of all men?

There is another thing:—young men of the richer classes, who have not much to do, come about me of their own accord; they like to hear the pretenders examined, and they often imitate me, and examine others themselves; there are plenty of persons, as they soon enough discover, who think that they know something, but really know little or nothing: and then those who are examined by them instead of being angry with themselves are angry with me: This confounded Socrates, they say; this villainous misleader of youth!—and then if somebody asks them, Why, what evil does he practice or teach? they do not know, and cannot tell; but in order that they may not appear to be at a loss, they repeat the ready-made charges which are used against all philosophers about teaching things up in the clouds and under the earth, and having no gods, and making the worse appear the better cause; for they do not like to confess that their pretense of knowledge has been detected—which is the truth: and as they are numerous and ambitious and energetic, and are all in battle array and have persuasive tongues, they have filled your ears with their loud and inveterate calumnies. And this is the reason why my three accusers, Meletus and Anytus and Lycon, have set upon me; Meletus, who has a quarrel with me on behalf of the poets; Anytus, on behalf of the craftsmen; Lycon, on behalf of the rhetoricians: and as I said at the beginning, I cannot expect to get rid of this mass of calumny all in a moment. And this, O men of Athens, is the truth and the whole truth; I have concealed nothing, I have dissembled nothing. And yet I know that this plainness of speech makes them hate me, and what is their hatred but a proof that I am speaking the truth?—this is the occasion and reason of their slander of me, as you will find out either in this or in any future inquiry.

ASK YOURSELF

2.22. How did young, upper-class Athenian men contribute to Socrates unpopularity?

Socrates Refutes the New Accusers. Socrates turns next to his present accusers. The charges Meletus brings against him are those of corrupting the youth and atheism. Socrates turns the tables and cross-examines Meletus, and here we have two classic examples of Socratic elenchus. As noted earlier, elenchus is the technique of questioning and answering, the purpose of which is to point out that the views of one's opponent lead to ridiculous or contradictory conclusions.

I have said enough in my defense against the first class of my accusers; I turn to the second class, who are headed by Meletus, that good and patriotic man, as he calls himself. And now I will try to defend myself against them: these new accusers must also have their affidavit read. What do they say? Something of this sort:— That Socrates is a doer of evil, and corrupter of the youth, and he does not believe in the gods of the state, and has other new divinities of his own. That is the sort of charge; and now let us examine the particular counts. He says that I am a doer of evil, who corrupt the youth; but I say, O men of Athens, that Meletus is a doer of evil, and the evil is that he makes a joke of a serious matter, and is too ready at bringing other men to trial from a pretended zeal and interest about matters in which he really never had the smallest interest. And the truth of this I will endeavor to prove.

Come hither, Meletus, and let me ask a question of you. You think a great deal about the improvement of youth?

MELETUS   Yes, I do.

SOCRATES   Tell the judges, then, who is their improver; for you must know, as you have taken the pains to discover their corrupter, and are citing and accusing me before them. Speak, then, and tell the judges who their improver is. Observe, Meletus, that you are silent, and have nothing to say. But is not this rather disgraceful, and a very considerable proof of what I was saying, that you have no interest in the matter? Speak up, friend, and tell us who their improver is.

MELETUS   The laws.

SOCRATES   But that, my good sir, is not my meaning. I want to know who the person is, who, in the first place, knows the laws.

MELETUS   The judges, Socrates, who are present in court.

SOCRATES   What do you mean to say, Meletus, that they are able to instruct and improve youth?

MELETUS   Certainly they are.

SOCRATES   What, all of them, or some only and not others?

MELETUS   All of them.

SOCRATES   By the goddess Here, that is good news! There are plenty of improvers, then. And what do you say of the audience,—do they improve them?

MELETUS   Yes, they do.

SOCRATES   And the senators?

MELETUS   Yes, the senators improve them.

SOCRATES   But perhaps the members of the citizen assembly corrupt them?—or do they too improve them?

MELETUS   They improve them.

SOCRATES   Then every Athenian improves and elevates them; all with the exception of myself; and I alone am their corrupter? Is that what you affirm?

MELETUS   That is what I stoutly affirm.

SOCRATES   I am very unfortunate if that is true. But suppose I ask you a question: Would you say that this also holds true in the case of horses? Does one man do them harm and all the world good? Is not the exact opposite of this true? One man is able to do them good, or at least not many;—the trainer of horses, that is to say, does them good, and others who have to do with them rather injure them? Is not that true, Meletus, of horses, or any other animals? Whether you and Anytus say yes or no, that is no matter. Happy indeed would be the condition of youth if they had one corrupter only, and all the rest of the world were their improvers. And you, Meletus, have sufficiently shown that you never had a thought about the young: your carelessness is seen in your not caring about matters spoken of in this very indictment.

 ASK YOURSELF

2.23. In the first exchange between Socrates and Meletus, what view of Meletus's does Socrates show to be ridiculous?

SOCRATES   And now, Meletus, I must ask you another question: Which is better, to live among bad citizens, or among good ones? Answer, friend, I say; for that is a question which may be easily answered. Do not the good do their neighbors good, and the bad do them evil?

MELETUS   Certainly.

SOCRATES   And is there anyone who would rather be injured than benefited by those who live with him? Answer, my good friend; the law requires you to answer— does anyone like to be injured?

MELETUS   Certainly not.

SOCRATES   And when you accuse me of corrupting and deteriorating the youth, do you allege that I corrupt them intentionally or unintentionally?

MELETUS   Intentionally, I say.

SOCRATES   But you have just admitted that the good do their neighbors good, and the evil do them evil. Now is that a truth which your superior wisdom has recognized thus early in life, and am I, at my age, in such darkness and ignorance as not to know that if a man with whom I have to live is corrupted by me, I am very likely to be harmed by him, and yet I corrupt him, and intentionally, too;—that is what you are saying, and of that you will never persuade me or any other human being. But either I do not corrupt them, or I corrupt them unintentionally, so that on either view of the case you lie. If my offense is unintentional, the law has no cognizance of unintentional offenses: you ought to have taken me privately, and warned and admonished me; for if I had been better advised, I should have left off doing what I only did unintentionally—no doubt I should; whereas you hated to converse with me or teach me, but you indicted me in this court, which is a place not of instruction, but of punishment.

 ASK YOURSELF

2.24. What view of Meletus's is shown to be false in the second exchange?

SOCRATES   I have shown, Athenians, as I was saying, that Meletus has no care at all, great or small, about the matter. But still I should like to know, Meletus, in what I am affirmed to corrupt the young. I suppose you mean, as I infer from your indictment, that I teach them not to acknowledge the gods which the state acknowledges, but some other new divinities or spiritual agencies in their stead. These are the lessons which corrupt the youth, as you say.

MELETUS   Yes, that I say emphatically.

SOCRATES   Then, by the gods, Meletus, of whom we are speaking, tell me and the court, in somewhat plainer terms, what you mean! for I do not as yet understand whether you affirm that I teach others to acknowledge some gods, and therefore do believe in gods and am not an entire atheist—this you do not lay to my charge; but only that they are not the same gods which the city recognizes—the charge is that they are different gods. Or, do you mean to say that I am an atheist simply, and a teacher of atheism?

MELETUS   I mean the latter—that you are a complete atheist.

SOCRATES   That is an extraordinary statement, Meletus. Why do you say that? Do you mean that I do not believe in the godhead of the sun or moon, which is the common creed of all men?

MELETUS   I assure you, judges, that he does not believe in them; for he says that the sun is stone, and the moon earth.

SOCRATES   Friend Meletus, you think that you are accusing Anaxagoras; and you have but a bad opinion of the judges, if you fancy them ignorant to such a degree as not to know that those doctrines are found in the books of Anaxagoras the Clazomenian, who is full of them. And these are the doctrines which the youth are said to learn of Socrates, when there are not infrequently exhibitions of them at the theater (price of admission one drachma at the most); and they might cheaply purchase them, and laugh at Socrates if he pretends to father such eccentricities. And so, Meletus, you really think that I do not believe in any god?

MELETUS   I swear by Zeus that you believe absolutely in none at all.

SOCRATES   You are a liar, Meletus, not believed even by yourself. For I cannot help thinking, O men of Athens, that Meletus is reckless and impudent, and that he has written this indictment in a spirit of mere wantonness and youthful bravado. Has he not compounded a riddle, thinking to try me? He said to himself:—I shall see whether this wise Socrates will discover my ingenious contradiction, or whether I shall be able to deceive him and the rest of them. For he certainly does appear to me to contradict himself in the indictment as much as if he said that Socrates is guilty of not believing in the gods, and yet of believing in them—but this surely is a piece of fun.

I should like you, O men of Athens, to join me in examining what I conceive to be his inconsistency; and do you, Meletus, answer. And I must remind you that you are not to interrupt me if I speak in my accustomed manner.

Did ever man, Meletus, believe in the existence of human things, and not of human beings? . . . I wish, men of Athens, that he would answer, and not be always trying to get up an interruption. Did ever any man believe in horsemanship, and not in horses? or in flute-playing, and not in flute-players? No, my friend; I will answer to you and to the court, as you refuse to answer for yourself. There is no man who ever did. But now please to answer the next question: Can a man believe in spiritual and divine agencies, and not in spirits or demigods?

MELETUS   He cannot.

SOCRATES   I am glad that I have extracted that answer, by the assistance of the court; nevertheless you swear in the indictment that I teach and believe in divine or spiritual agencies (new or old, no matter for that); at any rate, I believe in spiritual agencies, as you say and swear in the affidavit; but if I believe in divine beings, I must believe in spirits or demigods;—is not that true? Yes, that is true, for I may assume that your silence gives assent to that. Now what are spirits or demigods? are they not either gods or the sons of gods? Is that true?

MELETUS   Yes, that is true.

SOCRATES   But this is just the ingenious riddle of which I was speaking: the demigods or spirits are gods, and you say first that I don't believe in gods, and then again that I do believe in gods; that is, if I believe in demigods. For if the demigods are the illegitimate sons of gods, whether by the Nymphs or by any other mothers, as is thought, that, as all men will allow, necessarily implies the existence of their parents. You might as well affirm the existence of mules, and deny that of horses and asses. Such nonsense, Meletus, could only have been intended by you as a trial of me. You have put this into the indictment because you had nothing real of which to accuse me. But no one who has a particle of understanding will ever be convinced by you that the same man can believe in divine and superhuman things, and yet not believe that there are gods and demigods and heroes.

 ASK YOURSELF

2.25. How does Socrates show that he is not an atheist?

Socrates' Final Defense.   After dispensing with Meletus's invented charges, Socrates begins a serious defense of his life.

I have said enough in answer to the charge of Meletus; any elaborate defense is unnecessary; but as I was saying before, I certainly have many enemies, and this is what will be my destruction if I am destroyed; of that I am certain;—not Meletus, nor yet Anytus, but the envy and detraction of the world, which has been the death of many good men, and will probably be the death of many more; there is no danger of my being the last of them.

Someone will say: And are you not ashamed, Socrates, of a course of life which is likely to bring you to an untimely end? To him I may fairly answer: There you are mistaken: a man who is good for anything ought not to calculate the chance of living or dying; he ought only to consider whether in doing anything he is doing right or wrong—acting the part of a good man or of a bad. Whereas, according to your view, the heroes who fell at Troy were not good for much, and the son of Thetis above all, who altogether despised danger in comparison with disgrace; and when his goddess mother said to him, in his eagerness to slay Hector, that if he avenged his companion Patroclus, and slew Hector, he would die himself—"Fate," as she said, "waits upon you next after Hector"; he, hearing this, utterly despised danger and death, and instead of fearing them, feared rather to live in dishonor, and not to avenge his friend. "Let me die next," he replies, "and be avenged of my enemy, rather than abide here by the beaked ships, a scorn and a burden of the earth." Had Achilles any thought of death and danger? For wherever a man's place is, whether the place which he has chosen or that in which he has been placed by a commander, there he ought to remain in the hour of danger; he should not think of death or of anything, but of disgrace. And this, O men of Athens, is a true saying.

 ASK YOURSELF

2.26. What is Socrates' response to those who ask if he is ashamed of living his life as he did, considering that he is on trial for his life?

Strange, indeed, would be my conduct, O men of Athens, if I who, when I was ordered by the generals whom you chose to command me at Potidaea and Amphipolis and Delium, remained where they placed me, like any other man, facing death; if, I say, now, when, as I conceive and imagine, God orders me to fulfill the philosopher's mission of searching into myself and other men, I were to desert my post through fear of death, or any other fear; that would indeed be strange, and I might justly be arraigned in court for denying the existence of the gods, if I disobeyed the oracle because I was afraid of death: then I should be fancying that I was wise when I was not wise. For this fear of death is indeed the pretense of wisdom, and not real wisdom, being the appearance of knowing the unknown; since no one knows whether death, which they in their fear apprehend to be the greatest evil, may not be the greatest good. Is there not here conceit of knowledge, which is a disgraceful sort of ignorance? And this is the point in which, as I think, I am superior to men in general, and in which I might perhaps fancy myself wiser than other men,—that whereas I know but little of the world below, I do not suppose that I know: but I do know that injustice and disobedience to a better, whether God or man, is evil and dishonorable, and I will never fear or avoid a possible good rather than a certain evil. And therefore if you let me go now, and reject the counsels of Anytus, who said that if I were not put to death I ought not to have been prosecuted, and that if I escape now, your sons will all be utterly ruined by listening to my words—if you say to me, Socrates, this time we will not mind Anytus, and will let you off, but upon one condition, that you are to inquire and speculate in this way no more, and that if you are caught doing this again you shall die;—if this was the condition on which you let me go, I should reply: Men of Athens, I honor and love you; but I shall obey God rather than you, and while I have life and strength I shall never cease from the practice and teaching of philosophy, exhorting anyone whom I meet after my manner, and convincing him, saying: O my friend, why do you who are a citizen of the great and mighty and wise city of Athens, care so much about laying up the greatest amount of money and honor and reputation, and so little about wisdom and truth and the greatest improvement of the soul, which you never regard or heed at all? Are you not ashamed of this? And if the person with whom I am arguing says: Yes, but I do care; I do not depart or let him go at once; I interrogate and examine and cross-examine him, and if I think that he has no virtue, but only says that he has, I reproach him with undervaluing the greater, and overvaluing the less. And this I should say to everyone whom I meet, young and old, citizen and alien, but especially to the citizens, inasmuch as they are my brethren. For this is the command of God, as I would have you know; and I believe that to this day no greater good has ever happened in the state than my service to the God. For I do nothing but go about persuading you all, old and young alike, not to take thought for your persons and your properties, but first and chiefly to care about the greatest improvement of the soul. I tell you that virtue is not given by money, but that from virtue come money and every other good of man, public as well as private. This is my teaching, and if this is the doctrine which corrupts the youth, my influence is ruinous indeed. But if anyone says that this is not my teaching, he is speaking an untruth. Wherefore, O men of Athens, I say to you, do as Anytus bids or not as Anytus bids, and either acquit me or not; but whatever you do, know that I shall never alter my ways, not even if I have to die many times.

 ASK YOURSELF

2.27. Supposing that the jury would let him off if he promised to remain silent in the future, why does Socrates say he would reject this offer?

What Is and Is Not Truly Harmful and Truly Fearful

Men of Athens, do not interrupt, but hear me; there was an agreement between us that you should hear me out. And I think that what I am going to say will do you good: for I have something more to say, at which you may be inclined to cry out; but I beg that you will not do this. I would have you know that, if you kill such a one as I am, you will injure yourselves more than you will injure me. Meletus and Anytus will not injure me: they cannot; for it is not in the nature of things that a bad man should injure a better than himself. I do not deny that he may, perhaps, kill him, or drive him into exile, or deprive him of civil rights; and he may imagine, and others may imagine, that he is doing him a great injury: but in that I do not agree with him; for the evil of doing as Anytus is doing—of unjustly taking away another man's life— is greater far.

 ASK YOURSELF

2.28. What does Socrates think constitutes real injury?

Socrates as a Valuable Gadfly

And now, Athenians, I am not going to argue for my own sake, as you may think, but for yours, that you may not sin against the God, or lightly reject his boon by condemning me. For if you kill me you will not easily find another like me, who, if I may use such a ludicrous figure of speech, am a sort of gadfly, given to the state by the God; and the state is like a great and noble steed who is tardy in his motions owing to his very size, and requires to be stirred into life. I am that gadfly which God has given the state and all day long and in all places am always fastening upon you, arousing and persuading and reproaching you. And as you will not easily find another like me, I would advise you to spare me. I dare say that you may feel irritated at being suddenly awakened when you are caught napping; and you may think that if you were to strike me dead, as Anytus advises, which you easily might, then you would sleep on for the remainder of your lives, unless God in his care of you gives you another gadfly. And that I am given to you by God is proved by this:—that if I had been like other men, I should not have neglected all my own concerns, or patiently seen the neglect of them during all these years, and have been doing yours, coming to you individually, like a father or elder brother, exhorting you to regard virtue; this I say, would not be like human nature. And had I gained anything, or if my exhortations had been paid, there would have been some sense in that: but now, as you will perceive, not even the impudence of my accusers dares to say that I have ever exacted or sought pay of anyone; they have no witness of that. And I have a witness of the truth of what I say; my poverty is a sufficient witness.

 ASK YOURSELF

2.29. A "gadfly" is a person who acts as a provocative stimulus. Since Socrates considers himself a gadfly to the state, why does he advise his jury to spare him?

Someone may wonder why I go about in private, giving advice and busying myself with the concerns of others, but do not venture to come forward in public and advise the state. I will tell you the reason of this. You have often heard me speak of an oracle or sign which comes to me, and is the divinity which Meletus ridicules in the indictment. This sign I have had ever since I was a child. The sign is a voice which comes to me and always forbids me to do something which I am going to do, but never commands me to do anything, and this is what stands in the way of my being a politician. And rightly, as I think. For I am certain, O men of Athens, that if I had engaged in politics, I should have perished long ago and done no good either to you or to myself. And don't be offended at my telling you the truth: for the truth is that no man who goes to war with you or any other multitude, honestly struggling against the commission of unrighteousness and wrong in the state, will save his life; he who will really fight for the right, if he would live even for a little while, must have a private station and not a public one.

I can give you as proofs of this, not words only, but deeds, which you value more than words. Let me tell you a passage of my own life, which will prove to you that I should never have yielded to injustice from any fear of death, and that if I had not yielded I should have died at once. I will tell you a story—tasteless, perhaps, and commonplace, but nevertheless true. The only office of state which I ever held, O men of Athens, was that of senator; the tribe Antiochis, which is my tribe, had the presidency at the trial of the generals who had not taken up the bodies of the slain after the battle of Arginusae; and you proposed to try them all together, which was illegal, as you all thought afterwards; but at the time I was the only one of the Prytanes who was opposed to the illegality, and I gave my vote against you; and when the orators threatened to impeach and arrest me, and have me taken away, and you called and shouted, I made up my mind that I would run the risk, having law and justice with me, rather than take part in your injustice because I feared imprisonment and death. This happened in the days of the democracy. But when the oligarchy of the Thirty was in power, they sent for me and four others into the rotunda, and bade us bring Leon the Salaminian from Salamis, as they wanted to execute him. This was a specimen of the sort of commands which they were always giving with the view of implicating as many as possible in their crimes; and then I showed, not in words only, but in deed, that, if I may be allowed to use such an expression, I cared not a straw for death, and that my only fear was the fear of doing an unrighteous or unholy thing. For the strong arm of that oppressive power did not frighten me into doing wrong; and when we came out of the rotunda the other four went to Salamis and fetched Leon, but I went quietly home. For which I might have lost my life, had not the power of the Thirty shortly afterwards come to an end. And to this many will witness.

Now do you really imagine that I could have survived all these years, if I had led a public life, supposing that like a good man I had always supported the right and had made justice, as I ought, the first thing? No, indeed, men of Athens, neither I nor any other. But I have been always the same in all my actions, public as well as private, and never have I yielded any base compliance to those who are slanderously termed my disciples or to any other. For the truth is that I have no regular disciples: but if anyone likes to come and hear me while I am pursuing my mission, whether he be young or old, he may freely come. Nor do I converse with those who pay only, and not with those who do not pay; but anyone, whether he be rich or poor, may ask and answer me and listen to my words; and whether he turns out to be a bad man or a good one, that cannot be justly laid to my charge, as I never taught him anything. And if anyone says that he has ever learned or heard anything from me in private which all the world has not heard, I should like you to know that he is speaking an untruth.

But I shall be asked, Why do people delight in continually conversing with you? I have told you already, Athenians, the whole truth about this: they like to hear the cross-examination of the pretenders to wisdom; there is amusement in this. And this is a duty which the God has imposed upon me, as I am assured by oracles, visions, and in every sort of way in which the will of divine power was ever signified to anyone. This is true, O Athenians; or, if not true, would be soon refuted. For if I am really corrupting the youth, and have corrupted some of them already, those of them who have grown up and have become sensible that I gave them bad advice in the days of their youth should come forward as accusers and take their revenge; and if they do not like to come themselves, some of their relatives, fathers, brothers, or other kinsmen, should say what evil their families suffered at my hands. Now is their time. Many of them I see in the court. There is Crito, who is of the same age and of the same deme with myself; and there is Critobulus his son, whom I also see. Then again there is Lysanias of Sphettus, who is the father of Aeschines—he is present; and also there is Antiphon of Cephisus, who is the father of Epignes; and there are the brothers of several who have associated with me. There is Nicostratus the son of Theosdotides, and the brother of Theodotus (now Theodotus himself is dead, and therefore he, at any rate, will not seek to stop him); and there is Paralus the son of Demodocus, who had a brother Theages; and Adeimantus the son of Ariston, whose brother Plato is present; and Aeantodorus, who is the brother of Apollodorus, whom I also see. I might mention a great many others, any of whom Meletus should have produced as witnesses in the course of his speech; and let him still produce them, if he has forgotten—I will make way for him. And let him say, if he has any testimony of the sort which he can produce. Nay, Athenians, the very opposite is the truth. For all these are ready to witness on behalf of the corrupter, of the destroyer of their kindred, as Meletus and Anytus call me; not the corrupted youth only—there might have been a motive for that—but their uncorrupted elder relatives. Why should they too support me with their testimony? Why, indeed, except for the sake of truth and justice, and because they know that I am speaking the truth, and that Meletus is lying.

 ASK YOURSELF

2.30. Considering that he was so concerned about the affairs of others, what reason does Socrates give the jury for why he never took a public office?

Well, Athenians, this and the like of this is nearly all the defense which I have to offer. Yet a word more. Perhaps there may be someone who is offended at me, when he calls to mind how he himself, on a similar or even a less serious occasion, had recourse to prayers and supplications with many tears, and how he produced his children in court, which was a moving spectacle, together with a posse of his relations and friends; whereas I, who am probably in danger of my life, will do none of these things. Perhaps this may come into his mind, and he may be set against me, and vote in anger because he is displeased at this. Now if there be such a person among you, which I am far from affirming, I may fairly reply to him: My friend, I am a man, and like other men, a creature of flesh and blood, and not of wood or stone, as Homer says; and I have a family, yes, and sons. O Athenians, three in number, one of whom is growing up, and the two others are still young; and yet I will not bring any of them hither in order to petition you for an acquittal. And why not? Not from any self-will or disregard of you. Whether I am or am not afraid of death is another question, of which I will not now speak. But my reason simply is that I feel such conduct to be discreditable to myself, and you, and the whole state. One who has reached my years, and who has a name for wisdom, whether deserved or not, ought not to debase himself. At any rate, the world has decided that Socrates is in some way superior to others. And if those among you who are said to be superior in wisdom and courage, and any other virtue, demean themselves in this way, how shameful is their conduct! I have seen men of reputation, when they have been condemned, behaving in the strangest manner: they seemed to fancy that they were going to suffer something dreadful if they died, and that they could be immortal if you only allowed them to live; and I think that they were a dishonor to the state, and that any stranger coming in would say of them that the most eminent men of Athens, to whom the Athenians themselves give honor and command, are no better than we. And I say that these things ought not to be done by those of us who are of reputation; and if they are done, you ought not to permit them; you ought rather to show that you are more inclined to condemn, not the man who is quiet, but the man who gets up a doleful scene, and makes the city ridiculous.

But, setting aside the question of dishonor, there seems to be something wrong in petitioning a judge, and thus procuring an acquittal instead of informing and convincing him. For his duty is, not to make a present of justice, but to give judgment; and he has sworn that he will judge according to the laws, and not according to his own good pleasure; and neither he nor we should get into the habit of perjuring ourselves—there can be no piety in that. Do not then require me to do what I consider dishonorable and impious and wrong, especially now, when I am being tried for impiety on the indictment of Meletus. For if, O men of Athens, by force of persuasion and entreaty, I could overpower your oaths, then I should be teaching you to believe that there are no gods, and convict myself, in my own defense, of not believing in them. But that is not the case; for I do believe that there are gods, and in a far higher sense than that in which any of my accusers believe in them. And to you and to God I commit my cause, to be determined by you as is best for you and me.

 ASK YOURSELF

2.31. Socrates finished his defense, but refused to appeal to pity from the judges by crying or bringing in his children (as was usually done in Athenian courts). What does he believe is wrong with asking a favor of the judges by appealing to pity?

By a slim margin, the jury of 501 reached a verdict of guilty. It was customary in Athenian courts for the accused to recommend an alternative punishment once a guilty verdict had been reached.

There are many reasons why I am not grieved, O men of Athens, at the vote of condemnation. I expected it, and am only surprised that the votes are so nearly equal; for

I had thought that the majority against me would have been far larger; but now, had thirty votes gone over to the other side, I should have been acquitted. And I may say that I have escaped Meletus. And I may say more; for without the assistance of Anytus and Lycon, he would not have had a fifth part of the votes, as the law requires, in which case he would have incurred a fine of a thousand drachmae, as is evident.

And so he proposes death as the penalty. And what shall I propose on my part, O men of Athens? Clearly that which is my due. And what is that which I ought to pay or to receive? What shall be done to the man who has never had the wit to be idle during his whole life; but has been careless of what the many care about—wealth, and family interests, and military offices, and speaking in the assembly, and magistracies, and plots, and parties. Reflecting that I was really too honest a man to follow in this way and live, I did not go where I could do no good to you or to myself; but where I could do the greatest good privately to everyone of you, thither I went, and sought to persuade every man among you that he must look to himself, and seek virtue and wisdom before he looks to his private interests, and look to the state before he looks to the interests of the state; and that this should be the order which he observes in all his actions. What shall be done to such a one? Doubtless some good thing, O men of Athens, if he has his reward; and the good should be of a kind suitable to him. What would be a reward suitable to a poor man who is your benefactor, who desires leisure that he may instruct you? There can be no more fitting reward than maintenance in the Prytaneum, O men of Athens, a reward which he deserves far more than the citizen who has won the prize at Olympia in the horse or chariot race, whether the chariots were drawn by two horses or by many. For I am in want, and he has enough; and he only gives you the appearance of happiness, and I give you the reality. And if I am to estimate the penalty justly, I say that maintenance in the Prytaneum is the just return.

 ASK YOURSELF

2.32. Why did Socrates think he deserved a reward instead of a punishment?

Perhaps you may think that I am braving you in saying this, as in what I said before about the tears and prayers. But that is not the case. I speak rather because I am convinced that I never intentionally wronged anyone, although I cannot convince you of that—for we have had a short conversation only; but if there were a law at Athens, such as there is in other cities, that a capital cause should not be decided in one day, then I believe that I should have convinced you; but now the time is too short. I cannot in a moment refute great slanders; and, as I am convinced that I never wronged another, I will assuredly not wrong myself. I will not say of myself that I deserve any evil, or propose any penalty. Why should I? Because I am afraid of the penalty of death which Meletus proposes? When I do not know whether death is a good or an evil, why should I propose a penalty which would certainly be an evil? Shall I say imprisonment? And why should I live in prison, and be the slave of the magistrates of the year—of the Eleven? Or shall the penalty be a fine, and imprisonment until the fine is paid? There is the same objection. I should have to lie in prison, for money I have none, and I cannot pay. And if I say exile (and this may possibly be the penalty which you will affix), I must indeed be blinded by the love of life if I were to consider that when you, who are my own citizens, cannot endure my discourses and words, and have found them so grievous and odious that you would gladly have done with them, others are likely to endure me. No, indeed, men of Athens, that is not very likely. And what a life should I lead, at my age, wandering from city to city, living in ever-changing exile, and always being driven out! For I am quite sure that into whatever place I go, as here so also there, the young men will come to me; and if I drive them away, their elders will drive me out at their desire: and if I let them come, their fathers and friends will drive me out for their sakes.

 ASK YOURSELF

2.33. Why didn't Socrates recommend his imprisonment until a fine could be paid?

Someone will say: Yes, Socrates, but cannot you hold your tongue, and then you may go into a foreign city, and no one will interfere with you? Now I have great difficulty in making you understand my answer to this. For if I tell you that this would be a disobedience to a divine command, and therefore that I cannot hold my tongue, you will not believe that I am serious; and if I say again that the greatest good of man is daily to converse about virtue, and all that concerning which you hear me examining myself and others, and that the life which is unexamined is not worth living—that you are still less likely to believe.

Socrates is famous for the claim that the unexamined life is not worth living. But what kind of examination does he have in mind? In the last century or so a great deal of self-examination has gone on in the offices of psychotherapists and counselors of various sorts. People discuss everything from the way they were treated by their parents to how they *really* feel about the boss. The stress has often been on things that have happened to *me*, on how *I* feel.

 ASK YOURSELF

2.34. Is this the kind of self-examination Socrates has in mind? Justify your answer by refererring to statements in the preceding paragraph.

And yet what I say is true, although a thing of which it is hard for me to persuade you. Moreover, I am not accustomed to think that I deserve any punishment. Had I money I might have proposed to give you what I had, and have been none the worse. But you see that I have none, and can only ask you to proportion the fine to my means. However, I think that I could afford a minae, and therefore I propose that penalty; Plato, Crito, Critobulus, and Apollodorus, my friends here, bid me say thirty minae, and they will be the sureties. Well then, say thirty minae, let that be the penalty; for that they will be ample security to you.

ASK YOURSELF

2.35. Why didn't Socrates request to be exiled to a foreign city?

Socrates did offer to pay a fine with money donated to him by his followers. The amount, which was equivalent to a small dowry, might have been a few thousand dollars by today's standards. But the jury turned the offer down, condemning Socrates to death.

Not much time will be gained, O Athenians, in return for the evil name which you will get from the detractors of the city, who will say that you killed Socrates, a wise man; for they will call me wise even although I am not wise when they want to reproach you. If you had waited a little while, your desire would have been fulfilled in the course of nature. For I am far advanced in years, as you may perceive, and not far from death. I am speaking now only to those of you who have condemned me to death. And I have another thing to say to them: You think that I was convicted through deficiency of words—I mean, that if I had thought fit to leave nothing undone, nothing unsaid, I might have gained an acquittal. Not so; the deficiency which led to my conviction was not of words—certainly not. But I had not the boldness or impudence or inclination to address you as you would have liked me to address you, weeping and wailing and lamenting, and saying and doing many things which you have been accustomed to hear from others, and which, as I say, are unworthy of me. But I thought that I ought not to do anything common or mean in the hour of danger: nor do I now repent of the manner of my defense, and I would rather die having spoken after my manner, than speak in your manner and live. For neither in war nor yet at law ought any man to use every way of escaping death. For often in battle there is no doubt that if a man will throw away his arms, and fall on his knees before his pursuers, he may escape death; and in other dangers there are other ways of escaping death, if a man is willing to say and do anything. The difficulty, my friends, is not in avoiding death, but in avoiding unrighteousness; for that runs faster than death. I am old and move slowly, and the slower runner has overtaken me, and my accusers are keen and quick, and the faster runner, who is unrighteousness, has overtaken them. And now I depart hence condemned by you to suffer the penalty of death, and they, too, go their ways condemned by the truth to suffer the penalty of villainy and wrong; and I must abide by my award—let them abide by theirs. I suppose that these things may be regarded as fated,—and I think that they are well.

And now, O men who have condemned me, I would gladly prophesy to you; for I am about to die, and that is the hour in which men are gifted with prophetic power. And I prophesy to you who are my murderers, that immediately after my death punishment far heavier than you have inflicted on me will surely await you. Me you have killed because you wanted to escape the accuser, and not to give an account of your lives. But that will not be as you suppose: far otherwise. For I say that there will be more accusers of you than there are now; accusers whom hitherto I have restrained: and as they are younger they will be more severe with you, and you will be more offended at them. For if you think that by killing men you can avoid the accuser censuring your lives, you are mistaken; that is not a way of escape which is either possible or honorable; the easiest and noblest way is not to be crushing others, but to be improving yourselves. This is the prophecy which I utter before my departure, to the judges who have condemned me.

 ASK YOURSELF

2.36. What was the prophecy Socrates pronounced against those who voted for his condemnation?

Socrates continues by consoling his friends. A famous myth about Socrates was that he was possessed by a spirit that would occasionally force him to pause in the middle of a sentence, thereby warning him that something bad would soon take place.

Friends, who would have acquitted me, I would like also to talk with you about this thing that has happened, while the magistrates are busy, and before I go to the place at which I must die. Stay then awhile, for we may as well talk with one another while there is time. You are my friends, and I should like to show you the meaning of this event that has happened to me. O my judges—for you I may truly call judges—I should like to tell you of a wonderful circumstance. Hitherto the familiar oracle within me has constantly been in the habit of opposing me even about trifles, if I was going to make a slip or error about anything; and now as you see there has come upon me that which may be thought, and is generally believed to be, the last and worst evil. But the oracle made no sign of opposition, either as I was leaving my house and going out in the morning, or when I was going up into this court, or while I was speaking, at anything which I was going to say; and yet I have often been stopped in the middle of a speech; but now in nothing I either said or did touching this matter has the oracle opposed me. What do I take to be the explanation of this? I will tell you. I regard this as a proof that what has happened to me is a good, and that those of us who think that death is an evil are in error. This is a great proof to me of what I am saying, for the customary sign would surely have opposed me had I been going to evil and not to good.

 ASK YOURSELF

2.37. Since Socrates did not have a spiritual encounter with his oracle after his conviction, what does he take this as a sign for?

In his final remarks Socrates argues further that he should not be afraid of his impending execution.

Let us reflect in another way, and we shall see that there is great reason to hope that death is a good, for one of two things:—either death is a state of nothingness and utter unconsciousness, or, as men say, there is a change and migration of the soul from this world to another. Now if you suppose that there is no consciousness, but a sleep like the sleep of him who is undisturbed even by the sight of dreams, death will be an unspeakable gain. For if a person were to select the night in which his sleep was undisturbed even by dreams, and were to compare with this the other days and nights of his life, and then were to tell us how many days and nights he had passed in the course of his life better and more pleasantly than this one, I think that any man, I will not say a private man, but even the great king, will not find many such days or nights, when compared with the others. Now if death is like this, I say that to die is gain; for eternity is then only a single night. But if death is the journey to another place, and there, as men say, all the dead are, what good, O my friends and judges, can be greater than this? If indeed when the pilgrim arrives in the world below, he is delivered from the professors of justice in this world, and finds the true judges who are said to give judgment there, Minos and Rhadamanthus and Aeacus and Triptolemus, and other sons of God who were righteous in their own life, that pilgrimage will be worth making. What would not a man give if he might converse with Orpheus and Musaeus and Hesiod and Homer? Nay, if this be true, let me die again and again. I, too, shall have a wonderful interest in a place where I can converse with Palamedes, and Ajax the son of Telamon, and other heroes of old, who have suffered death through an unjust judgment; and there will be no small pleasure, as I think, in comparing my own sufferings with theirs. Above all, I shall be able to continue my search into true and false knowledge; as in this world, so also in that; I shall find out who is wise, and who pretends to be wise, and is not. What would not a man give, O judges, to be able to examine the leader of the great Trojan expedition; or Odysseus or Sisyphus, or numberless others, men and women too! What infinite delight would there be in conversing with them and asking them questions! For in that world they do not put a man to death for this; certainly not. For besides being happier in that world than in this, they will be immortal, if what is said is true.

Socrates argues that death is not something to be feared; the argument can be reconstructed like this:

a. If death is endless sleep, then death is good.
b. If death means seeing the heroes of old, then death is good.
c. Death is endless sleep *or* death means seeing the heroes of old.
d. Therefore, death is good.

 ASK YOURSELF

2.38. Criticize this argument by showing how premise (a), (b), or (c) may be false.

2.39. What is it about death as a case of seeing the heroes of old that appeals to Socrates, and how would he spend the afterlife with them?

Wherefore, O judges, be of good cheer about death, and know this of a truth—that no evil can happen to a good man, either in life or after death. He and his are not neglected by the gods; nor has my own approaching end happened by mere chance. But I see clearly that to die and be released was better for me; and therefore the oracle gave no sign. For which reason also, I am not angry with my accusers, or my condemners; they have done me no harm, although neither of them meant to do me any good; and for this I may gently blame them.

Still I have a favor to ask of them. When my sons are grown up, I would ask you, O my friends, to punish them; and I would have you trouble them, as I have troubled you, if they seem to care about riches, or anything, more than about virtue; or if they pretend to be something when they are really nothing,—then reprove them, as I have reproved you, for not caring about that for which they ought to care, and thinking that they are something when they are really nothing. And if you do this, I and my sons will have received justice at your hands.

The hour of departure has arrived, and we go our ways—I to die, and you to live. Which is better God only knows.

Execution Scene from the Phaedo. The execution of Socrates is described with great poignance by Plato in the dialogue *Phaedo*, the concluding portions of which follow. (More selections from the *Phaedo* are included later in this chapter in the discussion of Plato.) Socrates's death is being described to several of his friends by Phaedo.

Now the hour of sunset was near, for a good deal of time had passed while he was within. When he came out, he sat down with us again after his bath, but not much was said. Soon the jailer, who was the servant of the Eleven, entered and stood by him, saying: To you, Socrates, whom I know to be the noblest and gentlest and best of all who ever came to this place, I will not impute the angry feelings of other men, who rage and swear at me when, in obedience to the authorities, I bid them drink the poison—indeed, I am sure that you will not be angry with me; for others, as you are aware, and not I, are the guilty cause. And so fare you well, and try to bear lightly what must needs be; you know my errand. Then bursting into tears he turned away and went out. Socrates looked at him and said: I return your good wishes, and will do as you bid. Then, turning to us, he said, How charming the man is: since I have been in prison he has always been coming to see me, and at times he would talk to me, and was as good as could be to me, and now see how generously he sorrows for me. But we must do as he says, Crito; let the cup be brought, if the poison is prepared: if not, let the attendant prepare some. Yet, said Crito, the sun is still upon the hilltops, and many a one has taken the draught late, and after the announcement has been made to him, he has eaten and drunk, and indulged in sensual delights; do not hasten then, there is still time. Socrates said: Yes, Crito, and they of whom you speak are right in doing thus, for they think that they will gain by the delay; but I am right in not doing thus, for I do not think that I should gain anything by drinking the poison a little later. I should be sparing and saving a life which is already gone: I could only laugh at myself for this. Please then do as I say, and do not refuse me.

Crito, when he heard this, made a sign to the servant, and the servant went in, and remained for some time, and then returned with the jailer carrying a cup of poison. Socrates said: You, my good friend, who are experienced in these matters, shall give me directions how I am to proceed. The man answered: You have only to walk about until your legs are heavy, and then to lie down, and the poison will act. At the same time, Echecrates, he handed the cup to Socrates, who in the easiest and gentlest manner, without the least fear or change of color or feature, looking at the man with all his eyes, as his manner was, took the cup and said: What do you say about making a libation out of this cup to any god? May I, or not? The man answered: We only prepare, Socrates, just so much as we deem enough. I understand, he said: yet I may and must pray to the gods to prosper my journey from this to that other world—may this, then, which is my prayer, be granted to me. Then holding the cup to his lips, quite readily and cheerfully he drank off the poison. And hitherto most of us had been able to control our sorrow; but now when we saw him drinking, and saw too that he had finished the draught, we could no longer forbear, and in spite of myself my own tears were flowing fast, so that I covered my face and wept over myself, for certainly I was not weeping over him, but at the thought of my own calamity in having lost such a companion. Nor was I the first, for Crito, when he found himself unable to restrain his tears, had got up and moved away, and I followed. And at that moment Apollodorus, who had been weeping all the time, broke out in a loud cry which made cowards of us all. Socrates alone retained his calmness: What is this strange outcry? he said. I sent away the women mainly in order that they might not offend in this way, for I have heard that a man should die in peace. Be quiet, then, and have patience. When we heard that, we were ashamed, and refrained our tears. He walked about until, as he said, his legs began to fail, and then he lay on his back, according to the directions, and the man who gave him the poison looked at his feet and legs now and then; and after a while he pressed his foot hard and asked him if he could feel; and he said, no; and then his leg, and so upwards and upwards, and showed us that he was cold and stiff. And he felt them himself, and said: When the poison reaches the heart, that will be the end. He was beginning to grow cold about the groin, when he uncovered his face, for he had covered himself up, and said (they were his last words)—he said: Crito, I owe a cock to Asclepius; will you remember to pay the debt? The debt shall be paid, said Crito; is there anything else? There was no answer to this question, but in a minute or two a movement was heard, and the attendants uncovered him. His eyes were set, and Crito closed his eyes and mouth. Such was the end, Echecrates, of our friend, whom I may truly call the wisest, and justest, and best of all the men whom I have ever known.

 ## ASK YOURSELF

2.40. A New Testament scholar, Oscar Cullmann, wrote a long essay comparing the death of Socrates to the death of Jesus. In what ways do they seem to you to differ?

PLATO

Introduction to the Theory of Forms

Plato apparently developed ideas that Socrates had anticipated, and at some point began to add views that were distinctively his. One of his most distinctive and important theories is the *theory of forms*. Plato's views on knowledge, the good life, the good community, the nature of language, and much else are a function of his theory of forms.

We have seen some of the basic assumptions behind that theory already expressed in the *Euthyphro*. There Socrates argued that all the various actions called "holy" must be so called because of a single "form." Socrates was making a point about how general terms (terms that apply to more than one thing) have meaning. Consider another example: Suppose you have two triangles, A and B. A is obtuse and red, B is pink and right-angled. But A is a triangle and B is a triangle. So whatever "triangle" means, it cannot include being right-angled or pink, otherwise B would be a triangle but A wouldn't! Whatever "triangle" means when applied to B, it must have the same meaning when applied to A. That meaning will be its essence. We might say that the meaning of "triangle" or the essence of triangularity is being a three-sided figure with interior angles equal to 180 degrees. It will be what a *triangle itself* is, or it will be *the form triangularity*, or it will be *the triangular itself*. Plato uses all of these expressions when speaking of the *form of triangularity*. Obviously there are many triangles (A, B, and countless others), but there is only one *form* of triangularity. "Triangle itself," the form, is in fact a "one over the many."

 ASK YOURSELF

2.41. Mention two thinkers before Plato who struggled with some version of the problem of the one over the many.

It is important to note that the considerations about meaning we have just discussed actually supply us with an argument for the existence of forms. We could lay the argument out like this:

a. The meaning of a word is what it refers to. (This assumption is crucial to Plato's argument.)

b. Each word has a single meaning (normally).

c. Therefore each word refers to a single thing [by (a) and (b)].

d. Therefore "triangle" refers to a single thing [by (c) and the fact that it is a single word].

e. There are *many* particular empirical triangles (triangles drawn on boards, in books, etc.).

f. Therefore "triangle" cannot refer to any empirical triangle (otherwise the other empirical triangles would not be triangles) [from (d) and (e)]

g. Therefore "triangle" refers to something that is *not* empirical. Let us call that one thing which is the single meaning of "triangle" "triangularity itself" or "the form of triangularity."

h. Therefore there is such a thing as the form of triangularity, and it is not identical with any empirical triangle.

A similar argument could be produced using (just about) any word or general term.

If Plato has proved in this way that there are forms, that still does not tell us much about what they are like. We might be inclined to think that a form is merely a definition, a convention about using words that could be changed. In that case it would have no permanent existence, but would depend upon the existence of minds to think it and the conventions of a language. Plato, on the contrary, thought definitions were extremely important. He thought they gave us access to something independently real, namely, forms. But again, what are forms, and how and where do they exist? Plato's characteristic claim is that they exist "apart" (from particular things) and are eternal. That is, they are not part of this familiar world about which we develop opinions through the senses. The senses give us some awareness of particular things of this world (a particular triangle). But "triangularity itself"(for instance) must exist apart from the world familiar to the senses.

 ASK YOURSELF

2.42. To what, according to Plato, do definitions give us access?

Plato will go on to argue that the only real knowledge is knowledge of forms. Since they are not known through the senses then real knowledge does not come through the senses. The most that can be acquired through the senses is *opinion*. This view of knowledge is a version of *rationalism*, and we will run into various versions of it throughout the history of philosophy. These and other important Platonic notions are clearly expressed in the dialogue *Phaedo*.

Phaedo

Plato's Rationalism: The Body and Desire as Obstacles to Knowledge and Immortality. In Plato's *Phaedo*, Socrates explains the nature of the forms in a conversation with Simmias and Cebes.

 From PLATO: *Phaedo* ──────────────

[SOCRATES]   Well, but there is another thing, Simmias: Is there or is there not an absolute justice?

[SIMMIAS]   Assuredly there is.

[SOCRATES]   And an absolute beauty and absolute good?

[SIMMIAS]   Of course.

[SOCRATES]   But did you ever behold any of them with your eyes?

[SIMMIAS]   Certainly not.

[SOCRATES]   Or did you ever reach them with any other bodily sense? (And I speak not of these alone, but of absolute greatness, and health, and strength, and of the essence or true nature of everything.) Has the reality of them ever been perceived by you through the bodily organs? Or rather, is not the nearest approach to the knowledge of their several natures made by him who so orders his intellectual vision as to have the most exact conception of the essence of that which he considers?

[SIMMIAS]   Certainly.

[SOCRATES]   And he attains to the knowledge of them in their highest purity who goes to each of them with the mind alone, not allowing when in the act of thought the intrusion or introduction of sight or any other sense in the company of reason. Rather, with the very light of the mind in her clearness he penetrates into the very light of truth in each. He has got rid, as far as he can, of eyes and ears and of the whole body, which he conceives of only as a disturbing element which hinders the soul from the acquisition of knowledge when in company with her. Is not this the sort of man who, if ever man did, is likely to attain the knowledge of existence?

[SIMMIAS]   There is admirable truth in that, Socrates.

[SOCRATES]   And when they consider all this, must not true philosophers make a reflection, of which they will speak to one another in such words as these: We have found, they will say, a path of speculation which seems to bring us and the argument to the conclusion that while we are in the body, and while the soul is mingled with this mass of evil, our desire will not be satisfied, and our desire is of the truth. For the body is a source of endless trouble to us by reason of the mere requirement of food. It is also liable to diseases which overtake and impede us in the search after truth. Moreover by filling us so full of loves, and lusts ,and fears, and fancies, and idols, and every sort of folly, the body prevents our ever having, as people say, so much as a thought.

If bodily senses cannot give knowledge, then we might expect a seeker of knowledge to downplay the body and elevate the mind or something mindlike, such as the soul. That is exactly what Plato does, as the preceding dialogue clearly indicates. But it is not only the senses that belong to the body. There are also "loves, and lusts, and fears, and fancies, and idols, and every sort of folly." On Plato's view, these also interfere with true knowledge and thus prevent contact with what is eternal and perfect.

Consider this example: I will never grasp what true justice is (the form of justice) if I am slave to the desire for possessions or to the fear of being unpopular. So Plato's thinking about the body versus the soul has an ethical and religious dimension. In fact, he recommends a kind of asceticism.

 ASK YOURSELF

2.43. How might a fear, such as the fear of being unpopular, interfere with someone's ability to understand what justice is?

Plato's notion of the body is not just the notion of a physical thing, but rather the notion of something corrupted by impure desires and fears, as well as by too much reliance on the senses in the quest for knowledge. Opposed to the body in this sense is the soul.

ASK YOURSELF

2.44. Do Plato's views on the relation of soul to body remind you of any teachings from another context? Explain your answer.

The contrast between the body and the soul upon which Plato lays such great stress makes him a certain kind of body/soul dualist

Plato's Body/Soul Dualism. Socrates continues by arguing that only by complete separation from the body can anyone achieve perfect immortality.

[SOCRATES]   And are we to suppose that the soul, which is invisible, in passing to the true Hades, which like her is invisible, and pure, and noble, and on her way to the good and wise God,—whither, if God will, my soul is also soon to go—that the soul, I repeat, if this be her nature and origin, is blown away and perishes immediately on quitting the body, as the many say? That can never be, dear Simmias and Cebes. The truth rather is that the soul which is pure at departing draws after her no bodily taint, having never voluntarily had connection with the body, which she is ever avoiding, herself gathered into herself (for such abstraction has been the study of her life). And what does this mean but that she has been a true disciple of philosophy and has practised how to die easily? And is not philosophy the practice of death?

[CEBES]   Certainly.

[SOCRATES]   That soul, I say, herself invisible, departs to the invisible world, to the divine and immortal and rational: thither arriving, she lives in bliss and is released from the error and folly of men, their fears and wild passions and all other human ills, and forever dwells, as they say of the initiated, in company with the gods. Is not this true, Cebes?

[CEBES]   Yes, beyond a doubt.

[SOCRATES]   But the soul which has been polluted, and is impure at the time of her departure, and is the companion and servant of the body always, and which is in love with and fascinated by the body and by the desires and pleasures of the body, until she is led to believe that the truth only exists in a bodily form, which a man may touch and see and taste and use for the purposes of his lusts—the soul, I mean, accustomed to hate and fear and avoid the intellectual principle, which to the bodily eye is dark and invisible, and can be attained only by philosophy—do you suppose that such a soul as this will depart pure and unalloyed?

[CEBES]   That is impossible, he replied.

[SOCRATES]   She is engrossed by the corporeal, which the continual association and constant care of the body have made natural to her.

[CEBES]   Very true.

[SOCRATES]   And this, my friend, may be conceived to be that heavy, weighty, earthy element of sight by which such a soul is depressed and dragged down again into the visible world, because she is afraid of the invisible and of the world below—prowling about tombs and sepulchres, in the neighborhood of which, as they tell us, are seen certain ghostly apparitions of souls which have not departed pure, but are cloyed with sight and therefore visible.

Two religious teachings would be in agreement with the preceding remarks. One is the teaching about the transmigration of souls, such as is found in Hinduism, but also among the Pythagoreans and others. The other is that pure souls go to a kind of heaven after death. Plato, however, does not present these teachings simply as doctrines to be believed, but rather tries to argue for their rational plausibility. Much of the *Phaedo*, which has as its setting the jail where Socrates is executed, is devoted to those arguments. Socrates is able to depart this life fearlessly because he is confident that his soul cannot be overcome by death.

Knowledge as Recollection. If only the soul can have true knowledge, then how is that knowledge acquired? We tend to think that learning takes place through "experience," or through the senses. Plato denies that the senses play any role in acquiring real knowledge, so what is his alternative? The answer once more depends upon the conception of the soul's immortality. The soul must come into existence already equipped with knowledge, which implies that the soul existed before birth and perhaps also that it has the capacity to survive death. In the dialogue *Meno* Socrates asks an uneducated slave boy if he knows how to double the area of a square. With some probing, the slave boy delivers the correct answer (draw a second square around the diagonal of the first square). Since the boy has never studied geometry, and since Socrates purportedly does not give him the answer, it follows that the answer must have already been *in him* to begin with. He only needed a little prompting in order to recollect the truth already contained in his soul. The same idea of *knowledge as recollection* is expressed in the *Phaedo*.

[SOCRATES]　For this is clear, that when we perceived something, either by the help of sight or hearing, or some other sense, there was no difficulty in receiving from this a conception of some other thing like or unlike which had been forgotten and which was associated with this. Therefore, as I was saying, one of two alternatives follows: either we had this knowledge at birth, and continued to know through life; or, after birth, those who are said to learn only remember, and learning is recollection only.

[SIMMIAS]　Yes, that is quite true, Socrates.

[SOCRATES]　And which alternative, Simmias, do you prefer? Had we the knowledge at our birth, or did we remember afterwards the things which we knew previously to our birth?

The Connection between Recollection, Knowledge, the Forms, and the Soul's Immortality. Plato's principal ideas are closely connected to one another.

[SOCRATES]　And shall we proceed a step further, and affirm that there is such a thing as equality, not of wood with wood, or of stone with stone, but that, over and above this, there is equality in the abstract? Shall we affirm this?

[SIMMIAS]　Affirm, yes, and swear to it, with all the confidence in life.

[SOCRATES]　And do we know the nature of this abstract essence?

[SIMMIAS] To be sure.

[SOCRATES] And whence did we obtain this knowledge? Did we not see equalities of material things, such as pieces of wood and stones, and gather from them the idea of an equality which is different from them?—you will admit that? Or look at the matter again in this way: Do not the same pieces of wood or stone appear at one time equal, and at another time unequal?

[SIMMIAS] That is certain.

[SOCRATES] But are real equals ever unequal? or is the idea of equality ever inequality?

[SIMMIAS] That surely was never yet known, Socrates.

[SOCRATES] Then these (so-called) equals are not the same with the idea of equality?

[SIMMIAS] I should say, clearly not, Socrates.

[SOCRATES] And yet from these equals, although differing from the idea of equality, you conceived and attained that idea?

[SIMMIAS] Very true, he said.

[SOCRATES] Which might be like, or might be unlike them? And must we not allow that when I or anyone look at any object, x, and perceive that the object aims at being some other thing, A, but falls short of being A,—must not whoever makes this observation have had previous knowledge of that A to which, as he says, the other thing, x, although similar, was inferior?

[SIMMIAS] Certainly.

[SOCRATES] And has not this been our case in the matter of equals and of absolute equality?

[SIMMIAS] Precisely.

[SOCRATES] Then we must have known absolute equality previously to the time when we first saw the material equals, and reflected that all these apparent equals aim at this absolute equality, but fall short of it? But that makes no difference; whenever from seeing one thing you conceived another, whether like or unlike, there must surely have been an act of recollection?

[SIMMIAS] Very true.

[SOCRATES] But what would you say of equal portions of wood and stone, or other material equals? And what is the impression produced by them? Are they equals in the same sense as absolute equality? Or do they fall short of this in a measure?

[SIMMIAS] Yes, in a very great measure, too.

[SOCRATES] And must we not allow that when I or anyone look at any object, and perceive that the object aims at being some other thing, but falls short of, and cannot attain to it—he who makes this observation must have had previous knowledge of that to which, as he says, the other, although similar, was inferior?

[SIMMIAS] Certainly.

Take two sticks or pencils of equal length and set one on the middle of the other, perpendicular to it. Do they still *appear* equal? Most will agree that they do not. Plato has tried to show that we do not get the idea of equality itself from observing those sticks. But how then does our perception of them function in our knowledge? The answer is that when set side by side they *remind* us of equality itself, or the *form* of equality. The equality of the two sticks is like an inadequate version of the real thing. In that sense equality itself is like a standard to which particular equal things can only partially measure up. Particular things, even a pair of sticks, are thought of as striving to be as like the absolute standard, the form, as possible. This same idea was lurking in the *Euthyphro*. A standard is a particular thing to which we look for the sake of comparison.

 ASK YOURSELF

2.45. Use an example like the one presented earlier in the discussion of the *Euthyphro* to illustrate the idea of a standard as a particular thing to which we look when making judgments.

If we could only know of equality (justice, beauty, etc.) through some "previous knowledge" then we must have existed in some form prior to our present existence. Our ability to judge two sticks to be equal requires familiarity with the form "equality itself" and that familiarity requires the preexistence of the soul.

[SOCRATES]   There can be no doubt that if these absolute ideas existed before we were born, then our souls must have existed before we were born, and if not the ideas, then not the souls.

[SIMMIAS]   Yes, Socrates; I am convinced that there is precisely the same necessity for the existence of the soul before birth, and of the essence [form] of which you are speaking: and the argument arrives at a result which happily agrees with my own notion. For there is nothing which to my mind is so evident as that beauty, goodness, and other notions of which you were just now speaking have a most real and absolute existence; and I am satisfied with the proof.

 ASK YOURSELF

2.46. If Goodness itself has a "most real and absolute existence," does it follow that relativism is false? Explain.

2.47. Explain the relation between the possibility of knowledge, the existence of the forms, and the immortality of the soul.

Once again it is important to see that there is an argument for the existence of forms implicit in this discussion:

a. We do sometimes make the true judgment that two things are equal.

b. If we did not understand or grasp the form (triangularity itself) or essence of triangularity, we could not make those judgments.

    c. Therefore we must understand the form "triangularity itself."

    d. Therefore there must be forms.

 ASK YOURSELF

2.48. The preceding argument starts from the fact of knowledge. The other argument for the existence of forms that was mentioned at the beginning of the section on Plato starts from what fact?

In the next section Socrates (speaking for Plato, no doubt) lays out some of the main characteristics of the forms.

The Forms Are Eternal, Unchanging, and Apart from the World of the Senses. Socrates provides a positive description of the forms.

[SOCRATES]   Now let us return to the previous discussion. Is that form or essence, which in the dialectical process we define as essence of true existence—whether essence of equality, beauty, or anything else—are these essences, I say, liable at times to some degree of change? Or are they each of them always what they are, having the same simple, self-existent and unchanging forms, and not admitting of variation at all, in any way, or at any time?

[CEBES]   They must be always the same, Socrates.

[SOCRATES]   And what would you say of the many beautiful—whether men or horses or garments or any other things which may be called equal or beautiful—are they all unchanging and the same always, or quite the reverse? May they not rather be described as almost always changing and hardly ever the same either with themselves or with one another?

[CEBES]   The latter; they are always in a state of change.

[SOCRATES]   And these you can touch and see and perceive with the senses, but the unchanging things you can only perceive with the mind—they are invisible and are not seen?

[CEBES]   That is very true.

[SOCRATES]   Well, then, let us suppose that there are two sorts of existences, one seen, the other unseen.

The unseen existences are, of course, the forms. So far we have seen two of Plato's arguments for believing there are forms and that he thinks their characteristics include (1) immateriality: the forms are not physical or visible; (2) the forms are the objects of genuine knowledge; (3) they are known by the soul prior to birth, and recollected afterwards; (4) they are eternal and unchanging. In addition we have seen that Plato is a body/soul dualist and a rationalist.

ASK YOURSELF

2.49. Define: form; body/soul dualism; rationalism; Platonic recollection.

The *Republic*

In the *Republic*, Plato's most famous dialogue, he expands on the conceptions of dualism, rationalism, and recollection and further explains the nature of knowledge. At the same time he applies his ideas to ethics and politics. Key to his discussion is the relation between the world of appearances and the realm of the forms (especially the form of the good), and between knowledge and its objects. He illustrates these relations with two well-known analogies: the divided line and the parable of the cave. The selections here are presented in topical order rather than in the order found in the dialogue itself.

The Divided Line: Different Cognitive Conditions and Their Objects. The main speaker, Socrates, is conversing with Glaucon.

 From PLATO: the *Republic*, Book IV ——————————

[SOCRATES] Now take a line which has been cut into two unequal parts, and divide each of them again in the same proportion, and suppose the two main divisions to answer, one to the visible and the other to the intelligible, and then compare the subdivisions in respect of their clearness and want of clearness, and you will find that the first section in the sphere of the visible consists of images. And by images I mean, in the first place, shadows, and in the second place, reflections in water and in solid, smooth and polished bodies and the like: Do you understand?

[GLAUCON] Yes, I understand.

Plato uses the following chart:

VISIBLE   INTELLIGIBLE

section 1 ——————— /section 2——— | section 3——————— /section 4 ———

 ASK YOURSELF

2.50. What kind of images are in section 1 of the line?

[SOCRATES] Imagine, now, the other section, of which this is only the resemblance, to include the animals which we see, and everything that grows or is made.

[GLAUCON] Very good.

[SOCRATES]   Would you not admit that both the sections of this division have different degrees of truth, and that the copy is to the original as the sphere of opinion is to the sphere of knowledge?

[GLAUCON]   Most undoubtedly.

[SOCRATES]   Next proceed to consider the manner in which the sphere of the intellectual is to be divided.

[GLAUCON]   In what manner?

[SOCRATES]   Thus:—There are two subdivisions, in the lower of which [section 3] the soul uses the figures given by the former division [section 2] as images; the inquiry can only be hypothetical, and instead of going upwards to a principle descends to the other end; in the higher of the two sections [section 4] of the intelligible, the soul passes out of hypotheses, and goes up to a principle which is above hypotheses, making no use of images as in the former case, but proceeding only in and through the ideas themselves.

[GLAUCON]   I do not quite understand your meaning.

[SOCRATES]   Then I will try again; you will understand me better when I have made some preliminary remarks. You are aware that students of geometry, arithmetic, and the kindred sciences assume the odd and the even and the figures and three kinds of angles and the like in their several branches of science; these are their hypotheses, which they and everybody are supposed to know, and therefore they do not deign to give any account of them either to themselves or others; but they begin with them, and go on until they arrive at last, and in a consistent manner, at their conclusion?

[GLAUCON]   Yes, I know.

[SOCRATES]   And do you not know also that although they make use of the visible forms and reason about them, they are thinking not of these, but of the ideals which they resemble? They are not thinking of the figures which they draw, but of the absolute square and the absolute diameter, and so on—the forms which they draw or make, and which have shadows and reflections in water of their own. They are converted by them into images, but they are really seeking to behold the things themselves, which can only be seen with the eye of the mind.

[GLAUCON]   That is true.

[SOCRATES]   And of this kind I spoke as the intelligible, although in the search after it the soul is compelled to use hypotheses; not ascending to a first principle, because she is unable to rise above the region of hypothesis, but employs as images the objects of which the shadows below are resemblances in their turn, they having, in relation to the shadows and reflections of them, a greater distinctness, and therefore a higher value.

[GLAUCON]   I understand that you are speaking of the province of geometry and the sister arts.

Plato is here suggesting that particular geometrical things, for example, a particular triangle constructed of sticks, which a geometer might use for illustrative purposes or as a learning aid, have a relation to triangularity itself (the form) which is similar to the relation between a reflection or a mirror image of that stick triangle and the stick triangle itself. Plato's allegory is thus suggesting a useful way of thinking about the relation between forms and particular empirical objects, a relationship that is indeed puzzling. How, for example, is the form "dogness itself" related to my dog Fido, or the form "beauty itself" related to a particular beautiful thing, say, the Parthenon? This is a difficult problem for Plato. He claims that particulars "participate in" the forms, but what does that mean? The relation between images or reflections in water or in a mirror, and the things they are images of, provides a fruitful analogy for thinking about this matter.

Consider the following facts about such images. First, the images are in a sense *less real* than that of which they are the image. Moreover, the *existence* of the image *depends upon* the existence of the things that they image. And finally, the images are at best only *incomplete and inaccurate guides* to the objects that produce them. All of these are true of the relations of forms to empirical things. The forms are more real, the empirical things would not exist if the forms did not, and the real things only give us a partial and inadequate idea of the original forms. So particular things (a particular empirical stick triangle, for instance) is something like a mirror image of the form "triangularity itself."

 ASK YOURSELF

2.51. What are the three characteristics of the relation of forms to particulars mentioned in the preceding discussion?

[SOCRATES]   And when I speak of the other division of the intelligible, you will understand me to speak of that other sort of knowledge which reason herself attains by the power of dialectic, using the hypotheses not as first principles, but only as hypotheses—that is to say, as steps and points of departure into a world which is above hypotheses, in order that she may soar beyond them to the first principle of the whole; and clinging to this and then to that which depends on this, by successive steps she descends again without the aid of any sensible object, from ideas, through ideas, and in ideas she ends.

[GLAUCON]   I understand you; not perfectly, for you seem to me to be describing a task which is really tremendous; but, at any rate, I understand you to say that knowledge and being, which the science of dialectic contemplates, are clearer than the notions of the arts, as they are termed, which proceed from hypotheses only: these are also contemplated by the understanding, and not by the senses: yet, because they start from hypotheses and do not ascend to a principle, those who contemplate them appear to you not to exercise the higher reason upon them, although when a first principle is added to them they are cognizable by the higher reason. And the habit which is concerned with geometry and the cognate sciences I suppose that you would term understanding and not reason, as being intermediate between opinion and reason.

[SOCRATES]   You have quite conceived my meaning; and now, corresponding to these four divisions, let there be four faculties in the soul—reason answering to the highest, understanding to the second, belief to the third, and picture thinking to the last—and let there be a scale of them, and let us suppose that the several faculties have clearness in the same degree that their objects have truth.

[GLAUCON]   I understand, and give my assent, and accept your arrangement.

 ASK YOURSELF

2.52. Review the kinds of things in section 2 of the line.

2.53. What is the relation between sections 1 and 2?

2.54. What things are in sections 3 and 4 of the line?

2.55. What are the four faculties of the soul that correspond to the four divisions of the line?

2.56. Based on Plato's definition, give an example of each of the following: picture thinking; belief; understanding; reason.

The divided line indicates that Plato thinks there are different levels of cognition, ranging all the way from something that is almost pure ignorance, to that which is absolute knowledge. Corresponding to these different levels of thought are different kinds or degrees of being. In the next section it becomes clear, if it is not already, that the kinds of being that correspond to the lowest level, picture thinking, are less real than that which corresponds to the next level. The most real being is that which is most knowable. The idea that the *real is the rational or knowable* is another feature of rationalism.

It also becomes clear in what follows that Plato thinks that some forms are higher, more real, than others. Plato sets forth these ideas in terms of another allegory, *The Allegory of the Cave*. He argues that we do not get a satisfactory explanation of any thing or concept until we reach that which mentions what is good. Since all explanations refer to the forms, the ultimate explanation of anything must be in terms of some sort of direct or indirect participation in the *form of the good*.

The Allegory of the Cave. Plato describes the struggle for knowledge and the form of the Good

 From PLATO: the *Republic*, Book VII ———————

[SOCRATES]   And now, I said, let me show in a figure how far our nature is enlightened or unenlightened:—Behold! human beings living in a underground den, which has a mouth open towards the light and reaching all along the den; here they have been from their childhood, and have their legs and necks chained so that they cannot move, and can only see before them, being prevented by the chains from turning round their heads. Above and behind them a fire is blazing at a distance, and between the fire and the prisoners there is a raised way; and you will see, if you look, a low wall built along the way, like the screen which marionette players have in front of them, over which they show the puppets.

[GLAUCON]   I see.

[SOCRATES]   And do you see, men passing along the wall carrying all sorts of vessels, and statues and figures of animals made of wood and stone and various materials, which appear over the wall? Some of them are talking, others silent.

[GLAUCON]   You have shown me a strange image, and they are strange prisoners.

[SOCRATES]   Like ourselves; and they see only their own shadows, or the shadows of one another, which the fire throws on the opposite wall of the cave?

[GLAUCON]   True; how could they see anything but the shadows if they were never allowed to move their heads?

[SOCRATES]   And of the objects which are being carried in like manner they would only see the shadows?

[GLAUCON]   Yes.

[SOCRATES]   And if they were able to converse with one another, would they not suppose that they were naming what was actually before them?

[GLAUCON]   Very true.

[SOCRATES]   And suppose further that the prison had an echo which came from the other side, would they not be sure to fancy when one of the passers-by spoke that the voice which they heard came from the passing shadow?

[GLAUCON]   No question.

[SOCRATES]   To them, the truth would be literally nothing but the shadows of the images.

[GLAUCON]   That is certain.

[SOCRATES]   And now look again, and see what will naturally follow if the prisoners are released and disabused of their error. At first, when any of them is liberated and compelled suddenly to stand up and turn his neck round and walk and look towards the light, he will suffer sharp pains; the glare will distress him, and he will be unable to see the realities of which in his former state he had seen the shadows. Next imagine someone saying to him, that what he saw before was an illusion, but that now, when he is approaching nearer to being and his eye is turned towards more real existence, he has a clearer vision,—what will be his reply? And you may further imagine that his instructor is pointing to the objects as they pass and requiring him to name them,—will he not be perplexed? Will he not fancy that the shadows which he formerly saw are truer than the objects which are now shown to him?

[GLAUCON]   Far truer.

[SOCRATES]   And if he is compelled to look straight at the light, will he not have a pain in his eyes which will make him turn away and take in the objects of vision which he can see, and which he will conceive to be in reality clearer than the things which are now being shown to him?

[GLAUCON]   True.

[SOCRATES]   And suppose once more, that he is reluctantly dragged up a steep and rugged ascent, and held fast until he is forced into the presence of the sun himself, is he not likely to be pained and irritated? When he approaches the light his eyes will be dazzled, and he will not be able to see anything at all of what are now called realities.

[GLAUCON]   Not all in a moment.

[SOCRATES]   He will require to grow accustomed to the sight of the upper world. And first he will see the shadows best, next the reflections of men and other objects in the water, and then the objects themselves; then he will gaze upon the light of the moon and the stars and the spangled heaven; and he will see the sky and the stars by night better than the sun or the light of the sun by day?

[GLAUCON]   Certainly.

[SOCRATES]   Last of all he will be able to see the sun, and not mere reflections of him in the water, but he will see him in his own proper place, and not in another; and he will contemplate him as he is.

[GLAUCON]   Certainly.

[SOCRATES]   He will then proceed to argue that this [the Sun] is he who gives the season and the years, and is the guardian of all that is in the visible world, and in a certain way the cause of all things which he and his fellows have been accustomed to behold?

[GLAUCON]   Clearly, he would first see the Sun and then reason about him.

[SOCRATES]   And when he remembered his old habitation, and the wisdom of the den and his fellow-prisoners, do you not suppose that he would be happy with the change in himself, and pity them?

[GLAUCON]   Certainly, he would.

[SOCRATES]   And if they were in the habit of conferring honors among themselves on those who were quickest to observe the passing shadows and to remark which of them went before, and which followed after, and which were together, and who were therefore best able to draw conclusions as to the future, do you think that he would care for such honors and glories, or envy the possessors of them? Would he not say with Homer, "Better to be the poor servant of a poor master," and to endure anything, rather than think as they do and live after their manner?

[GLAUCON]   Yes, I think that he would rather suffer anything than entertain these false notions and live in this miserable manner.

[SOCRATES]   Imagine once more, such a one coming suddenly out of the Sun to be replaced in his old situation; would he not be certain to have his eyes full of darkness?

[GLAUCON]   To be sure.

[SOCRATES]   And if there were a contest, and he had to compete in measuring the shadows with the prisoners who had never moved out of the den, while his sight was still weak, and before his eyes had become adjusted (and the time which would be needed to acquire this adjustment might be very considerable) would he not be ridiculous? Men would say of him that up he went and down he came without his eyes, and that it was better not even to think of ascending. And if any one tried to release another and lead him up to the light, let them only catch the offender, and they would put him to death.

[GLAUCON]   No question.

[SOCRATES]   This entire allegory you may now append, dear Glaucon, to the previous argument; the prison-house is the world of sight, the light of the fire is the Sun, and you will not misapprehend me if you interpret the journey upwards to be the ascent of the soul into the intellectual world according to my poor belief, which, at your desire, I have expressed, whether rightly or wrongly God knows.

But, whether true or false, my opinion is that in the world of knowledge the idea of good appears last of all, and is seen only with an effort; and, when seen, is also inferred to be the universal author of all things beautiful and right, parent of light and of the lord of light in this visible world, and the immediate source of reason and truth in the intellectual; and that this is the power upon which he who would act rationally, either in public or private life, must have his eye fixed.

 ASK YOURSELF

2.57. Compare each section of the line to some part of the cave allegory. For instance, the first section of the line corresponds to the condition of seeing shadows on the cave wall. The second section corresponds to _____? The third to _____? The fourth to _____?

It is clear from the cave allegory that Plato thinks that acquisition of knowledge requires discipline and is painful. "No pain, no gain" is even more true in the realm of knowledge than it is in the realm of physical training and improvement. So if you find studying painful sometimes, do not be surprised!

We have already seen that Plato thinks people contain the truth in them. But in his view life in the body has made them forget what they know and has led them to focus their lives on what is perceptible and satisfies their bodily desires. It is very difficult to turn away from the body, and someone who prodded people into making that turn or conversion might not be too popular. Moreover, such a person might be thought a crackpot by some, since he claims that the familiar world is not fully real or worthy of our attention.

 ASK YOURSELF

2.58. Who might Plato have in mind when he speaks of the unpopularity of those who encourage people to seek wisdom?

2.59. The other notable feature of this allegory is the status of the Sun. The Sun is being compared to what?

It may still be far from clear why Plato would accord the form of the good such preeminent status. If so, it may help to think a little about the relation between knowledge, understanding, and explanation. Often to fully know something requires being able to explain it. I may see that a plant's leaves are green, but I do not fully understand, and thus in a sense have full knowledge of the world of plants, until I can explain *why* they are green, which would require knowledge of chlorophyll and how it functions. Generally properly functioning things function the way they do in order to bring about some goal that is beneficial or *good*, and that is of course the case with the chlorophyll in the leaves of the plant.

 ASK YOURSELF

2.60. What good is brought about by the function of the chlorophyll?

So even in terms of this example you can see that the ultimate explanation for the greenness of the leaves refers to what is good. Of course, some things may be good instrumentally, that is, good for something else. For example, money may be good, but not in itself (it is just paper) but for the sake of something else (a new Lexus, perhaps). But Plato thinks there must be something that is entirely good in itself. All instrumental goods would ultimately exist for the sake of that "good in itself." And of course in Plato's view that would be the form of the Good itself. Plato apparently thinks that *all* explanations, thus all understanding and knowledge, terminate in references to what is the ultimate Good, the Good itself.

The idea that understanding something requires grasping its function, purpose, or goal is the idea that understanding is *teleological* in form. The Greek word for "goal" or "function" is *telos*; teleological reasoning will come up for consideration at many points in this text.

 ASK YOURSELF

2.61. What is teleological in Plato's thinking about the form of the Good?

It is instructive to compare Plato's thought here to the thought of the Atomists. Democritus, as we have pointed out, thought that what explains the world is simply a swirling vortex of atoms. There was no purpose served by that swirl. It just happens, by accident so to speak, and produces a chain of causal reactions that are just as without purpose as the swirl is. That chain of causal reactions constitutes the entire history of the universe. Thus there is a sense in which Democritus pictures the universe as being through and through *meaningless*. That is because we almost naturally think of something as having meaning when it has a point or serves a purpose (*telos*).

Plato, on the other hand, thinks that the entire universe is absolutely permeated with meaning and purpose. That is what it amounts to when he says that the form of the Good is over all and the source of all, just as the physical Sun is over all and the source of all in the physical world (maybe the Sun isn't the source of everything, but even in modern views of the cosmos there would not be much of the earth as we know it were it not for the relation between it and the Sun). In Plato's view it is for the sake of what is good that everything exists and is as it is.

ASK YOURSELF

2.62. Give an example of something that is good insofar as it serves the purpose of enabling something to flourish.

The Structure of the Soul: Three Parts Corresponding to Three Types of People. In the *Republic* Plato presents a more complex account of the soul than that found in the *Phaedo.*

 From PLATO: the *Republic*, Book IX _____

[SOCRATES] . . . the individual soul . . . has been divided by us into three principles. . . . It seems to me that to these three principles three pleasures correspond; also three desires and governing powers.

[GLAUCON] How do you mean?

[SOCRATES] There is one principle with which, as we were saying, a man learns, another with which he is angry; the third, having many forms, has no special name, but is denoted by the general term appetitive, from the extraordinary strength and vehemence of the desires of eating and drinking and the other sensual appetites which are the main elements of it; also money-loving, because such desires are generally satisfied by the help of money.

[GLAUCON] That is true.

[SOCRATES] If we were to say that the loves and pleasures of this third part were concerned with gain, we should then be able to fall back on a single notion, and might truly and intelligibly describe this part of the soul as loving gain or money.

[GLAUCON] I agree with you.

[SOCRATES] Again, is not the spirited element wholly set on ruling and conquering and getting fame?

[GLAUCON] True.

[SOCRATES] Suppose we call it the contentious or ambitious—would the term be suitable?

[GLAUCON] Extremely suitable.

[SOCRATES] On the other hand, every one sees that the principle of knowledge is wholly directed to the truth, and cares less than either of the others for gain or fame.

[GLAUCON] Far less.

[SOCRATES] "Lover of wisdom," "lover of knowledge," are titles that we may fitly apply to that part of the soul?

[GLAUCON] Certainly.

[SOCRATES] One principle prevails in the souls of one class of men, another in others, as may happen?

[GLAUCON] Yes.

[SOCRATES]   Then we may begin by assuming that there are three classes of men—lovers of wisdom, lovers of honor, lovers of gain?

 ## ASK YOURSELF

2.63. What are the three parts of the soul?

Plato supposes that any of the three parts of the soul can predominate in a person. So if my appetites (the appetitive part of my soul) pretty much determine who I am, then I will be a "lover of gain" and the other parts of my soul will have to take a back seat. But what sort of person would I be in that case?

Perhaps many will agree that I would not be a very good person. Plato would say such a person would be "unjust," since a person enslaved to their appetites would no doubt be quite willing to lie, cheat, and even murder, and that is what is meant by being unjust in the sense of the term Plato is considering.

What Is the Advantage of Being Just? But this matter of injustice raises an interesting question that is at the heart of much of the discussion in the *Republic*. The sophist Thrasymachus is involved in the discussion in this dialogue, and he argues that justice is nothing but the interest of the stronger. In his view if I am strong enough to get away with cheating and murder, then I should cheat and murder whenever it is to my advantage to do so. I would come out ahead. There would be no advantage in being consistently just. I would be a person in whom the appetites dominated, but that would not lead to any harm for me, since I am strong enough to get away with crimes of all sorts in the pursuit of my desires. In the following passage Glaucon is voicing the views of Thrasymachus.

 ## From PLATO: the *Republic*, Book II

[GLAUCON]   Now that those who practice justice do so involuntarily and because they have not the power to be unjust will best appear if we imagine something of this kind: having given both to the just and the unjust the power to do what they will, let us watch and see whither desire will lead them. Then we shall discover the just man to be resorting to the same conduct as the unjust man, proceeding along the same road, grasping for their own advantage, which all natures deem to be their good. Only by the force of law do they honor equality.

The liberty which we are supposing may be most completely given to them in the form of such a power as is said to have been possessed by Gyges the ancestor of Croesus the Lydian. According to the tradition, Gyges was a shepherd in the service of the king of Lydia. There was a great storm, and an earthquake made an opening in the earth at the place where he was feeding his flock. Amazed at the sight, he descended into the opening, where, among other marvels, he beheld a hollow brazen horse, having doors, at which he, stooping and looking, in saw a dead body of more than human stature, as appeared to him, and having nothing on but a gold ring. He took this ring from the finger of the dead and went back up.

Now the shepherds met together, according to custom, that they might send their monthly report about the flocks to the king. Gyges came into their assembly with the ring on his finger, and as he was sitting among them he chanced to turn the collet of the ring inside his hand. Instantly he became invisible to the rest of the company and they began to speak of him as if he were no longer present. He was astonished at this, and again touching the ring he turned the collet outwards and always with the same result—when he turned the collet inwards he became invisible, when outwards he reappeared. Whereupon he contrived to be chosen one of the messengers who were sent to the court. As soon as he arrived he seduced the queen, and with her help conspired against the king and slew him, and took the kingdom.

Suppose now that there were two such magic rings, and the just put on one of them and the unjust the other; no man can be imagined to be of such an iron nature that he would stand fast in justice. No man would keep his hands off what was not his own when he could safely take what he liked out of the market, or go into houses and lie with any one at his pleasure, or kill or release from prison whom he would, and in all respects be like a God among men. Then the actions of the just would be as the actions of the unjust; they would both come at last to the same point. And this we may truly affirm to be a great proof that a man is just, not willingly or because he thinks that justice is any good to him individually, but of necessity, for wherever any one thinks that he can safely be unjust, there he is unjust. For all men believe in their hearts that injustice is far more profitable to the individual than justice, and he who argues as I have been supposing, will say that they are right. If you could imagine any one obtaining this power of becoming invisible, and never doing any wrong or touching what was another's, he would be thought by the on-lookers to be a most wretched idiot.

 ## ASK YOURSELF

2.64. If you had the ring of Gyges, do you think you would have any reason to not be immoral? Explain your answer.

Thrasymachus is in effect proposing the following argument:

a. Everyone wants to be happy. (That seems like a pretty fair assumption!)

b. Therefore it would be irrational to act in any way that would not contribute to one's own happiness.

c. Therefore if someone could be happy through injustice it would be irrational for them to stick to being just. People would rightly think such a person to be an "idiot."

Certainly Thrasymachus's position is still a popular one. There is in fact a widespread tendency to picture good people as being rather stupid, whereas evil people are often portrayed as very clever and shrewd. Many would agree with Thrasymachus that the person who tries to be just is indulging in "high-minded foolishness" or some other form of stupidity. Consider just the following points:

From PLATO: the *Republic*, Book I _____

[THRASYMACHUS]   First of all, in private contracts: wherever the unjust is the partner of the just you will find that, when the partnership is dissolved, the unjust man has always more and the just less. Secondly, in their dealings with the State: when there is an income tax, the just man will pay more and the unjust less on the same amount of income; and when there is anything to be received the one gains nothing and the other much. Observe also what happens when they take an office; there is the just man neglecting his affairs and perhaps suffering other losses, and getting nothing out of the public, because he is just; moreover he is hated by his friends and acquaintance for refusing to serve them in unlawful ways.

 ASK YOURSELF

2.65. Does anything sound familiar in that? Mention a contemporary example that in your opinion illustrates what Thrasymachus is talking about.

Plato wants to refute Thrasymachus's position. But he agrees with (a) and (b) in the preceding argument. So he must show that being just pays, that it leads to greater happiness. He must show that someone with the ring of Gyges would actually be better off if she did *not* rob, murder and so on even when doing so would get her what she "wants."

Does Being Just (Being Good) Pay? Plato uses various strategies in tackling this tough challenge. One of them consists in asking what would become of a community (any group of people) if justice was completely ignored.

[SOCRATES]   . . . would you have the goodness also to inform me, whether you think that a state, or an army, or a band of robbers and thieves, or any other gang of evil-doers could act at all if they injured one another?

[THRASYMACHUS]   No indeed, he said, they could not.

[SOCRATES]   But if they abstained from injuring one another, then they might act together better?

[THRASYMACHUS]   Yes.

[SOCRATES]   And this is because injustice creates divisions and hatreds and fighting, and justice imparts harmony and friendship; is not that true, Thrasymachus?

[THRASYMACHUS]   I agree, because I do not wish to quarrel with you.

[SOCRATES]   How good of you; but I should like to know also whether injustice, having this tendency to arouse hatred, wherever existing, among slaves or among freemen, will not make them hate one another and set them at variance and render them incapable of common action?

[THRASYMACHUS]   Certainly.

[SOCRATES]   And even if injustice be found in two only, will they not quarrel and fight, and become enemies to one another and to the just?

[THRASYMACHUS]   They will.

[SOCRATES]   And suppose injustice abiding in a single person, would your wisdom say that she loses or that she retains her natural power? Let us assume that she retains her power. Yet is not the power which injustice exercises of such a nature that wherever she takes up her abode, whether in a city, in an army, in a family, or in any other body, that body is, to begin with, rendered incapable of united action by reason of sedition and distraction? And does it not therefore become its own enemy and at variance with all that opposes it, and with the just? Is not this the case?

[THRASYMACHUS]   Yes, certainly.

[SOCRATES]   And is not injustice equally fatal when existing in a single person? For in the first place it renders him incapable of action because he is not at unity with himself, and in the second place it makes him an enemy to himself and the just? Is not that true, Thrasymachus?

[THRASYMACHUS]   Yes.

[SOCRATES]   And O my friend, I said, surely the gods are just?

[THRASYMACHUS]   Granted that they are.

[SOCRATES]   But if so, the unjust will be the enemy of the gods, and the just will be their friend?

[THRASYMACHUS]   Feast away in triumph, and take your fill of the argument; I will not oppose you, lest I should displease the company.

 ASK YOURSELF

2.66. What does Plato think will happen when any group of people ignores the rules of justice?

Thrasymachus's grouchy retort may indicate that he feels Socrates has scored a point against him. But has he? Socrates argument is this:

    a. Injustice creates conflict and strife.

    b. Justice enables harmony and peace.

    c. Therefore, justice is preferable to injustice.

Is this a good argument? Try to imagine a case where injustice would *not* create conflict. The problem is to imagine people living peacefully together without anyone following any rules, without any agreement as to how to live. It is indeed difficult to imagine such a possibility. A later philosopher, Thomas Hobbes (seventeenth century CE) argued that a condition in which everyone did as they pleased would be "nasty, brutish and short." But Hobbes thought the necessary order could be imposed by force by a sufficiently powerful monarch. Even such a monarch, however, would have to impose something like the traditional rules of justice. If he made it a rule that people should kill other people whenever they thought it would be to their advantage, he would soon be without a community to rule.

However, even if Plato's argument shows the implausibility of a peaceful or thriving community in which there is no heed paid to justice, has he also succeeded in showing that an *individual* might not be better off by ignoring the requirements of justice?

What Is Justice? What Makes a Political Community or State Just? Notice that Plato claims that the same argument does in fact apply to an individual. But does it? Part of the difficulty here is that we still have not determined exactly what justice is. In Plato's view, to know that you would have to grasp the form of Justice. You might expect that it is connected in some way with reason. We have already seen the idea that virtue is knowledge or wisdom. Justice is a virtue, so perhaps justice is a matter of reason or wisdom being in control.

In fact that is exactly Plato's view. Whether we are speaking of the state or of the individual, the essence of justice will be that each thing is fulfilling its proper function. In Plato's view it is the function of reason in the individual to rule, the function of the appetites to obey, and spirit to assist reason. In the community it is the function of the reasonable element, the educated (especially the philosophers!) to rule, the function of the great masses of people (the craftsmen, workers, farmers) to follow the reasonable commands of the rulers, and the function of the spirited types, such as soldiers and police, to assist the rulers in carrying out their reasonable commands. The following brings out the comparison:

INDIVIDUAL	STATE
just individual:	just state
reason rules:	the educated rule
spirit assists reason:	soldiers assist the educated rulers
appetites obey:	the masses of ordinary people willingly follow the rules set down by the educated elite

You should be able to guess to some extent why Plato thinks that reason should rule. He certainly thinks that only through reason can anyone discover or know what is real. Without reason people are chained down like the inhabitants of the cave, not really knowing what is what. Would you want such ignorant, deluded people in charge of the community in which you live?

Just why Plato thinks the other parts have the functions he claims they have will not be treated here, but you can get the flavor of his thinking from the passage that follows.

 From PLATO: the *Republic*, Book IV

[SOCRATES] But when the cobbler or any other man whom nature designed to be a trader, having his heart lifted up by wealth or strength or the number of his followers, or any like advantage, attempts to force his way into the class of warriors, or a warrior into that of legislators and guardians, for which he is unfitted, and either to take the implements or the duties of the other, or when one man is trader, legislator, and warrior all in one, then I think you will agree with me in saying that this interchange and this meddling of one with another is the ruin of the State.

[GLAUCON]   Most true.

[SOCRATES]   Seeing then, I said, that there are three distinct classes, any meddling of one with another, or the change of one into another, is the greatest harm to the State, and may be most justly termed evil-doing?

[GLAUCON]   Precisely.

[SOCRATES]   And the greatest degree of evil-doing to one's own city would be termed by you injustice?

[GLAUCON]   Certainly.

[SOCRATES]   This then is injustice; and on the other hand when the trader, the auxiliary, and the guardian each do their own business, that is justice, and will make the city just.

So the answer to the question, "What is justice" is this: In the state (or "city") justice is each person performing their proper function. We have all heard complaints about politicians trying to do the work of soldiers. There have also been complaints about soldiers trying to be politicians, as when Gen. Douglas MacArthur defied the orders of president Harry Truman during the Korean War. Some people also worry when businessmen become too prominent in political leadership, for fear they will bend government to their own private profit. And so on.

 ASK YOURSELF

2.67. Give an example of your own of harm done to a community when someone does not tend to their own business but, even with the best of intentions, tries to do someone else's job.

Though we may not agree with all the details of Plato's view, we can probably feel some sympathy with the general point that a good and just community will be one in which each person fulfills that role for which they are best suited. But we may wonder about the suggestion made in the passage just quoted that some people "by nature" have a certain function, so that someone who is "naturally" a cobbler should stick to making shoes and keep his nose out of politics and police work. It is not clear that anyone is by nature a cobbler, and most of us probably think that there might be cobblers out there who would make good presidents. Nonetheless, it does seem that some people might not be fit by nature to do certain jobs (for instance, someone with an IQ of 70 is by nature not a good candidate for doing the work of a rocket scientist).

Justice in the Individual.   Since in Plato's view the different parts of the soul of any individual also have by nature certain jobs, then the unjust individual will be someone in whom the parts of the soul are not doing their proper job, just as the unjust state is one in which the parts do not do their proper job.

[SOCRATES]   We must recollect that the individual in whom the several qualities of his nature do their own work will be just, and will do his own work?

[GLAUCON]   Yes, we must remember that too.

[SOCRATES]   And ought not the rational principle, which is wise, and has the care of the whole soul, to rule, and the passionate or spirited principle to be the subject and ally?

[GLAUCON]   Certainly.

[SOCRATES]   And, as we were saying, the united influence of music and gymnastic will bring them into accord, nerving and sustaining the reason with noble words and lessons, and moderating and soothing and civilizing the wildness of passion by harmony and rhythm?

[GLAUCON]   Quite true.

[SOCRATES]   And these two, thus nurtured and educated, and having learned truly to know their own functions, will rule over the concupiscent, which in each of us is the largest part of the soul and by nature most insatiable of gain; over this they will keep guard, lest, waxing great and strong with the fullness of bodily pleasures, as they are termed, the concupiscent soul, no longer confined to her own sphere, should attempt to enslave and rule those who are not her natural born subjects, and overturn the whole life of man?

[GLAUCON]   Very true.

   ASK YOURSELF

2.68. What part of the soul rules in a just individual?

Some thinkers have found the idea that reason has some specific function to be itself very suspect. Reason can be used to mastermind a bank robbery, solve a math problem, find a cure for a disease, or find a way to spread a disease. In which cases would it be functioning properly and in which not, and why? Someone might insist that a perfectly planned bank robbery is an example of reason functioning perfectly. Plato obviously would not agree, but why not?

Although this criticism undoubtedly has some force, it is important to remember that the arguments already given, in which we are reminded of the difficulties that beset individuals or communities that pay no heed to justice, also have some force. They in effect suggest that there is something irrational in injustice because it is not in accord with well-informed self-interest. But Plato's argument ultimately requires a deeper rationale, for perfectly functioning reason grasps something beyond this world, namely, the form of the Good. And only when we have grasped that form can we even begin to know what constitutes our self-interest.

The Best State and the Arts.   In Plato's view, as we have seen, the best state will be governed by those who have true knowledge. True knowledge is contrasted with mere opinion, and in particular with the lowest form of opinion, which consists in mistaking images for reality. That being the case, we might wonder about the status of the arts in the best state. Consider the following example.

According to Plato, when a carpenter makes a bed, he consults the idea of a bed, the form of "bedness itself." The empirical bed made by the artist is less real than that form. Now suppose an artist were to make a painting of the bed. It would be less real than the bed made by the carpenter, being a mere image. So it is even further than the empirical bed from the form. It is an image of an image. Since knowledge consists in the grasp of what is real, art must be worthless to the ideal state. Similarly the work of the poets or playwrights presents us not with truths but with imitations or reflections of real life. As such it could play no useful role in the ideal state.

 From PLATO: the *Republic*, Book X

[SOCRATES]   But would you call the painter a creator and maker?

[GLAUCON]   Certainly not.

[SOCRATES]   Yet if he is not the maker, what is he in relation to the bed?

[GLAUCON]   I think, he said, that we may fairly designate him as the imitator of that which the others make.

[SOCRATES]   Good; then you call him who is third in the descent from nature an imitator?

[GLAUCON]   Certainly.

[SOCRATES]   And the tragic poet is an imitator, and therefore, like all other imitators, he is thrice removed from the king and from the truth?

[GLAUCON]   That appears to be so.

[SOCRATES]   Then about the imitator we are agreed. And what about the painter?— I would like to know whether he may be thought to imitate that which originally exists in nature, or only the creations of artists [i.e., artisans, such as carpenters]?

[GLAUCON]   The latter.

[SOCRATES]   As they are or as they appear? You have still to determine this.

[GLAUCON]   What do you mean?

[SOCRATES]   I mean that you may look at a bed from different points of view, obliquely or directly or from any other point of view, and the bed will appear different, but there is no difference in reality. And the same of all things.

[GLAUCON]   Yes, the difference is only apparent.

[SOCRATES]   Now let me ask you another question: Which is the art of painting designed to be—an imitation of things as they are, or as they appear—of appearance or of reality?

[GLAUCON]   Of appearance.

[SOCRATES]   Then the imitator is a long way off the truth, and can do all things because he lightly touches on a small part of them, and that part is only an image.

Phaedrus

In this dialogue we find continuity as well as development in Plato's analysis of the nature of the soul; he continues to argue that the soul is immortal and has three primary divisions. But most remarkably, he also portrays the soul's struggle for knowledge in a way that allows passions or desires to play a positive, even a necessary, role. Thus this dialogue contrasts with the *Phaedo* and the *Republic*. Recall, for instance, the insistence in the *Phaedo* that passions and desires always obstruct the grasp of the forms. Plato's argument for immortality follows.

 From PLATO: the *Phaedrus*

[SOCRATES]   Let us view the affections and actions of the soul divine and human, and try to ascertain the truth about them. The beginning of our proof is as follows:

The soul through all her being is immortal, for that which is ever in motion is immortal; but that which moves another and is moved by another, in ceasing to move ceases also to live. Only the self-moving, never leaving self, never ceases to move, and is the fountain and beginning of motion to all that moves besides. Now, the beginning is unbegotten, for that which is begotten has a beginning; but the beginning is begotten of nothing, for if it were begotten of something, then the begotten would not come from a beginning. But if unbegotten, it must also be indestructible; for if beginning were destroyed, there could be no beginning out of anything, nor anything out of a beginning; and all things must have a beginning. And therefore the self-moving is the beginning of motion; and this can neither be destroyed nor begotten, else the whole heavens and all creation would collapse and stand still, and never again have motion or birth. But if the self-moving is proved to be immortal, he who affirms that self-motion is the very idea and essence of the soul will not be put to confusion. For the body which is moved from without is soulless; but that which is moved from within has a soul, for such is the nature of the soul. But if this be true, must not the soul be the self-moving, and therefore of necessity unbegotten and immortal? Enough of the soul's immortality.

The Latin word for "soul" is *anima*, which is found in the English "animated." "Soul" in this ancient usage is always associated with motion. According to Plato, something that initiates motion could not have had a beginning, since if it did whatever got it started would have to be self-moving, and so we start on an infinite regress.

 ASK YOURSELF

2.69. Therefore, we might as well admit from the outset that each source of motion (each soul) is itself without a beginning, or, in Plato's terms, is _____.

Plato continues by describing the three-part nature of the soul. He illustrates the divisions with an analogy of a charioteer drawn by two horses.

[SOCRATES]   Let me speak briefly, and in a figure, and let the figure be composite: a pair of winged horses and a charioteer. Now the winged horses and the charioteers of the gods are all of them noble and of noble descent, but those of other races are mixed; the human charioteer drives his in a pair; and one of them is noble and of noble breed, and the other is ignoble and of ignoble breed; and the driving of them of necessity gives a great deal of trouble to him. I will endeavor to explain to you in what way the mortal differs from the immortal creature.

The soul in her totality has the care of inanimate being everywhere, and traverses the whole heaven appearing in divers forms—when perfect and fully winged she soars upward, and orders the whole world. But the imperfect soul, losing her wings and drooping in her flight at last settles on the solid ground—there, finding a home, she receives an earthly frame which itself appears to be self-moved, but is really moved by her power; and this composition of soul and body is called a living and mortal creature. For no such union can be reasonably believed to be immortal; although fancy, not having seen nor surely known the nature of God, may imagine an immortal creature having both a body and also a soul which are united throughout all time.

. . . And now let us ask the reason why the soul loses her wings! . . . As I said at the beginning of this tale, I divided each soul into three—two horses and a charioteer; and one of the horses was good and the other bad: the division may remain, but I have not yet explained in what the goodness or badness of either consists, and to that I will proceed.

The right-hand horse is upright and cleanly made; he has a lofty neck and an aquiline nose; his color is white, and his eyes dark; he is a lover of honor and modesty and temperance, and the follower of true glory. He needs no touch of the whip, but is guided by word and admonition only. The other is a crooked lumbering animal, put together anyhow; he has a short thick neck; he is flat-faced and of a dark color, with gray eyes and blood-red complexion; the mate of insolence and pride, shag-eared and deaf, hardly yielding to whip and spur.

Now when the charioteer beholds the vision of love, and has his whole soul warmed through sense, and is full of the prickings and ticklings of desire, the obedient steed, then as always under the government of shame, refrains from leaping on the beloved; but the other, heedless of the goads and of the blows of the whip, plunges and runs away, giving all manner of trouble to his companion and the charioteer, whom he forces to approach the beloved and to remember the joys of love. They at first indignantly oppose him and will not be urged on to do terrible and unlawful deeds. But at last, when he persists in plaguing them, they yield and agree to do as he bids them.

 ASK YOURSELF

2.70. Plato's allegorical picture of the soul expresses very aptly the inner conflict that many people feel between that in them which is _____ and that which is _____.

In the *Phaedo*, Plato portrays the soul as intrinsically unified, intellectual and untroubled by desire except when attached to a body. But in the *Phaedrus* Plato presents the highest part of the soul as itself a source of desire. Thus desires or passions are no longer "merely" bodily and no longer necessarily obstacles to the search for truth.

 ASK YOURSELF

2.71. Using Plato's division of the soul into charioteer and two steeds, state what part of the soul actually feels "desire" for the beloved first.

The dualism, rationalism, and asceticism of the *Phaedo* and the *Republic* seem to have been moderated in the *Phaedrus*. Perhaps Plato began to think that his analysis of self and knowledge was too simplistic. Bodily life, with its passions and changes, is perhaps not so devoid of value. We can perhaps infer that, given the views expressed in the *Phaedrus*, there might even be room for "the poets" in his ideal state.

SUGGESTIONS FOR FURTHER READING

Primary Sources

Cooper, John M., ed. *Plato: Complete Works* (Indianapolis: Hackett Publishing Company, 1997). Includes all of the works attributed to Plato in antiquity, including some (e.g., *Sisyphus, Second Alcibiades*) not included in Hamilton and Cairns. Many recent translations.

Hamilton, Edith, ed. *The Collected Dialogues of Plato, including the Letters* (New York: Pantheon Books, 1961). A variety of translators; a long-time standard edition.

Critical Analyses and Discussions

Allen, R. E. *Plato's Parmenides* (Minneapolis: University of Minnesota Press, 1983). An advanced book, but very interesting for those who wish to see the subtle details of Plato's criticisms of his own theory of forms, and his responses.

Annas, Julia. *An Introduction to Plato's Republic* (Oxford: Clarendon Press, 1981). A fine introduction to Plato's central work.

Benson, Hugh H., ed. *Essays on the Philosophy of Socrates* (New York: Oxford University Press, 1992). Recent work on Socrates dealing with philosophical issues in the early dialogues, as well as the historicity of the dialogues as a source.

Grube, G.M.A. *Plato's Thought* (Indianapolis: Hackett Publishing Company, 1980). Accessible general introduction.

Irwin, T. H. *Classical Thought* (Oxford: Oxford University Press, 1989). A general discussion by a premier philosopher/scholar.

Kraut, Richard. *The Cambridge Companion to Plato* (Cambridge: Cambridge University Press, 1992). Recent scholarship on the continuing philosophical challenge of Plato. Excellent extensive bibliography.

Vlastos, Gregory. *Plato's Universe* (Seattle: University of Washington Press, 1975). This and the following two works are by one of the foremost interpreters of ancient philosophy.

———. *Socrates: Ironist and Moral Philosopher* (Ithaca, NY: Cornell University Press, 1991).

———. *Socratic Studies* (Cambridge: Cambridge University Press, 1994).

CHAPTER 3

ARISTOTLE

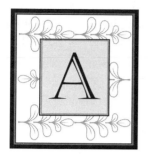

ristotle was born in 384 BCE in Macedonia—northern Greece—where his father was a physician to the king. Undoubtedly the empirical nature of his father's studies influenced him to take an interest in observable details. That interest is evident in a lifetime of collecting observations on plants and animals. Aristotle traveled to Athens at the age of eighteen and became a member of Plato's academy. He remained there twenty years, did some traveling, and returned to Macedonia, where for a short time he was tutor to the king's son Alexander, later known as "the great" for his military exploits and his establishment of a great empire. Eventually Aristotle returned to Athens and set up his own school, called the Lyceum. He was in the habit of walking around while he lectured, a habit that earned him and his followers the name "peripatetic"—from the Greek word meaning "to walk around."

The most general difference between Aristotle and his great teacher Plato is that Aristotle regarded the familiar world revealed by the senses to be fully real. In Plato's view a particular dog is less real than the "form" of dogness, and the forms are transempirical, eternal, and unchanging. For Aristotle, on the contrary, the particular observable thing is the most real thing. Aristotle is working out his views on this matter in the following selections from his work *Categories*. Like Plato he thinks language contains clues to what is real. But his account of the way words work is more complex and subtle than Plato's.

 ASK YOURSELF

3.1. What is the most general difference between Aristotle and Plato?

LOGICAL WORKS

Categories

Aristotle discusses different kinds of "predication." For example, when I predicate "blue" of the sky, I ascribe, or predicate, a quality. If I say, "The Parthenon is north of the Lyceum," I predicate a relationship. The different kinds of predication mark different "categories."

The Category of Substance. The idea of substance is naturally associated with the idea of what is most basic or most real. We speak of the "substance" of a book, or the "substances" that make up the world. Aristotle's concept of substance arises in part from thoughts about grammar. In a sentence such as "George is clever," the subject is George and cleverness is "predicated of" George (the grammatical predicate is "is clever"). We can talk about all sorts of things, that is, make all sorts of things the "subject" of our talk. For example, I can say (1) "Mary is beautiful" and I can say (2) "The color pink is beautiful." But Aristotle wants to show that there is a very fundamental difference between these two cases of "talking about." In the one case we are talking about a substance, in the other we are not.

 ASK YOURSELF

3.2. In which, (1) or (2), are we talking about a "substance," do you suppose?

 From ARISTOTLE: *Categories*, Chapter 5 ——————

Substance, in the truest and primary and most definite sense of the word, is that which is neither predicable of a subject nor present in a subject; for instance, the individual man or horse.

If you fill in the "x" in "George is x" with all sorts of predicates (e.g., "clever," "to the left of Bill," and so forth) what you say will make sense, but you cannot sensibly fill in "x" in "x is George" with all sorts of predicate or subject terms.

But in a secondary sense those things are called substances within which, as species, the primary substances are included; also those which, as genera, include the species. For instance, the individual man is included in the species "man," and the genus to which the species belongs is "animal"; these, therefore—that is to say, the species "man" and the genus "animal"—are termed secondary substances.

The kinds of things that "are neither predicable of nor present in a subject" are exactly the things that are classified or sorted by such terms as "man," "animal," "fish," "arachnid," and the like. Terms like "white," "clever," or "to the left of" do not, on the other hand, classify things in the sense of independently existing entities at all.

It is plain from what has been said that both the name and the definition of the predicate must be predicable of the subject. For instance, "man" is predicted of the individual man. Now in this case the name of the species "man" is applied to the individual, for we use the term "man" in describing the individual; and the definition of "man" will also be predicated of the individual man, for the individual man is both man and animal. Thus, both the name and the definition of the species are predicable of the individual.

With regard, on the other hand, to those things that are present in a subject, it is generally the case that neither their name nor their definition is predicable of that in which they are present. Though, however, the definition is never predicable, there is nothing in certain cases to prevent the name being used. For instance, "white" being present in a body is predicated of that in which it is present, for a body is called white: the definition, however, of the color "white" is never predicable of the body.

Suppose the definition of "man" is "rational featherless biped." Then if George is a man it will also be the case that "rational featherless biped" can be predicated of him. Now suppose the definition of "white" is "the color produced by the refraction of rays x and y" (we will not quibble over whether that is a correct schema, or even whether one can define "white" at all). Now you cannot sensibly say "George is the color produced by the refraction of rays x and r." George is not a color, though he may have a color. So you cannot predicate the definition of "white" of George. We can predicate "white" of George but not its definition, and that is one grammatical way to distinguish terms that tell us what George is, substance terms such as "man" or "animal," from terms that merely ascribe some property, like whiteness, which someone could lack without ceasing to be a man.

Everything except primary substances is either predicable of a primary substance or present in a primary substance. This becomes evident by reference to particular instances which occur. "Animal" is predicated of the species "man," therefore of the individual man, for if there were no individual man of whom it could be predicated, it could not be predicated of the species "man" at all. Again, color is present in body, therefore in individual bodies, for if there were no individual body in which it was present, it could not be present in body at all. Thus everything except primary substances is either predicated of primary substances, or is present in them, and if these last did not exist, it would be impossible for anything else to exist.

Doesn't this last remark amount to the claim that the most basic entities in the universe are precisely individuals like George? Not water or "seeds" or earth, water, fire, and air (Thales, Anaxagoras, Empedocles); not the One (Parmenides); not numbers (the Pythagoreans); not the forms (Plato); but ordinary persons and dogs and cats and trees are the ultimate furniture of the universe!

 ASK YOURSELF

3.3. Give an example of your own of each of the following: primary substance; secondary substance; something found in a subject but not predicated of it.

Of secondary substances, the species is more truly substance than the genus, being more nearly related to primary substance. For if any one should render an account of what a primary substance is, he would render a more instructive account, and one more proper to the subject, by stating the species than by stating the genus. Thus, he would give a more instructive account of an individual man by stating that he was man than by stating that he was animal, for the former description is peculiar to the individual in a greater degree, while the latter is too general. Again, the man who gives an account of the nature of an individual tree will give a more instructive account by mentioning the species "tree" than by mentioned the genus "plant." Moreover, primary substances are most properly called substances in virtue of the fact that they are the entities which underlie everything else, and that everything else is either predicated of them or present in them. Now the same relation which subsists between primary substance and everything else subsists also between the species and the genus: for the species is to the genus as subject is to predicate, since the genus is predicated of the species, whereas the species cannot be predicated of the genus. Thus we have a second ground for asserting that the species is more truly substance than the genus. Of species themselves, except in the case of such as are genera, no one is more truly substance than another. We should not give a more appropriate account of the individual man by stating the species to which he belonged, than we should of an individual horse by adopting the same method of definition. In the same way, of primary substances, no one is more truly substance than another; an individual man is not more truly substance than an individual ox.

It is, then, with good reason that of all that remains, when we exclude primary substances, we concede to species and genera alone the name "secondary substance," for these alone of all the predicates convey a knowledge of primary substance. For it is by stating the species or the genus that we appropriately define any individual man; and we shall make our definition more exact by stating the former than by stating the latter. All other things that we state, such as that he is white, that he runs, and so on, are irrelevant to the definition. Thus it is just that these alone, apart from primary substances, should be called substances.

 ASK YOURSELF

3.4. Plato argued that reality comes in degrees. Does Aristotle agree? Justify your answer.

3.5. So, Aristotle says, "white" and "running" do not name or denote substances. That seems like common sense. But what would Plato have said "white" names or refers to?

3.6. Does Plato's view imply that what "white" refers to is just as basic and real as what "man" refers to? Explain.

Further, primary substances are most properly so called, because they underlie and are the subjects of everything else. Now the same relation that subsists between primary substance and everything else subsists also between the species and the genus to which the primary substance belongs, on the one hand, and every attribute which is not included within these, on the other. For these are the subjects of the genus.

The concept of substance has provoked controversy among philosophers for millennia. It is not always easy to tack down the subject of the controversies. For example, there is a common way of thinking about substance as that which underlies various properties. Substances are precisely things that have properties or characteristics. After all, you couldn't have a bunch of properties or traits without something that had those traits, could you? Wouldn't that be like the smile of the Cheshire cat, which stays around after the cat is gone? But some philosophers, such as David Hume in the eighteenth century (CE) argued, "We have no idea of substance distinct from that of a collection of particular qualities" (*Treatise*, 1.1.16). So in Hume's view a particular man is just a collection of properties, such as the property of being white, six feet tall, rational, clever, and so forth. None of these properties tell us what a man is. They are all on the same level, so to speak.

 ASK YOURSELF

3.7. What does Hume say a particular man is, and how does what he says differ from Aristotle's account?

Hume's view has a difficulty that Aristotle avoids. If you asked Hume, "What holds the various properties that make up George together, that is, how do you specify the collection that is George?" he would have to reply in one of two ways: (1) He could say that what holds them together is the subject, George. But in that case he seems to have returned to the idea of George as a substance. Or (2) he could say that George can be specified simply by enumerating all the properties that make him up. But in that case, every time a new property showed up (e.g., George's nose turns red) you would have a different item, no longer the same old George! But then we would have no way of talking about or thinking about things that persist through time and that we can come to understand better as time passes. We could not even think of ourselves as the "same" person we were one second ago, since in the last second we are bound to have changed in some way, even if only by having a speck of dust on an eyelid that was not there a second ago. If you think about it a bit, you can see that the ability to talk and think in terms of subjects that persist through time is very basic. How could we do without it? Aristotle is depending upon these very facts in presenting his claim that particular things like George are basic in a way that a bit of white or a particular instance of cleverness are not. In his view terms like "man" or "animal" do not just name properties on the same level as whiteness or having a red nose, but are fundamental for sorting out or classifying the basic particular things. And if there were not those basic particular things, there couldn't be anything else, either.

Another way to put some of these points is this: George cannot be true of something in the way that white or clever can. You cannot sensibly say, "It is true of clever that it is George," but you can say, "It is true of George that he is clever." Thus the very structure of language seems to support the notion that "substance in the truest and primary and most definite sense of the word" refers to individual men, horses, carrots, and so forth. Everything else that exists is just qualities of substances, such as where they are located, what their color is, whether they are to the left or right of something else, whether they are equal to or smaller than something else, and so forth.

 ASK YOURSELF

3.8. Plato thought that there is a "form," equality itself, which is more real than any two equal things. That is, he though "equality" named an enduring particular. What would Aristotle say to Plato about this?

Aristotle's thinking about substance is further developed in his book *Physics*, in which he takes up the subjects that concerned the Presocratics as well as Plato. What is the relation of the one to the many, of that which changes to that which stays the same?

NATURE AND THE SOUL

Physics

Aristotle undertakes a critical inquiry into nature and the explanation of change.

On "Nature" (Physis). Aristotle takes up the discussion of *physis* that was begun by the Presocratics.

 From ARISTOTLE: *Physics*, Book 2, Chapter 1 _____

Of things that exist, some exist by nature, some from other causes. "By nature" the animals and their parts exist, and the plants and the simple bodies (earth, fire, air, water) for we say that these and the like exist "by nature." All the things mentioned present a feature in which they differ from things that are not constituted by nature. Each of them has within itself a principle of motion and of stationariness (in respect of place, or of growth and decrease, or by way of alteration).

On the other hand, a bed and a coat and anything else of that sort, qua receiving these designations—i.e., insofar as they are products of art—have no innate impulse to change. But insofar as they happen to be composed of stone or of earth or of a mixture of the two, they do have such an impulse, and just to that extent, which seems to indicate that nature is a source or cause of being moved and of being at rest in that to which it belongs primarily, in virtue of itself and not in virtue of a concomitant attribute. . . .

When Aristotle speaks of "motion" he is referring to any kind of change. So a change in color would be an example of motion. Now a coat might change color by being dyed. But that change would not be a change "from within." On the other hand, if a coat changes on its own or from within, it will do so not because it is a coat but, say, because it is made of wool, which changes naturally in various ways. The same kind of change in a piece of wool would be found in a wool sweater or on the sheep itself. So that kind of change in the coat has nothing to do with the fact that it is a coat.

 From ARISTOTLE: *Physics*, Book 3, Chapter 2 _____

Some identify the nature or substance of a natural object with that immediate constituent of it which taken by itself is without arrangement, e.g. the wood is the "nature" of the bed, and the bronze the "nature" of the statue. As an indication of this Antiphon points out that if you planted a bed and the rotting wood acquired the power of sending up a shoot, it would not be a bed that would come up, but wood—which shows that the arrangement in accordance with the rules of the art is merely an incidental attribute, whereas the real nature [of the wood] is the other, which, further, persists continuously through the process of making.

 ASK YOURSELF

3.9. Give an example of something that exists by nature.

3.10. What is Antiphon's argument to show that a bed does not exist "by nature?"

"Nature," then, refers to that which has a principle of change within itself. But there are different kinds of changes, for example, changes in color, changes in location, or the change from being alive to being dead. Aristotle realizes that in trying to understand a changing world we are trying to understand various kinds of change. Rather than denying change any reality (Parmenides) or confining it to the realm of opinion (Plato), Aristotle supposes that we can understand and have real knowledge of a changing world. We attempt to understand by looking for answers to questions that start "Why . . . ?" In Book 3 of the *Physics* Aristotle says, "Men do not think they know a thing till they have grasped the 'why' of (which is to grasp its primary cause)."

For example, if we wanted to know "why" the wood bed buried in the ground rotted, the answer would be in terms of the "nature" of wood. Wood is the kind of stuff or nature that rots when exposed to moisture for a long time. Thus we explain the change in the wood in terms of its "material." Aristotle calls this an explanation in terms of "material causes." He thinks there are four basic kinds of explanations, and he calls them explanations in terms of "causes." This use of the word "cause" is a bit unusual. Aristotle identifies four such causes: material, formal, efficient, and final.

Material Causes. Aristotle begins with a discussion of the way in which the "stuff" of something may contribute to and explain various changes that it undergoes.

 From ARISTOTLE: *Physics*, Book 2, Chapter 1 ____

But if the material of each of these objects has itself the same relation to something else, say bronze (or gold) to water, bones (or wood) to earth and so on, that (they say) would be their nature and essence [i.e., water would be the nature of bronze, earth of bones or wood]. Consequently some assert earth, others fire or air or water or some or all of these, to be the nature of the things that are. For any object any one of these [philosophers] supposed to have this character—whether one thing or more than one thing—this or these he declared to be the whole of substance, all else being its affections, states, or dispositions. Every such thing [e.g., earth] they held to be eternal (for it could not turn into anything else and cease to be earth), but other things [e.g., bones or wood] they held comes into being and ceases to be times without number.

This then is one account of "nature," namely that it is the immediate material substratum of things which have in themselves a principle of motion or change.

ASK YOURSELF

3.11. Did Thales try to explain the changes in nature in terms of material causes? Explain.

There are, however, other kinds of "why questions" that are answered in terms of other kinds of "causes."

Formal Causes. Sometimes we answer a "why" question by citing a formal feature of a thing or process.

Another account is that "nature" is the shape or form that is specified in the definition of the thing. For the word "nature" is applied to what is according to nature and the natural in the same way as "art" is applied to what is artistic or a work of art. We should not say in the latter case that there is anything artistic about a thing, if it is a bed only potentially, not yet having the form of a bed; nor should we call it a work of art. The same is true of natural compounds. What is potentially flesh or bone has not yet its own "nature," and does not exist until it receives the form specified in the definition, which we name in defining what flesh or bone is. Thus in the second sense of "nature" it would be the shape or form (not separable except in statement) of things which have in themselves a source of motion. (The combination of the two, e.g., man, is not "nature" but "by nature" or "natural.") The form indeed is "nature" rather than the matter; for a thing is more properly said to be what it is when it has attained to fulfillment than when it exists potentially. Again man is born from man, but not bed from bed. That is why people say that the figure is not the nature of a bed, but the wood is—if the bed sprouted not a bed but wood would come up. But even if the figure is art, then on the same principle the shape of man is his nature. For man is born from man.

The essential characteristics of bone, or of a man, are a function, so to speak, of organization. In one sense, what makes something a piece of bone is not, say, its calcium, but the particular arrangement of its elements. A bit of calcium may be potentially bone, but it is potentially a lot of other things, too. Not until it gets in a certain arrangement or shape does it count as bone. Aristotle is close to the spirit of Plato when he calls the particular character of a thing, its shape or organization or essence, "form." Look back at the beginning of this passage and then answer the following question:

ASK YOURSELF

3.12. Plato thought that the form or essence of a thing (a particular man, for instance) existed apart from that particular thing. Cite evidence from the preceding passage that shows that Aristotle disagrees.

If we want to know "why something is a man" one kind of answer will consist in specifying the form, or essence, or essential definition, of man. For example, something is a man because it walks upright on two legs, is featherless, and has opposable thumbs. That would be an explanation or answer to a "why question" in terms of a "formal cause."

Efficient Causes. But there are still other "why questions."

 From ARISTOTLE: *Physics*, Book 2, Chapter 3 ____

. . . there are several causes of the same thing . . . e.g. both the art of the sculptor and the bronze are causes of the statue. These are causes of the statue qua statue, not in virtue of anything else that it may be—only not in the same way, the one being the material cause, the other the cause whence the motion comes.

If we want to know why a certain statue exists, it would not help to be told "because it is bronze" (although if we wanted to know why its surface was hard, that would be an explanation of sorts). We may want to know what brought it into existence, what caused it to exist, in the sense of "cause" that is most familiar to English speakers. The sculptor would be the cause in that sense. He shaped the bronze into, say, a likeness of Venus; he "effected" a change in the bronze and thus might be called the "efficient cause" of the statue. When a thrown rock breaks a window, when a drop of acid puts a hole in the carpet, or when an lineman knocks down a quarterback, they are all acting as "efficient causes." The study of efficient causes is largely what science has been for several hundred years. Even when twenty-first century scientists invoke materials, or definitions, or purposes, they may often think of these as reducible to causes in the efficient sense. It is in this sense of "cause" that we are interested in what caused a disease, or what caused my automobile to stall, or what causes the planets to move in elliptical orbits.

Final Causes. There is a still further sense of cause, however, corresponding to a further kind of "why" question.

Again (4) in the sense of end or "that for the sake of which" a thing is done, e.g. health is the cause of walking about. ("Why is he walking about?" we say. "To be healthy," and, having said that, we think we have assigned the cause.) The same is true also of all the intermediate steps which are brought about through the action of something else as means towards the end, e.g. reduction of flesh, purging, drugs, or surgical instruments are means towards health. All these things are "for the sake of" the end, though they differ from one another in that some are activities, others instruments.

When we ask, "Why is George walking about?" we are asking for an explanation in terms of purpose or goal. We want to know what the walking is a means toward, whether it might have as its goal better health, or to try out new shoes, or to get to the drugstore, and so forth. We are especially inclined to explain human actions in terms of purposes or goals. The Greek word for purpose or goal is *telos*, so this kind of explanation is called "teleological." The Latin term for "goal" or "end" is *finis*, so these kinds of explanations are also sometimes called "final cause" explanations. Aristotle sums up his ideas in the following passage.

 From ARISTOTLE: *Physics*, Book 2, Chapter 7 ____

It is clear then that there are causes, and that the number of them is what we have stated. The number is the same as that of the things comprehended under the question "why." The "why" is referred ultimately either (1), in things which do not involve motion, e.g. in mathematics, to the "what" (to the definition of "straight line" or "commensurable", &c.), or (2) to what initiated a motion, e.g. "why did they go to war?—because there had been a raid"; or (3) we are inquiring "for the sake of what?"—"that they may rule"; or (4), in the case of things that come into being, we are looking for the matter. The causes, therefore, are these and so many in number.

Now, the causes being four, it is the business of the physicist to know about them all, and if he refers his problems back to all of them, he will assign the "why" in the way proper to his science—the matter, or the form, or the mover, or "that for the sake of which." The last three often coincide; for the "what" and "that for the sake of which" are one, while the primary source of motion is the same in species as these (for man generates man), and so too, in general, are all things which cause movement by being themselves moved. . . .

The last sentence could be rephrased as follows: The formal cause, the final cause, and the efficient cause often coincide. For example, the efficient cause of a child is the father and mother, but they also supply the "nature" or form, that is, the human essence (the formal cause), and it is for the sake of having a human child that they act to produce one (the final cause).

 ASK YOURSELF

3.13. Do Plato's forms act as "causes" in more than one of Aristotle's senses? Explain your answer, thinking particularly about the form of the *Good* as you do.

3.14. What might be the material, formal, efficient, and final causes of a piece of sculpture familiar to you?

3.15. What Aristotelian "cause" is most likely being asked for in each of the following "why questions?" (1) Why is this liquid bitter tasting? (2) Why are the newspapers all over the floor? (3) Why do the leaves of plants turn toward the light? (4) Why does 2 + 2 = 4? (5) Why does low atmospheric pressure often bring bad weather? (6) Why do skiers throw their weight downhill when executing a turn?

On the Soul

Plato and Socrates apparently conceived of the soul as something distinct from the body, capable of existing before the birth and after the death of the body. Aristotle's conception is, once again, very different from his old teacher's view. In fact, Aristotle does not confine "souls" to human beings. Understanding why will illuminate his conception of the human soul.

Kinds of Soul. Not only humans have souls.

 From ARISTOTLE: *On the Soul*, Book 1, Chapter 1 _

We must consider also whether soul is divisible or is without parts, and whether it is everywhere homogeneous or not; and if not homogeneous, whether its various forms are different specifically or generically: up to the present time those who have discussed and investigated soul seem to have confined themselves to the human soul. We must be careful not to ignore the question whether soul can be defined in a single unambiguous formula, as is the case with animal, or whether we must not give a separate formula for each of it, as we do for horse, dog, man, god (in the latter case the "universal" animal—and so too every other "common predicate"—being treated either as nothing at all or as a later product).

 From ARISTOTLE: *On the Soul*, Book 2, Chapter 2 _

We resume our inquiry from a fresh starting-point by calling attention to the fact that what has soul in it differs from what has not, in that the former displays life. Now this word has more than one sense, and provided any one alone of these is found in a thing we say that thing is living. Living, that is, may mean thinking or perception or local movement and rest, or movement in the sense of nutrition, decay and growth. Hence we think of plants also as living, for they are observed to possess in themselves an originative power through which they increase or decrease in all spatial directions; they grow up and down, and everything that grows increases its bulk alike in both directions or indeed in all, and continues to live so long as it can absorb nutriment. This power of self-nutrition can be isolated from the other powers mentioned, but not they from it—in mortal beings at least. The fact is obvious in plants; for it is the only "soul" power they possess. This is the originative power the possession of which leads us to speak of things as living at all. But it is the possession of sensation that leads us for the first time to speak of living things as animals; for even those beings which possess no power of local movement but do possess the power of sensation we call animals and not merely living things.

Certain kinds of animals possess in addition the power of locomotion, and still another order of animate beings, i.e. man and possibly another order like man or superior to him, the power of thinking, i.e. mind. It is now evident that a single definition can be given of soul only in the same sense as one can be given of figure. For, as in that case there is no figure distinguishable and apart from triangle, &c., so here there is no soul apart from the forms of soul just enumerated. It is true that a highly general definition can be given for figure which will fit all figures without expressing the peculiar nature of any figure. So here in the case of soul and its specific forms.

The notion of soul is strongly connected with life. You could almost say "soul = life." But there are many kinds of living things, plants, animals, viruses, and so forth. Aristotle is raising the question whether there should be one account of soul for all of these different kinds of living things.

Aristotle is pointing out that the "kind" of life a plant has consists simply in nutritive (vegetative) functions. On the other hand, what we call animals, while they have nutritive functions, also have the capacity for sensation. So they have "life" in a somewhat expanded sense. Aristotle is thus arguing that there are different kinds of soul (different "ways" of being alive).

So there must be different definitions for different types of soul. We could give a general definition of soul, just as we can define "figure" in general, even though there is no such thing as a figure in general, but only particular figures, such as the triangle, the square, and so forth. The general definition of "soul" would be "anything that is alive" or "whatever it is that makes living things alive." But there are differences in the way plants are alive, animals are alive, and humans are alive.

 ASK YOURSELF

3.16. In what way does the life of humans differ from the life of other animals?

How the Soul and the Body Are Related. The difference between Aristotle's conception of the soul and Plato's is particularly marked in his account of the relation of soul to body.

 From ARISTOTLE: *On the Soul*, Book 2, Chapter 1

Suppose that the eye were an animal—sight would have been its soul, for sight is the substance or essence of the eye which corresponds to the formula, the eye being merely the matter of seeing; when seeing is removed the eye is no longer an eye, except in name—it is no more a real eye than the eye of a statue or of a painted figure. . . . [A]s the pupil plus the power of sight constitutes the eye, so the soul plus the body constitutes the animal. From this it indubitably follows that the soul is inseparable from its body. . . .

Aristotle is drawing an analogy: If an eyeball could live on its own, then the power of sight would be to an eyeball as the soul is to the body. Obviously you cannot have the power of sight all by itself. The power must be realized in something. Likewise, you cannot have a soul all by itself. It is simply a kind of "power" or capacity, and you cannot have capacities all by themselves. Capacities are always capacities of something. For example, you cannot have the capacity to run all by itself. You can only have it in a dog, a man, an ant, and so forth.

ASK YOURSELF

3.17. Since humans have (1) vegetative capacities, (2) the capacity for sensation and movement, and (3) the capacity for thought, would it follow that human beings have three different souls?

3.18. Could an individual human soul be immortal, given the correctness of Aristotle's account? Why or why not?

ETHICS

The work by Aristotle set for examination here is meant to be a "practical" work. That is, it is meant for people who are serious about putting its ideas into practice. A merely theoretical inquiry into ethical goodness does not interest Aristotle (see, for example, *Nicomachean Ethics*, Book 2, Chapter 2, section 1). Although in his view arguments by themselves cannot make a person good, the person who is serious about leading a good life will want to consider carefully arguments about what that life is and what leading it involves, provided they have time to do so (and some people are so consumed just by the need to survive that they will not have time). He or she will want to learn to avoid bad arguments and views in particular. Even though arguments by themselves will not make a person good, people can be misled and corrupted by *bad* reasoning.

As you study this work, therefore, you will want to keep asking, "How does what Aristotle says connect up with my own conception of the good life and my own acting out of that conception? Can I learn anything from him that will make a practical difference to me, that will enable me to live better or, at least, avoid ways of living or views about living that are ultimately hurtful"? Anyone who has no concern about these sorts of practical questions will not likely find much in this work of interest, and certainly will not find what Aristotle wanted them to find. Aristotle's work is divided up into books consisting of many short chapters, which makes it easy to refer to particular spots in the text. The chapter headings included here are not part of Aristotle's text.

Book 1

Chapter 1. The Good as the Aim of All Action. Aristotle's thinking about ethics stresses the idea of a good life, not just particular good actions.

 From ARISTOTLE: *Nicomachean Ethics*, Book 1 ____

Every art and every scientific inquiry, and similarly every action and purpose, may be said to aim at some good. Hence the good has been well defined as that at which all things aim. But it appears that there is a difference in the ends; for the ends are sometimes activities, and sometimes results beyond the mere activities. Also, where there are certain ends beyond the actions, the results are naturally superior to the activities.

ASK YOURSELF

3.19. Is there anything at all that you do that is not done for the sake of some "good"? If you think there is, name it here.

You might have heard a proverb that goes something like this: "There is nothing worse than getting all the way to the top and then discovering you are on the wrong ladder."

 ASK YOURSELF

3.20. This proverb is a way of saying that we need to think about the _____ of action, not just the means.

3.21. Now try to think of an example of a good thing you want that is (1) an activity and one that is (2) some result of an activity.

As there are various actions, arts, and sciences, it follows that the aims or ends are also various. Thus health is the aim of medicine, a vessel of shipbuilding, victory of strategy, and wealth of domestic economy. It often happens that there are a number of such arts or sciences which fall under a single discipline, as the art of making bridles, and all such other arts as make the instruments of horsemanship, fall under horsemanship, and this again as well as every military action under strategy, and in the same way other arts or sciences under other disciplines. But in all these cases the ends of the higher arts or sciences, whatever they may be, are more desirable than those of the subordinate arts or sciences, as it is for the sake of the former that the latter themselves are sought. It makes no difference to the argument whether the activities themselves are the ends of the actions, or something else beyond the activities as in the above mentioned sciences.

Chapter 2. The Science of the Highest Good Is "Political." Political science is knowledge of what is required for a good community. It includes more than "politics" as we may understand that word.

If it is true that (a) in our actions there is an end which we wish for its own sake, and on account of which we wish everything else, and (b) that we do not desire all things for the sake of something else (for, if that were so, the process would go on ad infinitum, and our desire would be idle and futile) then (c) it is clear that this will be the good or the supreme good.

Aristotle is here asking if there is some single end that we *all* seek, some ultimate goal which we seek for its own sake and not as a means to something else. (It will become evident as we proceed in what sense such an ultimate goal might be "one" or "single.")

ASK YOURSELF

3.22. Do you think there is an ultimate goal we all seek? If you answer "yes," what, at this stage of your thoughts, do you think it is? If "no," then does everything that you aim at serve as a means to something else?

3.23. What is Aristotle's objection to the idea that everything done is a means to something (answer this no matter whether you said yes or no in the previous answer)?

Does it not follow then that the knowledge of this supreme good is of great importance for the conduct of life, and that, if we know it, we shall have a better chance of attaining what we want, like archers who have a target to aim at? But, if this is the case we must endeavor to understand, at least in outline, its nature, and the branch of knowledge or the discipline to which it belongs.

It would seem that it would be the most authoritative or overarching science or discipline, and such is evidently the *political;* for it is political science or the discipline of politics which determines what sciences are necessary in states, and what kind of sciences should be learnt, and who in the state should learn them and to what extent. We perceive too that the most honored disciplines, e.g., generalship, domestic economy, and rhetoric, are subordinate to it. But as it makes use of the other practical sciences, and also legislates upon the things to be done and to be avoided, it follows that its end will include the ends of all other sciences, and will therefore be the true good of humans. For although the good of an individual is identical with the good of the state, it is evidently greater and more perfect to attain and preserve the good of the state. Though it is worth something to do this for an individual, it is nobler and more divine to do it for a nation or state. These then are the objects at which the present inquiry aims, and so it is in a sense a political inquiry.

 ASK YOURSELF

3.24. Why does Aristotle think that inquiry into the highest good for humans must in a sense be "political"?

Chapter 3. The Methods for This Inquiry. Ethical reasoning is not like many other sorts of reasoning, such as that required for geometry or the construction of a watch. It does not have that kind of precision.

But our statement of the case will be adequate, if it be made with all such clearness as the subject-matter admits; for it would be wrong to expect the same degree of accuracy in all reasonings just as it would with respect to the products of the various crafts. Noble and just things, which are the subjects of investigation in political science, show so much variety and uncertainty that they are sometimes thought to have only a conventional, and not a natural, existence. There is the same sort of uncertainty in regard to good things, as it often happens that injuries result from them; thus people have been ruined by wealth, or again by courage. As our subjects then and our premises are of this nature, we must be content to indicate the truth roughly and in outline; and as our subjects and premises are true generally but not universally, we must be content to arrive at conclusions which are generally true. It is right to receive the particular statements which are made in the same spirit; for an educated person will expect accuracy in each subject only so far as the nature of the subject allows; he might as well accept probable reasoning from a mathematician as require demonstrative proofs from a rhetorician.

But everyone is capable of judging the subjects that he understands, and is a good judge of them. It follows that in particular subjects it is a specialist who is a good judge. Hence the young are not proper students of political science, as they have no experience of the actions of life which form the premises and subjects of [practical] reasonings. Also it may be added that from their tendency to follow their emotions they will not study the subject to any purpose or profit, for the purpose of ethical science is not knowledge but action.

 ASK YOURSELF

3.25. Does Aristotle think that the subject matter of ethics is precise? Does he think it is a bad thing if it is not? Why?

The claim that the aim of ethical knowledge is action, not just contemplation of truth, is crucial to Aristotle. Nonetheless in Book 10 of this work it seems that Aristotle does deviate from this claim.

It makes no difference whether a person is young in years or youthful in character; for the defect of which I speak is not one of time but is due to the emotional character of his life and pursuits. Knowledge is as useless to such a person as it is to an intemperate person. But where the desires and actions of people are regulated by reason the knowledge of these subjects will be extremely valuable.

But having said so much by way of preface as to the students of political science, the spirit in which it should be studied, and the object which we set before ourselves, let us resume our argument as follows. . . .

 ASK YOURSELF

3.26. Give two of Aristotle's reasons for saying that a young person might not come up with the best answers to questions about the good for humans.

Chapter 4. Common Beliefs about the Highest Good Are Inaccurate. Aristotle takes everyday beliefs about the good life seriously, but he also is critical of some of them.

As every knowledge and moral purpose aspires to some good, what is in our view the good at which the political science aims, and what is the highest of all practical goods? As to its name, there is I may say, a general agreement. The masses and the cultured classes agree in calling it *happiness* (*eudaimonia*), and conceive that "to live well" or "to do well" is the same thing as "to be happy." But as to the *nature* of happiness, they do not agree, nor do the masses give the same account of it as the philosophers. The former describe it as something visible and palpable, e.g., pleasure, wealth or honour. People give various definitions of it, and often the same person gives different definitions at different times; for when a person has been ill, it is health, when he is poor, it is wealth.

 ASK YOURSELF

3.27. List the common conceptions of happiness mentioned so far.

3.28. Can you think of a few others to list here?

3.29. Can you see any problem with any of these conceptions? Explain.

If someone is conscious of his own ignorance, he envies people who use grand language above his own comprehension. Some philosophers on the other hand have held that, besides these various goods, there is an absolute good which is the cause of goodness in them all.

 ASK YOURSELF

3.30. Who might Aristotle be thinking of?

It would perhaps be a waste of time to examine all these opinions; it will be enough to examine such as are most popular or as seem to be more or less reasonable.

But we must not fail to observe the distinction between the reasonings which proceed from first principles and the reasonings which lead up to first principles. For Plato was right in raising the difficult question whether the true way was *from* first principles or *to* first principles, as in the race-course from the judges to the goal, or vice versa. We must begin with such facts as are known. But facts may be known in two ways, i.e. either relatively to ourselves or absolutely. It is probable then that we must begin with such facts as are known to us, i.e. relatively. It is necessary therefore, if a person is to be a competent student of what is noble and just and of politics in general, that he should have received a good moral training. For the fact that a thing is so is a first principle or starting point, and, if the fact is sufficiently clear it will not be necessary to go on to ask the reason of it. But a person who has received a good moral training either possesses first principles, or will have no problem in acquiring them. But if he does not possess them, and cannot acquire them, he had better lay to heart Hesiod's lines:

"Far best is he who is himself all-wise,
And he, too, good who listens to wise words;
But whoever is not wise nor lays to heart
Another's wisdom is a useless man."

ASK YOURSELF

3.31. In the study of ethics, Aristotle is saying, we must start from some true opinions or views, and those can only be gotten through a good upbringing. Does this imply that people with a bad upbringing (for example, abused people) will not be able to get a good start at studying these matters?

3.32. Do you think he is right? Why?

Chapter 5. An Analysis of the Common Views. Aristotle sets out some objections to common views on what constitutes that good, or those goods, at which all our actions aim.

But to return from our digression: it seems not unreasonable that people should derive their conception of good or of happiness from men's lives. Thus ordinary or vulgar people conceive it to be pleasure, and accordingly approve a life of enjoyment. For there are exactly three prominent lives, the sensual, the political, and, thirdly, the speculative.

Now the mass of men present an absolutely slavish appearance, as choosing the life of brute beasts, but they meet with consideration because so many persons in authority share the tastes of Sardanapalus.

Cultivated and practical people, on the other hand, identify happiness with honor, as honor is the general end of political life. But this appears too superficial for our present purpose; for honor seems to depend more on the people who pay it rather than the upon the person to whom it is paid, and we have an intuitive feeling that the good is something that is proper to a man himself and cannot be easily taken away from him. It seems too that the reason why men seek honor is that they may be confident of their goodness. Accordingly they seek it at the hands of the wise and those who know them well, and they seek it on the ground of virtue; hence it is clear that in their judgment at any rate virtue is superior to honor.

It would perhaps be right then to look upon virtue rather than honor as being the end of the political life. Yet virtue again, it appears, lacks completeness; for it seems that a man may possess virtue and yet be asleep or inactive throughout life, and, not only so, but he may experience the greatest calamities and misfortunes. But nobody would call such a life a life of happiness, unless he were maintaining a paradox. It is not necessary to dwell further on this subject, as it is sufficiently discussed in the popular philosophical treatises. The third life is the speculative which we will investigate hereafter.

The life of money-making is in a sense a life of constraint, and it is clear that wealth is not the good of which we are in quest; for it is useful in part as a means of something else. It would be a more reasonable view therefore that the things mentioned before, namely sensual pleasure, honor and virtue, are ends rather than wealth is, as they are things which are desired on their own account. Yet these too are apparently not ends, although much argument has been employed to show that they are.

ASK YOURSELF

3.33. List four common views on the good that are discussed, and mention a problem with each.

The notion that "calamities and misfortunes" could interfere with ethical goodness is a theme to which we return repeatedly.

Chapter 7. Making More Precise the Idea of a Highest Good. Aristotle now attempts to reason his way toward an account of the good that can withstand the kinds of objections he has brought against some popular accounts (see Chapter 5).

But leaving this subject for the present let us revert to the good of which we are in quest and consider what its nature might be. For it is clearly different in different actions or arts: it is one thing in medicine, another in strategy, and so on. What then is the good in each of these instances? It is presumably that for the sake of which all else is done. Thus in medicine it is health, in strategy, victory, in domestic architecture, a house, and so on. But in every action and purpose it is for the sake of the end [goal, purpose] that all people do everything else. If then there is a certain end of *all* action, this would be the practicable good, and if there are several such ends it will be these. Thus our argument has arrived by a different path at the same conclusion as before; but we must endeavor to elucidate it still further.

As it appears that there are more ends than one and some of these, e.g., wealth, flutes, and instruments generally we desire as means to something else, it is evident that they are not all final ends. But the highest good is clearly something final. Hence if there is only one final end, this will be the object we are looking for, and if there are more than one, it will be the most final of them. We speak of that which is sought after for its own sake as more final than that which is sought after as a means to something else; we speak of that which is never desired as a means to something else as more final than the beings which are desired both in themselves and as a means to something else; and we speak of a thing as absolutely final, if it is always desired in itself and never as a means to something else.

It seems that *happiness* preeminently answers to this description, as we always desire happiness for its own sake and never as a means to something else, whereas we desire honour, pleasure, intellect, and every virtue, partly for their own sakes (for we should desire them independently of what might result from them) but partly also as being means to happiness, because we suppose they will prove the instruments of happiness. Nobody desires happiness, on the other hand, for the sake of these things, nor indeed as a means to anything else at all.

ASK YOURSELF

3.34. Aristotle thinks that happiness is always desired _____, and never _____. Moreover, other things that we desire partly for their own sake are also wanted because they seem to contribute to _____.

The following comments once more stress that humans are "political" beings.

We come to the same conclusion if we start from the consideration of self-sufficiency, if it may be assumed that the final good is self-sufficiency. But when we speak of self-sufficiency, we do not mean that a person leads a solitary life all by himself, but that he has parents, children, wife, and friends, and fellow-citizens in general, as man is naturally a social being.

But it is necessary to prescribe some limit; for if the circle be extended so as to include parents, descendants, and friends' friends, it will go on indefinitely. Leaving this point, however, for further investigation, we define the self-sufficient as that which, taken by itself, makes life desirable, and wholly free from want, and this is our conception of happiness.

Again we conceive happiness to be the most desirable of all things, and that not merely as one among other good things. If it were one among other good things, the addition of the smallest good would increase its desirableness; for the accession makes a superiority of goods, and the greater of two goods is always the more desirable. It appears then that happiness is something final and self-sufficient, being the end of all action.

Perhaps, however, no one would ever disagree with the claim that happiness is the supreme good; what is wanted is to *define* its nature a little more clearly. The best way of arriving at such a definition will probably be to ascertain the function of Man. For, as with a flute player, a statuary, or any artisan, or in fact anybody who has a definite function and action, his goodness, or excellence, seems to lie in his function, so it would seem to be with Man, if indeed he has a definite function. Can it be said then that, while a carpenter and a cobbler have a definite function and action, Man, unlike them, is naturally functionless? The reasonable view is that, as the eye, the hand, the foot, and similarly each several part of the body has a definite function, so Man may be regarded as having a definite function apart from these.

ASK YOURSELF

3.35. Aristotle argues that happiness is the supreme good since it is _____ and because it is not just _____ among _____.

Aristotle's view that there is a "function" common to all humans, or at any rate to all "men," is quite crucial to his argument. Yet he seems aware that some people might find his idea odd or contestable. People can generally "function" in so many ways, fill so many roles, that it seems odd to suggest that there is *one* function that they have. Even though we can ask a quarterback in football what his function is, it almost seems insulting to ask someone what their "function" is simply as a human being. A doorknob has a function. A human being does not. Or so it might seem. Read on.

What then, can this function be? It is not life; for life is apparently something which man shares with the plants; and it is something peculiar to him that we are looking for. We must exclude therefore the life of nutrition and increase. There is next what may be called the life of sensation. But this too, is apparently shared by humans with horses, cattle, and all other animals. There remains what I may call the practical life of the rational part of human being. But the rational part is twofold; it is rational partly in the sense of being obedient to reason, and partly in the sense of possessing reason and intelligence. The practical life too may be conceived in two ways, namely, either as a moral state, or as a moral activity: but we must understand by it the life of activity, as this seems to be the truer form of the conception. The function of a human being then is the activity of soul in accordance with reason, or not independently of reason.

 ASK YOURSELF

3.36. Aristotle determines the function of human beings by asking what is unique about people. Consider the following comparison. Suppose I wonder what the *function* of the quarterback in football is. I notice that he contributes to winning the game, so perhaps that is his function. But so do the others players. If I want to know what his _____ is, the function that distinguishes him from all other players, I must learn what his _____ contribution to playing and winning is. Right? That is, those actions, roles, or tasks that *distinguish* him from others will tell me what his function is. So, we must determine what trait or characteristic distinguishes human beings from other beings in order to see what the function of human beings is. Aristotle thinks that _____ is the distinguishing trait.

3.37. Does that seem like a good suggestion to you? Try coming up with an alternative distinguishing trait.

Now the function of any x and of a *good* x will be the same (thus the function of a harpist and of a *good* harpist are the same, and likewise for all classes of things). This being so, *if* we (a) define the function of Man as a kind of life, and (b) this life as an activity of soul or a course of action in conformity with reason, and (c) if the function of a good man is to perform such activities well and finely, and (d) if a function is performed well and finely when it is performed in accordance with its proper excellence (virtue, *arete*), *then* it follows that the good of human beings is an activity of soul [or a course of action] in accordance with [human beings'] proper excellence or virtue or if there are more virtues than one, in accordance with the best and most complete virtue. But it is necessary to add the words "in a complete life." For as one swallow or one day does not make a spring, so one day or a short time does not make a blessed or happy man.

Remember that we are inquiring into the good life for human beings. For Aristotle that comes to inquiring into what a good human being is. You might disagree. Perhaps you know someone who seems quite happy but is not a good (honest, etc.) person. But could a person who is not good be fully happy?

☞ ASK YOURSELF

3.38. However, if you mean by a "good person" a person who is functioning optimally, and if you think that "happiness" consists precisely in functioning optimally, then of course you will have to conclude that a _____ person is a _____ person and vice versa. That is what Aristotle wants to prove. But he thinks the notion of the best, happiest life as the optimally functioning life has intuitive plausibility.

This may be taken as a sufficiently accurate sketch of the good; for it is right, I think, to draw the outlines first and afterwards to fill in the details. It would seem that anybody can carry on and complete what has been satisfactorily sketched in outline, and that time is a good inventor or cooperator in so doing. This is the way in which the arts have made their advances, as anybody can supply a deficiency.

But bearing in mind what has been already said, we must not look for a greater degree of accuracy than the subject matter allows, and to such an extent as is proper to the inquiry. . . . [T]here are various ways of discovering first principles; some are discovered by induction, others by perception, others by what is known as habituation, and so on. We must try to apprehend all in the natural or appropriate way, and must take pains to define them satisfactorily, as they have a vital influence upon all that follows from them. For it seems that the first principle or beginning is more than half the whole, and is the means of arriving at a clear conception of many points which are under investigation.

Again, Aristotle has stressed that ethics necessarily has a kind of natural imprecision. Plato would disagree. This disagreement is important.

Chapter 8. This Account of the Good Squares with Common Beliefs. Although Aristotle has criticized common ideas about the good (see Chapter 5), he still thinks it important to show that his own views are not so different from widely held views. One reason he thinks it important emerges in what follows, namely, correct views on the good derive from experiences that all people have.

In considering the first principle we must pay regard not only to the conclusion and the premises of our argument, but also to such views as are popularly held about it. For while all experience harmonizes with the truth, it is never long before truth clashes with falsehood. Goods have been divided into three classes, namely external goods as they are called, goods of the soul and goods of the body. Of these three classes we consider the goods of the soul to be goods in the strictest or most literal sense. But it is to the soul that we ascribe psychical actions and activities. Thus our definition is a good one, at least according to this theory, which is not only ancient but is accepted by students of philosophy at the present time. It is right too, insofar as certain actions and activities are said to be the end; for thus it appears that the end is some good of the soul and not an external good. It is in harmony with this definition that the happy man should live well and do well since happiness, as has been said, is in fact a kind of living and doing well [or, a kind of optimal functioning].

It appears too that the requisite characteristics of happiness are all contained in the definition; for some people hold that happiness is virtue, others that it is prudence, others that it is wisdom of some kind, others that it is these things or one of them conjoined with pleasure or not dissociated from pleasure, others again include external prosperity. Some of these views are held by many ancient thinkers, others by a few thinkers of high repute. It is probable that neither side is altogether wrong, they are both right.

Now the definition is in harmony with the view of those who hold that happiness is virtue or excellence of some sort; for activity in accordance with virtue implies virtue. But it would seem that there is a considerable difference between taking the supreme good to consist in a moral state (a disposition to be moral or a capacity to be so) or in an activity. For a moral state, although it exists, may produce nothing good, e.g., if a person is asleep, or has in any way become inactive. But this cannot be the case with an activity since activity implies action and good action. As in the Olympian games it is not the most beautiful and strongest persons who receive the crown but they who actually enter the lists as combatants—for it is some of these who become victors—so it is they who *act* rightly that attain to what is noble and good in life, and their life is pleasant in itself. For pleasure is a psychical fact, and whatever a man is said to be fond of is pleasant to him, e.g., a horse to one who is fond of horses, a spectacle to one who is fond of spectacles, and similarly just actions to a lover of justice, and virtuous actions in general to a lover of virtue. Now most men find a sense of discord in their pleasures, because their pleasures are not such as are naturally pleasant.

But to the lovers of nobleness natural pleasures are pleasant. It is actions in accordance with virtue that are naturally pleasant both relatively to these people and in themselves.

Nor does their life require that pleasure should be attached to it as a sort of amulet; it possesses pleasure in itself. For it may be added that a person is not good, if he does not take delight in noble actions, as nobody would call a person just if he did not take delight in just actions or generous if he did not take delight in generous actions and so on. But if this is so, it follows that actions in accordance with virtue are pleasant in themselves. But they are also good and noble, and good and noble in the highest degree, if the judgment of the virtuous man upon them is right (his judgment being such as we have described). Happiness then is the best and noblest and most pleasant thing in the world, nor is there any such distinction between goodness, nobleness, and pleasure as the epigram as Delos suggests:

> "Justice is noblest, Health is best,
> To gain one's end is most pleasant."

For these are all essential characteristics of the best activities, and we hold that happiness consists in these or in one and the noblest of these.

ASK YOURSELF

3.39. Can you think of two pleasures, one of which would clash with the other?

3.40. Common views of happiness include several elements. Judging by the amount of discussion he gives to it Aristotle is most concerned to show that *his* account of happiness is consistent with the common idea that happiness includes _____.

Still it is clear that happiness requires the addition of external goods, as we said; for it is impossible, or at least difficult for a person to do what is noble unless he is furnished with external means. For there are many things which can only be done through the instrumentality of friends or wealth or political power, and there are some things the lack of which must mar felicity, e.g., noble birth, a prosperous family, and personal beauty. For a person is incapable of happiness if he is absolutely ugly in appearance, or low born, or solitary and childless, and perhaps still more so, if he has exceedingly bad children or friends and has lost them by death. As we said, then, it seems that prosperity of this kind is an indispensable addition to virtue. It is for this reason that some persons identify good fortune, and others, virtue, with happiness.

ASK YOURSELF

3.41. This passage contains claims that many people will deny. Mention one.

Chapter 9. Happiness Is Acquired Primarily through Effort of Some Sort, Rather Than through "Good Luck." We see as the discussion continues in this section that Aristotle is ambivalent about the place of luck or good fortune (chance) in the constitution of an ethically good life. He seems on the verge of taking back what he just said at the end of Chapter 8.

The question is consequently raised whether happiness is something that can be learnt or acquired by habit or discipline of any other kind, or whether it comes by some divine dispensation or even by chance.

Now if there is anything in the world that is a gift of the Gods to men, it is reasonable to suppose that happiness is a divine gift, especially as it is the best of human things. This however is perhaps a point which is more appropriate to another investigation than the present. But even if happiness is not sent by the Gods but is the result of virtue and of learning or discipline of some kind, it is apparently one of the most divine things in the world; for it would appear that that which is the prize and the end of virtue is the supreme good and is in its nature divine and blessed. It will also be widely extended; for it will be capable of being produced in all persons, except such as are morally deformed, by a process of study or care. And if it is better that happiness should be produced in this way than by chance, it may reasonably be supposed that it is so produced, since everything is ordered in the best possible way in Nature and so too in art, and in causation generally and most of all in the highest kind of causation. But it would be altogether inconsistent to leave what is greatest and noblest to chance.

 ASK YOURSELF

3.42. Aristotle is arguing that happiness is the greatest and noblest end, and the greatest and noblest cannot be left to _____. But he seems uncertain.

3.43. Try to think of a case where *luck* played a role in a person's becoming a *good* person, an optimally functioning person, and describe it.

But the definition of happiness itself helps to clear up the question; for happiness has been defined as a certain kind of activity of the soul in accordance with virtue or excellence. Of the other goods, i.e., of goods besides those of the soul, some are necessary as antecedent conditions of happiness, others are in their nature co operative and serviceable as instruments of happiness.

The conclusion at which we have arrived agrees with our original position. For we laid down that the end of political science is the supreme good; and political science is concerned with nothing so much as with producing a certain character in the citizens or in other words with making them good, and capable of performing noble actions.

Aristotle is saying that if happiness consists in an activity, as he originally claimed, then it cannot be, or be the result of, something that simply "happens to you" but must rather be more like an achievement.

 ASK YOURSELF

3.44. How would the assumption that happiness is simply the result of _____ conflict with Aristotle's original position?

It is reasonable then not to speak of an ox, or a horse, or any other animal as happy; for none of them is capable of participating in activity as so defined.

To which we might say "why not?" If happiness is a kind of optimal functioning (activity in accord with excellence), then why can't a horse or dog be happy "as so defined"? A happy horse, we might say, is an optimally functioning horse, exercising to the full those capacities that make a horse a good horse.

 ASK YOURSELF

3.45. Has Aristotle simply defined happiness in such a way as to exclude animals? Try to defend his definition.

For the same reason no child can be happy; as the age of a child makes it impossible for him to display this activity at the present, and if a child is ever said to be happy, the grounds for saying so is his potential, rather than his actual performance. For happiness demands, as we said, a complete virtue and a complete life. For there are all sorts of changes and chances in life, and it is possible that the most prosperous of men will, in his old age, fall into extreme calamities, as is told of Priam in the heroic legends. But if a person has experienced such chances, and has died a miserable death, nobody calls him happy.

 ASK YOURSELF

3.46. We do of course speak of children as being "happy." But if we stick with the idea that happiness is optimal (human) functioning and that optimal functioning involves developed _____ (see question 3.37), then we can appreciate Aristotle's point, since children are not developed much in that way.

3.47. There is another point made in this passage, which relates to Aristotle's point in Book 1, Chapter 7. State that point and say whether, and why, you agree or do not agree.

Chapter 10. Under What Conditions Can Someone Be Called Happy? Must They Be Immune to Changes of Fortune? Or Is Happiness Necessarily within a Person's Control? Once again Aristotle is ambivalent (see again Chapters 7 and 9) in his answer to these questions. To his puzzlement so far he adds questions about the extent to which a person's happiness will be affected by the fortunes of his descendants or other things that may happen after death.

Is it the case then that nobody in the world may be called happy as long as he is alive? Must we adopt Solon's rule of looking to the end? And, if we follow Solon, can it be said that a man is really happy after his death? Surely such a view is wholly absurd, especially for us who define happiness as a species of activity. But if we do not speak of one who is dead as happy, and if Solon's meaning is not this but rather that it is only when a person is dead that it is safe to call him fortunate, since then he is exempt at last from evils and calamities, this again is a view which is open to some objection. For it seems that one who is dead is capable of being affected both by good and by evil in the same way as one who is living but not conscious; for example such a one can be affected by honors and dishonors even though he does not yet know it, and the prosperity or misfortunes of a person's descendants might bear on how happy we take them to be.

But here a difficulty occurs. For if a person has lived a fortunate life up to old age, and has died a good death, it is possible that he may experience many vicissitudes of fortune in the persons of his descendants. Some of them may be good and may enjoy such a life as they deserve; others may be good and may have a bad life. It is clear too, that descendants may stand in all sorts of different degrees of relationship to their ancestor. It would be an extraordinary result, if the dead man were to share the vicissitudes of their fortune and to become happy or miserable when they are. But it would be equally extraordinary, if the fortune of future descendants should not affect their parents at all or just for a certain time.

Could you be happy now if you knew that your children or grandchildren would live in misery, due, let us say, to environmental disasters?

It will be best, however, to revert to the difficulty which was raised before, as it will perhaps afford an answer to the present question. If it is right to look to the end, and when the end comes to count a person blessed not because they are fortunate at that moment, but as having been so before, then would it not be odd, at the time when he is happy, not to speak the truth about him just because we do not wish to call the living happy in view of the vicissitudes to which they are liable, and because we have formed a conception of happiness as something that is permanent and exempt from the possibility of change, and because the same persons are liable to many revolutions of fortune? For it is clear that if we follow the changes of fortune, we shall often call the same person happy at one time and miserable at another, representing the happy man as "a sort of chameleon" and "a temple on rotting foundations."

It cannot be right to follow the changes of fortune. It is not upon these that good or evil depends; they are necessary accessories of human life, as we said; but it is a man's activities in accordance with virtue that constitute his happiness and the opposite activities that constitute his misery. The difficulty which has now been discussed is itself a witness that this is the true view. For there is no human function so constant as activities in accordance with virtue; they seem to be more permanent than the sciences themselves. Among these activities, too, it is the most honorable which are the most permanent, as it is in them that the life of the fortunate chiefly and most continuously consists. For this is apparently the reason why such activities are not liable to be forgotten.

The element of permanency which is required will be found in the happy man, and he will preserve his character throughout life; for he will constantly or in a preeminent degree pursue such actions and speculations as accord with virtue; nor is there anybody who will bear the chances of life so nobly, with such a perfect and complete harmony, as he who is truly good and "foursquare without a flaw."

Now the events of chance are numerous and of different magnitudes. It is clear then that small incidents of good fortune, or the reverse, do not turn the scale of life, but that such incidents as are great and numerous augment the felicity of life if they are fortunate, since they tend naturally to embellish it where the use of them is noble and virtuous, but frequent reversals can hem in and mar our happiness both by causing pains and by hindering various activities. Still even in these circumstances nobility shines out, when a person bears the weight of accumulated misfortunes with calmness, not because he does not really feel them, but from innate dignity and magnanimity.

Aristotle is once again (see Chapters 8 and 9) addressing what might be called the "problem of moral luck." The problem is, how can fortune, good or bad, determine the goodness of a life when the best kind of life has already been described as activity in accordance with reason, optimal functioning? Yet we can hardly say that when terrible things happen even to the best person, that that has no effect upon their "happiness."

 ASK YOURSELF

3.48. In the previous passage Aristotle suggests a sort of solution to this problem; the good person, he says, will bear misfortune with _____.

But if it is the activities that determine the life, as we said, nobody who is fortunate can become miserable; for he will never do what is hateful and mean. For our conception of the truly good and sensible man is that he bears all the chances of life with decorum and always does what is noblest in the circumstances, as a good general uses the forces at his command to the best advantage in war, a good cobbler makes the best shoe with the leather that is given him, and so on through the whole series of the arts. If this is so, it follows that the happy man can never become miserable; I do not say that he will be fortunate if he meets such chances of life as Priam. Yet he will not be variable or liable to frequent change, as he will not be moved from his happiness easily or by ordinary misfortunes but only by such misfortunes as are great and numerous, and after them it will not be soon that he will regain his happiness but, if he regains it at all, it will be only in a long and complete period of time and after attaining great and noble results.

We may safely then define a happy man as one whose activities accord with perfect virtue and who is adequately furnished with external goods, not for a brief period of time but for a complete or perfect lifetime. But perhaps we ought to add that he will always live so, and will die as he lives; for it is not given us to foresee the future. But we take happiness to be an end, and to be altogether perfect and complete, and, this being so, we shall call people fortunate during their lifetime, if they possess and will possess these characteristics, but fortunate only so far as men may be fortunate. So much for the determination of this matter.

Aristotle does not want to deny the importance of luck, but he does wants to resist the idea that personal goodness is just a function of luck. Can you appreciate the difficulty here? In speaking of the good person as "fortunate only so far as men may be fortunate" does Aristotle suggest that there are real limits to ethical endeavor, so that no matter how hard we try and how well we act, our lives may still go down in defeat?

In Chapter 11 (omitted here) Aristotle again expresses some skepticism about the idea that the dead are affected by what happens among the living and concludes that what happens to our descendants or friends after we die should not have too great an impact on our own happiness. In Chapter 12 (omitted here) Aristotle argues that the fact that we praise virtue shows that it involves activity or effort, but just for that reason some have argued that it is not the highest state of blessedness. For it might seem that the highest blessedness would be a kind of gift, which did not require struggle on our part. Even if that is so, however, it does not show that virtue is not necessary for happiness.

Chapter 13. An Introduction to the Concept of Virtue. The notion of a *virtue* as Aristotle and the Greeks generally employed it is the notion of an excellence (some trait necessary for optimal functioning). So speed would be a virtue in a sprinter. What then are the *moral* virtues like?

Since happiness is (defined as) activity of soul in accordance with complete or perfect excellence (virtue), it is necessary to consider virtue, for that will perhaps be a better way of studying happiness.

It appears that true statesmen [those dealing with "politics"] expend the largest amount of trouble on virtue, as it is their wish to make the citizens virtuous and obedient to the laws. We have instances of such statesmen in the legislators of Crete and Lacedaemon and others that have resembled them. But if this inquiry is proper to political science, it will clearly accord with our original purpose to pursue it. But it is clear that it is human virtue which we have to consider; for the good of which we are in search is, as we said, the human good, and the happiness, human happiness. By human virtue or excellence we mean not that of the body, but that of the soul, and by happiness we mean an activity of the soul.

If this is so, it is clearly necessary for statesmen to have some knowledge of the nature of the soul in the same way as it is necessary for one who is to treat the eye or any part of the body, to have some knowledge of it, and even more so since political science is better and more honorable than medical science. The more cultivated doctors take a great deal of trouble to acquire knowledge of the body, and likewise the statesman must make a study of the soul. But he must study it with a view to his particular object and so far only as his object requires; for to elaborate the study of it further would, I think, be to aggravate unduly the labor of our present undertaking.

There are some facts concerning the soul which we have adequately stated in our popular works as well, and these we may rightly use. It is stated for example that the soul has two parts, one irrational and the other possessing reason. But whether these parts are distinguished like the parts of the body and like everything that is itself divisible, or whether they are distinct only in our account, but in fact inseparable, as convex and concave in the circumference of a circle, does not matter to the present inquiry.

Again, it seems that of the irrational part of the soul one part is common, i.e. shared by man with all living things; I mean the part which is the cause of nutrition and growth. . . . It is clear then that the virtue or excellence of this faculty is not distinctively human but is shared by man with all living things; for it seems that this part and this faculty are especially active in sleep, whereas good and bad people are never so little distinguishable as in sleep—whence the saying that there is no difference between the happy and the miserable during half their lifetime. And this is only natural; for sleep is an inactivity of the soul in respect of its virtue or vice, except insofar as certain impulses affect it to a slight extent, and make the visions of the virtuous [i.e., dreams] better than those of ordinary people. But enough has been said on this point, and we must now leave the principle of nutrition, as it possesses no natural share in human virtue.

Aristotle's account of "soul" here as well as his earlier uses of the term may be somewhat confusing, since many people tend to think of the soul as a separable thing, and it is clear that he does not think of it that way. But if you are unfamiliar with Aristotle's psychology, this passage amounts to a little introduction. Here he speaks of the soul as having a "vegetative part." What that means is that a human being has a vegetative aspect, that is, capacities for digestion and the like.

 ASK YOURSELF

3.49. Vegetative capacities are clearly not "rational." Mention here some capacities that *are* rational.

It seems that there is another natural principle of the soul that is irrational and yet in a sense partakes of reason. For in a continent or incontinent person we praise the reason, and that part of the soul that possesses reason, as it exhorts men rightly and exhorts them to the best conduct. But it is clear that there is in them another principle that is naturally different from reason and fights and contends against reason. For just as the paralyzed parts of the body, when we intend to move them to the right, are drawn away in a contrary direction to the left, so it is with the soul; the impulses of incontinent people run counter to reason. But there is this difference, however, that while in the body we see the part that is drawn astray, in the soul we do not see it. But it is probably right to suppose with equal certainty that there is in the soul too something different from reason, which opposes and thwarts it, although the sense in which it is distinct from reason is immaterial. But it appears that this part too partakes of reason, as we said; at all events in a continent person it obeys reason, while in a temperate or courageous person it is probably still more obedient, as being absolutely harmonious with reason.

It appears then that the irrational part of the soul is itself twofold; for the vegetative faculty does not participate at all in reason but the faculty of desire participates in it more or less, in so far as it is submissive and obedient to reason. But it is obedient in the sense in which we speak of paying attention to a father or to friends, but not in the sense in which we speak of paying attention to mathematics. All correction, rebuke and exhortation are a witness that the irrational part of the soul is in a sense subject to the influence of reason. But if we are to say that this part too possesses reason, then the part that possesses reason will have two divisions, one possessing reason absolutely and in itself, the other listening to it as a child listens to its father.

It seems natural to say of certain desires, or emotions, that they are rational or irrational. For example, the desire for pain, except in very unusual circumstances, would seem to be irrational. Fear of being in a crowd would seem to be irrational. Yet our desires and emotions do not belong to reason per se, in Aristotle's view, but are capable of being organized or trained by reason.

Virtue or excellence again, admits of a distinction that depends on this difference. For we speak of some virtues as intellectual and of others as ethical; thus wisdom, intelligence and prudence are intellectual virtues, while liberality and temperance are moral or ethical virtues. For when we describe a person's character, we do not say that he is wise or intelligent but that he is a gentle or temperate. Yet we praise a wise man too in respect of his mental state, and such mental states as deserve to be praised we call virtuous.

ASK YOURSELF

3.50. Aristotle is interested in "character." Character is something acquired through training. He thinks that good character is acquired through training in which reason plays a fundamental role. His way of putting this has been to say that there must be a part of the _____ that is subject to _____.

3.51. Now try to fill out the following summary of Aristotle's argument so far. The concern of "ethics" is with determining what is the best kind of life for a human being. A "good" person will be one who has achieved that kind of life.

a. All actions aim at some _____

b. There must be a highest good, which is the ultimate _____ of all our actions, which is desired for its own sake, not merely as a _____ to something else.

c. Knowledge of this supreme good will obviously be important for the conduct of life, if we wish to lead a good life or live in such a way as to achieve the highest goal.

d. Common opinion holds that this highest good is _____ and that seems correct insofar as it is desired for _____, not for the sake of something else.

e. But there is no common agreement on the correct account of happiness. Some common notions are that happiness is _____, or _____, or _____. But all of these are open to strong objections as definitions.

f. Since happiness is universally agreed to be equivalent to the good for humans, we can arrive at a good definition of happiness by considering what the specific good of humans might be, and we can do that by discovering the _____ of humans, since a "good x" is one that is _____ well, that is, working and developing according to its own inmost nature.

g. We can determine the unique function of humans by considering what makes them _____ or different from other being .

h. Thus we can see that the unique function of humans is to act in accord with _____, since the ability to so act is what distinguishes humans from other _____.

i. Now a *good* thing of any kind (and thus a good human being) is one that performs its particular function well.

j. It follows from (f) through (i) that a *happy* person will be a good person, that is, a person who is performing their particular function well.

k. Thus the end of human life, the _____ at which all human actions ultimately aim, is excellent activity in accordance with _____.

Something that functions optimally or operates in an excellent way is said to have a virtue or virtues, since a virtue is a trait required for excellent operation. So to be a good person is to be a virtuous person, and vice versa.

3.52. Now, can you think of some objections to all of this? For instance, can you imagine a person who is using reason to guide all of their actions, who is doing an excellent job of it, but who is nonetheless not "good" or virtuous and might even be evil? Try to describe such a case.

Book 2

Aristotle turns to a more precise account of virtue and the means of acquiring it.

Chapter 1. Virtue, Character, and Training. Aristotle now provides an analysis of the concept of a virtue or excellence (*arete* in Greek).

 From ARISTOTLE: *Nicomachean Ethics*, Book II ____

Virtue or excellence being twofold, partly intellectual and partly moral, intellectual virtue is both originated and fostered mainly by teaching; it therefore demands experience and time. Moral virtue on the other hand is the outcome of habit, and accordingly its name is derived by a slight deflection from habit. From this fact it is clear that no moral virtue is implanted in us by nature; a law of nature cannot be altered by habituation. Thus a stone naturally tends to fall downwards, and it cannot be habituated or trained to rise upwards, even if we were to [try to] habituate it by throwing it upwards ten thousand times; nor again can fire be trained to sink downwards, nor anything else that follows one natural law be habituated or trained to follow another. It is neither by nature then nor in defiance of nature that virtues are implanted in us. Nature gives us the *capacity* of receiving them, and that capacity is perfected by *habit*.

Again, if we take the various natural powers that belong to us, we first acquire the proper faculties and afterwards display the activities. It is clearly so with the senses. It was not by seeing frequently or hearing frequently that we acquired the senses of seeing or hearing; on the contrary it was because we possessed the senses that we made use of them, not by making use of them that we obtained them.

But we acquire the virtues by first exercising them, as is the case with all the arts, for it is by doing what we ought to do when we have learnt the arts that we learn the arts themselves; for example we become builders by building and harpists by playing the harp. Similarly it is by doing just acts that we become just, by doing temperate acts that we become temperate, by doing courageous acts that we become courageous.

ASK YOURSELF

3.53. Aristotle is saying that everyone has the capacity to be, say, courageous, but only those become courageous who get in the _____ of acting courageously, and only those get in the _____ who repeatedly act courageously.

3.54. Does what Aristotle says seem to imply that you have to already be courageous in order to become courageous? Explain.

The experience of governments is a witness to this truth, for it is training in habits that legislators have at heart; if a legislator does not succeed in it, he fails of his purpose, and it constitutes the distinction between a good polity [form of government] and a bad one.

Again, the causes and means by which any virtue is produced and by which it is destroyed are the same; and it is equally so with any art; for it is by playing the harp that both good and bad harpists are produced and the case of builders and all other artisans is similar, as it is by building well that they will be good builders and by building badly that they will be bad builders. If it were not so, there would be no need of anybody to teach them; they would all be born good or bad in their several trades. The case of the virtues is the same. It is by acting in such transactions as take place between man and man that we become either just or unjust. It is by acting in the face of danger and by habituating ourselves to fear or courage that we become either cowardly or courageous. It is much the same with our desires and angry passions. Some people become temperate and gentle, others become intemperate and angry, according as they conduct themselves in one way or another way in particular circumstances.

To sum up then, states of character are the results of repeated acts corresponding to those states. So it is necessary for us to produce on demand those activities that will produce the corresponding [ethical] states. It makes no small difference then how we are trained up from our youth; rather it is a serious, even an all-important matter.

 ASK YOURSELF

3.55. Does Aristotle's account imply that if you have not been brought up properly you have very little or no chance of becoming a good (i.e., optimally functioning, virtuous, and thus happy) person?

Chapter 2. Reminders on the (Inexact) Nature of This Subject. Some Points about Virtues and Their Acquisition or Loss. Aristotle introduces the notion of a virtue as a kind of mean state, in which excess or deficiency is avoided.

Our present study is not, like other studies, purely speculative in its intention; for the object of our enquiry is not to know the nature of virtue but to become ourselves virtuous, as that is the sole benefit which it conveys. It is necessary therefore to consider the right way of performing actions, for it is actions, as we have said, that determine the character of the resulting ethical states.

That we should act in accordance with right reason is a common general principle, which may here be taken for granted. The nature of right reason, and its relation to the virtues generally, will be subjects of discussion hereafter. But it must be admitted at the outset that all reasoning upon practical matters must be like a sketch in outline for it cannot be scientifically exact. We began by laying down the principle that the kind of reasoning demanded in any subject must be such as the subject-matter itself allows; and questions of practice and expediency no more admit of invariable rules than questions of health.

But if this is true of general reasoning upon Ethics, still more true is it that scientific exactitude is impossible in reasoning upon particular ethical cases. They do not fall under any art or any law, but the agents themselves are always bound to pay regard to the circumstances of the moment, just as in medicine or navigation.

Still, although such is the nature of the present argument, we must try to make the best of it. The first point to be observed then is that in such matters as we are considering deficiency and excess are equally fatal. It is so, as we observe, in regard to health and strength; for we must judge of what we cannot see by the evidence of what we do see. Excess or deficiency of gymnastic exercise is fatal to strength. Similarly an excess or deficiency of meat and drink is fatal to health, whereas a suitable amount produces, augments and sustains it. It is the same then with temperance, courage, and the other virtues. A person who avoids and is afraid of everything and faces nothing becomes a coward; a person who is not afraid of anything but is ready to face everything becomes foolhardy. Similarly he who enjoys every pleasure and never abstains from any pleasure is licentious; he who eschews all pleasures like a boor is an insensible sort of person. For temperance and courage are destroyed by excess and deficiency but preserved by the mean state.

 ASK YOURSELF

3.56. Aristotle is making a point here that he treats in considerable detail in later chapters of this book and that is thought by some to be his most characteristic idea, namely, that virtues are midpoints between extremes. For example, courage is midway between being _____ and being _____.

Again, not only are the causes and the agencies of production, increase and destruction in the ethical states the same, but the sphere of their activity will be proved to be the same also. It is so in other instances which are more conspicuous, e.g. in strength; for strength is produced by taking a great deal of food and undergoing a great deal of labor, and it is the strong man who is able to take most food and to undergo most labor.

The same is the case with the virtues. It is by abstinence from pleasures that we become temperate, and, when we have become temperate, we are best able to abstain from them. So too with courage; it is by habituating ourselves to despise and face alarms that we become courageous, and, when we have become courageous, we shall be best able to face them.

Chapter 3. Virtue, Pleasure, and Pain. Aristotle shows that virtues are traits that are connected in some way with our ability to manage pleasures and pains in a reasonable way.

The pleasure or pain which follows upon actions may be regarded as a test of a person's moral state. He who abstains from physical pleasures and feels delight in so doing is temperate but he who feels pain at so doing is licentious. He who faces dangers with pleasure, or at least without pain, is courageous; but he who feels pain at facing them is a coward.

 ASK YOURSELF

3.57. Put the preceding point about courage in your own words.

For moral virtue is concerned with pleasures and pains. [This can be seen from the following facts:] (a) It is pleasure which makes us do what is base, and pain which makes us abstain from doing what is noble. Hence the importance of having had a certain training from very early days, as Plato says, namely such a training as produces pleasure and pain at the right objects; for this is the true education.

 ASK YOURSELF

3.58. Would someone who takes pleasure in watching someone else being tortured be an example of a person who has been improperly "trained"?

3.59. Does it seem odd to speak of "training" the emotions?

3.60. Name an example of an emotion of yours that your parents or someone else has tried to "train."

(b) Again, if the virtues are concerned with actions and emotions, and every action and every emotion is attended by pleasure and pain, this will be another reason why virtue should be concerned with pleasures and pains. (c) There is also a proof of this fact in the use of pleasure and pain as means of punishment; for punishments are in a sense medical measures, and the means employed as remedies are naturally the opposites of the diseases to which they are applied. (d) Again, as we said before, every moral state of the soul is in its nature relative to, and concerned with, the thing by which it is naturally made better or worse. But pleasures and pains are the causes of vicious states of character when we pursue and avoid such pleasures and pains as are wrong, or pursue and avoid them at the wrong time or in the wrong manner, or in any other of the various ways in which it is logically possible to do wrong. Hence it is that people actually define the virtues as ways of being unaffected and undisturbed [by pleasures and pains]; but they are wrong in using this absolute language, and not qualifying it by speaking of being affected in the right or wrong manner, time and so on.

It may be assumed then that moral virtue tends to produce the best action in respect of pleasures and pains, and that vice is its opposite. But the same points will be evident from the following considerations: (f) There are three things which influence us to desire them, namely the noble, the expedient, and the pleasant; and three opposite things which influence us to eschew them, namely the shameful, the injurious and the painful. The good man then will be likely to take a right line, and the bad man to take a wrong one, with respect to all these, but especially in respect to pleasure; for pleasure is felt not by humans only but by the lower animals, and is associated with all things that are matters of desire, as the noble and the expedient alike appear pleasant. (g) Pleasure too develops in us all from early childhood, so that it is difficult to get rid of the emotion of pleasure, as it is deeply ingrained in our life. (h) Again, we make pleasure and pain in a greater or less degree the standard of our actions. So our entire study should be concerned from first to last with pleasures and pains; for right or wrong feelings of pleasure or pain have a material influence upon actions. (i) Again, it is more difficult to contend against pleasure than against anger, as Helaclitus says, and both art and virtue are constantly concerned with what is more difficult. For a good result [or product] is even better by virtue of this [the difficulty involved in producing it]. So for this reason pleasure and pain are the whole business of both virtue and politics [management of communities], since the one who makes good use of them is good, the one who makes a bad use is evil.

So we have pointed out that virtues are concerned with pleasures and pains; the actions from which it originates increase it, or if differently performed destroy it, and those from which it arose are those in which it is exercised.

 ASK YOURSELF

3.61. List as briefly as possible Aristotle's eight reasons for his claim that virtue (excellence) has to do with pleasures and pains.

3.62. Think about your own assessments of other people. Do you tend to think badly of people who are addicted to certain pleasures? Give one example.

3.63. Do you think badly of people who are so afraid of a little pain (whether the pain be physical or emotional) that they will do nearly anything to avoid it? Give one example.

3.64. Give an example of the sort of thing a person might do to avoid pain that you would call "immoral."

Chapter 4. The Distinction between a Virtuous Act and a Virtuous Person. Aristotle now addresses a problem raised earlier.

A difficulty may be raised as to what is meant by saying that in order to become just we must do just actions, and in order to become temperate we must do temperate actions. For [someone might argue], if they do such actions they must be just already, just as if they spell correctly or play in tune they are scholars or musicians.

 ASK YOURSELF

3.65. State the problem in your own words here.

Aristotle's solution is given in what follows.

. . . acts done in conformity with the virtues are not done justly or temperately if they themselves are of a certain kind, but only if the one who acts is in a certain state of mind when he does them; first, he must act with knowledge, secondly he must deliberately choose the act, and choose it or its own sake; and thirdly it must spring from a fixed disposition of character. . . . Thus although actions are called just and temperate when they are such acts as just and temperate people would do, the agent is just and temperate not when he simply does these acts, but when he does them in the *way* just and temperate people do. It is correct then to say that a person becomes just by doing just actions and temperate by doing temperate actions, and no one has any chance of becoming good without doing them.

 ASK YOURSELF

3.66. So the solution is as follows: Suppose I do a courageous act, but (1) I do not fully understand the situation I am in (do not fully understand the danger, for instance, or do not have an accurate idea of my own abilities to handle the situation); and/or (2) I cannot be said to have deliberately chosen to so act (since perhaps I did not have enough knowledge to deliberate) and thus, since I do not fully appreciate what I am doing, cannot be said to have chosen this act "for its own sake"; and/or (3) I have not become accustomed or habituated to acting in this way. Where any of these three conditions hold, then we would *not* say that I was a _____ person, even though my *act* was a _____ act.

3.67. What are the three conditions that must be met before we will say that a person who performs a virtuous act is themselves virtuous?

But the mass of people, instead of doing virtuous actions, have recourse to discussing virtue and think that they are pursuing philosophy and that this will make them good. In so doing they act like sick people who listen carefully to the doctors' instructions but completely neglect to carry out his orders. That sort of philosophy will no more lead to a healthy state of soul than will the mode of treatment produce health of body.

Chapter 5. The Genus of Virtue. Virtue is a "state of the soul." Exactly what kind of state?

We have next to consider the formal definition of virtue.

A state of the soul is either an emotion, a capacity, or a disposition; virtue must be one of these three then. By emotions I mean desire, anger, fear, confidence, envy, joy, friendship, hatred, longing, jealousy, pity; and such states of mind accompanied by pleasure or pain. The capacities are the faculties in virtue of which we can be said to be liable to emotions, e.g. capable of releasing anger or pain or pity. Dispositions are formed states of character in virtue of which we are well or badly disposed in respect of the mentioned; for instance, we have a bad disposition in regard to anger if we are disposed to get angry too violently or not enough, a good disposition if we habitually feel moderate anger; and similarly with respect to other emotions.

Now virtues and vices are not emotions because we are not called good or bad according to our emotions; nor are we praised or blamed for our emotions—no one is praised for being frightened or angry or blamed for being angry merely, but only for being angry in a particular way—but we are praised or blamed for our virtues and vices. Again, we are not angry or afraid from choice, but the virtues are certain modes of choice, or involve choice.

The same considerations show that virtues and vices are not capacities, since we are not called good or bad, praised or blamed, because of our capacity for emotion.

If then the virtues are neither emotions nor capacities, it remains that they are dispositions. Thus we have said what the genus of virtue is [it is a disposition].

☞ ASK YOURSELF

3.68. Aristotle's strategy in his attempt to distinguish virtue from emotions is to point out that we do not _____ people for their emotions but we do _____ them for their _____.

Chapter 6. The Species of Virtue. A virtue is a disposition (a tendency). But what specific kind of disposition? Remember, a good person is a happy person (and vice versa) since to be good is to be functioning well and that is what happiness is. But functioning well requires "excellence" (of course!). Moreover, we have already learned that excellence in human living requires the use of reason. Now read on.

Now in everything, whether it be continuous or discrete, it is possible to take a greater, a smaller, or an equal amount, and this either absolutely or in relation to ourselves, the equal being a mean between excess and deficiency. By the mean in respect of the thing itself, or the absolute mean, I understand that which is equally distinct from both extremes; and this is one and the same thing for everybody. By the mean considered relatively to ourselves I understand that which is neither too much nor too little; but this is not one thing, nor is it the same for everybody.

Thus if 10 be too much and 2 too little we take 6 as a mean in respect of the thing itself; for 6 is as much greater than 2 as it is less than 10, and this is a mean in arithmetical proportion. But the mean considered relatively to ourselves must not be ascertained in this way. It does not follow that if 10 pounds of meat be too much and 2 too little for a man to eat, a trainer will order him 6 pounds, as this may itself be too much or too little for the person who is to take it; it will be too little e.g. for Milo [a very big Greek athlete], but too much for a beginner in gymnastics. It will be the same with running and wrestling; the right amount varies with the individual.

This being so, everybody who understands his business avoids alike excess and deficiency; he seeks and chooses the mean, not the absolute mean, but the mean considered relatively to himself.

Every science then performs its function well, if it regards the mean and refers the works which it produces to the mean. This is the reason why it is usually said of successful works that it is impossible to take anything from them or to add anything to them, which implies that excess or deficiency is fatal to excellence but that the mean state ensures it . . . virtue therefore will aim at the mean.

 ASK YOURSELF

3.69. If you choose the mean relative to yourself, then assuming that you have the virtue of courage, would your choice whether, for example, to run or stand firm when attacked by an armed enemy have to be the same if you were heavily armed or not?

3.70. Is a person who runs away from danger always a coward? Explain.

I speak of moral virtue, as it is moral virtue which is concerned with emotion and actions, and it is these which admit of excess and deficiency and the mean. Thus it is possible to go too far, or not to go far enough, in respect of fear, courage, desire, anger, pity, and pleasure and pain generally, and the excess and the deficiency are alike wrong; but to experience these emotions at the right times and on the right occasions and towards the right persons and for the right causes and in the right manner is the mean or the supreme good, which is characteristic of virtue.

Similarly there may be excess, deficiency, or the mean, in regard to actions. But virtue is concerned with emotions and actions, and here excess is an error and deficiency a fault, whereas the mean is successful and laudable, and success and merit are both characteristics of virtue. It appears then that virtue is a mean state, so far at least as it aims at the mean.

 ASK YOURSELF

3.71. So having a virtue is not just having a disposition to *act* in a certain way, but it is also having dispositions to *feel* in certain ways. And of course the two are closely connected. Give an example from your own life of a tendency to feel in inappropriate ways that leads you to act badly (you will be unable to answer this question only if you are a perfect person).

Again, error is many formed (for evil is a form of the unlimited and good of the limited, as the Pythagoreans imaged it), while success is possible in only one way, which is why it is easy to fail and difficult to succeed, as it is easy to miss the mark and difficult to hit it. This is another reason why excess and deficiency are marks of vice, and observance of the mean a mark of virtue: Goodness is simple, badness is manifold.

Virtue then is a disposition with respect to choice, i.e. the disposition to choose a mean that is relative to ourselves, the mean being determined by reasoned principle, that is, as a prudent man would determine it.

 ## ASK YOURSELF

3.72. So here is Aristotle's definition of *virtue*. You should try now to define the terms he uses in the definition, in particular, "disposition," "choice," "reasoned principle," and "prudence."

Virtue is a mean state lying between two vices, the vice of excess on the one hand, and the vice of deficiency on the other, and whereas the vices either fall short of or go beyond what is proper in the emotions and actions, virtue not only discovers but embraces the mean. Accordingly, virtue, if regarded in its essence or theoretical conception, is a mean state, but, if regarded from the point of view of the highest good, or of excellence, it is extreme.

But it is not every action or every emotion that admits of a mean state. There are some whose very name implies wickedness, as e.g. malice, shamelessness, and envy, among emotions, or adultery, theft, and murder, among actions. All these, and others like them, are censured as being intrinsically wicked, not merely the excesses or deficiencies of them. It is never possible then to be right in respect of them; they are always wrong. Right or wrong in such actions as adultery does not depend on our committing them with the right person, at the right time or in the right manner; on the contrary it is wrong to do anything of the kind at all. It would be equally wrong then to suppose that there can be a mean state or an excess or deficiency in unjust, cowardly or licentious conduct. For, if it were, there would be a mean state of an excess or of a deficiency, an excess of an excess and a deficiency of a deficiency [which is nonsense].

 ## ASK YOURSELF

3.73. Here it looks as though Aristotle is taking away what he just gave us. If virtue consists in choosing _____ relative to us, then any vicious action, on Aristotle's account, ought to be a deficiency or a corresponding excess of some sort. But it makes no sense to say that such vicious actions as murder or adultery fall at the ends of some scale with a virtuous action in the middle. What would murder be the excess of? Just killing someone a little bit?

Perhaps the idea of virtue as the "mean" comes to Aristotle from certain strong currents in Greek culture, but is not essential to his analysis. At any rate one can still see that in many cases, at least, virtuous actions and feelings are those that avoid various kinds of excess and deficiency, both in action and in feeling and desire.

Chapter 7. A Catalogue of the Virtues. What follows is an outline of some of the main virtues and vices. We can imagine Aristotle pointing to a chart, with three divisions, one for excesses, one for virtues, and one for defects.

But it is not enough to lay down this as a general rule; it is necessary to apply it to particular cases, as in reasonings upon actions generally, statements, although they are broader are less exact than particular statements. For all action refers to particulars, and it is essential that our theories should harmonize with the particular cases to which they apply.

We must take particular virtues then from the catalogue of virtues. In regard to feelings of fear and confidence, courage is a mean state. On the side of excess, he whose fearlessness is excessive has no name, as often happens, but he whose confidence is excessive is foolhardy, while he whose timidity is excessive and whose confidence is deficient is a coward.

In respect of pleasures and pains, although not indeed of all pleasures and pains, and to a less extent in respect of pains than of pleasures, the mean state is temperance, the excess is licentiousness. We never find people who are deficient in regard to pleasure; accordingly such people again have not received a name, but we may call them insensible [dull, listless].

As regards the giving and taking of money, the mean state is liberality, the excess and deficiency are prodigality and illiberality [stinginess]. Here the excess and deficiency take opposite forms; for while the prodigal man is excessive in spending and deficient in taking, the illiberal man is excessive in taking and deficient in spending.

(For the present we are giving only a rough and summary account of the virtues, and that is sufficient for our purpose; we will hereafter determine their character more exactly.)

In respect of money there are other dispositions as well. There is the mean state which is magnificence; for the magnificent man, who is one who deals with large sums of money, differs from the liberal man who has to do only with small sums; and the excess corresponding to it is bad taste or vulgarity, the deficiency is meanness. These are different from the excess and deficiency of liberality; what the difference is will be explained hereafter.

When modern people hear the word "ethics" they think of such questions as whether it is ever right to tell a lie or to cheat, whether it is ever right to remove a respirator from a terminally ill person, and so forth. Many of us do not typically think about "character traits" when we hear "ethics," but even if we do, we would probably not include all the traits Aristotle is discussing here, such as being a big (and vulgar) spender on the one hand, or stingy on the other, as opposed to being "just right" (knowing how to spend, buy presents, or throw a party with just the right degree of opulence). So, not only is Aristotle more concerned with character traits than with criteria for right actions, he is also concerned with character traits that we might not think of as having anything to do with ethics.

ASK YOURSELF

3.74. But remember, he is raising the question, what is the _____ kind of life, or what is the _____ of all our actions, and he has concluded that the answer is happiness. And surely all sorts of character traits have a bearing on how happy we are, not just the "ethical" ones as *we* tend to think of as "ethics." For example, how clever, or pleasant, or artistic a person is can obviously have a bearing on the quality of their life.

In respect of honor and dishonor the mean state is high mindedness, the excess is what is called vanity, the deficiency little mindedness.

Corresponding to liberality, which, as we said, differs from magnificence as having to do not with great but with small sums of money, there is a moral state which has to do with petty honor and is related to high mindedness which has to do with great honor; for it is possible to aspire to honor in the right way, or in a way which is excessive or insufficient, and if a person's aspirations are excessive, he is called ambitious, if they are deficient, he is called unambitious, while if they are between the two, he has no name. The dispositions too are nameless, except that the disposition of the ambitious person is called ambition. The consequence is that the extremes lay claim to the mean or intermediate place. We ourselves speak of one who observes the mean sometimes as ambitious and at other times as unambitious; we sometimes praise an ambitious, and at other times an unambitious person. The reason for our doing so will be stated in due course, but let us now discuss the other virtues in accordance with the method which we have followed hitherto.

 ASK YOURSELF

3.75. Aristotle is evidently having some difficulty getting all of the virtues (vices) mapped onto his scheme of _____, (the virtue) and _____. This again suggests that this scheme is somewhat artificial and perhaps not central to his aims, although it may well be useful for instructional purposes.

Anger, like other emotions, has its excess, it deficiency, and its mean state. It may be said that they have no names, but as we call one who observes the mean gentle, we will call the mean state gentleness.

Among the extremes, if a person errs on the side of excess, he may be called passionate and his vice passionateness, if on that of deficiency he may be called impassive and his deficiency impassivity. There are also three other mean states with certain resemblances to each other, and yet with a difference. For while they are all concerned with intercourse in speech and action, they are different in that one of them is concerned with truth in such intercourse, and the others with pleasantness, one with pleasantness in amusement and the other with pleasantness in the various circumstances of life.

We must therefore discuss these states in order to make it clear that in all cases it is the mean state which is an object of praise, and the extremes are neither right nor laudable but blamable. It is true that these mean and extreme states are generally nameless, but we must do our best here as elsewhere to give them a name, so that our argument may be clear and easy to follow. In the matter of truth then, he who observes the mean may be called truthful, and the mean state truthfulness. Pretence, if it takes the form of exaggeration, is boastfulness, and one who is guilty of pretence is a boaster; but if it takes the form of depreciation it is understatement, and he who is guilty of it is a self-depreciator [guilty of false humility].

With respect to pleasantness in social pastimes, he who observes the mean is witty, and his disposition wittiness; the excess is buffoonery, and he who is guilty of it a buffoon, whereas he who is deficient in wit may be called a boor and his moral state boorishness.

As to the other kind of pleasantness, namely pleasantness in life, he who is pleasant in a proper way is friendly, and his mean state friendliness; but he who goes too far, if he has no ulterior object in view, is obsequious, while if his object is self-interest, he is a flatterer, and he who does not go far enough and always makes himself unpleasant is a quarrelsome and morose sort of person.

There are also mean states in the emotions and in the expression of the emotions. For although modesty is not a virtue, yet a modest person is praised as if he were virtuous; for here too one person is said to observe the mean and another to exceed it, as e.g. the bashful man who is never anything but modest, whereas a person who has insufficient modesty or no modesty at all is called shameless, and one who observes the mean modest.

Righteous indignation, again, is a mean state between envy and malice. They are all concerned with the pain and pleasure that we feel at the fortunes of our neighbors. A person who is righteously indignant is pained at the prosperity of the undeserving; but the envious person goes further and is pained at anybody's prosperity, and the malicious person is so far from being pained that he actually rejoices at misfortunes. We shall have another opportunity however of discussing these matters.

 ASK YOURSELF

3.76. In his discussion of truthfulness Aristotle evidently has in mind truthfulness about oneself, not just truthfulness about anything whatsoever. Is that sort of truthfulness important to the kind of lives people lead? Why or why not?

Notice that Aristotle's discussion of virtues and vices includes much that we might include under the emotions or temperament. But of course an emotion such as envy tends to go with certain dispositions to act in certain ways. So Aristotle's claim that the species of virtue is dispositions not only to act but to *feel* certain ways is still pertinent.

 ASK YOURSELF

3.77. Is the presence of envy and malice in the world at least as responsible for the miseries of life as what we call immoral actions, such as lying or murder or theft?

3.78. Are the people who have these vices as likely to be miserable as the people who are their victims? Explain briefly.

But in regard to justice, as the word is used in various senses, we will afterwards define those senses and explain how each of them is a mean state. And we will follow the same course with the intellectual virtues.

There are then three dispositions, two being vices, namely one the vice of excess and the other that of deficiency, and one virtue, which is the mean state between them; and they are all in a sense mutually opposed. . . . Thus the courageous man appears foolhardy as compared with the coward, but cowardly as compared with the foolhardy. Similarly, the temperate person appears licentious as compared with the insensible person but insensible as compared with the licentious, and the liberal man appears prodigal compared to the stingy man, but stingy compared to a prodigal one. . . .

Again, while some extremes exhibit more or less similarity to the mean, as foolhardiness resembles courage [more than cowardice does] and prodigality resembles liberality [more than stinginess does], there is the greatest possible dissimilarity between the extremes. But things which are furthest removed from each other are defined to be opposites; hence the further things are removed, the greater is the opposition between them. It is in some cases the deficiency and in others the excess which is the more opposite to the mean. Thus it is not foolhardiness (the excess), but cowardice (the deficiency) which is the more opposed to courage, nor is it insensibility (the deficiency), but licentiousness (the excess) which is the more opposed to temperance.

There are two reasons why this should be so. One lies in the nature of the thing itself; for as one of the two extremes is the nearer and more similar to the mean, it is not this extreme, but its opposite, that we chiefly set against the mean. For instance, as it appears that foolhardiness is more similar and nearer to courage than cowardice, it is cowardice that we chiefly set against courage; for things which are further removed from the mean seem to be more opposite to it.

. . . there is a second reason which lies in our own nature. It is the things to which we ourselves are naturally more inclined that appear more opposed to the mean. Thus we are ourselves naturally more inclined to pleasures than to their opposites, and are more prone therefore to licentiousness than to decorum. Accordingly we speak of those things, in which we are more likely to run to great lengths, as being more opposed to the mean. Hence it follows that licentiousness, which is an excess, is more opposed to temperance than dullness.

It has now been sufficiently shown that moral virtue is a mean state, and in what sense it is a mean state; it is a mean state as lying between two vices, a vice of excess on the one side and a vice of deficiency on the other, and as aiming at the mean in the emotions and actions.

That is the reason why it is so hard to be virtuous; for it is always hard work to find the mean in anything. For example, it is not everybody, but only a man of science, who can find the mean or center of a circle. So too anybody can get angry, that is an easy matter, and anybody can give or spend money, but to give it to the right persons, to give the right amount of it and to give it at the right time and for the right cause and in the right way, this is not what anybody can do, nor is it easy. That is the reason why it is rare and laudable and noble to do well. Accordingly one who aims at the mean must begin by departing from that extreme which is the more contrary to the mean; he must act in the spirit of Calypso's advice, "Far from this spray and swell keep thou the ship," for of the two extremes one represents a greater failure than the other.

As it is difficult then to hit the mean exactly, we must take the second best course, as the saying is, and choose the lesser of two evils, and this we shall best do in the way that we have described, i.e. by steering clear of the evil which is further from the mean.

ASK YOURSELF

3.79. Briefly, why is it that we tend to think of certain extremes as being closer to the right and virtuous actions (or dispositions) than others? For example, why do we think rashness closer to courage than cowardice? Remember, there are two reasons. Give both.

3.80. It follows then that in situations of danger, it would be better to act rashly then to show lots of caution. But is a timid person likely to end up happier? Why or why not?

We must also observe the things to which we are ourselves particularly prone, as different natures have different inclinations, and we may ascertain what these are by a consideration of our feelings of pleasure and pain. And then we must drag ourselves in the direction opposite to them; for it is by removing ourselves as far as possible from what is wrong that we shall arrive at the mean, as we do when we pull a crooked stick straight.

ASK YOURSELF

3.81. If you tend to be stingy, you should try to recognize that fact, and then err on the side of _____ . If you tend to be lustful (intemperate with respect to sex) you should err in the direction of being _____. Does this sound like a recipe for happiness to you?

3.82. Some people, in Aristotle's day and ever since, have thought that the best life is one of excess (eat drink and be merry, *a lot*). Mention a few things here that you might say to someone against such a view (or to yourself, if you have such a view).

But in all cases we must especially be on our guard against what is pleasant and against pleasure, as we are not impartial judges of pleasure. Hence our attitude towards pleasure must be like that of the elders of the people in the *Iliad* towards Helen, and we must never be afraid of applying the words they used; for if we dismiss pleasure as they dismissed Helen, we shall be less likely to go wrong.

ASK YOURSELF

3.83. (1) Do Aristotle's concerns with pleasure show that he has puritanical and repressive tendencies? (2) Mention some examples of your own of people who have made themselves miserable through their inability or refusal to manage and control their desires for pleasure (you do not need to mention names, and you should certainly consider including yourself among the examples). Try to make your answers to (1) and (2) consistent.

It is by action of this kind, to put it summarily, that we shall best succeed in hitting the mean. It may be admitted that this is a difficult task, especially in particular cases. For example, it is not easy to determine the right manner, objects, occasions, and duration of anger. There are times when we ourselves praise people who are deficient in anger, and call them gentle, and there are other times when we speak of people who exhibit a savage temper as spirited. It is not however one who deviates a little from what is right, but one who deviates a great deal, whether on the side of excess or of deficiency, that is censured; for he is sure to be found out.

Again, it is not easy to decide theoretically how far and to what extent a man may go before he becomes blamable, but neither is it easy to define theoretically anything else within the region of perception; such things fall under the head of particulars, and our judgment of them depends upon our perception.

Aristotle is claiming something here that is quite central to his way of thinking about ethics. He is saying that in order to achieve a good life, a life of virtue and happiness, we must have something like what we would now call "perceptiveness." We use this word to describe a sensitivity to particular persons and particular situations.

 ASK YOURSELF

3.84. But couldn't a person still be a good person who lacked perceptiveness, provided only that they followed such rules as "do not lie, do not cheat, do not inflict unnecessary pain, be kind," and so forth? If you can think of a reason why such a person might *not* succeed in being or at any rate doing good, state it here. If you cannot, think about it a little more.

3.85. Some philosophers have argued that reading certain novels (although certainly not just *any* novel) may help remind us of the complexities of the moral life. Say here why they might think this (relate to the previous question).

3.86. Does what Aristotle says about rearing and training at the end of Book 2, Chapter 1 and near the beginning of Book 2, Chapter 3 have any bearing on this matter of perceptiveness? Can you train someone to be perceptive? Explain, and give an example from some non-ethical domain (e.g., sports, the arts).

Book 3

Aristotle's concept of virtue is further clarified by his account of choice. Choice, you may remember, was essential to virtue in the definition he gave earlier.

Chapter 2. What Choice Is Not. Aristotle begins by distinguishing choice from related concepts.

 From ARISTOTLE: *Nicomachean Ethics*, Book III

. . . we must next discuss choice; for it is thought to be most closely bound up with virtue and to discriminate characters better than actions do. Choice, then, seems to be voluntary, but not the same thing as the voluntary; the latter extends more widely. For both children and the lower animals share in voluntary action, but not in choice, and acts done on the spur of the moment we describe as voluntary, but not as chosen.

It is already clear that Aristotle's notion of choice is somewhat technical. We would ordinarily say that children do make choices. Aristotle would probably not disagree with us about the facts, but only about what words to use in describing them.

Those who say choice is appetite or anger or wish or a kind of opinion do not seem to be right. For choice is not common to irrational creatures as well, but appetite and anger are. Again, the incontinent man [person who lacks self-control] acts with appetite, but not with choice; while the continent man on the contrary acts with choice, but not with appetite. Again, appetite is contrary to choice, but not appetite to appetite. Again, appetite relates to the pleasant and the painful, choice neither to the painful nor to the pleasant. Still less is it anger; for acts due to anger are thought to be less objects of choice than any others. But neither is it wish, though it seems near to it; for choice cannot relate to impossibles, and if any one said he chose them [impossible things, such as to be to be twenty again at the age of fifty] he would be thought silly; but there may be a wish even for impossibles, e.g. for immortality. And we may wish for things that could in no way be brought about by one's own efforts, e.g. that a particular actor or athlete should win in a competition; but no one chooses such things, but only the things that he thinks could be brought about by his own efforts. Again, wish relates rather to the end, choice to the means; for instance, we wish to be healthy, but we choose the acts which will make us healthy, and we wish to be happy and say we do, but we cannot well say we choose to be so; for, in general, choice seems to relate to the things that are in our own power. For this reason, too, it cannot be opinion; for opinion is thought to relate to all kinds of things, no less to eternal things and impossible things than to things in our own power; and it is distinguished by its falsity or truth, not by its badness or goodness, while choice is distinguished rather by these. Now with opinion in general perhaps no one even says it is identical. But it is not identical even with any kind of opinion; for by choosing what is good or bad we are men of a certain character, which we are not by holding certain opinions.

 ASK YOURSELF

3.87. It appears that some people *do* think that they are good partly because they have the "right" opinions, for example, right opinions about some political matter or socially divisive issue (give your own examples). Aristotle would laugh at that, since he thinks personal goodness is a matter of _____.

. . . What, then, or what kind of thing is it, since it is none of the things we have mentioned? It seems to be voluntary, but not all that is voluntary seems to be an object of choice. Is it, then, what has been decided on by previous deliberation? At any rate choice involves a rational principle and thought. Even the name seems to suggest that it is what is chosen before other things. [The Greek word translated as "choice" here literally means "to take before."]

Chapter 3. Choice and Deliberation. Aristotle points out that we do not deliberate about what is impossible (for example, whether to jump five hundred feet into the air or draw a square circle) or about other matters that are not under our control. His positive account follows.

. . . things that are brought about by our own efforts, but not always in the same way, are the things about which we deliberate, e.g. questions of medical treatment or of money-making. And we do so more in the case of the art of navigation than in that of gymnastics, inasmuch as the art of navigation has been less exactly worked out, and again about other things in the same ratio, and more also in the case of the arts than in that of the sciences; for we have more doubt about the former. Deliberation is concerned with things that happen in a certain way for the most part, but in which the event is obscure, and with things in which it is indeterminate.

 ASK YOURSELF

3.88. Aristotle is explaining what choice is partly by reference to a point stressed in Book 1, Chapter 3 and elsewhere. What is that point?

We call in others to aid us in deliberation on important questions, distrusting ourselves as not being equal to deciding. We deliberate not about ends but about what pertains to the end. . . . [I]f a thing [which we want to do] appears possible we try to do it. By "possible" things I mean things that might be brought about by our own efforts; and these in a sense include things that can be brought about by the efforts of our friends, since the moving principle is in ourselves. The subject of investigation is sometimes the instruments, sometimes the use of them; and similarly in the other cases—sometimes the means, sometimes the mode of using it or the means of bringing it about.

It seems, then, as has been said, that man is a moving principle of actions. Now deliberation is about the things to be done by the agent himself, and actions are for the sake of things other than themselves. For the end cannot be a subject of deliberation, but only what promotes the end; nor indeed can the particular facts be a subject of it, as whether this is bread or has been baked as it should; for these are matters of perception. If we are to be always deliberating, we shall have to go on to infinity.

The same thing is deliberated upon and is chosen, except that the object of choice is already determinate, since it is that which has been decided upon as a result of deliberation that is the object of choice. For every one ceases to inquire how he is to act when he has brought the moving principle back to himself and to the ruling part of himself; for this is what chooses. . . . The object of choice being one of the things in our own power which is desired after deliberation, *choice will be deliberate desire of things in our own power*; for when we have decided as a result of deliberation, we desire in accordance with our deliberation. We may take it, then, that we have described choice in outline, and stated the nature of its objects and the fact that it is concerned with means.

Here is Aristotle's definition of choice: deliberate desire of things in our power. It is notable for the way in which it combines reason and desire. Choice is not construed as the exercise of a raw faculty of will, nor as the output of pure rationality.

Aristotle's general definition of choice may still leave us wondering whether there is some standard for distinguishing good from bad choice, correct from incorrect. Here is his answer.

the excellent man judges each class of things rightly, and in each the truth appears to him. For each state of character has its own ideas of the noble and the pleasant, and perhaps the excellent man differs from others most by seeing the truth in each class of things, for he is as it were the norm and measure of [what is true] in them. In most things the error seems to be due to pleasure; for it appears a good when it is not. We therefore choose the pleasant as a good, and avoid pain as an evil.

The excellent man is, of course, one who is not so swayed by love of pleasure or fear of pain that he chooses badly or foolishly. Unfortunately, if we are not acquainted with any such people we will have not have a standard for good or correct choice. For the standard must be embodied, so to speak. Manuals on how to live are not suitable means to achieving personal development, which is a matter of training, of good upbringing and good models.

Aristotle's "Naturalism." Aristotle's ethics is sometimes described as a "virtue" ethics since the concept of a virtue functions so centrally in his thought. A "virtue" in his thinking is simply an excellence or excellent quality of something that enables it to fulfill its function in a superior way.

 ASK YOURSELF

3.89. What then would be the most obvious virtue of a knife?

Thus, in order to know what the virtues of a human being are, you must know what the function of a human being is. Obviously you could not know what traits make a knife a good knife (or a human a good human) if you didn't know what its function was. If you thought the function of a knife was to pick up peas from your plate, you would think a good knife was one shaped like a spoon. Well, try cutting a loaf of bread with a spoon, even a "sharp" one.

As already pointed out, there is a difficulty in the idea that humans have some one central function. Suppose, however, that they do. Then a good human will be one who fulfills that function well. What makes a human a good human will then be a matter of *fact*, not just a matter of someone's subjective opinion, or someone's "values," just as what makes a knife a good knife is a matter of fact, not open to dispute among reasonable people. This idea conflicts with the very common notion that ethics is a matter of subjective opinion, and that there is no way to argue rationally about ethical differences (for example, the difference between those who oppose and those who support euthanasia).

So, for Aristotle, there is no gap between "facts" and "values." Such a position in ethics is sometimes called "naturalism." Until fairly recently naturalism was thought by perhaps the majority of modern philosophers to be mistaken for the following sort of reason: When we say someone is good we might mean that they "function well" in some capacity or other. But, in ethics, when we say someone is good, we mean they are *morally* good, and moral goodness can only be made to look like a natural trait such as functioning well if we sneak in the idea that the kind of functioning we mean is "*moral*" functioning.

 ASK YOURSELF

3.90. What would be wrong with defining "morally good" as "functioning well" and then defining "functioning well" as "functioning well morally"?

Recently more philosophers have begun to think that Aristotle is not so easily refuted and that his views on the virtues, moral psychology, moral luck, human happiness, and many other related topics deserve careful consideration. If reading Aristotle has led you to question the popular idea that there must be a gap between "facts" and "values" or that ethical matters are "subjective" or merely "relative to" individuals or cultures, it will have served a useful purpose. If it has merely alerted you to the place of character in thinking about ethics, it will have served a useful purpose. And of course, whenever we do something, we want it to serve some useful purpose!

SUGGESTIONS FOR FURTHER READING

Primary Sources

Barnes, Jonathan, ed. *The Complete Works of Aristotle: The Revised Oxford Translation* (Princeton, NJ: Princeton University Press, 1984). Some recent and very fine translations.

Cohen, S. M., Curd, P., and Reeve, C. D. C. *Readings in Ancient Greek Philosophy* (Indianapolis: Hackett Publishing Company, 1995). A fuller selection from the Presocratics, Plato, and Aristotle than that contained in this present volume. Useful and quite up-to-date bibliography and a particularly helpful glossary of Aristotle's main terms.

McKeon, Richard, ed. *The Basic Works of Aristotle* (New York: Random House 1941). Many older but still very serviceable translations.

Critical Analyses and Discussions

Ackrill, J. L. *Aristotle the Philosopher* (Oxford: Oxford University Press, 1981). Discussion of central issues by a well-known translator.

Barnes, Jonathan. *Aristotle* (Oxford: Oxford University Press, 1982). An engaging general discussion.

———, ed. *The Cambridge Companion to Aristotle* (Cambridge: Cambridge University Press, 1995). Excellent representation of recent scholarship on principal facets of Aristotle's thought.

Cooper, John. *Reason and Human Good in Aristotle* (Cambridge, MA: Harvard University Press, 1975). A classic work on Aristotle's ethics.

Kraut, Richard. *Aristotle on the Human Good* (Princeton, NJ: Princeton University Press, 1989). Defends the view that Aristotle's claims about the highest good being contemplative (in his *Nicomachean Ethics* Book 10) is his considered view rather than an aberration.

Nussbaum, Martha. *The Fragility of Goodness: Luck and Ethics in Greek Tragedy and Philosophy* (Cambridge: Cambridge University Press, 1986). Takes a view opposed to Kraut on Aristotle's idea of the highest good. Interesting discussions of relevant literary texts (e.g., Sophocles).

Nussbaum, M. C., and Rorty, A. O., eds. *Essays on Aristotle's De Anima* (Oxford: Oxford University Press, 1992). A collection of fairly recent work on Aristotle's remarkable thinking about the soul.

Ross, W. D. *Aristotle* (New York: Barnes and Noble, 1949). A classic general introduction to Aristotle's life and works.

Sherman, N. *Aristotle's Ethics: Critical Essays* (London: Rowman and Littlefield, 1999). A very good representation of work on Aristotle's seminal ethics over the last twenty years; Sherman includes work on feminism and Aristotle and on mistaken ideas of the mean in action.

CHAPTER 4

HELLENISTIC PHILOSOPHY

everal social and political factors impacted philosophy after the time of Aristotle. Alexander the Great died in 323 BCE with no heir to his new empire. His territories were initially peacefully divided between four of his generals. But in 275 unity was no longer possible, and the four Hellenistic dynasties warred among themselves. The Greek city-states were under the rule of the Selucid dynasty and were no longer of political significance in the larger scheme of things. Eventually, the Greek city-states lost independence entirely.

During this time, there was a freer mingling of races and nationalities, a greater freedom of thought, and rapid trade expansion. Wages did not keep pace with rapidly rising inflation, so many people barely managed subsistence-level living. All of these changes brought about cultural upheaval and widespread feelings of uncertainty and alienation, and several popular philosophies developed to address these problems. Plato's and Aristotle's writings were too specialized and abstract for popular tastes. Instead, philosophers emphasized individual contentment or happiness, the Greek word for which is *eudaimonia*. Four eudaimonian schools emerged, each offering different views of how to attain happiness: Epicureanism, Stoicism, Cynicism, and Skepticism.

 ASK YOURSELF

4.1 Why did philosophers after Aristotle emphasize individual contentment?

The social climate changed once again when power passed from the Hellenistic dynasties to the Roman Empire. The Romans admired classic Greek culture, and many Roman philosophers remained faithful to the basic doctrines of their Greek predecessors. Thus this period saw loyal proponents of Plato and Aristotle, as well as defenders of the four eudaimonian philosophies. Other philosophers, such as the Roman orator Cicero, took bits and pieces from all of the philosophical schools and are accordingly dubbed *eclectics*.

 ASK YOURSELF

4.2. What was philosophy like in the Roman period?

EPICUREANISM

Epicurus (342–271 BCE) founded the philosophical school named after him, Epicureanism, which emphasized the view that pleasure is the ultimate good in life. Born on the island of Samoa, Epicurus visited Athens at the age of eighteen and briefly studied under a follower of Plato. In his mid-thirties he returned to Athens and founded a school at a garden he purchased, where he and his students lived. He remained there for the rest of his life. Ancient historians report that Epicurus composed three hundred scrolls of writing, but unfortunately, almost none of it survives.

Atoms and Free Will

Epicurus was heavily influenced by Atomistic philosophy, which maintained that the only things that exist are atoms in a vacuum of empty space. Like Democritus, Epicurus believed that larger objects are made from collections of tiny, indivisible atoms that collide and then stick to each other. However, Epicurus was unhappy with two key aspects of Democritus's theory. First, Epicurus found a conceptual problem with Democritus's explanation of colliding atoms. Suppose that we emptied a box of atoms off a cliff. Since the atoms would all fall in the same line, then they would never collide with each other, and we'd never get any larger objects. Epicurus's solution to this puzzle was that something about the atoms themselves makes them deviate off their course, a feature of the atoms that he called the *slight swerve*. Once off their initial paths, atoms can then collide with other atoms and make the things that we see around us.

 ASK YOURSELF

4.3. What is the function of the "swerve" in Epicurus's thought?

A second problem that Epicurus had with Democritus's theory was its rejection of free will. According to Democritus, if everything is composed of atoms, and atoms operate according to fixed and regulated principles, then everything that happens in the universe is the result of fixed and regulated principles. This is also true of humans and human activity. Since I am only an object composed of atoms, then anything I do will be the outcome of fixed principles that regulate the physical world of atoms. In contemporary vocabulary, *materialism* implies *determinism*. Although Epicurus endorsed atomistic materialism, he resisted the conclusion that our behavior is determined and that we have no free will. According to Epicurus, free will is a fact of experience that can't be denied. The scientific explanation of free will rests on his notion of the slight swerve. Atoms have the power of occasional free movement. Since we humans are composed of atoms, this undetermined feature of atoms forms the basis of the free and undetermined decisions that we make.

 ASK YOURSELF

4.4. Although inspired by Democritus, Epicurus opposed the Atomistic view of determinism and argued instead that humans have _____.

Epicurus's insightful solution to the materialistic problem of determinism sounds much like solutions that some defenders of free will have offered in our own time. In the early twentieth century, physicists proposed a theory of indeterminacy about the behavior of subatomic particles. According to this theory, there are no fixed laws that regulate the movement of electrons around an atom's nucleus. Although we can make some predictions about where a given electron might be, we cannot pinpoint its exact location at a point in time. Inspired by the indeterminacy theory, some philosophers argued that subatomic indeterminacy supports free will. However, there are problems with both Epicurus's slight swerve defense of free will and its contemporary counterparts. First, even if some events at the atomic level are undetermined, this does not seem to carry over to events at larger levels of physical reality. When my car stops running, I believe that there is a precise mechanical cause for this problem, and I don't blame it on atomic slight swerves or subatomic indeterminacy. Human behavior operates at this higher level of physical reality, not the subatomic one. A second problem with Epicurus's solution is that it fails to distinguish between (1) a random, uncaused event and (2) a purposeful and undetermined choice. Atomic slight swerves appear to be random and uncaused events. Even if we grant that such uncaused events occur, at best it will only explain abrupt and random bodily movements, such as seizures and jitters. It will not form the basis of a purposeful and intentioned human action, which is what we need for genuine, freely willed actions.

 ## ASK YOURSELF

4.5. Give an example of a human bodily movement that might be a random, and contrast that with an example of a purposeful human choice.

Fearing the Gods

Epicurus's account of the atoms and free will is only one of his many philosophical contributions. His lasting fame rests on his view that the good life consists of minimizing life's pains and increasing life's pleasures. Although later Epicureans focused more on the mandate to increase pleasure, Epicurus himself stressed the need to minimize pain. Pain comes in a variety of forms, both physical and emotional. One type of emotional pain is that which comes from the fear of the unknown. If I am constantly worrying about what God thinks of me and what will happen to me after I die, then I will be unhappy. To be truly happy, we must conquer these fears. To this end, Epicurus explains that we should not fear the gods. In the following selection, Epicurus urges us to believe that God is immortal and happy. However, we should not hold to common views about the Gods, which are based on false suppositions. The selections in this section are from Epicurus's *Letter to Menoeceus*, a short and revealing work preserved by third-century CE biographer Diogenes Laertius in his work *Lives of Eminent Philosophers*.

From EPICURUS: *Letter to Menoeceus*

Do and practice those things to which I constantly exhort you, embracing them as the very principles of the good life. First, reckoning in accordance with the idea of God engraved on the common mind, namely that God is immortal and blessed, attribute to him neither what is alien to his immortality nor removed from his blessedness. Believe about him all that preserves his immortality and blessedness. Gods exist, for the knowledge of them is by distinct intellectual perception. But they are not as the vulgar crowd, which is unable to maintain a consistent conception of them, supposes. The impious person is not the one who denies the Gods of the crowd. Rather, the impious person is the one who saddles the Gods with the opinions of the crowd. For the declarations of the crowd concerning the Gods are not divinely infused concepts but false opinions, [such as the idea that] it is from the Gods that the worst misfortunes fall upon the evil, and profits upon [the good]. For since they are always accustomed to their own character traits, they endorse those similar to their own [that is, they attribute them to the gods], but consider all others alien.

 ASK YOURSELF

4.6. According to Epicurus, what is a problem with what people commonly believe about the gods?

4.7. Give an example of something about your own view of God that might give you fear.

Epicurus argues that, ultimately, we are freed from the fear of Gods since they have nothing to do with human affairs. As seen in the previous quote, he believes that they exist. Elsewhere he argues that we know that they exist since they appear to us in dreams. Nevertheless, they are happy in their own realm and don't disturb us.

Fear of Death

Fear of death also disrupts our lives and prevents us from being happy. Epicurus argues that we should be free from the fear of death because there is no afterlife and thus we can't experience any pain after death. There is no afterlife because everything in the world is material, including ourselves, and we disintegrate when we die. From one perspective, Epicurus's solution may seem to produce more anxiety than he hopes to resolve. However, Epicurus precisely explains the psychological stakes involved in the issue of life after death. Consider the state of death itself. For Epicurus, all of life's goods and evils presuppose consciousness, and death eliminates that. Thus, there can't be anything about death itself that is painful, and it makes no sense to fear what isn't painful. Consider next the anticipation of death. While I am alive and anticipate my death, this may cause me discomfort. However, Epicurus argues, it is senseless to have a painful anticipation of death when the state of death is not to be feared.

Accustom yourself to the thought that death is nothing to us. For all good and evil reside in sensation, but death is the removal of all sensation. Therefore the correct understanding, that death is nothing to us, makes the mortality of life enjoyable not by adding infinite time, but by removing the yearning for immortality. Nothing is terrible in life to one who has truly grasped that nothing terrible belongs to not living. So that one is foolish who says that he fears death not because it will be painful when it arrives but is painful because of its inevitable approach. For that which is no trouble when it arrives is, in expectation, an empty pain. Death, the most chilling of evils, is nothing to us, since really when we are, death is not, and on the other hand when death arrives, we are not. It is nothing either to the living or the dead since for the former it is not, and the latter are no longer.

But at one moment the crowd flees from death as the greatest of evils, at another moment longs for it as repose from the evils of life. But the wise person neither deprecates life nor fears its cessation. Life neither offends him nor does he believe cessation of life to be any evil. Just as he does not seek the greatest quantity of food, but rather the most pleasing food, so also he plucks the sweetest fruits of time, not the longest span of time.

He who exhorts the young to live beautifully but the old to make a fine end is simple minded, not only because of the desirability of life but because the practice of living well and dying well are the same. But that one is much worse who says it would be better not to be born, "Once born most swiftly to pass right through Hades' gates." For if he says this from conviction why does he not depart from life? For such a course of action is available, had he firmly wished it. But if he is joking, it amounts to idle chatter among folks who ignore him.

 ASK YOURSELF

4.8. Why according to Epicurus should we not fear the anticipation of death?

4.9. According to Epicurus, what is wrong with the view that we should "depart from life," that is, kill ourselves?

Pleasure and Pain

According to Epicurus, pleasure is the goal that nature has ordained for us. It is also the standard by which we judge everything good. However, we need to be cautious in pursuing pleasures. Specifically, we should seek a pleasure only when it pains us when we don't have it.

We should keep bearing in mind that the future is neither wholly ours nor wholly not ours, so that we neither entirely expect its sure occurrence, nor give up hope as though it were entirely beyond reach.

We must consider that some desires are inborn, some vain, and of those inborn some are necessary and others inborn only. Of those which are necessary some are necessary for *eudaimonia*, some for bodily repose, others for life itself. Now undisturbed contemplation of these matters enables us to bring back all choice and avoidance into the service of bodily health and *ataraxia* [mental repose], for such is the goal of the blessed life. Thanks to these we perform all our actions, so as to feel neither distress nor fright. Once this is the case for us, the tempest of the soul is dispersed so that the living being does not have to proceed as though lacking something nor seek something different by which he might fulfill the good of body and soul. For we have need of pleasure when we feel distress at its absence, but when we are not distressed we are no longer addicted to pleasure. Accordingly we count pleasure as the originating principle and the goal of the blessed life. For we recognize pleasure as the first and fitting good, for from it proceeds all choice and avoidance, and we return to it as the feeling-standard by which we judge every good.

 ASK YOURSELF

4.10. Give an example of a pleasure that we should forego, since the absence of that pleasure would cause us no pain.

Even though we should gravitate toward pleasure and reduce pain, we should not actively pursue every pleasure, nor actively avoid every pain. Sometimes, we get a greater pleasure from enduring a pain, such as trips to the dentist. The fewer desires we have, the easier we can be pleased.

But since pleasure is the first and natural good, for this very reason we do not choose every pleasure, but pass over many where great discomfort for us follows from them. And we consider many pains to be better than pleasure, since a greater pleasure comes to us after enduring distress for a long time. Every pleasure is good by natural kinship to us, yet not all are to be chosen, even as all distress is bad, yet not all is of such a nature as to be avoided. By calculating the advantages and disadvantages one will look to make a judgment on all these things. For sometimes we treat the good as bad, and conversely the bad as good. Therefore habituation to plain things rather than luxuries produces complete health, and makes a person fit for the exigencies of life and disposes us better when approaching luxuries after long intervals [without them], and prepares us to be without fear in the face of contingency.

We consider self sufficiency a great good not because we always prefer having few things, but so that, where we lack plenty, we may use what little we have in the genuine conviction that those enjoy the sweetest luxuries who need them least, and that all that is natural is easily obtained, while vain things are difficult to attain. So, when all the pain of need is removed, plain flavors bring us pleasure equal to that of gourmet dining. Bread and water give the highest pleasure when set before one who needs them.

When therefore we declare pleasure to be the goal, we do not refer to the pleasures of profligates and those at ease in enjoyments, as some think who are ignorant and disagree or scarcely get the point, but rather we refer to the absence of bodily pain and mental disturbance. For it is not continuous drinking and reveling or indulgences in boys and women, nor fish and all the rest born by a rich table, which produce a pleasant life, but rather sober reasoning, searching out the grounds of all choice and avoidance, and extirpating opinion, from which the greatest disturbance of the soul proceeds.

ASK YOURSELF

4.11. Since pleasure is "our first and native good" it might seem that we should eat, drink, and be merry, and really live it up. Would Epicurus agree?

Prudence and Freedom

Despite the emphasis that Epicurus places on the pursuit of pleasure, he argues that prudence is the greatest good. Prudence is the ability to make careful decisions; if we are prudent, then we will live pleasantly, honorably, and justly.

The origin and greatest good of all these things is prudence. Hence prudence is more prized than philosophy, for from it springs all the rest of the virtues, and prudence teaches us that it is not possible to live pleasantly without living prudently, finely and justly, nor to live prudently, finely and justly without pleasure. For the virtues are by nature bound up with living pleasantly; it is inseparable from them. For that reason you think no one better than that one who believes piously about the Gods, maintains a fearless attitude towards death, has by reason determined the naturally ordained end, and understands the (properly) delimited goods to be easily fulfilled and attained (whereas the course of distress is short), and who laughs at the allotments of fate, whom some have brought in as mistress of all. [Such a prudent one thinks that the chief power in determining events lies with us] for on the one hand some things happen by necessity, on the other some are by chance, and some are within our control.

For while necessity cannot be persuaded from its course, and he sees chance to be unstable, that which is within our control is without a master, and blame and its opposite naturally attach to it. So it is better to follow the myths about the Gods than to be enslaved to the fated dealings posited by the determinists. For the former suggests a possibility of placating the Gods by worship, but the latter suggests implacable necessity. The prudent one does not entertain the idea that, as the crowd supposes, chance is a God (for God's acts are fixed) or an uncertain cause. He does not think good or evil are given to people by chance for blessed living, but that opportunities for great good or evil are supplied by it. He considers it better to incur bad luck while acting rationally than to be lucky while acting irrationally. For it is better to fail in well chosen actions than to succeed in badly chosen actions through luck.

Therefore, practice these and related matters on your own, day and night, and do the same with one like yourself, and, whether awake or asleep you will never be disturbed but will live as a God among men. For one living among immortal blessings is not like a mortal being.

ASK YOURSELF

4.12. What are the marks of a prudent person?

4.13. According to Epicurus, the determinism of natural philosophers is worse than the superstitious belief in controlling divine forces. Why?

STOICISM

Philosophers often contrast Epicureanism with a second eudaimonian school, Stoicism. Whereas Epicureanism recommends that we attain happiness by pursuing pleasure and avoiding pain, Stoics recommend that we attain happiness by resigning ourselves to our fated place in the ordered cosmos; this means denying the pleasures and luxuries of life and living as an ascetic. Not only are Stoicism and Epicureanism conceptually at odds with each other, but, as both schools competed for members, Stoics and Epicureans saw themselves as rivals to each other. Given its emphasis on pleasure, we might think that Epicureanism would have been the more popular of the two schools. In point of fact, however, Stoicism had the greater following.

Zeno of Citium: Logic, Physics, and Ethics

The founder of Stoicism was Zeno of Citium (331–232 BCE), who was from a small Phoenician-Greek city in Cyprus. The Phoenicians were a Semitic people, which means that they were linguistically related to the ancient Canaanites and Israelites. According to legend, Zeno had a slightly twisted neck, was severe in manner, ate raw food, drank mostly water, wore thin clothes, and was oblivious to rain, heat, and pain. At age twenty-two, he arrived in Athens as the result of a shipwreck. Once there he was exposed to the teachings of various philosophical schools, including Epicureanism. He supposedly developed his own theories in reaction to these, which he publicly presented on the Painted Porch in the marketplace of Athens. The Greek work for "porch" is *stoa*, and it is from this that Stoicism derives its name. There are several anecdotes about Zeno's life, each of which highlights some aspect of Stoicism. On one occasion, Zeno whipped a slave for stealing. When the slave said that it was his destiny to steal, Zeno said it was also the slave's destiny to be whipped. This story shows the consistency between destiny and just deserts. On another occasion, Zeno heard someone criticize a minor work by the writer Antisthenes. Zeno objected that the critic ignored a major and more superior writing by Antisthenes. This story shows that the presence of natural evil in the world does not disprove a larger orderly creation. A final and somewhat depressing anecdote reports that one day Zeno broke his toe while walking down a road. Seeing this as a sign, he then killed himself by holding his breath. This story shows that natural events express God's will.

 ASK YOURSELF

4.14. What are the Stoic lessons in the three anecdotes about Zeno?

There are no surviving writings of Zeno, and what we know of his teachings comes to us from later Stoic writers. He apparently emphasized three things—logic, physics, and ethics. The relation between them is explained in a garden metaphor. Picture a walled garden containing a single fruit-bearing tree. The wall represents logic, the tree represents physics, and the fruit represents ethics. Accordingly, the wall of logic protects physics and ethics by laying down rules for pursuing truth. The tree of physics involves a study of cosmic order. Ethics is the fruit that directly results from physics—it instructs us how to live in the natural order. We will briefly consider key features of each of these three areas.

One part of Stoic logic involved criteria of truth. Think about the following statements: There is life on earth; there is life elsewhere in the universe; there is life on Mars; there is life on the Sun. We have differing degrees of conviction about each of these four statements. We have the highest degree of conviction about life on earth, mainly because we can see life on earth with our own eyes. However, we have the lowest degree of conviction about life on the Sun, since the sun is just too hot to support living things. Stoics articulated four degrees of conviction. At the lowest level we have a *mind picture* (*phantasia*), which merely gives us an impression of some thing; at this level of conviction, we do not even judge whether our impression is true or false. Next is *casual assent* (*synkatathesis*), which is a rough acknowledgment that a conception is either true or false. Next is *comprehension* (*katalepsis*), which involves a deepened assent and commonsense recognition that a conception is infallibly true. Finally, there is *knowledge* (*episteme*), which is an especially strong scientific knowledge that is possessed only by the wise. Zeno demonstrated these differing degrees of conviction by successively closing his fist, tighter and tighter, finally reaching knowledge, which "takes hold of us by the hair and drags us to assent!"

 ASK YOURSELF

4.15. Give examples of beliefs with differing degrees of conviction that illustrate the Stoic notions of mind picture, casual assent, comprehension, and science.

In addition to devising criteria of truth, another part of Stoic logic involved devising formal systems of argumentation. In this area, the Stoic contribution is best seen by comparison with the older system of logic proposed by Aristotle. Aristotle's logic stressed the relation of classes to each other; for example, the statement "all humans are mortal" states that things that fall in the class of "human" are also contained in the class of "mortal things." If "Socrates is a human" is true, then he belongs to class of humans and we can infer that "Socrates is mortal." Stoic logic, on the other hand, stressed the notion of an if-then relation between statements, rather than class relations. For example, we could infer from the truth of "If Bill is here then Mary will be glad" and "Bill is here" to "Mary is glad." That sort of inference cannot be accounted for properly in Aristotelian logic. The difference between the two approaches to logic is subtle. However, when followed consistently, each results in differing methods of proof. Although Aristotle's system dominated the study of logic for two thousand years, since the twentieth century logicians have developed more powerful systems that depend, in part, upon the sentential logic of the Stoics.

 ASK YOURSELF

4.16. Give an example of a sentence that fits into an if-then structure.

Turning next to physics, the Stoic's most important contribution is their discussion of *cosmic order*, which Stoic texts variously describe as God, Zeus, creative fire, aether, *logos*, reason of the world, soul of the world, law of nature, providence, destiny, and order. Regardless of the descriptive title used, the meaning is the same: Every aspect of the universe is fixed in an orderly fashion, follows rigid laws, and has a strict design. Technically, there is no real difference between the universe itself and the cosmic order behind it. Cosmic order is the most cohesive and creative aspect of the universe, and the rest of the universe is simply more relaxed. A second aspect of Stoic physics is their theory of the *eternal recurrence*, which is that the history of the universe is cyclical, going through endless cycles of creation and destruction. In modern terminology, it is as though the universe experiences a big bang, then big crunch, then another big bang, then another big crunch, on to infinity. Each cycle is identical, since the same cosmic ordering principle produces the same creation. This means not only that I will exist in each of these creative cycles, but also that I will have the same job, own the same car, and even scratch the same itch on my right shoulder that I am scratching right now. Each cycle begins with creative fire. Creation is then organized according to the four elements of earth, air, fire, and water, and everything ends in the same fire that started it all.

 ASK YOURSELF

4.17. Explain the two aspects of Stoic physics.

Stoic ethics is a logical outcome of the physical fact that everything in the universe is fixed by cosmic order. This means that everything that happens to me in life is the result of predetermined order. So, it useless for me to strive for things in life that are not part of this order. I need to accept my lot in life and approach life with resignation or apathy (*apatheia*). I will then be able to accept everything that happens to me, without any emotional upset. Thus, in view of the fact that each person is assigned a particular role in life, we should each play our parts to the best of our abilities. We are responsible for correcting ourselves, but we cannot judge others. To fulfill our destiny in the best way we need to develop four particular virtues. Through intelligence I know what is good and bad; through bravery I know what to fear and what not to fear; through justice I know how to give what is deserved; and through self-control I know what emotions to extinguish.

Stoic ethics involves a paradox: If everything in life is beyond my control, then it is not in my power to accept or reject the Stoic's recommendation. If I in fact resign myself to life's events, it is because I am fated to adopt that attitude, and not because I choose to do so. Stoic philosophers were aware of this problem, but made recommendations anyway. Recommending things to people seems to be a natural way of communicating, even if it is not actually in our power to act on the recommendations.

 ASK YOURSELF

4.18. According to Stoics, why should I resign myself to fate?

Epictetus

Although most Stoics writings did not survive, we have records of the teachings of the Stoic philosopher Epictetus (50–138 CE). Epictetus was born a Greek slave to a high-ranking Roman administrator. Epictetus had some kind of physical handicap, which, some historians speculate, he might have gotten from being abused as a slave. In his teens he was sent to study under a famous Stoic master. He was freed from slavery at about age eighteen, but was banished from society at about age forty. For the next fifty years he taught in humble surroundings. He lived in a house with only a straw mat, a simple pallet, and a clay lamp. His followers report that he was a simple, sweet, and charitable man with strong moral and religious convictions. His teachings were recorded by his pupil Arrian in two works: the *Discourses* and the *Manual*. The selections here are from the *Manual*. Epictetus opens this short work by distinguishing between things that are within our control and those that are outside of our control.

 From EPICTETUS: *Manual*

1. Some things are in our control and others not. Things in our control are opinion, pursuit, desire, aversion, and, in a word, whatever are our own actions. Things not in our control are body, property, reputation, command, and, in one word, whatever are not our own actions.

The things in our control are by nature free, unrestrained, unhindered; but those not in our control are weak, slavish, restrained, belonging to others. Remember, then, that if you suppose that things which are slavish by nature are also free, and that what belongs to others is your own, then you will be hindered. You will lament, you will be disturbed, and you will find fault both with gods and men. But if you suppose that only to be your own which *is* your own, and what belongs to others such as it really is, then no one will ever compel you or restrain you. Further, you will find fault with no one or accuse no one. You will do nothing against your will. No one will hurt you, you will have no enemies, and you not be harmed.

Aiming therefore at such great things, remember that you must not allow yourself to be carried, even with a slight tendency, towards the attainment of lesser things. Instead, you must entirely quit some things and for the present postpone the rest. But if you would both have these great things, along with power and riches, then you will not gain even the latter, because you aim at the former too: but you will absolutely fail of the former, by which alone happiness and freedom are achieved.

Work, therefore to be able to say to every harsh appearance, "You are but an appearance, and not absolutely the thing you appear to be." And then examine it by those rules which you have, and first, and chiefly, by this: whether it concerns the things which are in our own control, or those which are not; and, if it concerns anything not in our control, be prepared to say that it is nothing to you.

ASK YOURSELF

4.19. Describe the things that are within and not within our control and Epictetus's attitude about them.

4.20. According to Epictetus, what do I need to do to guarantee my own happiness?

2. Remember that following desire promises the attainment of that of which you are desirous; and aversion promises the avoiding that to which you are averse. However, he who fails to obtain the object of his desire is disappointed, and he who incurs the object of his aversion wretched. If, then, you confine your aversion to those objects only which are contrary to the natural use of your faculties, which you have in your own control, you will never incur anything to which you are averse. But if you are averse to sickness, or death, or poverty, you will be wretched. Remove aversion, then, from all things that are not in our control, and transfer it to things contrary to the nature of what is in our control. But, for the present, totally suppress desire: for, if you desire any of the things which are not in your own control, you must necessarily be disappointed; and of those which are, and which it would be laudable to desire, nothing is yet in your possession. Use only the appropriate actions of pursuit and avoidance; and even these lightly, and with gentleness and reservation.

 ASK YOURSELF

4.21. What things should we neither desire nor find averse?

For Epictetus, some of the greatest unhappinesses in life results from the death of loved ones, such as our spouses and children. Like other sources of unhappiness, we can eliminate these, too, by suppressing our desires and adjusting our mental attitudes toward them. In a series of graphic and sometimes shocking analogies, Epictetus coaches us on how to emotionally distance ourselves from our loved ones. If they then unexpectedly die, we will not experience unhappiness.

3. With regard to whatever objects give you delight, are useful, or are deeply loved, remember to tell yourself of *what general nature they are*, beginning from the most insignificant things. If, for example, you are fond of a specific ceramic cup, remind yourself that it is only ceramic cups in general of which you are fond. Then, if it breaks, you will not be disturbed. If you kiss your child, or your wife, say that you only kiss things that are human, and thus you will not be disturbed if either of them dies.

4. When you are going about any action, remind yourself what nature the action is. If you are going to bathe, picture to yourself the things that usually happen in the bath: some people splash the water, some push, some use abusive language, and others steal. Thus you will more safely go about this action if you say to yourself, "I will now go bathe, and keep my own mind in a state conformable to nature." And do this in the same manner with regard to every other action. For thus, if any hindrance arises

in bathing, you will have it ready to say, "It was not only to bathe that I desired, but to keep my mind in a state conformable to nature; and I will not keep it if I am bothered at things that happen."

5. People are disturbed, not by things, but by the principles and notions which they form concerning things. Death, for instance, is not terrible, else it would have appeared so to Socrates. But the terror consists in our notion of death that it is terrible. When therefore we are hindered, or disturbed, or grieved, let us never attribute it to others, but to ourselves; that is, to our own principles. An uninstructed person will lay the fault of his own bad condition upon others. Someone just starting instruction will lay the fault on himself. Some who is perfectly instructed will place blame neither on others nor on himself.

 ASK YOURSELF

4.22. As with ceramic cups, how should we value our spouses and children?

4.23. Whenever things go wrong in life, we typically find someone to blame for the problem. According to the previous passage, how should we view such blame?

6. Don't be prideful with any excellence that is not your own. If a horse should be prideful and say, " I am handsome," it would be supportable. But when you are prideful, and say, " I have a handsome horse," know that you are proud of what is, in fact, only the good of the horse. What, then, is your own? Only your reaction to the appearances of things. Thus, when you behave conformably to nature in reaction to how things appear, you will be proud with reason; for you will take pride in some good of your own.

7. Consider when, on a voyage, your ship is anchored; if you go on shore to get water you may along the way amuse yourself with picking up a shell fish, or an onion. However, your thoughts and continual attention ought to be bent towards the ship, waiting for the captain to call on board; you must then immediately leave all these things, otherwise you will be thrown into the ship, bound neck and feet like a sheep. So it is with life. If, instead of an onion or a shellfish, you are given a wife or child, that is fine. But if the captain calls, you must run to the ship, leaving them, and regarding none of them. But if you are old, never go far from the ship: lest, when you are called, you should be unable to come in time.

8. Don't demand that things happen as you wish, but wish that they happen as they *do* happen, and you will go on well.

9. Sickness is a hindrance to the body, but not to your ability to choose, unless that is your choice. Lameness is a hindrance to the leg, but not to your ability to choose. Say this to yourself with regard to everything that happens, then you will see such obstacles as hindrances to something else, but not to yourself.

10. With every accident, ask yourself what abilities you have for making a proper use of it. If you see an attractive person, you will find that self-restraint is the ability you have against your desire. If you are in pain, you will find fortitude. If you hear unpleasant language, you will find patience. And thus habituated, the appearances of things will not hurry you away along with them.

11. Never say of anything, "I have *lost* it"; but say instead that "I have *returned* it." Is your child dead? It is returned. Is your wife dead? She is returned. Is your estate taken away? Is that not also returned? [Don't say] "The person who took these away is a bad." What difference is it to you who the giver assigns to take it back? While he gives it to you to possess, take care of it; but don't view it as your own, just as travelers view a hotel.

 ASK YOURSELF

4.24. In the analogy in section 7, what does the captain represent?

4.25. According to the previous passage, how should we view the particular human who takes our property or kills our loved ones?

12. If you want to improve, reject such reasonings as these: "If I neglect my affairs, I'll have no income; if I don't correct my servant, he will be bad." For it is better to die with hunger, exempt from grief and fear, than to live in affluence with perturbation; and it is better your servant should be bad, than you unhappy.

Begin therefore from little things. Is a little oil spilt? A little wine stolen? Say to yourself, "This is the price paid for apathy, for tranquility, and nothing is to be had for nothing." When you call your servant, it is possible that he may not come; or, if he does, he may not do what you want. But he is by no means of such importance that it should be in his power to give you any disturbance.

13. If you want to improve, be content to be thought foolish and stupid with regard to external things. Don't wish to be thought to know anything; and even if you appear to be somebody important to others, distrust yourself. For, it is difficult to both keep your faculty of choice in a state conformable to nature, and at the same time acquire external things. But while you are careful about the one, you must of necessity neglect the other.

14. If you wish your children, and your wife, and your friends to live forever, you are stupid; for you wish to be in control of things which you cannot, you wish for things that belong to others to be your own. So likewise, if you wish your servant to be without fault, you are a fool; for you wish vice not to be vice, but something else. But, if you wish to have your desires undisappointed, this is in your own control. Exercise, therefore, what is in your control. He is the master of every other person who is able to confer or remove whatever that person wishes either to have or to avoid. Whoever, then, would be free, let him wish nothing, let him decline nothing, which depends on others else he must necessarily be a slave.

15. Remember that you must behave in life as at a dinner party. Is anything brought around to you? Put out your hand and take your share with moderation. Does it pass by you? Don't stop it. Is it not yet come? Don't stretch your desire towards it, but wait till it reaches you. Do this with regard to children, to a wife, to public posts, to riches, and you will eventually be a worthy partner of the feasts of the gods. And if you don't even take the things which are set before you, but are able even to reject them, then you will not only be a partner at the feasts of the gods, but also of their empire. For,

by doing this, Diogenes, Heraclitus and others like them, deservedly became, and were called, divine.

51. The first and most necessary topic in philosophy is that of the use of moral theorems, such as, "We ought not to lie;" the second is that of demonstrations, such as, "What is the origin of our obligation not to lie;" the third gives strength and articulation to the other two, such as, "What is the origin of this demonstration." For what is demonstration? What is consequence? What contradiction? What truth? What falsehood? The third topic, then, is necessary on the account of the second, and the second on the account of the first. But the most necessary, and that whereon we ought to rest, is the first. But we act just on the contrary. For we spend all our time on the third topic, and employ all our diligence about that, and entirely neglect the first. Therefore, at the same time that we lie, we are immediately prepared to show how it is demonstrated that lying is not right.

 ASK YOURSELF

4.26. Epictetus thinks that the happy life is one with as little disturbances as possible. How do we achieve this?

4.27. Based on the Epictetus's dinner party analogy, how should we act when presented with the opportunity to have a spouse, children, a good job, or wealth?

4.28. In the previous passage, Epictetus explains that philosophers typically discuss ethics at three different levels. What are the three levels, and which is the most important?

CYNICISM

One of the strangest movements in all of philosophy is that of the Cynics, who held that we attain happiness and tranquillity by denying established convention. Known as the "dog philosophers" (the Greek for "dog" is *kuon* from which *kuneios*, shameful, is derived), the Cynics denied conventions of wealth, reputation, pleasure, property, family duty, and religion. They were typically ascetics, since they viewed money as an artificial convention. Of all the eudaimonian schools, Cynicism was the least systematized, having no official treatises; the descriptions we have were authored by people outside the school itself. Rather than making their points in written argument form, the Cynics attempted to teach by example, and the examples they gave often involved deliberately shocking speech and conduct. Their goal was to grab attention and vividly illustrate the shortcomings of established convention. Cynics used several metaphors to describe their self-appointed task. For example, they considered themselves as messengers of God, the watchdogs of humanity who would bark at illusion, the surgeons whose knives would slice the cancer of pretentiousness from people's minds.

 ASK YOURSELF

4.29. By defying convention, what did the Cynics hope to achieve?

Antisthenes and Diogenes

The founding father of the school was an Athenian named Antisthenes (440–370 BCE), who first studied rhetoric under the sophist Gorgias. Dissatisfied with Gorgias, Antisthenes soon gravitated to Socrates, bringing several of Gorgias's students with him. While a student of Socrates, Antisthenes wore tattered clothes, had a matted beard, and carried around a bag like a beggar. According to one anecdote, Socrates commented to him, "Why are you so pretentious? Through your rags I see your vanity." Nevertheless, Antisthenes continued with this manner of appearance. After Socrates' execution, Antisthenes started his own school, which captured some of the flavor of Socrates' teachings in extreme form. Following Socrates, he focused on moral concerns and taught that virtue is needed for true happiness. Achieving virtue, however, involves mental and physical toil. In our quest for virtue, we need to exercise self-control, deny pleasures, and study the names of things and their definitions. Also like Socrates, as suggested by the anecdote, Antisthenes saw foolishness in the established views of the many and was bold in exposing his discontent. Antisthenes' attacks on conventional politics were so strong that his school became increasingly unpopular, and many of his more scholarly students abandoned him.

 ASK YOURSELF

4.30. What did Antisthenes have in common with Socrates?

The second great Cynic was a loyal pupil of Antisthenes named Diogenes (fourth century BCE). Nicknamed "The Dog," Diogenes imitated Antisthenes's manner of appearance and contempt for convention. A highly visible ascetic in Athens, Diogenes was said by Plato to be "Socrates gone mad." Events of Diogenes' life are sketchy. He was exiled from his home country of Sinope when he and his banker father defaced a coin. He arrived in Athens and sought to be a disciple of Antisthenes. Annoyed by Diogenes' persistence, Antisthenes hit Diogenes with a stick, to which Diogenes replied: "Strike me, Antisthenes, but you will never find a stick sufficiently hard to remove me from your presence, while you speak anything worth hearing." Impressed by this, Antisthenes accepted him into his school. Diogenes' behavior was no less strange than that of his teacher. He once embraced a cold statue in winter, illustrating how even our perceptions of pain are conventional. During the daytime he carried a lit oil lantern, holding it up to people, illustrating his search for a virtuous person. Another anecdote describes how Alexander the Great sought to meet the strange Diogenes fellow that he heard so much about. Finding Diogenes living in a tub, Alexander said, "I am Alexander the Great," to which Diogenes replied, "I am Diogenes the Cynic." Alexander then asked if Diogenes needed any special favor from him. Diogenes replied, "You might stand aside, you are blocking the sunlight." Alexander then said, "If I wasn't Alexander, I'd want to be Diogenes."

ASK YOURSELF

4.31. Give an example of Diogenes' shocking behavior.

4.32. Give an example of a modern-day person who, like the Cynics, does shocking things to expose the enslaving qualities of established conventions.

SKEPTICISM

The last of the four eudaimonian schools is skepticism, which held that we achieve happiness by doubting everything. Each of the four eudaimonian schools focused on things that make us unhappy. Epicureans argued that pains, such as fear, make us unhappy. Stoics argued that unhappiness comes from desiring things beyond what fate has in store for us. Cynics argued that unhappiness comes from falling under the spell of conventions. Skeptics, by contrast, held that we become unhappy when we commit ourselves to any theory. Suppose, for example, that I hear someone defend capital punishment. I become persuaded by the arguments, and now people who oppose the death penalty agitate me. The same thing happens when I take strong stands on other moral issues such as abortion, homosexuality, or health care controversies. It's not only moral issues that make us agitated, but *any* controversial issue, such as whether God exists, whether the subatomic particles decay over time, or even whether my dog Rover is larger than your dog Fido. If I can take a stand on an issue, then I risk becoming agitated and, consequently, unhappy.

 ASK YOURSELF

4.33. What did skeptics hope to accomplish by doubting everything?

Academics and Pyrrhonians

Two distinct skeptical traditions emerged in Hellenistic philosophy. One tradition arose within Plato's Academy shortly after the death of Plato and is commonly called *Academic skepticism*. Although Plato himself had strong convictions about our ability to know truths, ironically, his followers abandoned this view. Instead, they held that we have no self-evidently true perceptions. All of our perceptions are subjective, and we don't know if they accurately copy the world that we see. This skeptical approach of the new Academy continued for generations.

The second skeptical tradition is called *Pyrrhonism*, after its founder Pyrrho of Elea (360–270 BCE). In his youth, Pyrrho studied painting, but later turned to philosophy. He accompanied Alexander on his campaign through Asia and India, and historians speculate that he might have picked up some skeptical tendencies from the ascetics there. Anecdotes about Pyrrho relate that he was careless about all external objects and was saved from danger only by friends who steered him clear of "carts, precipices, dogs and what not." He was apparently insensitive to pain, and could withstand surgical operations without flinching. The only surviving summary of his philosophical views is this:

> Pyrrho shows that objects are equally indifferent and unfathomable and undeterminable because neither our senses nor our judgments are true or false. So for that reason we should not trust in them but should be without judgment and without inclination and unmoved, saying about each thing that it no more is than is not or both is and is not or neither is nor is not.

From our perspective, the philosophical differences between Academic and Pyrrhonian skepticism seem insignificant. At the time, however, the differences were great. Unlike the Academics, Pyrrhonians emphasized that tranquillity is the goal of skepticism. Pyrrhonian skepticism was not just a theoretical exercise, but a way of moderating our ordinary beliefs. To this end, followers of Pyrrho perfected skeptical methods of argumentation by which they could show the falsehood of any belief, particularly beliefs about external objects. By advancing these skeptical arguments, the Pyrrhonians avoided fanaticism about the issue at hand and, hence, were content with ordinary life.

 ASK YOURSELF

4.34. Who were the founders of the Academic and Pyrrhonian schools of skepticism, respectively?

Like most of the writings of the eudaimonian schools, few texts of the Greek skeptics have come down to us. But one surviving text, *Outlines of Pyrrhonism* by Sextus Empiricus (second century CE), is exceptional both for its clarity and completeness. The following selections are taken from Book 1 of that work.

The Goal and Criterion of Skepticism

According to Sextus, there are three kinds of philosophers: (1) dogmatics, who claim to have found truth, such as Aristotle and the Stoics; (2) Academic skeptics, who are still partially dogmatic; and (3) Pyrrhonian skeptics, who make no claims about truth at all. Sextus emphasizes that we can achieve tranquillity only if we stop dogmatizing completely.

 From SEXTUS EMPIRICUS: *Outlines of Pyrrhonism* —

The way of the Skeptical School is an ability to place appearances in opposition to judgments in any way whatever, and thus through the equilibrium of the reasons and things opposed to each other, to reach, first the state of suspension of judgment, and afterwards that of tranquility. . . . "Suspension of judgment" is a holding back of the opinion, in consequence of which we neither deny nor affirm anything. "Tranquility" is repose and calmness of soul. We shall explain how tranquility accompanies suspension of judgment when we speak of the aim. [1.4]

Skepticism arose in the beginning from the hope of attaining tranquility; for men of the greatest talent were perplexed by the contradiction of things, and being at a loss what to believe, began to question what things are true, and what false, hoping to attain tranquility as a result of the decision. The fundamental principle of the Skeptical system is especially this, namely, to oppose every argument by one of equal weight, for it seems to us that in this way we finally reach the position where we have no dogmas.

 ASK YOURSELF

4.35. What does Sextus mean by *tranquility*, and how do we attain it?

It is evident that we pay careful attention to appearances from what we say about the criterion of the Skeptical School. The word criterion is used in two ways. First, it is understood as a proof of existence or non-existence, in regard to which we shall speak in the opposing argument. Secondly, when it refers to action, meaning the criterion to which we give heed in life, in doing some things and refraining from doing others, and it is about this that we shall now speak. We say, consequently, that the criterion of the Skeptical School is the appearance, and in calling it so, we mean the idea of it. It cannot be doubted, as it is based upon susceptibility and involuntary feeling. Hence no one doubts, perhaps, that an object appears so and so, but one questions if it is as it appears. Therefore, as we cannot be entirely inactive as regards the observances of daily life, we live by giving heed to appearances, and in an unprejudiced way.

 ASK YOURSELF

4.36. What is the main point of dispute concerning reality and appearance?

Sextus explains that, even though the skeptic suspends judgment about things, the skeptic must also act in the world. For example, if the skeptic simply did nothing, he might starve to death.

But this observance of what pertains to the daily life appears to be of four different kinds. Sometimes it is directed by the guidance of nature, sometimes by the necessity of the feelings, sometimes by the tradition of laws and of customs, and sometimes by the teaching of the arts. It is directed by the guidance of nature, for by nature we are capable of sensation and thought; by the necessity of the feelings, for hunger leads us to food, and thirst to drink; by the traditions of laws and customs, for according to them we consider piety a good in daily life, and impiety an evil; by the teaching of the arts, for we are not inactive in the arts we undertake. We say all these things, however, without expressing a decided opinion.

 ASK YOURSELF

4.37. As active people, what are the four areas of regulation that skeptics follow?

It follows naturally to next treat of the aim of the Skeptical School. An aim is that for which as an end all things are done or thought, itself depending on nothing, or in other words, it is the ultimatum of things to be desired. We say, then, that the aim of the Skeptic is tranquility in those things which pertain to the opinion, and moderation in the things that life imposes. For as soon as he began to philosophize he wished to discriminate between ideas, and to understand which are true and which are false, in order to attain tranquility. He met, however, with contradictions of equal weight, and, being unable to judge, he withheld his opinion; and while his judgment was in suspension tranquility followed, as if by chance, in regard to matters of opinion. For he who is of the opinion that anything is either good or bad by nature is always troubled, and when he does not possess those things that seem to him good he thinks that he is tortured by the things which are by nature bad, and pursues those that he thinks to be good. Having acquired them, however, he falls into greater perturbation, because he is excited beyond reason and without measure from fear of a change, and he does everything in his power to retain the things that seem to him good. But he who is undecided, on the contrary, regarding things that are good and bad by nature, neither seeks nor avoids anything eagerly, and is therefore in a state of tranquility.

For that which is related of Apelles the painter happened to the Skeptic. It is said that as he was once painting a horse he wished to represent the foam of his mouth in the picture, but he could not succeed in doing so, and he gave it up and threw the sponge at the picture with which he had wiped the colors from the painting. As soon, however, as it touched the picture it produced a good copy of the foam. The Skeptics likewise hoped to gain tranquility by forming judgments in regard to the anomaly between appearances and the things of thought, but they were unable to do this, and so they suspended their judgment; and while their judgment was in suspension tranquility followed, as if by chance, as the shadow follows a body. Nevertheless, we do not consider the Skeptic wholly undisturbed, but he is disturbed by some things that are inevitable. We confess that sometimes he is cold and thirsty, and that he suffers in such ways. But in these things even the ignorant are beset in two ways, from the feelings themselves, and not less also from the fact that they think these conditions are bad by nature. The Skeptic, however, escapes more easily, as he rejects the opinion that anything is in itself bad by nature. Therefore we say that the aim of the Skeptic is tranquility in matters of opinion, and moderation of feeling in those things that are inevitable. Some notable Skeptics have added also suspension of judgment in investigation.

 ASK YOURSELF

4.38. According to Sextus, ordinary people are afflicted by (1) a circumstance itself, and (2) the belief that this circumstance is evil by nature. The skeptic, however, is only afflicted by the first of these. Give an example of (1) and (2).

The Ten Modes of Skepticism

The Ten Modes of Skepticism are perhaps the most important contribution of the Pyrrhonian skeptics. The Modes are systematic argument techniques that skeptics use to show how we must suspend judgment on virtually every conceivable issue. The Ten

Modes were initially devised by the Pyrrhonian philosopher Aenesidemus (first century BCE), are presented here by Sextus. Sextus begins by briefly listing the Ten Modes.

Certain Modes were commonly handed down by the older Skeptics, by means of which suspended judgment seems to take place. They are ten in number, and are called synonymously arguments and points. They are these: The first is based upon the differences in animals; the second upon the differences in men; the third upon the difference in the constitution of the organs of sense; the fourth upon circumstances; the fifth upon position, distance, and place; the sixth upon mixtures; the seventh upon the quantity and constitution of objects; the eighth upon relation; the ninth upon frequency or rarity of occurrences; the tenth upon systems, customs, laws, mythical beliefs, and dogmatic opinions. We make this order ourselves.

Although Sextus gives detailed accounts of each of these modes, we will look only at the first, which is representative of the rest. Briefly, the first Mode contends that animals of different species perceive things differently. For example, they different animals see, taste, smell, hear, or feel the same thing in a different manner. Since we can't prefer one species over the other, we can't say for sure what the reality is behind their respective perceptions. We can state this argument more formally as this:

  a. An object appears to have quality X to a dog.

  b. The same object appears to have quality Y to a cow.

  c. We cannot prefer the dog to the cow.

  d. Hence, we suspend judgment as to whether the object has quality X or Y.

The first Mode, we said, is the one based upon the differences in animals, and according to this Mode, different animals do not get the same ideas of the same objects through the senses. This we conclude from the different origin of the animals, and also from the difference in the constitution of their bodies. . . .

We may see this more clearly in the things that are sought for and avoided by animals. For example, myrrh appears very agreeable to men and intolerable to beetles and bees. Oil also, which is useful to men, destroys wasps and bees if sprinkled on them; and sea-water, while it is unpleasant and poisonous to men if they drink it, is most agreeable and sweet to fishes. Swine also prefer to wash in vile filth rather than in pure clean water. Furthermore, some animals eat grass and some eat herbs; some live in the woods, others eat seeds; some are carnivorous, and others lactivorous; some enjoy putrefied food, and others fresh food; some raw food, and others that which is prepared by cooking; and in general that which is agreeable to some is disagreeable and fatal to others, and should be avoided by them. Thus hemlock makes the quail fat, and henbane the hogs, and these, as it is known, enjoy eating lizards; deer also eat poisonous animals, and swallows, the cantharid. Moreover, ants and flying ants, when swallowed by men, cause discomfort and colic, but the bear, on the contrary, whatever sickness he may have, becomes stronger by devouring them. The viper is benumbed if one twig of the oak touches it, as is also the bat by a leaf of the plane-tree. The elephant flees before the ram, and the lion before the cock, and seals from the rattling of beans that are being pounded, and the tiger from the sound of the drum. Many other examples could be given, but that we may not seem to dwell longer than is necessary on this subject, we conclude by saying that since the same things are pleasant to some and unpleasant to others, and the pleasure and displeasure depend on the ideas, it must be that different animals have different ideas of objects.

And since the same things appear different according to the difference in the animals, it will be possible for us to say how the external object appears to us, but as to how it is in reality we shall suspend our judgment. For we cannot ourselves judge between our own ideas and those of other animals, being ourselves involved in the difference, and therefore much more in need of being judged than being ourselves able to judge. And furthermore, we cannot give the preference to our own mental representations over those of other animals, either without evidence or with evidence, for besides the fact that perhaps there is no evidence, as we shall show, the evidence so called will be either manifest to us or not. If it is not manifest to us, then we cannot accept it with conviction; if it is manifest to us, since the question is in regard to what is manifest to animals, and we use as evidence that which is manifest to us who are animals, then it is to be questioned if it is true as it is manifest to us. It is absurd, however, to try to base the questionable on the questionable, because the same thing is to be believed and not to be believed, which is certainly impossible. The evidence is to be believed insofar as it will furnish a proof, and disbelieved insofar as it is itself to be proved. We shall therefore have no evidence according to which we can give preference to our own ideas over those of so-called irrational animals. Since therefore ideas differ according to the difference in animals, and it is impossible to judge them, it is necessary to suspend the judgment in regard to external objects.

 ASK YOURSELF

4.39. What are some examples that Sextus gives to show how animals of different species perceive things differently?

SUGGESTIONS FOR FURTHER READING

Primary Sources

Epicurean Texts

Bailey, C. *Epicurus: The Extant Remains* (Oxford: Clarendon, 1926). Standard translation.

Inwood, Brad *Hellenistic Philosophy: Introductory Readings* (Indianapolis: Hackett Publishing Company, 1988). A very useful collection of works and testimonia from all of the Hellenistic philosophers.

Lucretius. *On the Nature of Things*, trans. W. H. D. Rouse (Cambridge, MA: Harvard University Press, 1975). Latin text with English translation. The most important single source for Epicurean ideas outside of the few remains of Epicurus's own writings.

Skepticism

Sextus Empiricus. *Against the Professors*, trans. R. G. Bury (Cambridge, MA: Harvard University Press, 1935–1949). Three-volume parallel Greek text and English translation with minimal notes.

———. *Outlines of Pyrrhonism*, trans. J. Annas and J. Barnes (Cambridge: Cambridge University Press, 1994). Good translation with introduction and notes.

———. *Selections from the Major Writings on Scepticism, Man, & God*, ed. Philip P. Hallie (Indianapolis: Hackett Publishing Company, 1985).

Stoic Texts

Cicero, M. T. *On Fate*, trans. R. W. Sharples (Warminster: Aris & Phillips, 1991). Latin text with English translation; includes much of our best information on the Stoic doctrine of fate.

Epictetus. *The Handbook of Epictetus*, trans. N. White (Indianapolis: Hackett Publishing Company, 1983). The best available translation, with a good introduction to Epictetus.

Inwood, B., and Gerson, L. P. *Hellenistic Philosophy, Introductory Readings* (Indianapolis: Hackett Publishing Company, 1988). Includes a large body of primary texts on Stoicism in translation.

Long, A. A., and Sedley, D. N. *The Hellenistic Philosophers* (Cambridge: Cambridge University Press, 1987). Volume 1 contains Stoic sources in translation with commentary; volume 2 has the original texts.

Marcus Aurelius. *The Meditations*. trans. G. M. A. Grube (Indianapolis: Hackett Publishing Company, 1985).

Critical Analyses and Discussions

Epicureanism

Cooper, John. *Reason and Emotion: Essays on Ancient Moral Psychology and Ethical Theory*. (Princeton, NJ: Princeton University Press, 1999). Includes excellent discussion of Epicurus's "normative" hedonism.

Long, A. A. *Hellenistic Philosophy* (London: Duckworth, 1974). Widely regarded as the best introduction to Hellenistic philosophy.

Mitsis, P. *Epicurus' Ethical Theory* (Ithaca, NY: Cornell University Press, 1988).

Nussbaum, M. *The Therapy of Desire* (Princeton, NJ: Princeton University Press, 1994). Interesting recent work on Hellenistic philosophy and literature, stressing the idea, common in this period, of the practice of philosophy as analogous to medical practice, designed to heal souls made sick by false beliefs and corrupting influences.

Skepticism

Diogenes Laertius. *Lives of Eminent Philosophers* (Cambridge, MA: Harvard University Press, 1925). Two-volume parallel Greek text and English translation; IX 61–116 is devoted to Pyrrhonism.

House, D. K. "The Life of Sextus Empiricus." *Classical Quarterly* 30: 227–238, 1980. Stresses how little we actually know about Sextus Empiricus.

Stoicism

Hershbell, J. P. "The Stoicism of Epictetus: Twentieth Century Perspectives," in W. Haase, ed., *Aufstieg und Niedergang der römischen Welt* (Berlin: de Gruyter, II 36.3: 2, 148–63, 1989). Excellent review of the literature; includes discussion of Epictetus's relation to other philosophers.

Inwood, B. *Ethics and Human Action in Early Stoicism* (Oxford: Oxford University Press, 1985). Excellent study of Stoic ethics.

Long, A. A. *Hellenistic Philosophy* (London: Duckworth, 1974). Includes a very good introductory study of Stoicism; very accessible.

———. *Stoic Studies* (Cambridge: Cambridge University Press. 1996). Collection of articles by the leading postwar specialist in Stoicism.

Nussbaum, M. *The Therapy of Desire* (Princeton, NJ: Princeton University Press, 1994). A colorful defense of the Stoic treatment of emotions, with citations from Seleca's drama.

CHAPTER 5

MEDIEVAL PHILOSOPHY

T he Roman Empire was breaking up at the time of the death of Saint Augustine (430 CE), bishop of Hippo in North Africa. The year after Augustine's death Hippo was partly burned by Vandal invaders. At the same time, barbarian tribes invaded Europe. Subsequently, urban life and the elements of civilization that depend upon urban life declined. The era following these devastations, which lasted until about 1500 CE, came to be known as the "dark ages." The name is particularly appropriate for the six hundred years or so up to 1100 CE, apart from a brief period of flourishing from about 750–850 known as the Carolingian Renaissance (associated with the ruler Charlemagne, whose Latin name is "Carolus"). That brief renaissance was followed by further invasions, this time from the Scandinavian north. Some of the men of the north (thus, "nor-mans") eventually settled in territories they had conquered, including "Normandy" in northern France. Anselm, whose *Proslogion* is excerpted in this chapter, was a Norman abbot. The cessation of the Viking invasions by about 1000 enabled a pattern of revival during the later part of the eleventh century, of which Anselm was a part. The twelfth and thirteenth centuries were a time of true cultural flourishing, with developments in philosophy and theology being particularly notable. It would not be at all accurate to think of this period as part of a "dark age." In much of the rest of the Mediterranean world the expansion of Islam (from about 600 CE onward) was accompanied by the growth of a high civilization that can only be mentioned here.

The most characteristic feature of this period in Europe is certainly the dominance of the Christian church. For example, one major theme of the medieval period is the contest between the church and secular rulers (emperors, kings, and so on) over control of political affairs. It is difficult for people today, particularly Americans, to imagine the extent of the political and cultural influence of the Christian church during this era. Education too was almost entirely in the hands of the church, as was the preservation, out of the ruins of the Roman Empire, of at least some of the learning of the ancient world.

It comes as no surprise, then, to find that medieval philosophers in the West were virtually all churchmen, priests, bishops, and monastic theologians, who tried to reconcile Platonic, neo-Platonic, and Aristotelian concepts with Christian doctrine. In the Arabic world too (which by the twelfth century extended from Persia to Spain) and among Jews the bearings of philosophical teachings on religious doctrine were a primary concern. Continued preoccupation with such issues as the status of universals, the relation of goodness to being, and the relation of nature to convention (*physis* versus *nomos*) showed the grip of the ancient world on the medieval era. But a largely new concern with the existence of a personal God, the origin of evil, and the freedom of the will marked a turn that was motivated by the increasing influence of monotheistic religion in all domains of life.

ASK YOURSELF

5.1. Mention three topics that medieval thinkers treated extensively that are *not* central to ancient thought.

AUGUSTINE

Augustine might be thought of as the first major figure in the medieval period for he stood, so to speak, with one foot in the ancient world and one in the medieval. He was born in 354 in Tagaste (modern Souk Aras) in Algeria. He relates the story of his life in his *Confessions*, which has become a classic of Western literature. In that work we see typical philosophical puzzlement and argument combined with religious fervor, a sense of unsatisfied yearning that besets human life, and a profound sense of both intellectual and moral sin. Here are the opening lines of the *Confessions*.

 From AUGUSTINE: *Confessions*

GREAT art Thou, O Lord, and greatly to be praised; great is Thy power, and of Thy wisdom there is no end. And man, being a part of Thy creation, desires to praise Thee, man, who bears about with him his mortality, the witness of his sin, even the witness that Thou "resistest the proud,"—yet man, this part of Thy creation, desires to praise Thee. Thou movest us to delight in praising Thee; for Thou hast formed us for Thyself, and our hearts are restless till they find rest in Thee.

Augustine was educated as a rhetorician (speech maker, lawyer) and was marked out, by his brilliance, for an impressive career in the Roman imperial administration. But a long preoccupation with religious questions culminated in a conversion experience that was followed shortly thereafter (in 387) by baptism into the Christian church. About the same time he became deeply involved in the study of Platonist philosophy. In fact it was his study of the Platonists that contributed, he claimed, to his openness to Christian truth. This combination of philosophical speculation with religious teaching and authority in Augustine's life and thought provided a forecast of the most characteristic medieval concerns.

Augustine became bishop of Hippo in North Africa and, despite the heavy administrative duties that fall on a bishop, managed to produce a body of literature larger than any to come down to us from any other ancient writer. His works include philosophy, theology, and polemical tracts (i.e., writings devoted to attacking positions and views on religious matters that he believed were mistaken).

Augustine's early work *On Free Choice of the Will* takes up many of the problems which concerned later medieval figures. The central issue is the *origin of evil*, which is always a problem for religious believers, since the existence of evil seems to conflict with the belief in an all-good, all-powerful, and all-knowing God. Augustine's solution depends upon the idea that evil is the result of free choices of the will on the part of free creatures, and thus is not traceable to God. Many other matters are taken up in this work, however, such as (1) the relation of faith and reason, (2) the relations between divine and human law, (3) the nature of the soul, (4) the possibility of proving the existence of God, and (5) the problem of the compatibility of God's foreknowledge and free will. This little work, then, contains much of the agenda for philosophy during the next thousand years. Notice, for example, how often this work is cited in the selections in this chapter from Aquinas, where it is referred to as "de Lib. Arb." The work is written as a dialogue or conversation between Augustine and his friend Evodius. All selections in this section are excerpted from *On Free Choice of the Will*.

Book 1. God and Evil

Book 1 discusses the origin of evil, the nature of evildoing as rooted in disordered desire, the relation of divine to earthly law, and, briefly, some other related topics.

The Origin of Evil. The key question for the entire work is stated at the outset. What is the origin of evil? This is a puzzling matter for those who believe in an all-good and all-powerful creator God.

 From AUGUSTINE: *On Free Choice of the Will*, Book 1

EVODIUS.   Please tell me: isn't God the cause of evil?

AUGUSTINE.   I will tell you once you have made clear what kind of evil you are asking about. For we use the word "evil" in two senses: first, when we say that someone has done evil; and second, when we say that someone has suffered evil.

EVOD.   I want to know about both.

AUG.   But if you know or believe that God is good—and it is not right to believe otherwise—then he does no evil. On the other hand, if we acknowledge that God is just—and it is impious to deny it—then he rewards the good and punishes the wicked. Those punishments are certainly evils for those who suffer them. Therefore, if no one is punished unjustly—and we must believe this, since we believe that this universe is governed by divine providence—it follows that God is a cause of the second kind of evil, but in no way causes the first kind.

EVOD.   Then is there some other cause of the evil that God does not cause?

AUG.   There certainly is. Such evil could not occur unless someone caused it. But if you ask who that someone is, it is impossible to say. For there is no single cause of evil; rather, everyone who does evil is the cause of his own evildoing. If you doubt this, recall what I said earlier: Evil deeds are punished by the justice of God. They would not be punished justly if they had not been performed voluntarily.

 ASK YOURSELF

5.2. What is the question that is raised in this dialogue?

5.3. Does Augustine begin by assuming that a good creator God exists, or not? If your answer is "yes," is that a sensible thing to do or not? Why?

Augustine is particularly concerned with the origin of the first kind of evil, evil "that someone has done" and that is not itself a just punishment for sin. Fill in the blanks in the following argument, which concerns that kind of evil. This argument is implicit in the opening dialogue.

    a. God exists.

    b. God is perfectly good.

    c. A perfectly good being would not _____.

    d. There is evil.

    e. Therefore God is not _____.

    f. Therefore, something else must be _____.

This argument, when completed correctly, is valid. Certainly some people will deny the truth of (a). Hardly anyone would want to deny premise (b). There might be some argument about (c). Probably no one would deny (d).

 ASK YOURSELF

5.4. Assuming all four are true, is it the case that the second conclusion, (f), *must* be true?

EVOD.   It seems that no one could sin unless he had first learned how to sin. And if that is the case, I must ask this: From whom did we learn to sin?

AUG.   Do you think learning is a good thing?

EVOD.   Who would dare to say that learning is a bad thing?

AUG.   What if it is neither good nor bad?

EVOD.   I think it is good.

AUG.   Indeed it is, since knowledge is given or awakened through learning, and no one comes to know anything except through learning. Don't you agree?

EVOD.   Of course not.

AUG.   Well then, if all understanding is good, and no one who does not understand learns, then everyone who learns is doing good. For everyone who learns, understands; and everyone who understands is doing good. So someone who wants to know the cause of our learning something really wants to know the cause of our doing good. So let's have no more of your wanting to hunt down this mysterious evil teacher. If he is evil, he is no teacher; and if he is a teacher, he is not evil.

EVOD.   Now that you have convinced me that we do not learn to do evil, please explain to me what is the source of our evildoing.

AUG.   You have hit upon the very question that worried me greatly when I was still young, a question that wore me out, drove me into the company of heretics, and knocked me flat on my face.

ASK YOURSELF

5.5. Augustine claims that "we simply cannot come to know evil things." He is trying to show that there is a close connection between what is knowable and what is good and between ignorance and evil. The idea that there is such a connection should remind you of a famous statement made by Socrates and seconded by Plato. What was that statement?

5.6. Does the position taken by Socrates and Augustine imply that a person who does evil is in some way *stupid*?

5.7. The "heretics" mentioned in the passage were the Manicheans, who believed in two Gods of equal power, one good and one evil. Restate "the question" here (see question 5.2) and try to say why "the question" might drive someone into the company of people with that particular belief.

Believing Must Precede Understanding.   In this section Augustine states a fundamental assumption that guides all of his thinking.

AUG.   I was so hurt by this fall, buried under a mountain of silly fairy tales, that if my love of finding the truth had not secured divine help, I would not have been able to get out from under them to breathe freely and begin to seek the truth. And since such pains were taken to free me from this difficulty, I will lead you on the same path that I followed in making my escape. God will be with us, and he will make us understand what we have believed. For we are well aware that we are at the stage described by the prophet, who says, "Unless you believe, you will not understand" (Isaiah 7:9).

We believe that everything that exists comes from the one God, and yet we believe that God is not the cause of sins. What is troubling is that if you admit that sins come from the souls that God created, and those souls come from God, pretty soon you'll be tracing those sins back to God.

EVOD.   You have stated plainly what bothers me in thinking about this question. That is the problem that has compelled me and drawn me into this inquiry.

 ASK YOURSELF

5.8. The principle ("Unless you believe you will not understand") is fundamental for Augustine. Is it the case that there are some things which I must simply believe, by accepting someone's testimony or depending upon some authority? Would it be possible to refuse to believe anything whatsoever prior to having good evidence for its truth? Explain your answers.

Many contemporary philosophers believe that accepting the testimony of others, or relying on the authority of others in various ways, is necessary for us to even get started in getting to know and understand the world. It does not follow, however, that we should never question the truth of those things that we at some point simply accepted or seek to "understand" them better. "Understanding" might include such things as being able to explain concepts in detail or being able to cite relevant evidence.

 ASK YOURSELF

5.9. Are there any things that you believe but do not understand? The author of this study guide believes that a well-functioning gallbladder is necessary for good health, but does not really understand why (his concept of a gallbladder is fuzzy, and he is not sure what evidence supports this belief). Give some examples of things you believe but do not fully understand.

5.10. Most of us have moral or religious beliefs that we do not fully understand. Would it be better if we did understand these things, rather than just believing them? Why or why not?

5.11. State plainly what Augustine has "stated plainly."

The Nature of Evildoing. Augustine here explores what it is that makes evil deeds evil. Here too a methodological principle is at work that requires believing before understanding. We inevitably begin with certain beliefs about what is evil or wrong, but we may not understand those beliefs fully. We may, for instance, give inadequate accounts of them, as Evodius does in the following passage.

AUG.   You want to know the source of our evildoing. So we must first discuss what evildoing is. State your view on the matter. If you cannot explain the whole thing at once in a few words, you can at least show me your view by naming particular evil deeds.

EVOD.   Adultery, murder, and sacrilege, not to mention others that time and memory do not permit me to enumerate. Who could fail to recognize these as evil deeds?

AUG.   Tell me first, why do you think adultery is evil? Because the law forbids it?

EVOD.   On the contrary. Clearly, it is not evil because the law forbids it; rather, the law forbids it because it is evil.

AUG.   But suppose someone were to make things difficult for us by extolling the pleasures of adultery and asking why we think adultery evil and deserving of condemnation. Surely you do not think that people who want to understand, and not merely to believe, would have to take refuge in an appeal to the authority of the law? Now like you I do believe, and believe most firmly, and cry out that all peoples and nations should believe, that adultery is evil. But now we are attempting to know and hold firmly by understanding what we have already accepted by faith. So think this over as carefully as you can, and tell me what reason you have by which you know that adultery is evil.

EVOD.   I know that it is evil because I would not tolerate it if someone tried to commit adultery with my own wife. Anyone who does to another what he does not want done to himself does evil.

AUG.   What if someone's lust is so great that he offers his wife to another and willingly allows him to commit adultery with her, and is eager to enjoy the same freedom with the other man's wife? Do you think that this man has done nothing evil?

EVOD.   Far from it!

AUG.   But by your rule he does not sin, since he is not doing anything that he is unwilling to have done to himself. You must therefore look for some other argument to show that adultery is evil.

Moral beliefs may well be among those beliefs that we do not fully understand, in the sense of being able to give a good account or explanation of them or of their foundations. Augustine is here seeking out such foundations, and he first wishes to eliminate wrong or inadequate accounts. Here he argues that the "golden rule" (do unto others as you would have them do unto you) cannot be the basis of our particular moral beliefs.

 ASK YOURSELF

5.12. State Augustine's argument against the golden rule as an explanation for the wrongness of adultery.

Evildoing as Disordered Desire. Augustine's positive account of what makes evildoing evil focuses on the role of desire in human life. Desires of all sorts are not necessarily evil in themselves. What then makes them evil? Here is his answer.

AUG.   Then perhaps what makes adultery evil is *"disordered* desire," whereas so long as you look for the evil in the external, visible act, you are bound to encounter difficulties. In order to understand that disordered desire is what makes adultery evil, consider this: if a man is unable to sleep with someone else's wife, but it is somehow clear that he would like to, and would do so if he had the chance, he is no less guilty than if he were caught in the act.

EVOD.   Nothing could be clearer. Now I see that there is no need for a long discussion to persuade me that this is the case with murder and sacrilege and every sin whatsoever. For it is clear now that *disordered* desire is what drives every kind of evildoing.

Augustine's emphasis on interior motivation is undoubtedly influenced in part by Christian teachings (cf. the sayings of Jesus in Matthew 5). In the following text Augustine considers some counterexamples to the claim that "disordered desire" is what makes evil acts evil. He argues that the desire to live without fear is not disordered. So it is not sinful. Therefore, someone who kills because they desire to live without fear would not be sinning. But surely in some cases at least it *would* be sinning (would, in fact, be murder). For example, a slave who killed his master because he feared punishment for some reason would surely be committing a sin.

AUG.   It follows that, since the master is killed by the slave as a result of this desire, he is not killed as a result of a blameworthy desire. And so we have not yet figured out why this deed is evil. For we are agreed that all wrongdoing is evil only because it results from *disordered* desire, that is, from blameworthy cupidity.

EVOD.   At this point it seems to me that the slave is unjustly condemned, which I would not dream of saying if I could think of some other response.

AUG.   You have let yourself be persuaded that this great crime should go unpunished, without considering whether the slave wanted to be free of the fear of his master in order to satisfy his own disordered desires. All wicked people, just like good people, desire to live without fear. The difference is that the good, in desiring this, turn their love away from things that cannot be possessed without the fear of losing them. The wicked, on the other hand, try to get rid of anything that prevents them from enjoying such things securely. Thus they lead a wicked and criminal life, which would better be called death.

 ASK YOURSELF

5.13. Both the good and the wicked desire to live without fear. What then is the difference between them that enables the good to avoid evil?

We may cringe at Augustine's example, for he seems to assume that slavery itself is morally permissible. However, the main point of the preceding discussion depends upon the definition of disordered desire as "excessive love of those things which one can lose against one's will." A personal example would be excessive love of my daughter. Someone could kidnap her, and that would obviously be against what I want or will.

 ASK YOURSELF

5.14. List some examples of your own of things that you love but which could be taken from you against your will.

5.15. Now, mention something that could *not* be taken from you against your will. A personal example would be honesty. If my honesty is "taken away" it can only be because I have given it away, for example, by giving in to the temptation to lie.

Human (Civil) Law and Divine Law. It appears that many things that are forbidden by divine law are permitted by the typical laws of civil communities. Augustine applies the distinction between what can be taken away against my will and what cannot in the following way: Suppose someone abducted my daughter. They would be taking her away against my will. Now it follows from the definition that I should not be too attached to things that can by taken away against my will since such attachment is "disordered" and therefore evil. What then could justify my killing someone if that were the only way I could prevent them from abducting my daughter? Perhaps most of us would think that to be a permissible action, but it is important to keep alive a sense of the extreme gravity of taking life in any circumstance. It is also important to try to appreciate Augustine's strong resistance to anything like idolatry (i.e., putting some other loyalty before loyalty to God). It would seem that a law that allows me to kill in order to hang on to some worldly thing is actually too lenient, allowing me to do something that the law of God would not allow. For God's law would never justify acts that arise out of evil or disordered desire. Yet civil law might permit killing in such instances.

 ASK YOURSELF

5.16. Does this show that civil law is seriously defective? Explain.

EVOD.   Now I've come to my senses. I am glad that I understand so clearly the nature of that blameworthy desire which is called *disordered* desire. Obviously it is the love of those things that one can lose against one's will.

So, if you don't mind, why don't we go on to consider whether *disordered* desire is also the driving force in acts of sacrilege, most of which, as we see, are committed out of superstition?

AUG.   I think you're being too hasty. First, I think, we should discuss whether an attacking enemy or an ambushing murderer can be killed without any *disordered* desire, for the sake of preserving one's life, liberty, or chastity.

EVOD.   How can I think that people are without *disordered* desire when they fight fiercely for things that they can lose against their will? Or if those things cannot be lost, what need is there to resort to killing for their sake?

AUG.   Then the law is unjust that permits a traveler to kill a highway robber in order to keep from being killed himself, or that permits anyone who can, man or woman, to kill a sexual assailant, before he or she is harmed. The law also commands a soldier to kill the enemy; and if he refuses, he is subject to penalties from his commander. Surely we will not dare to say that these laws are unjust, or rather, that they are not laws at all. For it seems to me that an unjust law is no law at all.

EVOD.   I see that the law is quite secure against this sort of objection, for it permits lesser evils among the people that it governs in order to prevent greater evils. It is much better that one who plots against another's life should be killed rather than one who is defending his own life. And it is much worse for someone unwillingly to suffer a sexual assault, than for the assailant to be killed by the one he was going to assault.

A soldier who kills the enemy is acting as an agent of the law, so he can easily perform his duty without *disordered* desire. Furthermore, the law itself, which was established with a view to protecting the people, cannot be accused of any *disordered* desire. As for the one who enacted the law, if he did so at God's command—that is, if he did what eternal justice prescribes—he could do so without any *disordered* desire at all. But even if he did act out of *disordered* desire, it does not follow that one must be guilty of *disordered* desire in obeying the law; for a good law can be enacted by one who is not himself good. For example, suppose that someone who had gained tyrannical power accepted a bribe from some interested party to make it illegal to take a woman by force, even for marriage. The law would not be bad merely in virtue of the fact that the one who made it was unjust and corrupt. Therefore, the law that commands that enemy forces be repulsed by an equal force for the protection of the citizens can be obeyed without *disordered* desire. The same can be said of all officials who by lawful order are subject to some higher power. But as for those other men, I do not see how they can be excused, even if the law itself is just.

 ASK YOURSELF

5.17. Evodius has argued that civil laws that do not conform perfectly to divine law may be justified on the grounds that they prevent _____ evils.

5.18. Evodius offers a further argument for laws that allow killing in order to prevent the loss of things that can be lost against one's own will. What is the argument?

5.19. The "other men" mentioned in the last sentence of the preceding passage would be people who act on their own (the fearful slave, for instance), outside of the law. It appears then that civil law, law of the kind devised by earthly communities, can legitimately permit actions that the law of God does not strictly permit. Two reasons are given. State them one more time.

EVOD. For the law does not force them to kill; it merely leaves that in their power. They are free not to kill anyone for those things which can be lost against their will, and which they should therefore not love. Perhaps one might doubt whether life is somehow taken from the soul when the body is slain. But if it can be taken away, it is of little value; and if it cannot, there is nothing to fear. As for chastity, who would doubt that it is located in the soul itself, since it is a virtue? So it cannot be taken away by a violent assailant. Whatever the one who is killed was going to take away is not completely in our power, so I don't understand how it can be called ours. I don't blame the law that allows such people to be killed; but I can't think of any way to defend those who do the killing.

AUG. And I can't think why you are searching for a defense for people whom no law condemns.

EVOD. No law, perhaps, of those that are public and are read by human beings; but I suspect that they are condemned by a more powerful, hidden law, if indeed there is nothing that is not governed by divine providence. How can they be free of sin in the eyes of that law, when they are defiled with human blood for the sake of things that ought to be held in contempt? It seems to me, therefore, that the law written to govern the people rightly permits these killings and that divine providence avenges them. The law of the people merely institutes penalties sufficient for keeping the peace among ignorant human beings, and only to the extent that their actions can be regulated by human government. But those other faults deserve other penalties that I think Wisdom alone can repeal.

One of Augustine's most famous books is called *The City of God*. In that book he makes a distinction between civil communities here on earth, the *earthly city* (such as the United States), and the *heavenly city*. Only in the latter is there the highest form of justice. Nonetheless, the earthly community is not entirely worthless. Similar ideas are at work here, but instead of referring to a heavenly and an earthly city, Augustine here speaks of two types of law.

ASK YOURSELF

5.20. One type is public or civil law, which is suitable for the _____ city. The other is _____ and would be appropriate for the _____ city.

In *The City of God* Augustine tries to show that we must not expect the earthly city to be very satisfying. By the true standards of the heavenly city it is always a miserable failure. Some of its laws may allow what is immoral. But how far should this idea be taken? Some people today argue that even though abortion is in their view a violation of divine law we should not expect civil law to condemn it. They argue that such a civil law would cause more evil than it would prevent.

 ASK YOURSELF

5.21. Assuming for the sake of argument that they are right about that, do you think Augustine would agree in this case? Explain your answer.

Summary. The summary of the argument so far is this. The problem is: What is the origin of evil? It seems that everything comes from God, but does evil, too? Surely not. Perhaps then evil comes from humans. But how could humans learn evil, since learning is good? Perhaps then evil originates in "disordered desire" (rather than in something that has been "learned"), which somehow gets control in a person. If all evil actions come from disordered desire, then any action produced by disordered desire would be justly condemned. But some such actions (e.g., killing someone to prevent the abduction of my daughter) are not condemned by civil law. So there must be a distinction between divine law and civil law. The latter might allow things that the former does not allow.

Relativism, Temporal Law, and Eternal Law. Relativism is discussed in various places in this text, including the Glossary. In Augustine's view, variations in laws and moral beliefs between different earthly communities are to be expected given the limitations imposed on those communities by fallen human nature. But there should be no variation in eternal law.

AUG.   I praise and approve your distinction, for although it is tentative and incomplete, it boldly aims at lofty heights. You think that the law that is established to rule cities allows considerable leeway, leaving many things unpunished that divine providence avenges; and rightly so. And just because that law doesn't do everything, it doesn't follow that we should disapprove of what it does do. But, if you wish, let us carefully examine to what extent evildoing is punished by the law that rules peoples in this life. Whatever is left is punished inevitably and secretly by divine providence.

EVOD.   I would like to, if only it were possible to get to the end of such matters; for I think this issue is infinite.

AUG.   Take heart, and set out confidently and piously in the paths of reason. There is nothing so abstruse or difficult that it cannot become completely clear and straightforward with God's help. And so, depending on him and praying for his aid, let's look into the question that we have posed. First, tell me this: is the law that is promulgated in writing helpful to human beings living this present life?

EVOD.   Of course, for they are the ones who make up peoples and cities.

AUG.   Do these human beings and peoples belong to the class of things that are eternal, and can neither change nor perish? Or are they changeable and subject to time?

EVOD.   Who could doubt that they are changeable and bound by time?

AUG.   Therefore, if a people is well-ordered and serious-minded, and carefully watches over the common good, and every one in it values private affairs less than the public interest, is it not right to enact a law that allows this people to choose their own magistrates to look after their interest—that is, the public interest?

EVOD.   It is quite right.

AUG.   But suppose that the same people becomes gradually depraved. They come to prefer private interest to the public good. Votes are bought and sold. Corrupted by those who covet honors, they hand over power to wicked and profligate men. In such a case would it not be right for a good and powerful man (if one could be found) to take from this people the power of conferring honors and to limit it to the discretion of a few good people, or even to one?

EVOD.   Yes, it would.

 ASK YOURSELF

5.22. Augustine has just argued that a more or less democratic form of government might be right in one time and/or place, a totalitarian dictatorship right in another time and/or place. Does this sound "relativistic" to you? Explain your answer.

AUG.   Now these two laws appear to be contradictory, for one of them gives the people the power to confer honors, while the other takes it away; and the second one is established in such a way that the laws cannot both be in force in one city at the same time. Shall we therefore conclude that one of them is unjust and should not be enacted?

EVOD.   Not at all.

AUG.   Then, if you like, let us call a law "temporal" if, although it is just, it can justly be changed in the course of time.

EVOD.   Agreed.

AUG.   Then consider the law that is called the highest reason, which must always be obeyed, and by which the wicked deserve misery and the good deserve a happy life, and by which the law that we agreed to call "temporal" is rightly enacted and rightly changed. Can anyone of sense deny that this law is unchangeable and eternal? Or can it sometimes be unjust for the wicked to be miserable and the good happy, or for a well-ordered and serious-minded people to choose their own magistrates, while a licentious and worthless people is deprived of this power?

EVOD.   I see that this law is indeed eternal and unchangeable.

AUG.   I think you also see that nothing is just and legitimate in the temporal law except that which human beings have derived from the eternal law. For if at one time a people can justly confer honors, and at another time cannot justly do so, this temporal change can be just only because it is derived from the eternal law, according to which it is always just for a serious-minded people to confer honors, but unjust for a frivolous people to do so. Or do you think otherwise?

 ## ASK YOURSELF

5.23. The foregoing arguments are meant to show that what appears to be relativism is not so. The fact that a law or institution is right in one set of circumstances and wrong in another only shows that the rightness in question applies to what is temporal and changing. Yet something which is eternal and unchanging is behind all genuine laws and institutions. What is it?

5.24. Do you think Augustine would say that in some circumstances a dictatorship could not be just?

5.25. Various reformers (e.g., Martin Luther King) have argued that laws that are not grounded in the law of God cannot be just. It is doubtful that King would have thought a dictatorship could be just. Do Augustine and King have the same conception of justice? Explain your answer.

Orderly Desire and the Nature of the Human Soul. Sometimes one way to see what something is, such as disordered desire, is to see what its opposite, orderly desire, is. In the following section Augustine begins a discussion of what it is that makes a person's desires, and self in general, orderly.

AUG.   Well then, let us now consider what it is for a human being to be perfectly ordered within, since human beings united under one law—a temporal law, as we have said—constitute a people. . . . Here is what I want to say. Whatever this thing is in virtue of which human beings are superior to animals, whether we should call it "mind" or "spirit" or both (for both terms are used in Scripture), if it rules and controls the other things that constitute a human being, then that human being is perfectly ordered. For we see that we have many characteristics in common not only with animals but even with trees and plants. We know that trees, which are at the lowest level of life, take in nourishment, grow, reproduce, and flourish. We recognize and acknowledge that animals can see and hear, and can sense material objects by touch, taste, and smell, often better than we can. Consider also strength, health, and bodily vigor, ease and swiftness of motion. In all of these respects we are superior to some animals, equal to others, and inferior to quite a few. Yet we have these sorts of traits in common with animals, although the life of the lower animals consists entirely in the pursuit of physical pleasures and the avoidance of pains.

There are other qualities that do not appear to exist in animals but are not the highest human attributes: for example, joking and laughing. Anyone with a proper understanding of human nature will consider these things distinctively human, to be sure, but of lesser importance. Then there are traits like the love of praise and fame, and the will to power. Animals do indeed lack these traits, but it should not be thought that a *disordered* desire for such things makes us superior to animals. When that drive is not subject to reason it makes us wretched, and no one considers himself superior to another because of his wretchedness. When these impulses of the soul are ruled by reason, a human being is said to be ordered. For we should not call it right order, or even order at all, when better things are subjected to worse. Don't you agree?

EVOD.   It is obvious.

 ASK YOURSELF

5.26. Augustine tries to get at an answer to the question "What is orderly desire?" by first considering the differences between human beings and _____.

5.27. His procedure here is reminiscent of an ancient thinker who thought it important to know the distinctive function of a person in order to know what a well-functioning (i.e., well-ordered) person would be. That thinker was _____, and his view on what distinguishes animals from humans and makes the latter better is about the same as Augustine's, namely, it is _____.

5.28. Augustine's discussion is also reminiscent of that same ancient thinker since Augustine distinguishes three kinds of life (or soul)—_____, _____, and _____—just as that ancient thinker did.

Augustine goes on to argue that the right ordering of the mind could not have been overcome by disordered desire, since that desire is inferior to reason, and the inferior cannot overcome the superior. He also argues that something that is equal to or superior to reason could not have been responsible for putting disordered desire in control of the self, since that would imply that, since disordered desire is unjust, reason is itself unjust.

 ASK YOURSELF

5.29. Augustine assumes then that reason cannot be unjust. Why do you suppose he assumes that? Think again about what you have learned from Plato.

AUG.   The conclusions that we have reached thus far indicate that a mind that is in control, one that possesses virtue, cannot be made a slave to *disordered* desire by anything equal or superior to it, because such a thing would be just, or by anything inferior to it, because such a thing would be too weak. Just one possibility remains: only its own will and free choice can make the mind a companion of evil desire. . . .

ASK YOURSELF

5.30. The conclusion Augustine reaches here is of course fundamental for the structure of this book and for his thought generally. State that conclusion here.

Vice Is Its Own Punishment. People pay a price for their disordered desires, namely, a confused and unhappy life.

EVOD.   I can't see any other alternative.

AUG.   Then you must also think that the mind justly suffers punishment for so great a sin.

EVOD.   I cannot deny it.

AUG.   Surely the very fact that *disordered* desire rules the mind is itself no small punishment. Stripped by opposing forces of the splendid wealth of virtue, the mind is dragged by *disordered* desire into ruin and poverty; now taking false things for true, and even defending those falsehoods repeatedly; now repudiating what it had once believed and nonetheless rushing headlong into still other falsehoods; now withholding assent and often shying away from clear arguments; now despairing completely of finding the truth and lingering in the shadows of folly; now trying to enter the light of understanding but reeling back in exhaustion.

In the meantime cupidity carries out a reign of terror, buffeting the whole human soul and life with storms coming from every direction. Fear attacks from one side and desire from the other; from one side, anxiety; from the other, an empty and deceptive happiness; from one side, the agony of losing what one loved; from the other, the passion to acquire what one did not have; from one side, the pain of an injury received; from the other, the burning desire to avenge it. Wherever you turn, avarice can pinch, extravagance squander, ambition destroy, pride swell, envy torment, apathy crush, obstinacy incite, oppression chafe, and countless other evils crowd the realm of disordered desire and run riot. In short, can we consider this punishment trivial—a punishment that, as you realize, all who do not cleave to wisdom must suffer?

 ASK YOURSELF

5.31. Is the punishment a person receives when their minds become "companions of evil desire" something that comes only after death, or does some of it come sooner? If it comes sooner, mention ten things that constitute that punishment here (number them).

5.32. Would you consider all of these things to be like punishments? Explain your answer.

It is very characteristic of Augustine that he thinks the origin of evil to be in the *will* rather than in a corrupted reason or appetite. Socrates, Plato, and Aristotle do not appear to have had any such conception. We have seen that Augustine is very indebted to those ancient thinkers. Yet his views about the will puts a considerable strain on his relationship to their thought. In the following portion of the text he discusses what might account for the fact that while everyone wills to be happy not everyone is. He concludes that the reason lies in the *way* some people will their happiness. There are basically two ways, which correspond to two kinds of desire and to two kinds of law.

The Two Laws Again, and the Two Kinds of Desire.   Augustine combines his insights into the differences between civil and eternal law and disordered and well-ordered desire.

AUG.   Very well. First, tell me something about those who delight in living rightly, and take such pleasure in it that they find it not merely right but actually sweet and joyful. Do they love and cherish the law that, as they see, confers a happy life upon a good will and an unhappy life upon an evil will?

EVOD.   They love it intensely, for it is by following that law that they live as they do.

AUG.   Now when they love this, are they loving something changeable and temporal, or something stable and eternal?

EVOD.   Clearly, something eternal and unchangeable.

AUG.   What about those who persevere in an evil will but nonetheless desire to be happy? Can they love the law by which such people are justly punished with unhappiness?

EVOD.   Not at all, I think.

AUG.   Do they love something else?

EVOD.   A number of things—whatever their evil will is bent on getting or keeping.

AUG.   I believe you mean things like wealth, honors, pleasures, physical beauty, and everything else that one cannot get or keep simply by willing.

We see here that the evil will is closely connected to, if not exactly the same thing as, disordered desire, which was defined as excessive love of those things that can be lost against one's will.

EVOD.   That is exactly what I meant.

AUG.   You surely do not think that these things are eternal, subject as they are to the ravages of time.

EVOD.   Only a complete fool could think that.

AUG.   Then it is clear that some human beings love eternal things while others love temporal things; and we have also found that there are two laws, one eternal and one temporal. Now if you know anything about justice, which human beings do you think should be subject to the eternal law, and which should be subject to the temporal?

EVOD.   The answer to that is obvious. I think that those who are happy on account of their love for eternal things live under the eternal law, while those who are unhappy are subject to the temporal law.

AUG.   You're correct, provided that you remain firm in holding what our argument clearly demonstrated: that those who serve the temporal law cannot be free from the eternal law, from which is derived, as we said, everything that is just and yet can justly be changed. But I believe you realize that those who cleave to the eternal law by their good will have no need of the temporal law.

EVOD.   I agree.

AUG.   So the eternal law demands that we purify our love by turning it away from temporal things and toward what is eternal.

EVOD.   Yes.

AUG.   But when human beings in their evil desires cleave to things that can be called ours only for a time, the temporal law demands that they possess those things in accordance with the law by which peace and human society are preserved—insofar as they can be preserved on the basis of such things. The first such good is this body, along with all of the things associated with it that are called goods, such as health, keen senses, strength, beauty, and other qualities, some of which are necessary for good deeds and are therefore to be regarded highly, and others of which are less valuable. The second such good is freedom. Now the only genuine freedom is that possessed by those who are happy and cleave to the eternal law; but I am talking about the sort of freedom that people have in mind when they think they are free because they have no human masters, or that people desire when they want to be set free by their masters. Then come parents, brothers and sisters, a spouse, children, neighbors, relatives, friends, and anyone who is bound to us by some need. Next is the city itself, which frequently takes the place of the parents, together with honors and praise and what is called popular acclaim. And finally comes property, which includes anything over which the law gives us control and which we have a recognized right to sell or give away.

To explain how the law distributes all of these things to their rightful owners is a long and difficult task, and one that is clearly irrelevant to the matter at hand. It is enough to see that the temporal law can punish evildoing only by taking away one or another of these goods from the one being punished.

So it is by fear that the temporal law coerces human beings and bends the souls of its subjects in whatever direction it pleases. As long as they are afraid of losing these things, they use them with the kind of moderation necessary to maintain whatever sort of city can be built out of such people. They are punished, not because they love temporal goods [which is itself a violation to the divine law], but because they wrongfully take them away from others.

 ASK YOURSELF

5.33. Give an example of a temporal good that is taken away from someone when they are punished by the state.

Using and Enjoying.   In the following section Augustine introduces a distinction that is fundamental through much of his writing, namely, the distinction between *using* something, on the one hand, and *enjoying* or *being attached* to it, on the other.

ASK YOURSELF

5.34. Study his remarks; then give some examples of things that should be used but that we should not be attached to.

AUG.   Therefore, the very same things are used in different ways by different people; some use them badly and others use them well. Someone who uses them badly clings to them and becomes entangled with them. He serves things that ought to serve him, fixing on goods that he cannot even use properly because he is not himself good. But one who uses these things rightly shows that they are good, although not good for himself. For those things do not make the one who uses them good or better; in fact, they become good by being put to good use. And so someone who uses them well does not become attached to them. They don't become limbs of his soul, as it were (which is what happens when one loves them), so that when these things begin to be amputated he is not disfigured by any pain or decay. He is completely above such things, ready to possess and make use of them when there is need, and even readier to lose them and do without them. Since this is the case, you must realize that we should not find fault with silver and gold because of the greedy, or food because of gluttons, or wine because of drunkards, or womanly beauty because of fornicators and adulterers, and so on, especially since you know that fire can be used to heal and bread to poison.

EVOD.   Clearly we must not blame the things themselves but the people that use them wrongly.

 ASK YOURSELF

5.35. There are echoes here of an ancient school of philosophy that flourished during the Roman period, which stressed the importance of "detachment." That school was _____.

Summary. Augustine now puts down a summary of his ideas about the two kinds of law, the two kinds of desire, and the importance of the will in the explanation of evil.

AUG.   That's right. We have now, I think, begun to see what the eternal law can do. We have found out how far the temporal law can go in punishing evildoing. We have clearly and carefully distinguished between two sorts of things—eternal and temporal; and in turn between two sorts of human beings—those who pursue and love eternal things, and those who pursue and love temporal things. We have determined that the choice to follow and embrace one or the other lies with the will, and that only the will can depose the mind from its stronghold of power and deprive it of right order. And it has become clear that we should not blame anything when someone uses it wrongly; we should blame the one who uses it wrongly. Given all of that, why don't we return to the question we posed at the beginning of this discussion and see whether it has been answered.

We set out to discover what evildoing is. This whole discussion was aimed at answering that question. So we are now in a position to ask whether evildoing is anything other than neglecting eternal things, which the mind perceives and enjoys by means of itself and which it cannot lose if it loves them; and instead pursuing temporal things—which are perceived by means of the body, the least valuable part of a human being, and which can never be certain—as if they were great and marvelous things. It seems to me that all evil deeds—that is, all sins—fall into this one category. But I want to know what you think about this.

EVOD.   I agree; all sins come about when someone turns away from divine things that truly persist and toward changeable and uncertain things. These things do have their proper place, and they have a certain beauty of their own; but when a perverse and disordered soul pursues them it becomes enslaved to the very things that divine order and law command it to rule over.

And I think that we have answered another question. After we asked what evildoing is, we set out to discover the source of our evildoing. Now unless I am mistaken, our argument showed that we do evil by the free choice of the will. . . .

 ASK YOURSELF

5.36. In the preceding passage Augustine produces a summary of the argument so far. Review it and reproduce it in outline form.

Evodius and Augustine agree that all sins come about when someone turns away from divine things that truly persist and toward changeable and uncertain things. The contrast between the unchanging eternal and the changeable was fundamental in ancient Greek philosophy from the Presocratics onward, as you know. Plato also thought that true knowledge, which is also true virtue, was only possible when we focus on the eternal. This contrast also seems to be fundamental for Augustine.

 ASK YOURSELF

5.37. Has Augustine substituted Greek philosophical notions for Christian ideas, or are these ideas also Christian, as well as Greek and philosophical? Explain your answer.

Book 2. More on the Origin of Evil

Much of Book 2 is devoted to a proof for the existence of God. Augustine's proof is similar to a proof developed by Aquinas that will be mentioned later. In Book 2 the question that was raised toward the end of Book 1—What might explain the evil will itself?—is also taken up again. Where did the evil will itself come from?

The Source of the Evil Will. If evil comes from the will of people, so that God cannot be blamed for it, there is still the question, where did the evil will come from?

From AUGUSTINE: *On Free Choice of the Will*, Book II

AUG.   But perhaps you are going to ask what is the source of this movement by which the will turns away from the unchangeable good toward a changeable good. This movement is certainly evil, even though free will itself is to be counted among good things, since no one can live rightly without it. For if that movement, that turning away from the Lord God, is undoubtedly sin, surely we cannot say that God is the cause of sin. So that movement is not from God. But then where does it come from? If I told you that I don't know, you might be disappointed; but that would be the truth. For one cannot know that which is nothing.

You must simply hold with unshaken faith that every good thing that you perceive or understand or in any way know is from God. For any nature you come across is from God. So if you see anything at all that has measure, number, and order, do not hesitate to attribute it to God as craftsman. If you take away all measure, number, and order, there is absolutely nothing left. Even if the rudiments of a form remain, in which you find neither measure nor number nor order—since wherever those things are there is a complete form—you must take that away too, for it seems to be like the material on which the craftsman works. For if the completion of form is a good, then the rudiments of a form are themselves not without goodness. So if you take away everything that is good, you will have absolutely nothing left. But every good thing comes from God, so there is no nature that does not come from God. On the other hand, every defect comes from nothing, and that movement of turning away, which we admit is sin, is a defective movement. So you see where that movement comes from; you may be sure that it does not come from God.

 ASK YOURSELF

5.38. What ancient thinker argued that reality consists of numbers?

In the portions of Book 2 cited in the preceding passage and in many other places in this work a fundamental aspect of Augustine's ontology (i.e., conception of what really exists) is very much in view, in which being is associated with goodness, whereas nonbeing or nothingness is associated with evil. Remember, he is trying to explain the *origin of evil*. He has located it in the will, when it turns away from the unchangeable to a changeable good. But now the question is: What makes it possible for the will to turn that way? Augustine answers, "If I told you I don't know, that would be the truth."

 ASK YOURSELF

5.39. Why does he think you cannot *know* where evil comes from? In answering this you should once again think about Plato's views on knowledge and goodness.

Book 3. God's Foreknowledge and Freedom: The Great Chain of Being

Despite Augustine's efforts so far, the problem of the source of the evil will seems to resist easy solution. The discussion continues in Book 3.

More on the Source of the Evil Will and the Dilemma of Free Will versus Determinism or Fate. Free will is a good thing and comes from a good God. But what about the movement of the will away from God? Where does it come from? And how could it be really "free" if God knows everything that will happen beforehand?

 From AUGUSTINE: *On Free Choice of the Will*, Book III

EVOD.   It has been demonstrated to my satisfaction that free will is to be numbered among good things, and indeed not among the least of them, and therefore that it was given to us by God, who acted rightly in giving it. So now, if you think that this is a good time, I would like you to explain the source of the movement by which the will turns away from the common and unchangeable good toward its own good, or the good of others, or lower goods, all of which are changeable.

AUG.   Why do we need to know that?

EVOD.   Because if the will was given to us in such a way that it had this movement naturally, then it turned to changeable goods by necessity, and there is no blame involved when nature and necessity determine an action. . . .

AUG.   . . . If that movement existed by nature or necessity, it could in no way be blameworthy. But you are so firmly convinced that this movement is indeed blameworthy that you think it would be ridiculous to entertain doubts about something so certain. Why then did you affirm, or at least tentatively assert, something that now seems to you clearly false? For this is what you said: "If the will was given to us in such a way that it had this movement naturally, then it turned to changeable goods by necessity, and there is no blame involved when nature and necessity determine an action." Since you are sure that this movement was blameworthy, you should have been quite sure that the will was not given to us in such a way.

EVOD.   I said that this movement was blameworthy and that therefore it displeases me. And I am surely right to find fault with it. But I deny that a soul ought to be blamed when this movement pulls it away from the unchangeable good toward changeable goods, if this movement is so much a part of its nature that it is moved by necessity.

AUG.   You admit that this movement certainly deserves blame; but whose movement is it?

EVOD.   I see that the movement is in the soul, but I don't know whose it is.

AUG.   Surely you don't deny that the soul is moved by this movement.

EVOD.   No.

AUG.   Do you deny that a movement by which a stone is moved is a movement of the stone? I'm not talking about a movement that is caused by us or some other force, as when it is thrown into the air, but the movement that occurs when it falls to the earth by its own weight.

EVOD.   I don't deny that this movement, by which the stone seeks the lowest place, is a movement of the stone. But it is a natural movement. If that's the sort of movement the soul has, then the soul's movement is also natural. And if it is moved naturally, it cannot justly be blamed; even if it is moved toward something evil, it is compelled by its own nature. But since we don't doubt that this movement is blameworthy, we must absolutely deny that it is natural, and so it is not similar to the natural movement of a stone.

AUG.   Did we accomplish anything in our first two discussions?

EVOD.   Of course we did.

 ASK YOURSELF

5.40. In contemporary terms, the debate here is over freedom of the will versus the influence of natural law. We often deny that someone is to be blamed for their actions when we think those actions were entirely due to the influence upon them of _____ and environment. Since such influences are simply part of its _____, as Evodius puts it, the result cannot be blameable.

5.41. The next paragraph contains a summary of what has been achieved in Books 1 and 2. Study it and outline the summary.

AUG.   I'm sure you recall that in Book 1 we agreed that nothing can make the mind a slave to *disordered* desire except its own will. For the will cannot be forced into such iniquity by anything superior or equal to it, since that would be unjust; or by anything inferior to it, since that is impossible. Only one possibility remains: the movement by which the will turns from enjoying the Creator to enjoying his creatures belongs to the will itself. So if that movement deserves blame (and you said it was ridiculous to entertain doubts on that score), then it is not natural, but voluntary. This movement of the will is similar to the downward movement of a stone in that it belongs to the will just as that downward movement belongs to the stone. But the two movements are dissimilar in this respect: the stone has no power to check its downward movement, but the soul is not moved to abandon higher things and love inferior things unless it wills to do so. And so the movement of the stone is natural, but the movement of the soul is voluntary. If someone were to say that a stone is sinning because its weight carries it downward, I would not merely say that he was more senseless than the stone itself; I would consider him completely insane. But we accuse a soul of sin when we are convinced that it has abandoned higher things and chosen to enjoy inferior things. Now we admit that this movement belongs to the will alone, and that it is voluntary and therefore blameworthy; and the only useful teaching on this topic is that which condemns and checks this movement and thus serves to rescue our wills from their fall into temporal goods and turn them toward the enjoyment of the eternal good. Therefore, what need is there to ask about the source of the movement by which the will turns away from the unchangeable good toward changeable good?

EVOD.   I see that what you are saying is true, and in a way I understand it. There is nothing I feel so firmly and so intimately as that I have a will by which I am moved to enjoy something. If the will by which I choose or refuse things is not mine, then I don't know what I can call mine. So if I use my will to do something evil, whom can I hold responsible but myself? For a good God made me, and I can do nothing good except through my will; therefore, it is quite clear that the will was given to me by a good God so that I might do good. If the movement of the will by which it turns this way or that were not voluntary and under its own control, a person would not deserve praise for turning to higher things or blame for turning to lower things, as if swinging on the hinge of the will. Furthermore, there would be no point in admonishing people to forget about lower things and strive for what is eternal, so that they might refuse to live badly but instead will to live rightly. And anyone who does not think that we ought to admonish people in this way deserves to be banished from the human race.

 ASK YOURSELF

5.42. If the "movement of the will by which we turn this way or that (to good or to evil) were not voluntary," several things would follow. List them.

The Problem of God's Foreknowledge and Free Will. If God knows exactly what you are going to do one minute from now, how could you be free to do otherwise, that is, how could you have free will?

AUG.   Since these things are true, I very much wonder how God can have fore-knowledge of everything in the future, and yet we do not sin by necessity. It would be an irreligious and completely insane attack on God's foreknowledge to say that something could happen otherwise than as God foreknew. So suppose that God foreknew that the first human being was going to sin. Anyone who admits, as I do, that God foreknows everything in the future will have to grant me that. Now I won't say that God would not have made him—for God made him good, and no sin of his can harm God, who not only made him good but showed His own goodness by creating him, as He also shows His justice by punishing him and His mercy by redeeming him—but I will say this: since God foreknew that he was going to sin, his sin necessarily had to happen. How, then, is the will free when such inescapable necessity is found in it?

 ASK YOURSELF

5.43. Here a problem about free will and God's foreknowledge is stated. Fill in the blanks:

     a. What God foreknows will happen _____.

     b. What happens _____ cannot have been freely chosen.

     c. God foreknows our actions.

     d. Therefore, our actions _____.

5.44. It should be obvious why this last conclusion is disastrous for Augustine's entire project in this work. Nonetheless, state briefly why it is.

Augustine goes on to question the motives of those who are bothered by this problem. He proposes a solution, which he briefly summarizes as follows.

AUG.   . . . Thus, we believe both that God has foreknowledge of everything in the future and that nonetheless we will whatever we will. Since God foreknows our will, the very will that he foreknows will be what comes about. Therefore, it will be a will, since it is a will that he foreknows. And it could not be a will unless it were in our power. Therefore, he also foreknows this power. It follows, then, that his foreknowledge does not take away my power; in fact, it is all the more certain that I will have that power, since he whose foreknowledge never errs foreknows that I will have it.

EVOD.   I agree now that it is necessary that whatever God has foreknown will happen, and that he foreknows our sins in such a way that our wills remain free and are within our power.

 ## ASK YOURSELF

5.45. Augustine's solution can be summarized as follows. Fill in the blanks:

    a. God foreknows what we shall will.

    b. What someone wills is, by definition, in their own _____.

    c. Therefore, God foreknows that what we will do in the future will be in our own _____.

    d. When we do what is in our own _____ we are _____.

    e. Therefore, God's foreknowledge does not cancel our _____.

The crucial step in this argument may appear to be step (b). The point is that you would not say of someone who was acting out of necessity (i.e., unable to do anything other than what they are doing) that he or she freely chose to do what he or she did. Augustine goes on to consider whether *anyone's* foreknowledge would constrain freedom. If somehow I know that you are going to tell a lie two minutes from now, and since I cannot know what is false, then it must be the case that you will tell a lie in two minutes. So when two minutes are up it would seem that you have no possibility of choosing *not* to lie. Augustine points out that my knowing what you will do does not itself determine you to do what you do, or is not the cause of your doing it. Likewise then, God, in foreknowing what we shall do, does not cause us to do whatever we end up doing.

ASK YOURSELF

5.46. Augustine's main point is that knowing ahead of time what someone is going to do (whether the knowing is God's or anyone else's) does not _____ them to act as they do.

The Great Chain of Being. Much of the remainder of Book 3 depends upon a notion of great historical importance. Augustine says, "There is so great a variety of parts in the earth that we cannot conceive of any earthly form that God has not created. By intermediate steps one passes gradually from the most fertile and pleasant land to the briniest and most barren. . . ." He is stating a familiar idea that has permeated the thinking of philosophers, theologians, poets, and others for centuries, which is often referred to as "the great chain of being."

Augustine applies this idea to the problem of evil in the following way: Suppose someone were to argue (as many have and still do) that even though evil comes from the free will of people, God is responsible insofar as he could have refrained from creating such free beings. The strategy in replying to this would be to show that God's goodness required the creation of such free beings. So Augustine argues,

a. Even an evil person (soul) is better than a stone (or some other merely material object).

b. If A is better than B, then A has a higher degree of reality than B (for the origin of this assumption, you can go all the way back to Plato).

c. A universe in which *all* degrees of reality are included is better than one that lacked some degree of reality. (Or, a universe that is a "great chain" is better than one with "gaps.")

d. Therefore, a world with evil people is better than one without them.

e. Conclusion: Therefore, God, being good, would create a world that ends up having evil people in it (although he does not create the evil itself).

This argument raises many difficulties, and an adequate discussion of them would require considerable labor in an attempt to understand just how the "great chain" idea functions for Augustine. It may appear that these claims in Book 3 are not consistent with the free will argument stated in Book 1. If God created beings who would inevitably will evil, then is God not the ultimate source of evil? Suffice it to say here that the idea of a great chain of being has played a very significant role in the thinking of many writers, including poets and philosophers, and the influence of Plato in this conception is very pronounced.

 ASK YOURSELF

5.47. What are the main elements in the idea of the great chain of being?

The *Confessions:* Augustine on Time

The bulk of Augustine's *Confessions* are autobiographical, but in Book 11 of that work he begins reflecting on God's timelessness, and that leads him to question the nature of time itself. He argues that the past and future do not exist in any real sense and the present is so fleeting as to be beyond our grasp. His discussion sets the foundation for virtually all further discussions of the philosophy of time. The following passages are from the *Confessions,* Book 11, Sections 14–20.

Section 14: The Nonexistence of Time-Past and Time-Future. Do the present and future "exist"? It seems not.

 From AUGUSTINE: *Confessions,* Book II

At no time had you [O God] not made anything, because time itself was made by you. And no times are coeternal with you, because you remain unchanged, and if time did not change it would not be time. For what is time? Who can readily and briefly explain this? Who can even in thought comprehend it so as to utter a word about it? But, when talking, what do we mention with more familiarity and knowledge than time? Further, we understand it when we speak of it, and we understand also when someone else speaks of it.

What then is time? If no one asks me, I know. If I wish to explain it to someone that asks, I do not know. Yet I say boldly that I know that if nothing passed away, there would be no time-past. And if nothing were coming, there would be no time-future.

These two times then, past and future, how can they exist since the past is gone and the future is not yet here? But if the present stayed present, and never passed into time-past, then, truly, it would not be time, but eternity. Suppose that time-present (if it is to be time) only comes into existence because it passes into time-past. How, then, can we say that it exists, since its existence is caused by the fact that it will not exist? We can't truly say that time is, then, except because it tends towards non-being.

 ASK YOURSELF

5.48. Strictly speaking, why is there no time-past or time-future? There is no time-past because when any portion of time has past it _____. There is no time-future because _____.

Section 15: Problems with Determining Past, Present, and Future Lengths of Time. How can something that does not exist be "long" or "short"?

Yet we say, "a long time" and "a short time," speaking only of time-past or time-future. For example, we call a hundred years past "a long time past," and a hundred years hence "a long time future." But a short time past, we call, for example, ten days ago, and a short time future ten days hence. But in what sense is that long or short, if it doesn't exist? For the past is not now, and the future is not yet here. Let us not then say of the past "it *is* long," but instead that "it *has* been long." And of the future, [let us say] "it *will be* long." But, O my Lord, my light, doesn't your truth mock us here too? For if a past time *was* long, was it long when it became the past, or when it was still in the present? It can be long only when it existed and *could* be long. But when past, it was no longer exists; for this reason, neither could that be long, which did not exist. Let us not then say, "time past *has been* long" for we will not find what has been long. For, since it was past, it is no more. Let us say instead, that "that present time was long" since, when it was present, it was long. This is so since it had not yet passed away, so as to not exist. Therefore, there was what could be long, but after it was past, that ceased also to be long, which ceased to exit.

 ASK YOURSELF

5.49. What is wrong with saying that a given stretch of time-past *"has been long"*?

5.50. What is wrong with saying that a given stretch of time-past *"is long"*?

Let us see then, human soul, whether *present* time can be long since you have been given the ability to feel and measure lengths of time. What will you answer me? In the present, are a hundred years a long time? Examine first whether a hundred years can be present. If the first of these years is now current, then it is present; however, the other ninety-nine are future, and therefore do not yet exist. If, instead, the second year is current, the first is now past, another present, and the rest future. Thus, if we assume any middle year of this hundred to be present, all years before it are past, and all after it are future. For this reason, a hundred years can't be present. But examine now whether that one year which is now current is *itself* in the present. For, if the current month is present, then the rest are in the future. If the second month is present, then the first is already past, and the rest don't yet exist. Therefore, neither is the year now current existing in present. And, if it is not present as a whole, then is not the *year* present? For a year is twelve months, and which ever month is current, it is in the present, and the rest are past or future. Still further, the current month also doesn't exist in the present, but one day only. The rest are in the future (if they are first), the past (if they are last), or if any in the middle, then between past and future.

 ASK YOURSELF

5.51. We can't say that the current century, year, month, or day exists in the present because _____.

See how the present time (which alone we found could be called "long") is shortened to the length scarcely of one day! But let us examine this also, since neither is *one day* present as a whole. It is made up of twenty-four hours of night and day. The first sees the rest as the future, the last sees the previous as the past, and any in the middle has those before it past, those behind it future. Indeed, that one hour passes away in vanishing minutes. Whatever of it has vanished away is past, and whatever remains is the future. If we conceive of an instant of time which can't be divided into the smallest particles of moments, then that alone is we may be called the *present*. Yet this flies with such speed from future to past, that it can't be extended at all. For if it is extended, it is divided into past and future. Thus, the present takes up no space. Where, then, is the time which we may call long? Is it in the future? We don't say of it that "it is long," since it is not yet here, so as to be long. But we say, "it *will be* long." When, though, will that be?

For if even it is in the future, it will not be long (because it does not yet exist and cannot thereby be long). Perhaps it will only be long when in the future (which is not yet here) it will come into being and become present that so there should exist what may be long. But the present time cries out in the words above, that *it can't be long!*

 ASK YOURSELF

5.52. How short is the present moment?

Section 16: Problems with Measuring Time. If past and future do not exist, how can they be measured?

And yet, Lord, we indeed perceive intervals of time, and compare them, and say that some are shorter and others longer. We also measure how much longer or shorter this time is than that. We say, "This is double, triple, single, or only just the same as that." But we measure times as they are passing by perceiving them. As for the past times (which now do not exist) or the future times (which do not yet exist), who is able to measure them? No one can, unless, perchance, someone would presume to say that something can be measured which does not exist. Therefore, while time is passing, it may be observed and measured: but when it is once past, it can't, because it does not exit.

Section 17: But the Past and Future Must Exist. But the ability to foretell the future and relate the past requires that they exist in some sense.

I am asking, Father, not affirming. O my God, teach me and guide me. We learned and taught each other when young that there are three times: past, present, and future. Who will tell me, then, that there is only the present because the other two do not exist? Or do they also exist by coming into the present from some secret in the future, or retiring from the present into some secret pace of the past? Where did the prophets see future events if these events do not yet exist? For that which doesn't exist can't be seen. Similarly, those who relate past events could not do so without mentally discerning these events; and such discernment is not possible if the events themselves didn't exist.

Section 18: How Time Past and Future Are Now Present. Augustine now argues that time is dependent upon the mind.

Permit me, Lord, to seek further. O my hope, do not let my purpose be confounded. For if the past and future do exist, I would know where they are. And even if I don't, I at least know that, wherever they are, they are not in the future or past, but in the present. For if they are there in the future, then they are not yet there, and if they are there in the past, then they are not there still. Wherever they are and whatever they are, they exist only as present. When past facts are related, they are drawn out of the memory—not the events themselves which are past, but the words. These words are conceived by the images of the passing events which, through the senses, left traces in the mind. Thus my childhood, which now does not exist, is in time-past, which now also does not exist. But now when I recall these images and speak of them, I view them in the present because they are still in my memory. I confess, O my God, that I do not know whether there is a similar cause of foretelling future events—of things which do not yet exist—whereby the images are perceived before the events exist. However, I do know that we generally reflect on our future actions, and that fore-thinking is present, even though the action in question does not yet exist because it is in the future. Once we set upon and begin to do what which we were forethinking, the action will exist because it is no longer future but present.

However this secret fore-perceiving of future events works, we can only see that which exists. And what exists now is not the future, but the present. When the future is seen, we do not see the events themselves since these as yet do not exist. Instead, we see their causes or signs which already exist. Therefore they are not future but present to those who now see and foretell the future events as fore-conceived in the mind. Again, such fore-conceptions exist now, and those who foretell those things hold present conceptions. An illustration can be drawn from the wide variety of experience. I consider daybreak and predict that the sun is about to rise. What I consider is present; what I predict future—not the sun, which already exists, but the sun rising, which does not yet exist. Yet I certainly did imagine in my mind the sun itself rising (as now while I speak of it), otherwise I could not foretell it. But the day-break which I see in the sky is not the sun rising, although it precedes it. Neither is the day-break the image I have of it in my mind. The day-break and image are both seen now present, the sun rise which is to come may be foretold. Future things, then, do not yet exist, and if they do not *yet* exist, then they *don't* exist. If they don't exist, then they can't be seen, although they may be foretold from present things which exist not and can be seen.

 ASK YOURSELF

5.53. How are the past and future contained in the present?

Section 20: How We Should Refer to the Past, Present, and Future. Augustine now shows exactly how past and future depend upon the mind.

It is now plain and evident that neither future nor past things exist. Nor can we properly say, "there are three times: past, present, and future." Instead, it we might properly say "there are three times: a *present-of-things-past*, a *present-of-things-present*, and a *present-of-things-future*." For these three do exist in the mind in some way, but any other way I cannot see them. The present-of-things-past involves memory, the present-of-things-present involves perception, and the present-of-things-future involves expectation. If I am permitted to speak, I see and confess that there are three times. I also say that there are three times, past, present, and future, according to our misapplied custom. However, I will not object or find fault with this custom as long as it is understood neither the future or past exist. We speak properly of few things, and improperly of most things, although we understand what we mean.

ASK YOURSELF

5.54. How does Augustine recommend that we refer to the past, present and future?

ANSELM

Saint Anselm of Canterbury (1033–1109) was a Benedictine monk from Normandy, France, who became prior of the Abbey of Bec in Normandy and later Archbishop of Canterbury (in England). He lived at the time of William the Conqueror's invasion of England in 1066, which explains how a Norman monk could become England's foremost churchman. William, a Norman, installed his friends in positions of power after the conquest. Anselm also lived at the time of the first crusade (1096). His book, *Cur Deus Homo* (Why Did God become Human?), had enormous influence on the subsequent history of theology. Anselm is in many respects solidly in the Augustinian tradition. Augustine believed that God's existence could be confirmed through rational argumentation, but only to those who first believe in God. Reason thus depends upon faith, in some sense. Some later medieval theologians and philosophers maintained that God's existence could be established by reason operating independently of faith, but Anselm follows Augustine, as is evidenced by the fact that the original title for his work excerpted here was "Fides Quaerens Intellectum"(Faith Seeking Understanding). This is of course very close to the idea that was so central to Augustine (see question 5.8).

 ASK YOURSELF

5.55. State in Augustine's words what that idea was.

Proslogion 1

In his *Monologion* Anselm presents several proofs found in the writings of earlier philosophers. He is most famous, however, for his brief ontological argument for God's existence, which appears in his *Proslogion*. The ontological argument assumes the correctness of the (or "a") Judaeo-Christian conception of God and proceeds to show the implications of that conception. In a sense, then, it is simply an explanation or "spelling out" of what is believed, rather than an attempt to start from scratch and arrive at belief through argument. One must begin with belief (cf. Augustine) in any case. It turns out that more than one ontological argument appears in Anselm's text. These arguments were anticipated in several places by Augustine.

Chapter 2: Truly There Is a God, although the Fool Has Said in His Heart, There Is No God. Anyone who has the concept of God (that is, for whom God exists "in the understanding") will run into difficulties if he tries to deny that such a being exists also outside of his mind or understanding.

From ANSELM: *Proslogion 1*, Chapter 2

And so, Lord, do you, who gives understanding to faith, give me, so far as you know it to be profitable, to understand that you are as we believe; and that you are that which we believe. And, indeed, we believe that you are a being than which nothing greater can be conceived. Or is there no such nature, since the fool has said in his heart, there is no God? (Psalms 14:1). But, at any rate, this very fool, when he hears of this being of which I speak—a being than which nothing greater can be conceived— understands what he hears, and what he understands is in his understanding; although he does not understand it to exist.

For, it is one thing for an object to be in the understanding, and another to understand that the object exists. When a painter first conceives of what he will afterwards perform, he has it in his understanding, but he does not yet understand it to be, because he has not yet performed it. But after he has made the painting, he both has it in his understanding, and he understands that it exists, because he has made it.

Hence, even the fool is convinced that something exists in the understanding, at least, than which nothing greater can be conceived. For, when he hears of this, he understands it. And whatever is understood, exists in the understanding. And assuredly that, than which nothing greater can be conceived, cannot exist in the understanding alone. For, suppose it exists in the understanding alone: then it can be conceived to exist in reality; which is greater.

Therefore, if that, than which nothing greater can be conceived, exists in the understanding alone, the very being, than which nothing greater can be conceived, is one, than which a greater can be conceived. But obviously this is impossible. Hence, there is no doubt that there exists a being, than which nothing greater can be conceived, and it exists both in the understanding and in reality.

In its most simple form, this first version of the ontological argument is as follows:

a. We have the concept of God (i.e., we can conceive God, and in that sense God exists "in the understanding").

b. The concept of "God" is the concept of the greatest conceivable being.

c. Real existence (existence in reality) is greater than mere existence "in the understanding."

d. Therefore, God must exist in reality, not just in the understanding.

The first premise simply means that we understand and can consistently think about the concept of God (whereas we could not think about the concept of a square sphere, for instance). The second premise seems pretty obviously true. The third means that a real x is greater than an imaginary or merely conceived x of the same kind (e.g., a real $100 is greater than an imaginary $100).

ASK YOURSELF

5.56. If you are not sure about this argument ask yourself this: Suppose that God does not exist in reality, but only in the understanding. Would that entail that there must be something greater than God? If so, which of premises (a)–(c) would be contradicted?

In Chapter 3 of the *Proslogion* Anselm continues by arguing that not only does God exist, but he has necessary existence. This argument, it seems, has a different structure from the first.

Chapter 3: God Cannot Be Conceived Not To Exist. God Is That, Than Which Nothing Greater Can Be Conceived. That Which Can Be Conceived Not to Exist Is Not God. The conception of God is peculiar, unique. It is the conception of a being that cannot fail to exist.

 From ANSELM: *Proslogion 1*, Chapter 3

And it assuredly exists so truly, that it cannot be conceived not to exist. For, it is possible to conceive of a being which cannot be conceived not to exist; and this is greater than one which can be conceived not to exist. Hence, if that, than which nothing greater can be conceived, can be conceived not to exist, it is not that, than which nothing greater can be conceived. But this is an irreconcilable contradiction. There is, then, so truly a being than which nothing greater can be conceived to exist, that it cannot even be conceived not to exist; and this being you are, O Lord, our God.

So truly, therefore, do you exist, O Lord, my God, that you cannot be conceived not to exist; and rightly. For, if a mind could conceive of a being better than you, the creature would rise above the Creator; and this is most absurd. And, indeed, whatever else there is, except you alone, can be conceived not to exist. To you alone, therefore, it belongs to exist more truly than all other beings, and hence in a higher degree than all others. For, whatever else exists does not exist so truly, and hence in a less degree it belongs to it to exist. Why, then, has the fool said in his heart, there is no God (Psalms 14:1), since it is so evident, to a rational mind, that you do exist in the highest degree of all? Why, except that he is dull and a fool?

Anselm's first argument treats existence in ordinary reality as a perfection or great-making quality (e.g., an actually existing $100 is greater than a merely imaginary $100). His second argument treats *necessary* existence as a great-making quality, for only of something that exists necessarily would it be true to say that it "cannot be conceived not to exist." You can see why necessary existence might be considered a great-making property if you look next to the discussion of necessary existence and eternity.

But a few remarks about necessity are in order here. The concept contains many difficulties, but it is obviously connected with the notion of possibility and impossibility. The following example may give some help in thinking about it. Spheres are round *necessarily*. If someone claimed they had found a sphere that was not round we would say that was impossible. A sphere *has* to be round. If, for example, you are trying to think of something as being both a sphere and square, you are contradicting yourself in your own thoughts. Now you might think of Anselm as saying something like this: If you are thinking of something as being God and also as not existing, you are contradicting yourself in your own thoughts. For God exists necessarily. It simply belongs to the definition of God that God has necessary existence.

Gaunilo's Criticism of Anselm. Gaunilo, a monk who was a contemporary of Anselm, wrote an attack on Anselm's argument titled "On Behalf of the Fool." He offers several criticisms, the most well known being a parody on Anselm's argument in which he proves the existence of the *greatest possible island*. If we replaced "something than which nothing greater can be conceived" in Anselm's argument with "an island than which none greater can be conceived" then we could prove the existence of that island, Guanilo claimed. If someone denied that our most perfect island existed we could say that they must not be conceiving the most perfect island, since, as Anselm argues, existence in reality is a perfection or great-making quality, and so the most perfect island would have to have that quality, too. In Anselm's kind of reasoning, it seems, the most perfect island would have to have existence in reality (as well as a nice climate, etc.). Gaunilo's point was that we could prove the existence of *almost anything* using Anselm's style of argument (for example, the most perfect rock, the most perfect automobile). A form of argument that can be used to prove the existence of any perfect thing is obviously defective. Guanilo thus tries to show that Anselm's reasoning leads to absurd consequences and must be rejected.

 ASK YOURSELF

5.57. We said earlier that there is more than one argument in Anselm's text. Does Guanilo's argument apply to only one of Anselm's arguments? If so, which one? Explain and justify your answer.

Anselm's Reply to Guanilo. In an essay five times longer than his original argument, Anselm responded to Guanilo's criticisms. The following is his reply to the island argument.

 From ANSELM: *Apologian*, Chapter 3

You say, it is as if one should suppose an island in the ocean, which surpasses all lands in its fertility, and which, because of the difficulty, or rather the impossibility, of discovering what does not exist, is called a lost island; and should say that there can be no doubt that this island truly exists in reality, for this reason, that one who hears it described easily understands what he hears.

Now I promise confidently that if any man shall devise anything existing either in reality or in concept alone (except that than which a greater cannot be conceived) to which he can adapt the sequence of my reasoning, I will discover that thing, and will give him his lost island, not to be lost again.

But it now appears that this being than which a greater is inconceivable cannot be conceived not to be, because it exists on so assured a ground of truth; for otherwise it would not exist at all.

Hence, if any one says that he conceives this being not to exist, I say that at the time when he conceives of this either he conceives of a being than which a greater is inconceivable, or he does not conceive at all. If he does not conceive, he does not conceive of the non-existence of that of which he does not conceive. But if he does conceive, he certainly conceives of a being which cannot be even conceived not to exist. For if it could be conceived not to exist, it could be conceived to have a beginning and an end. But this is impossible.

He, then, who conceives of this being conceives of a being which cannot be even conceived not to exist; but he who conceives of this being does not conceive that it does not exist; else he conceives what is inconceivable. The non-existence, then, of that than which a greater cannot be conceived is inconceivable.

 ASK YOURSELF

5.58. Yes or no: Would something that did come into existence or could go out of existence fail to be God *by definition*, just as something that was square would fail to be spherical by definition?

5.59. Yes or no: If something has neither beginning nor end, has neither come into existence nor can go out of existence, would you say that it was *eternal*?

5.60. Would eternal existence be better than ordinary existence in reality? Explain your answer.

5.61. At first, Anselm's reply to Guanilo appears to be a mere reiteration of *one* of his original arguments. Which version of the ontological argument is he restating (i.e., that in *Proslogion* Chapter 2 or in *Proslogion* Chapter 3)?

5.62. The upshot of Anselm's reply is that his argument cannot apply to any being whose nonexistence is conceivable (such as an island). Suppose that Guanilo should reply that the most perfect island is by definition one that not only exists, but also exists necessarily (since necessary existence is a perfection or good-making property). Can you answer on Anselm's behalf? Remember, whatever counts as a definition of a most perfect island must be a definition of an island. Think about what goes into the definition of island (or look it up in a dictionary). Think about what goes into the definition of God (or check a dictionary). Now compare the definitions, and see if you can spot something that favors Anselm's argument and works against Guanilo.

The ontological argument is still vigorously discussed by contemporary philosophers. It has been given many formulations, some of them quite technical. While few if any philosophers believe that it could be used to convert an atheist, it prompts reflection on a host of issues, including the nature of necessity, possibility, and other "modal" notions.

AVERROËS

Islamic civilization in the medieval period was culturally far ahead of the that in west, by almost every measure of what constitutes "culture" or "civilization." The flourishing of philosophy, medicine, and the practical and fine arts in such centers of Islamic civilization as Baghdad (Persia) or Cordova (Spain) was enabled in part by a generous mixing of Greek, Persian, Islamic, and even Christian scholarship in an atmosphere that was often remarkably tolerant of religious and intellectual diversity. Arab scholars did a great deal to keep intact or revive ancient learning. For example, by the time of Charlemagne (ca. 800 CE) Arab scholars were translating the works of Aristotle into their own language, whereas Aristotle's writings were still largely unknown in the West. This particular translation project had far-reaching consequences for the development of Western philosophy as well as for the flourishing of Arabic thought.

Many important Arabic and Jewish thinkers shared with Augustine and later Christian philosophers the belief that philosophical categories and methods could be employed in attempts to think through religious teachings. We have seen that in Augustine and Anselm faith has a certain priority in the relationship between reason (or philosophy) and faith, even though both thinkers were deeply immersed in philosophical learning and reasoning. But some religious believers resisted *any* intrusion of philosophy into the religious domain. These believers often doubted the intrinsic value of philosophy and saw "reason" as a potential enemy of "faith." One of them, al-Ghazali (1058–1111) wrote an attack on the philosophers titled *The Incoherence of Philosophy*. One of the philosophers, Averroës, whose work is excerpted in this section, replied with a work titled *The Incoherence of the Incoherence*. One can only imagine what the title of al-Ghazali's reply to *that* might have been!

Abu al-Walid Muhammad Ibn Ahmad Ibn Rushd, better known as Averroës (1126–1198) was a lawyer and physician who wrote so much commentary on Aristotle's works that he became known in the Latin West as simply "the commentator." Aristotle seemed to hold truths incompatible with Muslim teaching, such as that the world is eternal, that God has no knowledge of the world, and that individual souls cannot exist after death. Yet Aristotle represented the supreme development of philosophical reason, so on these matters at least there must be a real conflict between religion and reason, faith and philosophy.

 ASK YOURSELF

5.63. What teachings of Aristotle seem to conflict with religious teachings such as are found in the Old Testament or the Koran?

To some readers Averroës avoided outright conflict with religious faith in his Aristotelian philosophizing only by proposing that there are two types or levels of truth, so that what is true in philosophy could be false in religion and vice versa. Latin thinkers (i.e., medieval philosophers from Europe) who asserted similar Aristotelian ideas or endorsed any kind of double-truth doctrine were identified as "Averroists" and became the object of a series of condemnations issued by church authorities. Most notable was one Siger of Brabant (1235–1282), whose views were condemned in 1277 by the bishop of Paris. The views condemned included some held by Aquinas (discussed later in this chapter), who was in fact Siger's adversary on most matters. It is understandable that religious authorities would be made uncomfortable by the idea of a double standard of truth. For example, if reason tells me that the world has always existed and religion tells me that God created it, how can I honestly say that I accept *both* of these claims?

You may be able to see from the following selection that Averroës himself had rather subtle views on these matters, although it is possible to see how his remarks might have been taken in a way that excited worries among the orthodox. In fact Averroës, Siger, Aquinas, and many others were immersed in philosophical studies and were not about to dismiss the claims of philosophy in the way that some religious believers thought necessary.

 ASK YOURSELF

5.64. Who were the Latin Averroists, and why did they get in trouble?

5.65. Some people still think that there is no room for philosophy in the thought of a religious believer, or that, more generally, reason conflicts with faith. Name someone (it could be yourself) who you think might hold such a view.

The following selection is from a work that was not known to Aquinas or the Latin Averroists, but it contains ideas familiar from Averroës' best-known works, including the idea that the truth must be presented to different people in different forms, depending upon their intellectual capacity. Only the most intelligent should be exposed to the truth in philosophical form. One can imagine how the elitism of such ideas might have offended some "ordinary believers." The following selections are taken from *The Decisive Treatise Determining the Nature of the Connection between Religion and Philosophy*.

Chapter 2: Philosophy and Religion Belong Together

In this chapter Averroës tries to show that philosophical study is actually commanded by the Koran, or Qur'an (the Islamic scriptures). (Citations from the Qur'an are given in Roman and Arabic numerals in the following translation.)

Reason and Scripture. Averroës first shows how allegorical interpretation can be used to eliminate apparent conflicts between reason (philosophical or demonstrative knowledge) and the teachings of scripture.

 From AVERROËS: *The Decisive Treatise*

Demonstrative truth and scriptural truth cannot conflict.

Now since this religion is true and summons to the study which leads to knowledge of the Truth, we the Muslim community know definitely that demonstrative study does not lead to [conclusions] conflicting with what Scripture has given us; for truth does not oppose truth but accords with it and bears witness to it.

If the apparent meaning of Scripture conflicts with demonstrative conclusions it must be interpreted allegorically, i.e., metaphorically.

This being so, whenever demonstrative study leads to any manner of knowledge about any being, that being is inevitably either unmentioned or mentioned in Scripture. If it is unmentioned there is no contradiction, and it is in the same case as an act whose category is unmentioned, so that the lawyer has to infer it by reasoning from Scripture. If Scripture speaks about it, the apparent meaning of the words inevitably either accords or conflicts with the conclusions of demonstration about it. If this [apparent meaning] accords there is no argument. If it conflicts there is a call for allegorical interpretation of it. The meaning of "allegorical interpretation" is: extension of the significance of an expression from real to metaphorical significance, without forsaking therein the standard metaphorical practices of Arabic, such as calling a thing by the name of something resembling it or a cause or consequence or accompaniment of it, or other things such as are enumerated in accounts of the kinds of metaphorical speech.

 ASK YOURSELF

5.66. Averroës is saying that something that can be demonstrated to be true by reason (e.g., "2 + 2 = 4") must be consistent with scriptural truth. If you agree with this, does it have any bearing on your answer to question 5.65? Explain.

5.67. "2 + 2 = 4" is not mentioned in the Scriptures, so there can be no conflict there. But suppose some scientist thinks he can demonstrate that the variety of living things developed from something very primitive and undifferentiated through a long natural process (e.g., natural selection), even though the Scriptures teach that God created many different kinds of things almost instantaneously. What does Averroës recommend that we do in such a case?

If the lawyer can do this, the religious thinker certainly can. Indeed these allegorical interpretations always receive confirmation from the apparent meaning of other passages of Scripture.

Now if the lawyer does this in many decisions of religious law, with how much more right is it done by the possessor of demonstrative knowledge! For the lawyer has at his disposition only reasoning based on opinion, while he who would know [God] [has at his disposition] reasoning based on certainty. So we affirm definitely that whenever the conclusion of a demonstration is in conflict with the apparent meaning of Scripture, that apparent meaning admits of allegorical interpretation according to the rules for such interpretation in Arabic. This proposition is questioned by no Muslim and doubted by no believer. But its certainty is immensely increased for those who have had close dealings with this idea and put it to the test, and made it their aim to reconcile the assertions of intellect and tradition. Indeed we may say that whenever a statement in Scripture conflicts in its apparent meaning with a conclusion of demonstration, if Scripture is considered carefully, and the rest of its contents searched page by page, there will invariably be found among the expressions of Scripture something which in its apparent meaning bears witness to that allegorical interpretation or comes close to bearing witness.

 ASK YOURSELF

5.68. Is Averroës saying that whenever philosophy or reason conflict with Scripture that Scripture must then be construed as allegorical? Wouldn't that make religious truth secondary to, dependent upon, philosophical truth?

All Muslims accept the principle of allegorical interpretation; they only disagree about the extent of its application.

In the light of this idea the Muslims are unanimous in holding that it is not obligatory either to take all the expressions of Scripture in their apparent meaning or to extend them all from their apparent meaning by allegorical interpretation. They disagree [only] over which of them should and which should not be so interpreted: the Ash'arites for instance give an allegorical interpretation to the verse about God's directing Himself and the Tradition about His descent, while the Hanbalites take them in their apparent meaning.

The double meaning has been given to suit people's diverse intelligence. The apparent contradictions are meant to stimulate the learned to deeper study.

The reason why we have received a Scripture with both an apparent and an inner meaning lies in the diversity of people's natural capacities and the difference of their innate dispositions with regard to assent. . . . But it is recorded in Tradition that many of the first believers used to hold that Scripture has both an apparent and an inner meaning, and that the inner meaning ought not to be learned by anyone who is not a man of learning in this field and who is incapable of understanding it. Thus, for example, Bukhari reports a saying of 'Ali Ibn Ab-i Tdlib, may God be pleased with him, "Speak to people about what they know. Do you want God and His Prophet to be accused of lying?" Other examples of the same kind are reported about a group of early believers. So how can it possibly be conceived that a unanimous agreement can have been handed down to us about a single theoretical question, when we know definitely that not a single period has been without scholars who held that there are things in Scripture whose true meaning should not be learned by all people?

The situation is different in practical matters: everyone holds that the truth about these should be disclosed to all people alike, and to establish the occurrence of unanimity about them we consider it sufficient that the question [at issue] should have been widely discussed and that no report of controversy about it should have been handed down to us. This is enough to establish the occurrence of unanimity on matters of practice, but on matters of doctrine the case is different.

ASK YOURSELF

5.69. Fill in the blank: Averroës' distinction between the apparent and the inner meaning of Scripture is, he claims, traditional, but he argues that there has never been unanimity among scholars as to where the distinction should be applied, at least where we are dealing with theoretical matters. Where _____ matters are concerned unanimity is more important.

5.70. What do you suppose might be an example of each kind, that is, of theoretical matters and of the kind mentioned in the blank in the previous question?

Ghazali's charge of unbelief against Farabi and Ibn Sina, for asserting the world's eternity and God's ignorance of particulars and denying bodily resurrection, is only tentative, not definite.

You may object: "If we ought not to call a man an unbeliever for violating unanimity in cases of allegorical interpretation, because no unanimity is conceivable in such cases, what do you say about the Muslim philosophers, like Abu Nasr and Ibn Sina? For Abu Hamid called them both definitely unbelievers in the book of his known as *The Disintegration*, on three counts: their assertions of the pre-eternity of the world and that God the Exalted does not know particulars" (may He be Exalted far above that [ignorance]!), "and their allegorical interpretation of the passages concerning the resurrection of bodies and states of existence in the next life."

We answer: It is apparent from what he said on the subject that his calling them both unbelievers on these counts was not definite, since he made it clear in *The Book of Distinction* that calling people unbelievers for violating unanimity can only be tentative.

Such a charge cannot be definite, because there has never been a consensus against allegorical interpretation. The Qur'an itself indicates that it has inner meanings which it is the special function of the demonstrative class to understand.

Moreover, it is evident from what we have said that a unanimous agreement cannot be established in questions of this kind, because of the reports that many of the early believers of the first generation, as well as others, have said that there are allegorical interpretations which ought not to be expressed except to those who are qualified to receive allegories. These are "those who are well grounded in science"; for we prefer to place the stop after the words of God the Exalted "and those who are well grounded in science" (iii: 7), because if the scholars did not understand allegorical interpretation, there would be no superiority in their assent which would oblige them to a belief in Him not found among the unlearned. God has described them as those who believe in Him, and this can only be taken to refer to the belief which is based on demonstration; and this [belief] only occurs together with the science of allegorical interpretation. For the unlearned believers are those whose belief in Him is not based on demonstration; and if this belief which God has attributed to the scholars is peculiar to them, it must come through demonstration, and if it comes through demonstration it only occurs together with the science of allegorical interpretation. For God the Exalted has informed us that those [verses] have an allegorical interpretation which is the truth, and demonstration can only be of the truth. That being the case, it is not possible for general unanimity to be established about allegorical interpretations, which God has made peculiar to scholars. This is self-evident to any fair-minded person.

 ASK YOURSELF

5.71. Do you think that Averroës' appeal to the lack of unanimity among scholars respecting allegorical interpretations might leave it open to people to read the Scriptures in any way they want?

Some Examples of the Function of Allegorical Interpretation. Averroës applies the points just made about allegorical interpretation to two philosophical views that seem to conflict with Scripture: (1) the view that God does not know the world and (2) the view that the world or universe had no temporal beginning. Both views were thought by some to be held by Aristotle.

On the question of the world, the ancient philosophers agree with the Ash'arites that it is originated and coeval with time. The Peripatetics only disagree with the Ash'arites and the Platonists in holding that past time is infinite. This difference is insufficient to justify a charge of unbelief.

Concerning the question whether the world is pre-eternal or came into existence, the disagreement between the Ash'arite theologians and the ancient philosophers is in my view almost resolvable into a disagreement about naming, especially in the case of certain of the ancients. For they agree that there are three classes of beings: two extremes and one intermediate between the extremes. They agree also about naming the extremes; but they disagree about the intermediate class.

[1] One extreme is a being which is brought into existence from something other than itself and by something, i.e. by an efficient cause and from some matter; and it, i.e. its existence, is preceded by time. This is the status of bodies whose generation is apprehended by sense, e.g. the generation of water, air, earth, animals, plants, and so on. All alike, ancients and Ash'arites, agree in naming this class of beings "originated."

[2] The opposite extreme to this is a being which is not made, from or by anything and not preceded by time; and here too all members of both schools agree in naming it "preeternal." This being is apprehended by demonstration; it is God, Blessed and Exalted, Who is the Maker, Giver of being and Sustainer of the universe; may He be praised and His Power exalted!

[3] The class of being which is between these two extremes is that which is not made from anything and not preceded by time, but which is brought into existence by something, i.e. by an agent. This is the world as a whole. Now they all agree on the presence of these three characters in the world. For the theologians admit that time does not precede it, or rather this is a necessary consequence for them since time according to them is something which accompanies motion and bodies. They also agree with the ancients in the view that future time is infinite and likewise future being. They only disagree about past time and past being: the theologians hold that it is fi-

nite (this is the doctrine of Plato and his followers), while Aristotle and his school hold that it is infinite, as is the case with future time.

Thus it is clear that [3] this last being bears a resemblance both to [1] the being which is really generated and to [2] the pre-eternal Being. So those who are more impressed with its resemblance to the pre-eternal than its resemblance to the originated name it "pre-eternal," while those who are more impressed with its resemblance to the originated name it "originated." But in truth it is neither really originated nor really pre-eternal, since the really originated is necessarily perishable and the really pre-eternal has no cause. Some—Plato and his followers—name it "originated and coeval with time," because time according to them is finite in the past.

Thus the doctrines about the world are not so very far apart from each other that some of them should be called irreligious and others not. For this to happen, opinions must be divergent in the extreme, i.e. contraries such as the theologians suppose to exist on this question; i.e. [they hold] that the names "pre-eternity" and "coming into existence" as applied to the world as a whole are contraries. But it is now clear from what we have said that this is not the case.

 ASK YOURSELF

5.72. List the three kinds of being.

5.73. Pay special attention to what follows in order to answer this question. Which of the three kinds of being might be identified with the "deep" in the first verses of Genesis (the first book of the Old Testament, where it says that "the Spirit of God moved upon the face of the deep")?

Anyhow, the apparent meaning of Scripture is that there was a being and time before God created the present being and time. Thus the theologians' interpretation is allegorical and does not command unanimous agreement.

Over and above all this, these opinions about the world do not conform to the apparent meaning of Scripture. For if the apparent meaning of Scripture is searched, it will be evident from the verses which give us information about the bringing into existence of the world that its form really is originated, but that being itself and time extend continuously at both extremes, i.e. without interruption. Thus the words of God the Exalted, "He it is Who created the heavens and the earth in six days, and His throne was on the water" (xi:7), taken in their apparent meaning imply that there was a being before this present being, namely the throne and the water, and a time before this time, i.e. the one which is joined to the form of this being, namely the number of the movement of the celestial sphere. And the words of the Exalted, "On the day when the earth shall be changed into other than earth, and the heavens as well" (xiv:48) also in their apparent meaning imply that there will be a second being after this being. And the words of the Exalted, "Then He directed Himself towards the sky, and it was smoke" (xli:11), in their apparent meaning imply that the heavens were created from something.

Thus the theologians too in their statements about the world do not conform to the apparent meaning of Scripture but interpret it allegorically. For it is not stated in Scripture that God was existing with absolutely nothing else: a text to this effect is nowhere to be found. Then how is it conceivable that the theologians' allegorical interpretation of these verses could meet with unanimous agreement, when the apparent meaning of Scripture which we have mentioned about the existence of the world has been accepted by a school of philosophers! . . .

Different Ways of Reading for Different People. Averroës tries to show that whether a passage of Scripture should be interpreted allegorically or not depends in part upon who is reading, the learned or the unlearned.

With regard to things which by reason of their recondite character are only knowable by demonstration, God has been gracious to those of His servants who have no access to demonstration, on account of their natures, habits or lack of facilities for education: He has coined for them images and likenesses of these things, and summoned them to assent to those images, since it is possible for assent to those images to come about through the indications common to all men, i.e. the dialectical and rhetorical indications. This is the reason why Scripture is divided into apparent and inner meanings: the apparent meaning consists of those images which are coined to stand for those ideas, while the inner meaning is those ideas [themselves], which are clear only to the demonstrative class. These are the four or five classes of beings mentioned by Abu Hdmid in The Book of the Distinction.

But when it happens, as we said, that we know the thing itself by the three methods, we do not need to coin images of it, and it remains true in its apparent meaning, not admitting allegorical interpretation. If an apparent text of this kind refers to principles, anyone who interprets it allegorically is an unbeliever, e.g. anyone who thinks that there is no happiness or misery in the next life, and that the only purpose of this teaching is that men should be safeguarded from each other in their bodily and sensible lives, that it is but a practical device, and that man has no other goal than his sensible existence.

A twentieth-century writer on the philosophy of religion, R. B. Braithwaite, has argued that religious teachings are in fact simply stories that function to orient people ethically in their everyday lives by giving them pictures or models that will assist them in molding character; there is simply nothing more to religion than that. Just as a story about a fictional hero might inspire someone to be courageous, so religious stories inspire us to better lives. In his view there is no need that the stories be *true*, since they only function as "practical devices" (Averroës' words).

 ASK YOURSELF

5.74 What would Averroës say about such a view as Braithwaite's, and what would he call its author?

If this is established, it will have become clear to you from what we have said that there are [1] apparent texts of Scripture which it is not permitted to interpret allegorically; to do so on fundamentals is unbelief, on subordinate matters, heresy.

There are also [2] apparent texts which have to be interpreted allegorically by men of the demonstrative class; for such men to take them in their apparent meaning is unbelief, while for those who are not of the demonstrative class to interpret them allegorically and take them out of their apparent meaning is unbelief or heresy on their part.

 ASK YOURSELF

5.75 Do these last remarks sound like a doctrine of "double truth" to you? Justify your answer.

Of this [latter] class are the verse about God's directing Himself and the Tradition about His descent. That is why the Prophet, peace on him, said in the case of the black woman, when she told him that God was in the sky, "Free her, for she is a believer." This was because she was not of the demonstrative class; and the reason for his decision was that the class of people to whom assent comes only through the imagination, i.e. who do not assent to a thing except in so far as they can imagine it, find it difficult to assent to the existence of a being which is unrelated to any imaginable thing. This applies as well to those who understand from the relation stated merely [that God has] a place; these are people who have advanced a little in their thought beyond the position of the first class, [by rejecting] belief in corporeality. Thus the [proper] answer to them with regard to such passages is that they belong to the ambiguous texts, and that the stop is to be placed after the words of God the Exalted, "And no one knows the interpretation thereof except God" (iii:7). The demonstrative class, while agreeing unanimously that this class of text must be interpreted allegorically, may disagree about the interpretation, according to the level of each one's knowledge of demonstration.

There is also [3] a third class of Scriptural texts falling uncertainly between the other two classes, on which there is doubt. One group of those who devote themselves to theoretical study attachs them to the apparent texts which it is not permitted to interpret allegorically, others attach them to the texts with inner meanings which scholars are not permitted to take in their apparent meanings. This [divergence of opinions] is due to the difficulty and ambiguity of this class of text. Anyone who commits an error about this class is excused, I mean any scholar.

An Example: Texts about the Future Life. The texts about the future life fall into category [3] mentioned in the preceding passage, since demonstrative scholars do not agree whether to take them in their apparent meaning or interpret them allegorically. Either is permissible. But it is inexcusable to deny the fact of a future life altogether.

If it is asked, "Since it is clear that scriptural texts in this respect fall into three grades, to which of these three grades, according to you, do the descriptions of the future life and its states belong?" we reply: The position clearly is that this matter belongs to the class [3] about which there is disagreement. For we find a group of those who claim an affinity with demonstration saying that it is obligatory to take these passages in their apparent meaning, because there is no demonstration leading to the impossibility of the apparent meaning in them—this is the view of the Ash'arites; while another group of those who devote themselves to demonstration interpret these passages allegorically, and these people give the most diverse interpretations of them. In this class must be counted Abu Hdmid and many of the Safis; some of them combine the two interpretations of the passages, as Abu Hdmid does in some of his books.

 ASK YOURSELF

5.76. Do you think that belief in the resurrection should be taken literally or allegorically? If literally, what would the resurrection literally be like?

5.77 Do you think "literal" and "allegorical" are the only possibilities here?

Chapter 3: The Elite and Ordinary Believers

In Chapter 3 Averroës considers the following claim: "Philosophical interpretations of scripture should not be taught to the majority. The law provides other methods of instructing them."

Scripture Has a Twofold Purpose. Averroës argues for a distinction between practical and theoretical elements in scriptural teaching. The latter has to do with bringing people to true judgments, and there is more than one way to do that.

The purpose of Scripture is to teach true theoretical and practical science and right practice and attitudes.

You ought to know that the purpose of Scripture is simply to teach true science and right practice. True science is knowledge of God, Blessed and Exalted, and the other beings as they really are, and especially of noble beings, and knowledge of happiness and misery in the next life. Right practice consists in performing the acts which bring happiness and avoiding the acts which bring misery; and it is knowledge of these acts that is called "practical science." They fall into two divisions: (1) outward bodily acts; the science of these is called "jurisprudence"; and (2) acts of the soul such as gratitude, patience and other moral attitudes which the Law enjoins or forbids; the science of these is called "asceticism" or "the sciences of the future life." To these Abu Hdmid turned his attention in his book: as people had given up this sort [of act] and become immersed in the other sort, and as this sort [2] involves the greater fear of God, which is the cause of happiness, he called his book *The Revival of the Sciences of Religion*. But we have digressed from our subject, so let us return to it.

Scripture teaches concepts both directly and by symbols, and uses demonstrative, dialectical and rhetorical arguments. Dialectical and rhetorical arguments are prevalent because the main aim of Scripture is to teach the majority. In these arguments concepts are indicated directly or by symbols, in various combinations in premises and conclusion.

We say: The purpose of Scripture is to teach true science and right practice; and teaching is of two classes, [of] concepts and [of] judgments, as the logicians have shown. Now the methods available to men of [arriving at] judgments are three: demonstrative, dialectical and rhetorical; and the methods of forming concepts are two: either [conceiving] the object itself or [conceiving] a symbol of it. But not everyone has the natural ability to take in demonstrations, or [even] dialectical arguments, let alone demonstrative arguments which are so hard to learn and need so much time [even] for those who are qualified to learn them. Therefore, since it is the purpose of Scriptures simply to teach everyone, Scripture has to contain every method of [bringing about] judgments of assent and every method of forming concepts.

Dialectical methods of arriving at judgment are methods that involve simply accepting that something is true, and then inferring further truths from what is accepted. Rhetorical methods depend upon picturesque language, analogies, and the like. Demonstrative methods provide abstract proofs that are purportedly free of contestable assumptions.

 ASK YOURSELF

5.78. Which of these three methods would you say are considered acceptable or are practiced by Augustine and Anselm? Justify your answer with citations or references to your answers to questions in the section on Augustine.

5.79. Does Averroës agree with Augustine and Anselm? Justify your answer.

Now some of the methods of assent comprehend the majority of people, i.e. the occurrence of assent as a result of them [is comprehensive]: these are the rhetorical and the dialectical [methods]—and the rhetorical is more comprehensive than the dialectical. Another method is peculiar to a smaller number of people: this is the demonstrative. Therefore, since the primary purpose of Scripture is to take care of the majority (without neglecting to arouse the elite), the prevailing methods of expression in religion are the common methods by which the majority comes to form concepts and judgments.

 ASK YOURSELF

5.80. Essay question: Compare and contrast Augustine and Averroës on the relation of reason and faith (religion and philosophy).

MOSES MAIMONIDES

We have seen how a concern about possible conflicts between faith and philosophy led Averroës to a consideration of the nature of religious language, in his case the language of the Qur'an and the Old Testament Scripture. This same preoccupation with language is central to *The Guide for the Perplexed*, the great work of Jewish philosopher Moses Maimonides (1135–1204). Born in Cordova, Spain, Maimonides' family left that country when he was still a boy rather than give up their Jewish faith when a new and not-so-tolerant Muslim dynasty came to power. He spent most of his life in Egypt. Maimonides established an international reputation as a philosopher and theologian, and many came to him for help. Maimonides had an enormous influence upon various Christian thinkers, most notably Thomas Aquinas, whose proofs for the existence of God are very close to some proposed by Maimonides.

"In this work I address those who have studied philosophy . . . and who while firm in religious matters are perplexed and bewildered on account of the ambiguous and figurative expressions employed in the holy writings," says Maimonides in the introduction to *The Guide for the Perplexed.*

 ASK YOURSELF

5.81. Have you ever been perplexed as to how to understand some passage of the Bible or some religious teaching? Give an example if you have.

The following selections from *The Guide for the Perplexed* shows how Maimonides approached some of the problems posed for philosophical reason by religious language. Notice that he does not simply draw a rough distinction between "literal" and "metaphorical" uses of language. Rather, he shows that there are many different kinds of uses of terms, a great many of which could just as well be said to be literal. The important thing is to see how those uses differ. If you have ever been perplexed about how to take certain passages of the bible, Maimonides has some interesting suggestions in this "guide for the perplexed."

God and Biblical Language

Maimonides shows how the use of various Hebrew terms in the Torah or Old Testament does not imply that God has a body.

Chapter 3: Language about God and the Image of God. What is implied by various scriptural references to God? Maimonides discusses this matter as it arises in connection with Genesis 1, where it says, "Let us make man in our own image." (The Hebrew for "image" is *zelem.*)

 From MAIMONIDES: *The Guide for the Perplexed*

Some have been of opinion that by the Hebrew *zelem*, the shape and figure of a thing is to be understood, and this explanation led men to believe in the corporeality [of the Divine Being]: for they thought that the words "Let us make man in our *zelem*" (Gen. 1:26), implied that God had the form of a human being, i.e., that He had figure and shape, and that, consequently, He was corporeal. They adhered faithfully to this view, and thought that if they were to relinquish it they would eo ipso reject the truth of the Bible: and further, if they did not conceive God as having a body possessed of face and limbs, similar to their own in appearance, they would have to deny even the existence of God. The sole difference which they admitted, was that He excelled in greatness and splendor, and that His substance was not flesh and blood. Thus far went their conception of the greatness and glory of God. The incorporeality of the Divine Being, and His unity, in the true sense of the word—for there is no real unity without incorporeality—will be fully proved in the course of the present treatise (Part 2, chapter 1). In this chapter it is our sole intention to explain the meaning of the words *zelem* and *demut*. I hold that the Hebrew equivalent of "form" in the ordinary acceptation of the word, viz., the figure and shape of a thing, is *toar*. Thus we find "[And Joseph was] beautiful in *toar* ('form'), and beautiful in appearance" (Gen. 39:6): "What form (*toar*) is he of?" (I Sam. 28:14): "As the form (*toar*) of the children of a king" (Judges 8:18). It is also applied to form produced by human labor, as "He makes its form (*toar*) with a line," and "he makes its form (*toar*) with the compass" (Isa. 44:13). This term is not at all applicable to God. The term *zelem* on the other hand, signifies the specific form, viz., that which constitutes the essence of a thing, whereby the thing is what is; the reality of a thing in so far as it is that particular being. In man the "form" is that constituent which gives him human perception: and on account of this intellectual perception the term *zelem* is employed in the sentences "In the *zelem* of God he created him" (Gen. 1:27). It is therefore rightly said, "You despise their *zelem*" (Ps. 63:20); the "contempt" can only concern the soul—the specific form of man, not the properties and shape of his body. I am also of opinion that the reason why this term is used for "idols" may be found in the circumstance that they are worshipped on account of some idea represented by them, not on account of their figure and shape. For the same reason the term is used in the expression, "the forms (*zalme*) of your emerods" (I Sam. 6:5), for the chief object was the removal of the injury caused by the emerods, not a change of their shape. As, however, it must be admitted that the term *zelem* is employed in these two cases, viz. "the images of the "emerod" and "the idols" on account of the external shape, the term *zelem* is either a homonym [a term with two completely different and disconnected meanings] or a hybrid term, and would denote both the specific form and the outward shape, and similar properties relating to the dimensions and the shape of material bodies; and in the phrase, "Let us make man in our *zelem*" (Gen. 1:26), the term signifies "the specific form" of man, viz., his intellectual perception, and does not refer to his "figure" or "shape." Thus we have shown the difference between *zelem* and *toar*, and explained the meaning of *zelem*.

Demut is derived from the verb *damah*, "he is like." This term likewise denotes agreement with regard to some abstract relation: comp. "I am himself to the pelican of the wilderness" (Ps. 102:7); the author does not compare himself to the pelican in point of wings and feathers, but in point of sadness, "Nor any tree in the garden of God was like unto him in beauty" (Ezek. 31:8); the comparison refers to the idea of beauty. "Their poison is like the poison of a serpent" (Ps. 58:5); "He is like unto a lion" (Ps. 17:12); the resemblance indicated in these passages does not refer to the figure and shape, but to some abstract idea. In the same manner is used "the likeness of the throne" (Ezek. 1:26); the comparison is made with regard to greatness and glory, not, as many believe, with regard to its square form, its breadth, of the length of its legs: this explanation applies also to the phrase "the likeness of the hayyot" ("living creatures," Ezek. 1:13).

As man's distinction consists in a property which no other creature on earth possesses, viz., intellectual perception, in the exercise of which he does not employ his senses, nor move his hand or his foot, this perception has been compared—though only apparently, not in truth—to the Divine perception which requires no corporeal organ. On this account, i.e., on account of the Divine intellect with which man has been endowed, he is said to have been made in the form and likeness of the Almighty, but far from it be the notion that the Supreme Being is corporeal, having a material form.

ASK YOURSELF

5.82. Quote one passage from Genesis that uses the word *zelem* and explain why this passage might lead someone to believe that God must have a body.

5.83. Maimonides makes several points in the course of showing that people who infer that God must have a body from the use of *zelem* and *demut* are mistaken. Mention two of his points with respect to each of these terms (four in all).

5.84. According to Maimonides, the Scriptures are comparing man and God with respect to what characteristics, when they say that man is created in the "image" (*zelem* or *demut*) of God?

It might be thought that the Hebrew words *temunah* and *tabnit* have one and the same meaning, but this is not the case. *Tabnit*, derived from the verb *banah* (he built), signifies the build and construction of a thing—that is to say, its figure, whether square, round, triangular, or of any other shape. Comp. "the pattern (*tabnit*) of the Tabernacle and the pattern (*tabnit*) of all its vessels" (Exod. 25:9); "according to the pattern (*tabnit*) which you were shown upon the mount" (Exod. 25:40); "the form of any bird" (Deut. 4:17); "the form (*tabnit*) of a hand" (Ezek. 8:3); "the pattern (*tabnit*) of the porch" (I Chron. 28:II). In all these quotations it is the shape which is referred to. Therefore the Hebrew language never employs the word *tabnit* in speaking of the qualities of God Almighty.

ASK YOURSELF

5.85. Maimonides is claiming that if the Scriptures had meant to suggest that God has a shape, it would have used the word "_____."

The term *temunah*, on the other hand, is used in the Bible in three different senses. It signifies, first, the outlines of things which are perceived by our bodily senses, i.e., their shape and form; as, e.g., "And you make an image the form (*temunat*) of some likeness" (Deut. 4:16); "for you saw no likeness" (*temunah*) (Deut. 4:15). Secondly, the forms of our imagination, i.e., the impressions retained in imagination when the objects have ceased to affect our senses. In this sense it is used in the passage which begins "In thoughts from the visions of the night" (Job 4:13), and which concludes "it remained but I could not recognize its sight, only an image—*temunah*—was before my eyes," i.e., an image which presented itself to my sight during sleep. Thirdly, the true form of an object, which is perceived only by the intellect: and it is in this third signification that the term is applied to God. The words "And the similitude of the Lord shall he behold" (Num. 12:8) therefore mean " he shall comprehend the true essence of the Lord."

Chapter 4: Seeing and Seeing God. This chapter continues the theme of Chapter 3, this time with a focus on terms that might seem to imply that God has a body since God is "visible." In various places the Torah speaks of people "seeing" God. What does this imply?

The three verbs *raah*, *hibbit*, and *hazah*, which denote "he perceived with the eye," are also used figuratively in the sense of intellectual perception. As regards the first of these verbs this is well known, e.g., "And he looked (*va-yar*) and beheld a well in the field" (Gen. 29:2): here it signifies ocular perception; "yea, my heart has seen (*raah*) much of wisdom and of knowledge" (Eccles. 1:16); in this passage it refers to the intellectual perception.

In this figurative sense the verb is to be understood, when applied to God; e.g., "I saw (*raiti*) the Lord" (I Kings 22:19); "And the Lord appeared (*va-yera*) unto him" (Gen. 18:1); "And God saw (*va-yar*) that it was good" (Gen. 1:10); "I beseech you, show me (*hareni*) your glory" (Exod. 33:18); "And they saw (*va-yiru*) the God of Israel" (Exod. 24:10). All these instances refer to intellectual perception, and by no means to perception with the eye as in its literal meaning: for, on the one hand, the eye can only perceive a corporeal object, and in connection with it certain accidents, as color, shape, etc.; and, on the other hand, God does not perceive by means of a corporeal organ, as will be explained.

In the same manner the Hebrew *hibbit* signifies "he viewed" with the eye; comp. "Look (*tabbit*) not behind you" (Gen. 19:26); "And if one look (*ve-nibbat*) unto the land" (Isa. 5:30); and figuratively, "to view and observe" with the intellect, "to contemplate" a thing till it be understood. In this sense the verb is used in passages like the following: "He has not beheld (*hibbit*) iniquity in Jacob" (Num. 23:21); for "iniquity" cannot be seen with the eye. The words, "And the looked (*ve-hibbitu*) after Moses" (Exod. 33:8)—in addition to the literal understanding of the phrase—were explained by our Sages in a figurative sense. According to them, these words mean that the Israelites examined and criticized the actions and sayings of Moses. Compare also "Contemplate (*habbet*), I pray you, the heaven" (Gen. 15:5); for this took place in a prophetic vision. This verb, when applied to God, is employed in this figurative sense; e.g., "to look (*me-habbit*) upon God" (Exod. 3:6); "And the similitude of the Lord shall he behold" (*yabbit*) (Num. 12:8); "And you cannot look (*habbet*) on iniquity" (Hab. 1:13).

The same explanation applies to *hazah*. It denotes to view with the eye, as: "And let our eye look (*ve-tahaz*) upon Zion" (Mic. 4:11); and also figuratively, to perceive mentally: "which he saw (*hazah*) concerning Judah and Jerusalem" (Isa. 1:1); "The word of the Lord came unto Abraham in a vision" (*mahazeh*) (Gen. 15:1): in this sense *hazah* is used in the phrase, "Also they saw (*va-yehezu*) God" (Exod. 24:11). Note this well.

 ASK YOURSELF

5.86. Certain things are said to be seen that do not have shape or form or physical being. For example, when God sees someone's sin or iniquity, he does not see a physical thing with a certain shape. Give three other examples from those given in the preceding passage and explain what point Maimonides is making with these examples.

Chapter 5: The Prerequisites to Philosophical Understanding and to True Seeing of God.
Here Maimonides argues that those who would like to see God physically are infected
by a kind of bodily craving that is opposed to true spiritual seeing. Understanding
the language of Scripture may require more than linguistic knowledge.

When the chief of philosophers [Aristotle] was about to inquire into some very profound subjects, and to establish his theory by proofs, he commenced his treatise with
an apology, and requested the reader to attribute the author's inquiries not to presumption, vanity, egotism, or arrogance, as though he were interfering with things of
which he had no knowledge, but rather to his zeal and his desire to discover and establish true doctrines, as far as lay in human power. We take the same position, and
think that a man, when he commences to speculate, ought not to embark at once on
a subject so vast and important; he should previously adapt himself to the study of
the several branches of science and knowledge, should most thoroughly refine his
moral character and subdue his passions and desires, the offspring of his imagination;
when, in addition, he has obtained a knowledge of the true fundamental propositions,
a comprehension of the several methods of inference and proof, and the capacity of
guarding against fallacies, then he may approach the investigation of this subject. He
must, however, not decide any question by the first idea that suggests itself to his
mind, or at once direct his thoughts and force them to obtain a knowledge of the Creator, but he must wait modestly and patiently, and advance step by step.

In this sense we must understand the words, "And Moses hid his face, for he was
afraid to look upon God" (Exod. 3:6), though retaining also the literal meaning of the
passage, that Moses was afraid to gaze at the light which appeared to his eye; but it
must on no account be assumed that the Being which is exalted far above every imperfection can be perceived by the eye. This act of Moses was highly commended by
God, who bestowed on him a well deserved portion of His goodness, as it is said:
"And the similitude of the Lord shall he behold" (Num. 12:8). This, say our Sages,
was the reward for having previously hidden his face, lest he should gaze at the Eternal. (Talm. B. Berakot Fa.) [A reference to the Jewish Talmud]

But "the nobles of the Children of Israel" were impetuous, and allowed their
thoughts to go unrestrained: what they perceived was but imperfect. Therefore it is
said of them, "And they saw the God of Israel, and there was under his feet," etc.
(Exod. 24:10); and not merely, "and they saw the God of Israel"; the purpose of the
whole passage is to criticize their act of seeing and not to describe it. They are blamed
for the nature of their perception, which was to a certain extent corporeal—a result
which necessarily followed, from the fact that they ventured too far before being perfectly prepared. They deserved to perish, but at the intercession of Moses this fate was
averted by God for the time. They were afterwards burnt at Taberah, except Nadab
and Abihu, who were burnt in the Tabernacle of the congregation, according to what
is stated by authentic tradition. (Midr. Rabba ad locum.) [A reference to the "midrash"]

If such was the case with them, how much more is it incumbent on us who are inferior, and on those who are below us, to persevere in perfecting our knowledge of
the elements, and in rightly understanding the preliminaries which purify the mind
from the defilement of error; then we may enter the holy and divine camp in order
to gaze: as the Bible says, "And let the priests also, which come near to the Lord, sanc-

tify themselves, lest the Lord break forth upon them" (Exod. 19:22). Solomon, also, has cautioned all who endeavor to attain this high degree of knowledge in the following figurative terms, "Keep your foot when you go to the house of God" (Eccles. 4:17).

I will now return to complete what I commenced to explain. The nobles of the Children of Israel, besides erring in their perception, were, through this cause, also misled in their actions; for in consequence of their confused perception, they gave way to bodily cravings. This is meant by the words, "Also they saw God and did eat and drink" (Exod. 24:11). The principal part of that passage, viz., "And there was under his feet as it were a paved work of a sapphire stone" (Exod. 24:10), will be further explained in the course of the present treatise (Chapter 28). All we here intend to say is, that wherever in a similar connection any one of the three verbs mentioned above occurs, it has reference to intellectual perception, not to the sensation of sight by the eye; for God is not a being to be perceived by the eye.

It will do no harm, however, if those who are unable to comprehend what we here endeavor to explain should refer all the words in question to sensuous perception, to seeing lights created [for the purpose], angels, or similar beings.

 ASK YOURSELF

5.87. Do you agree that in a study of religious and philosophical matters good moral character might be required? Why or why not?

5.88. Maimonides argues that those who insist upon the idea that one can "see" God in the sense of "ocular perception" may be at fault in more than an intellectual sense. How does he argue that?

THOMAS AQUINAS

The twelfth and thirteenth centuries were a time of great philosophical ferment throughout much of Europe and the Muslim world. Muslim thinkers such as Avicenna and al Farabi and Christian thinkers such as Abelard, Robert Grosseteste, and Albert the Great brought philosophical and theological debate to a level of high sophistication. But surely the supreme figure from this period was one of Albert the Great's pupils who remarkably was sometimes called "the dumb Ox," Thomas Aquinas. One of the clearest things about Aquinas is that he was by no means "dumb" in any sense of the word.

Aquinas was a Dominican friar (a kind of itinerant monk); the Dominicans became heavily involved in educational endeavors in the universities that began to arise and flourish in the twelfth and thirteenth centuries. That suited Aquinas very well, and he spent much of his life, which spans almost exactly the middle half of the thirteenth century (1225–1274), teaching in the university in Paris. That university was the center of intellectual life in thirteenth-century Europe. As already noted, Aquinas was familiar with and deeply influenced by the writings of both Averroës and Maimonides. Since neither were Christians it might be expected that such interests would get him in some trouble with church authorities, and indeed that was the case. Some of his ideas were included in the bishop of Paris's condemnation of 1277 (see the introduction to the section on Averroës earlier in this chapter).

Aquinas was very heavy, which, it seems, a monk should not be, but he was in fact very devout, the author of some famous hymns still sung in churches, and ultimately very modest. At the end of his life he remarked that everything he had written was nothing but "straw."

The Existence of God

Unlike Augustine and Anselm, Aquinas argued that some, but not all, basic religious truths, such as that God exists, can be proven without faith and through reason alone. The following selections are from *Summa Theologica* (1a, Q.2, "The Existence of God"). This work is written in a medieval literary form, known as *quaestio*, which explores issues using a series of questions, objections, and replies. This form reflects the atmosphere of debate between faculty members and between students and faculty members that was at the center of university education. (Imagine that tomorrow in class your task will be to debate the professor on some philosophical question!)

Whether the Existence of God is Self-Evident? In the first article in this section Aquinas considers whether knowledge of God is naturally implanted in all of us, that is, is "self evident." He presents some arguments for the claim that it is self-evident (Objections 1–3), states his own view, and replies to the objections.

 ASK YOURSELF

5.89. If God's existence were self-evident, would it be a waste of time to try to find a "proof" of it?

 From AQUINAS: *Summa Theologica*

Objection 1. It seems that the existence of God is self-evident. Now those things are said to be self-evident to us the knowledge of which is naturally implanted in us, as we can see in regard to first principles. But as Damascene says (De Fide Orth. i, 1, 3), "the knowledge of God is naturally implanted in all." Therefore the existence of God is self-evident.

Objection 2. Further, those things are said to be self-evident which are known as soon as the terms are known, which the Philosopher (1 Poster. iii) says is true of the first principles of demonstration. Thus, when the nature of a whole and of a part is known, it is at once recognized that every whole is greater than its part. But as soon as the signification of the word "God" is understood, it is at once seen that God exists. For by this word is signified that thing than which nothing greater can be conceived. But that which exists actually and mentally is greater than that which exists only mentally. Therefore, since as soon as the word "God" is understood it exists mentally, it also follows that it exists actually. Therefore the proposition "God exists" is self-evident.

Objection 3. Further, the existence of truth is self-evident. For whoever denies the existence of truth grants that truth does not exist: and, if truth does not exist, then the proposition "Truth does not exist" is true: and if there is anything true, there must be truth. But God is truth itself: "I am the way, the truth, and the life" (Jn. 14:6) Therefore "God exists" is self-evident.

On the contrary, no one can mentally admit the opposite of what is self-evident, as the Philosopher (Metaph. iv, lect. vi) states concerning the first principles of demonstration. But the opposite of the proposition "God is" can be mentally admitted: "The fool said in his heart, There is no God" (Ps. 52:1). Therefore, that God exists is not self-evident.

I answer that, A thing can be self-evident in either of two ways: on the one hand, self-evident in itself, though not to us; on the other, self-evident in itself, and to us. A proposition is self-evident because the predicate is included in the essence of the subject, as "Man is an animal," for animal is contained in the essence of man. If, therefore the essence of the predicate and subject be known to all, the proposition will be self-evident to all; as is clear with regard to the first principles of demonstration, the terms of which are common things that no one is ignorant of, such as being and non-being, whole and part, and such like. If, however, there are some to whom the essence of the predicate and subject is unknown, the proposition will be self-evident in itself, but not to those who do not know the meaning of the predicate and subject of the proposition. Therefore, it happens, as Boethius says (Hebdom., the title of which is: "Whether all that is, is good"), "that there are some mental concepts self-evident only to the learned, as that incorporeal substances are not in space." Therefore I say that this proposition, "God exists," of itself is self-evident, for the predicate is the same as the subject, because God is His own existence as will be hereafter shown (3, 4). Now because we do not know the essence of God, the proposition is not self-evident to us; but needs to be demonstrated by things that are more known to us, though less known in their nature—namely, by effects.

Reply to Objection 1. To know that God exists in a general and confused way is implanted in us by nature, inasmuch as God is man's beatitude. For man naturally desires happiness, and what is naturally desired by man must be naturally known to him. This, however, is not to know absolutely that God exists; just as to know that someone is approaching is not the same as to know that Peter is approaching, even though it is Peter who is approaching; for many there are who imagine that man's perfect good which is happiness, consists in riches, and others in pleasures, and others in something else.

Reply to Objection 2. Perhaps not everyone who hears this word "God" understands it to signify something than which nothing greater can be thought, seeing that some have believed God to be a body. Yet, granted that everyone understands that by this word "God" is signified something than which nothing greater can be thought, nevertheless, it does not therefore follow that he understands that what the word signifies exists actually, but only that it exists mentally. Nor can it be argued that it actually exists, unless it be admitted that there actually exists something than which nothing greater can be thought; and this precisely is not admitted by those who hold that God does not exist.

Reply to Objection 3. The existence of truth in general is self-evident but the existence of a Primal Truth is not self-evident to us.

In answering this issue, Aquinas argues that there are two ways that something can be self-evident: self-evident in itself and self-evident to us.

ASK YOURSELF

5.90. What is the difference between these two kinds of self-evidence, and in which of these two ways is God's existence self-evident?

In Objection 2, Aquinas presents what appears to be a version of Anselm's ontological argument as an example of an argument maintaining that God's existence is self-evident.

 ASK YOURSELF

5.91. What is Aquinas's reply to Anselm's argument?

Whether It Can Be Demonstrated That God Exists? Aquinas continues with his second article discussing faith, reason, and the existence of God.

Objection 1. It seems that the existence of God cannot be demonstrated. For it is an article of faith that God exists. But what is of faith cannot be demonstrated, because a demonstration produces scientific knowledge; whereas faith is of the unseen (Heb. 11:1). Therefore it cannot be demonstrated that God exists.

Objection 2. Further, the essence is the middle term of demonstration. But we cannot know in what God's essence consists, but solely in what it does not consist; as Damascene says (De Fide Orth. i, 4). Therefore we cannot demonstrate that God exists.

Objection 3. Further, if the existence of God were demonstrated, this could only be from His effects. But His effects are not proportionate to Him, since He is infinite and His effects are finite; and between the finite and infinite there is no proportion. Therefore, since a cause cannot be demonstrated by an effect not proportionate to it, it seems that the existence of God cannot be demonstrated.

On the contrary, the Apostle says: "The invisible things of Him are clearly seen, being understood by the things that are made" (Rm. 1:20). But this would not be unless the existence of God could be demonstrated through the things that are made; for the first thing we must know of anything is whether it exists.

I answer that, demonstration can be made in two ways: One is through the cause, and is called "a priori," and this is to argue from what is prior absolutely. The other is through the effect, and is called a demonstration "a posteriori"; this is to argue from what is prior relatively only to us. When an effect is better known to us than its cause, from the effect we proceed to the knowledge of the cause. And from every effect the existence of its proper cause can be demonstrated, so long as its effects are better known to us; because since every effect depends upon its cause, if the effect exists, the cause must pre-exist. Hence the existence of God, in so far as it is not self-evident to us, can be demonstrated from those of His effects which are known to us.

Reply to Objection 1. The existence of God and other like truths about God, which can be known by natural reason, are not articles of faith, but are preambles to the articles; for faith presupposes natural knowledge, even as grace presupposes nature, and perfection supposes something that can be perfected. Nevertheless, there is nothing to prevent a man, who cannot grasp a proof, accepting, as a matter of faith, something which in itself is capable of being scientifically known and demonstrated.

Reply to Objection 2. When the existence of a cause is demonstrated from an effect, this effect takes the place of the definition of the cause in proof of the cause's existence. This is especially the case in regard to God, because, in order to prove the existence of anything, it is necessary to accept as a middle term the meaning of the word, and not its essence, for the question of its essence follows on the question of its existence. Now the names given to God are derived from His effects; consequently, in demonstrating the existence of God from His effects, we may take for the middle term the meaning of the word "God."

Reply to Objection 3. From effects not proportionate to the cause no perfect knowledge of that cause can be obtained. Yet from every effect the existence of the cause can be clearly demonstrated, and so we can demonstrate the existence of God from His effects; though from them we cannot perfectly know God as He is in His essence.

The first objection to this article maintains that God's existence is a matter of faith, and not something which can be demonstrated.

 ASK YOURSELF

5.92. What is Aquinas's reply to this objection?

5.93. Aquinas maintains that there are two kinds of demonstration, the second of which applies to proof of God. In what way can God's existence be demonstrated?

Whether God Exists. Objections to Belief in the Existence of God. In the third and final article, Aquinas begins by presenting two arguments for atheism. He concludes this article by attacking the two opening arguments for atheism.

Objection 1. It seems that God does not exist; because if one of two contraries be infinite, the other would be altogether destroyed. But the word "God" means that He is infinite goodness. If, therefore, God existed, there would be no evil discoverable; but there is evil in the world. Therefore God does not exist.

Objection 2. Further, it is superfluous to suppose that what can be accounted for by a few principles has been produced by many. But it seems that everything we see in the world can be accounted for by other principles, supposing God did not exist. For all natural things can be reduced to one principle which is nature; and all voluntary things can be reduced to one principle which is human reason, or will. Therefore there is no need to suppose God's existence.

We place Aquinas's replies to these objections and a discussion of them here instead of at the end of the *quaestio*, as Aquinas himself did.

Reply to Objection 1. As Augustine says (Enchiridion xi): "Since God is the highest good, He would not allow any evil to exist in His works, unless His omnipotence and goodness were such as to bring good even out of evil." This is part of the infinite goodness of God, that He should allow evil to exist, and out of it produce good.

Reply to Objection 2. Since nature works for a determinate end under the direction of a higher agent, whatever is done by nature must needs be traced back to God, as to its first cause. So also whatever is done voluntarily must also be traced back to some higher cause other than human reason or will, since these can change or fail; for all things that are changeable and capable of defect must be traced back to an immovable and self-necessary first principle, as was shown in the body of the Article.

The first argument for atheism presented at the outset is the classic *problem of evil*, which maintains that the existence of God is incompatible with the presence of evil (or suffering) in the world. For further discussion of this problem, see Augustine's discussion of free will earlier in this chapter.

 ASK YOURSELF

5.94. What is Aquinas's reply to the problem of evil?

The second argument for atheism presented at the outset may be referred to as *the argument from parsimony*. The argument can be reconstructed as follows:

  a. All aspects of the universe can be explained by two principles: nature and human will.

  b. The rule of parsimony states that we should adopt the smallest number of principles needed.

  c. Therefore, there is no need to suppose God's existence as a further principle of explanation.

 ASK YOURSELF

5.95. What is Aquinas's reply to the criticism based on the principle of parsimony?

The *quaestio* continues as follows.

Proofs for the Existence of God: Cosmological Arguments. Aquinas presents his famous "five ways" or proofs of God's existence. Cosmological arguments start from some observable fact about the universe (the "cosmos") and reason to the existence of God. The first three of Aquinas's five "ways" are cosmological arguments.

On the contrary, it is said in the person of God: "I am Who am" (Ex. 3:14).

I answer that, the existence of God can be proved in five ways.

The first and more manifest way is the argument from motion. It is certain, and evident to our senses, that in the world some things are in motion. Now whatever is in motion is put in motion by another, for nothing can be in motion except it is in potentiality to that towards which it is in motion; whereas a thing moves inasmuch as it is in act. For motion is nothing else than the reduction of something from potentiality to actuality. But nothing can be reduced from potentiality to actuality, except by something in a state of actuality. Thus that which is actually hot, as fire, makes wood, which is potentially hot, to be actually hot, and thereby moves and changes it.

Another example of reduction from potentiality to actuality would be a student who is potentially an A student actually getting an A at the end of the semester. That would be an example of a "motion" in Aquinas's sense.

 ASK YOURSELF

5.96. Give an example of your own of something being reduced from potentiality to actuality.

Now it is not possible that the same thing should be at once in actuality and potentiality in the same respect, but only in different respects. For what is actually hot cannot simultaneously be potentially hot; but it is simultaneously potentially cold. It is therefore impossible that in the same respect and in the same way a thing should be both mover and moved, i.e. that it should move itself. Therefore, whatever is in motion must be put in motion by another. If that by which it is put in motion be itself put in motion, then this also must needs be put in motion by another, and that by another again. But this cannot go on to infinity, because then there would be no first mover, and, consequently, no other mover; seeing that subsequent movers move only inasmuch as they are put in motion by the first mover; as the staff moves only because it is put in motion by the hand. Therefore it is necessary to arrive at a first mover, put in motion by no other; and this everyone understands to be God.

The argument from motion can be summarized as follows: Some things are in motion; if X is in motion, then X must have been put in motion by Y. If Y is in motion, then it, too, must have been put in motion by some Z. But there cannot be an infinite chain of motion producers. Hence there must be some first unmoved mover (and that unmoved mover would be God).

The second way is from the nature of the efficient cause. In the world of sense we find there is an order of efficient causes. There is no case known (neither is it, indeed, possible) in which a thing is found to be the efficient cause of itself; for so it would be prior to itself, which is impossible. Now in efficient causes it is not possible to go on to infinity, because in all efficient causes following in order, the first is the cause of the intermediate cause, and the intermediate is the cause of the ultimate cause, whether the intermediate cause be several, or only one. Now to take away the cause is to take away the effect. Therefore, if there be no first cause among efficient causes, there will be no ultimate, nor any intermediate cause. But if in efficient causes it is possible to go on to infinity, there will be no first efficient cause, neither will there be an ultimate effect, nor any intermediate efficient causes; all of which is plainly false. Therefore it is necessary to admit a first efficient cause, to which everyone gives the name of God.

The argument from efficient cause is as follows: Some things have been caused to exist by something else. If X has been caused to exist, then X must have been caused by Y. If Y has been caused to exist, then it too must have been caused by some Z. But there cannot be an infinite chain of efficient causes. Hence there is a first cause, which we call God. The second of the first three ways, from efficient cause, is the most famous.

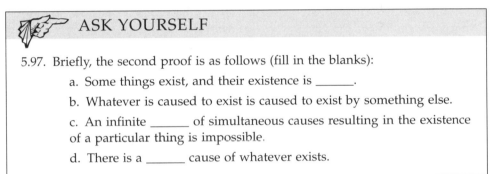

ASK YOURSELF

5.97. Briefly, the second proof is as follows (fill in the blanks):

  a. Some things exist, and their existence is _____.

  b. Whatever is caused to exist is caused to exist by something else.

  c. An infinite _____ of simultaneous causes resulting in the existence of a particular thing is impossible.

  d. There is a _____ cause of whatever exists.

Premise (a) is obviously true: The world is full of causes and effects. Premise (b) is a fact we all assume: If you have an effect, then you must have a cause, the converse of which states, if you do not have a cause, then you do not have an effect. Premise (c) states that there cannot be an infinite regress of causes. Aquinas's defense for this premise in this argument is that without a first cause, there would be no ultimate effect. Unfortunately, this is not a particularly clear explanation.

The explanation rests on a distinction Aquinas makes between two kinds of efficient causes: an essential cause (*per se*) and an accidental cause (*per accidens*). The standard example of a cause *per se* is a stone which is moved by a stick, which is moved by one's hand, which is moved by one's arm. This example exhibits three features that denote the presence of causes *per se*: (1) the stone, stick, hand, and arm have one property in common, namely, motion; (2) the motion of all four objects is simultaneous; and (3) the existence and motion of the first three objects are directly required to produce the motion of the stone. In contrast to this, the standard example of a cause *per accidens* is Abraham begetting Isaac who, in turn, begets Jacob. Here, neither Abraham's immediate existence nor his reproductive activity is required in the producing his grandson Jacob. This example lacks the three features of causes *per se*, and, for this reason, denotes the presence of causes *per accidens*.

Returning to Aquinas's argument from efficient cause, Aquinas implies that the chain of causes in question (i.e., X, which is caused by Y, which is caused by Z) be causes *per se*. If he tried to argue for the existence of a first cause on the basis of a chain of causes *per accidens*, it simply would not work, since it is possible for a series of causes *per accidens* to be infinite. A chain of causes *per se*, on the other hand, cannot regress infinitely. Since, using the earlier example, the hand and stick merely transfer motion to the stone, an infinite regress of causes would eliminate the possibility of *explaining* the motion that is being transferred ultimately to the stone. Without an initial cause of the motion, there would be no motion to transfer. There is more than one obscurity in Aquinas's account, but at least it should be clear that his argument does not depend upon the purported impossibility of an infinite temporal series.

Given, then, that the type of cause Aquinas is dealing with in premise (a) is an efficient cause *per se*, premise (c) ("there cannot be an infinite chain of efficient causes") seems more plausible. It is possible, incidentally, to see Aquinas's Averroistic tendencies in this discussion, for one of the condemned Aristotelian teachings that Averroës did not deny firmly enough for some religious believers was the teaching that the world had no beginning. Aquinas seems to agree with Aristotle that philosophy cannot prove whether or not the world has a beginning in time. There *could* be an infinite chain of causes *per accidens*, that is, no beginning in time to all the causal activities that make up the universe.

 ASK YOURSELF

5.98. State in your own words Aquinas's second way. Make sure you employ the distinction between causes *per se* and causes *per accidens*.

The third way is taken from possibility and necessity, the fourth from the gradation to be found in things. The fourth way shows the influence of the idea of the great chain of being, discussed earlier, and is in effect an argument used by Augustine. It consists of the claim that there must be a highest degree of everything, which is a way of saying that a logically complete system of reality must include a perfect God. We will omit these two ways or proofs in this discussion.

The Argument from Design (the Teleological Argument). This argument is also cosmological but is distinctive in ways that warrant giving it separate treatment. Some versions of this argument are still much discussed.

The fifth way is taken from the governance of the world. We see that things which lack intelligence, such as natural bodies, act for an end, and this is evident from their acting always, or nearly always, in the same way, so as to obtain the best result. Hence it is plain that not fortuitously, but designedly, do they achieve their end. Now whatever lacks intelligence cannot move towards an end, unless it be directed by some being endowed with knowledge and intelligence; as the arrow is shot to its mark by the archer. Therefore some intelligent being exists by whom all natural things are directed to their end; and this being we call God.

The argument from design is as follows: Objects without intelligence act toward some end (for example, a tree grows and reproduces its own kind). Moving toward an end or acting purposively requires intelligence. If X is unintelligent, yet acts for a some end, then X must be guided to this end by something which is intelligent. And this "something" is God.

ASK YOURSELF

5.99. One modern scientific theory may seem to explain the sorts of things Aquinas has in mind in the fifth way without assuming the existence of a divine designer. What is that theory, and how would it explain the sorts of things Aquinas thinks require a divine designer? (Remember, the "fifth way" depends upon the fact that things in nature, such as plants and animals, act, grow, develop, in ways that are best for them or help to ensure their flourishing and survival.)

5.100. Essay question: If we grant that Aquinas has established that there is some sort of first cause, or supreme designer, do we have to grant that the being in question is *God*? Would it have to have *all* of the various traits we think something must have to be God? What are some of those traits?

Natural Law

Aquinas is one of the strongest and most influential defenders of the view that morality is grounded in natural laws that exist independently of human convention.

Natural Law and Laws of Nature. Following Aristotle Aquinas holds that things in nature are guided by a built-in purpose. For example, the purpose of rain is to nourish plants. He argues further that the laws of nature describe the way things *ought* to be. Drought, for example, is fundamentally wrong—and constitutes a natural evil—since it is contrary to the natural purpose of rain. (If this seems like an odd view of a law of nature, see the following discussion.) Like other natural things, humans too have purposes which are reflected in other laws of nature. To name a few, we are rational, we are social, and we are naturally inclined to produce offspring. These natural laws govern the way things ought to be and thus how we ought to behave. So irrational behavior, asocial behavior, and sexual behavior that is completely disconnected from a desire for procreation would be contrary to natural law. Aquinas describes these morally binding natural laws most fully in his "Treatise on Law" (*Summa Theologica*, 1a2ae, Questions 90–144). The following selections are from 1a–2ae, Question 91, Articles 1–4; Question 93, Articles 1–3; Question 94, Articles 4–5.

ASK YOURSELF

5.101. Does it seem to you that in Aquinas's view the law of gravitation would be one of God's laws, and thus not so different from one of the ten commandments? Explain.

The Various Kinds of Law. There are four kinds of law: eternal law, natural law, human law, and divine law. Eternal law, the broadest type of law, is the unchanging divine governance over the universe. This covers the "laws of nature" and both *general* moral rules of conduct, such as "murder is wrong," and *particular* cases, such as "people should not poison their rich aunts." Natural law is a subset of eternal law that is obtainable by humans through reflection, but covers only *general* rules of conduct. Human law is an interpolation of natural law that is extended to *particular* cases. Finally, divine law (contained in the Bible) is a specially revealed subset of the eternal law that is meant to check possible errors in our attempts to both obtain natural law through reflection and derive more particular human laws. All moral laws, whether discovered through reflection, interpolated by legislators, or found in the Scriptures, are ultimately grounded in an objective, universal, and unchanging eternal law. In Question 91 Aquinas argues that, indeed, these four kinds of laws exist.

 ASK YOURSELF

5.102. What are the four kinds of law?

Is There an Eternal Law? Aquinas begins by trying to show that there must be an eternal law governing the entire universe.

 From AQUINAS: *Summa Theologica*

. . . a law is nothing else but a dictate of practical reason emanating from the ruler who governs a perfect community. Now it is evident, granted that the world is ruled by Divine Providence, as was stated in the I, 22, A1,2, that the whole community of the universe is governed by Divine Reason. Wherefore the very Idea of the government of things in God the Ruler of the universe, has the nature of a law. And since the Divine Reason's conception of things is not subject to time but is eternal, according to Prov. 8:23, therefore it is that this kind of law must be called eternal.

 ASK YOURSELF

5.103. (1) Would what we call the "laws of physics" be "eternal" according to this reasoning? Explain. (2) If someone claimed they were eternal would that not contradict the teaching that the universe had a beginning in time (since nothing eternal has a beginning in time)? (3) How does Aquinas get around this problem?

Is There a Natural Law in Us? The next question has to do with a human grasp of the eternal law.

Objection 1. It would seem that there is no natural law in us. Because man is governed sufficiently by the eternal law: for Augustine says (De Lib. Arb. i) that "the eternal law is that by which it is right that all things should be most orderly." But nature does not abound in superfluities as neither does she fail in necessaries. Therefore no law is natural to man.

Objection 2. Further, by the law man is directed, in his acts, to the end, as stated above (90, 2). But the directing of human acts to their end is not a function of nature, as is the case in irrational creatures, which act for an end solely by their natural appetite; whereas man acts for an end by his reason and will. Therefore no law is natural to man.

 ASK YOURSELF

5.104. Pay special attention to this objection and the next one. They seem to imply that there is a fundamental difference between, say, the (physical) law of gravitation and a law like "do not commit adultery." And there is such a difference, isn't there? Explain your answer.

Objection 3. Further, the more a man is free, the less is he under the law. But man is freer than all the animals, on account of his free-will, with which he is endowed above all other animals. Since therefore other animals are not subject to a natural law, neither is man subject to a natural law.

On the contrary, a gloss on Rm. 2:14: "When the Gentiles, who have not the law, do by nature those things that are of the law," comments as follows: "Although they have no written law, yet they have the natural law, whereby each one knows, and is conscious of, what is good and what is evil."

I answer that, as stated above (90, 1, ad 1), law, being a rule and measure, can be in a person in two ways: in one way, as in him that rules and measures; in another way, as in that which is ruled and measured, since a thing is ruled and measured, in so far as it partakes of the rule or measure. Wherefore, since all things subject to Divine providence are ruled and measured by the eternal law, as was stated above (1); it is evident that all things partake somewhat of the eternal law, insofar as, namely, from its being imprinted on them, they derive their respective inclinations to their proper acts and ends. Now among all others, the rational creature is subject to Divine providence in the most excellent way, in so far as it partakes of a share of providence, by being provident both for itself and for others. Wherefore it has a share of the Eternal Reason, whereby it has a natural inclination to its proper act and end: and this participation of the eternal law in the rational creature is called the natural law. Hence the Psalmist after saying (Ps. 4:6): "Offer up the sacrifice of justice," as though someone asked what the works of justice are, adds: "Many say, Who shows us good things?" in answer to which question he says: "The light of Your countenance, O Lord, is signed upon us": thus implying that the light of natural reason, whereby we discern what is good and what is evil, which is the function of the natural law, is nothing else than an imprint on us of the Divine light. It is therefore evident that the natural law is nothing else than the rational creature's participation of the eternal law.

Reply to Objection 1. This argument would hold, if the natural law were something different from the eternal law: whereas it is nothing but a participation thereof, as stated above.

Reply to Objection 2. Every act of reason and will in us is based on that which is according to nature, as stated above (10, 1): for every act of reasoning is based on principles that are known naturally, and every act of appetite in respect of the means is derived from the natural appetite in respect of the last end. Accordingly the first direction of our acts to their end must needs be in virtue of the natural law.

Reply to Objection 3. Even irrational animals partake in their own way of the Eternal Reason, just as the rational creature does. But because the rational creature partakes thereof in an intellectual and rational manner, therefore the participation of the eternal law in the rational creature is properly called a law, since a law is something pertaining to reason, as stated above (90, 1). Irrational creatures, however, do not partake thereof in a rational manner, wherefore there is no participation of the eternal law in them, except by way of similitude.

Aquinas uses the expression "participation of the law in" to refer to actions or features of something that do instantiate some (divine) law. Thus a plant leaf that turns toward light (phototropism) participates in law, that is, in the divine order established by God in creating that plant. But the plant does not "know what it is doing" and therefore is not in a sense "following a law." Only where a creature "knows what it is doing" in following a law is it strictly proper to say that there is a "participation of the eternal law in them." So even though divine law determines the movements of the plant's leaves, the plant is related to divine law and reason in a way that is merely similar in some respects to the way in which human actions can be related to divine law. Only in the case of rational creatures is there, strictly speaking, a following of natural law.

 ASK YOURSELF

5.105. What is the difference between the way a plant, say, "follows" divine law, and the way a human being does?

Many have criticized Aquinas's conception of natural law and other similar conceptions in the following way: Aquinas conflates the notion of law as a "description" of what actually goes on in nature, which is the notion of law found in modern natural science, with the notion of law as something promulgated by a legislature of some sort. State laws require that I drive on the right side of the road. Such laws tell me how things ought to be, not how they always in fact are. If we catch someone driving on the left side we do not suppose that the law is thus invalid or doesn't exist, whereas if we found something violating a supposed law of nature (such as the gravitational law) we might have to conclude that there is no such law after all. Aquinas supposedly conflates these two different senses of "law" and thus his account of law is fundamentally confused.

ASK YOURSELF

5.106. In the light of Aquinas's remarks in Question 2, and our discussion, do you think that the criticism of Aquinas just mentioned is accurate? Explain why or why not.

Whether There Is a Human Law? Aquinas argues that there must be human law (passed by legislatures, for instance) even though divine law "covers everything" in a sense.

Objection 1. It would seem that there is not a human law. For the natural law is a participation of the eternal law, as stated above (2). Now through the eternal law "all things are most orderly," as Augustine states (De Lib. Arb. i, 6). Therefore the natural law suffices for the ordering of all human affairs. Consequently there is no need for a human law.

Objection 2. Further, a law bears the character of a measure, as stated above (90, 1). But human reason is not a measure of things, but vice versa, as stated in Metaph. x, text. 5.

Therefore no law can emanate from human reason.

 ASK YOURSELF

5.107. What view of the relation of law to human reason did Aristotle and this objector reject?

5.108. Aquinas's remarks here should remind you of a famous statement by the ancient Greek philosopher Protagoras. What was the statement?

Objection 3. Further, a measure should be most certain, as stated in Metaph. x, text. 3. But the dictates of human reason in matters of conduct are uncertain, according to Wis. 9:14: "The thoughts of mortal men are fearful, and our counsels uncertain." Therefore no law can emanate from human reason.

On the contrary, Augustine (De Lib. Arb. i, 6) distinguishes two kinds of law, the one eternal, the other temporal, which he calls human.

I answer that, as stated above (90, 1, ad 2), a law is a dictate of the practical reason. Now it is to be observed that the same procedure takes place in the practical and in the speculative reason: for each proceeds from principles to conclusions, as stated above (De Lib. Arb. i, 6). Accordingly we conclude that just as, in the speculative reason, from naturally known indemonstrable principles, we draw the conclusions of the various sciences, the knowledge of which is not imparted to us by nature, but acquired by the efforts of reason, so too it is from the precepts of the natural law, as from general and indemonstrable principles, that the human reason needs to proceed to the more particular determination of certain matters. These particular determinations, devised by human reason, are called human laws, provided the other essential conditions of law be observed, as stated above (90, A2,3,4). Wherefore Tully says in his

Rhetoric (De Invent. Rhet. ii) that "justice has its source in nature; thence certain things came into custom by reason of their utility; afterwards these things which emanated from nature and were approved by custom, were sanctioned by fear and reverence for the law."

 ASK YOURSELF

5.109. Once again the notion of "custom" (what people customarily believe is right and wrong) is said to be rooted in nature, in the way things are independently of custom, and thus custom is *not* king. Name a Presocratic writer who said it *is* king. It is clear that some laws (e.g., "drive on the right side of the road") are simply a matter of custom (*nomos*) or convention. Such laws could be changed and no one would be any worse off. There is nothing particularly "natural" about such laws. But what about laws against murder or theft? Are they somehow rooted in nature, or, to put it another way, are they rooted in the way things were "meant to be"? (And if so, *who* meant them to be that way?)

5.110. What is your own view on the relation of law to custom and nature? If you think laws prohibiting murder are rooted in nature, you may be close to Aquinas's view.

5.111. Try to give some other account of such laws as those prohibiting murder and theft that does *not* rely on the idea of a natural order of some sort. In other words, what would account for the wrongness of murder or theft or lying, if not that they violate God's design?

Whether There Was Any Need for a Divine Law? Aquinas goes on to argue that even though human law is needed, it is not sufficient. He gives four reasons why is it not.

Objection 1. It would seem that there was no need for a Divine law. Because, as stated above (2), the natural law is a participation in us of the eternal law. But the eternal law is a Divine law, as stated above (1). Therefore there was no need for a Divine law in addition to the natural law, and human laws derived therefrom.

Objection 2. Further, it is written (Sirach 15:14) that "God left man in the hand of his own counsel." Now counsel is an act of reason, as stated above (14, 1). Therefore man was left to the direction of his reason. But a dictate of human reason is a human law as stated above (3). Therefore there is no need for man to be governed also by a Divine law.

Objection 3. Further, human nature is more self-sufficing than irrational creatures. But irrational creatures have no Divine law besides the natural inclination impressed on them. Much less, therefore, should the rational creature have a Divine law in addition to the natural law.

On the contrary, David prayed God to set His law before him, saying (Ps. 118:33): "Set before me for a law the way of Your justifications, O Lord."

I answer that, besides the natural and the human law it was necessary for the directing of human conduct to have a Divine law. And this for four reasons. First, because it is by law that man is directed how to perform his proper acts in view of his last end. And indeed if man were ordained to no other end than that which is proportionate to his natural faculty, there would be no need for man to have any further direction of the part of his reason, besides the natural law and human law which is derived from it. But since man is ordained to an end of eternal happiness which is disproportionate to man's natural faculty, as stated above (5, 5), therefore it was necessary that, besides the natural and the human law, man should be directed to his end by a law given by God.

Secondly, because, on account of the uncertainty of human judgment, especially on contingent and particular matters, different people form different judgments on human acts; whence also different and contrary laws result. In order, therefore, that man may know without any doubt what he ought to do and what he ought to avoid, it was necessary for man to be directed in his proper acts by a law given by God, for it is certain that such a law cannot err.

Thirdly, because man can make laws in those matters of which he is competent to judge. But man is not competent to judge of interior movements, that are hidden, but only of exterior acts which appear: and yet for the perfection of virtue it is necessary for man to conduct himself aright in both kinds of acts. Consequently human law could not sufficiently curb and direct interior acts; and it was necessary for this purpose that a Divine law should supervene.

Fourthly, because, as Augustine says (De Lib. Arb. i, 5,6), human law cannot punish or forbid all evil deeds: since while aiming at doing away with all evils, it would do away with many good things, and would hinder the advance of the common good, which is necessary for human intercourse. In order, therefore, that no evil might remain unforbidden and unpunished, it was necessary for the Divine law to supervene, whereby all sins are forbidden.

And these four causes are touched upon in Ps. 118:8, where it is said: "The law of the Lord is unspotted," i.e. allowing no foulness of sin; "converting souls," because it directs not only exterior, but also interior acts; "the testimony of the Lord is faithful," because of the certainty of what is true and right; "giving wisdom to little ones," by directing man to an end supernatural and Divine.

In the Judaeo-Christian Scriptures such expressions of "divine law" as the following can be found: (1) You shall have no other Gods before you (none other than the God of Israel, who is identified by his deeds, etc.); (2) Whoever looks on a woman lustfully has already committed adultery in his heart; (3) Turn the other cheek, do not return violence with violence.

 ASK YOURSELF

5.112. Try to associate each of the Scriptures just cited with one of Aquinas's four reasons for the need for divine law, given in the previous passage. For example if you think his first reason would go with (2), write "I, 2."

Three Points about Human and Divine Law. In Question 93 Aquinas discusses the nature of the eternal law that is the ultimate source of all moral laws. First, he argues that eternal law is instituted by God as God's way of governing all actions. Second, when considering whether the knowledge of the eternal law is available to everyone, Aquinas argues that the complete list of eternal laws is known only to God. However, humans have access to a subset of eternal law that is discovered through reflection (i.e., natural law). Third, Aquinas considers whether all laws, including human laws of governments, are derived from eternal law. He argues that, as long as governing bodies carefully and rationally derive their laws from natural law, then these laws will also be part of eternal law. However, even the slightest error of reasoning may result in an improper human law. Moreover, human law does not cover everything covered by divine law. In this connection notice Augustine's earlier discussion (pp. 184–89) as well as question 5.112.

 ## ASK YOURSELF

5.113. What four points about law does Aquinas make in Question 93?

Whether the Natural Law Is the Same in All People. In Question 94 Aquinas directly addresses the concept of natural law. First, when considering whether natural law is the same in all people, he argues that the more general or *primary* principles of natural law are common to all, such as "do not harm others." However, more particular or *secondary* derivations from these are not, such as "do not poison people." Second, as to whether the natural law can be changed, Aquinas argues that, although new primary principles may be added, none that are already there can be subtracted. Further, the formulation of secondary principles, as noted earlier, may not be consistently derived by all people and in that sense may change.

Objection 1. . . . (omitted)

Objection 2. Further, "Things which are according to the law are said to be just," as stated in Ethic. v. But it is stated in the same book that nothing is so universally just as not to be subject to change in regard to some men. Therefore even the natural law is not the same in all men.

Objection 3. Further, as stated above (2, 3), to the natural law belongs everything to which a man is inclined according to his nature. Now different men are naturally inclined to different things; some to the desire of pleasures, others to the desire of honors, and other men to other things. Therefore there is not one natural law for all.

The objections imagined here would all seem to support some kind of relativism in morals. Relativists believe that all moral rules are a matter of convention or at any rate are not grounded in anything permanent either in human nature or divine nature. Relativists are likely to say "what is right for one culture (or person) might be wrong for another culture (or person)."

 ## ASK YOURSELF

5.114. Are you a relativist? If so, why; if not, why not?

On the contrary, Isidore says (Etym. v, 4): "The natural law is common to all nations."

I answer that, As stated above (2, 3), to the natural law belongs those things to which a man is inclined naturally: and among these it is proper to man to be inclined to act according to reason. Now the process of reason is from the common to the proper, as stated in Phys. i. The speculative reason, however, is differently situated in this matter, from the practical reason. For, since the speculative reason is busied chiefly with the necessary things, which cannot be otherwise than they are, its proper conclusions, like the universal principles, contain the truth without fail. The practical reason, on the other hand, is busied with contingent matters, about which human actions are concerned: and consequently, although there is necessity in the general principles, the more we descend to matters of detail, the more frequently we encounter defects. Accordingly then in speculative matters truth is the same in all men, both as to principles and as to conclusions: although the truth is not known to all as regards the conclusions, but only as regards the principles which are called common notions. But in matters of action, truth or practical rectitude ["rectitude" = "rightness or correctness"] is not the same for all, as to matters of detail, but only as to the general principles: and where there is the same rectitude in matters of detail, it is not equally known to all.

It is therefore evident that, as regards the general principles whether of speculative or of practical reason, truth or rectitude is the same for all, and is equally known by all. As to the proper conclusions of the speculative reason, the truth is the same for all, but is not equally known to all: thus it is true for all that the three angles of a triangle are together equal to two right angles, although it is not known to all. But as to the proper conclusions of the practical reason, neither is the truth or rectitude the same for all, nor, where it is the same, is it equally known by all. Thus it is right and true for all to act according to reason: and from this principle it follows as a proper conclusion, that goods entrusted to another should be restored to their owner. Now this is true for the majority of cases: but it may happen in a particular case that it would be injurious, and therefore unreasonable, to restore goods held in trust; for instance, if they are claimed for the purpose of fighting against one's country. And this principle will be found to fail the more, according as we descend further into detail, e.g. if one were to say that goods held in trust should be restored with such and such a guarantee, or in such and such a way; because the greater the number of conditions added, the greater the number of ways in which the principle may fail, so that it be not right to restore or not to restore.

Consequently we must say that the natural law, as to general principles, is the same for all, both as to rectitude and as to knowledge. But as to certain matters of detail, which are conclusions, as it were, of those general principles, it is the same for all in the majority of cases, both as to rectitude and as to knowledge; and yet in some few cases it may fail, both as to rectitude, by reason of certain obstacles (just as natures subject to generation and corruption fail in some few cases on account of some obstacle), and as to knowledge, since in some the reason is perverted by passion, or evil habit, or an evil disposition of nature; thus formerly, theft, although it is expressly contrary to the natural law, was not considered wrong among the Germans, as Julius Caesar relates (De Bello Gall. vi).

The main support for relativism seems to reside in the fact that different peoples and cultures have somewhat different ideas about what is right and wrong. Aquinas has just addressed this point and tried to show that these facts about differences do not show that there is no single natural law.

ASK YOURSELF

5.115. Aquinas shows how differences in moral beliefs or customs might be due to either of two factors. What are those factors, and what would be an example of each?

Reply to Objection 2. The saying of the Philosopher is to be understood of things that are naturally just, not as general principles, but as conclusions drawn from them, having rectitude in the majority of cases, but failing in a few.

Reply to Objection 3. As, in man, reason rules and commands the other powers, so all the natural inclinations belonging to the other powers must needs be directed according to reason. Wherefore it is universally right for all men, that all their inclinations should be directed according to reason.

ASK YOURSELF

5.116. Aquinas claims that it is according to practical reason that we restore to the rightful owner anything we have borrowed, and so this principle is part of natural law. Suppose we borrowed a gun from a friend and then discovered that he had become suicidal. (1) Should we return the gun? (2) What would Aquinas say? (3) How does his answer bear on the general question whether the natural law is the same for all? (4) How does it bear on the issue of relativism?

Whether the Natural Law Can Be Changed? Someone who believes, as Aquinas does, that all genuine law is rooted in the eternal unchanging will of God must give an account of the way in which laws seem to change and vary with time and circumstance.

Objection 1. It would seem that the natural law can be changed. Because on Sirach 17:9, "He gave them instructions, and the law of life," the gloss says: "He wished the law of the letter to be written, in order to correct the law of nature." But that which is corrected is changed. Therefore the natural law can be changed.

Objection 2. Further, the slaying of the innocent, adultery, and theft are against the natural law. But we find these things changed by God: as when God commanded Abraham to slay his innocent son (Gen. 22:2); and when he ordered the Jews to borrow and purloin the vessels of the Egyptians (Ex. 12:35); and when He commanded Osee to take to himself "a wife of fornications" (Osee 1:2). Therefore the natural law can be changed.

Objection 3. Further, Isidore says (Etym. 5:4) that "the possession of all things in common, and universal freedom, are matters of natural law." But these things are seen to be changed by human laws. Therefore it seems that the natural law is subject to change.

On the contrary, it is said in the Decretals (Dist. v): "The natural law dates from the creation of the rational creature. It does not vary according to time, but remains unchangeable."

I answer that, a change in the natural law may be understood in two ways. First, by way of addition. In this sense nothing hinders the natural law from being changed: since many things for the benefit of human life have been added over and above the natural law, both by the Divine law and by human laws.

Secondly, a change in the natural law may be understood by way of subtraction, so that what previously was according to the natural law, ceases to be so. In this sense, the natural law is altogether unchangeable in its first principles: but in its secondary principles, which, as we have said (4), are certain detailed proximate conclusions drawn from the first principles, the natural law is not changed so that what it prescribes be not right in most cases. But it may be changed in some particular cases of rare occurrence, through some special causes hindering the observance of such precepts, as stated above (4).

 ASK YOURSELF

5.117. Consult the previous passage and give an example to illustrate the point about "cases of rare occurrence."

Reply to Objection 1. The written law is said to be given for the correction of the natural law, either because it supplies what was wanting to the natural law; or because the natural law was perverted in the hearts of some men, as to certain matters, so that they esteemed those things good which are naturally evil; which perversion stood in need of correction.

Reply to Objection 2. All men alike, both guilty and innocent, die the death of nature: which death of nature is inflicted by the power of God on account of original sin, according to 1 Kgs. 2:6: "The Lord kills and makes alive." Consequently, by the command of God, death can be inflicted on any man, guilty or innocent, without any injustice whatever. In like manner adultery is intercourse with another's wife; who is allotted to him by the law emanating from God. Consequently intercourse with any woman, by the command of God, is neither adultery nor fornication. The same applies to theft, which is the taking of another's property. For whatever is taken by the command of God, to Whom all things belong, is not taken against the will of its owner, whereas it is in this that theft consists. Nor is it only in human things, that whatever is commanded by God is right; but also in natural things, whatever is done by God, is, in some way, natural, as stated in the I, 105, 6, ad 1.

Reply to Objection 3. A thing is said to belong to the natural law in two ways. First, because nature inclines thereto: e.g. that one should not do harm to another. Secondly, because nature did not bring in the contrary: thus we might say that for man to be naked is of the natural law, because nature did not give him clothes, but art invented them. In this sense, "the possession of all things in common and universal freedom" is said to be of the natural law, because, to wit, the distinction of possessions and slavery were not brought in by nature, but devised by human reason for the benefit of human life. Accordingly the law of nature was not changed in this respect, except by addition.

Aquinas's concern to establish the unchangeableness of natural law is to be expected for several reasons, one of them being that if it were changeable even with respect to its first principles, it might not be possible to be sure what those principles were.

 ASK YOURSELF

5.118. Why would that be a problem, do you think?

Aquinas makes some remarkable claims in this connection, such as that theft, murder, and so on would be compatible with natural law.

 ASK YOURSELF

5.119. Under what circumstances might theft be permissible, and how would it not violate natural law in those circumstances?

5.120. Aquinas also seems to argue (in the last reply) that slavery might be justified in terms of its benefit for human life. Does this imply that it is consistent with natural law, and thus with God's eternal law, that there be slavery?

5.121. How does Aquinas meet Objection 2? Does his reply satisfy you? Would his reply leave it open to someone to justify any act whatsoever, no matter how horrible, by simply claiming that God has commanded it? Why, or why not?

5.122. Should anyone ever do something simply because someone, including God, has commanded it? Or should we only do what we can see is right, apart from what anyone commands? Explain your answers, and refer in your discussion to Plato's *Euthyphro*.

SUGGESTIONS FOR FURTHER READING

Primary Sources

Anselm

Anselm. *Cur deus homo* (*Why God Became a Man*), trans. J. Hopkins and H. Richardson, in *Anselm of Canterbury*, vol. 3 (New York: Mellen, 1976). Important work for the history of Western theology.

————. *De libertate arbitrii* (*Freedom of Choice*), trans. J. Hopkins and H. Richardson, in *Anselm of Canterbury*, vol. 2 (New York: Mellen,, 1976). Searches for a definition of free choice.

————. *De veritate* (*On Truth*), trans. J. Hopkins and H. Richardson, in *Anselm of Canterbury*, vol. 2 (New York: Mellen, 1976). Contains Anselm's definition of truth as identical with God.

———. *Proslogion*, trans. J. Hopkins, in *An Interpretive Translation of St. Anselm's Monologion and Proslogion* (Minneapolis: Banning, 1986). Includes Gaunilo's "On Behalf of the Fool" and Anselm's reply to Gaunilo.

Aquinas

Aquinas. *Basic Writings of St. Thomas Aquinas*, ed. Anton Pegis (New York: Random House, 1945). A good selection.

———. *Summa Theologiciae*, ed. Thomas Gilby (London: 1963–1975). Sixty-volume complete edition of Aquinas's main work.

Augustine

Many English translations of Augustine's best-known work, *Confessions*, are available in separate editions. A recent one by Henry Chadwick is available from Oxford University Press (1991).

English translations of Augustine's major works are to be found in P. Schaff, ed., *A Select Library of the Nicene and Post-Nicene Fathers of the Christian Church*, First Series (Edinburgh: T. & T. Clark, 1886–1888; reprinted, Grand Rapids, MI: Eerdmans, 1971–1974).

Augustine. *Basic Writings of Saint Augustine*, ed. W. Oates (New York: Random House, 1948). Two volumes.

———. *De civitate Dei* (*The City of God*), trans. J. O'Meara (Harmondsworth: Penguin, 1972). One of the best English translations of this core work.

Averroës (Ibn Rushd)

Averroës. *Averroës on Plato's 'Republic.'* ed. R. Lerner (Ithaca, NY: Cornell University Press, 1974). The most modern translation of Averroës commentary on Plato's *Republic*. Includes commentary.

———. *Averroës on the Harmony of Religion and Philosophy*, ed. G. Hourani (London: Luzac, 1961; reprinted 1976). Translation and discussion of the *Fasl al-maqal* and two related works.

———. *Averroës' Tahafut al-Tahafut* (*The Incoherence of the Incoherence*), ed. S. Vanden Bergh (London: Luzac, 1954; reprinted 1978). The standard translation of Averroës' response to al-Ghazali. Includes the latter's text.

———. *Averroës' Three Short Commentaries on Aristotle's 'Topics', 'Rhetoric' and 'Poetics,'* ed. C. Butterworth (Albany, NY: State University of New York Press, 1977). Translation and commentary on three of Averroës' principal discussions of different forms of language.

Maimonides

Maimonides. *The Guide for the Perplexed*, trans. M. Friedlander (New York: Dover Publications, 1956). Complete translation from the Arabic, in paperback format.

Analyses and Discussions

Anselm

Barth, Karl. *Anselm: Fides Quaerens Intellectum* (New York: Meridian Books, 1960). A study of Anselm's theological strategy and proof by a major twentieth-century theologian.

Hick, John, and McGill, Arthur C, eds. *The Many-Faced Argument* (New York: Macmillan. 1967). A collection of essays up to 1967, pro and con, on the ontological argument. Includes a famous article my Norman Malcolm distinguishing two arguments in the *Proslogion*.

Rowe, W. "The Ontological Argument and Question-Begging," *International Journal for Philosophy of Religion* 7: 425–432, 1976. Makes a case for regarding the argument of *Proslogion* 2 as question-begging.

Aquinas

Copleston, F. C. *Aquinas* (London: Penguin Books, 1955). A standard introduction to Aquinas's life and works.

Gilson, Etienne. *The Christian Philosophy of St. Thomas Aquinas* (New York: Random Rouse, 1956). A classic resource by a philosopher sympathetic to the Thomist tradition.

Kenny, Anthony, ed. *Aquinas: A Collection of Critical Essays* (New York: Anchor Doubleday, 1969).

———. *The Five Ways. St. Thomas Aquinas' Proofs of God's Existence* (London: Routledge & Kegan Paul, 1969).

Kretzman, Norman, and Stump, Eleonore, eds. *The Cambridge Companion to Aquinas* (Cambridge: Cambridge University Press, 1993). Recent essays on various facets of Aquinas's thought.

Augustine

Brown, Peter. *Augustine of Hippo* (Berkeley: University of California Press, 1967). A distinguished, very readable biography.

Chadwick, H. *Augustine* (New York: Oxford University Press. 1986). A first introduction to Augustine.

Dihle, A. *The Theory of Will in Classical Antiquity* (Berkeley, CA: University of California Press, 1982). One chapter of this important work is devoted to Augustine's theory.

Gilson, Etienne. *The Christian Philosophy of Saint Augustine* (New York: Random House, 1961). A learned Thomist expounds Augustine.

Kirwin, Christopher. *Augustine* (London: Routledge, 1989). An analytical philosopher probes Augustine's thought.

Averroës

Leaman, O. "Averroës and the West," in M. Wahba and M. Abousenna, eds. *Averroës and the Enlightenment* (New York: Prometheus, 1995, 53–67). Connects Averroës both to later Averroism and to modern developments.

———. "Averroës," in F. Niewöhner, ed. *Klassiker der Religionsphilosophie* (Munich: Beck, 142–162). Concise account of Averroës' contribution to philosophy.

Wolfson, H. "The Twice-Revealed Averroës, *Speculum* 36: 373–392, 1961. Influential summary of Averroës' place in the history of philosophy.

Maimonides

Katz, S., ed., *Maimonides: Selected Essays* (New York: Arno Press, 1980). Includes some classic essays.

Kraemer, J., ed., *Perspectives on Maimonides: Philosophical and Historical Studies* (Oxford: Oxford University Press, 1991). Essays on Maimonides's logic, theology, and jurisprudence and historical studies of his environment.

CHAPTER 6

RENAISSANCE
AND EARLY MODERN
PHILOSOPHY

he Renaissance, a European intellectual movement from roughly the fourteenth through the sixteenth centuries, marked the close of the middle ages and the beginning of the modern period. "Renaissance" comes from the French word for rebirth and specifically signifies a rebirth of classical Greek culture. Originally "the Renaissance" referred to a rebirth of ancient Greek artistic style but later was expanded to encompass all cultural achievement of this time, including art, literature, philosophy, navigation, and science. This revived interest was in part the result of a rediscovery of lost Greek and Roman texts; interest was further propelled by the invention of the movable type printing press in 1450, which allowed for wide distribution of affordable books, both classical and modern. Although the Renaissance produced world-class artists, theologians, essayists, and scientists, the philosophers of this period did not approach the stature of Plato, Aristotle, Augustine, or Aquinas. However, several aspects of Renaissance thought were especially influential in the early modern period of philosophy that followed. These developments are traced in the following sections of this chapter: humanism; the Reformation; fideism and skepticism; astronomy; and the scientific method.

HUMANISM

Renaissance humanism was the philosophical view emphasizing human worth and secular studies in contrast with religious belief. Humanists consciously rejected medieval religious authority, returned to classical ideals, and maintained that the ideal person embodies all human excellences, including music, art, poetry, science, and virtue. These secular studies became known as the "humanities." Despite their emphasis on secular ideals, humanists were devout religious believers and only advocated those values that they thought consistent with Christianity. Founded by the Italian poet Petrarch (1304–1374), Renaissance humanism remained an Italian phenomenon for a century.

Pico's *Oration*

The best remembered humanist of the Italian Renaissance was Pico della Mirandola (1463–1494), an eclectic philosopher who drew from Greek, scholastic, Kabbalistic, and Arabic philosophical traditions. In 1486 he planned to publicly defend nine hundred propositions drawn from these sources and for the occasion composed his *Oration on Human Dignity* (1480). However, the Pope declared thirteen of the propositions heretical, and the public presentation was prohibited. Pico wrote an *Apology* in defense of the propositions and quickly fled to France. Under the protection of Lorenzo de' Medici, he was brought back to Italy and became influential in Florence's Platonic

Academy. He was absolved of heresy by a new Pope in 1493, and died the next year at the early age of thirty-one. The selections in this section are from Pico's *Oration on Human Dignity*.

Common Explanations of Human Uniqueness. Pico opens his *Oration* by examining what specifically makes human beings so unique and remarkable. He considers several common explanations.

 From PICO: *Oration on Human Dignity*

Reverend Fathers: In the writings of the Arabians, I have read that Abdula the Saralen was asked what on the "world's stage," as they say, is the most wondrous. He replied, "There is no greater wonder than humanity." And Mercury agrees with this opinion: "A magnificent miracle is humanity!" (Asclepius 1:6). But I am dissatisfied when considering the reasons for these assertions [such as the following]. Man intermediates between all creatures, being familiar with the gods, yet rulers of inferior creatures. We interpret nature by the sharpness of our senses, the judgment of our reason, and the light of our intelligence. We are the moment between eternity's permanence, and the passage of time. As the Persians say, we are the binding force, no, the marriage union of the world. According to David, we are "just a little beneath the angels" (Psalms 8:5). These reasons are great, but not the principal ones. That is, they do not possess the privilege of the highest admiration. For, why should we not have more admiration for the angels and the beautiful heavenly choirs? Ultimately, it seems to me, I now understand why man is the most fortunate of creatures, and worthy of complete admiration. I understand what their allotted position is in the great chain of being, which is a role envied by the animals, and the stars, and the minds beyond the world. It is something wonderful beyond faith. And why not? It is for this reason that man is justly deemed a great miracle, and truly wonderful creature. So, with receptive ears, Fathers, listen attentively to what I say.

 ASK YOURSELF

6.1. What are some of the stock reasons given for why human beings are so wondrous?

The Place of Humans in Creation. Pico continues by giving his own explanation of human greatness, which rests on our place in creation.

By the laws of his hidden wisdom, God the father and master architect built this worldly home which we observe, a most sacred temple of his divinity. The areas above the heavens he gave minds. He gave animated souls to the celestial spheres. He filled the dregs of the lower world with a variety of animals. But when finished, the architect wished that there would be someone to appreciate the work, to love its beauty, and marvel at its size. Thus, all other things finished, as Moses and Timaeus report, he finally considered creating man. But there was nothing in his archetypes from which he could form new progeny, nor anything in his supply house which he might bequeath to a new son, nor was there an empty chair in which this new being could sit and contemplate the world. All places were filled. Everything had been assigned in the highest, middle, and lowest orders. But in this last task, it was not part of the Father's power to give up as though exhausted. It was not part of his wisdom to waver because of a lack of a clear plan. It was not part of his living kindness that he should be praised for his generosity to others, but condemned for lack of it on himself. Finally, the master architect declared that this creature, to whom nothing unique could be given, should be a composite, and have that which belonged exclusively to all other things.

 ASK YOURSELF

6.2. What problem did God run into when assigning humanity a spot in the great chain of being?

Thus, God took humanity, creatures of indeterminate form, placed them in a middle place in the world, and said the following: "I have given you, Adam, neither a fixed place nor a fixed form of your own. You may possess any place or any form as you desire. The laws ordained by me establish a limited nature for all other creatures. In accord with your free will, your destiny is in your own hands and you are confined to no bounds. You will fix the limits of your nature yourself. I have put you in the world's center so that you may look around and examine the world's content. I have made you neither heavenly nor earthly, neither mortal nor immortal. You may freely and honorably mold, make, and sculpt yourself into any shape you prefer. You can degenerate into the forms of the lower animals, or climb upward by your soul's reason, to a higher nature which is divine." What great generosity of God the Father! What great and wonderful happiness of humanity!

 ASK YOURSELF

6.3. What is Pico's explanation for why human beings are such extraordinary creations?

More's *Utopia*

A dominant theme in humanist writings was the Christianizing of Epicureanism—much the way Augustine Christianized Plato and Aquinas Christianized Aristotle. Erasmus, for example, argued that the Christian virtues are actually Epicurean since the Christian is to have a life full of true pleasure. One of the clearest expressions of humanistic Epicureanism is given by English statesman Thomas More (1478–1535). In his famous *Utopia* (1516), literally "no place," More describes an ideal island containing a society founded on reason. The work has been variously interpreted as a satire on the evils of his times, a dream world for scholars, or a forecast of communism. The selections in the section are from More's *Utopia*.

The Island of Utopia. More opens *Utopia* with a geographical description of this perfect island and an account of their social customs.

 From MORE: *Utopia*

The island of Utopia is in the middle 200 miles broad, and holds almost at the same breadth over a great part of it; but it grows narrower toward both ends. . . . Utopus that conquered it (whose name it still carries, for Abraxa was its first name) brought the rude and uncivilized inhabitants into such a good government, and to that measure of politeness, that they now far excel all the rest of mankind. . . . There are fifty-four cities in the island, all large and well built: the manners, customs, and laws of which are the same, and they are all contrived as near in the same manner as the ground on which they stand will allow. They have built over all the country, farm-houses for husbandmen, which are well contrived, and are furnished with all things necessary for country labor. Inhabitants are sent by turns from the cities to dwell in them. No country family has fewer than forty men and women in it, besides two slaves. There is a master and a mistress set over every family; and over thirty families there is a magistrate. . . . Agriculture is that which is so universally understood among them that no person, either man or woman, is ignorant of it. They are instructed in it from their childhood, partly by what they learn at school and partly by practice. . . . Besides agriculture, which is so common to them all, every man has some peculiar trade to which he applies himself, such as the manufacture of wool, or flax, masonry, smith's work, or carpenter's work; for there is no sort of trade that is not in great esteem among them. Throughout the island they wear the same sort of clothes without any other distinction, except what is necessary to distinguish the two sexes, and the married and unmarried. The fashion never alters. And as it is neither disagreeable nor uneasy, so it is suited to the climate, and calculated both for their summers and winters.

 ASK YOURSELF

6.4. What is the makeup of the "country family"?

Happiness, Pleasure, and Religion. More continues running through all the social institutions of the Utopian people. He then describes their various schools of philosophy, giving particular emphasis to the one with Epicurean elements.

As to moral philosophy, they have the same disputes among them as we have here. They examine what are properly good both for the body and the mind, and whether any outward thing can be called truly good, or if that term belong only to the endowments of the soul. They inquire likewise into the nature of virtue and pleasure. But their chief dispute is concerning the happiness of a human, and wherein it consists. Whether in some one thing, or in a great many? They seem, indeed, more inclinable to that opinion that places, if not the whole, yet the chief part of a person's happiness in pleasure. And, what may seem more strange, they make use of arguments even from religion, notwithstanding its severity and roughness, for the support of that opinion so indulgent to pleasure. For they never dispute concerning happiness without fetching some arguments from the principles of religion, as well as from natural reason, since without the former they reckon that all our inquiries after happiness must be but conjectural and defective.

 ASK YOURSELF

6.5. For More, what constitutes the chief point of human happiness?

More briefly discusses the Utopian religious beliefs and the rational foundation of hedonism.

These are their religious principles, that the soul of man is immortal, and that God of his goodness has designed that it should be happy; and that he has therefore appointed rewards for good and virtuous actions, and punishments for vice, to be distributed after this life. Though these principles of religion are conveyed down among them by tradition, they think that even reason itself determines a man to believe and acknowledge them, and freely confess that if these were taken away no person would be so insensible as not to seek after pleasure by all possible means, lawful or unlawful. [They say this] using only this caution, that a lesser pleasure might not stand in the way of a greater, and that no pleasure ought to be pursued that should draw a great deal of pain after it. For they think it the maddest thing in the world to pursue virtue, that is a sour and difficult thing; and not only to renounce the pleasures of life, but willingly to undergo much pain and trouble, if a man has no prospect of a reward. And what reward can there be for one that has passed his whole life, not only without pleasure, but in pain, if there is nothing to be expected after death? Yet they do not place happiness in all sorts of pleasures, but only in those that in themselves are good and honest.

 ASK YOURSELF

6.6. More argues that pursuing a life without pleasure makes no sense. Suppose we shun pleasure in this life in hopes of a future reward. More asks rhetorically: "What reward can there be?" What is his point?

Advancing Pleasure for Others. According to More, the pleasure we pursue is not simply for ourselves, but for others.

There is a party among them who place happiness in bare virtue; others think that our natures are conducted by virtue to happiness, as that which is the chief good of man. They define virtue thus, that it is a living according to nature, and think that we are made by God for that end. They believe that a person then follows the dictates of nature when he pursues or avoids things according to the direction of reason. They say that the first dictate of reason is the kindling in us of a love and reverence for the Divine Majesty, to whom we owe both all that we have and all that we can ever hope for. In the next place, reason directs us to keep our minds as free from passion and as cheerful as we can, and that we should consider ourselves as bound by the ties of good-nature and humanity to use our utmost endeavors to help forward the happiness of all other persons. For there never was any person such a morose and severe pursuer of virtue (such an enemy to pleasure, that though he set hard rules for people to undergo much pain, many watchings, and other rigors) yet did not at the same time advise them to do all they could, in order to relieve and ease the miserable, and who did not represent gentleness and good-nature as amiable dispositions. And from thence they infer that if a man ought to advance the welfare and comfort of the rest of mankind, there being no virtue more proper and peculiar to our nature, than to ease the miseries of others, to free from trouble and anxiety, in furnishing them with the comforts of life, in which pleasure consists, nature much more vigorously leads them to do all this for himself.

 ASK YOURSELF

6.7. More describes one Utopian philosophical school that emphasizes "living according to nature." What are the two "dictates of reason" concerning this?

Although we are to secure pleasure for others, we do this by beginning with ourselves.

A life of pleasure is either a real evil, and in that case we ought not to assist others in their pursuit of it, but on the contrary, to keep them from it all we can, as from that which is most hurtful and deadly; or if it is a good thing, so that we not only may, but ought to help others to it, why, then, ought not a man to begin with himself? Since no man can be more bound to look after the good of another than after his own. For nature cannot direct us to be good and kind to others, and yet at the same time to be unmerciful and cruel to ourselves. Thus, as they define virtue to be living according to nature, so they imagine that nature prompts all people on to seek after pleasure, as the end of all they do. They also observe that in order to our supporting the pleasures of life, nature inclines us to enter into society; for there is no man so much raised above the rest of mankind as to be the only favorite of nature who, on the contrary, seems to have placed on a level all those that belong to the same species. Upon this they infer that no man ought to seek his own conveniences so eagerly as to prejudice others. And therefore they think that not only all agreements between private persons ought to be observed, but likewise that all those laws ought to be kept (which either a good prince has published in due form, or to which a people that is neither oppressed with tyranny nor circumvented by fraud, has consented, for distributing those conveniences of life which afford us all our pleasures).

ASK YOURSELF

6.8. According to this school of Utopians, why shouldn't we seek out our conveniences at the prejudice (or expense) of others?

They think it is an evidence of true wisdom for a man to pursue his own advantages as far as the laws allow it. They account it piety to prefer the public good to one's private concerns. But they think it unjust for a person to seek for pleasure by snatching another person's pleasures from him. And on the contrary, they think it a sign of a gentle and good soul, for a man to dispense with his own advantage for the good of others; and that by this means a good man finds as much pleasure one way as he parts with another. For as he may expect the like from others when he may come to need it, so if that should fail him, yet the sense of a good action, and the reflections that he makes on the love and gratitude of those whom he has so obliged, gives the mind more pleasure than the body could have found in that from which it had restrained itself. They are also persuaded that God will make up the loss of those small pleasures, with a vast and endless joy, of which religion easily convinces a good soul.

 ASK YOURSELF

6.9 According to this school of Utopians, what consolations do we have when our bodily pleasures are minimal?

Types of Pleasure. More distinguishes between bodily pleasures and mental pleasures—a distinction that is central to nineteenth-century philosopher J. S. Mill in his *Utilitarianism.*

Thus, upon an inquiry into the whole matter, they reckon that all our actions, and even all our virtues, terminate in pleasure as our chief end and greatest happiness. They call every motion or state a pleasure (either of body or mind) in which man has a natural delectation. Thus they cautiously limit pleasure to those appetites which nature leads us to. For, they say that nature leads us only to those delights to which reason as well as sense carries us, and by which we neither injure any other person nor lose the possession of greater pleasures, and of such as draw no troubles after them. But they view those delights which men by a foolish though common mistake call pleasure, as if they could change as easily the nature of things as the use of words; as things that greatly obstruct their real happiness instead of advancing it, because they so entirely possess the minds of those that are once captivated by them with a false notion of pleasure, that there is no room left for pleasures of a truer or purer kind.

ASK YOURSELF

6.10. What is More's attitude about bodily pleasures?

More continues by satirizing those who derive an artificial pleasure from luxuries or misguided etiquette.

There are many things that in themselves have nothing that is truly delightful. On the contrary, they have a good deal of bitterness in them. And yet from our perverse appetites after forbidden objects, [these] are not only ranked among the pleasures, but are made even the greatest designs of life. Among those who pursue these sophisticated pleasures, they reckon such as I mentioned before, who think themselves really the better for having fine clothes; in which they think they are doubly mistaken, both in the opinion that they have of their clothes, and in that they have of themselves. For if you consider the use of clothes, why should a fine thread be thought better than a coarse one? And yet these men, as if they had some real advantages beyond others, and did not owe them wholly to their mistakes, look big, seem to fancy themselves to be more valuable, and imagine that a respect is due to them for the sake of a rich garment, to which they would not have pretended if they had been more meanly clothed. And [these people] even resent it as an affront, if that respect is not paid them. It is also a great folly to be taken with outward marks of respect, which signify nothing. For what true or real pleasure can one man find in another's standing bare, or making legs to him? Will the bending another man's knees give ease to yours? And will the head's being bare cure the madness of yours? And yet it is wonderful to see how this false notion of pleasure bewitches many who delight themselves with the fancy of their nobility, and are pleased with this conceit, that they are descended from ancestors who have been held for some successions rich, and who have had great possessions; for this is all that makes nobility at present; yet they do not think themselves a whit the less noble, though their immediate parents have left none of this wealth to them, or though they themselves have squandered it away.

ASK YOURSELF

6.11. What are some rules of etiquette that More finds groundless?

THE REFORMATION

The Protestant Reformation was born on October 31, 1517, when German priest Martin Luther (1483–1546) nailed a revolutionary document to the door of Wittenberg Castle. The situation was ripe in the surrounding German states to revolt in mass against both the religious and political domination of the Catholic church. Several factors in the centuries preceding the Reformation contributed to its realization. Early less successful attempts at reform by John Wycliffe (d. 1384) and John

Hus (d. 1415) provided a starting point for voicing discontent. Renaissance mystics such as Meister Eckhardt (d. 1327) and Thomas à Kempis (d. 1471) reacted against the dogmas of rationalistic scholastic theology and offered a more inward and personalized approach to religious truth. Renaissance humanism challenged the ill-gotten power of church leaders, ridiculed superstitious religious practices, and emphasized the spiritual significance behind religious rituals. Finally, papal interference in European politics set Germany's political leaders against the entire institution of Catholicism.

Luther's *Appeal*

As a young man Luther intended to go into law, but after a frightening experience during a thunderstorm he became an Augustinian monk. Luther had inward struggles about religious hypocrisy and what was necessary to become righteous. In time he became professor of theology at the University of Wittenberg, in Saxony, where he had a religious experience in the tower room of the Augustinian Friary. Studying Romans 1:17, "The just shall live by faith," Luther was persuaded that God's forgiveness comes through faith alone. Like Erasmus, Luther was also bothered by the sale of indulgences, which was on the rise to pay for the rebuilding of Saint Peter's Basilica. He was particularly offended by Johann Tetzel, an indulgence peddler who came to the borders of Saxony. Local churches competed by offering similar opportunities for remitting divine punishment. Wittenberg Castle Church itself contained eighteen thousand relics, collected by Frederic of Saxony, which, when viewed for a fee, could shorten one's stay in purgatory by as many as two million years. Included among the relics were a baby slain by Herod's soldiers, a twig from Moses' burning bush, pieces of Mary's girdle, feathers dropped by angels, and a tear shed by Jesus. In protest to all these practices, Luther nailed a document containing ninety-five theses to the door of Wittenberg Castle (which functioned as a public bulletin board). Among the propositions, Luther maintained that God gives full remission of punishment and guilt to all who ask; that indulgences are fraudulent and foster deceit, immorality, skepticism, and irreverence; and that if the Pope cared for people, he would empty purgatory out of love, not for money. Luther was excommunicated by the Pope, but he quickly became a folk hero. To gain support for his proposed reforms, he published his *Appeal to the German Nobility* (1520), which urged the nobility to correct the abuses of the church. The selections in this section are from Luther's *Appeal*.

 ASK YOURSELF

6.12. Name three practices to which Luther objected.

Against Aristotle. In his *Appeal*, Luther lists several points of church doctrine that need reform. He then notes that further reform is needed in other areas of society, including university curriculum. In particular, he criticizes the heavy reliance on Aristotle's teaching in universities.

From LUTHER: *Appeal to the German Nobility*

The universities also require a good, sound reformation. I must say this, let it bother whom it may. The fact is that whatever the papacy has ordered or instituted is only designed for the propagation of sin and error. What is the present state of universities, but, as the book of Maccabees says, "schools of 'Greek fashion' and 'heathenish manners' " (2 Macc. 4:12–13)? They are full of dissolute living, where very little is taught of the Holy Scriptures and of the Christian faith, and the blind heathen teacher, Aristotle, rules even more than Christ. My advice is that the books of Aristotle, the *Physics*, the *Metaphysics*, *On the Soul*, and the *Ethics*, which have up till the present been considered the best, be altogether abolished along with all others that claim to examine nature, though nothing can be learned from them, either of natural or spiritual things. Besides, no one has been able to understand his meaning, and much time has been wasted and many noble souls bothered with much useless labor, study, and expense. I venture to say that any potter has more knowledge of natural things than is to be found in these books. My heart is saddened to see how many of the best Christians have been fooled and led astray by the false words of this cursed, proud, and dishonest heathen. God sent him as a plague for our sins.

Doesn't the wretched man in his best book, *On the Soul*, teach that the soul dies with the body, though many have tried to save him with vain words? It is as if we didn't have the Holy Scriptures to teach us everything completely of which Aristotle had not the slightest perception. Yet this dead heathen has conquered, and has hindered and almost suppressed the books of the living God. Thus, when I see all this misery, I cannot help but think that the evil spirit has introduced this study.

 ASK YOURSELF

6.13. What problem does Luther find with Aristotle's *On the Soul*?

Then there is the *Ethics*, which is accounted one of the best, though no book is more directly contrary to God's will and the Christian virtues. Oh that such books could be kept out of the reach of all Christians! Let no one object that I say too much, or speak without knowledge. My friend, I know what I'm talking about. I know Aristotle as well as you or people like you. I have read him with more understanding than St. Thomas or Scotus, which I may say without arrogance, and can prove this if I need to. It doesn't matter that so many great minds have exercised themselves in these topics for hundreds of years. Such objections do not affect me as they might have done once, since it is plain as day that many more errors have existed for hundreds of years in the world and the universities. I would, however, gladly consent that Aristotle's books on *Logic*, *Rhetoric*, and *Poetics*, should be retained, or they might be usefully studied in a condensed form so that young people can practice speaking and preaching. But the notes and comments should be eliminated. Just as Cicero's *Rhetoric* is read without note or comment, Aristotle's *Logic* should be read without such long commentaries. But now neither speaking nor preaching is taught out of them, and they are used only for argumentation and toil.

ASK YOURSELF

6.14. What problem does Luther find with Aristotle's *Ethics*?

6.15. What purpose should Aristotle's *Logic, Rhetoric*, and *Poetics* serve?

Calvin's *Institutes*

John Calvin (1509–1564), a French theologian and early Protestant reformer, was raised Catholic, studied theology and law in Paris, and in his early years followed the intellectual path of Renaissance humanism. By 1534 Calvin allied himself with the Reformation movement and quickly became influential among French reformers. For safety, he left Paris, and eventually moved to Geneva, Switzerland, where, after a shaky start, he established a strict, almost theocratic local government. One of his laws, for example, prohibited any labor on Sunday—including stoking one's fireplace in winter. He soon became the leader of the Reformation in Switzerland (Presbyterianism) and in France (Huguenotism). Calvin authored several theological works, the most important of which is *The Institutes of the Christian Religion*. First published in 1536, the *Institutes* went through several revisions and by the final edition of 1559 was four times its original length. The work is in four books, following the succession of doctrines in the Apostles' Creed: (1) God the creator, and our knowledge of him; (2) God the redeemer, through Christ's atoning sacrifice, (3) the holy spirit who leads us to faith, and (4) the church, which is God's instrument to assist us in our weakness. Fifty years after Calvin's death, followers of Calvin presented his theology in five points, known as the "five points of Calvinism." They are (1) total depravity: humanity's complete nature is innately corrupted; (2) unconditional election: God predestines some to salvation; (3) limited atonement: salvation is restricted to those elected; (4) irresistible grace: the elect must accept God's favor; (5) perseverance of the saints: God sustains the elect despite their weakness. The selections in this section are from Calvin's *Institutes*.

Christian Philosophy. In addition to being a theological treatise, Calvin's *Institutes* offers a "Christian philosophy" intended to replace both classical and scholastic philosophy.

 From CALVIN: *Institutes of the Christian Religion*

Preface. Although the holy scriptures contain a perfect doctrine to which nothing can be added . . . still every person, not intimately acquainted with them, stands in need of some guidance and direction. Such guidance informs him as to what he ought to look for in the scriptures, so that he may not wander up and down, but pursue a certain path, and attain the end to which the Holy Spirit invites him.

Hence it is the duty of those who have received from God more light than others to assist the simple in this matter, and, as it were, lend them their hand to guide and assist them in finding the sum of what God has been pleased to teach us in his word.

Now, this cannot be better done in writing than by treating in succession of the principal matters which are comprised in Christian philosophy. For he who understands these will make more progress in the school of God in one day than any other person in three months. This, of course, assumes that he knows to what he should refer each sentence, and has a rule by which to test whatever is presented to him.

 ASK YOURSELF

6.16. In presenting his "Christian philosophy," for whom is Calvin writing: those who have received more light from God or those who have received less light from God?

Sense of Divinity.   Calvin argues that each person is born with a sense of divinity (*sensus divinitatis*), that is, an instinctive knowledge of God. This knowledge, he argues, escapes no one.

1.3.1 We hold to be beyond dispute that there exists in the human minds and indeed by natural instinct, some sense of divinity. This is so since, to prevent any person from pretending ignorance, God himself has given all people some idea of his Godhead. He constantly renews and occasionally enlarges our memory of this. Thus, being aware that there is a God, and that he is their Maker, people may be condemned by their own conscience when they neither worship him nor consecrate their lives to God's service. Certainly, if there is any quarter where it may be supposed that God is unknown, the most likely for such an instance to exist is among the dullest tribes farthest removed from civilization. But, as a heathen writer tells us, there is no nation so barbarous, no race so brutish, as not to be endowed with the conviction that there is a God. Even those who in other respects seem to differ very little from the lower animals, constantly retain some sense of religion. This common conviction is thoroughly possessed in the mind and firmly stamped on the breasts of all people. Since, then, there never has been, from the very first, any quarter of the globe, any city, any household even, without religion, this amounts to a tacit confession, that a sense of divinity is inscribed on every heart. No, even idolatry is ample evidence of this fact. For we know how reluctant humans are to lower themselves, in order to set other creatures above them. Therefore, when he chooses to worship wood and stone rather than be thought to have no God, it is evident how very strong this impression of a Deity must be. For, it is more difficult to obliterate it from the minds of people, than to break down the feelings of his nature. These feelings are certainly being broken down, though, when, in opposition to his natural haughtiness, he spontaneously humbles himself before the meanest object as an act of reverence to God.

 ASK YOURSELF

6.17. How is the sense of divinity reflected in "heathen" religious belief?

1.3.2 It is most absurd, therefore, to maintain, as some do, that religion was devised by the cunning and craft of a few individuals. Supposedly, these cunning individuals did this as a means of keeping the body of the people in due subjection; and, while teaching others to worship God, they themselves could not have believed less in the existence of God. I readily acknowledge, that cunning people have introduced a vast number of fictions into religion, with the view of inspiring the populace with reverence or striking them with terror, and thereby rendering them more submissive. But they never could have succeeded in this, had the minds of men not been previously imbued with that uniform belief in God, from which, as from its seed, the religious propensity springs. . . .

 ASK YOURSELF

6.18. Some argue that religion was invented by clever politicians. How does Calvin's theory presuppose the sense of divinity?

1.3.3 All people of sound judgment will therefore hold that a sense of divinity is permanently etched on the human heart. This belief is naturally brought out in all, and thoroughly fixed as it were in our very bones. This is strikingly attested by the insubordination of the wicked, who, though they struggle furiously, are unable to untangle themselves from the fear of God. Though Diagoras, and others of like minds, make themselves merry with whatever has been believed in all ages concerning religion, and Dionysus scoffs at the judgment of heaven, it is only a cynical grin. For, the worm of conscience, keener than burning steel, is gnawing them within. . . . It follows that this is not a doctrine which is first learned at school, but one as to which every man is his own master, from birth. One which nature herself allows no individual to forget, though many, with all their might, strive to do so. Moreover, all are born and live for the express purpose of learning to know God; and if the knowledge of God fails to fulfill this purpose, then it is fleeting and vain. Thus, it is clear that all those who do not direct the whole thoughts and actions of their lives to this end fail to fulfill the law of their being. This did not escape the observation even of philosophers. For it is exactly what Plato meant in the Phaedrus and the Theatetus when he taught (as he often does) that the chief good of the soul consists in resemblance to God. That is, the soul resembles God when, by means of knowing him, it is completely transformed into God. . . .

 ASK YOURSELF

6.19. What is the purpose of our lives?

The Soul: Consciousness of Ethics. In describing the nature of humans, Calvin examines the soul. He begins by arguing that the soul is made of an immaterial substance, and it is wrong to reduce the soul to bodily activities as some philosophers do. An important aspect of our soul is a consciousness of ethics, or righteousness.

1.15.6 It is pointless to seek a definition of the soul from philosophers, not one of whom, with the exception of Plato, distinctly maintained its immortality. Others of the school of Socrates, indeed, lean the same way, but still without teaching distinctly a doctrine of which they were not fully persuaded. Plato, however, advanced still further, and regarded the soul as an image of God. Others so attach its powers and faculties to the present life, that they leave nothing external to the body. It was already shown from Scripture that the substance of the soul is incorporeal. We must now add that, though it is not properly enclosed by space, it however occupies the body as a kind of habitation. It not only animates all its parts, and makes the organs fit and useful for their actions, but it also holds the first place in regulating the conduct. It does this not merely in regard to the function of a terrestrial life, but also in regard to the service of God. This, though not clearly seen in our corrupt state, yet the impress of its remains is seen in our very vices. From what source do humans have such a thirst for glory but from a sense of shame? And what is the source of this sense of shame but from a respect for what is honorable? Of this, the first principle and source is a consciousness that they were born to cultivate righteousness,—a consciousness akin to religion. But as people were undoubtedly created to meditate on the heavenly life, so it is certain that the knowledge of it was etched on the soul. And, indeed, people would lack the principal use of their understanding if they were not able to discern their happiness, the perfection of which consists in being united to God. Hence, the principal action of the soul is to aspire to that higher level, and, accordingly, the more a person studies to approach God, the more he proves himself to be endued with reason.

 ASK YOURSELF

6.20. One aspect of our soul is to provide us with a consciousness of ethics, or righteousness. For Calvin, what does the perfection of our happiness consist in?

The Parts of the Soul. Calvin criticizes those who say that the soul must have several parts since it is often at odds with itself.

There is some plausibility in the opinion of those who maintain that humans have more than one soul, namely, a sentient and a rational. However, if there is no soundness in their arguments, we must reject their views, unless we would torment ourselves with things frivolous and useless. They tell us, there is a great repugnance between organic movements and the rational part of the soul. They say this as if reason also were not at variance with herself, and her counsels sometimes conflicting with each other like hostile armies. But since this disorder results from the depravation of nature, it is erroneous to infer that there are two souls, because the faculties do not accord so harmoniously as they ought.

 ASK YOURSELF

6.21. According to Calvin, why can't we infer that there are different parts of the soul, based on its internal inconsistencies?

But I leave it to philosophers to discourse more subtilely of these faculties. For the edification of the pious, a simple definition will be sufficient. I admit, indeed, that what they ingeniously teach on the subject is true, and not only pleasant, but also useful to be known. Nor do I forbid any who are inclined to pursue the study. First, I admit that there are five senses, which Plato (in *Theaeteto*) prefers calling organs, by which all objects are brought into a common sensorium, as into a kind of receptacle. Next comes the imagination or the fancy (phantasia), which distinguishes between the objects brought into the sensorium. Next there is reason, to which the general power of judgment belongs. And, lastly, there is intellect, which contemplates with fixed and quiet look whatever reason discursively revolves. In like manner, to intellect, fancy, and reason, the three cognitive faculties of the soul, correspond three appetite faculties. There is the will, whose office is to choose whatever reason and intellect propound. Next are the irascible (quick-tempered) appetites which seize on what is set before it by reason and fancy. Finally there is the concupiscible (even-tempered) appetites which lay hold of the objects presented by sense and fancy.

 ASK YOURSELF

6.22. Tentatively following Plato, Calvin divides the soul into three initial divisions: the senses, the cognitive faculties, and the appetitive faculties. What are the three cognitive faculties?

6.23. What are the three appetitive faculties?

Calvin recognizes, however, that there are other possible divisions of the faculties.

Though these things are true, or at least plausible, still (as I fear they are more fitted to entangle by their obscurity than to assist us) I think it best to omit them. If anyone chooses to distribute the powers of the mind in a different manner, calling one appetitive, which, though devoid of reason, yet obeys reason, if directed from a different quarter, and another intellectual, as being by itself participant of reason, I have no great objection. Nor am I disposed to quarrel with the view, that there are three principles of action, viz., sense, intellect, and appetite. But let us rather adopt a division adapted to all capacities—a thing which certainly is not to be obtained from philosophers. For they, when they would speak most plainly, divide the soul into appetite and intellect, but make both double. To the latter they sometimes give the name of contemplative, as being contented with mere knowledge and having no active powers (which circumstance makes Cicero designate it by the name of intellect, ingenii; De Fin. Book 5.) At other times they give it the name of practical, because it variously moves the will by the apprehension of good or evil. Under this class is included the art of living well and justly. The former viz., appetite, they divide into will and concupiscence, calling it "boulesis," so whenever the appetite, which they call "horme," obeys the reason. But when appetite, casting off the yoke of reason, runs to intemperance, they call it "pathos." Thus they always presuppose in man a reason by which he is able to guide himself aright.

Intellect and the Will. Calvin next revises his division of the soul's faculties. Now he sees the initial division between intellect and the will.

1.15.7 We are forced somewhat to dissent from the method of teaching of the philosophers. For philosophers, being unacquainted with the corruption of nature, which is the punishment of revolt, erroneously confound two states of human which are very different from each other. Let us therefore hold, for the purpose of the present work, that the soul consists of two parts, the intellect and the will (Book 2 chap. 2 sec. 2, 12)—the office of the intellect being to distinguish between objects, according as they seem deserving of being approved or disapproved; and the office of the will, to choose and follow what the intellect declares to be good, to reject and shun what it declares to be bad (Plato, in the *Phaedrus*). We dwell not on the subtlety of Aristotle, that the mind has no motion of itself; but that the moving power is choice, which he also terms the appetite intellect. Not to lose ourselves in superfluous questions, let it be enough to know that the intellect is to us, as it were, the guide and ruler of the soul. The will always follows its beck, and waits for its decision, in matters of desire. For this reason Aristotle truly taught, that in the appetite there is a pursuit and rejection corresponding in some degree to affirmation and negation in the intellect (Aristotle, *Ethics*, Book 6, Sec. 2). Moreover, it will be seen in another place, (Book 2, Chap. 2, see. 12–26), how surely the intellect governs the will. Here we only wish to observe, that the soul only possesses those faculties which are duly referred to one or other of these members. And in this way we comprehend sense under intellect. Others distinguish thus: They say that sense inclines to pleasure in the same way as the intellect to good; that hence the appetite of sense becomes concupiscence and lust, while the affection of the intellect becomes will. For the term appetite, which they prefer, I use that of will, as being more common.

 ASK YOURSELF

6.24. What is the relation between the intellect and the will?

Human Faculties Before and after the Fall. Calvin contends that we must understand our present human nature by seeing what it became after the fall of Adam, not by considering what it was like in its original and perfect state.

1.15.8 Therefore, God has provided the human soul with intellect, by which he might distinguish good from evil, just from unjust, and might know what to follow or to shun, reason going before with her lamp. For this reason, philosophers, in reference to her directing power, have called her "to hegemonikon." To this he has joined will, to which choice belongs. People excelled in these noble endowments in his primitive condition [i.e., before the fall of Adam]. At that time, reason, intelligence, prudence, and judgment, not only sufficed for the government of his earthly life, but also enabled him to rise up to God and eternal happiness. Thereafter choice was added to direct the appetites, and temper all the organic motions. The will was thus perfectly submissive to the authority of reason. In this upright state, human nature possessed freedom of will, by which, if he chose, he was able to obtain eternal life.

ASK YOURSELF

6.25. What was the state of the human will before the fall?

It is unreasonable to introduce here the question concerning the secret predestination of God, because we are not considering what might or might not happen, but what human nature truly was. Adam, therefore, might have stayed in this original state if he chose, since it was only by his own will that he fell. But it was because his will was pliable in either direction (and he had not received constancy to keep going) that he so easily fell. Still he had a free choice of good and evil. And not only so, but in the mind and will there was the highest integrity, and all the organic parts were duly framed to obedience, until humans corrupted its good properties, and destroyed himself. Hence we see the great darkness of philosophers who looked for a complete building within a the rubble of ruins, and fit arrangement in disorder. The principle they set out with was that people could not be rational animals unless they had a free choice of good and evil. They also imagined that the distinction between virtue and vice was destroyed, if man did not of his own counsel arrange his life. So far well, had there been no change in human nature. This being unknown to them, it is not surprising that they throw everything into confusion.

ASK YOURSELF

6.26. Ignorant of the fall of humans, what do classical philosophers say about our present human nature with respect to reason, free will, and morality?

However, some, while they profess to be the disciples of Christ, still seek for free-will in human nature, notwithstanding that humans are lost and drowned in spiritual destruction, labor in various delusions. This approach makes for a heterogeneous mixture of inspired doctrine and philosophical opinions, and so erring as to both. But it will be better to leave these things to their own place (see Book 2 chap. 2). At present it is necessary only to remember, that human nature, at its first creation, was very different from what it has become. It derives its origin from its later state, after it became corrupted, and received a hereditary taint. At first every part of the soul was formed to decency. There was soundness of mind and freedom of will to choose the good.

ASK YOURSELF

6.27. What aspect of human will became tainted at the fall?

Calvin next addresses the claim that humanity fell because God didn't give the first humans a strong enough will in the first place.

If anyone objects that it was placed, as it were, in a slippery position, because its power was weak, I answer, that the degree conferred was sufficient to take away every excuse. For surely the Deity could not be tied down to this condition,—to make humans such that they either could not or would not sin. Such a nature might have been more excellent. But to expostulate with God as if he had been bound to confer this nature on man, is more than unjust, seeing he had full right to determine how much or how little He would give. Why He did not sustain humans by the virtue of steadfastness is hidden in his own purpose. It is our purpose to keep within the bounds of composure. Humanity had received the power, if it had the will, but it had not the will which would have given the power. For this will would have been followed consistently. Still, after humans had received so much, there is no excuse for them having spontaneously brought death upon themselves. No necessity was laid upon God to give humanity more than an intermediate and even transient will, so that out of humanity's fall God might extract materials for his own glory.

 ASK YOURSELF

6.28. For Calvin, God gave original humans faculties strong enough to resist evil if they chose. From God's perspective, why isn't the fall of humans so bad?

Human Reason Partly Preserved after the Fall. Although, according to Calvin, human free will became tainted with the fall of Adam, what about human reason? Calvin suggests that this remained somewhat more intact, as evidenced by the intellectual achievements of nonbelievers.

2.2.15 In reading profane authors, the admirable light of truth displayed in them should remind us, that the human mind, however much fallen and perverted from its original integrity, is still adorned and invested with admirable gifts from its Creator. If we reflect that the Spirit of God is the only fountain of truth, we will be careful, so not to insult him, to avoid rejecting or condemning truth wherever it appears. In despising the gifts, we insult the Giver. How, then, can we deny that truth must have beamed on those ancient lawgivers who arranged civil order and discipline with so much equity? Should we say that the philosophers, in their exquisite researches and skillful description of nature, were blind? Should we deny the possession of intellect to those who drew up rules for discourse, and taught us to speak in accordance with reason? Should we say that those who, by the cultivation of the medical art, expended their industry in our behalf were only raving? What should we say of the mathematical sciences? Should we deem them to be the dreams of madmen? No, we cannot read the writings of the ancients on these subjects without the highest admiration. It is an admiration which their excellence will not allow us to withhold. But should we deem anything to be noble and praiseworthy, without tracing it to the hand of God? Such ingratitude is far from us. This is an ingratitude not chargeable even on heathen poets, who acknowledged that philosophy and laws, and all useful arts were the inventions of the gods. Therefore, since it is manifest that people whom the Scriptures term carnal, are so acute and clear-sighted in the investigation of inferior things, their example should teach us how many gifts the Lord has left in possession of human nature, notwithstanding of its having been despoiled of the true good.

 ASK YOURSELF

6.29. What disciplines or areas of human reason remained relatively intact after the fall?

God Gives Particular Unique Abilities. Calvin also notes that God's spirit works through nonbelievers so that their intellectual contributions can benefit believers.

2.2.16 Moreover, let us not forget that there are most excellent blessings which the Divine Spirit dispenses to whom he will for the common benefit of mankind. Consider the skill and knowledge required for the construction of the Tabernacle which was imparted to Bezaleel and Aholiab [both unbelievers], by the Spirit of God (Exod. 31:2; 35:30). It is not strange, then, that the knowledge of those things which are of the highest excellence in human life is said to be communicated to us by the Spirit. Nor, is there any ground for asking what path the Spirit can have with the ungodly, who are altogether alienated from God? For what is said as to the Spirit dwelling in believers only, is to be understood of the Spirit of holiness by which we are consecrated to God as temples. Notwithstanding of this, He fills, moves, and invigorates all things by the virtue of the Spirit, and that according to the peculiar nature which each class of beings has received by the Law of Creation. But if the Lord has been pleased to assist us by the work and ministry of the ungodly in physics, dialectics, mathematics, and other similar sciences, let us avail ourselves of it. Otherwise, by neglecting the gifts of God spontaneously offered to us, we would be justly punished for our sloth. However, no one should imagine a person is very happy merely because, with reference to the things of this world, he has been endowed with great talents for the investigation of truth. We should add that the whole power of intellect thus given is, in the sight of God, fleeting and vain whenever it is not based on a solid foundation of truth. Augustine . . . says most correctly that as the gratuitous gifts given to people were withdrawn, so the natural gifts which remained were corrupted after the fall. Not that they can be polluted in themselves in so far as they proceed from God, but that they have ceased to be pure to polluted man, unless he should by their means obtain any praise.

 ASK YOURSELF

6.30. According to Augustine, why did our natural gifts, such as reason, become corrupt after the fall?

2.2.17 The sum of the whole is this: From a general survey of the human race, it appears that one of the essential properties of our nature is reason, which distinguishes us from the lower animals, just as these by means of sense are distinguished from inanimate objects. For although some individuals are born without reason, that defect does not impair the general kindness of God, but rather serves to remind us, that whatever we retain ought justly to be ascribed to the Divine indulgence. Had God not so spared us, our revolt would have carried along with it the entire destruction of nature. God shows his favor to us in that some excel in acuteness, and some in judgment, while others have greater readiness in learning some peculiar art. He gives such a variety to prevent anyone from presuming to usurp to himself that which flows from God's mere liberality. From this basis it is that one is more excellent than another, but that in a common nature the grace of God is specially displayed in passing by many and thus proclaiming that it is under obligation to none. We may add, that each individual is brought under particular influences according to his calling. Many examples of this occur in the Book of Judges, in which the Spirit of the Lord is said to have come upon those whom he called to govern his people (Judges 6:34.) In short, in every distinguished act there is a special inspiration. . . .

 ASK YOURSELF

6.31. What is the source of someone's unique intellectual ability?

Predestination. One of the most controversial aspects of Calvin's philosophy is the doctrine of predestination: God selects some people to be saved and selects others to be condemned to hell. This position is sometimes called *double predestination* since the fates of both the saved and unsaved are predetermined.

3.21.1 The covenant of [eternal] life is not preached equally to all, and among those to whom it is preached, it does not always meet with the same reception. This diversity reception displays the unsearchable depth of the divine judgment, and is without doubt a part of God's purpose of eternal election. But if it is plainly owing to God's *mere pleasure* that salvation is spontaneously offered to some, while others have no access to it, great and difficult questions immediately arise. These questions are inexplicable, when proper views are not entertained concerning election and predestination. To many this seems a perplexing subject, because they deem it most incompatible that, of the great totality of mankind, some should be predestined to salvation, and others to destruction. . . . However, until we are made acquainted with his eternal election, we will never feel persuaded (as we ought) that our salvation flows from the free mercy of God. . . . It is plain how ignorance of this principle greatly detracts from the glory of God, and impairs true humility. . . . To make it evident that our salvation flows entirely from the good mercy of God, we must be carried back to the origin of election. Thus, those who would extinguish it, wickedly do as much as in them lies to obscure what they ought most loudly to extol, and pluck up humility by the very roots. . . .

ASK YOURSELF

6.32. How does the doctrine of predestination highlight God's glory?

Some theologians maintain that predestination is simply a consequence of God's foreknowledge. That is, since God knows ahead of time whether we will accept him or reject him, then our path of acceptance or rejection is already fixed. Calvin argues that predestination is not merely an offshoot of foreknowledge in this manner. Instead, predestination involves an overt, deliberate choice on God's part. This becomes clear when we closely define both foreknowledge and predestination.

3.21.5 No pious person could simply deny the predestination by which God adopts some to the hope of life, and pronounces others to eternal death. But it is greatly undermined especially by those who make foreknowledge its cause. We, indeed, ascribe both foreknowledge and predestination to God. But we say, that it is absurd to make the latter subordinate to the former. When we attribute *foreknowledge* to God, we mean that all things always were, and ever continue, under his eye. To God's knowledge there is no past or future, but all things are present. Indeed, all things are so present, that it is not merely the idea of them that is before God (such as objects which we retain in our memories) but that he truly sees and contemplates them as actually under his immediate inspection. This foreknowledge extends to the whole circuit of the world, and to all creatures.

ASK YOURSELF

6.33. How does Calvin define "foreknowledge"?

By predestination we mean the eternal decree of God, by which he determined with himself whatever he wished to happen with regard to every person. All are not created on equal terms, but some are preordained to eternal life, others to eternal damnation. Accordingly, as each has been created for one or other of these ends, we say that each person has been predestined to life or to death. God has testified this not only in the case of single individuals, but with communities too. This was so of all future generations of Abraham, to make it plain that the future condition of each nation lives entirely at his disposal.

ASK YOURSELF

6.34. How does Calvin define "predestination"?

In summary, the key elements of Calvin's understanding of human nature are these: The first created humans had pure intellects, genuinely free wills, and were not predestined to fall. After the fall, however, humans lost their freedom of choice, their intellects became compromised to at least some extent, and their salvation and condemnation became predestined by God. Both before and after the fall, humans had and continue to have an instinctive sense of God's existence and a consciousness of morality.

FIDEISM AND SKEPTICISM

In the philosophy of religion, the term "fideism" (literally "faith-ism") refers to the view that religious knowledge is initially obtained through faith alone, and not through reason. The champion of this view in early Christian theology was Augustine, who maintained that "I believe in order that I may know." During the middle ages, Augustine's faith approach to religion was quickly overshadowed by Aquinas, Scotus, Ockham, and others who offered rational proofs for God's existence. The dominance of this rationalistic approach continued through the Renaissance and early modern period. So strong was this tendency that during the eighteenth century it was sometimes a worse offense to reject rational proofs for God than to reject the divine status of Jesus. However, beginning in the Renaissance, a vocal minority of philosophers and theologians opposed such rationalism and returned to the fideism of Augustine. These new defenders of fideism not only ridiculed the authority of reason in religious belief, but some also maintained that their views were compatible with the skepticism of the ancient Greeks. As the Renaissance witnessed a new appreciation for ancient Greek classics, the skeptical writings of Sextus Empiricus—the best surviving example of the Pyrrhonian skeptical tradition—were also revived and endorsed by several philosophers. For Sextus, *complete* skepticism entailed doubting God's existence—a recommendation that fideists certainly rejected. However, the point of commonality was their respective beliefs in the overall bankruptcy of reason.

Montaigne's *Apology*

An early defense of fideist skepticism is found in Michel Montaigne's *Apology for Raymond Sebond* (1580). Montaigne (1533–1592) was a French lawyer, diplomat, and creator of the literary form known as the "essay." His collected writings, the *Essay*, is a chronological arrangement of 107 chapters on various topics presented in three books. The second book represents the more skeptical phase in his writings, the running theme of which is, "What do I know?" (*Que sais-je?*). His skeptical approach comes to a head in his *Apology* (first published separately and later included in the *Essay*), in which he makes specific use of Sextus's ten modes of skepticism to explain his discontent with reason. All selections in this section are from Montaigne's *Apology*.

Sebond's Natural Theology. Montaigne opens his *Apology* with a description of Raymond Sebond's book *Natural Theology*. Sebond (d. 1432) was a fifteenth-century Catholic theologian from Catalonia, Spain. Montaigne's first published work was a translation of this text (1568–1569), done at his father's request.

From MONTAIGNE: *Apology for Raymond Sebond*

Learning is indeed a very great and considerable quality. Those who despise it invariably discover their own lack of understanding. However, I do not prize it as excessively as others do. For example, Heril the philosopher argued that only the Sovereign Good can make us wise and content. I do not believe this any more than I do the claim made by others that learning is the mother of all virtue, and all vice results from ignorance. Even if it is true, it is subject to a very long interpretation. . . . Shortly before my father's death he accidentally found this book [i.e., the *Natural Theology* by Raymond Sebond] under a pile of other neglected papers and commanded me to translate it into French for him. . . . Sebond's purpose is strong and bold. By human and natural reasoning he undertakes to establish all the articles of Christian religion, contrary to the atheists. He is, in truth, so firm and successful, that I doubt it is possible to do better on that subject, and I doubt that he has been equaled. To me, the work seemed too beautiful and rich for such an unknown author, of whom all we know is that he was a Spanish physics professor at Thoulouse about 200 years ago. I asked Adrian Turnebus, who knows everything, what he thought of the book. He answered that he thought it was an abstract drawn from St. Thomas Aquinas since only Aquinas's wit, learning, and subtlety could produce those thoughts. So, whoever was the author and inventor (without more argument it is not reasonable to deprive Sebond of that title), he was a person of great sufficiency and admirable abilities. The first thing they attack in his work is that Christians should not base their belief upon human reasoning, as it is only the result of faith and the particular inspiration of divine grace. This objection contains a certain zeal for piety and, thus, with courtesy and respect we should address those who offer it. This is a task more proper for a person well-read in divinity than for me who knows nothing of it. . . .

 ASK YOURSELF

6.35. Assuming that Sebond's reasoning resembled Aquinas's, what arguments for God's existence might he offer, and what implications do they have regarding the domain of reason in religious matters?

Faith. Against Sebond's rationalistic approach to religious belief, Montaigne argues that our reason cannot be relied upon and that religious truth is arrived at through faith.

Nevertheless, it is faith alone that grasps the deep mysteries of our religion. I do not say, though, that it is not a brave and admirable attempt to use our God-given natural and human abilities to the service of our faith. It is undoubtedly the most noble use we can put them to. . . . I know an important, well educated person who confessed to me that Sebond's arguments saved him from serious error. . . . Let us see, then, if man has in his power some more forcible and convincing reasons than those of Sebond—especially people who are inclined to arrive at certainty by arguments and reasons. St. Augustine, disputing against such people, justly criticizes them for maintaining that our beliefs must be false if they cannot be established by reason. He cleverly offers specific experiments to show that a great variety of known and indubitable things cannot be demonstrated by our natural reason, such as when people confess that they see nothing. Without drawing from unusual examples (as Augustine does) we must do more than this so they will see the weakness of their reason. Consider: reason is so blind that there is no faculty clear enough to distinguish the easy and the hard; nature in general challenges reason's authority and rejects its mediation in all subjects equally; what does Truth mean when she preaches to us to reject worldly philosophy, or when she so frequently dictates to us that our wisdom is folly in the sight of God? The vainest of all vanities is humanity; the person who presumes upon his wisdom does not yet know what wisdom is; a person seduces and deceives himself if he thinks himself to be something when in fact he is nothing. These sentences of the Holy Ghost clearly and vividly express what I am saying, and I need no other proof against people who would submit to the Holy Spirit's authority with humility and obedience. But those others will not tolerate anyone to oppose their reasoning, except by reasoning itself; thus they will be punished at their own expense.

 ASK YOURSELF

6.36. What is the message of the "Holy Ghost" concerning the use of reason?

Pyrrhonism. Montaigne continues by describing the skeptical position of Pyrrho, the ancient Greek philosopher.

Suppose that learning and knowledge actually produced the effects they speak of. That is, they could blunt and soften the sharpness of the misfortunes that follow us. Does it do this any better than what ignorance accomplishes much more clearly and simply? The philosopher Pyrrho was at sea, and because of a violent storm was in great danger of being thrown overboard. He offered no comfort to those that were with him in the ship except to follow the example of a pig that was on board. For, nothing at all dismayed the pig, who seemed to watch and outstare the storm. Philosophy, after all her principles, ultimately has us follow the examples of a wrestler or a muleteer. For in them we see less feeling of death, pain, grief, and other inconveniences. They exhibit a more courageous consistency than learning or knowledge could ever give someone, unless, through an inborn habit, he prepared for it. . . .

That ignorance which knows, judges, and condemns itself is not an absolute ignorance. For to be so, it must be completely ignorant of itself. Thus, the profession of the Pyrrhonians is to waver, to doubt, to inquire, and never be assured of anything nor explain himself. Of the three functions or faculties of the soul (i.e. the imaginative, the appetite, and the consenting), they follow the first two, but the last they believe is ambiguous and hold neither one side nor the other with approval or inclination. . . . This straight and inflexible attitude of their judgment, receiving all objects without adoption or consent, leads them to their tranquillity. This is the condition of a quiet and settled life, which is exempt from the agitations which we receive by the impression of the opinion and knowledge which we imagine to have of things.

ASK YOURSELF

6.37. What is the end result of skepticism for Pyrrhonian skeptics?

From such knowledge we get fear, avarice, envy, passionate desires, ambition, pride, superstition, love of novelty, rebellion, disobedience, obstinacy, and a great number of bodily evils. Indeed, by with this attitude they exempt themselves from jealousy within their own discipline. For, they argue only mildly. They do not fear rebuttal or contradiction in their arguments. When they say that heavy things fall downward, they would hate to be believed and wish to be contradicted. This, in turn, brings about doubt and suspense of judgment, which is their purpose. They put forward their propositions only to criticize those they imagine we believe in. If you take their side, then they will try to maintain the opposite view. It is all the same to them, nor do they have a preference. If you propose that snow is black, they will argue on the other side that snow is white. If you say it is neither one nor the other, they will maintain that it is both.

ASK YOURSELF

6.38. How do Pyrrhonians typically engage in disputes?

. . . I understand why the Pyrrhonian philosophers cannot by any manner of speech express their general conception. To do so, they would need a new language. Our language is completely composed of affirmative propositions, which are directly against the Pyrrhonians. Thus, when they say "I doubt" you have them by the throat to make them admit that they doubt; at least you are assured of and know this. So they have been compelled to save themselves with the following comparison from medicine, without which their attitude would be inexplicable. When they say, "I don't know," or "I doubt," they say, that this proposition expels itself along with other propositions, just as rhubarb [i.e., a laxative] purges one of bad humors and is itself purged. This attitude is more clearly seen in the question "What do I know?" I bear these words as inscribed on a pair of balances.

ASK YOURSELF

6.39. According to the Pyrrhonians' "laxative" metaphor, what becomes of the skeptic's very claim that everything should be doubted?

Bayle's *Dictionary*

Another illustration of the unusual marriage between fideism and skepticism is the following from Pierre Bayle (1647–1706). Bayle, a French philosophy and history professor, is most remembered for his monumental *Historical and Critical Dictionary* (1692). The multivolume work contains entries on over 2,500 people—from Adam and Eve to Spinoza—and nearly two hundred entries on nonperson topics. Bayle sheltered himself from political repercussions by making conservative statements in the main entries of his articles, but indirectly and obliquely criticized those views in the extended notes which were several times longer than the initial entries. This approach was adopted by the eighteenth-century encyclopedists. Critics of Bayle saw through this concealment and accused him of endorsing Manicheanism, Pyrrhonism, Epicureanism, and atheism. Of particular importance were his entries on Eve, David, Pyrrho, the Manicheans, the Paulicans, Zeno, Pomponazzi, Xenophanes, Spinoza, Nicole, and Pellison. The following are selections from his article on Pyrrho. He begins with a harmless description of Pyrrho's skepticism.

 From BAYLE: *Historical and Cultural Dictionary* ——

. . . Pyrrho found reasons to both affirm and deny everything; thus he suspended his assent after he had well examined the arguments pro and con, and reduced all his conclusions to a non *liquet*, that is, let the matter be further inquired into. So, he sought truth as long as he lived, but he viewed the matter in such a way that he never would grant that he found it. Though he is not the creator of that method of philosophizing, yet it goes by his name. It is commonly called Pyrrhonism (or skepticism) and is the art of disputing everything, without doing anything else but suspending one's judgment. It is justly detested in the schools of Divinity, where some try to give it a new, though an illusory, strength. However, it may be useful to compel a person out of a sense of ignorance, to call for the help of God, and to submit to the authority of faith.

Bayle elaborates on the final point in a footnote.

When a person is able to apprehend all the ways of suspending his judgment, which have been explained by Sextus Empiricus, he may then see that logic is the greatest effort of subtlety that the human mind is capable of. But he will also see that such a subtlety will give him no satisfaction. It confuses itself; for if it were solid, it would necessarily prove that we must doubt. Therefore there would be some certainty, there would be a certain rule of truth. However, that system itself would be destroyed by it. But you need not fear that things would come to that: the reasons for doubting are doubtful themselves: one must therefore doubt whether he ought to doubt. What chaos! What torment for the mind! It seems, therefore, that this unhappy state is the fittest of all to convince us, that our reason is the way to wander, since when it displays itself with the greatest subtlety, it throws us into such emptiness. What naturally follows from this is to renounce that guide, and appeal to the cause of all things to give us a better guide. It is a great step towards the Christian religion, which requires us to expect from God the knowledge of what we are to believe and do, and that we should attach our understanding to the obedience of faith. If a person is first convinced that he can expect no satisfaction from his philosophical studies, he will be more inclined to pray to God; he will ask God for the conviction of the truths which he ought to believe, rather than flattering himself with the success of his reasoning and disputing. It is therefore a welcomed inclination to faith to know the defects of reason. Hence it is that Pascal and some others have said, that to convert Libertines, they must be made sensible of the weakness of reason, and taught to mistrust it.

 ASK YOURSELF

6.40. According to Bayle, what is the problem of circularity with the Pyrrhonian method of skepticism as advanced by Sextus Empiricus?

6.41. For Bayle, how is skepticism "a great step toward the Christian religion"?

Pascal's Wager

Blaise Pascal (1623–1662) is remembered for both his scientific and theological contributions to the seventeenth century. He devoted himself to science in the early part of his life and invented the first calculating machine, which was one of the first applied achievements of the scientific revolution. He also conducted experiments on air pressure and, contrary to the accepted views at the time, concluded that "nature has no abhorrence of a vacuum." After a religious experience in 1654, Pascal joined the ascetic Jansenist religious order and devoted most of his writing to theology. He continued writing in the field of mathematics, however, making contributions in probability theory, number theory, and geometry. After his death, an unfinished book of his titled *Pensées*, that is, *Thoughts* was published. Although Pascal is a harsh critic of Pyrrhonian skepticism in this work, he nevertheless denies that science can improve the human condition—presumably a conclusion based on the limits he found to his own scientific inquiries. And, even though he strongly attacks religious skepticism, he nevertheless believes that the traditional arguments for God's existence fail: There is "too much to deny, yet too little to be sure." Religious belief, then, is a matter of faith and not reason. The most famous part of the work is the "wager": When reason is neutral on the issue of God's existence, the balance of positive and negative consequences of believing versus disbelieving in God should psychologically compel us to believe that God exists. The following selections are from Pascal's *Thoughts*.

Reason Is Neutral Concerning God. Pascal begins his discussion of the wager by discussing the limitations of reason in proving God's existence.

From PASCAL: *Thoughts*

By faith we know God's existence. In the glorious state of heaven we will know his nature. Now, I have already shown that we may easily know the existence of a thing without knowing its nature. Let us speak now according to the light of nature. If there is a God he is infinitely incomprehensible, since, having neither parts nor limits, he has no proportion to us. We are then incapable of knowing either what he is, or whether he is. This being true, who will dare to undertake to resolve this question? It cannot be we who have no proportion to him.

Who, then, will blame those Christians who are not able to give a reason for their belief insofar as they profess a religion for which they can give no reason? In exposing it to the world, they declare that it is a folly *stultitiam* (1 Corinthians 1:18). And then you complain that they do not prove it! If they proved it, they would not keep their word. It is in lacking proofs that they do not lack sense. Yes, but though this may excuse those who offer it such, and take away the blame for producing it without reason, this does not excuse those who receive it.

 ASK YOURSELF

6.42. What does the "light of nature" or reason alone tell us about God's nature and existence?

Let us examine this point then, and say "God is, or he is not." But to which side shall we incline? Reason cannot decide it at all. There is an infinite chaos that separates us. A game is being played at the extremity of this infinite distance in which heads or tails must come up. Which will you take? By reason you can wager on neither. By reason you can hinder neither from winning.

Do not, then, charge those with falsehood who have made a choice. For you know nothing about it. "No. But I blame them for having made, not *this* choice, but *a* choice. For although he who takes heads, and the other, are in the same fault, they are both in fault. The proper way is simply not to wager."

 ASK YOURSELF

6.43. Given that our reason cannot prove God's existence, what is wrong with just flipping a coin to decide what we should believe?

Stakes of the Wager. Even though we can't just flip a coin, Pascal believes that ultimately a choice must be made. In William James's terms, we face a "forced option" where even not choosing constitutes a choice. Not only is our choice forced, but there are tremendous differences in consequences depending on what side we choose.

Yes, but you must wager. This is not voluntary. You have set sail. Which will you take? Let's see. Since a choice must be made, let's see which interests you the least. You have two things to lose: the true and the good. And you have two things to stake: your reason and your will; that is, your knowledge and your complete happiness. And your nature has two things to shun: error and misery. Your reason is not more wounded, since a choice must necessarily be made in choosing one rather than the other. Here a point is eliminated. But what about your happiness? Let us weigh the gain and the loss in taking heads that God exists. Let us weigh these two cases. If you gain, you gain all. If you lose, you lose nothing. Wager without hesitation, then, that he is. "This is admirable. Yes, it is necessary to wager, but perhaps I wager too much." Let us see. Since there is equal risk of gaining or losing, if you had to gain but two lives for one, still you might wager. But if there were three lives to gain, it would be required to play (since you are under the necessity of playing). And, when you are forced to play, you would be imprudent not to risk your life in order to gain three in a play where there is equal hazard of loss and gain. But there is an eternity of life and happiness. And this being true, even if there were an infinity of chances (only one of which might be for you) you would still be right in wagering one in order to have two. And being obliged to play, if there was an infinity of life infinitely happy to gain, you would act foolishly to refuse to play one life against three in a game where among an infinity of chances there is one for you. But there is here an infinity of life infinitely happy to gain. And there is a chance of gain against a finite number of chances of loss, and what you play is finite.

 ASK YOURSELF

6.44. How much do we stand to gain if we wager in favor of belief in God?

This [the balance of gain over loss] is quite settled. Wherever the infinite is, and where there is not an infinity of chances of loss against the chance of gain, there is nothing to weigh, and we must give all. And thus, when we are forced to play, we must renounce reason in order to keep life, rather than to risk it for the infinite gain, which is as likely to occur as the loss of nothingness.

The stakes of the wager are illustrated in the following chart:

	WAGER HE EXISTS	WAGER HE DOESN'T
God exists	Infinite happiness	Nothing
God doesn't exist	Nothing	Nothing

The point of the wager is to prove neither that God exists nor that belief in God is a rational belief. Instead, the wager aims to show that belief in God is a *rational act*. An *act* is rational if it achieves a reasonable end; by contrast, *beliefs* are rational when they meet certain standards (e.g., consistency, due consideration of the relevant evidence).

Whether Future Happiness is Infinitely Uncertain. Pascal continues voicing a potential criticism to his previous reasoning. My happiness in this life is certain, but my alleged future happiness is actually infinitely uncertain. So why gamble on that which is infinitely uncertain, regardless of how great its possible gain?

For there is no use in saying that it is uncertain whether we shall gain, and that it is certain that we risk. And there is no use in saying that, [a] the infinite distance between the certainty of what we risk and, [b] the uncertainty of what we shall gain, raises the finite good which we certainly risk to a level of equality with the uncertain infinite gain. It is not so. Every player, without violating reason, risks a certainty to gain uncertainty, and nevertheless he risks a finite certainty to gain a finite uncertainty. The distance is not infinite between this certainty of what we risk, and the uncertainty of gain. This is false. There is, in truth, an infinity between the certainty of gaining and the certainty of losing. But the uncertainty of gaining is proportioned to the certainty of what we risk, according to the proportion of the chances of gain and loss. It follows from this that if there are as many chances on one side as there are on the other, the game is playing even. And then the certainty of what we risk is equal to the uncertainty of the gain. This is quite far from being infinitely distant. And thus our proposition [of infinite gain] is of infinite force when there is the finite to hazard in a play where the chances of gain and loss are equal, and the infinite to gain. This is demonstrative, and if people are capable of any truths, this is one of them.

Pascal's response to this criticism is to deny that our future gain is infinitely uncertain. The odds are the same as to whether we will gain happiness or we won't.

Faith. Pascal continues by considering those who say that they are not psychologically capable of making such a belief commitment.

"I confess it, I admit it. But, still, are there no means of seeing the truth behind the game?" Yes, the scriptures and the rest.

"Yes, but my hands are tied and my mouth is dumb. I am forced to wager, and I am not free. I am chained and so constituted that I cannot believe. What will you have me do then?" It is true. But at least learn your inability to believe, since reason brings you to such belief [given the previous reasoning], and yet you cannot believe. Try then to convince yourself not by the addition of proofs for the existence of God, but by the reduction of your own passions. You would have recourse to faith, but don't know the ways. You wish to be cured of infidelity, and you ask for the remedy. Learn it from those who have been bound like yourself, and who would wager now all their goods. These know the road that you wish to follow, and are cured of a disease that you wish to be cured of. Follow their course, then, from its beginning. It consisted in doing all things *as if* they believed in them, in using holy water, in having masses said, etc. Naturally this will make you believe and stupefy you at the same time. "But this is what I fear." And why? What have you to lose?

 ASK YOURSELF

6.45. Pascal's solution to those who claim an inability to believe is to reduce one's passions and rely on faith. What steps should we take to have such faith?

No Loss in This Life. Pascal argues that a life of belief in God is not a loss in this life, but is in fact a gain.

> But to show you that this leads to it [i.e., belief], this will diminish the passions, which are your great obstacles. Now, what harm will come to you in taking this course? You would be faithful, virtuous, humble, grateful, beneficent, a sincere friend, truthful. Truly, you would not be given up to poisonous pleasures, to false glory, or false joys. But would you not have other pleasures?
>
> I say to you that you will gain by it in this life. And, each step you take in this direction, you will see so much of the certainty of gain, and so much of the nothingness of what you hazard, that you will acknowledge in the end that you have wagered something certain, infinite for which you have given nothing.

James's Criticisms of Pascal's Wager. In his essay "The Will to Believe," early twentieth-century American philosopher William James criticized Pascal's wager on two accounts. James first argues that the calculating nature of the wager is too cold and impersonal and cannot produce sincere belief:

> We feel that a faith in masses and holy water adopted willfully after such a mechanical calculation—would lack the inner soul of faith's reality; and if we were ourselves in the place of the Deity, we should probably take particular pleasure in cutting off believers of this pattern from their infinite reward. It is evident that unless there be some pre-existing tendency to believe in masses and holy water, the option offered to the will by Pascal is not a living option.

James's second criticism is that the same argument in the wager applies to belief in other deities since different religions claim to give eternal life:

> As well might the Mahdi write to us, saying, "I am the Expected One whom God has created in his effulgence. You shall be infinitely happy if you confess me; otherwise you shall be cut off from the light of the sun. Weigh, then, your infinite gain if I am genuine against your finite sacrifice if I am not!"

 ASK YOURSELF

6.46. Illustrate James's point using either a real or invented world religion.

ASTRONOMY

Two distinct types of contributions characterize the scientific revolution: (1) particular discoveries, such as calculus, the sun-centered view of the heavens, and the theory of gravity; and (2) methods of scientific investigation, particularly those by Francis Bacon and René Descartes. This section deals with the first of these, focusing particularly on the contributions to the field of astronomy. Although the connection between astronomy and philosophy during the scientific revolution may not be immediately obvious, there are at least two important points of overlap. First, a branch of philosophy called the *philosophy of science* critically examines a range of scientific issues, one of which involves the credibility of scientific hypotheses. How do we show that one scientific hypothesis is better than another? Astronomers during the scientific revolution grappled with this very question as they sought to overturn the older earth-centered system of the universe in favor of newer Sun-centered ones. The earth-centered/Sun-centered controversy is now a standard illustration in the philosophy of science for exploring how we move from an older faulty hypothesis to a newer and better one. Second, perhaps more than any other area of scientific inquiry, advances in astronomy during this time redefined how people saw themselves in relation to the larger scheme of things. Laws of nature were more precisely articulated and the mechanistic structure of the heavens became a model for understanding how things operate here on earth. For many philosophical theologians, by understandings these laws we better understand the mind of God and his role in creating and sustaining the universe.

The Earth-Centered System of the Universe

The medieval earth-centered view of the universe is based on a progression of ideas in ancient Greek astronomy. The dialogue began with Thales (636–546 BCE), who believed that the earth was a flat disk floating on water. More sophisticated systems were soon proposed. Followers of Pythagoras (fl. 530 BCE) suggested that the earth was round and encircled by several heavenly spheres, similar to the layers of an onion that surround its core. The moon was attached to the innermost sphere, and all the stars to the outer sphere. Attached to the middle spheres were Mercury, Venus, the Sun, Mars, Jupiter, and Saturn. The spheres were perfectly round and moved in a perfectly uniform shape. The faster spheres were closer to the center (Mercury being the fastest) and the slower ones further away (Saturn being the slowest). A Pythagorean named Philolaus (fl. 425 BCE) suggested an alternative scheme. A fiery watchtower of the Gods was at the center of things, and the earth, the Sun, and the planets rotated around the fiery watchtower. This view never took hold. Following the earlier Pythagorean model, Eudoxus (fl. 370 BCE) offered a system with twenty-seven spheres rotating around the fixed earth. A similar picture of the universe emerges with Aristotle (384–322 BCE) in "On the Heavens" and Book 8 of the *Physics*. Aristotle held that the spheres were perfectly shaped solids and totaled fifty-five in number, resulting from the fifty-five distinct observable motions in the sky. Each sphere is also accompanied by its own God, and the spheres move with joy in the presence of its God. The Gods are eternal, so this produces circular motion, which for him is the only kind of perfect and eternal motion.

An underlying problem with the earth-centered schemes of the universe was explaining the retrograde, or apparent backward motion of the planets. This appears when observing over a period of years the movement of planets against the backdrop of the stars. A theory of perfectly circular spheres in perfectly circular motion could not account for these observations. To bring the models of the universe in line with observed phenomena, different changes were proposed. Aristarchus (fl. 240 BCE) maintained that the Sun was at the center of the universe and that the planets—along with the earth—were attached to their own encircling spheres. Aristarchus also proposed that the earth rotated on its axis. Unfortunately, his views were not adopted. A second modification was a system of epicycles. Epicycles are smaller pinwheel-like spheres attached to the larger spheres. The earth remains at the center of surrounding spheres. The planets, then, move around on the smaller epicycles, while the epicycles move around on the larger spheres. This view was developed by Hipparchus (fl. 140 BCE). A third modification was a system of *eccentric* circles. In this view, all of the heavenly spheres surround the earth. However, the earth is not at the exact center, but slightly off to one side. As the planetary spheres rotate, the spheres are tugged slightly off center, then on center, then off again. A combination of the rotation and the tugging presents the illusion of retrograde motion from the earth's perspective.

The eccentric and epicycle models were combined by Ptolemy (fl. 120 CE), a Greco-Egyptian mathematician and geographer. In his thirteen volume *Almagest*, he presents the accumulated data from years of astronomical observations. He then shows that Hipparchus's simple account of epicycles cannot be made to fit the data. Instead, he argues that the data are better explained when the planets are attached to epicycles *and* the earth is slightly off center. Ptolemy's explanation dominated European astronomy for the next thirteen hundred years. However, as more astronomical data accumulated during the middle ages, refinements were made to both the pure epicycle system of Hipparchus and Ptolemy's combination epicycle-eccentric system. Some epicycle systems proposed that there were epicycles within epicycles. The most sophisticated of these had over two hundred epicycles. Developments of Ptolemy's combination system retained a single epicycle; however, they introduced a reference point (called the "equant") on the other side of the off-centered earth. The larger planetary spheres would then speed up and slow down in relation to the area swept by this reference point.

Medieval systems of the universe retained and further developed the metaphysical aspects of the heavens. Since crystals on earth have a natural symmetry, many believed that the perfect heavenly spheres were a spherical variety of crystals. The heavens were still seen as a place of perfection where spiritual beings dwelled. The universe was *finite*, extending no further than the final crystalline sphere containing the stars. Following Aristotle, God is the prime mover who starts all motion, which then moves down through the spheres, ultimately producing the tides, the winds, the seasons, and the generation of plants and animals. Virtually every astronomer was an astrologer, given that everything in the heavens had significance.

Copernicus

Piece by piece, Renaissance astronomers rejected the medieval systems of the universe. Polish clergyman Nicholas Copernicus (1473–1543) proposed the Sun-centered system in his *On the Revolutions of the Heavenly Spheres* (1543). In his view, the Sun was encircled by a series of perfectly circular spheres that moved the planets. To make his theory match his actual observations of planetary motion, he still needed to postulate forty-five epicycles and eccentric planetary orbits. His theory was no more accurate in prediction than either of the earth-centered systems (that is, the elaborate epicycle system or the modified epicycle-eccentric circle system). It also carried over the belief in celestial spheres and a finite universe. Copernicus died shortly after the publication of his work, and thus did not witness the official backlash to his theory from the Catholic church, which condemned his theory in 1616. Nevertheless, astronomers of the time accepted it over rival medieval systems because of its unity and harmony. Many accepted his view as simply a helpful calculating device, without making a commitment to its truth. The following selections are from his "Dedication" to the Pope in *On the Revolutions of the Heavenly Spheres*.

Problems with Traditional Theories. Copernicus explains the two existing systems of the universe and notes their respective faults.

 From COPERNICUS: *On the Revolutions of the* _____
Heavenly Spheres

But perhaps Your Holiness will see better why I published these studies after seeing the pains I've taken in elaborating them, and have not hesitated to commit my views of the motion of the Earth to writing. You may similarly be curious to hear how it occurred to me to form a conception of any terrestrial motion in the first place—contrary to both the accepted view of mathematicians and common sense. Therefore I will have it known to Your Holiness that the only thing which induced me to look for another way of reckoning the movements of the heavenly bodies was that I knew that mathematicians by no means agree in their investigations of this subject. For, in the first place, they are so much in doubt concerning the motion of the sun and the moon, that they can not even demonstrate and prove by observation the constant length of a complete year. And in the second place, in determining the motions both of these and of the five other planets, they fail to employ consistently one set of first principles and hypotheses; instead, they use methods of proof based only on the apparent revolutions and motions. For some employ concentric circles only [with many epicycles]. Others use eccentric circles and [a single] epicycles. And even by these means they do not completely attain the desired end. For, although those who have depended upon concentric circles [and many epicycles] have shown that certain diverse motions can be deduced from these. Yet they have not succeeded thereby in laying down any sure principle, corresponding indisputably to the phenomena.

 ASK YOURSELF

6.47. What is the problem with the system of concentric circles and many epicycles?

Those, on the other hand, who have devised systems of eccentric circles, seem in great part to have solved the apparent movements by calculations which by these eccentrics are made to fit. However, they have nevertheless introduced many things which seem to contradict the first principles of the uniformity of motion. Nor have they been able to discover or calculate from these the main points, which is the shape of the world and the fixed symmetry of its parts. Their procedure has been as if someone were to collect hands, feet, a head, and other members from various places, all very fine in themselves, but not proportionate to one body, and no single one corresponding in its turn to the others; from these, then, a monster rather than a man would be formed. Thus in their process of demonstration which they term a "method," they are found to have omitted something essential, or to have included something foreign and not pertaining to the matter in hand. This certainly would never have happened to them if they had followed fixed principles. For if the hypotheses they assumed were not false, all that resulted therefrom would be verified indubitably. Those things which I am saying now may be obscure, yet they will be made clearer in their proper place.

 ASK YOURSELF

6.48. What is the problem with the system of eccentric circles?

Advantages of the Sun-Centered System. Copernicus explains how he got the idea of a Sun-centered system from ancient writers. Further, by working out the details of this new system, he explains that there is a symbiotic compatibility among all the parts of the system.

I turned over in my mind for a long time this uncertainty of the traditional mathematical methods of calculating the motions of the celestial bodies. I began to grow disgusted that no more consistent scheme of the movements of the mechanism of the universe (set up for our benefit by that best and most law abiding Architect of all things) was agreed upon by philosophers who otherwise investigate so carefully the most minute details of this world. Thus, I undertook the task of re-reading the books of all the philosophers I could get access to, to see whether anyone ever was of the opinion that the motions of the celestial bodies were other than those postulated by the people who taught mathematics in the schools. And I found first, indeed, in Cicero, that Niceta perceived that the Earth moved. After that, in Plutarch, I found that some others were of this opinion, whose words I have seen fit to quote here, that they may be accessible to all.

Some maintain that the Earth is stationary, but Philolaus the Pythagorean says that it revolves in a circle about the fire of the ecliptic, like the sun and moon. Heraklides of Pontus and Ekphantus the Pythagorean make the Earth move, not changing its position, however, confined in its falling and rising around its own center in the manner of a wheel.

 ASK YOURSELF

6.49. Which ancient writers proposed a Sun-centered system?

Taking this as a starting point, I began to consider the mobility of the Earth. And although the idea seemed absurd, yet because I knew that the liberty had been granted to others before me to postulate all sorts of little circles for explaining the phenomena of the stars, I thought I also might easily be permitted to try whether by postulating some motions of the Earth, more reliable conclusions could be reached regarding the revolution of the heavenly bodies, than those of my predecessors.

So, I postulated movements which (further on in the book) I ascribe to the Earth, and through many and long observations I discovered the following. I assumed that the movements of the other planets are applied also to the circular motion of the Earth, and are also substituted for the revolution of each star. From this, not only do their phenomena follow logically, but the relative positions and magnitudes both of the stars and all their orbits, and of the heavens themselves, become closely related. So closely related are they that nothing can be changed in any of its parts without causing confusion in the other parts and in the whole universe. Therefore, in the course of the work I have followed this plan: I describe in the first book all the positions of the orbits together with the movements which I ascribe to the Earth, in order that this book might contain, as it were, the general scheme of the universe. In the remaining books, I establish the motions of the other stars and of all their orbits together with the movement of the Earth. This is done so that one may see from this to what extent the movements and appearances of the other stars and their orbits can be saved, if they are transferred to the movement of the Earth.

 ASK YOURSELF

6.50. According to Copernicus, how can some of the apparent motion of the stars be explained?

Why exactly did Copernicus reject traditional earth-centered systems in favor of his Sun-centered system? His discussion here tells us how his thoughts on the subject progressed over time. The underlying thrust of his discussion, however, is that we must adapt our theories about reality to the actual appearances of things, using the sparsest theory that we can to account for those appearances. In short, the Sun-centered system was more theoretically simple than the various earth-centered systems. Since Copernicus, the notion of simplicity has become one of the central points of discussion in the philosophy of science. Another philosophically important implication of Copernicus's discussion is this: How we observe the world ultimately rests on the theoretical presuppositions that we make. We learn little about reality by simply observing flickering stars and planets across the sky. Knowledge of the heavens is only attained when we interpret our observations from within the context of some theory, such as earth-centered or Sun-centered ones. Whether our presuppositions are good or bad, they are nevertheless assumptions that we cannot avoid making.

After Copernicus, the next key contribution to Sun-centered theory was Johannes Kepler (1571–1603), a German teacher of mathematics and astronomy. Influenced by neo-Platonists who honored the Sun, Kepler followed Copernicus's Sun-centered account. He also held that the solar system contained a series of enveloping "regular solids." Regular solids are three-dimensional shapes that have equal edges, equal angles, equal faces, and equal corners. Each planetary orbit circled around one of these huge regular solids. The order is as follows: a sphere for Saturn, a cube, a sphere for

Jupiter, a tetrahedron, a sphere for Mars, a dodecahedron, a sphere for Earth. Two additional solids rested within earth's sphere for Venus and Mercury. Excited by this concept, he worked as an assistant to the Danish astronomer Tycho Brahe (1546–1601) in the hopes of gaining access to Brahe's state-of-the-art observational data. Kepler experimented with different configurations of circular planetary orbits. However, he was dissatisfied because of an observational discrepancy of eight minutes (where sixty minutes equals one degree). In his *On the Motion of Mars* (1609) he solved the riddle with his proposed three laws of planetary motion: (1) Planets travel in elliptical orbits; (2) the radius vector connecting Sun and planet sweeps over equal areas in equal times; and (3) the squares of the periods of any two planets are in the same ratio as the cubes of their mean distances from the Sun (i.e., the farther away from the Sun, the slower a planet moves). Despite his advances, Kepler's religious mysticism made him hesitant to abandon the notion of perfect crystalline spheres in the heavens.

Galileo

The son of a musician, Galileo Galilei (1564–1642) was born near Florence and later studied medicine at the University of Pisa. Legend has it that he observed a swinging lamp in the university cathedral, and noted that it took the same amount of time for it to complete its swing cycle, regardless of how wide the swing was. This inspired him to study mathematics. Galileo took on various teaching posts and made a name for himself by publishing scientific treatises. In 1592 he was awarded the chair of mathematics at Padua, where he remained for eighteen years and did his most important work. In a letter to Kepler during this time (April 4, 1597) he notes that he had for some time been an advocate of the Copernican system, but said nothing of it for fear of ridicule.

The Telescope. Telescopes were invented by Dutch spectacle makers who brought them to sell in Venice. The invention appealed to businesspeople since it could detect cargo ships two hours before they could otherwise be observed, thus giving the businessperson an advantage in the market. Galileo heard of the invention while visiting Venice in the spring of 1609. On his return to Padua, in one night he thought the idea out himself and made a telescope that had a power of three. In *The Assayer* (1623) he explains his thought process.

 From GALILEO: *The Assayer*

On the simple information of the effect obtained, I discovered the telescope, not by chance [as was the case with the original Dutch inventor], but by the way of pure reasoning. Here are the steps. The artifice of the instrument depends either on one glass or on several. It cannot depend on one, for that must be either convex, or concave, or plain. The last form neither augments nor diminishes visible objects. The concave diminishes them, and the convex increases them, but both show them blurred and indistinct. Passing then to the combination of two glasses, and knowing that glasses with plain surfaces change nothing, I concluded that the effect could not be produced by combining a plain glass with a convex or a concave one. I was thus left with the two other kinds of glasses, and after a few experiments I saw how the effect sought could be produced. Such was the march of my discovery, in which I was not assisted in any way by the knowledge that the conclusion at which I aimed was a fact.

Galileo explains how he made another telescope with a power of thirty and pointed it at the sky. His findings were published in *The Starry Messenger* (1610). He recounts that he saw more stars through the telescope than one could with the naked eye. He discovered the moons of Jupiter and suggested that the earth was just another planet, like moons of the Sun.

The Moon's Surface. In *The Starry Messenger*, he also published the first map of the Moon; its rough surfaces—seen especially on the boundaries between shadow and light—suggested that it was made of the same general stuff as the earth and was not a perfect, heavenly substance. He writes, "On earth, before the rising of the sun, are not the highest peaks of the mountains illuminated by the sun's rays while the plains remain in shadow?" The publication of *The Starry Messenger* prompted numerous exchanges between Galileo and scientists of the day. In the following selection from Galileo's letter to Giacomo Muti (February 28, 1616), the implications of the Moon's rough surface are discussed, particularly as regards life on the Moon.

 From GALILEO: *"Letter to Muti"*

A few days ago, when paying my respects to the illustrious Cardinal Muti, a discussion arose on the inequalities of the moon's surface. Signor Alessandro Capoano argued to disprove the fact [of its rough surfaces]. He argued that if the lunar surfaces be unequal and mountainous, and since nature has made our earth mountainous for the benefit of plants and animals beneficial to mankind, one may say as a consequence that on the moon there must be other plants and other animals beneficial to other intellectual creatures. Since such a consequence is most false, he said, then the fact from which it is drawn must also be false; therefore lunar mountains do not exist! To this I replied as follows. As to the inequalities of the moon's surface we have only to look through a telescope to be convinced of their existence. As to the "consequences," I said, they are not only unnecessary, but absolutely false and impossible. For I was in a position to prove that neither mankind, nor animals, nor plants as on this earth, nor anything at all like them can exist on the moon. I said then, and I say now, that I do not believe that the body of the moon is composed of earth and water, and wanting these two elements we must necessarily conclude that it wants all the other things which without these elements cannot exist or subsist. I added further that even allowing that the matter of the moon may be like that of the earth (a most improbable supposition), still not one of those things which the earth produces can exist on the moon. For, to their production other things besides earth and water are necessary, namely, the sun—the greatest agent in Nature—and the resulting variance of heat and cold, and of day and night. Now, such variances are on the moon very different from those on the earth. In the latter case, to produce a diversity of seasons, the sun rises and falls more than 47 degrees (in passing from one tropic to the other). In the former case the variation is only 5 degrees on each side of the ecliptic. While, therefore, on the earth the sun in every 24 hours illuminates all parts of its surface, each half of the moon is alternately in sunshine and darkness for 15 continuous days of 24 hours. Now, if our plants and animals were exposed to ardent sunshine every month for 360 consecutive hours, and then for a similar time were plunged in cold and darkness, they could not possibly preserve themselves, much less produce and multiply. We must, therefore, conclude that what would be impossible on our earth under the circumstances we have *supposed* to exist, must be impossible on the moon where those conditions *do* exist.

 ASK YOURSELF

6.51. For Galileo, what are the similarities and differences between the surface of the earth and the surface of the Moon?

Conflicts with the Bible. In 1611 Galileo went to Rome to demonstrate his telescope to church officials. He was initially well received and was thereby encouraged to publish his *Letters on the Sunspots* (1613), which more directly advocates the Copernican system. However, traditional Aristotelian professors soon lobbied against him, contending that his Copernican views contradicted the Bible. Galileo disagreed and composed a series of letters intended to be read by Roman officials. One such letter was to his student, Benedetto Castelli (December 21, 1613), in which he argues that the domain of Scripture and religious authority does not cross over into areas of scientific study.

 From GALILEO: *"Letter to Castelli"*

The Bible, although dictated by the Holy Spirit, admits . . . in many passages of an interpretation other than the literal one. And, moreover, we cannot maintain with certainty that all interpreters are inspired by God. Therefore, I think it would be the part of wisdom not to allow any one to apply passages of Scripture in such a way as to force them to support as true any conclusions concerning nature, the contrary of which may afterwards be revealed by the evidence of our senses, or by actual demonstration. Who will set bounds to human understanding? Who can assure us that everything that can be known in the world is known already? . . . I am inclined to think that Holy Scripture is intended to convince people of those truths which are necessary for their salvation, and which being far above human understanding cannot be made credible by any learning, or by any other means than revelation.

 ASK YOURSELF

6.52. For Galileo, what was God's intended purpose of Scripture?

But it seems to me that I am not bound to believe that the same God who has endowed us with senses, reason, and understanding, does not permit us to use them, and desires to acquaint us in another way [that is, through revelation or religious authority] with such knowledge as we are in a position to acquire for ourselves by means of those faculties. This is especially so concerning those sciences about which the Holy Scriptures contain only small fragments and varying explanations. And this is precisely the case with astronomy, of which there is so little that the planets are not all enumerated, only the sun and moon, and once or twice Venus under the name of Lucifer. This, therefore, being granted, I think that in discussing natural phenomena we ought not to begin with texts from Scripture, but with experiment and demonstration. For, from the Divine Word, both Scripture and Nature do alike proceed. And I can see that that which experience sets before our eyes concerning natural effects, or which demonstration proves to us, ought not on any account to be called in question, much less condemned, upon the testimony of Scriptural texts, which may (under their mere words) have meanings of a contrary nature. . . .

 ASK YOURSELF

6.53. For Galileo, what should be our source of knowledge about astronomy?

To command professors of astronomy that they must themselves see to disproving their own observations and demonstrations is to ask the impossible. For it is not only to command them not to see what they do see, and not to understand what they do understand, but to seek for and to find the contrary. I would beg these wise and prudent Fathers to consider diligently the difference between opinionative and demonstrative doctrines, to the end that they may assure themselves that it is not in the power of professors of demonstrative sciences to change their opinions at pleasure, and adopt first one side and then the other. For, there is a great difference between ordering a mathematician, or a philosopher, as to what opinion to hold, and doing the same with a merchant, or a lawyer. For, demonstrated conclusions touching things of nature and of the heavens cannot be changed with the same facility as opinions touching what is lawful, or not, in a contract, bargain, or bill of exchange.

Therefore, let such people apply themselves to the study of the arguments of Copernicus and others, and leave the condemning of them as erroneous and heretical to whom it belongs. Yet, as to this latter, they must not hope to find such rash and hurried determinations in the vigilant Holy Fathers, or in the absolute wisdom of him who cannot err [that is, the Pope], as those into which they permit themselves to be hurried by some particular affection or interest of their own. In these, and such like opinions which are not directly articles of faith, certainly no one doubts that his Holiness has always an absolute power of admitting or condemning them. But it is not in the power of any creature to make them to be true or false, otherwise than as, in fact, they are.

 ASK YOURSELF

6.54. What is Galileo's distinction between opinionative and demonstrative doctrines?

6.55. What is not within the Pope's power?

Galileo developed this line of argumentation further and published it in his *Letter to the Grand Duchess Christina* (1615). In this work he directly addresses the criticism that the Bible says that the Sun moves and the earth stands still. He replies that this principle of literal interpretation would have us assign to God feet, hands, eyes, anger, repentance, hatred, and ignorance. The Bible was written in a language that condescends to popular capacity. He writes that, "It is necessary for the Bible, in order to be accommodated to the understanding of every person, to speak many things which appear to differ from the absolute truth so far as the bare meaning of the words is concerned." He also contends that "the Bible intentionally forbore to speak of these things." He continues in his letter to Benedetto Castelli that church officials should not presume to tell scientists what they are to believe. Unfortunately, his various defenses failed. In 1616 Galileo was called before Cardinal Bellarmine, who ordered him to neither hold nor defend the Copernican world system since it was contrary to Scripture. However, he was permitted to discuss it as a mathematical hypothesis. He was also forewarned that Copernicus's system was soon to be officially condemned by the church. Indeed, the following year, in 1616, the church decreed the following: "Propositions to be forbidden: that the Sun is immovable at the center of the heaven; that the earth is not at the center of the heaven, and is not immovable, but moves by a double motion."

Dialogues on the Two Chief Systems of the World. Galileo waited for an intellectual Pope to take office before publishing further defenses of the Copernican theory. He thought he found such a person in his friend Pope Urban VIII, who was a lover of the arts. Galileo visited Pope Urban six times in 1624 hoping that he would let his new ideas slowly replace the old. Galileo was permitted to noncommittally discuss both the Ptolemaic and Copernican systems. He was also required to conclude that God could have created the world in any number of ways and that we cannot know which God chose. In accordance, Galileo published his *Dialogues on the Two Chief Systems of the World* (1632). The work defends the Sun-centered system against criticisms from defenders of the earth-centered system. Publishing the work was difficult, but it was immediately successful. In the following selections from the Introduction to the *Dialogue*, Galileo delicately balances the interests of the church with his own scientific concerns. He concedes that the church's earlier condemnation of Copernicus was made with full knowledge of the scientific facts. In this context, he explains that he is only advancing the Copernican system as a calculating tool.

 From GALILEO: *Dialogues on Two Chief Systems*

Some years ago a beneficial edict was proclaimed at Rome, which, in order to hinder the dangerous scandals of the present age, commanded a fitting silence on the Pythagorean opinion of the earth's motion. Some were uninhibited who rashly asserted that this decree originated, not from a judicious examination, but from an ill-informed passion. Complaints were heard that counselors totally inexperienced in astronomical observations ought not by hasty prohibitions to clip the wings of speculative minds. My zeal could not keep silence when I heard these rash lamentations, and I thought it proper, as being fully informed with regard to that most prudent edict, to appear publicly as a witness of the actual truth. At that time I happened to be in Rome. I was admitted to the audiences, and enjoyed the approval of the most distinguished prelates of that Court. Nor did the publication of the aforesaid decree occur without my receiving some prior indication of it. For that reason, . . . collecting together all my own speculations on the Copernican system, it is my intention in this present work to show to foreign nations that the knowledge of this preceded the Roman censures. Thus, from this country proceeded not only dogmas for the salvation of the soul, but also inventive discoveries for the gratification of the understanding. With this object I have taken up in the dialogue the Copernican side of the question, treating it as a pure mathematical hypothesis. I try in every artificial manner to represent it as having the advantage, not over the opinion of the stability of the earth absolutely, but over it as taught and defended by some who profess to be peripatetics [that is, followers of Aristotle]. For they retain only the name ["peripatetic"], and are content, without improvement, to worship shadows, not philosophizing with their own reason, but only from the recollection of four principles imperfectly understood.

 ASK YOURSELF

6.56. Galileo explains that he is not defending the Copernican system over the contention itself that the earth is stable. Instead, what is he defending the Copernican system against?

Unfortunately, Galileo's presentation of the Copernican theory was still too direct. Pope Urban felt betrayed and Galileo was forced to appear before a tribunal of the universal inquisition. Under threat of torture, he signed a recantation of his position and in 1633 was placed under house arrest for his eight remaining years. During these years, he continued publishing and corresponding with scientists. He died in 1642.

Newton

As the scientific revolution continued, medieval conceptions of the universe were buried even deeper. Such was the result of the contributions by Isaac Newton (1642–1727), who is considered to be among the greatest figures in the history of science. Newton's childhood years were somewhat unstructured; his father died before he was born, and he was later pulled from school to work on his mother's farm. Ultimately he continued his education and was awarded the mathematics professorship at Cambridge when he was twenty-six. During these early years, Newton made his three chief scientific discoveries, which he refined and published much later. The first was the development of calculus, a mathematical innovation that he termed "fluxions." The second was his experiments with prisms showing how white light is composed of colored light. The third was the idea of universal gravitation, which explained the orbits of the Moon and planets. Newton did not publish much, but as his works appeared, he quickly achieved an almost unparalleled fame both within the scientific community and in society at large. He was briefly a member of Parliament and resigned his professorship in 1701 when appointed master of the British mint. Soon after he was elected president of the Royal Society, Great Britain's oldest scientific society, and was reelected each year until his death in 1727.

Gravity. Newton's definitive discussion of universal gravity appeared in *Principia Mathematica* (1687), in which he showed how the laws of gravity explain planetary motion. In addition to his law of universal gravitation, he also proposed three laws of mechanics (inertia; the relation between force, mass, and acceleration; and the relation between action and reaction). In the following selections from the Preface to his *Principia*, Newton explains his plan.

 From NEWTON: *Principia Mathematica*

In the third book we give an example of this in the explication of the system of the world. For, by the propositions mathematically demonstrated in the first book, we there derive from the celestial phenomena the forces of gravity with which bodies tend to the sun and the several planets. Then, from these forces, by other propositions which are also mathematical, we deduce the motions of the planets, the comets, the moon, and the sea. I wish we could derive the rest of the phenomena of nature by the same kind of reasoning from mechanical principles. For I am induced by many reasons to suspect that they may all depend upon certain forces by which the particles of bodies, by some causes hitherto unknown, are either mutually impelled towards each other and cohere in regular figures, or are repelled and recede from each other. Which forces being unknown, philosophers have hitherto attempted the search of nature in vain. But I hope the principles here laid down will afford some either to that or some truer method of philosophy.

 ASK YOURSELF

6.57. Newton proposes to show how the force of gravity directs celestial phenomena. What else does he hope can be demonstrated at some future time?

God's Role in the Physical Universe. Historians of science today debate about whether Newton believed that God created a completely self-sustaining universe or whether God was still needed as an active regulating force. In any event, Newton argues that God went to great measures in making the universe as self-sustaining as it is, and this reflects intelligent design, rather than a blind natural force. For example, even though gravity alone could account for the formation of celestial bodies, God is still needed to explain why some are luminous, such as the Sun and stars, and others are not luminous, such as the planets. Newton describes this in the first of a series of four letters to Richard Bentley.

 From NEWTON: *"Letter to Bentley"*

But if the matter [of the universe] was [initially] evenly disposed throughout an infinite space, it could never convene into one mass. But some of it would convene into one mass and some into another, so as to make an infinite number of great masses, scattered at great distances from one to another throughout all that infinite space. And thus might the sun and fixed stars be formed, supposing the [original] matter were of a lucid nature. But how the matter should divide itself into two sorts, and the part of it which is fit to compose a shining body should fall down into one mass and make a sun and the rest which is fit to compose an opaque body should coalesce (not into one great body, like the shining matter, but into many little ones); or if the sun at first were an opaque body like the planets or the planets lucid bodies like the sun, how he alone should be changed into a shining body whilst all they continue opaque (or all they be changed into opaque ones whilst he remainst unchanged), I do not think explicable by mere natural causes, but am forced to ascribe it to the counsel and contrivance of a voluntary agent.

Newton argues further that God's creative abilities are also seen in the precise motion of the various planets. Only a few differences here or there would throw the planets into irregular orbits. Newton makes this case in a second letter to Bentley.

Were all the planets as swift as Mercury or as slow as Saturn or his satellites [i.e., its moons]; or were the several velocities otherwise much greater or less than they are (as they might have been had they arose from any other cause than their gravities); or had the distances from the centers about which they move been greater or less than they are (as they might have been had they arose from any other cause than their gravities); or had the quantity of matter in the sun or in Saturn, Jupiter, and the earth (and by consequence their gravitating power) been greater or less than it is; [then, in any of these cases,] the primary planets could not have revolved about the sun nor the secondary ones about Saturn, Jupiter, and the earth, in concentric circles as they do, but would have moved in hyperbolas or parabolas or in ellipses very eccentric. To make this system, therefore, with all its motions, required a cause which understood and compared together the quantities of matter in the several bodies of the sun and planets and the gravitating powers resulting from thence. . . . And to compare and adjust all these things together in so great a variety of bodies, [such a design] argues that cause to be, not blind and fortuitous, but very well skilled in mechanics and geometry.

 ASK YOURSELF

6.58. What kind of skills does God have that enable him to make the motion of the planets so perfect?

Implications of Modern Astronomy

There are several important implications of the Sun-centered system as developed by Copernicus, Kepler, Galileo, and Newton. First, the conception of the size of the universe shifted from being finite to being infinite. The universe, then, has no center and theologians lose an important symbol illustrating how humans are at the center of God's creative activity. Indeed, we seem insignificant when set against the infinite backdrop of celestial objects. Second, celestial bodies are no longer eternal, but made of the same stuff as earth. Thus, the heavens lose their otherworldly quality. Third, there are no more teleological explanations of the world: Mathematical explanations have us ask *how* something happens, not *why*. Finally, God is no longer an active participant in the daily functioning of the universe. He is the brilliant creator of everything, and evidence of His existence is seen in His creation, but He is now a passive spectator to the physical events He set in motion. The phrase "God of the gaps" is sometimes used to describe the tendency during the scientific revolution to look for divine activity in those areas that science cannot fully explain. As science filled in the knowledge gaps during the scientific revolution, the role for divine activity lessened.

SCIENTIFIC METHOD

As noted, there were two distinct contributions to the scientific revolution: particular discoveries and the development of the scientific method. This section deals with scientific method. Scientific method is a procedure by which we gain scientific knowledge. Strictly speaking, scientific method aims at discovering new *facts*. However, such methods were often mixed with methods of *proof*, which involved demonstrating the validity of one's conclusion. Methods of investigation and proof were so often combined that, in his *Dialogue* (1632), Galileo insisted that the two are distinct and the method of proof is not typically the same as the method of investigation. Today, method of investigation is what *defines* a science and distinguishes it from other academic disciplines, such as literature and fine art, and from pseudosciences such as parapsychology. But today's tools of precise scientific investigation developed slowly. Aristotle distinguished between two approaches to gaining scientific knowledge. The first is deduction, which involves a structure of demonstration akin to mathematics. For Aristotle, such demonstrations are achieved with a syllogism, the classic example of which is as follows:

  a. All men are mortal.
  b. Socrates is a man.
  c. Therefore, Socrates is mortal.

The second approach Aristotle notes is induction, in which specific instances are used as evidence for a universal conclusion. Aristotle's own descriptions of induction vary and are ultimately inadequate for purposes of scientific inquiry. Later philosophers describe induction as "ampliative" in the sense that the conclusion goes beyond what is contained in the premises. An example of ampliative induction is as follows:

  a. Rock 1 falls to the ground when I open my hand.
  b. Rock 2 falls to the ground when I open my hand.
  c. Therefore, all rocks similar to 1 and 2 will probably fall to the ground when I open my hand.

Three principal features distinguish deductive arguments from ampliative inductive arguments. First, inductive arguments add new information in their conclusions, unlike deductive arguments, where the conclusion is implicitly contained within the premises. Second, even good inductive arguments do not have absolute certainty and risk some chance of having a false conclusion; with valid deductive arguments, by contrast, the truth of all premises guarantees the truth of the conclusion. Third, deductive arguments are valid or invalid, with no middle ground; inductive arguments are considered strong or weak and anything in between.

Aristotle also argued that different fields of inquiry require different methods of investigation. The more formal sciences could attain certainty with deductive syllogistic logic. The more empirical sciences could not attain this. Following Aristotle, medieval science employed a disunified collection of scientific approaches. To the extent that formal sciences needed to rise to the level of mathematical certainty, syllogistic deduction was the preferred method. Dissatisfied with the status quo, Renaissance thinkers began almost from scratch in creating methods of scientific inquiry as they streamlined the process of discovery. Many proposed methods were vague, others were naive, and most turned out to be dead ends. Some were proposed as techniques exclusively for the physical sciences, and others more broadly for any rational inquiry. The Renaissance philosopher who parted company the most with the Aristotelian and medieval scientific tradition was Francis Bacon, who rejected both the deductive syllogistic method and the prevailing opinion that each discipline needed its own method.

Bacon and Induction

Francis Bacon (1561–1626) was born in London into an aristocratic family. Although he became a member of Parliament and a counselor to the queen, he was frustrated by his failure to acquire a political position of substantial influence. During his years of political service, Bacon published his famous collection of essays and several works on reorganizing the natural sciences. The most important of the latter was the *Novum Organum* (*New Organon*, 1620). In 1621 he was accused of bribery and corruption, to which he ultimately signed a confession of guilt. Although the initial punishment included fines and imprisonment, these were later reduced. Nevertheless, he was unable to return to politics. He spent the remaining five years of his life writing histories and refining his overhaul of the sciences. He died from bronchitis contacted while conducting a winter experiment to see if stuffing a dead fowl with snow would inhibit the rotting process.

Bacon's published and unpublished philosophical writings are best seen as part of his grandiose plan to organize the sciences. This involved a projected, and largely unfinished, six-part work called the *Instauratio*. The plan involved (1) a new division of the sciences, (2) a new method of scientific inquiry, (3) a collection of scientific observations and facts, (4) examples of the new method, (5) philosophical precursors to the new philosophy, and (6) the new philosophy itself, which results from applying the new method. The following selections are from Bacon's *New Organon*, a work that may be viewed as a preliminary of Division Two of the *Instauratio*. The title of the work is taken from Aristotle's *Organon* (logical works), and, accordingly, signals a radical departure from the traditional method of scientific inquiry. The text consists of a series of aphorisms that loosely revolve around common themes. The selections in this section are from Bacon's *New Organon*.

Induction versus Deduction. In the very first aphorism of the *New Organon*, Bacon grounds human understanding in observation and experience. This leads to a harsh rejection of Aristotle's *a priori* deductive method. The alternative he proposes is an *a posteriori* and inductive approach.

 From BACON: *New Organon*

1:1. Man, who is the servant and interpreter of nature, can act and understand no further than he has observed in either the operation or the contemplation of the method and order of nature.

1:12. The [deductive] logic now in use serves rather to fix and give stability to the errors which have their foundation in commonly received notions, rather than to help the search after truth. So it does more harm than good.

1:13. The syllogism is no match for the subtlety of nature. Thus, it is not applied to the first principles of sciences, and is applied in vain to intermediate axioms. It commands assent therefore to the [concluding] proposition, but does not take hold of the thing [in nature].

1:18. The discoveries which have previously been made in the sciences are such as lie close to common notions, scarcely beneath the surfaces. In order to penetrate into the inner and further recesses of nature, it is necessary that both notions and axioms be derived from things by a more sure and guarded way. It is necessary that a better and more certain method of intellectual operation be introduced altogether.

1:19. There are and can be only two ways of searching into and discovering truth. The one flies away from the senses and particulars, and instead starts with the most general principles. It simply assumes that the truth of these is settled and immovable. From these general principles it proceeds to judgment and to the discovery of middle principles. And this way is now in fashion. The other way derives general principles from the senses and particulars, rising gradually and continually, so that it arrives at the most general principles last of all. This is the true way, but as yet untried.

 ASK YOURSELF

6.59. For Bacon, which method (inductive or deductive) goes from general to particular, and which goes from particular to general?

1:20. The understanding left to itself follows the first way, which proceeds according to logical order. For the mind longs to spring up to positions of higher generality so that it may find rest there. After a little while it wearies of experiment. But this evil is increased by [deductive] logic, because of the order and solemnity of its disputations.

1:21. The understanding left to itself in a sober, patient, and grave mind, especially if it is not hindered by received doctrines, tries a little that other way [through induction], which is the right one. However, it has little progress since the understanding is uneven and quite unfit to contend with the obscurity of things—unless it is directed and assisted.

1:22. Both ways set out from the senses and particulars, and rest in the highest generalities. But the difference between them is infinite. For, the first way just glances at experiment and particulars in passing. The second way dwells duly and orderly among them. The first way, again, begins at once by establishing certain abstract and useless generalities. The second way rises by gradual steps to that which is prior and better known in the order of nature.

 ASK YOURSELF

6.20. For Bacon, why does the understanding naturally incline toward deductive reasoning?

The Four Idols. Bacon continues by describing four sources of bias in science. His treatment of these dominates Book One of the *New Organon* and indicates the importance he placed on the subject. He refers to these sources of bias as "idols" (*idola*) and lists them as idols of the tribe (from human nature), idols of the cave (from individual constitution), idols of the marketplace (from words), and idols of the theater (from accepted philosophers).

1:39. There are four classes of Idols which invade people's minds. To these for distinction's sake I have assigned names, calling the first class *Idols of the Tribe*, the second, *Idols of the Cave*, the third, *Idols of the Marketplace*, the fourth, *Idols of the Theater*.

1:40. The formation of ideas and axioms by true induction is no doubt the proper remedy to be applied for the keeping off and clearing away of idols. To point them out, however, is of great use. For the doctrine of Idols is to the Interpretation of Nature what the doctrine of the refutation of sophisms is to common logic.

1:41. The Idols of the Tribe have their foundation in human nature itself, and in the tribe or race of people. For it is a false assertion that the sense of man is the measure of things. On the contrary, all perceptions as well of the sense is of the mind are according to the measure of the individual and not according to the measure of the universe. And the human understanding is like a false mirror which, receiving rays irregularly, distorts and discolors the nature of things by mingling its own nature with it.

 ASK YOURSELF

6.61. Regarding the idols of the tribe, how does human nature affect our perception of the world?

1:42. The Idols of the Cave are the idols of the individual person. For everyone (besides the errors common to human nature in general) has a cave or den of his own, which refracts and discolors the light of nature. This owes either to his own proper and peculiar nature, or to his education and conversation with others, or to the reading of books, and the authority of those whom he esteems and admires, or to the differences of impressions, accordingly as they take place in a mind preoccupied and predisposed or in a mind indifferent and settled, or the like. So that the spirit of humanity (according as it is limited to different individuals) is in fact a variable thing and full of perturbation, and governed as it were by chance. For this reason, it was well observed by Heraclitus that people look for sciences in their own lesser worlds, and not in the greater or common world.

 ASK YOURSELF

6.62. Regarding idols of the cave, how does an individual's unique mental and physical makeup affect his perception of the world?

1:43. There are also Idols formed by the communication and association of people with each other. I call these Idols of the Marketplace because of the exchange and association of people there. For it is by discourse that people associate. And words are imposed according to the understanding of the common people. And therefore the ill and unfit choice of words wonderfully obstructs the understanding. The matter is not set right by the definitions or explanations of some things which educated people use to guard and defend themselves. But words plainly force and overrule the understanding, and throw all into confusion, and lead men away into numberless empty controversies and idle fancies.

 ASK YOURSELF

6.63. Why does Bacon refer to this third source of bias as idols of the "marketplace"?

1:44. Lastly, there are Idols which have immigrated into people's minds from the various dogmas of philosophies, and also from wrong laws of demonstration. These I call Idols of the Theater, because in my judgment all the received systems are but so many stage-plays, representing worlds of their own creation after an unreal and scenic fashion. Nor is it only of the systems now in vogue, or only of the ancient sects and philosophies, that I speak. For many more plays of the same kind may yet be composed and in like artificial manner set forth; since errors which are most widely different have nevertheless causes for the most part alike. Neither again do I mean this only of entire systems, but also of many principles and axioms in science, which by tradition, credulity, and negligence have come to be received.

 ASK YOURSELF

6.64. Why does Bacon refer to this fourth source of bias as idols of the "theater"?

The Forms of Things. Aristotle contended that science involves the discovery of a phenomenon's *causes*. For example, to understand the nature of heat, we must discover the causes of heat. For Aristotle, this involves uncovering all four of its causes: formal, material, efficient, and final. Despite Bacon's harsh rejection of Aristotle's deductive syllogism, Bacon follows Aristotle by seeing science as the discovery of causes and, specifically, formal causes. According to Bacon, the formal causes of a thing (or, more concisely, its "forms") are its physical properties. For example, the form of heat is the violent, irregular motion of particles. Thus, by discovering this form of heat, we reveal the scientific nature of heat itself.

2:3. If a person is acquainted with the [general] cause of any nature in certain subjects (such as whiteness or heat) his knowledge is imperfect. And if he is able to bring about an effect on certain substances only (of those susceptible of such an effect), then his power is similarly imperfect. Now, if a person's knowledge is confined to the efficient and material causes (which are unstable causes, and merely vehicles, or causes which convey the form in certain cases) he may arrive at new discoveries in reference to substances in some degree similar to one another, and selected beforehand. But he does not touch the deeper boundaries of things. But whoever is acquainted with forms, embraces the unity of nature in the most dissimilar substances. He is able therefore to detect and bring to light things never yet done. This could not be accomplished by innovation of nature, nor industry in experimenting, nor accident itself, and would never have occurred to the thought of man. Thus, truth in speculation and freedom in operation result from the discovery of forms.

For Bacon a good set of rules of scientific method will reveal the forms of a thing. He explains what we should expect from a good set of such rules.

2:4. The two roads to human practice and to human knowledge lie close together, and are nearly the same. Nevertheless, because of the dangerous and ingrained habit of dwelling on abstractions, it is more safe to begin with practice and raise the sciences from those foundations which have relation to practice. We should let our active part itself be the seal which prints and determines our contemplative counterpart. Suppose a person wanted to generate and impose a nature on a given object. We must consider what kind of rule or direction or guidance he would most wish for, and express this rule in the simplest and least intricate language. Suppose, for example, that a person wanted to impose the yellow color of gold upon a silver object, or an increase in weight (observing the laws of matter), or impose transparency on an opaque stone, or tenacity on glass, or vegetation on some substance that is not vegetable. We must therefore consider what kind of rule or guidance he would most desire. First, he will undoubtedly wish to be directed to something which will not deceive him in the result nor fail him in the experiment. Secondly, he will wish for a rule which will not tie him down to specific means and particular modes of operation. For it is possible that he might not have those means available, nor be able to conveniently procure them. And if there are other means and other methods for producing the required nature (besides the one recommended) these may perhaps be within his reach. And yet he will be excluded by the narrowness of the rule, and get no good from them.

Thirdly, he will desire something to be shown him, which is not as difficult as the thing proposed to be done, but comes nearer to practice.

Thus a true and perfect rule of operation and direction will be that it is *certain, free, and leads to action.*

 ASK YOURSELF

6.65. What are the three things that a good rule of scientific method should accomplish?

And this is the same thing with the discovery of the true form. For the form of a nature is such, that given the form the nature necessarily follows. Therefore it is always present when the nature is present, and universally applies it, and is consistently inherent in it. Again, the form is such that if it is taken away, then the nature necessarily disappears. Therefore it is always absent when the nature is absent, and implies its absence, and inheres in nothing else. A final feature [of a good rule of scientific investigation] is that the true form deduces the given nature [e.g., heat] from some source of being which is inherent in more natures, and which is better known in the natural order of things than the form itself. For a true and perfect axiom of knowledge and direction will be that *another nature will be discovered which is convertible with the given nature [e.g., heat], and yet is a limitation of a more general nature [e.g., violent, irregular motion], as of a true and real genus.*

In contemporary terminology, the fourth aspect of a good rule of scientific method is that it will lead to the discovery of the necessary and sufficient conditions of a given nature (such as heat). The forms, then, are those necessary and sufficient conditions (such as violent, irregular motion of particles).

Tables of Comparative Instances. Having maintained that the job of science is to uncover a thing's forms, Bacon finally explains the inductive method by which this is done. Bacon's specific inductive methodology is presented in what he describes as three "Tables of Comparative Instances," which involve presence, absence, and degree. The "Table of Presence" (agreement) involves examining instances in which the same phenomenon is present and noting what other circumstances are in common. For example, to understand the forms involved with heat, we examine all hot things and see what circumstance is in common (e.g., irregular motion of particles).

2:11. The investigation of forms proceeds as follows. A nature is given [e.g., heat], and we must first of all collect and present to our understanding all known instances which have this particular nature [e.g., all hot things], even in substances which are dissimilar. And such a collection must be made in the manner of a history, without premature speculation, or any great amount of subtlety. For example let the investigation be into the form of heat.

Instances agreeing in the nature of heat:
1. The rays of the sun, especially in summer and at noon.

2. The rays of the sun reflected and condensed, as between mountains, or on walls, and most of all in burning-glasses and mirrors.
3. Fiery meteors.
4. Burning thunderbolts.
5. Eruptions of flame from the cavities of mountains.

. . .

27. Even keen and intense cold produces a kind of sensation of burning.
28. Other instances.

This table I call the "Table of Essence and Presence."

The second table, the "Table of Absence," involves examining instances in which a phenomenon is absent and noting what circumstances are in common. Thus, to understand heat, for example, we must examine a list of cold things, too, and see what features are irrelevant to the production of heat (e.g., density).

2:12. Secondly, we must present to the understanding those instances in which a given nature is wanting. This is because, as stated above, the above form should no less to be absent when the given nature is absent, than present when it is present. But to note all these would be endless.

The negatives should therefore be attached to the affirmatives, and the absence of the given nature [e.g., heat] inquired of only in those subjects that are most close to the others in which it is present and forthcoming. This I call the "Table of Deviation," or of "Absence in Proximity."

Instances in proximity where the nature of heat is absent:

1. To the first [on the above chart]: The rays of the moon and of stars and comets are not found to be hot to the touch; indeed the severest colds are observed to be at the full moons.

. . .

32. To the 27th [on the above chart]: There are many actions common both to heat and cold, though in a very different manner. For children find that snow after a while seems to burn their hands. Cold preserves meat from rotting, no less than fire. Heat contracts bodies, which cold does also. But these and similar instances may more conveniently be addressed by an inquiry concerning cold.

 ASK YOURSELF

6.66. For the Table of Absence, why does Bacon suggest that we examine only those instances that are similar to those on the Table of Presence (yet lack the property in question, such as heat)?

Finally, the "Table of Degrees" involves examining instances in which a phenomenon is present in varying degrees, noting what circumstances also vary. For example, to understand heat, we must look at things that are at different temperatures and note what circumstances are present in varying degrees (e.g., slow to rapid irregular motion of particles).

2:13. Thirdly we must present to the understanding instances in which the nature under inquiry is found in different degrees, more or less. This must be done by making a comparison either of its increase and decrease in the same subject, or of its amount in different subjects, as compared one with another. For, the form of a thing is the very thing itself. And the thing itself differs from the form no differently than as the apparent differs from the real, or the external from the internal, or the thing in reference to mankind from the thing in reference to the universe. Thus, it necessarily follows that no nature can be assumed to be the true form unless it always decreases when the nature in question decreases, and in like manner always increases when the nature in question increases. Therefore, this Table I call the "Table of Degrees" or the "Table of Comparison."

Table of Degrees or Comparison in heat.

. . .

25. Some ignited bodies are found to be much hotter than some flames. Ignited iron, for instance, is much hotter and more consuming than flame of spirit of wine.
26. Of substances also which are not ignited but only heated by fire, as boiling water and air confined in furnaces, some are found to exceed in heat many flames and ignited substances.
27. Motion increases heat, as you may see in bellows, and by blowing. This is in view of the fact that harder metals are not dissolved or melted by a dead or quiet fire until it is made intense by blowing.

Inductive Inference. By constructing all three Tables of Instances, we thereby eliminate irrelevant properties (such as density) and pinpoint the essential properties (such as irregular motion of particles). This, for Bacon, is true induction.

2:15. The work and office of these three tables I call the "Presentation of Instances to the Understanding." Once this presentation is made, induction itself must be set at work. For, upon a review of each and every instance, the problem is to find such a nature that is always present or absent with the given nature [e.g., heat], and always increases and decreases with it, and which is (as I have said) a particular case of a more general nature. Now if the mind attempts this affirmatively from the beginning, as when left to itself as it always is inclined to do, the result will be fancies and guesses and poorly defined notions, and axioms that must be mended everyday. . . .

2:16. . . . Therefore, the first work of induction (as regards the discovery of forms) is the rejection or exclusion of the several natures which are not found in some instance where the given nature is present, or are found in some instance where the given nature is absent, or are found to increase some instance when the given nature decreases, or to decrease when the given nature increases. Then indeed after the rejection and exclusion has been duly made, there will remain at the bottom an affirmative, solid, true, and well defined form; all superficial opinions will have vanish into smoke. This is quickly said. But the way to come at it is winding and intricate.

 ASK YOURSELF

6.67. What is the first work of induction?

Bacon recognized that we cannot examine an endless number of instances for the three tables. At some point we must stop and survey the instances so far. This review he calls the "first vintage."

Although Bacon is considered the father of scientific method, his tables of instances were not adopted by the scientific community of his day. Further, over two hundred years passed before inductive reasoning was more precisely formulated by J. S. Mill in his *System of Logic* (1843). Meanwhile, other scientists and philosophers followed alternative methods of investigation.

Descartes's Methods

French philosopher and mathematician René Descartes (1596–1650) was an active participant in the scientific revolution in both scientific method and in particular discoveries. Descartes was educated at a Jesuit college that was firmly grounded in the scholastic tradition. After furthering his education in Paris, he enlisted in the Dutch and, later, the Barvarian militaries. In 1629 Descartes moved to Holland, where he lived in seclusion for twenty years, changing his residence frequently to preserve his privacy. During this period he produced the writings upon which his fame rests. His studies were first restricted to science; only later did he explore metaphysics. In 1649 Descartes moved to Stockholm at the request of Queen Christina of Sweden, who employed him as a philosophy tutor. Christina scheduled the lectures at 5 AM. The early hours and harsh climate took their toll on Descartes's already weakened condition. He died shortly after in 1650. During his life, Descartes's fame rose to such an extent that many Catholics believed he would be a candidate for sainthood. As his body was transported from Sweden back to France, anxious relic collectors along the path removed pieces of his body. By the time his body reached France, it was considerably reduced in size.

Descartes's first discussion of scientific method is in an unfinished work of 1628 titled *Rules for the Direction of the Mind*. The first twelve of the planned thirty-six rules deal with the general aspects of his proposed methodology and are considered early versions of principles that made their way into his later writings. In 1633 Descartes prepared for publication a work on physics called *Le Monde*, which defended a heliocentric view of the universe. That same year the Catholic church condemned Galileo's *Dialogue* (1632). Descartes did not think Galileo's views were prejudicial to religion, and he worried that his own views might be censured. Thus he suspended publication of *Le Morde*. In 1637 Descartes published a collection of essays titled *Optics, Meterology, and Geometry*. Prefaced to these essays was a work titled "Discourse on the Method of Rightly Conducting the Reason and Seeking Truth in the Sciences."

Most of the "Discourse" was written before the 1633 condemnation of Galileo's *Dialogue*. However, Descartes later added a concluding section that explained that he insisted on publishing, despite political risks. The simple reason was that he counted on the public to help confirm his scientific theories. In the "Discourse," Descartes offers a method of inquiry quite different from Bacon's. Whereas Bacon advocated induction, Descartes insists on a more deductive approach. The following selections are from Descartes's *Discourse*.

Aim of the "Discourse." Descartes opens by highlighting the value that his method of investigation has had in his own investigations.

 From DESCARTES: *Discourse*

. . . I shall not hesitate to say that I have had great good fortune from my youth up, in lighting upon and pursuing certain paths which have conducted me to considerations and maxims from which I have formed a Method. With the assistance of this method it appears to me I have the means of gradually increasing my knowledge and of little by little raising it to the highest possible point which the mediocrity of my talents and the brief duration of my life call permit me to reach. For I have already reaped from it fruits of such a nature that, even though I always try in the judgments I make on myself to lean to the side of self-depreciation rather than to that of arrogance, and though, looking with the eye of a philosopher on the diverse actions and enterprises of all mankind, I find scarcely any which do not seem to me vain and useless, I do not cease to receive extreme satisfaction in the progress which I seem to have already made in the search after truth, and to form such hopes for the future as to venture to believe that, if amongst the occupations of men, simply as men, there is some one in particular that is excellent and important, that is the one which I have selected.

It must always be recollected, however, that possibly I deceive myself, and that what I take to be gold and diamonds is perhaps no more than copper and glass. I know how subject we are to delusion in whatever touches ourselves, and also how much the judgments of our friends ought to be suspected when they are in our favor. But in this Discourse I shall be very happy to show the paths I have followed, and to set forth my life as in a picture, so that everyone may judge of it for himself; and thus in learning from the common talk what are the opinions which are held of it, a new means of obtaining self-instruction will be reached, which I shall add to those which I have been in the habit of using.

Thus my design is not here to teach the Method which everyone should follow in order to promote the good conduct of his Reason, but only to show in what manner I have endeavored to conduct my own. Those who set about giving precepts must esteem themselves more skillful than those to whom they advance them, and if they fall short in the smallest matter they must of course take the blame for it. But regarding this Treatise simply as a history, or, if you prefer it, a fable in which, amongst certain things which may be imitated, there are possibly others also which it would not be right to follow, I hope that it will be of use to some without being hurtful to any, and that all will thank me for my frankness.

ASK YOURSELF

6.68. Descartes notes that he is not teaching a method that everyone should follow. What, instead, is he doing?

Replacing the Old with the New. Most of the "Discourse" is autobiographical insofar as it traces Descartes's intellectual development and how his method assisted him in his investigations. Descartes realized that he needed to reject much of the teachings of his youth. This raised the question of exactly how he should proceed in replacing old theories with new ones. He found his answer by observing how old parts of cities are replaced with new.

I was then in Germany, to which country I had been attracted by the wars which are not yet at an end. And as I was returning from the coronation of the Emperor to join the army, the setting in of winter detained me in a quarter where, since I found no society to divert me, while fortunately I had also no cares or passions to trouble me, I remained the whole day shut up alone in a stove-heated room, where I had complete leisure to occupy myself with my own thoughts. One of the first of the considerations that occurred to me was that there is very often less perfection in works composed of several portions, and carried out by the hands of various masters, than in those on which one individual alone has worked. Thus we see that buildings planned and carried out by one architect alone are usually more beautiful and better proportioned than those which many have tried to put in order and improve, making use of old walls which were built with other ends in view. In the same way also, those ancient cities which, originally mere villages, have become in the process of time great towns, are usually badly constructed in comparison with those which are regularly laid out on a plain by a surveyor who is free to follow his own ideas. Even though, considering their buildings each one apart, there is often as much or more display of skill in the one case than in the other, the former have large buildings and small buildings indiscriminately placed together, thus rendering the streets crooked and irregular, so that it might be said that it was chance rather than the will of men guided by reason that led to such an arrangement. And if we consider that this happens despite the fact that from all time there have been certain officials who have had the special duty of looking after the buildings of private individuals in order that they may be public ornaments, we shall understand how difficult it is to bring about much that is satisfactory in operating only upon the works of others.

 ASK YOURSELF

6.69. Which kinds of cities are better and more organized than others?

Thus I imagined that those people who were once half-ravaged, and who have become civilized only by slow degrees, merely forming their laws as the disagreeable necessities of their crimes and quarrels constrained them, could not succeed in establishing so good a system of government as those who, from the time they first came together as communities, carried into effect the constitution laid down by some prudent legislator. Thus it is quite certain that the constitution of the true Religion whose ordinances are of God alone is incomparably better regulated than any other. And, to come down to human affairs, I believe that if Sparta was very flourishing in former times, this was not because of the excellence of each and every one of its laws, seeing that many were very strange and even contrary to good morals, but because, being drawn up by one individual, they all tended towards the same end. And similarly I thought that the sciences found in books—in those at least whose reasonings are only probable and which have no demonstrations—composed as they are of the gradually accumulated opinions of many different individuals—do not approach so near to the truth as the simple reasoning which a man of common sense can quite naturally carry out respecting the things which come immediately before him. Again I thought that since we have all been children before being men, and since it has for long fallen to us to be governed by our appetites and by our teachers (who often enough contradicted one another, and none of whom perhaps counseled us always for the best), it is almost impossible that our judgments should be so excellent or solid as they should have been had we had complete use of our reason since our birth, and had we been guided by its means alone.

 ASK YOURSELF

6.70. Which kinds of laws are better and more organized than others?

6.71. Which kinds of scientific theories are better and more organized than others?

It is true that we do not find that all the houses in a town are leveled to the ground for the sole reason that the town is to be rebuilt in another fashion, with streets made more beautiful; but at the same time we see that many people cause their own houses to be knocked down in order to rebuild them, and that sometimes they are forced so to do where there is danger of the houses falling of themselves, and when the foundations are not secure. From such examples I argued to myself that there was no plausibility in the claim of any private individual to reform a state by altering everything, and by overturning it throughout, in order to set it right again. Nor is it likewise probable that the whole body of the Sciences, or the order of teaching established by the Schools, should be reformed. But as regards all the opinions which up to this time I had embraced, I thought I could not do better than try once and for all to sweep them completely away, so that they might later on be replaced, either by others which were better, or by the same, when I had made them conform to the uniformity of a rational scheme. And I firmly believed that by this means I should succeed in directing my life much better than if I had only built on old foundations, and relied on principles of which I allowed myself to be in youth persuaded without having inquired into their truth.

ASK YOURSELF

6.72. For Descartes, what is the best way to replace old teachings with new ones?

For although in so doing I recognized various difficulties, these were at the same time not insurmountable, nor comparable to those which are found in reformation of the most insignificant kind in matters which concern the public. In the case of great bodies it is too difficult a task to raise them again when they are once thrown down, or even to keep them in their places when once thoroughly shaken. And their fall cannot be otherwise than very violent. Then as to any imperfections that they may possess (and the very diversity that is found between them is sufficient to tell us that these in many cases exist) custom has doubtless greatly lightened them, while it has also helped us to avoid, or insensibly corrected a number against which mere foresight would have found it difficult to guard. And finally the imperfections are almost always more supportable than would be the process of removing them, just as the great roads which wind about amongst the mountains become, because of being frequented, little by little so well-beaten and easy that it is much better to follow them than to try to go more directly by climbing over rocks and descending to the foot of precipices.

 ASK YOURSELF

6.73. What are some of the obstacles involved with replacing the old with the new?

Four Rules of Scientific Method. Descartes explains that he had learned a variety of methodological approaches in a variety of disciplines. They all had limits, however. Syllogistic logic, he believes, only communicates what we already know. Geometry and algebra are either too abstract in nature for practical application or too restricted to the shapes of bodies. However, he believes that a more condensed and universal list of methodological rules was better than a lengthy and varied list.

In my younger days, I had studied Logic, to a certain extent, among the different branches of Philosophy. I had also studied Mathematics, Geometrical Analysis and Algebra—three arts or sciences which seemed as though they ought to contribute something to the design I had in view. But in examining them I observed in respect to Logic that the syllogisms and the greater part of the other teaching served better in explaining to others those things that one knows (or like the art of Lully, in enabling one to speak without judgment of those things of which one is ignorant) than in learning what is new. And although in reality Logic contains many precepts which are very true and very good, there are at the same time mingled with them so many others which are hurtful or superfluous, that it is almost as difficult to separate the two as to draw a Diana or a Minerva out of a block of marble which is not yet roughly hewn. And as to the Analysis of the ancients and the Algebra of the moderns, besides the fact that they embrace only matters the most abstract, such as appear to have no actual use, the former is always so restricted to the consideration of symbols that it cannot exercise the Understanding without greatly fatiguing the imagination; and in the latter one is so subjected to certain rules and formulas that the result is the construction of an art which is confused and obscure, and which embarrasses the mind, instead of a science which contributes to its cultivation. This made me feel that some other Method must be found, which, comprising the advantages of the three, is yet exempt from their faults. And as a multiplicity of laws often furnishes excuses for evil-doing, and as a State is hence much better ruled when, having but very few laws, these are most strictly observed. So, instead of the great number of precepts of which Logic is composed, I believed that I should find the four which I shall state quite sufficient, provided that I adhered to a firm and constant resolve never on any single occasion to fail in their observance.

The first of these was to accept nothing as true which I did not clearly recognize to be so; that is to say, carefully to avoid precipitation and prejudice in judgments, and to accept in them nothing more than what was presented to my mind so clearly and distinctly that I could have no occasion to doubt it.

The second was to divide up each of the difficulties which I examined into as many parts as possible, and as seemed requisite in order that it might be resolved in the best manner possible.

The third was to carry on my reflections in due order, commencing with objects that were the most simple and easy to understand, in order to rise little by little, or by degrees, to knowledge of the most complex, assuming an order, even if a fictitious one, among those which do not follow a natural sequence relatively to one another.

The last was in all cases to make enumerations so complete and reviews so general that I should be certain of having omitted nothing.

 ASK YOURSELF

6.74. Briefly, what are the four rules Descartes offers?

Descartes's method, as expressed in these rules, rests on three mental operations: intuition, deduction, and enumeration. These three abilities constitute our human reason. *Intuition* involves directly apprehending the simplest components (or "simple natures") of a subject matter. *Deduction* is not syllogistic, but a process of inferring necessary relations between simple natures. *Enumeration* is a process of review that we use when deductions become so long that we risk error due to a faulty memory.

Descartes continues by explaining how use of this method in science led him to the discovery of analytic geometry and a system of the cosmos similar to Galileo's. In philosophy, he deduced God's existence, the existence of the external world, and the distinction between the human mind and body. As noted earlier, Bacon parted company with medieval scientists by offering a single scientific methodology that encompassed all sciences. Descartes goes one step further than Bacon and presents a method that can be used in any *rational* inquiry—including metaphysics—and not just the natural sciences.

Provisional Code of Morals. In tearing down old systems and replacing them with new ones, Descartes realized that he needed a provisional set of moral guidelines to carry him through the transition. He presents four such rules.

And finally, as it is not sufficient, before commencing to rebuild the house which we inhabit, to pull it down and provide materials and an architect (or to act in this capacity ourselves, and make a careful drawing of its design), unless we have also provided ourselves with some other house where we can be comfortably lodged during the time of rebuilding, so in order that I should not remain irresolute in my actions while reason obliged me to be so in my judgments, and that I might not omit to carry on my life as happily as I could, I formed for myself a code of morals for the time being which did not consist of more than three or four maxims, which maxims I should like to enumerate to you.

The first was to obey the laws and customs of my country, adhering constantly to the religion in which by God's grace I had been instructed since my childhood, and in all other things directing my conduct by opinions the most moderate in nature, and the farthest removed from excess in all those which are commonly received and acted on by the most judicious of those with whom I might come in contact. For since I began to count my own opinions as naught, because I desired to place all under examination, I was convinced that I could not do better than follow those held by people on whose judgment reliance could be placed. And although such persons may possibly exist amongst the Persians and Chinese as well as amongst ourselves, it seemed to me that it was most expedient to bring my conduct into harmony with the ideas of those with whom I should have to live; and that, in order to ascertain that these were their real opinions, I should observe what they did rather than what they said, not only because in the corrupt state of our manners there are few people who desire to say all that they believe, but also because many are themselves ignorant of their beliefs. For since the act of thought by which we believe a thing is different from that by which we know that we believe it, the one often exists without the other. And amongst many opinions all equally received, I chose only the most moderate, both because these are always most suited for putting into practice, and probably the best (for all excess has a tendency to be bad), and also because I should have in a less degree turned aside from the right path, supposing that I was wrong, than if, having chosen an extreme course, I found that I had chosen amiss. I also made a point of counting as excess all the engagements by means of which we limit in some degree our liberty. Not that I hold in low esteem those laws which, in order to remedy the inconstancy of feeble souls, permit, when we have a good object in our view, that certain vows be taken, or contracts made, which oblige us to carry out that object. This sanction is even given for security in commerce where designs are wholly indifferent. But because I saw nothing in all the world remaining constant, and because for my own part I promised myself gradually to get my judgments to grow better and never to grow worse, I should have thought that I had committed a serious sin against commonsense if, because I approved of something at one time, I was obliged to regard it similarly at a later time, after it had possibly ceased to meet my approval, or after I had ceased to regard it in a favorable light.

ASK YOURSELF

6.75. What is Descartes's first moral maxim?

My second maxim was that of being as firm and resolute in my actions as I could be, and not to follow less faithfully opinions the most dubious, when my mind was once made up regarding them, than if these had been beyond doubt. In this I should be following the example of travelers, who, finding themselves lost in a forest, know that they ought not to wander first to one side and then to the other, nor, still less, to stop in one place, but understand that they should continue to walk as straight as they can in one direction, not diverging for any slight reason, even though it was possibly chance alone that first determined them in their choice. By this means if they do not go exactly where they wish, they will at least arrive somewhere at the end, where probably they will be better off than in the middle of a forest. And thus since often enough in the actions of life no delay is permissible, it is very certain that, when it is beyond our power to discern the opinions which carry most truth, we should follow the most probable; and even although we notice no greater probability in the one opinion than in the other, we at least should make up our minds to follow a particular one and afterwards consider it as no longer doubtful in its relationship to practice, but as very true and very certain, inasmuch as the reason, which caused us to determine upon it is known to be so. And henceforward this principle was sufficient to deliver me from all the penitence and remorse which usually affect the mind and agitate the conscience of those weak and vacillating creatures who allow themselves to keep changing their procedure, and practice as good, things which they afterwards judge to be evil.

 ASK YOURSELF

6.76. What is Descartes's second moral maxim?

My third maxim was to try always to conquer myself rather than fortune, and to alter my desires rather than change the order of the world, and generally to accustom myself to believe that there is nothing entirely within our power but our own thoughts: so that after we have done our best in regard to the things that are without us, our ill-success cannot possibly be failure on our part. And this alone seemed to me sufficient to prevent my desiring anything in the future beyond what I could actually obtain, hence rendering me content; for since our will does not naturally induce us to desire anything but what our understanding represents to it as in some way possible of attainment, it is certain that if we consider all good things which are outside of us as equally outside of our power, we should not have more regret in resigning those goods which appear to pertain to our birth, when we are deprived of them for no fault of our own, than we have in not possessing the kingdoms of China or Mexico. . . .

ASK YOURSELF

6.77. What is Descartes's fourth moral maxim?

And last of all, to conclude this moral code, I felt it incumbent on me to make a review of the various occupations of men in this life in order to try to choose out the best. And without wishing to say anything of the employment of others, I thought that I could not do better than continue in the one in which I found myself engaged. That is to say, I occupy my whole life in cultivating my Reason, and in advancing myself as much as possible in the knowledge of the truth in accordance with the method which I had prescribed myself. I had experienced so much satisfaction since beginning to use this method, that I did not believe that any sweeter or more innocent could in this life be found, every day discovering by its means some truths which seemed to me sufficiently important, although commonly ignored by other men. . . .

 ASK YOURSELF

6.78. What is Descartes's last moral maxim?

Although Descartes's method had its advocates, it was also criticized by his contemporaries, such as the mathematician Pierre de Fermat, and ultimately dismissed. Leibniz says that Descartes's rules amount to saying "take what you need, and do what you should, and you will get what you want."

Newton's Method of Investigation

As noted, practicing scientists of the day had intuitions and even rules of thumb about how to advance scientific knowledge. Newton, too, had such rules that he clearly articulated in two separate writings.

Rules of Reasoning in Philosophy. At the outset of *Principia Mathematica*, Newton proposes "Four Rules of Reasoning in Philosophy," which are his first proposed rules of scientific method. Like Bacon, Newton appears to follow Aristotle's contention that science is the discovery of causes, as seen specifically in the first two rules below. The first rule advocates a version of Ockham's razor, insofar as we should not multiply explanatory causes beyond necessity. The second rule is that from the same effects we infer the same causes. This is a foundational notion in inductive arguments from analogy, and was extensively used by eighteenth-century Scottish philosopher David Hume (1711–1776). The following selections are from Newton's *Principia*.

From NEWTON: *Principia Mathematica* ——————

Rule 1: We are to admit no more causes of natural things than such as are both true and sufficient to explain their appearances.

To this purpose the philosophers say that nature does nothing in vain, and more is in vain when less will serve. For nature is pleased with simplicity and affects not the pomp of superfluous causes.

Rule 2: Therefore to the same natural effects we must, as far as possible, assign the same causes.

As to respiration in a man and in a beast, the descent of stones in Europe and in America, the light of our culinary fire and of the sun, the reflection of light in the earth and in the planets.

Rule 3. The qualities of bodies, which admit neither intensification nor remission of degrees, and which are found to belong to all bodies within the reach of our experiments, are to be esteemed the universal qualities of all bodies whatsoever.

For since the qualities of bodies are only known to us by experiments, we are to hold for universal all such as universally agree with experiments, and such as are not liable to diminution can never be quite taken away. . . .

Rule 4. In experimental philosophy we are to look upon propositions inferred by general induction from phenomena as accurately or very nearly true, notwithstanding any contrary hypotheses that may be imagined, till such time as other phenomena occur by which they may either be made more accurate or liable to exceptions.

This rule we must follow, that the argument of induction may not be evaded by hypotheses.

 ASK YOURSELF

6.79. In rule four, what is the only thing that can reverse a conclusion one arrives at through induction?

Method of Analysis. Newton's second, third, and fourth rules deal with aspects of inductive reasoning. In his *Optics* (1704) Newton amplified his account of induction, particularly as appears in rule four. He describes the inductive scientific process as a *method of analysis*. Newton first experimented with optics in 1666. The old view of optics, since Aristotle, was that light becomes modified when passing through a prism. Newton's explanation was that white light becomes separated into a spectrum. As a proof, he showed that once these colors were separated, they could not be further separated by passing it through other prisms. Further, he could recombine colored light into white light. He finally published his results in the *Optics*. For Newton, scientific reasoning of this sort underscores the importance of method for scientists. The following discussion of his method of analysis is from *Optics*, Book 3, Queries.

From NEWTON: *Optics*

As in mathematics, so in natural philosophy the investigation of difficult things by the method of analysis ought ever to precede the method of composition. This analysis consists in making experiments and observations, and in drawing general conclusions from them by induction, and admitting of no objections against the conclusions but such as are taken from experiments or other certain truths. For, hypotheses are not to be regarded in experimental philosophy. And although the arguing from experiments and observations by induction be no demonstration of general conclusions, yet it is the best way of arguing which the nature of things admits of, and may be looked upon as so much the stronger by how much the induction is more general. And if no exception occurs from phenomena, the conclusion may be pronounced generally. But if at any time afterwards any exception shall occur from experiments, it may then begin to be pronounced with such exceptions as occur. By this way of analysis we may proceed from compounds to ingredients, and from motions to the forces producing them, and, in general, from effects to their causes, and from particular causes to more general ones, until the argument ends in the most general. This is the method of analysis, and the synthesis consists in assuming the causes discovered and established as principles, and by them explaining the phenomena proceeding from them and proving the explanations.

 ASK YOURSELF

6.80. What is Newton's attitude about the use of hypotheses in scientific investigation?

In his essay "A Discourse on Descartes' Method," Contemporary philosopher Jaakko Hintikka summarizes Newton's method of analysis as follows: (1) the analysis of a complex phenomenon into ingredients; (2) the experimental or observational discovery of dependencies between different ingredients; (3) the inductive generalization of these dependencies to all similar cases; and (4) the deductive application of the generalization to other cases. According to Hintikka, this method of analysis is not unique to Newton. Indeed, many modern philosophers and scientists followed this procedure, including Galileo and even Descartes. He argues further that the method of analysis was initially used in Greek mathematics, specifically by Pappus (fl. fourth century CE) in his work *Mathematical Collections*.

Mathematics and Scientific Method

Another broad approach to both scientific method and scientific proof was simply to use *mathematics* as a means of expanding the boundaries of knowledge. In perhaps his most famous statement Galileo asserts that the "Book of Nature is written in mathematical characters" (*The Assayer*, 1623). Even here, there were two basic approaches to the use of mathematics. First, some scientists believed that mathematical reasoning alone could give us scientific knowledge. If we presume that physical things are mathematical in nature, then we simply start deducing mathematical consequences from this. Kepler, for example, never articulated a formal method of investigation, but was driven by the Pythagorean view that mathematical relationships determined the structure of the universe. Thus, for him, knowledge of the world was gained by making deductions from *a priori* numerical principles. A second approach was to make hypotheses about nature in a mathematical form, and then use mathematics to draw out consequences that might be tested through experiments. The difference between the two approaches is that, on the first, our experiences are somewhat irrelevant since truth is discovered in the mathematical relations themselves. On the second, though, our experiences confirm or refute our mathematically deduced conclusions. Newton takes this second approach in his methods of analysis, described earlier. Dutch scientist Christiaan Huygens (1629–1695) also adopts this methodology, and, in *The Laws of Chance* (1657), he emphasizes the value of mathematics in furthering our knowledge:

> There are very few things which we know which are not capable of being reduced to a mathematical reasoning. And when they cannot, it is a sign our knowledge of them is very small and confused. And where a mathematical reasoning can be had, it is as great folly to make use of any other as to grope for a thing in the dark when you have a candle standing by you.

In a variety of disciplines, books appeared regularly that used arithmetical calculations as a method of proof. William Petty applied mathematics to political science in his *Political Arithmetic* (1690). Francis Hutcheson adopted this method for ethics in his *Inquiry concerning Moral Good and Evil* (1725). Perhaps the most absurd illustration of this kind was John Craig's *Mathematical Principles of Christian Theology* (1699), in which he deduces the approximate time of the second coming of Christ:

> It is necessary that Christ come before 1454 years elapse. For it is necessary that Christ come before the probability of the Gospel story vanishes; but that probability will perish when 1454 years (=3150 − 1696) have elapsed from our time. . . . And in no time less than 1454 years is it necessary for him to come, insofar as his arrival depends upon the disappearance of the probability of his history.

SUGGESTIONS FOR FURTHER READING

Primary Sources

Astronomy

Galileo. *Dialogue concerning the Two Chief World Systems*, trans. S. Drake (Berkeley: University of California Press, 1953). Galileo's criticism of the Aristotelian system of the world.

———. *Letter to the Grand Duchess Christina*, in *Discoveries and Opinions of Galileo*, ed. and trans. S. Drake (New York: Doubleday, 1957). Discusses the relation between science and religion.

Fideism and Skepticism

Bayle, Pierre. *The Dictionary Historical and Critical of Mr. Peter Bayle* (London: Routledge/Thoemmes Press, 1997). Facsimile reprint of the five-volume 1734 English translation.

Pascal, Blaise. *Pensées*, trans. A. J. Krailsheimer (London: Penguin Books, 1995). Recent translation of Pascal's most famous philosophical text.

Humanism

Kraye, Jill, ed. *Cambridge Translations of Renaissance Philosophical Texts* (Cambridge: Cambridge University Press, 1997). Two-volume collection of new translation son key Renaissance moral and political philosophy.

Pico della Mirandola, Giovanni. *On the Dignity of Man* (Indianapolis: Hackett Publishing Company, 1998). Recent translation of Pico's most famous writing.

Reformation

Calvin, John. *Institutes of the Christian Religion*, ed. J. T. McNeill, trans. F. L. Battles (Philadelphia: Westminster, 1960). Standard two-volume translation of Calvin's famous work.

Scientific Method

Bacon, Francis. *The Oxford Francis Bacon* (Oxford: Clarendon Press, 1996). Twelve-volume edition of Bacon's writings; in progress.

———. *The Works of Francis Bacon*, ed. J. Spedding (London: Longmans, 1857–1874). Fourteen-volume standard edition of Bacon's works.

Descartes, Rene. *The Philosophical Writings of Descartes*, ed. and trans. J. Cottingham, R. Stoothoff, D. Murdoch, and A. Kenny (Cambridge: Cambridge University Press, 1984). Three-volume standard English translation of Descartes's key philosophical writings, including the *Discourse*.

Critical Analyses and Discussions

Astronomy

Machamer, Peter, ed. *The Cambridge Companion to Galileo*. (Cambridge: Cambridge University Press, 1998). Collection of essays on various topics.

Fideism and Skepticism

Krailsheimer, A. J. *Pascal* (New York: Oxford University Press, 1980). Brief survey of Pascal's philosophy.

Humanism

Kraye, Jill, ed. *The Cambridge Companion to Renaissance Humanism* (Cambridge: Cambridge University Press, 1996). Collection of essays on various topics.

Reformation

Dowey, E. A. *The Knowledge of God in Calvin's Theology* (New York: Columbia University Press, 1994). Recent discussion by a noted scholar.

Scientific Method

Cottingham, John, ed. *The Cambridge Companion to Descartes* (Cambridge: Cambridge University Press, 1992). Collection of essays on various topics.

———, ed. *Descartes* (New York: Oxford University Press, 1998). Collection of essays on various aspects of Descartes's philosophy.

Peltonen, Markku, ed. *The Cambridge Companion to Bacon* (Cambridge: Cambridge University Press, 1996). Collection of essays on various topics.

CHAPTER 7

CONTINENTAL RATIONALISM

ationalism" traditionally refers to a seventeenth-century philosophical movement begun by René Descartes that took place largely in Continental Europe. Rationalism is usually understood in relation to its rival eighteenth-century movement, Empiricism, founded by John Locke, which largely took place in Great Britain. Two key points distinguish Rationalism from Empiricism. The first involves differing theories about the origin of ideas. Rationalists believed that an important group of foundational concepts are known intuitively through reason, as opposed to being known through experience. Descartes describes such concepts as innate ideas, the most important of these including the ideas of oneself, infinite perfection, and causality. British Empiricists, as we will see, staunchly rejected this view and argued that all ideas ultimately trace back to experiences, such as sense perceptions and emotions. The second distinguishing feature between Rationalism and Empiricism concerns their differing methods of investigating problems. Rationalists maintained that we could deduce truths with absolute certainty from our innate ideas, much the way theorems in geometry are deduced from axioms. They saw mathematical proofs as the perfect method of demonstrating truth, and accordingly, mathematical proof became the model for all other kinds of demonstration. Although Empiricists also used deductive reasoning, they put a greater emphasis on the inductive method championed by fellow British countryman Francis Bacon.

Who were the Rationalists? After Descartes, several dozen scientists and philosophers continued his teachings throughout Continental Europe and, accordingly, were called "Cartesians." Some Cartesians strayed little from Descartes's scientific and metaphysical theories. Others incorporated his theories into Calvinistic theology. A handful of philosophers influenced by Descartes were more original in developing their own views; these philosophers are included under the more general title "Rationalists." In addition to Descartes, Rationalists covered in this chapter include Benedict Spinoza, Nicolas de Malebranche, Gottfried Wilhelm Leibniz, and Anne Conway.

RENÉ DESCARTES

Descartes's philosophy developed in the context of all of the features of Renaissance and early modern philosophy discussed in the previous chapter. Like the humanists, he rejected religious authority in the quest for scientific and philosophical knowledge. For Descartes, reason was both the foundation and guide for pursuing truth. Although Descartes was a devout Catholic, he was also influenced by the Reformation's challenge to church authority, particularly the challenge against medieval Aristotelianism. As noted in the previous chapter, he was an active participant in the scientific revolution in both scientific method and in particular discoveries. Finally, and perhaps most importantly, Descartes reacted strongly against the Renaissance resurgence of ancient Greek skepticism. Thus, we find in Descartes's writings a relentless pursuit of absolute certainty. Descartes's most famous and influential philosophical writing is his *Meditations*. The full title of the work is *Meditations on the First Philosophy: In Which the Existence of God and the Distinction between Mind and Body Are Demonstrated*. The work was first published in 1641 in Latin and was translated into French in the following year by the Duc de Luynes. Descartes was so pleased with the French translation that he made some additions and endorsed it for later publication. The following text of the *Meditations* is based on the Latin version, with additions from the French version contained in brackets. The complete text of Meditations 1 and 2 is presented, and selections from Meditations 3 and 6 are also presented.

Meditation 1: Concerning Those Things That Can Be Called into Doubt

Descartes opens his meditations indicating his desire to have only true beliefs. One way to accomplish this is to doubt everything he has learned that might be suspect of error.

Systematically Doubting the Foundations of Our Knowledge. The type of doubt that Descartes proposes is not what we would call a commonsense doubt. For example, common sense tells me that it is unreasonable to believe that black cats are harbingers of bad luck. Instead, his doubting process is a philosophical one and is sometimes called "hyperbolic" or "exaggerated" doubt, which means that he proposes to doubt anything that he has some reason to doubt. The goal of this doubting process is to arrive at a list of beliefs that are certain and indubitably true. It thus may be viewed as a systematic doubting experiment that consists in articulating reasons for doubting sensory information. When he presents the last of these reasons, there are virtually no items of knowledge in which he can have confidence.

 From DESCARTES: *"Meditation 1"* ————————

It is now some years since I detected how many were the false beliefs that I had from my earliest youth admitted as true, and how doubtful was everything I had since constructed on this basis. And from that time I was convinced that I must once for all seriously undertake to rid myself of all the opinions which I had formerly accepted, and commence to build anew from the foundation, if I wanted to establish any firm and permanent structure in the sciences. But as this enterprise appeared to be a very great one, I waited until I had attained an age so mature that I could not hope that at any later date I should be better fitted to execute my design. This reason caused me to delay so long that I should feel that I was doing wrong were I to occupy in deliberation the time that yet remains to me for action. Today, then, since very opportunely for the plan I have in view I have delivered my mind from every care [and am happily agitated by no passions] and since I have procured for myself an assured leisure in a peaceable retirement, I will at last seriously and freely address myself to the general upheaval of all my former opinions.

ASK YOURSELF

7.1 What reason does Descartes give in Meditation 1 for seriously undertaking to rid himself of his former opinions?

Now for this object it is not necessary that I should show that all of these are false—I will perhaps never arrive at this end. But inasmuch as reason already persuades me that I ought no less carefully to withhold my assent from matters which are not entirely certain and indubitable than from those which appear to me evidently to be false, if I am able to find in each one some reason to doubt, this will suffice to justify my rejecting the whole. And for that end it will not be requisite that I should examine each in particular, which would be an endless undertaking; for owing to the fact that the destruction of the foundations of necessity brings with it the downfall of the rest of the edifice, I will only in the first place attack those principles upon which all my former opinions rested.

All that up to the present time I have accepted as most true and certain I have learned either from the senses or through the senses; but it is sometimes proved to me that these senses are deceptive, and it is wiser not to trust entirely to anything by which we have once been deceived.

ASK YOURSELF

7.2. Descartes does not intend to doubt the truth of every specific idea that comes into his head. Rather, what does he plan to undermine?

7.3. What is the main assumption that he brings under suspicion?

Before turning to Descartes's reasons for doubt, some terminological background is needed. Descartes recognizes that some perceptions seem more genuine than others. For instance, we look at an apple and perceive qualities of redness, sweet smell, roundness, and singularity. Descartes recognized that the qualities of redness and sweet smell do not really belong to the apple. Instead, these qualities exist only in the mind of an observer and are then imposed onto the apple. These have been traditionally called *secondary qualities* and include color, sound, taste, odor, heat, and roughness. By contrast, the qualities of roundness and singularity belong to the apple itself and are not products of the observer's mind. These have been termed *primary qualities* and include quantity, shape, time, and magnitude. For Descartes, secondary qualities arise from what he calls "objects of the senses," primary qualities from "objects of mathematics." An apple would be a secondary object, or object of the senses, when we consider only its secondary qualities of redness and sweet smell. On the other hand, an apple is a primary object, or object of mathematics, when we consider only its primary qualities of shape and singularity (quantity). The root of the primary/secondary distinction is the attribute of *extension* (or existence in space). Primary qualities are features that necessarily belong to extended objects. All secondary qualities, by contrast, do not necessarily belong to extended objects and, thus, are spectator dependent. In view of this primary/secondary distinction, when Descartes doubts the reliability of his senses, he must find reason to doubt both his primary and secondary perceptions.

Optical Illusions. Descartes begins his systematic doubting experiment by pointing out an obvious credibility problem with our senses: optical illusions.

But it may be that although the senses sometimes deceive us concerning things which are hardly perceptible, or very far away, there are yet many others to be met with as to which we cannot reasonably have any doubt, although we recognize them by their means. For example, there is the fact that I am here, seated by the fire, attired in a dressing gown, having this paper in my hands and other similar matters. And how could I deny that these hands and this body are mine, were it not perhaps that I compare myself to certain persons, devoid of sense, whose cerebella are so troubled and clouded by the violent vapors of black bile, that they constantly assure us that they think they are kings when they are really quite poor, or that they are clothed in purple when they are really without covering, or who imagine that they have an earthenware head or are nothing but pumpkins or are made of glass. But they are mad, and I should not be any the less insane were I to follow examples so extravagant.

 ASK YOURSELF

7.4. Descartes begins doubting the reliability of his senses by noting that we perceive distant objects to be much smaller than they really are. This, however, does not undermine the general reliability of the senses. Why not?

Dream Hypothesis. Continuing his doubting experiment, Descartes suggests the possibility that he is dreaming.

At the same time I must remember that I am a man, and that consequently I am in the habit of sleeping, and in my dreams representing to myself the same things or sometimes even less probable things, than do those who are insane in their waking moments. How often has it happened to me that in the night I dreamt that I found myself in this particular place, that I was dressed and seated near the fire, whilst in reality I was lying undressed in bed! At this moment it does indeed seem to me that it is with eyes awake that I am looking at this paper; that this head which I move is not asleep, that it is deliberately and of set purpose that I extend my hand and perceive it; what happens in sleep does not appear so clear nor so distinct as does all this. But in thinking over this I remind myself that on many occasions I have in sleep been deceived by similar illusions, and in dwelling carefully on this reflection I see so evidently that there are no certain indications by which we may clearly distinguish wakefulness from sleep that I am lost in astonishment. And my astonishment is such that it is almost capable of persuading me that I now dream.

7.5. Why is Descartes almost convinced that he is sleeping?

Now let us assume that we are asleep and that all these particulars, for example, that we open our eyes, shake our head, extend our hands, and so on, are but false delusions; and let us reflect that possibly neither our hands nor our whole body are such as they appear to us to be. At the same time we must at least confess that the things which are represented to us in sleep are like painted representations which can only have been formed as the counterparts of something real and true, and that in this way those general things at least, that is, eyes, a head, hands, and a whole body, are not imaginary things, but things really existent. For, as a matter of fact, painters, even when they study with the greatest skill to represent sirens and satyrs by forms the most strange and extraordinary, cannot give them natures which are entirely new, but merely make a certain medley of the members of different animals; or if their imagination is extravagant enough to invent something so novel that nothing similar has ever before been seen, and that then their work represents a thing purely fictitious and absolutely false, it is certain all the same that the colors of which this is composed are necessarily real. And for the same reason, although these general things, to wit, [a body], eyes, a head, hands, and such like, may be imaginary, we are bound at the same time to confess that there are at least some other objects yet more simple and more universal, which are real and true; and of these just in the same way as with certain real colors, all these images of things which dwell in our thoughts, whether true and real or false and fantastic, are formed.

To such a class of things pertains corporeal nature in general, and its extension, the figure of extended things, their quantity or magnitude and number, as also the place in which they are, the time which measures their duration, and so on.

 ASK YOURSELF

7.6. What type of information (that is, primary or secondary) comes under doubt when Descartes considers that he may be dreaming?

That is possibly why our reasoning is not unjust when we conclude from this that Physics, Astronomy, Medicine and all other sciences which have as their end the consideration of composite things, are very dubious and uncertain; but that Arithmetic, Geometry and other sciences of that kind which only treat of things that are very simple and very general, without taking great trouble to ascertain whether they are actually existent or not, contain some measure of certainty and an element of the indubitable. For whether I am awake or asleep, two and three together always form five, and the square can never have more than four sides, and it does not seem possible that truths so clear and apparent can be suspected of any falsity [or uncertainty].

ASK YOURSELF

7.7. What type of knowledge remains incontestable (that is, primary or secondary), and what are the fields of study that examine this information?

The Evil Genius Hypothesis.   Taking his doubts further, Descartes initially speculates that God is deceiving him about all of the things that he believes or perceives, including primary objects.

Nevertheless I have long had fixed in my mind the belief that an all-powerful God existed by whom I have been created such as I am. But how do I know that he has not brought it to pass that there is no earth, no heaven, no extended body, no magnitude, no place, and that nevertheless [I possess the perceptions of all these things and that] they seem to me to exist just exactly as I now see them? And, besides, as I sometimes imagine that others deceive themselves in the things which they think they know best, how do I know that I am not deceived every time that I add two and three, or count the sides of a square, or judge of things yet simpler, if anything simpler can be imagined?

 ASK YOURSELF

7.8. What examples does he give to show that God could deceive him with mathematics?

This speculation causes Descartes problems, however, because according to traditional Christian theology, infinite goodness is one of God's necessary attributes. If backed into a corner, some might deny God's existence rather than admit that He is the cause of deception. With God out of the picture, however, Descartes argues that he would be even more vulnerable to deception.

But possibly God has not desired that I should be thus deceived, for he is said to be supremely good. If, however, it is contrary to his goodness to have made me such that I constantly deceive myself, it would also appear to be contrary to his goodness to permit me to be sometimes deceived, and nevertheless I cannot doubt that he does permit this.

There may indeed be those who would prefer to deny the existence of a God so powerful, rather than believe that all other things are uncertain. But let us not oppose them for the present, and grant that all that is here said of a God is a fable. They may suppose that I have arrived at the state of being that I have reached—attributing it to fate or to accident, or making out that it is by a continual succession of antecedents, or by some other method—since to err and deceive oneself is a defect. Nevertheless, as the Author to whom they assign my origin is said to be less powerful, it is clear that the probability increases that I deceive myself even more because of my imperfection. To these reasons I have certainly nothing to reply, but at the end I feel constrained to confess that there is nothing in all that I formerly believed to be true, of which I cannot in some measure doubt. This is so not merely through lack of thought or through frivolity, but for reasons which are very powerful and maturely considered. Thus, if I desire to arrive at any certainty [in the sciences], I should continue to refrain from giving credence to these opinions just as though they were evidently false.

 ASK YOURSELF

7.9. What is Descartes's response to those who would deny God's existence rather than admit that God is the cause of deception?

Descartes reflects on how far astray his doubts may take him and to what extent they are justified.

But it is not sufficient to have made these remarks, we must also be careful to keep them in mind. For these ancient and commonly held opinions still revert frequently to my mind, long and familiar custom having given them the right to occupy my mind against my inclination and rendered them almost masters of my belief. Nor will I ever lose the habit of deferring to them or of placing my confidence in them, so long as I consider them as they really are, that is, opinions in some measure doubtful, as I have just shown, and at the same time highly probable, so that there is much more reason to believe in than to deny them. That is why I consider that I will not be acting amiss, if, taking of set purpose a contrary belief, I allow myself to be deceived, and for a certain time pretend that all these opinions are entirely false and imaginary, until at last, having thus balanced my former prejudices with my latter [so that they cannot divert my opinions more to one side than to the other], my judgment will no longer be dominated by bad usage or turned away from the right knowledge of the truth. For I am assured that there can be neither peril nor error in this course, and that I cannot at present yield too much to distrust, since I am not considering the question of action, but only of knowledge.

 ASK YOURSELF

7.10. Discussions of skepticism during the modern period often drew a distinction between speculative and action-oriented skepticism. A speculative skeptic merely uncovers theoretical problems; an actional skeptic continues by recommending a course of action. With religious beliefs in particular, actional skepticism was viewed as more dangerous, as it might recommend that we act as though there were no God. What kind of doubt does Descartes propose here?

I will then suppose, not that God who is supremely good and the fountain of truth, but some evil genius not less powerful than deceitful, has employed his whole energies in deceiving me. I will consider that the heavens, the earth, colors, figures, sound, and all other external things are nothing but the illusions and dreams of which this genius has availed himself in order to lay traps for my credulity. I will consider myself as having no hands, no eyes, no flesh, no blood, nor any senses, yet falsely believing myself to possess all these things. I will remain obstinately attached to this idea, and if by this means it is not in my power to arrive at the knowledge of any truth, I may at least do what is in my power [that is, suspend my judgment], and with firm purpose avoid giving credence to any false thing, or being imposed upon by this arch deceiver, however powerful and deceptive he may be. But this task is a laborious one, and insensibly a certain lethargy leads me into the course of my ordinary life. And just as a captive who in sleep enjoys an imaginary liberty, when he begins to suspect that his liberty is but a dream, fears to awaken, and conspires with these agreeable illusions that the deception may be prolonged, so insensibly of my own accord I fall back into my former opinions, and I dread awakening from this slumber, lest the laborious wakefulness which would follow the tranquillity of this calmness should have to be spent not in daylight, but in the excessive darkness of the difficulties which have just been discussed.

 ASK YOURSELF

7.11. How does Descartes revise his doubt so not to run counter to traditional Christian belief?

7.12. What external things does Descartes take to be deceptive traps of the evil genius?

Synopsis. When it was first published, Descartes prefaced the Meditations with a synopsis of each of the six meditations. His synopsis of the first is as follows.

In the first Meditation I set forth the reasons for which we may, generally speaking, doubt about all things and especially about material things, at least so long as we have no other foundations for the sciences than those which we have until now possessed. But although the utility of a doubt which is so general does not at first appear, it is at the same time very great, inasmuch as it delivers us from every kind of prejudice, and sets out for us a very simple way by which the mind may detach itself from the senses; and finally it makes it impossible for us ever to doubt those things which we have once discovered to be true.

Meditation 2: Concerning the Nature of the Human Mind: That the Mind Is More Known Than the Body

Extent of His Doubt. Descartes opens Meditation 2 describing the extent of his doubt. Virtually every item of knowledge he previously believed is subject to some kind of doubt.

 From DESCARTES: *"Meditation 2"* ⎯⎯⎯⎯⎯

The Meditation of yesterday filled my mind with so many doubts that it is no longer in my power to forget them. And yet I do not see in what manner I can resolve them.

And, just as if I had all of a sudden fallen into very deep water, I am so baffled that I can neither make certain of setting my feet on the bottom, nor can I swim and so support myself on the surface. I will nevertheless make an effort and follow anew the same path as that on which I yesterday entered, that is, I will proceed by setting aside all that in which the least doubt could be supposed to exist, just as if I had discovered that it was absolutely false. And I will ever follow in this road until I have met with something which is certain, or at least, if I can do nothing else, until I have learned for certain that there is nothing in the world that is certain. Archimedes, in order that he might draw the terrestrial globe out of its place, and transport it elsewhere, demanded only that one point should be fixed and immovable. In the same way I will have the right to conceive high hopes if I am happy enough to discover one thing only which is certain and indubitable.

I suppose, then, that all the things that I see are false; I persuade myself that nothing has ever existed of all that my fallacious memory represents to me. I consider that I possess no senses; I imagine that body, figure, extension, movement and place are but the fictions of my mind. What, then, can be distinguished as true? Perhaps nothing at all, unless that there is nothing in the world that is certain.

 ASK YOURSELF

7.13. Archimedes was an ancient Greek engineer who said, "Give me a fulcrum and a firm point, and I alone can move the earth." Finish this analogy: Archimedes' ability to move the world is to a firm and immovable point just as a true philosophical system (that is, "high hopes") is to _____.

7.14. What are the various things that Descartes doubts at this point in his quest?

But how can I know there is not something different from those things that I have just considered, of which one cannot have the slightest doubt? Is there not some God, or some other being by whatever name we call it, who puts these reflections into my mind? That is not necessary, for is it not possible that I am capable of producing them myself? I myself, am I not at least something? But I have already denied that I had senses and body. Yet I hesitate, for what follows from that? Am I so dependent on body and senses that I cannot exist without these? But I was persuaded that there was nothing in all the world, that there was no heaven, no earth, that there were no minds, nor any bodies: was I not then likewise persuaded that I did not exist? Not at all; of a surety I myself did exist since I persuaded myself of something [or merely because I thought of something]. But there is some deceiver or other, very powerful and very cunning, who ever employs his ingenuity in deceiving me. Then without doubt I exist also if he deceives me, and let him deceive me as much as he will, he can never cause me to be nothing so long as I think that I am something. So that after having reflected well and carefully examined all things, we must come to the definite conclusion that this proposition: I am, I exist, is necessarily true each time that I pronounce it, or that I mentally conceive it.

ASK YOURSELF

7.15. The one thing Descartes recognizes that he can never doubt is the fact that he exists. Why is this?

In his *Discourse on the Method*, Descartes summarizes this line of reasoning in the famous phrase, "I think, therefore I am" (in Latin, "cogito ergo sum"). Descartes borrowed this strategy from Augustine's attempt to refute skepticism in his own day. Augustine writes, "On none of these points do I fear the arguments of the skeptics of the Academy who say: what if you are deceived? For if I am deceived, I am. For he who does not exist cannot be deceived. And if I am deceived, by this same token I am" (*City of God*, 11:26). Once Descartes recognizes the indubitable truth that he exists, he then attempts to further his knowledge by discovering the type of thing he is.

Rational Animal. Trying to understand what he is, Descartes recalls Aristotle's definition of a human as a rational animal.

But I do not yet know clearly enough what I am, I who am certain that I am; and hence I must be careful to see that I do not imprudently take some other object in place of myself, and thus that I do not go astray in respect of this knowledge that I hold to be the most certain and most evident of all that I have formerly learned. That is why I will now consider anew what I believed myself to be before I started upon these last reflections. And of my former opinions I will withdraw all that might even in a small degree be invalidated by the reasons which I have just brought forward, in order that there may be nothing at all left beyond what is absolutely certain and indubitable.

What then did I formerly believe myself to be? Undoubtedly I believed myself to be a human. But what is a human? Should I say a rational animal? Certainly not. For then I should have to inquire what an animal is, and what is rational. And thus from a single question I should insensibly fall into an infinitude of others more difficult; and I should not wish to waste the little time and leisure remaining to me in trying to unravel subtleties like these.

 ASK YOURSELF

7.16. Why is Descartes dissatisfied with the answer that he is a human or rational animal?

Body and Soul. Continuing his quest for identity, he recalls a more general view he previously had of his identity, which is that he is composed of both body and soul.

But I will rather stop here to consider the thoughts which of themselves spring up in my mind, and which were not inspired by anything beyond my own nature alone when I applied myself to the consideration of my being. In the first place, then, I considered myself as having a face, hands, arms, and all that system of members composed on bones and flesh as seen in a corpse which I designated by the name of body. In addition to this I considered that I was nourished, that I walked, that I felt, and that I thought, and I referred all these actions to the soul. But I did not stop to consider what the soul was, or if I did stop, I imagined that it was something extremely rare and subtle like a wind, a flame, or an ether, which was spread throughout my grosser parts. As to body I had no manner of doubt about its nature, but thought I had a very clear knowledge of it. And if I had desired to explain it according to the notions that I had then formed of it, I should have described it as follows. By the body I understand all that which can be defined by a certain figure. It is something which can be confined in a certain place, and which can fill a given space in such a way that every other body will be excluded from it. It can be perceived either by touch, or by sight, or by hearing, or by taste, or by smell. It can be moved in many ways, not, in truth, by itself, but by something which is foreign to it, by which it is touched [and from which it receives impressions]. For to have the power of self-movement, as also of feeling or of thinking, I did not consider to belonged to the nature of body. On the contrary, I was rather astonished to find that faculties similar to them existed in some bodies.

But what am I, now that I suppose that there is a certain genius which is extremely powerful, and, if I may say so, malicious, who employs all his powers in deceiving me? Can I affirm that I possess the least of all those things which I have just said pertain to the nature of body? I pause to consider, I revolve all these things in my mind, and I find none of which I can say that it pertains to me. It would be tedious to stop to enumerate them.

 ASK YOURSELF

7.17. Why can't Descartes refer to himself as a thing that has a body?

Let us pass to the attributes of soul and see if there is any one which is in me? What of nutrition or walking [the first mentioned]? But if it is so that I have no body it is also true that I can neither walk nor take nourishment. Another attribute is sensation. But one cannot feel without body, and besides I have thought I perceived many things during sleep that I recognized in my waking moments as not having been experienced at all. What of thinking? I find here that thought is an attribute that belongs to me; it alone cannot be separated from me. I am, I exist, that is certain. But how often? Just when I think; for it might possibly be the case if I ceased entirely to think, that I should likewise cease altogether to exist. I do not now admit anything which is not necessarily true: to speak accurately I am not more than a thing which thinks, that is to say a mind or a soul, or an understanding, or a reason, which are terms whose significance was formerly unknown to me. I am, however, a real thing and really exist; but what thing? I have answered: a thing which thinks.

ASK YOURSELF

7.18. According to classical philosophers such as Plato and Aristotle, the key attributes of the soul involve eating, movement, and sensation. Why can't he claim to have these attributes of the soul?

Other Possible Attributes. Descartes continues examining other theories of human existence and lists of human attributes.

And what more? I will exercise my imagination [in order to see if I am not something more]. I am not a collection of members which we call the human body: I am not a subtle air distributed through these members, I am not a wind, a fire, a vapor, a breath, nor anything at all which I can imagine or conceive; because I have assumed that all these were nothing. Without changing that supposition I find that I only leave myself certain of the fact that I am somewhat. But perhaps it is true that these same things which I supposed were non-existent because they are unknown to me, are really not different from the self which I know. I am not sure about this, I will not dispute about it now. I can only give judgment on things that are known to me. I know that I exist, and I inquire what I am, I whom I know to exist. But it is very certain that the knowledge of my existence taken in its precise significance does not depend on things whose existence is not yet known to me. Consequently it does not depend on those which I can feign in imagination. And indeed the very term *feign* in imagination proves to me my error, for I really do this if I imagine myself a something, since to imagine is nothing else than to contemplate the figure or image of a corporeal thing. But I already know for certain that I am, and that it may be that all these images, and, speaking generally, all things that relate to the nature of body are nothing but dreams [and chimeras]. For this reason I see clearly that I have as little reason to say, "I will stimulate my imagination in order to know more distinctly what I am," than if I were to say, "I am now awake, and I perceive somewhat that is real and true: but because I do not yet perceive it distinctly enough, I will go to sleep of express purpose, so that my dreams may represent the perception with greatest truth and evidence." And, thus, I know for certain that nothing of all that I can understand by means of my imagination belongs to this knowledge which I have of myself. It is necessary to withdraw the mind from this mode of thought with the utmost diligence in order that it may be able to know its own nature with perfect distinctness.

ASK YOURSELF

7.19. What are some of the theories of human existence that Descartes rejects?

7.20. Descartes can imagine various attributes he might have. What does he do with such imaginary considerations?

I Am a Thinking Thing. Descartes concludes that the attribute of thinking is the only quality that he can justifiably claim at this point. But he is quick to point out that thinking is the only attribute about which he is sure—not that thinking is the only attribute that he has. Nevertheless, this is the starting point of a radical ontological distinction that carries Descartes through his meditations. That distinction is between thinking substance (*res cogitans*) and extended substance (*res extensa*). The two substances are mutually exclusive. A thinking substance is nonphysical or spiritual in nature, and an extended substance is physical, but not capable of consciousness or thought.

But what then am I? A thing which thinks. What is a thing which thinks? It is a thing which doubts, understands, [conceives], affirms, denies, wills, refuses, which also imagines and feels. Certainly it is no small matter if all these things pertain to my nature. But why should they not so pertain? Am I not that being who now doubts nearly everything, who nevertheless understands certain things, who affirms that one only is true, who denies all the others, who desires to know more, is averse from being deceived, who imagines many things, sometimes indeed despite his will, and who perceives many likewise, as by the intervention of the bodily organs? Is there nothing in all this which is as true as it is certain that I exist, even though I should always sleep and though he who has given me being employed all his ingenuity in deceiving me? Is there likewise any one of these attributes which can be distinguished from my thought, or which might be said to be separated from myself? For it is so evident of itself that it is I who doubts, who understands, and who desires, that there is no reason here to add anything to explain it. And I have certainly the power of imagining likewise; for although it may happen (as I formerly supposed) that none of the things which I imagine are true, nevertheless this power of imagining does not cease to be really in use, and it forms part of my thought. Finally, I am the same who feels, that is to say, who perceives certain things, as by the organs of sense, since in truth I see light, I hear noise, I feel heat. But it will be said that these phenomena are false and that I am dreaming. Let it be so; still it is at least quite certain that it seems to me that I see light, that I hear noise and that I feel heat. That cannot be false; properly speaking it is what is in me called feeling; and used in this precise sense that is no other thing than thinking.

 ASK YOURSELF

7.21. What, for Descartes, does thinking entail?

7.22. What justifies Descartes in claiming that he is a thing that doubts?

Note Descartes's general strategy for adding to his knowledge. He is first concerned with the issue of personal identity and will only much later address the issue of external objects (in Meditation 6). He then anticipates the criticism that he is going about his investigation backward, for it seems that knowledge of external objects is more obvious and distinct than knowledge of personal identity. Everyone knows what an apple is (an external object), but few people can properly answer the question: "Who am I?" (an issue of personal identity). Thus, it seems that Descartes should tackle the easier problem of external objects first.

From this time I begin to know what I am with a little more clearness and distinction than before; but nevertheless it still seems to me, and I cannot prevent myself from thinking, that corporeal things, whose images are framed by thought, which are tested by the senses, are much more distinctly known than that obscure part of me which does not come under the imagination. Although really it is very strange to say that I know and understand more distinctly these things whose existence seems to me dubious, which are unknown to me, and which do not belong to me, than others of the truth of which I am convinced, which are known to me and which pertain to my real nature, in a word, than myself. But I see clearly how the case stands: my mind loves to wander, and cannot yet suffer itself to be retained within the just limits of truth. Very good, let us once more give it the freest rein, so that, when afterwards we seize the proper occasion for pulling up, it may the more easily be regulated and controlled.

Descartes does not agree that he proceeds in a backward fashion, and he argues that our personal identity is actually more clear and fundamental than perception of external objects. He makes his case by comparing our perceptions of a piece of wax at two times: once while the wax is in a solid state, and later after the wax has been melted by a fire.

The Wax Example and Our Senses. In arguing that knowledge of the mental realm precedes knowledge of the material realm, Descartes argues that our senses alone cannot inform us of the identity of the two states of the wax.

Let us begin by considering the most common matters, those which we believe to be the most distinctly comprehended, namely, the bodies which we touch and see; not indeed bodies in general, for these general ideas are usually a little more confused, but let us consider one body in particular. Let us take, for example, this piece of wax: it has been taken quite freshly from the hive, and it has not yet lost the sweetness of the honey which it contains; it still retains somewhat of the odor of the flowers from which it has been culled; its color, its figure, its size are apparent; it is hard, cold, easily handled, and if you strike it with the finger, it will emit a sound. Finally all the things which are requisite to cause us distinctly to recognize a body, are met within it. But notice that while I speak and approach the fire what remained of the taste is exhaled, the smell evaporates, the color alters, the figure is destroyed, the size increases, it becomes liquid, it heats, scarcely can one handle it, and when one strikes it, now sound is emitted. Does the same wax remain after this change? We must confess that it remains; none would judge otherwise. What then did I know so distinctly in this piece of wax? It could certainly be nothing of all that the senses brought to my notice, since all these things which fall under taste, smell, sight, touch, and hearing, are found to be changed, and yet the same wax remains.

 ASK YOURSELF

7.23. Why isn't the identity of the two states of wax established through the senses?

The Imagination. For Descartes, the continuity of the wax cannot be established through the faculty of the imagination, either.

Perhaps it was what I now think, namely, that this wax was not that sweetness of honey, nor that agreeable scent of flowers, nor that particular whiteness, nor that figure, nor that sound, but simply a body which a little while before appeared to me as perceptible under these forms, and which is now perceptible under others. But what, precisely, is it that I imagine when I form such conceptions? Let us attentively consider this, and, abstracting from all that does not belong to the wax, let us see what remains. Certainly nothing remains except a certain extended thing which is flexible and movable. But what is the meaning of flexible and movable? Is it not that I imagine that this piece of wax being round is capable of becoming square and of passing from a square to a triangular figure? No, certainly it is not that, since I imagine it admits of an infinitude of similar changes, and I nevertheless do not know how to compass the infinitude by my imagination, and consequently this conception which I have of the wax is not brought about by the faculty of imagination. What now is this extension? Is it not also unknown? For it becomes greater when the wax is melted, greater when it is boiled, and greater still when the heat increases; and I should not conceive [clearly] according to truth what wax is, if I did not think that even this piece that we are considering is capable of receiving more variations in extension than I have ever imagined.

 ASK YOURSELF

7.24. Why isn't the identity of the two states of the wax established through the imagination?

The Mind Alone. Descartes concludes that the identity of the two states of wax is established neither by sight, nor touch, nor imagination, but by an act of the mind alone.

We must then grant that I could not even understand through the imagination what this piece of wax is, and that it is my mind alone which perceives it. I say this piece of wax in particular, for as to wax in general it is yet clearer. But what is this piece of wax which cannot be understood except by the [understanding or] mind? It is certainly the same that I see, touch, imagine, and finally it is the same which I have always believed it to be from the beginning. But what must particularly be observed is that its perception is neither an act of vision, nor of touch, nor of imagination, and has never been such although it may have appeared formerly to be so, but only an intuition of the mind, which may be imperfect and confused as it was formerly, or clear and distinct as it is at present, according as my attention is more or less directed to the elements which are found in it, and of which it is composed.

Possible Criticisms. Descartes considers possible criticisms to his conclusion that we understand the physical world through an act of the mind. In common language we claim that we "see" the same wax in its two states (as opposed to "mentally intuit" the same wax in its two states). Thus, common language seems to suggest that the continuity of the wax is a function of "seeing" (i.e., the senses).

Yet in the meantime I am greatly astonished when I consider [the great feebleness of mind] and its proneness to fall [insensibly] into error. For although without giving expression to my thought I consider all this in my own mind, words often impede me and I am almost deceived by the terms of ordinary language. For we say that we see the same wax, if it is present, and not that we simply judge that it is the same from its having the same color and figure. From this I should conclude that I knew the wax by means of vision and not simply by the intuition of the mind; unless by chance I remember that, when looking from a window and saying I see men who pass in the street, I really do not see them, but infer that what I see is men, just as I say that I see wax. And yet what do I see from the window but hats and coats which may cover automatic machines? Yet I judge these to be men. And similarly solely by the faculty of judgment which rests in my mind, I comprehend that which I believed I saw with my eyes.

 ASK YOURSELF

7.25. When I look out the window, I conclude that we see people crossing the road. What, however, is all that appears to my senses?

Descartes considers again whether we understand the physical world through the senses and imagination together.

A man who makes it his aim to raise his knowledge above the common should be ashamed to derive the occasion for doubting from the forms of speech invented by the vulgar. I prefer to pass on and consider whether I had a more evident and perfect conception of what the wax was when I first perceived it, and when I believed I knew it by means of the external senses or at least by the common sense as it is called (that is to say by the imaginative faculty) or whether my present conception is clearer now that I have most carefully examined what it is, and in what way it can be known. It would certainly be absurd to doubt as to this. For what was there in this first perception which was distinct? What was there which might not as well have been perceived by any of the animals? But when I distinguish the wax from its external forms, and when, just as if I had taken from it its vestments, I consider it quite naked, it is certain that although some error may still be found in my judgment, I can nevertheless not perceive it thus without a human mind.

 ASK YOURSELF

7.26. How does the wax appear to us when we inspect it with our minds (as opposed to our senses or imagination)?

Even if Descartes is wrong and we understand the wax through our senses or our imagination, he argues that the mind is still prior to sensations. For even if he erroneously judges that the wax exists through sight or imagination, this presupposes that he himself exists.

But finally what will I say of this mind, that is, of myself, for up to this point I do not admit in myself anything but mind? What, then, I who seem to perceive this piece of wax so distinctly, do I not know myself, not only with much more truth and certainty, but also with much more distinctness and clearness? For if I judge that the wax is or exists from the fact that I see it, it certainly follows much more clearly that I am or that I exist myself from the fact that I see it. For it may be that what I see is not really wax, it may also be that I do not possess eyes with which to see anything; but it cannot be that when I see, or (for I no longer take account of the distinction) when I think I see, that I myself who think am nothing. So if I judge that the wax exists from the fact that I touch it, the same thing will follow, namely, that I am. And if I judge that my imagination, or some other cause, whatever it is, persuades me that the wax exists, I will still conclude the same. And what I have here remarked of wax may be applied to all other things which are external to me [and which are met with outside of me]. And further, if the [notion or] perception of wax has seemed to me clearer and more distinct, not only after the sight or the touch, but also after many other causes have rendered it quite evident to me, with how much more [evidence] and distinctness must it be said that I now know myself, since all the reasons which contribute to the knowledge of wax, or any other body whatever, are yet better proofs of the nature of my mind. And there are so many other things in the mind itself which may contribute to the elucidation of its nature, that those which depend on body such as these just mentioned, hardly merit being taken into account.

But finally here I am, having insensibly reverted to the point I desired, for, since it is now evident to me that even bodies are not properly speaking known by the senses or by the faculty of imagination, but by the understanding only, and since they are not known from the fact that they are seen or touched, but only because they are understood, I see clearly that there is nothing which is easier for me to know than my mind. But because it is difficult to rid oneself so promptly of an opinion to which one was accustomed for so long, it will be well that I should halt a little at this point, so that by the length of my meditation I may more deeply imprint on my memory this new knowledge.

 ## ASK YOURSELF

7.27. For Descartes, sensation and imagination are mental attributes that depend on the body. How important are they in defining the nature of the mind?

Synopsis. Descartes's synopsis of Meditation 2 (initially presented at the opening of his meditations) is as follows.

In the second Meditation, mind (which making use of the liberty which pertains to it) takes for granted that all those things are non-existent of whose existence it has the least doubt. Further, however, it recognizes that it is absolutely impossible that it does not itself exist. This point is likewise of the greatest moment, inasmuch as by this means a distinction is easily drawn between the things which pertain to mind—that is to say to the intellectual nature—and those which pertain to body.

Meditation 3: Of God: That He Exists

In the first paragraph of Meditation 3 Descartes summarizes his progress, and he indicates that he is ready to further his knowledge.

 From DESCARTES: *"Meditation 3"* ———————————

I will now close my eyes, I will stop my ears, I will call away all my senses, I will efface even from my thoughts all the images of corporeal things, or at least (for that is hardly possible) I will consider them as vain and false; and thus holding converse only with myself and considering my own nature, I will try little by little to reach a better knowledge of and a more familiar acquaintanceship with myself. I am a thing that thinks, that is to say, that doubts, affirms, denies, that knows a few things, that is ignorant of many [that loves, that hates], that wills, that desires, that also imagines and perceives; for as I remarked before, although the things which I perceive and imagine are perhaps nothing at all apart from me and in themselves, I am nevertheless assured that these modes of thought that I call perceptions and imaginations, inasmuch only as they are modes of thought, certainly reside [and are met with] in me.

Clarity and Distinctness. Descartes notes that when he contemplates the certainty of his existence, he knows the truth of his existence clearly and distinctly.

And in the little that I have just said, I think I have summed up all that I really know, or at least all that until now I was aware that I knew. In order to try to extend my knowledge further, I will now look around more carefully and see whether I cannot still discover in myself some other things which I have not until now perceived. I am certain that I am a thing which thinks. But do I not then likewise know what is requisite to render me certain of a truth? Certainly in this first knowledge there is nothing that assures me of its truth, except the clear and distinct perception of that which I state, which would not indeed suffice to assure me that what I say is true, if it could ever happen that a thing which I conceived so clearly and distinctly could be false; and accordingly it seems to me that already I can establish as a general rule that all things which I perceive very clearly and very distinctly are true.

 ASK YOURSELF

7.28. What is the general rule Descartes posits regarding clarity and distinctness?

Certainty of the World and Mathematics. Descartes would like to use this general rule and show both the existence of external objects and the truth of mathematics. For, to differing degrees, both of these are vivid concepts. Unfortunately, knowledge of external objects does not rise to the level of clarity and distinctness.

At the same time I have before received and admitted many things to be very certain and evident, which yet I afterwards recognized as being dubious. What then were these things? They were the earth, sky, stars and all other objects which I grasped by means of the senses. But what did I clearly [and distinctly] perceive in them? Nothing more than that the ideas or thoughts of these things were presented to my mind. And not even now do I deny that these ideas are met with in me. But there was yet another thing which I affirmed, and which, owing to the habit which I had formed of believing it, I thought I perceived very clearly, although in truth I did not perceive it at all, namely, that there were objects outside of me from which these ideas proceeded, and to which they were entirely similar. And it was in this that I erred, or, if perchance my judgment was correct, this was not due to any knowledge arising from my perception.

 ASK YOURSELF

7.29. What judgments about the external world at first seemed vivid, but later proved to be questionable?

By contrast, mathematical judgments are perceived clearly and distinctly.

But when I took anything very simple and easy in the sphere of arithmetic or geometry into consideration, for example, that two and three together made five, and other things of the sort, were not these present to my mind so clearly as to enable me to affirm that they were true? Certainly if I judged that since such matters could be doubted, this would not have been so for any other reason than that it came into my mind that perhaps a God might have endowed me with such a nature that I may have been deceived even concerning things which seemed to me most evident. But every time that this preconceived opinion of the sovereign power of a God presents itself to my thought, I am constrained to confess that it is easy to Him, if he wishes it, to cause me to err, even in matters in which I believe myself to have the best evidence. And, on the other hand, always when I direct my attention to things which I believe myself to perceive very clearly, I am so persuaded of their truth that I let myself break out into words such as these: Let who will deceive me, he can never cause me to be nothing while I think that I am, or some day cause it to be true to say that I have never been, it being true now to say that I am, or that two and three make more or less than five, or any such thing in which I see a evident contradiction.

However, an obstacle remains: God may be deceiving Descartes irrespective of how clearly and distinctly he perceives mathematical truths. To put the general rule of clarity and distinctness on sound footing, Descartes must (1) prove God's existence and then (2) show that God is not a deceiver.

And, certainly, since I have no reason to believe that there is a God who is a deceiver, and as I have not yet satisfied myself that there is a God at all, the reason for doubt which depends on this opinion alone is very slight, and so to speak metaphysical. But in order to be able altogether to remove it, I must inquire whether there is a God as soon as the occasion presents itself; and if I find that there is a God, I must also inquire whether he may be a deceiver. For without a knowledge of these two truths I do not see that I can ever be certain of anything.

Principle of Cause and Effect. In preparation for his proof for God's existence, Descartes discusses a principle of causality: "There must be as much in the total efficient cause as there is in the effect of that same cause." In short, there must be as much in any cause as there is in its effect.

Now it is evident by the natural light that there must at least be as much reality in the efficient and total cause as in its effect. For, I ask, from where can the effect derive its reality, if not from its cause? And in what way can this cause communicate this reality to it, unless it possessed it in itself? And from this it follows, not only that something cannot proceed from nothing, but likewise that what is more perfect, that is to say, which has more reality within itself, cannot proceed from the less perfect.

 ASK YOURSELF

7.30. How does Descartes know the truth of his principle of cause and effect?

7.31. What are two consequences that follow from the principle of cause and effect?

Descartes argues that the principle of cause and effect applies to ideas as well as to physical objects. That is, an idea with a moderate amount of objective reality (let's say, with five units of complexity) must be produced by something with at least that much objective reality (five or more units of complexity).

And this is not only evidently true of those effects which possess actual or formal reality, but also of the ideas in which we consider merely what is termed objective reality. To take an example, the stone which has not yet existed not only cannot now commence to be unless it has been produced by something which possesses within itself, either formally or eminently, all that enters into the composition of the stone [that is, it must possess the same things or other more excellent things than those which exist in the stone] and heat can only be produced in a subject in which it did not previously exist by a cause that is of an order [degree or kind] at least as perfect as heat, and so in all other cases.

 ASK YOURSELF

7.32. How does the principle of cause and effect apply to the causes of an actual stone or some actual heat?

But further, the idea of heat, or of a stone, cannot exist in me unless it has been placed within me by some cause which possesses within it at least as much reality as that which I conceive to exist in the heat or the stone. For although this cause does not transmit anything of its actual or formal reality to my idea, we must not for that reason imagine that it is necessarily a less real cause; we must remember that [since every idea is a work of the mind] its nature is such that it demands of itself no other formal reality than that which it borrows from my thought, of which it is only a mode [that is, a manner or way of thinking]. But in order that an idea should contain some one certain objective reality rather than another, it must without doubt derive it from some cause in which there is at least as much formal reality as this idea contains of objective reality. For if we imagine that something is found in an idea which is not found in the cause, it must then have been derived from nothing; but however imperfect may be this mode of being by which a thing is objectively [or by representation] in the understanding by its idea, we cannot certainly say that this mode of being is nothing, nor consequently, that the idea derives its origin from nothing.

 ASK YOURSELF

7.33. How does the principle of cause and effect apply to the causes of our ideas of heat or of a stone?

Origin of the Idea of Infinite Perfection. Finally, Descartes considers the idea of God that is in his mind. This idea is that of "an infinite and independent substance." More to the point, he has in his mind an idea of infinite perfection.

Hence there remains only the idea of God, concerning which we must consider whether it is something which cannot have proceeded from me myself. By the name God I understand a substance that is infinite [eternal, immutable], independent, all-knowing, all-powerful, and by which I myself and everything else, if anything else does exist, have been created. Now all these characteristics are such that the more diligently I attend to them, the less do they appear capable of proceeding from me alone; hence, from what has been already said, we must conclude that God necessarily exists.

 ASK YOURSELF

7.34. Since Descartes's idea of infinite perfection could not have been produced by himself, what must he conclude?

Formally, Descartes's argument for God's existence is as follows:

a. We have an idea of infinite perfection.

b. The idea we have of ourselves entails finitude and imperfection.

c. There must be as much reality in the cause of any idea as in the idea itself (the principle of cause and effect).

d. Therefore, the idea we have of infinite perfection originated from a being with infinite perfection, and this being is God.

God Is Not a Deceiver. Descartes closes Meditation 3 arguing that God is not a deceiver.

And one certainly ought not to find it strange that God, in creating me, placed this idea within me to be like the mark of the workman imprinted on his work; and it is likewise not essential that the mark will be something different from the work itself. For from the sole fact that God created me it is most probable that in some way he has placed his image and likeness upon me, and that I perceive this likeness (in which the idea of God is contained) by means of the same faculty by which I perceive myself. That is to say, when I reflect on myself I not only know that I am something [imperfect], incomplete and dependent on another, which incessantly aspires after something which is better and greater than myself, but I also know that he on whom I depend possesses in Himself all the great things towards which I aspire [and the ideas of which I find within myself]. And he possesses this not indefinitely or potentially alone, but really, actually and infinitely; and that thus he is God. And the whole strength of the argument which I have here made use of to prove the existence of God consists in this, that I recognize that it is not possible that my nature should be what it is, and indeed that I should have in myself the idea of a God—if God did not truly exist a God, I say, whose idea is in me, that is, who possesses all those supreme perfections of which our mind may indeed have some idea but without understanding them all, who is liable to no errors or defect [and who has none of all those marks which denote imperfection]. From this it is evident that he cannot be a deceiver, since the light of nature teaches us that fraud and deception necessarily proceed from some defect.

 ASK YOURSELF

7.35. When focusing on God's nature, why does Descartes conclude that God is not a deceiver?

Synopsis. Descartes's synopsis of Meditation 3 (initially presented at the opening of his meditations) is as follows.

In the third Meditation it seems to me that I have explained at sufficient length the principal argument of which I make use in order to prove the existence of God. But nonetheless, because I did not wish in that place to make use of any comparisons derived from corporeal things, so as to withdraw as much as I could the minds of readers from the senses, there may perhaps have remained many obscurities which, however, will, I hope, be entirely removed by the Replies which I have made to the Objections which have been set before me. Amongst others there is, for example, this one, "How the idea in us of a being supremely perfect possesses so much objective reality [that is to say participates by representation in so many degrees of being and perfection] that it necessarily proceeds from a cause which is absolutely perfect." This is illustrated in these Replies by the comparison of a very perfect machine, the idea of which is found in the mind of some workman. For as the objective contrivance of this idea must have some cause, that is, either the science of the workman or that of some other from whom he has received the idea, it is similarly impossible that the idea of God which is in us should not have God himself as its cause.

Meditation 6: Of the Existence of Material Things, and of the Real Distinction between the Soul and Body of Man

At this point in the meditations, Descartes has obtained certainty about a variety of topics: his existence, his essence, the causal principle, God's existence, that God made him, that God is not a deceiver, that clarity and distinctness are indicators of truth. Descartes sets two aims in Meditation 6: first, to show the existence of material objects, and second, to show that mind is distinct from body.

Identity as a Thinking Thing. Descartes recalls how he attained certainty that God would not deceive him about his clear and distinct ideas. One such idea concerns the identity as a thinking thing. Even though he may have a body, his true identity is that of a thinking thing alone.

 From DESCARTES: *"Meditation 6"*

But now that I begin to know myself better, and to discover more clearly the author of my being, I do not in truth think that I should rashly admit all the matters which the senses seem to teach us, but, on the other hand, I do not think that I should doubt them all universally.

And first of all, because I know that all things which I perceive clearly and distinctly can be created by God as I understand them, it suffices that I am able to perceive one thing apart from another clearly and distinctly in order to be certain that the one is different from the other, since they may be made to exist in separation at least by the omnipotence of God. And it does not signify by what power this separation is made in order to compel me to judge them to be different. And, therefore, just because I know certainly that I exist, and that meanwhile I do not remark that any other thing necessarily pertains to my nature or essence, except that I am a thinking thing, I rightly conclude that my essence consists solely in the fact that I am a thinking thing [or a substance whose whole essence or nature is to think]. And although possibly (or rather certainly, as I will say in a moment) I possess a body with which I am very intimately conjoined, it is certain that this I [that is to say, my soul by which I am what I am], is entirely and absolutely distinct from my body, and can exist without it. This is because, on the one hand, I have a clear and distinct idea of myself inasmuch as I am only a thinking and unextended thing, and as, on the other, I possess a distinct idea of body, inasmuch as it is only an extended and unthinking thing,

 ASK YOURSELF

7.36. What are the two reasons Descartes gives for concluding that his mind could exist without his body?

In Descartes's view of things, humans are spirits that occupy a mechanical body, and the essential attributes of humans are exclusively attributes of the spirit (such as thinking, willing, and conceiving) that do not involve the body at all. Attributes such as sense perception, movement, and appetite require a body, are attributes of our body and not of our spirit, and, hence, do not comprise our essence.

Faculties of Thinking. Descartes explains that we are designed with several mental faculties that are responsible for various ways of thinking. Descartes is most concerned here with the passive faculty of perception.

I further find in myself faculties employing modes of thinking peculiar to themselves, namely, the faculties of imagination and feeling, without which I can easily conceive myself clearly and distinctly as a complete being; while, on the other hand, they cannot be so conceived apart from me, that is without an intelligent substance in which they reside, for [in the notion we have of these faculties, or, to use the language of the Schools] in their formal concept, some kind of intellection is comprised, from which I infer that they are distinct from me as its modes are from a thing. I observe also in me some other faculties such as that of change of position, the assumption of different figures and such like, which cannot be conceived, any more than can the preceding, apart from some substance to which they are attached, and consequently cannot exist without it; but it is very clear that these faculties, if it be true that they exist, must be attached to some corporeal or extended substance, and not to an intelligent substance, since in the clear and distinct conception of these there is some sort of extension found to be present, but no intellection at all. There is certainly further in me a certain passive faculty of perception, that is, of receiving and recognizing the ideas of sensible things. But this would be useless to me [and I could in no way benefit from it], if there were not either in me or in some other thing another active faculty capable of forming and producing these ideas.

 ASK YOURSELF

7.37. What is the passive faculty of perception?

Existence of External Objects. Connected to the passive faculty of perception is an active source of the perceptions we receive. That is, if I passively (or nonwillfully) perceive a rock in front of me, then there is some active source feeding me that perception. Descartes sees only three possible explanations of that active source: The perceptions are actively produced either by himself, by God, or by external objects. He eliminates the first two options and concludes that external objects are the active source of such perceptions.

But this active faculty cannot exist in me [inasmuch as I am a thing that thinks] seeing that it does not presuppose thought, and also that those ideas are often produced in me without my contributing in any way to the same, and often even against my will. It is thus necessarily the case that the faculty resides in some substance different from me in which all the reality which is objectively in the ideas that are produced by this faculty is formally or eminently contained, as I remarked before. And this substance is either a body, that is, a corporeal nature in which there is contained formally [and really] all that which is objectively [and by representation] in those ideas, or it is God Himself, or some other creature more noble than body in which that same is contained eminently. But, since God is no deceiver, it is very evident that he does not communicate to me these ideas immediately and by Himself, nor yet by the intervention of some creature in which their reality is not formally, but only eminently, contained. For since he has given me no faculty to recognize that this is the case, but, on the other hand, a very great inclination to believe [that they are sent to me or] that they are conveyed to me by corporeal objects, I do not see how he could be defended from the accusation of deceit if these ideas were produced by causes other than corporeal objects. Hence we must allow that corporeal things exist. However, they are perhaps not exactly what we perceive by the senses, since this comprehension by the senses is in many instances very obscure and confused. But we must at least admit that all things which I conceive in them clearly and distinctly, that is to say, all things which, speaking generally, are comprehended in the object of pure mathematics, are truly to be recognized as external objects.

 ASK YOURSELF

7.38. Why does Descartes rule out himself as the active source of perceptions?

7.39. Why does Descartes rule out God as the active source of perception?

Stated briefly, Descartes's argument for the existence of external objects is as follows:

a. I know clearly and distinctly that there is in me a passive faculty that receives perceptions from an active source.

b. This active source of perception is either me, God, or external objects.

c. I am not that active source since such perceptions are not willfully produced and do not involve thinking (my true essence).

d. God does not implant ideas of perception in me since this would be deception.

e. Therefore, external objects are the active source of perceptions.

For Descartes, (d) is the crucial premise to his argument. Why does he believe that perceptions are not implanted in him by God? The answer is that, first, Descartes has no faculty by which he could know if such perceptions are implanted by God. Second, he has a strong inclination to believe that secondary perceptions are the result of secondary external objects. Third, Descartes argues that it would be deception on God's part if God (1) permitted Descartes to erroneously believe perceptions are caused by objects and (2) did not give him a faculty to know that such notions are actually caused by God. Descartes has here expanded on the notion of God not being a deceiver. In Meditation 3, God's quality of nondeception was commissive in that a perfect God could not commit any act that would deceive. Here, however,

Descartes argues that a perfect God cannot omit any preventative measures that would help Descartes understand the truth. God's nondeception, then, is also omissive. This commissive/omissive distinction is similar to the notion of sins of commission (such as the direct stabbing of an innocent person) and sins of omission (such as refusing to rescue a person from drowning). Descartes maintains, then, that a nondeceptive God can perform neither deceptions of commission nor deceptions of omission.

Four Sources of Error. Descartes argues that there are four sources of error that are inherently tied to the structure of our physical bodies. The first of these stems from the fact that the mind and body are distinct.

In order to begin this examination, then, I here say, in the first place, that there is a great difference between mind and body, inasmuch as body is by nature always divisible, and the mind is entirely indivisible. For, as a matter of fact, when I consider the mind, that is to say, myself inasmuch as I am only a thinking thing, I cannot distinguish in myself any parts, but understand myself to be clearly one and entire. And although the whole mind seems to be united to the whole body, yet if a foot, or an arm, or some other part, is separated from my body, I am aware that nothing has been taken away from my mind. And the faculties of willing, feeling, conceiving, etc. cannot be properly speaking said to be its parts, for it is one and the same mind which employs itself in willing and in feeling and understanding. But it is quite otherwise with corporeal or extended objects, for there is not one of these imaginable by me which my mind cannot easily divide into parts, and which consequently I do not recognize as being divisible; this would be sufficient to teach me that the mind or soul of man is entirely different from the body, if I had not already learned it from other sources.

 ASK YOURSELF

7.40. What key difference between mind and body results in error?

A second source of error results from the fact that the mind does not receive impressions directly from all parts of the body.

I further notice that the mind does not receive the impressions from all parts of the body immediately, but only from the brain, or perhaps even from one of its smallest parts, namely, from that in which the common sense is said to reside, which, whenever it is disposed in the same particular way, conveys the same thing to the mind, although meanwhile the other portions of the body may be differently disposed, as is testified by innumerable experiments which it is unnecessary here to recount.

 ASK YOURSELF

7.41. How does the mind receive impressions?

A third source of error arises from the fact that there are long nerves going to and from the brain. If we poke one of these at any place, we will have the same sensation.

I notice, also, that the nature of body is such that none of its parts can be moved by another part a little way off which cannot also be moved in the same way by each one of the parts which are between the two, although this more remote part does not act at all. As, for example, in the cord ABCD [which is in tension] if we pull the last part D, the first part A will not be moved in any way differently from what would be the case if one of the intervening parts B or C were pulled, and the last part D were to remain unmoved. And in the same way, when I feel pain in my foot, my knowledge of physics teaches me that this sensation is communicated by means of nerves dispersed through the foot, which, being extended like cords from there to the brain, when they are contracted in the foot, at the same time contract the inmost portions of the brain which is their extremity and place of origin, and then excite a certain movement which nature has established in order to cause the mind to be affected by a sensation of pain represented as existing in the foot. But because these nerves must pass through the tibia, the thigh, the loins, the back and the neck, in order to reach from the leg to the brain, it may happen that although their extremities which are in the foot are not affected, but only certain ones of their intervening parts [which pass by the loins or the neck], this action will excite the same movement in the brain that might have been excited there by a hurt received in the foot, in consequence of which the mind will necessarily feel in the foot the same pain as if it had received a hurt. And the same holds good of all the other perceptions of our senses.

 ASK YOURSELF

7.42. Give one of Descartes's examples of this long nerve phenomenon.

Finally, some bodily feelings are deceptive insofar as they give us exaggerated or misdirected sensations. These, however, are present for the benefit of self-preservation.

I notice finally that since each of the movements which are in the portion of the brain by which the mind is immediately affected brings about one particular sensation only, we cannot under the circumstances imagine anything more likely than that this movement, amongst all the sensations which it is capable of impressing on it, causes the mind to be affected by that one which is best fitted and most generally useful for the conservation of the human body when it is in health. But experience makes us aware that all the feelings with which nature inspires us are such as I have just spoken of; and there is therefore nothing in them which does not give testimony to the power and goodness of the God [who has produced them]. Thus, for example, when the nerves which are in the feet are violently or more than usually moved, their movement, passing through the medulla of the spine to the inmost parts of the brain, gives a sign to the mind which makes it feel somewhat, namely, pain, as though in the foot, by which the mind is excited to do its utmost to remove the cause of the evil as dangerous and hurtful to the foot. It is true that God could have constituted the nature of man in such a way that this same movement in the brain would have conveyed something quite different to the mind. For example, it might have produced consciousness of itself either insofar as it is in the brain, or as it is in the foot, or as it is in some other place between the foot and the brain, or it might finally have produced consciousness of anything else whatsoever. But none of all this would have contributed so well to the conservation of the body. Similarly, when we desire to drink, a certain dryness of the throat is produced which moves its nerves, and by their means the internal portions of the brain. And this movement causes in the mind the sensation of thirst, because in this case there is nothing more useful to us than to become aware that we have need to drink for the conservation of our health. And the same holds good in other instances.

  ASK YOURSELF

7.43. Give one of Descartes's examples of an exaggerated bodily feeling that is for the benefit of self-preservation.

Synopsis. Descartes's synopsis of Meditation 6 (initially presented at the opening of his meditations) is as follows.

Finally in the Sixth I distinguish the action of the understanding from that of the imagination; the marks by which this distinction is made are described. I here show that the mind of man is really distinct from the body, and at the same time that the two are so closely joined together that they form, so to speak, a single thing. All the errors which proceed from the senses are then surveyed, while the means of avoiding them are demonstrated, and finally all the reasons from which we may deduce the existence of material things are set forth. Not that I judge them to be very useful in establishing that which they prove, namely, that there is in truth a world, that men possess bodies, and other such things which never have been doubted by anyone of sense; but because in considering these closely we come to see that they are neither so strong nor so evident as those arguments which lead us to the knowledge of our mind and of God; so that these last must be the most certain and most evident facts which can fall within the cognizance of the human mind. And this is the whole matter that I have tried to prove in these Meditations, for which reason I here omit to speak of many other questions which I dealt incidentally in this discussion.

Supplementary Selections

The Cogito Is Not Deduced. Descartes published a lengthy set of objections and replies along with the *Meditations*. One of the more important exchanges from the "Second Set of Objections" concerned whether Descartes deduces the knowledge of his existence in the sense of a logical deduction.

From DESCARTES: *"Objections"*

Objection: [At the outset of Meditation 2] you are not yet certain of the aforesaid existence of God. Yet, according to your statement, you cannot be certain of anything or know anything clearly and distinctly unless previously you know certainly and clearly that God exists. Thus, you cannot clearly and distinctly know that you are a thinking thing, since, according to you, that knowledge depends on the clear knowledge of the existence of God, the proof of which you have not yet reached at that point where you draw the conclusion that you have a clear knowledge of what you are.

Reply: When I said that "we could know nothing with certainty unless we were first aware that God existed," I announced in express terms that I referred only to the science of understanding such conclusions "as can recur in memory without attending further to the proofs which led me to make them." Further, knowledge of the first principles is not usually called "science" by dialecticians. But when we become aware that we are thinking beings, this is a primitive act of knowledge derived from no syllogistic reasoning. He who says, "I think, hence I am, or exist," does not deduce existence from thought by a syllogism. But by a simple act of mental vision, he recognizes it as if it were a thing that is known *per se*. This is evident from the fact that if it were syllogistically deduced, the major premise, "that everything that thinks is, or exists" would have to be known previously. But yet that has rather been learned from the experience of the individual, that unless he exists he cannot think. For our mind is so constituted by nature that general propositions are formed out of the knowledge of particulars.

 ASK YOURSELF

7.44. Why don't we deduce the proposition "I exist"?

The Pineal Gland. As seen in Meditation 6, Descartes believes that humans are composed of two distinct parts: a physical body that moves about in the physical world, and a nonphysical or spiritual mind that does the thinking. This dualism presents a problem for Descartes insofar as an explanation is needed as to how our minds and bodies interact in their separate realms. For example, when my hand touches something hot, this sensation is registered in my mind. Also, if my mind decides to remove my hand, this decision must be transferred to my body, which results in motor activity. Thus, Descartes needs an explanation of both sensory and motor communication between our spirit minds and physical bodies. In the following, from Part One of *The Passions of the Soul* (1649), Descartes argues that the pineal gland in the brain is the gateway between the two realms. (Section titles are from Descartes.)

 From DESCARTES: *The Passions of the Soul*

31. That there is a small gland in the brain in which the soul exercises its function more particularly than in the other parts. It is likewise necessary to know that al-

though the soul is joined to the whole body, there is yet in that a certain part in which it exercises its functions more particularly than in all the others. And it is usually believed that this part is the brain, or possibly the heart. It is believed to be the brain because it is with it that the organs of sense are connected. And it is believed to be the heart because it is apparently in it that we experience the passions. But, in examining the matter with care, it seems as though I had clearly ascertained that the part of the body in which the soul exercises its functions immediately is in nowise the heart, nor the whole of the brain. Instead, it is merely the most inward of all its parts, namely, a certain very small gland which is situated in the middle of its substance and so suspended above the duct whereby the animal spirits in its anterior cavities have communication with those in the posterior. It is such that the slightest movements which take place in it may alter very greatly the course of these spirits. And, reciprocally, the smallest changes which occur in the course of the spirits may do much to change the movements of this gland.

 ASK YOURSELF

7.45. What are the two standard accounts of where the body and soul are connected?

32. How we know that this gland is the main seat of the soul. The reason which persuades me that the soul cannot have any other seat in all the body than this gland wherein to exercise its functions immediately, is that I reflect that the other parts of our brain are all of them double, just as we have two eyes, two hands, two ears, and finally all the organs of our outside senses are double. And inasmuch as we have but one solitary and simple thought of one particular thing at one and the same moment, it must necessarily be the case that there must somewhere be a place where the two images which come to us by the two eyes, where the two other impressions which proceed from a single object by means of the double organs of the other senses, can unite before arriving at the soul, in order that they may not represent to it two objects instead of one. And it is easy to see how these images or other impressions might unite in this gland by the intermission of the spirits which fill the cavities of the brain. But there is no other place in the body where they can be thus united unless they are so in this gland.

 ASK YOURSELF

7.46. What reason does Descartes give for holding that the pineal gland is the gateway between the brain and body?

34. How the soul and the body act on one another. Let us then conceive here that the soul has its principal seat in the little gland which exists in the middle of the brain. For, from this spot it radiates forth through all the remainder of the body by means of the animal spirits, nerves, and even the blood, which, participating in the impres-

sions of the spirits, can carry them by the arteries into all the members. Recall what has been said above about the machine of our body, that is, that the little filaments of our nerves are so distributed in all its parts, that on the occasion of the diverse movements which are there excited by sensible objects, they open in different ways the pores of the brain. This, in turn, causes the animal spirit contained in these cavities to enter in different ways into the muscles, by which means they can move the members in all the different ways in which they are capable of being moved. And also, recall all the other causes which are capable of moving the spirits in different ways and which suffice to conduct them into different muscles. Let us here add that the small gland which is the main seat of the soul is so suspended between the cavities which contain the spirits that it can be moved by them in as many different ways as there are sensible differences in the object.

 ASK YOURSELF

7.47. How does the soul receive perceptions from the body?

Further, it may also be moved in different ways by the soul, whose nature is such that it receives in itself as many different impressions, that is to say, that it possesses as many different perceptions as there are different movements in this gland. Reciprocally, likewise, the machine of the body is so formed that from the simple fact that this gland is differently moved by the soul (or by such other cause, whatever it is) it thrusts the spirits which surround it towards the pores of the brain, which conduct them by the nerves into the muscles, by which means it causes them to move the limbs.

 ASK YOURSELF

7.48. How does the soul send motor commands to the body?

BENEDICT SPINOZA

Benedict (Baruch) Spinoza (1632–1677) was the son of a Jewish merchant from Amsterdam. His father and grandfather were originally Spanish crypto-Jews—that is, Jews who were forced to adopt Christianity in post-Islamic Spain but secretly remained Jewish. He was educated in traditional Jewish Curriculum. His father died when he was twenty-one, after which he was embroiled in a lawsuit with his stepsister over his father's estate. Spinoza won the suit, but nevertheless handed virtually all of it over to his stepsister. Shortly after, Spinoza's budding theological speculations prompted conflict with Jewish leaders. Spinoza publicly contended that the Scriptures do not maintain that God has no body, that angels exist, or that the soul is immortal. After failed attempts to silence him, he was excommunicated in 1656. For a time Spinoza was associated with a former Jesuit who ran a school for children. Spinoza used this as an opportunity to further his own education and to supplement his income by teaching in the school. At this time he also learned the trade of lens grinding for glasses and telescopes.

In his late twenties, he supervised a discussion group on philosophical and theological issues. As his own ideas developed, he went on retreat from Amsterdam for three years to formulate them in writing. At a cottage in Rijnsburg, he wrote *A Short Treatise on God, Man and His Well-Being* and *On the Improvement of the Understanding*. He also composed a geometric version of Descartes's *Principles of Philosophy*, which friends encouraged him to publish. Part of the purpose of the work was to pave the way for publishing his own thoughts, which were critical of Cartesianism. By producing such a work, he could not be accused later of not understanding Descartes. The work appeared in 1663 and was the only writing of Spinoza's published with his name on it during his life. Further developing his own ideas, over the next two years Spinoza composed his greatest work, the *Ethics*. In 1663 Spinoza left Rijnsburg and moved near The Hague. Hoping to publish the *Ethics*, and anticipating controversy, he wrote and published anonymously his *Tractatus Theologico-Politicus* (1670), which defends the liberty to philosophize in the face of religious or political interference. After a self-initiated and failed diplomatic mission to France, Spinoza was forced to give up hopes of publishing the *Ethics*. He died in 1677 from a lung disease, the result of breathing dust from lens grinding.

As directed in Spinoza's will, the *Ethics* was published posthumously along with some of his other works (1677). The *Ethics* is about two hundred pages long, and its most visibly distinguishing feature is its style of composition modeled after Euclid's geometry. Each of its five parts opens with a brief list of definitions and axioms, and from these a series of propositions (or theorems) are deduced. Spinoza initially composed the first parts of the *Ethics* in dialogue form, but rejected this for the more precise—and unfortunately more difficult—geometric method. In general, geometric proofs are designed so that if we accept the definitions and axioms at the outset, and deductions from these are properly made, then we must accept the concluded propositions. However, as Leibniz observed, even though Spinoza's system follows this style, it nevertheless lacks mathematical rigor.

The most famous section of the *Ethics* is Part One, "Concerning God," in which Spinoza defends the position of pantheism—literally all-God, which is the view that God is identical to the universe as a whole. Other Western philosophers before Spinoza advocated pantheism, including Xenophanes, Parmenides, and Plotinus. However, the vast majority of Western philosophers and theologians strongly rejected this view in favor of a transcendent concept of God, which holds that God is distinct from his creation. Indeed, some theologians maintained that God has the attribute of *separateness*, thus being completely separate from the rest of the universe, including the physical world and humans. Spinoza articulates pantheism in the proposition: "Besides God, no substance can be granted or conceived." That is, for any substance or thing that we attempt to identify in the world around us, that thing will actually be part of God.

God Does Not Willfully Direct the Course of Nature

At the Close of Part One of the *Ethics*, Spinoza includes an Appendix that is written in normal pose style, rather than in his overformal geometry book style. The following selections are from the Appendix. He begins with a summary of his views about God.

From SPINOZA: *Ethics*

In the foregoing I have explained the nature and properties of God. I have shown that (1) he necessarily exists, (2) that he is one, (3) that he is, and acts solely by the necessity of his own nature, (4) that he is the free cause of all things, and how he is so, (5) that all things are in God, and so depend on him, that without him they could neither exist nor be conceived, and (6) that all things are predetermined by God, not through his free will or absolute fiat, but from the very nature of God or infinite power. I have further, where occasion offered, taken care to remove the prejudices which might impede the comprehension of my demonstrations. Yet there still remain misconceptions, not a few which might and may prove very grave hindrances to the understanding of the ordering of things, as I have explained it above. I have therefore thought it worthwhile to bring these misconceptions before the bar of reason.

The principal misconception about God that Spinoza wants to address in the Appendix is that God acts purposefully and directs events in nature toward a definite goal. For Spinoza, God does not do this.

☞ ASK YOURSELF

7.49. What three issues does Spinoza plan to address?

All such opinions spring from the notion commonly entertained, that all things in nature act as men themselves, act, namely, with an end in view. It is accepted as certain, that God himself directs all things to a definite goal (for it is said that God made all things for humans, and humans that he might worship him). I will, therefore, consider this opinion, asking first, why it obtains general credence, and why all men are naturally so prone to adopt it. Secondly, I will point out its falsity. And, lastly, I will show how it has given rise to prejudices about good and bad, right and wrong, praise and blame, order and confusion, beauty and ugliness, and the like.

Why People Think That God Acts with a Purpose. Turning to the first of the three points, Spinoza notes that individual humans do not act freely, but are under the illusion that they do. We are ignorant of the true causes of things and are only aware of our own desire to pursue what is useful to us.

However, this is not the place to deduce these misconceptions from the nature of the human mind. It will be sufficient here, if I assume as a starting point, what ought to be universally admitted, namely, that all people are born ignorant of the causes of things, that all have the desire to seek for what is useful to them, and that they are conscious of such desire. From here it follows, first, that people think themselves free inasmuch as they are conscious of their volitions and desires, and never even dream, in their ignorance, of the causes which have disposed them so to wish and desire. Secondly, that people do all things for an end, namely, for that which is useful to them, and which they seek.

ASK YOURSELF

7.50. Given our ignorance of the true mechanical causes of our own action, what two attitudes do humans adopt about our wills and goals?

Given this tendency to see human behavior as willful and purposeful, we continue by imposing willful purposes on events outside of us.

Thus it comes to pass that they only look for a knowledge of the final causes of events, and when these are learned, they are content, as having no cause for further doubt. If they cannot learn such causes from external sources, they are compelled to turn to considering themselves, and reflecting what end would have induced them personally to bring about the given event, and thus they necessarily judge other natures by their own. Further, as they find in themselves and outside themselves many means which assist them not a little in their search for what is useful, for instance, eyes for seeing, teeth for chewing, herbs and animals for yielding food, the sun for giving light, the sea for breeding fish, &c., they come to look on the whole of nature as a means for obtaining such conveniences. Now as they are aware that they found these conveniences and did not make them, they think they have cause for believing, that some other being has made them for their use. As they look upon things as means, they cannot believe them to be self-created. But, judging from the means which they are accustomed to prepare for themselves, they are bound to believe in some ruler or rulers of the universe endowed with human freedom, who have arranged and adapted everything for human use.

ASK YOURSELF

7.51. Why did humans conclude that a divine being or beings intentionally designed nature for our use?

Religious superstitions arose as humans found their own ways of worshiping God. Problems of consistency also arose as people insisted that everything in nature is done by God for a purpose.

They are bound to estimate the nature of such rulers (having no information on the subject) in accordance with their own nature, and therefore they assert that the gods ordained everything for the use of humans, in order to bind humans to themselves and obtain from him the highest honor. Hence also it follows that everyone thought out for himself, according to his abilities, a different way of worshipping God, so that God might love him more than his fellows, and direct the whole course of nature for the satisfaction of his blind cupidity and insatiable avarice. Thus the prejudice developed into superstition, and took deep root in the human mind; and for this reason everyone strove most zealously to understand and explain the final causes of things; but in their attempt to show that nature does nothing in vain, nothing which is useless to humans, they only seem to have demonstrated that nature, the gods, and men are all mad together. Consider, I pray you, the result: among the many helps of nature they were bound to find some hindrances, such as storms, earthquakes, diseases, &c.: so they declared that such things happen, because the gods are angry at some wrong done them by men, or at some fault committed in their worship. Day by day, experience protested and showed by infinite examples that good and evil fortunes fall to the circumstance of pious and impious alike. Still they would not abandon their inveterate prejudice, for it was more easy for them to class such contradictions among other unknown things of whose use they were ignorant, and thus to retain their actual and innate condition of ignorance, than to destroy the whole fabric of their reasoning and start afresh.

 ASK YOURSELF

7.52. What experiences conflict with the position that everything in nature is done by God for a purpose?

They therefore laid down as an axiom, that God's judgments far transcend human understanding. Such a doctrine might well have sufficed to conceal the truth from the human race for all eternity, if mathematics had not furnished another standard of truth in considering solely the essence and properties of figures without regard to their final causes. There are other reasons (which I need not mention here) besides mathematics, which might have caused men's minds to be directed to these general prejudices, and have led them to the knowledge of the truth.

 ASK YOURSELF

7.53. For Spinoza, what alternative standard of truth refutes the superstition that everything in nature is done by God for a purpose?

God Does Not Act from a Purpose. Spinoza continues with his second point and argues that everything in nature is done from necessity, not from God's willful purpose. He first argues that the concept of a perfect final goal is flawed. For Spinoza, the most perfect of God's acts are those closest to Him. Succeeding events further down the chain are more imperfect. Thus if a given chain of events culminated in sunny weather, for example, that would be less perfect than the initial events in the chain.

I have now sufficiently explained my first point. There is no need to show at length that nature has no particular goal in view, and that final causes are mere human figments. This, I think, is already evident enough, both from the causes and foundations on which I have shown such prejudice to be based, and also from Prop. xvi., and the Corollary of Prop. xxxii., and, in fact, all those propositions in which I have shown, that everything in nature proceeds from a sort of necessity, and with the utmost perfection. However, I will add a few remarks, in order to overthrow this doctrine of a final cause utterly. That which is really a cause it considers as an effect, and vice versa: it makes that which is by nature first to be last, and that which is highest and most perfect to be most imperfect. Passing over the questions of cause and priority as self-evident, it is plain from Props. xxi., xxii., xxiii. that that effect is most perfect which is produced immediately by God. The effect which requires for its production several intermediate causes is, in that respect, more imperfect. But if those things which were made immediately by God were made to enable him to attain his end, then the things which come after, for the sake of which the first were made, are necessarily the most excellent of all.

Further, this doctrine does away with the perfection of God: for, if God acts for an object, he necessarily desires something which he lacks. Certainly, theologians and metaphysicians draw a distinction between the object of want and the object of assimilation. Still they confess that God made all things for the sake of himself, not for the sake of creation. They are unable to point to anything prior to creation, except God himself, as an object for which God should act, and are therefore driven to admit (as they clearly must), that God lacked those things for whose attainment he created means, and further that he desired them.

 ASK YOURSELF

7.54. How does the doctrine of final cause compromise the perfection of God?

For Spinoza, the theologian's contention that God willfully directs all natural events amounts to a reduction to ignorance. That is, all natural events trace back to God's will, and we are all ignorant of God's will.

We must not omit to notice that the followers of this doctrine, anxious to display their talent in assigning final causes, have imported a new method of argument in proof of their theory—namely, a reduction, not to the impossible, but to ignorance; thus showing that they have no other method of exhibiting their doctrine. For example, if a stone falls from a roof onto someone's head, and kills him, they will demonstrate by their new method, that the stone fell in order to kill the man. For, if it had not by God's will fallen with that object, how could so many circumstances (and there are often many concurrent circumstances) have all happened together by chance? Perhaps you will answer that the event is clue to the facts that the wind was blowing, and the man was walking that way. "But why," they will insist, "was the wind blowing, and why was the man at that very time walking that way?" If you again answer, that the wind had then sprung up because the sea had begun to be agitated the day before, the weather being previously calm, and that the man had been invited by a friend, they will again insist: "But why was the sea agitated, and man invited at that time?" So they will pursue their questions from cause to cause, till at last you take refuge in the will of God—in other words, the sanctuary of ignorance. So, again, when they survey the frame of the human body, they are amazed; and being ignorant of the causes of so great a work of art, conclude that it has been fashioned, not mechanically, but by divine and supernatural skill, and has been so put together that one part will not hurt another.

Hence anyone who seeks for the true causes of miracles, and strives to understand natural phenomena as an intelligent being, and not to gaze at them like a fool, is set down and denounced as an impious heretic by those, whom the masses adore as the interpreters of nature and the gods. Such persons know that, with the removal of ignorance, the wonder which forms their only available means for proving and preserving their authority would vanish also. But I now quit this subject, and pass on to my third point.

 ASK YOURSELF

7.55. For Spinoza, what motivates such theologians to insist on this path of ignorance?

NICOLAS de MALEBRANCHE

The most influential and original of the Cartesian philosophers was Nicolas de Malebranche (1638–1715). Deformed and sickly, Malebranche was born in Paris and from his childhood preferred solitude. He studied theology at the Sorbonne and at age twenty-two entered the Congregation of the Oratory, where he spent the rest of his life in seclusion. He was ordained in 1664 and the same year became acquainted with Descartes's *Treatise on Man*, an unfinished work that explores the relation between the human mind and body. He subsequently devoted his studies to Cartesian philosophy and science and four years later published his greatest work, *The Search after Truth (De la Recherche de la vérité*, 3 vols., 1674–1675). In response to theological criticisms of this work he soon after published his *Treatise of Nature and Grace (Traité de la nature et de la grâce*, 1680), which attempts to reconcile God's power, knowledge, and goodness with the evil in the world. This work embroiled him in even more controversy, particularly with French Bishop Jacques Bénigne Bossuet and French theologian Antoine Arnauld. Malebranche's other philosophical writings include Dialogues on Metaphysics and on Religion (*Entretiens sur la métaphysique et sur la religion*, 1688), a work in fourteen dialogues that more informally covers much of the ground in his *Search after Truth*, and *A Treatise of Morality (Traité de morale*, 1683). In 1699 he was elected to the Académie des Sciences for his scientific writings. Near the end of his life, similarities between his views of God and those of Spinoza led to accusations that he followed Spinoza's heretical system. He defended himself against these charges in various letters and writings.

Two aspects of Malebranche's philosophy have been especially influential in the history of philosophy: (1) that we see all things through God and (2) occasionalism. Both of these doctrines are presented here. As to the first of these, Malebranche was concerned with explaining how our minds get perceptual images of external objects. His final answer to the question is that, within himself, God contains images of all external things and implants these ideas in our mind at the appropriate time. Thus, we see external objects by viewing their images as they reside in God. The following selections are from *The Search after Truth*, Book 3, Part 2, Chapters 1 and 6. Chapter titles are from Malebranche; subsection titles have been added.

Chapter 1, Section 1: What Is Meant by Ideas; That They Truly Exist, and That They Are Necessary to Perceive All Material Objects

Malebranche begins by setting out the problem he wishes to address.

The Definition of "Idea." We do not have direct access to the external objects, but only have ideas (or perceptions) that presumably resemble those objects.

 From MALEBRANCHE: *The Search after Truth*

I think everyone will confess that we do not perceive external objects by themselves. We see the sun, the stars, and many objects outside of us. And it is not probable that the soul should go out of the body and walk, as it were, through the heavens, to contemplate all those objects there. She does not, then, see them by themselves and as the immediate object of mind. When the soul sees the sun, for instance, it is not the sun, but something which is closely united to our soul. And it is that which I call "idea" so that here by this word "idea," I mean only what is the immediate object, or the nearest thing to the mind when it perceives anything.

 ASK YOURSELF

7.56. What does Malebranche mean by "idea"?

A central problem in modern philosophy concerns the connection between our perceptions and the external objects that supposedly produce our perceptions. For example, if I perceive a red ball in front of me, I may be tempted to assume that the object in front of me has *exactly* the properties as I perceive them (such as a particular shade of red). This view is called *direct realism*, and Malebranche immediately dismisses this theory. Instead, for Malebranche, ideas in some way represent the object in question. This view is called *representative realism*. Accordingly, when Malebranche uses the word "idea" he restricts its meaning to mental perceptions that represent or copy some original thing.

It must be observed, that to make the mind perceive any object, it is absolutely necessary that the idea of this object should be actually present, of which we can have no doubt. But it is not required that there should be some external object which resembles this idea. For it often happens that we perceive things which do not exist, and which never did exist. Thus, we often have in our minds real ideas of things which never were. For instance, when a person imagines a mountain of gold, it is absolutely necessary that the idea of this mountain should be really present to his mind. When a mad person, a person in a high fever, or a person that is asleep, sees any terrible animal before his eyes, it is certain that the idea of this animal truly exists. And yet this mountain of gold, and this animal, never were.

However, people being naturally inclined to believe that only corporeal objects exist, they judge the reality and existence of things quite differently than they should.

For as soon as they are sensible of any object, they will certainly maintain that this object exists, although, it often happens, there is nothing out there. And further, they affirm that this object is exactly the same as they see it, which never happens. But in respect to the idea which necessarily exists, and which can be nothing else besides what it appears to be, without any reflection, they commonly judge it to be nothing. They do this as if ideas had not a very great number of properties: as if the ideas of a square, for instance, were not very different from that of some number, and did not represent things perfectly distinct; which could never happen to nothing, since nothing has no propriety. It is therefore indisputable that ideas have a real existence. But let us examine their nature and essence, and see what it can be in the soul that is capable of representing all things.

 ASK YOURSELF

7.57. What mistakes do people typically make when they make judgments about external objects based on their ideas (or perceptions) of those objects?

Chapter 6: That We See All Things in God

Given the failure of these four theories, Malebranche argues that we obtain ideas of external things by viewing them within God Himself, for God houses ideas of all external things and, by His own choosing, allows us to see those ideas.

Spiritual Entities Reside in God. This theory rests on the contention that spiritual entities reside in God. Malebranche maintains this for two reasons. First, as indicated earlier, as creator, God must have the ideas or blueprints of all things. Second, all spirits (and spiritual things such as ideas) dwell within God, just as all physical things dwell in space.

We have examined in the preceding chapters four different manners in which the human mind may see external objects, and these do not appear probable to us. There only remains the fifth, which alone appears agreeable to reason and is the most proper, which is the dependence that spirits have on God in all their thoughts.

In order to understand it correctly, we must remember what has been said in the preceding chapter, that it is absolutely necessary that God should have in himself the ideas of all the beings he has created, since otherwise he could not have produced them. And, thus, he sees all those beings by considering the perfections that he includes in himself, and to which all beings are related. Moreover, it is necessary to know that God is very strictly united to our souls by his presence, so that we may say that he is the place of spirits, just as space is the place of bodies. These two things being supposed, it is certain that the mind may see what there is in God, which represents created beings, since that is very spiritual, very intelligible, and most present to the mind. Thus the mind may see in God the works of God, supposing God be willing to disclose to our minds what there is in God that represents those works. These are the reasons that seem to prove that he wills rather than creates an infinite number of ideas in every mind.

Efficiency Argument. Malebranche offers several proofs of his theory that we get ideas of external objects by viewing those ideas in God. He still is troubled, however, by the second rejected theory (that God innately planted ideas of external things in our minds), and he sees this as the principal rival to his own theory. His first defense of his own theory, then, is that it is a more efficient explanation than that offered by the rival theory.

First, although we do not absolutely deny that God was able to produce an infinitely infinite number of beings who represent objects with every mind he creates, yet we ought not to believe that he does so. For it is not only compatible with reason, but it also appears by the economy of nature, that God never does by very difficult means what may be done by a plain and easy way. God does nothing in vain and without reason. His wisdom and his power are not exhibited by doing little things by difficult means. That is repugnant to reason, and shows a limited knowledge. On the contrary, his greatness is seen by doing great things by plain easy means. It is thus that from extension alone he produces everything we see that is admirable in nature, and even that which gives life and motion to animals. For those who postulate substantial forms, faculties, and souls in animals different from their blood and from the organs of their body, in order to perform their functions, at the same time seem to argue that God wants understanding, or that he cannot do those admirable things by extension alone. They measure the power of God and his sovereign wisdom by the smallness of their own capacity. Then since God may make human minds see all things, by willing barely that they should see what is in themselves; that is, what is in him that has a relation to those things, and which represents them, there is no probability that he would do it otherwise; and that he should produce, in order thereunto, as many infinities of infinite numbers of ideas, as there are created spirits.

 ASK YOURSELF

7.58. Malebranche rejects the theory of innately implanted ideas of external things because it is less efficient than Malebranche's own theory. Malebranche illustrates God's efficiency by describing the variety of things that God created out of extension alone (i.e., out of physical substance alone). What does this include?

We must observe, however, that we cannot conclude that spirits see the essence of God insofar as they can see all things in God in that manner. This is because what they see is very imperfect, whereas God is very perfect. We see matter divisible and figured, etc., but there is nothing in God that is divisible or figured. For God is all beings, because he is infinite and comprehends all, but he is no being in particular. Nevertheless that which we see is but one, or several beings in particular, and we do not apprehend that perfect simplicity of God which includes all beings. Besides that it may be said, that we do not so much see the ideas of things, as the things which those ideas represent; for when we see a square, for instance, we do not say that we see the idea of that square, which is united to the mind, but only the square which is without us.

ASK YOURSELF

7.59. Given that we obtain ideas of external things by viewing them through God, this does not mean that we actually can see the inner nature of God Himself. What is the key difference between the ideas of external things that we see through God and God's nature itself?

Sovereignty Argument. A second argument for Malebranche's own theory is that it highlights God's sovereignty more than the alternative theory does.

There is a second reason which may induce us to believe that we see all objects because God wills that that which is in God and represents things should be discovered to us (rather than because we have as many ideas created with us as we can see things). For this puts all created spirits in an absolute dependence upon God, and the greatest spirits that can be. This being so, we cannot only see nothing except what God wills that we should see, but we can also see nothing, unless God himself shows it to us. *Non sumus sufficientes cogitare aliquid a nobis, tanquam ex nobis, sed sufficientia nostra ex deo est* (2 Cor. 3:5). It is God himself which instructs and enlightens philosophers in that knowledge which ungrateful people call natural, although it is an immediate gift from heaven: *deus enim illis manifestavit* (Rom. 1:19). It is he that is properly the light of the mind, and the father of light or knowledge. *Pater luminum* (James 1:17). It is he that teaches wisdom to people: *qui docet hominem scientiam* (Psalms 53). In a word, he is the true light, which enlightens all those that come into this world: *lux vera que illuminat omnem hominem venientem in hunc mundum* (John 1:9).

 ASK YOURSELF

7.60. How does Malebranche's theory emphasize God's sovereignty?

In short, it is pretty difficult to distinctly recognize the dependence which our minds have on God in all their particular actions (supposing that they have all that which we distinctly know to be necessary for them in order to act, or all the ideas of things present to their mind, and truly that general and confused word concurrence, by which people pretend to explain the dependence that creatures have on God, does not awaken any distinct idea in an attentive mind). Yet it is quite necessary that people should know distinctly that they can do nothing without God.

Abstract Idea Argument. Malebranche's third argument is based on how we acquire abstract or general ideas, such as the universal notion of a triangle. General ideas are initially formed in God, and we access these through God.

But the strongest of all reasons, is the manner in which the mind perceives all things. It is certain, and everybody knows by experience, that when we wish to think on anything in particular thing, we first cast our eyes on all beings. After that, we apply ourselves to the consideration of the object we design to think on. Now it is most certain that we see it already, though confusedly and in general. So, as we may desire to see all the beings, sometimes one and sometimes another, it is certain that all beings are present to our mind. And it appears that all beings can only be present to our mind because God is present to our minds, that is, he who includes all things in the simplicity of his being.

It seems, moreover, that the mind would not be capable of representing to itself universal ideas of kinds and species, *etc.*, unless it saw all beings included in one. Since every creature is a particular being, we cannot say that we see anything created when we see, for instance, a triangle in general. In short, I believe that it is impossible to give a good reason of the manner in which the mind comes to know several abstracted and general truths, unless it is by the presence of him [i.e., God] that can direct the mind in a world of different manners.

 ASK YOURSELF

7.61. Malebranche argues that we cannot conceive of universal abstract ideas unless we saw all beings included in one, which we as humans cannot do on our own accord. What ability does God have that allows for the creation of abstract ideas?

Using the abstract idea of "the infinite" as a starting point, Malebranche gives a variation of Descartes's proof of God's existence in Meditation 3. For Descartes, we have an innate idea of infinite perfection that must have been implanted in us by an infinitely perfect being (i.e., God). Malebranche's argument is as follows:

a. We have a concept of infinite being.

b. We do not comprehend "infinite being" in the way in which ideas copy objects.

c. Our comprehension of infinite being results from a union or direct acquaintance with God Himself.

d. Therefore, God exists.

It is from the idea of infinite being, with which we are directly acquainted, that we form our ideas of finite beings.

Thus, the chief proof of the existence of God which is the best, the most majestic, and the most solid (or that which supposes the fewest things) is the idea we have of infinity. For, the mind does not comprehend infinite being, and the mind has a very distinct idea of God which it can only have by the union it has with God. This is because it cannot be conceived that the idea of a being infinitely perfect, as that we have of God, should be anything that is created.

But not only does the mind have the idea of infinity, it has it even before that of the finite. For we conceive the infinite being, and from this alone that we conceive a being, without considering whether it is finite or infinite. But in order to conceive of a finite being, we must reduce something of that general notion of a being which, consequently, must precede it. Thus, the mind perceives nothing but an infinity, and that idea cannot be formed by the confused mixture of all the ideas of particular beings, as philosophers imagine. On the contrary, all those particular ideas are only participations of the general idea of infinity insofar as God does not derive his being from the creatures, but all creatures only subsist by him.

 ASK YOURSELF

7.62. How do we arrive at the notion of finite being?

Principle Purpose Argument. Malebranche turns to his final proof that we see all things in God. Since God creates all things for His own purpose, then as human creatures we cannot perceive anything without seeing God in those things.

The last proof, which perhaps will be a demonstration to those that are used to abstracted arguments, is this. It is impossible that God should have any other principal end of his actions but himself. This notion is common to all people that are capable of any reflection, and the holy scriptures do not allow us to doubt that God has made everything for himself. Therefore, it is necessary that our natural love (I mean the motion he produces in our mind) should tend towards him. Moreover, the knowledge and the light which he presents to our minds should make us know something that is in him. For whatever comes from God can only be for God. If God created a spirit, and gave it an idea of the sun (as the immediate object of its knowledge), in my opinion God would create that spirit, and the idea in that spirit, for the sun and not for him.

God cannot therefore create a spirit to know his works, unless that spirit sees God in some measure by looking at his works. So we may say that, unless we do see God in some measure, we would see nothing. Similarly, unless we do love God (I mean, unless God continually imprinted in us the love of good in general) we should love nothing. For since that love is our will, then we can love nothing, nor will anything without him. This is because we cannot love particular goods without directing towards those goods the inclination of love which God gives us towards himself. Thus, just as we love nothing except by the necessary love we have for God, so too we see nothing except by the natural knowledge we have of God. And all the particular ideas we have of creatures are only limitations of the idea of the creator, as all the motions of the will for the creatures, are only determinations of the motion for the creator.

 ASK YOURSELF

7.63. What is the main end toward which all love (or desire) is directed?

I believe that all theologians will grant that the impious love God with that natural love which I speak of. St. Augustine and some other fathers affirm as an undeniable thing that the impious see in God the rule of morality and necessary truths. So, the opinion I explain should not trouble anyone. Thus St. Augustine speaks:

> The mind is advised that it should turn to the Lord as to that light by which it was touched in some way, even when that mind turned away from him. For hence it is that even the godless think of eternity, and rightly condemn and rightly praise many things in the moral conduct of people. Bu what rules, pray, do they judge these things if not by those in which they see how each one ought to live, even though they themselves do not live in the same manners? Where do they see them? They do not see them in their own nature. For, these things are doubtless in the mind, and their minds are admittedly changeable. But it sees these rules as unchangeable, whoever can see even this in them. . . . Where, then, are they written except in the book of that light which is called Truth? From there every just law is transcribed and transferred to the heart of the person who works justice. . . . But he who does not work justice, and yet sees what is to be worked, he it is who is turned away from this light, but still touched by it. (*The Trinity*, 14:15)

There are many passages in St. Augustine similar to this by which he proves that we see God, even in this life, by the knowledge we have of eternal truths. Truth is uncreated, immutable, immense, eternal, and above all things. It is true by itself. It derives its perfection from nothing. It makes creatures more perfect, and all spirits naturally try to know it. Nothing but God can have all those perfections. Therefore truth is God. We see some of those immutable eternal truths. Therefore we see God. These are St. Augustine's reasons, and ours differ a little from them. And we are unwilling to unjustly use the authority of so great a person to confirm our opinion.

 ASK YOURSELF

7.64. For Augustine, what is truth?

Different Kinds of Ideas We See through God. Thus, we see God especially when we consider necessary truths, such as those of mathematics and ethics. Malebranche slightly modifies Augustine's position and argues instead that we see God in the *ideas* behind truths, not in the truths themselves.

We believe that truths, even those that are eternal (such as that two times two is four) are not so much absolute beings, and even less so do we believe that they *are* God. For it is clear that truth only consists in a relation of equality, such as between twice two and four. Therefore we do not say that we see God when seeing truths, as St. Augustine says. Instead, we see God when seeing the ideas of those truths. For ideas are real, but the equality between the ideas, which is truth, has no reality. For example, when people say that the cloth they measure contains three yards, the cloth and the yards are real, but the equality between three yards and the cloth is not a real thing. It is only a relation that is between the three yards and the cloth. When we say that twice two are four, the ideas of the numbers are real, but the equality which there is between them is only a relation. Thus, according to our opinion, we see God when we see eternal truths. Not that those eternal truths are God, but because the ideas on which those truths depend are *in* God. Perhaps St. Augustine understood it this way. We also believe that we know changeable and corruptible things in God as well, although St. Augustine only speaks of immutable and incorruptible things. This is because these do not require us to place any imperfection in God since, as we have already said, it is sufficient that God should show us what there is in him that is related to these things.

For Malebranche, we know both eternal truths and facts about the physical world by viewing them in God. When we see all things in God, however, it is not as if we ourselves are sensing them in God. Instead, God actively places these ideas in us by making the appropriate physiological modifications in our souls.

But though I say we see in God the things that are material and sensible, it must be observed that I do not say we have a sensation of them in God, but only that it is from God who acts in us. For God knows sensible things, but he does not feel them. When we perceive anything that is sensible, sensation and pure idea is in our perception. Sensation is a modification of our soul, and it is God that causes it in us. And he can cause the sensation even though he himself doesn't have the sensation. This is because, in the idea he has of our souls, he sees that our souls are capable of sensation. As for the idea which is joined to sensation, this is in God, and we see it because it is his pleasure to reveal it to us. And God joins sensation to the idea when objects are present, so that we may believe that the objects are as they are, and that we may have such sensations and passions as we ought to have in relation to them.

God, thus, is the source of all ideas, including facts about the physical world, necessary truths (such as $2 + 2 = 4$), and moral truths (such as that we must love good). The manner in which God gives us these ideas, however, differs. Ideas of necessary truths, for example, come from a union or direct acquaintance with God Himself.

Lastly, we believe that all spirits see the eternal laws as well as other [physical] things in God, but with some difference. We know eternal order and eternal truths, and even the objects which God has made according to such order and truths. This is done by the union which our spirits have necessarily with the word, or wisdom of God which directs us, as we have shown. But [as to natural moral laws], it is by the impression we receive continually from the will of God, which inclines us to him, and tries, so to speak, to make our wills absolutely like that of his. This is how we know order is a law, I mean, and that we know the eternal laws, such as these: we must love good, and shy from evil; we must love justice more than all riches; it is better to obey God than to command people; and many other natural laws. For the knowledge of all those laws is not different from the knowledge of the impression which we always feel in ourselves, though we do not always follow it by the free choice of our will, which we know to be common to all spirits, though it is not equally strong in all.

ASK YOURSELF

7.65. How do we obtain ideas of moral truths?

It is by that dependence, relation, and union of our mind to the word of God, and of our will to his love, that we are made after the image and likeness of God. And although this may be very much defaced by sin, yet it is necessary that it should subsist as long as we do. But if we bear the image of the word humbled upon earth; and if we follow the motions of the holy ghost, that primitive image of our first creation, that union of our mind with the word of the father, and to the love of the father and of the son, will be re-established, and made indelible. We will be like God, if we are like the person God. In short, God will be all in us, and we all in God, in a far more perfect manner than that by which it is necessary for us to subsist, that we should be in him, and he in us.

 ASK YOURSELF

7.66. In what way are we made in the image of God?

The Most Probable Theory. Malebranche concludes that this is the most probable of all the theories of how we acquire ideas of objects. He also notes how it makes God actively involved in all causal relations of which we are a part.

Here are some reasons which may persuade us that spirits perceive all things by the immediate presence of him who comprehends all in the simplicity of his being. Everyone will judge it according to the internal conviction he will receive of it, after having seriously considered it. But I do not think that there is any probability in all the other ways of explaining these things, and that this last appears more than probable. Thus our souls depend on God in all respects. For as it is he who makes them feel grief, pleasure, and all other sensations, by the natural union he has established between them and our body which is no other than his decree and general will. Thus it is he, who by the natural union which he has made between the will of humans, and the representation of the ideas which the immensity of the divine being includes, that makes them know whatever they do know. And that natural union is also nothing else but his general will. So, none but he can direct us, by representing all things to us; as none but he can make us happy, by making us taste all manner of pleasures.

Let us therefore keep to this opinion that God is the intelligible world, or the place of spirits, just as the material world is the place of bodies. Spirits receive all their modifications from his power. They find all their ideas in his wisdom. It is by his love that they are acted in all their regular motions. Since his power and love are nothing but himself, let us believe with St. Paul, that he is not far from everyone of us, and that it is in him that we have life, motion, and a being. *Non longe est ab unequoque nostrum, in ipso cnim vivimus, movemur, & sumius* (Acts 17:28).

Occasionalism

Occasionalism is the view that God is the principal force behind all causal events. For example, when a baseball bat strikes a baseball, God is the actual cause of the motion of the baseball. The bat is merely the occasional or incidental cause that signals God to actually move the ball. Hints of this position are first found in Descartes's *Principles on Philosophy* 2:36. In defending the view that "God is the primary cause of motion," Descartes argues as follows:

> [The cause of motion in nature] is in fact twofold: first, there is the universal and primary cause—the general cause of all the motions in the world. And second, there is the particular cause which produces in an individual piece of matter some motion which it previously lacked. Now as far as the general cause is concerned, it seems clear to me that this is no other than God himself. In the beginning in his omnipotence he created matter, along with its motion and rest. And now, merely by his regular concurrence, he preserves the same amount of motion and rest in the material universe as he put there in the beginning. . . . Thus, God imparted various motions to the parts of matter when he first created them, and he now preserves all this matter in the same way, and by the same process by which he originally created it. And it follows from what we have said that this fact alone makes it most reasonable to think that God likewise always preserves the same quantity of motion in matter.

Descartes's argument is this:

a. God first imparted things with motion at creation.

b. God preserves or maintains the existence of things after creation.

c. The act of preservation is indistinguishable from the act of creation (Meditation 3).

d. Thus, God continually imparts motion to things.

What Descartes hinted at his followers articulated more precisely. French historian and Cartesian philosopher Geraud de Cordemoy (d. 1684) drew a distinction between the "true cause" of an event, which is God, and its "occasional cause," such as the bat striking the ball. Malebranche further developed Cordemoy's reasoning and produced the definitive defense of the theory of occasionalism. His defense appears in the following selections from *The Search after Truth*, Book 6, Part 2, Chapter 3, titled, "Of the Most Dangerous Error in Philosophy; Of the Ancients."

Ancient Philosophy's Conception of Causal Power. Malebranche begins explaining how ancient philosophers postulated metaphysical entities as the basis of causal force. He refutes this position by pushing it to the point of absurdity. His first observation about their contention is that if something has power, it is to some degree divine.

From MALEBRANCHE: *The Search after Truth* _____

Ancient philosophers explained the effects of nature by certain entities which they had no particular idea of. In doing so they not only spoke what they did not conceive, but even established a principle from where may directly be drawn most false and dangerous consequences.

Let us suppose, according to their opinion, that in bodies there are some beings distinct from matter. Not having any distinct idea of these entities, we might easily imagine that they are the true, or principal causes of the effects that we see produced. This is indeed the common sentiment of most philosophers. For it is mainly to explain these effects, that they make use of the notions of substantial forms, real qualities, and other like entities. But when we attentively consider the idea we have of *cause* or *power* of acting, we cannot doubt that it represents something divine. For the idea of a sovereign power is the idea of sovereign divinity. And the idea of a subordinate power is the idea of an inferior. But a true divinity, at least, according to the opinion of the heathens, is the idea of a power or true cause. We admit therefore something divine in all bodies that encompass us, when we admit forms, faculties, qualities, virtues, and real beings, capable of producing certain effects, by the power of their own nature. And thus, they insensibly enter into the opinions of the heathens, by the respect they have for their philosophy. Faith indeed works it, but it may perhaps be said that if we are Christians in our hearts, we are heathens in our minds.

 ASK YOURSELF

7.67. According to ancient philosophers, what are some of the entities that are supposedly responsible for the causal power that exists between things (and are thereby to some extent divine)?

Malebranche continues his reduction to absurdity noting that anything with such power is superior to us and entitled to be worshiped.

Moreover, it is difficult to persuade ourselves that we ought neither to love or fear true powers and beings, who can act upon us, punish us with pain, or recompense us with pleasure. And as love and fear are a true adoration, it is also difficult to persuade ourselves that we ought not to adore them. For whatever can act upon us as a real and true cause is necessarily above us, according to St. Augustine and right reason. The same father (and the same reason) tells us it is an immutable law that inferior things should submit to superior. And from hence, this great father concludes, that the body cannot act upon the soul, and that nothing can be above the soul but God.

 ASK YOURSELF

7.68. Why, according to Saint Augustine, can't the body act upon the soul (as when my soul perceives something warm which my body touches)?

In the holy scriptures, when God proves to the Israelites that they ought to adore him, that is, that they ought to fear and love him, the chief reasons he brings are taken from his power to recompense and punish them. He represents to them the benefits they have received from him, the evils for which he has punished them, and that he has still the same power. He forbids them to adore the Gods of the heathens, because they have no power over them, and can do them neither harm nor good. He requires them to honor him only, because he only is the true cause of good and evil, and that there happens none in their city, according to the prophet, which he has not done; for natural causes are not the true causes of the evil that appears to be done to us. It is God alone that acts in them, and it is he only that we must fear and love: *soli deo honor & gloria*.

In short, this opinion (that we ought to fear and love whatever is the true cause of good and evil) appears so natural and just, that it is impossible to destroy it. Thus, if we suppose this false opinion of the philosophers (which we try here to confuse—that bodies which encompass us are the true causes of the pleasures and evils which we feel), then reason seems to justify a religion like to that of the heathens, and approves of the universal irregularity of manners.

It is true that reason does not tell us that we must adore onions and leeks as the sovereign divinity; because they cannot make us entirely happy when we have of them, or entirely unhappy when we want them. Nor have the heathens ever done to them so much honor as to the great Jupiter, upon whom all their divinities depend, or as to the sun, which our senses represent to us, as the universal cause which gives life and motion to all things. If with the heathen philosophers, we suppose the sun includes in its being the true causes of whatever it seems to produce, not only in our bodies and minds, but likewise in all beings which encompass us, we cannot prevent ourselves from regarding this as a sovereign divinity.

 ASK YOURSELF

7.69. Following the logic of the ancient philosophers, why does it make some kind of sense to worship the Sun as the sovereign divinity?

But if we must not pay a sovereign honor to leeks and onions, yet we may always give them some particular adoration. I mean, we may think of and love them in some manner. If it is true, that in some sort they can make us happy, we must honor them in proportion to the good they can do us. And certainly, people who give ear to the reports of their senses, think that lentils are capable of doing them good. Otherwise the Israelites, for instance, would not have regretted their absence in the defect, nor considered it as a misfortune to be deprived of them, if they did not, in some manner, look upon themselves happy in the enjoyment of them. These are the irregularities which our reason engages us in, when it is joined to the principles of the heathen philosophy, and follows the impressions of the senses.

ASK YOURSELF

7.70. Following the logic of the ancient philosophers, why does it make some kind of sense to worship leeks, onions, or lentils?

God Is the True Cause, Nature Is the Occasional Cause. Having rejected the ancient conception of the source of causation, Malebranche argues that God is the true cause of all motion. His argument is as follows:

a. Only physical bodies and spirits exist.

b. Physical bodies cannot causally move things themselves.

c. Therefore, only spirits can causally move things.

d. Finite minds cannot causally move things.

e. God, who is infinitely perfect, can causally move things.

f. Therefore, only God can causally move things.

To cast doubt on this miserable philosophy, the certainty of its principles, and clearness of the ideas we make use of, it is necessary to clearly establish those truths which are opposite to the errors of the ancient philosophy. In short, we must prove that there is only one true cause, because there is only one true God. Nature, or the power of everything, proceeds only from the will of God. All natural things are not true causes, but only occasional ones, and some other truths will be the consequences of these.

It is evident that all bodies, both great and small, have no power of removing themselves: a mountain, a house, a stone, a grain of sand. In short, the least or biggest bodies we can conceive, have no power of removing themselves. We have only two sorts of ideas, that of bodies, and that of spirits. Since we ought to speak only of those things that we conceive, we should reason according to these two ideas. Since therefore the idea we have of all bodies shows us that they cannot move themselves, it must be concluded that they are moved by spirits only. But when we examine the idea we have of all finite minds, we do not see the necessary connection between their wills and the motion of any body whatever it may be. On the contrary, we see that there is none, nor can there be any. From this we ought to conclude (if we will argue according to our knowledge) that as no body is able to move itself, so there is no created spirit that can be the true or principal cause of the motion of any body whatever.

ASK YOURSELF

7.71. In defense of premise (d) in the last argument, why does Malebranche conclude that finite minds cannot causally move things?

But when we think of the idea of God, of a being infinitely perfect, and consequently almighty, we know that there is such a connection between his will, and the motion of all bodies. It is impossible to conceive that he should will the motion of a body, and that would not be moved. Thus, if we speak things as we conceive them (and not as we feel them), we must say that only his will can move bodies. The moving force of bodies, therefore, is not in the bodies which move, since this power of motion is nothing else but the will of God.

 ## ASK YOURSELF

7.72. Why is God (who is spirit) capable of willing the motion of a body?

God, then, is the true cause of all motion. The natural causes we see around us are what Malebranche calls occasional or incidental causes.

Thus bodies have no action. When a bowl is moved and contacts another bowl which is in turn moved, it communicates nothing of its own. For in itself it does not have the impression that it communicates to the other. Yet a bowl is the natural cause of the motion which it communicates. A natural cause, then, is not a real and true cause, but only an occasional one, and which determined the author of nature to act after such and such a manner, in such and such an occurrence.

It is certain, that it is by the motion of visible or invisible bodies that all things are produced. For experience teaches us that bodies, whose parts are in greatest motion, always act more than others, and produce the greatest change in the world. All the powers of nature then proceed from the will of God. He has created the world because he willed it: *dixit & facta funt*: he moves all things, and so produces all the effects that we see happen. Because he has also willed certain laws, according to which bodies communicate their motions in their encounters; and because these laws are productive, they act, and bodies cannot act. There is therefore no force, power, or true cause, in the material and sensible world, nor must we admit of forms, faculties, and real qualities, to produce effects that bodies cannot, and to divide, with God, the force and power which is essential to him.

Just as God is the true cause of all physical motion, Malebranche continues explaining that God is also the true cause of all mental events that are nonphysical.

Not only bodies cannot be the true causes of anything, the most noble spirits are also under a like impotence. They can know nothing if God does not enlighten them. Nor can they have any sensation if he does not modify them. They are capable of willing nothing if God does not move them towards him. I confess they can determine the impression that God gives them towards him, to other objects. But I do not know whether that can be called a power. If the capability of sinning is a power, it would be a power which the almighty does not have. St. Augustine says in some of his works, if people had in themselves the power of loving good, we might say they had some power. But people can only love because God wills they should love, and because his will is effective. They love only because God continually inclines them to good in general, that is, towards himself. Since God created them only for himself, he never preserves them without turning them towards and inclining them to himself. They have no motion towards good in general, since it is God who moves them. They only follow by an entire free choice, this impression according to the law of God, or determine it towards a false good after the law of the flesh: they can only be determined by a prospect of good: for being able to do only what God makes them, they can love nothing but good.

ASK YOURSELF

7.73. What other types of mental events are caused by God, as suggested by Augustine?

God Is also the True Cause of Human Bodily Motion. Having maintained generally that God is the cause of most (if not all) mental events, Malebranche argues specifically that God is the true cause of human sensation and bodily motion. Suppose, for example, I wish to move my arm. My task is to *will* this event. This becomes the cue for God to physically move my arm through physiological causes.

But if we should suppose what is true in one sense, that spirits have in themselves the power of knowing truth and loving good, if their thoughts and wills produced nothing external, we might always say they were able to do nothing. Now it appears most certain to me, that the will of spirits is not capable of moving the smallest body in the world. For it is evident there is no necessary connection between the will we have of moving our arms, and the motion of them. It is true, they are moved when we please, and by that means we are the natural cause of their motion. But natural causes are not true causes; they are only occasional ones, which act merely through the power and efficacy of God, as I have already explained.

For how can we move our arms? To move them we must have animal spirits, and convey them by certain nerves, into such and such muscles to swell and contract them. For by this means the arms move. Or according to the opinion of some, we do not know yet how it is performed. And we see that people who do not even know they have spirits, nerves, and muscles to move their arms, yet move them with as much art and facility as those that understand anatomy best. It is then granted, that people *will* the motion of their arms, but it is only God that can and knows how to remove them. If a person cannot throw down a tower, at least he knows well what must be done in order to it. But there is no person that knows so much as what he must do to move one of his fingers by the help of his animal spirits. How then can people move their arms? These things appear evident to me, and to all those that will think of them, though perhaps they may be incomprehensible to such as will not consider them.

ASK YOURSELF

7.74. As illustrated by Malebranche's example of throwing down a tower, why aren't we the true cause of the movement of our arms?

Malebranche continues explaining why it is not conceivable that we should be the true cause of our bodily motion and also why God would not give us that kind of power.

Not only are people *not* the true causes of the motions produced in their bodies, it seems even a contradiction that they *should* be so. A true cause is such that the mind perceives a necessary connection between it and its effect. This is what I mean. Now it is only an infinitely perfect being whose mind can perceive a necessary connection between his will and the effects of it. It is only God, then, who is the true cause, and who has really the power of moving bodies. I say, moreover, that it is not probable that God would communicate this power he has of moving bodies either to humans or angels. And those who pretend the power we have of moving our arms is a true power, must confess that God could also give to spirits the power of creating, annihilating, and performing all possible things. In a word, this implies that he can make them almighty, as I will further show.

 ASK YOURSELF

7.75. Why is it incomprehensible that we could be the true cause of moving our arms?

God has no need of any instrument to act. It is sufficient if he wills a thing for it to be, because it is a contradiction to suppose he wills it, and that it should not be. His power then is his will, and the communicating of his power is a communication of his will. But to communicate his will to a person or an angel, can signify nothing else but willing. Some body, for instance, should be effectively moved when it is willed by a person or an angel. Now in this case I see two wills which concur when an angel would move a body, that of God, and that of the angel. And to know which of the two will be the true cause of the motion of this body, we must know which it is that is productive. There is a necessary connection between the will of God, and what he wills. God wills in this case, that a body should move when it is willed by an angel. There is a necessary connection therefore, between the will of God and the motion of this body. And consequently it is God who is the true cause of the motion of the body, and the will of the angel only an occasional one.

 ASK YOURSELF

7.76. Suppose that God gave an angel the power to move our arm. What would be the true cause and what would be the occasional cause?

Additional Arguments. Malebranche offers additional arguments showing why God must be the true cause of bodily motion, even if our wills are also involved. First, if God would make someone move contrary to his desire, the person's desire would clearly be only the occasional cause, and not the true cause. Second, if God makes a person's will the true cause of an event, then, in acts of creation and destruction, the person's will would be the true cause of this as well. This is especially absurd when considering nonhuman decisions in which the wills of animals and even the natural dispositions of matter may be present along with God's will. These, clearly, are not the true causes of the resulting motion, creation, or destruction. Third, if God could give such power to people, animals, or matter, He would be making them into Gods, which God cannot do.

But to show it yet more clearly, let us suppose that God wills that things should happen quite contrary to what some spirits desire, as we may think of devils, or some other spirits, who merit this punishment. We cannot say in this case that God communicates his power to them, since they can do nothing that they would do. Yet the wills of these spirits would be the natural causes of whatever effects should be produced. As such, bodies should be moved to the right hand, because these spirits would have them moved to the left; and the desire of these spirits would determine the will of God to act, as our wills to move the parts of our bodies, determine the first cause to move them. Accordingly, the wills of spirits are only occasional causes.

Yet if after all these reasons, we will still maintain, that the will of an angel, which moves any body, should be a true cause, and not an occasional one, it is plain that this same angel might be the true cause of the creation and annihilation of all things. For God could as well communicate to him his power of creating and destroying bodies, as that of moving them, if he willed that things should be created and annihilated. In a word, if he willed, all things would happen as the angel wishes them, even as he wills that bodies should move as the angel pleases. If it is said that an angel or a human would be the true movers, because God moves bodies when they will it, it may also be said, that a human and an angel may be true creators since God can create beings when they will it. No, perhaps it might be said, that the most vile animals, or matter of itself, should be the effective cause of the creation of any substance. This would be so if we supposed, as the philosophers do, that God produces substantial forms whenever the disposition of matter requires it. In short, because God has resolved from all eternity in certain times to create such and such things, we might also say that these times should be the causes of the creation of these beings, as reasonably as to pretend, that a bowl which meets another, is the true cause of the motion it communicates to it. This is because God has determined by his general will, which constituted the order of nature, that when two bodies should meet there should be such and such a communication of motion.

There is then but one only true God, and he the one only true cause. And we must not imagine that that which precedes an effect is the true cause of it. God cannot even communicate his power to the creatures, if we follow the light of reason. He cannot make them true causes, because he cannot make them Gods. Bodies, spirits, pure intelligences, can all do nothing. It is he who has made these spirits that illuminates and acts them. It is he who has created the heavens and the earth, which regulates the motions thereof. In short, it is the author of our being that executes our wills, *femel jussis, sewsper pares.* He even moves our arms when we make use of them against his orders, for he complains by his prophets, that we make him serve our unjust and criminal desires.

ASK YOURSELF

7.77. Who is the true cause of the movement of our arms when we go against God's orders?

For Malebranche, superstitions and Godless beliefs resulted from the failure to recognize God as the true cause of all. Just as proper religion teaches us that there is only one true God, proper philosophy teaches us that there is only one true cause of everything.

All these little heathen divinities, and all these particular causes of the philosophers, are only chimeras that the wicked spirit tries to establish to ruin the worship of the true God. It is not the philosophy they have received from Adam, which teaches these things. It is that which they have received from the serpent, for since the fall the mind of humans became perfectly heathenish. It is this philosophy which joined to the errors of the senses, has made them adore the sun, and which is still at this day, the universal cause of the irregularity of the mind, and corruption of the heart of humans. By their actions, and sometimes by their words, why do they say that we should love the body, since the body is capable of affording us all pleasures? And why do we laugh at the Israelites, which regretted the loss of the garlic and onions of Egypt since, in effect, they were unhappy by being deprived of what, in some measure, could make them happy? But the new philosophy, which they represent as a dismal thing to frighten weak minds, is despised and condemned without being understood. The new philosophy, I say, since they are pleased to call it so, destroys all the arguments of the libertines, by the establishment of the most chief of its principles, which perfectly agrees with the first principle of the Christian religion, that we must love and fear but one God, since there is only one God who can make us happy.

For if religion teaches us that there is but one true God, this philosophy shows us there is but one true cause. If religion informs us, that all the divinities of the heathens are only stones and metals without life and motion, this philosophy discovers to us, also, that all second causes, or all the divinities of their philosophy, are only matter and ineffective wills. In short, if religion teaches us that we must not bow our knees to false Gods, this philosophy also tells us that our imaginations and minds ought not to be prostituted to the imaginary greatness and power of causes, which are not true causes. We must neither love nor fear them, nor busy ourselves about them. Instead, we should think upon God only, see him, adore him, fear and love him in all things.

ASK YOURSELF

7.78. What do we learn from the "new" philosophy?

But this does not agree with the inclination of some philosophers. They will neither see nor think upon God. For, since the fall, there is a secret opposition between God and humans. People take pleasure in erecting Gods after their own imagination, and they voluntarily love and fear the fictions of their own imagination, as they heathens did the works of their own hands. They are like children who tremble at their companions, after they have daubed their faces. Or if they allow for a more noble comparison (although perhaps it be not so just) they resemble those famous Romans, who had some fear and respect for the fictions of their own minds, and foolishly adored their emperors after they had let loose the eagle when they deified them.

GOTTFRIED WILHELM LEIBNIZ

Gottfried Wilhelm Leibniz (1646–1716) was born into a Lutheran family in Germany, and in his early years was largely self-educated through his father's private library. In 1661 he entered the University of Leipzig, where he studied law, and later received his doctorate from the University of Nürnberg. He was variously employed as a councilor, historian, librarian, and diplomat, principally for the courts of Hanover and Brunswick. Throughout his life, and in all of his various areas of interest, he tried to mediate or reconcile disputing sides of controversies. As a political diplomat he tried to unite the nations of Europe. As a theological diplomat he tried to unify the churches. He promoted cooperative activity in scientific and medical research. Leibniz became influential within the scientific community through correspondences with noted scientists and his occasionally published scientific essays. His most noted scientific contribution was his invention of calculus, which created a controversy with Newton. Early in his life Newton invented calculus (which he called "fluxions") and privately used it in his scientific studies. For publications, however, Newton wrote the proofs out in conventional mathematics. But Leibniz published the theory first. Letters circulated among London scientists on the issue, and the consensus was reached that they each arrived at the discovery independently.

Leibniz wrote in fragments (letters, brief essays), and only after his death was it revealed that the vast majority of his literary output was unpublished. His only book published during his life was the *Theodicy* (1710), written for Queen Sophie Charlotte of Prussia, which attempts to explain the presence of evil in a world created by a benevolent God. He also composed a book-length critique of Locke's *Essay concerning Human Understanding*, which he titled "New Essays on Human Understanding." His critique covers all four books of Locke's *Essay* but is particularly noted for its defense of innate ideas in the face of Locke's attacks. After Locke's death in 1704, however, Leibniz chose not to publish it. In the years following Leibniz's own death in 1716, thirty or so of his philosophical essays and letters appeared slowly. Perhaps the most important of these is an untitled outline of the metaphysical doctrines in the *Theodicy*, which was written just before his death in 1714 and first published in 1840. This essay, since titled the "Monadology," is a systematic summary of the wide range of Leibniz's ideas in ninety brief propositions. The complete text of the "Monadology" is presented here.

Monads

Leibniz opens the "Monadology" by describing the essential features of monads and the role they play in the universe.

What Monads Are. Leibniz explains that monads are the true atoms of which all physical things are composed. They are simple substances without parts, indestructible, incorruptible, individual centers of force. Monads comes into being only through creation, end through annihilation, and, unlike atoms, exist in neither space nor time. He argues that, technically, monads do not have direct causal effects on other monads. That is, they contain no open windows that allow them entrance to influence other monads.

 From LEIBNIZ: *Monadology*

1. The monad, of which we will speak here, is nothing else than a simple substance, which goes to make up composites; by simple, we mean without parts.

2. There must be simple substances because there are composites; for a composite is nothing else than a collection or aggregatum of simple substances.

3. Now, where there are no constituent parts there is possible neither extension, nor form, nor divisibility. These monads are the true atoms of nature, and, in fact, the elements of things.

4. Their dissolution, therefore, is not to be feared and there is no way conceivable by which a simple substance can perish through natural means.

5. For the same reason there is no way conceivable by which a simple substance might, through natural means, come into existence, since it cannot be formed by composition.

6. We may say then, that the existence of monads can begin or end only all at once, that is to say, the monad can begin only through creation and end only through annihilation. Composites, however, begin or end gradually.

7. There is also no way of explaining how a monad can be altered or changed in its inner being by any other created thing, since there is no possibility of transposition within it, nor can we conceive of any internal movement which can be produced, directed, increased or diminished there within the substance, such as can take place in the case of composites where a change can occur among the parts. The monads have no windows through which anything may come in or go out. The Attributes are not liable to detach themselves and make an excursion outside the substance, as could *sensible species* of the Schoolmen. In the same way neither substance nor attribute can enter from without into a monad.

 ASK YOURSELF

7.79. Unlike monads, which come into being through divine creation and end through divine annihilation, how do composite things (i.e., things composed of monads) come into being?

The Identity of Indiscernibles and Changes within Monads. According to Leibniz, monads clearly differ from each other. His proof for this rests in a principle that philosophers refer to as the *Identity of Indiscernibles*: If any two beings have exactly the same set of intrinsic and nonrelational properties, then they are indiscernible (i.e., indistinguishable). Thus, according to Leibniz, monads must internally differ from each other in *some* way; otherwise there would only be one monad. Further on Leibniz explains two key qualities within monads that generate their differences: (1) the activity of perceiving the nature of surrounding monads and (2) the activity of representing (mirroring, mimicking) the nature of surrounding monads. Both of these activities range from being completely active to being almost inert.

8. Still monads need to have some qualities, otherwise they would not even be existences. And if simple substances did not differ at all in their qualities, there would be no means of perceiving any change in things. Whatever is in a composite can come into it only through its simple elements and the monads, if they were without qualities (since they do not differ at all in quantity) would be indistinguishable one from another. For instance, if we imagine a *plenum* or completely filled space, where each part receives only the equivalent of its own previous motion, one state of things would not be distinguishable from another.

9. Each monad, indeed, must be different from every other monad. For there are never in nature two beings which are exactly alike, and in which it is not possible to find a difference either internal or based on an intrinsic property.

10. I assume it as admitted that every created being, and consequently the created monad, is subject to change, and indeed that this change is continuous in each.

11. It follows from what has just been said, that the natural changes of the monad come from an internal principle, because an external cause can have no influence on its inner being.

12. Now besides this principle of change there must also be in the monad a variety which changes. This variety constitutes, so to speak, the specific nature and the variety of the simple substances.

13. This variety must involve a multiplicity in the unity or in that which is simple. For since every natural change takes place by degrees, there must be something which changes and something which remains unchanged, and consequently there must be in the simple substance a plurality of conditions and relations, even though it has no parts.

 ASK YOURSELF

7.80. The differences between monads results from the differing changes that they go through. How do natural changes take place?

The Doctrine of Minute Perception. Although monads perceive things, Leibniz argues that they are not conscious. This position is called the Doctrine of Minute Perception. For Leibniz, this is an important point since many errors in the history of philosophy result from failing to recognize that some unconscious things can perceive. In particular, this has led followers of Descartes to conclude that that animals (which lack consciousness) don't even have perceptive souls and that unconscious sleep is like death since all perception would also be annihilated.

14. The passing condition which involves and represents a multiplicity in the unity, or in the simple substance, is nothing else than what is called *perception*. This should be carefully distinguished from apperception or consciousness, as will appear in what follows. In this matter the Cartesians have fallen into a serious error, in that they deny the existence of those perceptions of which we are not conscious. It is this also which has led them to believe that spirits alone are monads and that there are no souls of animals or other entelechies, and it has led them to make the common confusion between a protracted period of unconsciousness and actual death. They have thus adopted the Scholastic error that souls can exist entirely separated from bodies, and have even confirmed ill-balanced minds in the belief that souls are mortal.

15. The action of the internal principle which brings about the change or the passing from one perception to another may be called appetition. It is true that the desire (*l'appetit*) is not always able to attain to the whole of the perception which it strives for, but it always attains a portion of it and reaches new perceptions.

16. We, ourselves, experience a multiplicity in a simple substance, when we find that the most trifling thought of which we are conscious involves a variety in the object. Therefore all those who acknowledge that the soul is a simple substance ought to grant this multiplicity in the monad, and Monsieur Bayle should have found no difficulty in it, as he has done in his *Dictionary* article "Rorarius."

 ASK YOURSELF

7.81. For Leibniz, what is the quality of "appetition" in a monad?

Whether Material Things Can Perceive. The issue of the monad's ability to perceive raises an important issue: Is a purely physical thing capable of perception? Philosophers today address this issue by considering whether advanced computerized robots could at some point be capable of mental perception. Philosophers of Leibniz's day were equally concerned with this issue and questioned whether any purely material machine could be capable of thinking. Leibniz answers no: Perception cannot be reduced to physical mechanisms. He has us imagine that a brain was the size of a mill house. If we could explore the inside, we could not locate the actual perception.

17. It must be confessed, however, that perception, and that which depends upon it, are inexplicable by mechanical causes, that is to say, by figures and motions. Supposing that there were a machine whose structure produced thought, sensation, and perception, we could conceive of it as increased in size with the same proportions until one was able to enter into its interior, as he would into a mill. Now, on going into it he would find only pieces working upon one another, but never would he find anything to explain perception. It is accordingly in the simple substance, and not in the composite nor in a machine that the perception is to be sought. Furthermore, there is nothing besides perceptions and their changes to be found in the simple substance. And it is in these alone that all the internal activities of the simple substance can consist.

18. All simple substances or created monads may be called entelechies, because they have in themselves a certain perfection. There is in them a sufficiency which

makes them the source of their internal activities, and makes them, so to speak, incorporeal Automatons.

19. If we wish to designate as soul everything which has perceptions and desires in the general sense that I have just explained, all simple substances or created monads could be called souls. But since feeling is something more than a mere perception I think that the general name of monad or entelechy should suffice for simple substances which have only perception, while we may reserve the term Soul for those whose perception is more distinct and is accompanied by memory.

20. We experience in ourselves a state where we remember nothing and where we have no distinct perception, as in periods of fainting, or when we are overcome by a profound, dreamless sleep. In such a state the soul does not sensibly differ at all from a simple monad. As this state, however, is not permanent and the soul can recover from it, the soul is something more.

 ASK YOURSELF

7.82. What types of human perception most closely resemble the kind of perception that monads exhibit?

21. Nevertheless it does not follow at all that the simple substance is in such a state without perception. This is so because of the reasons given above; for it cannot perish, nor on the other hand would it exist without some affection and the affection is nothing else than its perception. When, however, there are a great number of weak perceptions where nothing stands out distinctively, we are stunned; as when one turns around and around in the same direction, a dizziness comes on, which makes him swoon and makes him able to distinguish nothing. Among animals, death can occasion this state for quite a period.

22. Every present state of a simple substance is a natural consequence of its preceding state, in such a way that its present is big with its future.

23. Therefore, since on awakening after a period of unconsciousness we become conscious of our perceptions, we must, without having been conscious of them, have had perceptions immediately before; for one perception can come in a natural way only from another perception, just as a motion can come in a natural way only from a motion.

24. It is evident from this that if we were to have nothing distinctive, or so to speak prominent, and of a higher flavor in our perceptions, we should be in a continual state of stupor. This is the condition of monads which are wholly bare.

Human Perception

Having explained the nature of simple perception in monads, Leibniz moves on to discuss the more complex varieties of perception in humans.

Animal and Human Mental Activity. Whereas monads can only perceive, animals and humans have more complicated forms of mental activity. First, we have heightened perceptions from our sense organs. Second, we have memories associated with events.

25. We see that nature has given to animals heightened perceptions, having provided them with organs which collect numerous rays of light or numerous waves of air and thus make them more effective in their combination. Something similar to this takes place in the case of smell, in that of taste and of touch, and perhaps in many other senses which are unknown to us. I shall have occasion very soon to explain how that which occurs in the soul represents that which goes on in the sense organs.

26. The memory furnishes a sort of consecutiveness which imitates reason but is to be distinguished from it. We see that animals when they have the perception of something which they notice and of which they have had a similar previous perception, are led by the representation of their memory to expect that which was associated in the preceding perception, and they come to have feelings like those which they had before. For instance, if a stick be shown to a dog, he remembers the pain which it has caused him and he whines or runs away.

27. The vividness of the picture, which comes to him or moves him, is derived either from the magnitude or from the number of the previous perceptions. For, oftentimes, a strong impression brings about, all at once, the same effect as a long-continued habit or as a great many reiterated, moderate perceptions.

28. People act in like manner as animals, insofar as the sequence of their perceptions is determined only by the law of memory, resembling the *empirical physicians* who practice simply, without any theory, and we are empiricists in three-fourths of our actions. For instance, when we expect that there will be daylight tomorrow, we do so empirically, because it has always happened so up to the present time. It is only the astronomer who uses his reason in making such an affirmation.

Higher Human Reasoning. In addition to the kinds of perceptions that we share with animals, humans have additional mental faculties that make us unique. First, we have knowledge of eternal and necessary truths—specifically, knowledge of God—and reflective knowledge of ourselves. Second, we are capable of reasoning. Third, there are simple ideas of which no definition can be given, such as foundational tautologies.

29. But the knowledge of eternal and necessary truths is that which distinguishes us from mere animals and gives us reason and the sciences, thus raising us to a knowledge of ourselves and of God. This is what is called in us the Rational Soul or the Mind.

30. It is also through the knowledge of necessary truths and through abstractions from them that we come to perform Reflective Acts, which cause us to think of what is called the I, and to decide that this or that is within us. It is thus, that in thinking upon ourselves we think of *being*, of *substance*, of the *simple* and *composite*, of a *material* thing and of God himself, conceiving that what is limited in us is in him without limits. These reflective acts furnish the principal objects of our reasonings.

31. Our reasoning is based upon two great principles: first, that of contradiction, by means of which we decide that to be false which involves contradiction and that to be true which contradicts or is opposed to the false.

32. And second, the principle of sufficient reason, in virtue of which we believe that no fact can be real or existing and no statement true unless it has a sufficient reason why it should be thus and not otherwise. Most frequently, however, these reasons cannot be known by us.

ASK YOURSELF

7.83. What are the two principles of reasoning?

33. There are also two kinds of truths: those of reasoning and those of fact. The truths of reasoning are necessary, and their opposite is impossible. Those of fact, however, are contingent, and their opposite is possible. When a truth is necessary, the reason can be found by analysis in resolving it into simpler ideas and into simpler truths until we reach those which are primary.

34. It is thus that with mathematicians the speculative theorems and the practical canons are reduced by analysis to definitions, axioms, and postulates.

35. There are finally simple ideas of which no definition can be given. There are also the axioms and postulates or, in a word, the primary principles which cannot be proved and, indeed, have no need of proof. These are identical propositions whose opposites involve express contradictions.

ASK YOURSELF

7.84. What are the two kinds of truth?

God

Having briefly explained the rational nature of humans, Leibniz turns next to the issue of God's existence, His nature, and His creative activity.

Cosmological Argument and the Nature of God. Leibniz offers two proofs for God's existence in the "Monadology," the first of which is a reformulation of the classic cosmological argument for God's existence. Older versions of the cosmological argument begin with a given event, trace back the chain of causes of that event, and conclude that it is not possible to have an infinite chain of causes culminating in that event. Thus, a first cause exists that starts that chain. Leibniz, however, concedes that a causal chain of contingent facts can regress infinitely. Nevertheless, an explanation is still needed as to why this infinite chain of contingent causes exists in the first place. Thus, we must postulate the existence of a necessary being that explains the existence of this infinite chain of contingent beings.

36. But there must be also a sufficient reason for contingent truths or truths of fact; that is to say, for the sequence of the things which extend throughout the universe of created beings, where the analysis into more particular reasons can be continued into greater detail without limit because of the immense variety of the things in nature and because of the infinite division of bodies. There is an infinity of figures and of movements, present and past, which enter into the efficient cause of my present writing, and in its final cause there are an infinity of slight tendencies and dispositions of my soul, present and past.

37. And as all this detail again involves other and more detailed contingencies, each of which again has need of a similar analysis in order to find its explanation, no real advance has been made. Therefore, the sufficient or ultimate reason must needs be outside of the sequence or series of these details of contingencies, however infinite they may be.

38. It is thus that the ultimate reason for things must be a necessary substance, in which the detail of the changes shall be present merely potentially, as in the fountainhead, and this substance we call God.

39. Now, since this substance is a sufficient reason for all the above mentioned details, which are linked together throughout, *there is but one God, and this God is sufficient.*

Leibniz's argument can be formulated as follows:

a. The world contains an infinite sequence of contingent facts.

b. An explanation is needed as to the origin of this whole infinite series (which goes beyond an explanation of each member in the series).

c. The explanation of this whole series cannot reside in the series itself, since the very fact of its existence would still need an explanation (principle of sufficient reason).

d. Therefore, there is a necessary substance that produced this infinite series (and which is the complete explanation of its own existence as well).

The classic criticism of Leibniz's cosmological argument was given by Hume in Part 9 of his *Dialogues concerning Natural Religion*:

> In such a chain too, or succession of objects, each part is caused by that which preceded it, and causes that which succeeds it. Where then is the difficulty? But the *whole*, you say, wants a cause. I answer, that the uniting of these parts into a whole (like the uniting of several distinct countries into one kingdom, or several distinct members into one body) is performed merely by an arbitrary act of the mind, and has no influence on the nature of things. Did I show you the particular causes of each individual in a collection of twenty particles of matter, I should think it very unreasonable, should you afterwards ask me, what was the cause of the whole twenty. This is sufficiently explained in explaining the cause of the parts.

Leibniz continues discussing the various attributes of God, particularly his perfection.

40. We may hold that the supreme substance, which is unique, universal and necessary with nothing independent outside of it, which is further a pure sequence of possible being, must be incapable of limitation and must contain as much reality as possible.

41. From this it follows that God is absolutely perfect, perfection being understood as the magnitude of positive reality in the strict sense, when the limitations or the bounds of those things which have them are removed. There where there are no limits, that is to say, in God, perfection is absolutely infinite.

42. It follows also that created things derive their perfections through the influence of God, but their imperfections come from their own natures, which cannot exist without limits. It is in this latter that they are distinguished from God. An example of this original imperfection of created things is to be found in the natural inertia of bodies.

 ASK YOURSELF

7.85. Where do humans get their perfection and imperfection?

Ontological Argument. Leibniz offers a second proof for God's existence, which is a modification of Anselm's ontological argument for God's existence. For Anselm, God (defined as the greatest conceivable being) must have every attribute that would make him the greatest being. Necessary existence is one such greatness-making attribute. Thus, by definition, God must have the attribute of necessary existence. Leibniz begins his proof noting that, insofar as God is a necessary being, all other beings are contingent on God for their existence and for their natures. Like Malebranche, Leibniz believes that God has the master blueprint of all created things within Him, and this blueprint contains eternal truths (such as mathematical truths). Working from such a priori "eternal truths," Leibniz develops his argument without any appeal to *a posteriori* experience.

43. It is true, furthermore, that in God is found not only the source of existences, but also that of essences, in so far as they are real. In other words, he is the source of whatever there is real in the possible. This is because the understanding of God is in the region of eternal truths or of the ideas upon which they depend, and because without him there would be nothing real in the possibilities of things, and not only would nothing be existent, nothing would be even possible.

44. For it must needs be that if there is a reality in essences or in possibilities or indeed in the eternal truths, this reality is based upon something existent and actual, and, consequently, in the existence of the necessary Being in whom essence includes existence or in whom possibility is sufficient to produce actuality.

45. Therefore God alone (or the Necessary Being) has this prerogative that if he is possible he must necessarily exist, and, as nothing is able to prevent the possibility of that which involves no bounds, no negation and consequently, no contradiction, this alone is sufficient to establish *a priori* his existence. We have, therefore, proved his existence through the reality of eternal truths. But a little while ago we also proved it *a posteriori*, because contingent beings exist which can have their ultimate and sufficient reason only in the necessary being which, in turn, has the reason for existence in itself.

Leibniz's version of the ontological argument is a simple *modus ponens* argument:

    a. If it is possible that a necessary being exists, then a necessary being exists.

    b. It is possible that a necessary being exists.

    c. Therefore a necessary being exists.

The key to this argument is premise (a), especially what it means for a being to be "necessary." Using terminology that Leibniz introduces further on, a necessary being is one that exists in every "possible world." Consider every possible configuration of the universe: In one possible universe Lincoln did not become president, and in another there are no humans. For Leibniz, a necessary being is one that exists in every possible world, including the actual world. Suppose that there is a possible world W in which God exists necessarily. That means God would exist in every possible world that is relative to W, including our own actual world. This, then establishes premise (a): If in some possible world God exists necessarily, then God indeed exists necessarily (i.e., in all possible worlds). For Leibniz, premise (b) would be false only if it is contradictory. But it is not contradictory to suppose that God possibly exists in every possible world. From this, the conclusion in (c) validly follows. Given that his proof for God here is based on "eternal truths" (specifically, truths of necessity and contingency) Leibniz continues discussing that nature of eternal truths.

46. Yet we must not think that the eternal truths being dependent upon God are therefore arbitrary and depend upon his will, as Descartes seems to have held, and after him M. Poiret. This is the case only with contingent truths which depend upon fitness or the choice of the greatest good; necessarily truths on the other hand depend solely upon his understanding and are the inner objects of it.

 ASK YOURSELF

7.86. What was Descartes's view about eternal truths (such as mathematics), and what is Leibniz's response?

Creation. For Leibniz, God is the only uncreated monad (or original simple substance). All other monads come into being and are sustained by Him in an act Leibniz calls "fulguration." Without God, monads can neither come into being or be destroyed (paralleling the modern view of the conservation of energy). God has three principle attributes: power, knowledge, and will. These three attributes are exhibited in more limited form within monads as subject, perception, and appetition (i.e., the desire to perceive new things). As noted earlier, monads cannot causally affect each other, although they are influenced by perceiving surrounding monads. Such perception between monads is mediated by God.

47. God alone is the ultimate unity or the original simple substance. All created or derivative monads are the products of him, and arise, so to speak, through the continual outflashings (fulgurations) of the divinity from moment to moment, limited by the receptivity of the creature to whom limitation is an essential.

48. In God are present: power, which is the source of everything; knowledge, which contains the details of the ideas; and, finally, will, which changes or produces things in accordance with the principle of the greatest good. To these correspond in the created monad, the subject or basis, the faculty of perception, and the faculty of appetition. In God these attributes are absolutely infinite or perfect, while in the created

monads or in the entelechies (*perfectihabies,* as Hermolaus Barbarus translates this word), they are imitations approaching him in proportion to the perfection.

49. A created thing is said to act outwardly insofar as it has perfection, and to be acted upon by another insofar as it is imperfect. Thus action is attributed to the monad insofar as it has distinct perceptions, and passion or passivity is attributed insofar as it has confused perceptions.

50. One created thing is more perfect than another when we find in the first that which gives an a priori reason for what occurs in the second. This why we say that one acts upon the other.

 ASK YOURSELF

7.87. What makes one object more perfect than another?

51. In the case of simple substances, the influence which one monad has upon another is only ideal. It can have its effect only through the mediation of God, insofar as in the ideas of God each monad can rightly demand that God, in regulating the others from the beginning of things, should have regarded it also. For since one created monad cannot have a physical influence upon the inner being of another, it is only through the primal regulation that one can have dependence upon another.

52. It is thus that among created things action and passivity are reciprocal. For God, in comparing two simple substances, finds in each one reasons obliging him to adapt the other to it. And consequently what is active in certain respects is passive from another point of view. It is active insofar as what we distinctly know in it serves to give a reason for what occurs in another. It is passive insofar as the reason for what occurs in it is found in what is distinctly known in another.

Best of All Possible Worlds. Of all the possible worlds God could have created, His nature directed Him to create the best universe. Thus, His choice of creating this universe was determined in the sense that all alternatives were inferior and, thus, unacceptable.

53. Now as there are an infinity of possible universes in the ideas of God, and but only one of them can exist, there must be a sufficient reason for the choice of God which determines him to select one rather than another.

54. And this reason is to be found only in the fitness or in the degree of perfection which these worlds possess, each possible thing having the right to claim existence in proportion to the perfection which it involves.

55. This is the cause for the existence of the greatest good; namely, that the wisdom of God permits him to know it, his goodness causes him to choose it, and his power enables him to produce it.

 ASK YOURSELF

7.88. How is it that God's attributes direct Him to create the best of all possible worlds?

Every Monad Mirrors the Universe. In this best of all possible worlds, God completely filled the universe with monads, and all of these work together in carrying out God's perfect plan. No matter how disconnected the world might seem, there is an underlying master plan. All monads, then, are interconnected by virtue of this plan, and each one contains within itself an incomplete copy of this master plan. Thus, each monad mirrors the universe.

56. Now this interconnection, relationship, or this adaptation of all things to each particular one, and of each one to all the rest, brings it about that every simple substance has relations which express all the others and that it is consequently a perpetual living mirror of the universe.

57. And as the same city regarded from different sides appears entirely different, and is, as it were multiplied respectively, so, because of the infinite number of simple substances, there are a similar infinite number of universes which are, nevertheless, only the aspects of a single one as seen from the special point of view of each monad.

58. Through this means has been obtained the greatest possible variety, together with the greatest order that may be. That is to say, through this means has been obtained the greatest possible perfection.

59. This hypothesis, moreover, which I venture to call demonstrated, is the only one which fittingly gives proper prominence to the greatness of God. M. Bayle recognized this when in his dictionary (article "Rorarius") he raised objections to it. Indeed, he was inclined to believe that I attributed too much to God, and more than it is possible to attribute to him. But he was unable to bring forward any reason why it is impossible to suppose that this universal harmony causes every substance to express exactly all others through the relation which it has with them.

 ASK YOURSELF

7.89. What aspect of Leibniz's theory did Bayle object to?

60. Besides, in what has just been said, there are *a priori* reasons for why things cannot be otherwise than they are. It is because God, in ordering the whole, has had regard to every part and in particular to each monad. And since the monad is by its very *nature representative*, nothing can limit it to represent merely a part of things. It is nevertheless true that this representation is, as regards the details of the whole universe, only a confused representation, and is distinct only as regards a small part of them, that is to say, as regards those things which are nearest or greatest in relation to each monad. If the representation were distinct as to the details of the entire Universe, each monad would be a Deity. It is not in the object represented that the monads are limited, but in the modifications of their knowledge of the object. In a confused way they reach out to infinity or to the whole, but are limited and differentiated in the degree of their distinct perceptions.

61. In this respect composites are like simple substances, for all space is filled up; therefore, all matter is connected. And in a plenum or filled space every movement has an effect upon bodies in proportion to this distance, so that not only is every body

affected by those which are in contact with it and responds in some way to whatever happens to them, but also by means of them the body responds to, those bodies adjoining them, and their intercommunication reaches to any distance whatsoever. Consequently every body responds to all that happens in the universe, so that he who saw all could read in each one what is happening everywhere, and even what has happened and what will happen. He can discover in the present what is distant both as regards space and as regards time; "all things conspire" as Hippocrates said. A soul can, however, read in itself only what is there represented distinctly. It cannot all at once open up all its folds, because they extend to infinity.

 ASK YOURSELF

7.90. For Leibniz, another reason why every monad responds to what happens in the universe is because of the fact that all space is filled up. What is the connection between filled space and mirroring the universe?

Body and Soul

Leibniz next examines the differing natures of physical bodies and immaterial souls and how the two interconnect in living things.

Physical Bodies and the Infinite Divisibility of Matter. Leibniz borrows the term *entelechy* from Aristotle to designate a primary active force in things. The entelechy of an inorganic monad is its physical nature, such as the monads that make up a stone. Living things such as trees are composed of monads with a different entelechy, such an active nutritional force. Animals are composed of monads with yet a different entelechy, such as an active appetitive force; we call this entelechy the *soul* of the animal. As part of God's perfect plan, all of these objects are highly ordered both in themselves and in how we perceive them.

62. Thus although each created monad represents the whole universe, it represents more distinctly the body which specially pertains to it and of which it constitutes the entelechy. And as this body expresses all the universe through the interconnection of all matter in the plenum, the soul also represents the whole universe in representing this body, which belongs to it in a particular way.

63. The body belonging to a monad (which is its entelechy or soul) constitutes together with an entelechy what may be called a *living being*, and with a soul what is called an *animal*. Now this body of a living being or of an animal is always organic. For, since every monad is a mirror of the universe and is regulated with perfect order, then there also needs to be order in what represents it. That is to say there must be order in the perceptions of the soul and, consequently, in the body through which the universe is represented in the soul.

64. Therefore every organic body of a living being is a kind of divine machine or natural automaton, infinitely surpassing all artificial automatons. This is because a machine constructed by human skill is not a machine in each of its parts. For instance, the teeth of a brass wheel have parts or bits which to us are not

artificial products and contain nothing in themselves to show the use to which the wheel was destined in the machine. The machines of nature, however (that is to say, living bodies), are still machines in their smallest parts *ad infinitum.* Such is the difference between nature and art, that is to say, between divine art and ours.

 ASK YOURSELF

7.91. What is the difference between purely natural things (created by God) and artificial things (created by us)?

Like the ancient Greek philosopher Anaxagoras, Leibniz believes that matter is infinitely divisible. That is, for any given physical thing, one can divide it again and again, onto infinity. This position stands in contrast to the view of the ancient Greek Atomists and modern-day Newtonians, who contended that physical things are composed of indivisible, material particles that exist in a vacuum. Thus, as part of God's perfect universe, there are infinitely many, infinitely small monads that occupy all space.

65. The author of nature has been able to employ this divine and infinitely marvelous artifice, because each portion of matter is not only, as the ancients recognized, infinitely divisible, but also because it is really divided without end, every part into other parts, each one of which has its own proper motion. Otherwise it would be impossible for each portion of matter to express all the universe.

66. From this we see that there is a world of created things, of living beings, of animals, of entelechies, of souls, in the smallest particle of matter.

67. Every portion of matter may be conceived as like a garden full of plants and like a pond full of fish. But every branch of a plant, every member of an animal, and every drop of the fluids within it, is also such a garden or such a pond.

68. And although the ground and air which lies between the plants of the garden, and the water which is between the fish in the pond, are not themselves plants or fish, yet they nevertheless contain these, usually so small however as to be imperceptible to us.

69. There is, therefore, nothing uncultivated, or sterile or dead in the universe, no chaos, no confusion, save in appearance. This is somewhat as a pond would appear at a distance when we could see in it a confused movement, and so to speak, a swarming of the fish, without however discerning the fish themselves.

 ASK YOURSELF

7.92. For Leibniz, there is no real chaos or confusion in the universe. What is the basis of the chaos or confusion that we might see?

Souls of Animals. As noted, souls of animals are the larger active forces that direct the subcomponent parts. An animal's soul can retain its identity even though the material parts may slowly change over time. Thus, even birth and death are gradual processes of changing subcomponents.

70. It is evident, then, that every living body has a dominating entelechy, which in animals is the soul. The parts, however, of this living body are full of other living beings, plants and animals, which in turn have each one its entelechy or dominating soul.

71. This does not mean, as some who have misunderstood my thought have imagined, that each soul has a quantity or portion of matter appropriated to it or attached to itself for ever, and that it consequently owns other inferior living beings destined to serve it always. Because all bodies are in a state of perpetual flux like rivers, and the parts are continually entering in or passing out.

72. The soul, therefore, changes its body only gradually and by degrees, so that it is never deprived all at once of all its organs. There is frequently a metamorphosis in animals, but never metempsychosis or a transmigration of souls. Neither are there souls wholly separate from bodies, nor bodiless spirits. God alone is without body.

73. This is also why there is never absolute generation or perfect death in the strict sense, consisting in the separation of the soul from the body. What we call generation is development and growth, and what we call death is envelopment and diminution.

 ASK YOURSELF

7.93. How are birth and death gradual?

Pushing this point further, Leibniz maintains that animal souls are present before physical birth and are not destroyed with the disintegration of the physical body.

74. Philosophers have been much perplexed in accounting for the origin of forms, entelechies, or souls. Today, however, it has been learned through careful investigations made in plant, insect and animal life, that the organic bodies of nature are never the product of chaos or putrefaction, but always come from seeds in which there was without doubt some preformation. Thus, it has been decided that not only is the organic body already present before conception, but also a soul in this body, in a word, the animal itself. And it has been decided that, by means of conception, the animal is merely made ready for a great transformation, so as to become an animal of another sort. We can see cases somewhat similar outside of generation when grubs become flies and caterpillars butterflies.

75. These little animals, some of which by conception become large animals, may be called spermatic. Those among them which remain in their species, that is to say, the greater part, are born, multiply, and are destroyed, like the larger animals. There are only a few chosen ones which come out upon a greater stage.

76. This, however, is only half the truth. I believe, therefore, that if the animal never actually commences by natural means, no more does it by natural means come to an end. Not only is there no generation, but also there is no entire destruction or absolute death. These reasonings, carried on a *posteriori* and drawn

from experience, accord perfectly with the principles which I have above deduced *a priori*.

77. Therefore we may say that not only the soul (the mirror of the indestructible universe) is indestructible, but also the animal itself is indestructible, although its mechanism is frequently destroyed in parts and although it puts off and takes on organic coatings.

Union of Soul and Body. The difficulties involved in showing the union between the soul and body led Descartes to deny that animals could think and to postulate pineal gland as the gateway between the body and soul in humans. For Malebranche, God shuttles information back and forth between our bodies and souls. Leibniz's theory does not face these problems. Although the body and soul follow their own distinct laws in their own distinct realms, they operate in perfect synchronization since they are both part of God's perfect master plan.

78. These principles have furnished me the means of explaining on natural grounds the union, or rather the conformity between the soul and the organic body. The soul follows its own laws, and the body likewise follows its own laws. They are fitted to each other in virtue of the pre-established harmony between all substances since they are all representations of one and the same universe.

79. Souls act in accordance with the laws of final causes through their desires, ends and means. Bodies act in accordance with the laws of efficient causes or of motion. The two realms, that of efficient causes and that of final causes, are in harmony, each with the other.

 ASK YOURSELF

7.94. What are the laws that govern bodies and souls, respectively?

80. Descartes saw that souls cannot at all impart force to bodies, because there is always the same quantity of force in matter. Yet he thought that the soul could change the direction of bodies. This was, however, because at that time the law of nature which affirms also that conservation of the same total direction in the motion of matter was not known. If he had known that law, he would have fallen upon my system of pre-established harmony.

81. According to this system, bodies act as if (to suppose the impossible) there were no souls at all, and souls act as if there were no bodies, and yet both body and soul act as if the one were influencing the other.

The Human Spirit

Leibniz closes the "Monadology" by describing human rationality, our place in God's kingdom, and God's method of rewarding and punishing our actions.

Rational Minds. In primitive form, the souls of humans also existed from creation. However, they are later elected to take on the rational nature of a soul. The rational nature of the human soul is what we call our "spirit," and this mirrors the image of God Himself.

82. I find that essentially the same thing is true of all living things and animals, which we have just said (namely, that animals and souls begin from the very commencement of the world and that they no more come to an end than does the world). However, rational animals have this peculiarity, that their little spermatic animals (as long as they remain such) have only ordinary or sensuous souls, but those of them which are, so to speak, elected, attain by actual conception to human nature, and their sensuous souls are raised to the rank of reason and to the prerogative of spirits.

83. Among the differences that there are between ordinary souls and spirits (some of which I have already described) there is also this, that while souls in general are living mirrors or images of the universe of created things, spirits are also images of the Deity himself or of the author of nature. They are capable of knowing the system of the universe, and of imitating some features of it by means of artificial models, each spirit being like a small divinity in its own sphere.

 ASK YOURSELF

7.95. In what ways do we mirror the image of God?

The City of God and Suffering. Our rational abilities give us a social nature that enables us to have a relationship with God. The community of all rational beings with God constitutes a city of God, which is a moral world within a natural world. Just as there is a pre-ordered harmony between realms of the body and soul, there is a similar harmony between the natural world and the moral world. Thus, the suffering that we see in the world is part of this total harmony and is nevertheless part of the best of all possible worlds that God could create. Since we cannot comprehend God's master plan, we should simply be content with how the universe in fact is and recognize that it cannot be improved.

84. Therefore, spirits are able to enter into a sort of social relationship with God. With respect to them he is not only what an inventor is to his machine (as in his relation to the other created things), but be is also what a prince is to his subjects, and even what a father is to his children.

85. From this it is easy to conclude that the totality of all spirits must compose the city of God, that is to say, the most perfect state that is possible under the most perfect monarch.

86. This city of God, this truly universal monarchy, is a moral world within the natural world. It is what is noblest and most divine among the works of God. And in it consists in reality the glory of God, because he would have no glory were not his greatness and goodness known and wondered at by spirits. It is also in relation to this divine city that God properly has goodness. His wisdom and his power are shown everywhere.

87. As we established above that there is a perfect harmony between the two natural realms of efficient and final causes, it will be in place here to point out another

harmony which appears between the physical realm of nature and the moral realm of grace, that is to say, between God considered as the architect of the mechanism of the world and God considered as the monarch of the divine city of spirits.

88. This harmony brings it about that things progress of themselves toward grace along natural lines, and that this earth, for example, must be destroyed and restored by natural means at those times when the proper government of spirits demands it, for chastisement in the one case and for a reward in the other.

89. We can say also that God, the Architect, satisfies in all respects God the Law Giver, that therefore sins will bring their own penalty with them through the order of nature, and because of the very structure of things, mechanical though it is. And in the same way the good actions will attain their rewards in mechanical way through their relation to bodies, although this cannot and ought not always to take place without delay.

 ASK YOURSELF

7.96. What are some of the reasons that suffering might occur from natural (i.e., "mechanical") means?

90. Finally, under this perfect government, there will be no good action unrewarded and no evil action unpunished. Everything must turn out for the well-being of the good; that is to say, of those who are not dissatisfied in this great state, who, after having done their duty, trust in Providence and who love and imitate, as is meet, the Author of all Good, delighting in the contemplation of his perfections according to the nature of that genuine, pure love which finds pleasure in the happiness of those who are loved. It is for this reason that wise and virtuous persons work in behalf of everything which seems conformable to the presumptive or antecedent will of God. Such people are, nevertheless, content with what God actually brings to pass through his secret, consequent and determining will. They recognize that if we were able to understand sufficiently well the order of the universe, we should find that it surpasses all the desires of the wisest of us. They will also see that it is impossible to make it better than it is, not only for all in general, but also for each one of us in particular. This is on the condition that we have the proper attachment for the author of all, not only as the Architect and the efficient cause of our being, but also as our Lord and the Final Cause, who ought to be the whole goal of our will, and who alone can make us happy.

 ASK YOURSELF

7.97. What should our attitudes be toward instances of suffering that we do not fully understand?

Against Atoms and a Vacuum

Between 1715 and 1716 Leibniz exchanged a series of letters on the subject of Newonian science with theologian Samuel Clarke (1675–1792). Their debate became one of the most well-known scientific controversies of the eighteenth century and signaled the end of metaphysical approaches to science (as advanced by Leibniz) in favor of mathematical approaches (as advanced by Newton and Clarke). Leibniz's dispute with Newtonian science began ten years earlier over the issue of which of the two first invented calculus. Their dispute then expanded to a variety of more substantive issues. Newton held that planets and comets move freely through an aetherial substance around a fixed center. Leibniz thought that this would be a perpetual miracle since Leibniz denied that objects can act on each other at a distance. Instead, Leibniz followed Descartes's explanation that the motion of planets results from swirls of aether. Most importantly, Leibniz attacked Newton's view that a vacuum in space is possible. Followers of Newton held that matter was composed of tiny, yet indivisible particles, or "corpuscles," which existed in a vacuum of empty space. Earlier, Descartes argued against the theory of a vacuum, maintaining that extension and matter are equivalent; thus empty space was a contradiction in terms. Leibniz offers a different line of reasoning in his attack on both the vacuum and corpuscle theories.

Leibniz's Argument. In a postscript to his fourth letter to Clarke (June 2, 1716), presented here, Leibniz offers two distinct arguments against both vacuums and atoms. His first argument (paralleling arguments seen earlier in the *Monadology*) is that the more matter there is in the universe, the better. Hence God would have filled the whole universe with material stuff and made each particle of matter infinitely small.

 From LEIBNIZ: *"Letter to Clarke"* _____

All those who maintain a vacuum are more influenced by imagination than by reason. When I was a young man, I also gave into the notion of a vacuum and atoms. But reason brought me into the right way. It was a pleasing imagination. People carry their inquiries no farther than those two things [i.e., a vacuum and atoms]. They, as it were, nail down their thoughts to them. They fancy they have found out the first elements of things, a *non plus ultra*. We would have nature to go no farther and to be finite, as our minds are. But this is being ignorant of the greatness and majesty of the author of things. The least corpuscle is actually subdivided in *infinitum*, and contains a world of other creatures, which would be wanting in the universe, if that corpuscle was an atom (that is, a body of one entire piece without subdivision). In like manner, to admit a vacuum in nature is ascribing to God a very imperfect work. It is violating the grand principle of the necessity of a sufficient reason which many have talked of, without understanding its true meaning; as I have lately shown in proving, by that principle, that space is only an order of things, as time also is, and not at all an absolute being. To omit many other arguments against a vacuum and atoms, I shall here mention those which I ground upon God's perfection, and upon the necessity of a sufficient reason. I lay it down as a principle, that every perfection which God could impart to things without derogating from their other perfections, has actually been imparted to them. Now let us fancy a space wholly empty. God could have placed some matter in it, without derogating in any respect from all other things. Therefore he has actually placed some matter in that space. Therefore, there is no space wholly empty. Therefore all is full. The same argument proves that there is no corpuscle, but what is subdivided.

ASK YOURSELF

7.98. In arguing against the theory of a vacuum, why, according to Leibniz, was God compelled to fill all empty space?

7.99. Leibniz states that the argument against a vacuum can also be used to refute the theory of corpuscles (i.e., tiny indivisible particles of matter). Reconstruct that argument against the theory of corpuscles.

Leibniz continues with a second argument against the vacuum theory. Someone might hold that, to be harmonious, nature needs a special balance between matter and empty space. Leibniz opposes this view.

I shall add another argument grounded upon the necessity of a sufficient reason. It is impossible that there should be any principle to determine what proportion of matter there ought to be, out of all the possible degrees from a plenum to a vacuum, or from a vacuum to a plenum. Perhaps it will be said, that the one should be equal to the other. But, because matter is more perfect than a vacuum, reason requires that a geometrical proportion should be observed, and that there should be as much more matter than vacuum, as the former deserves to have the preference before the latter. But then there must be no vacuum at all. For the perfection of matter is to that of a vacuum, as something to nothing. And the case is the same with atoms. What reason can anyone assign for confining nature in the progression of subdivision? These are fictions.

 ASK YOURSELF

7.100. For Leibniz, why must there be more matter than empty space?

Clarke's Response. Clarke responds specifically to Leibniz's attack on the corpuscle theory. According to Clarke, a given piece of matter will be either perfectly solid (and thus indivisible), or it will consist of pores (or holes) designating its subparts. Suppose that it consists of parts with pores. Then those subparts will either be solid or have pores.

 From CLARKE: *"Letter to Leibniz"*

The arguments alleged in the postscript to Mr. Leibniz's fourth paper have been already answered in the foregoing replies. All that needs here to be observed is that his notion concerning the impossibility of physical atoms (for the question is not about mathematical atoms) is a manifest absurdity. For either there are or there are not any perfectly solid particles of matter. If there are any such, then the parts of such perfectly solid particles, taken of equal figure and dimensions (which is always possible in supposition) are physical atoms perfectly alike. But if there be no such perfectly solid particles, then there is no matter at all in the universe. For, the further the division and subdivision of the parts of any body is carried (before you arrive at parts perfectly solid and without pores) the greater is the proportion of pores to solid matter in that body. If, therefore, carrying on the division *in infinitum*, you never arrive at parts perfectly solid and without pores, it will follow that all bodies consist of pores only, without any matter at all, which is a manifest absurdity. And the argument is the same with regard to the matter of which any particular species of bodies is composed, whether its pores be supposed empty, or always full of extraneous matter.

 ASK YOURSELF

7.101. Why, according to Clarke, can't there be an infinite progression of material subparts with pores?

ANNE CONWAY

British philosopher Anne Conway (1631–1678) was educated privately by Henry More, a prominent member of a seventeenth-century intellectual movement known as Cambridge Platonism. Like More, members of the group were connected with Cambridge University—as either teachers or students—and appreciated Plato's emphasis on both reason and the spirit realm. Turned off by scientists of the time who offered purely mechanistic views of the universe, the Cambridge Platonists held that God and spirit were active components of the universe. In addition to the influence of Cambridge Platonists, Conway was also inspired by mystical writers of the Jewish Cabalistic tradition, who developed theories about female forces in the universe. Some years after her death, Conway's private notebook was translated into Latin and in 1690 was published in Holland—a country in which more controversial ideas could be disseminated without fear of political reprisal. Two years later the Latin work was translated back into English under the title *The Principles of the Most Ancient and Modern Philosophy* (1692).

Two themes stand out in Conway's work: (1) Things are capable of changing much more than we typically might think, and (2) body and soul are more or less the same thing, differing only in degree, and not in kind. Although Conway is not a Rationalist in the Continental European tradition of Descartes, her emphasis on soul and her resistance to mechanical scientific explanations place her more among rationalist philosophers than among Empiricists such as Francis Bacon. Leibniz himself noted an affinity between his and Conway's views. Selections here are from Chapters 6, 8, and 9 of Conway's *Principles*.

All Creatures Are Changeable

Conway divides all things in the universe into three categories. First, there is God, who, being infinitely perfect, is incapable of change. Second, there is Christ, who changes only for the better. Third, there are created things, which can change in innumerable ways, for the better or the worse. Conway argues that species of things can change; for example, a horse can become a human being. Although in theory any physical thing can become anything else, Conway argues that God does not do this in reality because of problems that would invariably arise regarding moral responsibility.

 From CONWAY: *Principles*

That all creatures in their own nature are changeable (the distinction between God and creatures duly considered) evidently evinces, and the same is by daily experience confirmed. Now if any creature be in its own nature changeable, it has this mutability (as it is a creature), and consequently all creatures will have the same, according to that rule: Whatsoever agrees to anything as placed under this or that species, agrees to all comprehended under the same species. But mutability agrees to a creature (which is the most general name of that species, under which all creatures are comprehended), and from thence it is manifest. For otherwise there would be no distinction between God and creatures. For if any creature were of itself, and in its own nature unchangeable, that creature would be God, because immutability is one of his incommunicable attributes.

Now let us consider how far this mutability may reach, or be extended, and, first, whether one individual can be changed into another of the same or a different species? This, I say, is impossible. For then the very essences of things would be changed, which would make a great confusion, not only in the creatures, but in the wisdom of God, which made all things. As for example, if this man could be changed into that, viz. Paul into Judas, or Judas into Paul, then he that sinned would not be punished for his sin, but another in his stead, who was both virtuous and innocent. So then a good man would not receive the reward of his virtue, but a vicious man in his stead. But if we suppose one good man to be changed into another, as Paul into Peter, and Peter into Paul, Paul would not receive his own proper reward, but Peter's nor Peter his, but Paul's, which would be a confusion, and unbecoming the wisdom of God.

 ASK YOURSELF

7.102. What is the moral problem with God changing one human being into another?

Moreover, if the very individual essences of things could be changed one into another, it would follow [that] creatures were not true in themselves. And so we could not be assured, nor have any certain knowledge of anything. And then all the inbred notions and dictates of truth, which men generally find in themselves, would be false, and by consequence the conclusions drawn from thence. For every true science, or certainty of knowledge, depends upon the truth of the objects, which are commonly called *veritates objectivæ*, or objective truths. If therefore these objective truths should be changed the one into the other, certainly the truth of the propositions depending thereon would be changed also; and so no proposition could be unchangeably true, no not the most clear and obvious as these are: the whole is greater than its part, and two halves make a whole.

ASK YOURSELF

7.103. If we could change the individual essences of things, what would we sacrifice?

Body and Soul Differ Only in Degree, Not in Kind. According to Conway, not only can one species change into another, but a thing made out of a material body can change into a soul, and vice versa. Her underlying reasoning is that body and soul are not essentially different kinds of things. With few exceptions, philosophers throughout history held that body and soul are radically different in nature. For example, bodies take up space, are incapable of moving by themselves, and are subject to decompose over time; none of this is so with souls. Conway disputes all of the conventional points of distinction between body and soul. Instead, she argues that bodies and souls fall into a spectrum and intermingle with each other in differing degrees. She offers a series of arguments for her position, one of which, presented here, is based on the intimate connection and interaction between bodies and souls.

To prove that spirit and body differ not essentially, but gradually, I shall deduce my fourth argument from the intimate band or union, which intercedes between bodies and spirits. [It is] by means whereof the spirits have dominion over the bodies with which they are united, that they move them from one place to another, and use them as instruments in their various operations. For if spirit and body are so contrary one to another (so that a spirit is only life, or a living and sensible substance, but a body a certain mass merely dead; a spirit penetrable and indiscerpible [i.e., indivisible into parts], which are all contrary attributes) what (I pray you) is that which does so join or unite them together? Or, what are those links or chains, whereby they have so firm a connection, and that for so long a space of time? Moreover also, when the spirit or soul is separated from the body, so that it has no longer dominion or power over it to move it as it had before, what is the cause of this separation?

 ASK YOURSELF

7.104. What are some of the problems involved with the connection between body and soul?

If it be said, that the vital agreement ([which] the soul has to the body) is the cause of the said union, and that the body being corrupted that vital agreement ceases, I answer, we must first inquire in what this vital agreement does consist. For if they cannot tell us wherein it does consist, they only trifle with empty words, which give a sound, but want a signification. For certainly in the sense which they take body and spirit in, there is no agreement at all between them. For a body is always a dead thing, void of life and sense, no less when the spirit is in it, than when it is gone out of it. Hence there is no agreement at all between them. And if there is any agreement, that certainly will remain the same, both when the body is sound, and when it is corrupted.

If they deny this, because a spirit requires an organized body (by means whereof it performs its vital acts of the external senses—moves and transports the body from place to place, which organical action ceases when the body is corrupted) certainly by this the difficulty is never the better solved. For why does the spirit require such an organized body? For example, Why does it require a corporeal eye so wonderfully formed and organized, that I can see by it? Why does it need a corporeal light to see corporeal objects? Or, why is it requisite that the image of the object should be sent to it, through the eye, that I may see it? If the same were entirely nothing but a spirit, and no way corporeal, why does it need so many several corporeal organs, so far different from the nature of it?

 ASK YOURSELF

7.105. Defenders of the body/soul distinction might argue that the two are connected by means of a "vital agreement" between the two. What, for Conway, is the problem with this explanation?

Furthermore, how can a spirit move its body, or any of its members, if a spirit (as they affirm) is of such a nature, that no part of its body can in the least resist it, even as one body is wont to resist another, when it is moved by it, by reason of its impenetrability? For if a spirit could also easily penetrate all bodies, wherefore does it not leave the body behind it when it is moved from place to place, seeing it can so easily pass out without the least resistance? For certainly this is the cause of all motions which we see in the world, where one thing moves another, viz. because both are impenetrable in the sense aforesaid. For, were it not for this impenetrability, one creature could not move another, because this would not oppose that, nor at all resist it. An example whereof we have in the sails of a ship, by which the wind drives the ship, and that so much the more vehemently, by how much the fewer holes, vents, and passages, the same finds in the sails against which it drives. When on the contrary, if, instead of sails, nets were expanded, through which the wind would have a freer passage, certainly by these the ship would be but little moved, although it blew with great violence. Hence we see how this impenetrability causes resistance, and this makes motion. But if there were no impenetrability, as in the case of body and spirit, then there would be no resistance, and by consequence the spirit could make no motion in the body. . . .

 ASK YOURSELF

7.106. Defenders of the body/soul distinction might similarly argue that souls move impenetrable bodies, just as the wind pushes a sail. However, Conway argues that—even in the dualist's view—souls can penetrate everything; thus, there is no resistance that might allow a soul to move a body. Explain how she makes this point with her analogy of the net.

How then should we visualize the interaction between souls and bodies? According to Conway, we should first recognize how light bodies impact heavy bodies—such as air pushing against a heavy windmill. Heavy spirits, then, interact with lighter bodies in the same way.

For we may easily understand how one body is united with another, by that true agreement that one has with another in its own nature. And so the most subtle and spiritual body may be united with a body that is very gross and thick, namely, by means of certain bodies partaking of subtlety and grossness, according to divers degrees consisting between two extremes. And these middle bodies are indeed the links and chains by which the soul, which is so subtle and spiritual, is conjoined with a body so gross—which middle spirits (if they cease, or are absent) the union is broken or dissolved. So from the same foundation we may easily understand how the soul moves the body, *viz.* as one subtle body can move another gross and thick body. And seeing body itself is a sensible life, or an intellectual substance, it is no less clearly conspicuous how one body can wound, or grieve, or gratify, or please another. [It is] because things of one, or alike nature can easily affect each other. . . .

I shall draw a fifth argument from what we observe in all visible bodies, as in earth, water, stones, wood, etc. What abundance of spirits is in all these things? For earth and water continually produce animals, as they have done from the beginning, so that a pool filled with water may produce fishes though none were ever put there to increase or breed. And seeing that all other things do more originally proceed from earth and water, it necessarily follows, that the spirits of all animals were in the water. And therefore it is said in Genesis, that the spirit of God moved upon the face of the waters, viz. that from hence he might produce whatsoever was afterwards created.

 ASK YOURSELF

7.107. Conway defends her view of body/soul similarity by describing an array of situations in which spirits interact with material things. Give some of her examples.

But if it be said, this argument does not prove that all spirits are bodies, but that all bodies have in them the spirits of all animals (so that every body has a spirit in it, and likewise a spirit and body, and although they are thus united, yet they still remain different in nature one from another, and so cannot be changed one into another) to this I answer. If every body, even the least, has in it the spirits of all animals, and other things, even as matter is said to have in it all forms, now I demand, whether a body has actually all those spirits in it, or potentially only? If actually, how is it possible that so many spirits essentially distinct from body can actually exist in their distinct essences in so small a body (even in the least that can be conceived) unless it be by intrinsic presence, which is not communicable to any creature, as already proved. For if all kinds of spirits are in any, even the least body, how comes it to pass that such an animal is produced of this body and not another? Yea, how comes it to pass that all kinds of animals are not immediately produced out of one and the same body, which experience denies. For we see that nature keeps her order in all operations, whence one animal is formed of another, and one species proceeds from another, as well when it ascends to a farther perfection, as when it descends to a viler state and condition.

But if they say, all spirits are contained in any body, not actually in their distinct essences, but only potentially as they term it, then it must be granted, that the body and all those spirits are one and the same thing. That is, that a body may be turned into them, as when we say wood is potentially fire (that is, can be turned into fire), water is potentially air (that is, may be changed into air). . . .

 ASK YOURSELF

7.108. Responding to Conway's previous argument, critics might argue that the presence of souls in the world does not show that bodies are souls; instead, it only shows bodies contain souls, either actually or potentially. What is her response to the claim that bodies might contain souls potentially?

Against Descartes, Hobbes, and Spinoza

Conway was aware that her theory of body and soul ran counter to views of the subject held by famous philosophers of her time. Descartes believed that bodies and souls were radically distinct things. Hobbes held that everything was composed of matter, including God himself. Spinoza held that God's creations were all part of God himself.

From what has been lately said, and from divers reasons alleged, that spirit and body are originally in their first substance but one and the same thing, it evidently appears that the philosophers (so called) which have taught otherwise, whether ancient or modern, have generally erred. . . .

And none can object, that all this philosophy is no other than that of Descartes or Hobbes under a new mask. For, first, as touching the Cartesian philosophy, this says that every body is a mere dead mass, not only void of all kind of life and sense, but utterly incapable thereof to all eternity. This grand error also is to be imputed to all those who affirm body and spirit to be contrary things, and inconvertible one into another, so as to deny a body all life and sense, but utterly incapable thereof to all eternity. This grand error also is to be imputed to all those who affirm body and spirit to be contrary things, and inconvertible one into another, so as to deny a body all life and sense, which is quite contrary to the grounds of this our philosophy. Wherefore it is so far from being a *Cartesian* principle, under a new mask, that it may be truly said it is *anti-Cartesian*, in regard of their fundamental principles—although, it cannot be denied that Descartes taught many excellent and ingenious things concerning the mechanical part of natural operations, and how all natural motions proceed according to rules and laws mechanical, even as indeed nature herself, i.e., the creature, as an excellent mechanical skill and wisdom in itself (given it from God, who is the fountain of all wisdom) by which it operates. But yet in nature, and her operations, they are far more than merely mechanical, and the same is not a mere organical body, like a clock, wherein there is not a vital principle of motion, but a living body, having life and sense, which body is far more sublime than a mere mechanism, or mechanical motion.

 ASK YOURSELF

7.109. According to Conway, what is Descartes's view of body?

But, secondly, as to what pertains to Hobbes's opinion, this is more contrary to this our philosophy, than that of Descartes. For Descartes acknowledged God to be plainly immaterial, and an incorporeal spirit. Hobbes affirms God himself to be material and corporeal—yea, nothing else but matter and body—and so confounds God and the creatures in their essences, and denies that there is any essential distinction between them. These and many more the worst of consequences are the dictates of Hobbes's philosophy, to which may be added that of Spinoza, for this Spinoza also confounds God and the creatures together, and makes but one being of both, all which are diametrically opposite to the philosophy here delivered by us.

 ASK YOURSELF

7.110. According to Conway, what is wrong with Hobbes's view that God is material?

SUGGESTIONS FOR FURTHER READING

Primary Sources

Conway

Conway, Anne. *The Principles of the Most Ancient and Modern Philosophy* (Cambridge: Cambridge University Press, 1996). Recent edition of the 1692 translation of Conway's sole philosophical work.

Descartes

Descartes, Rene. *The Philosophical Writings of Descartes*, ed. and trans. J. Cottingham, R. Stoothoff, D. Murdoch, and A. Kenny (Cambridge: Cambridge University Press, 1984). Three-volume standard English translation of Descartes's key philosophical writings, including the *Meditations*.

Leibniz

Leibniz, G. W. *Leibniz: Philosophical Essays*, ed. and trans. R. Ariew and D. Garber (Indianapolis: Hackett Publishing Company, 1989). Recent English translation of Leibniz's principal philosophical essays.

Malebranche

Malebranche, Nicolas. *The Search after Truth*, trans. Thomas M. Lennon and Paul J. Olscamp (Cambridge: Cambridge University Press, 1997). Translation of Malebranche's principal philosophical work.

Spinoza

Spinoza, Benedict. *The Chief Works of Benedict de Spinoza*, trans. R. H. M. Elwes (New York: Dover, 1951). Two-volume translation of Spinoza's principal philosophical works, the *Ethics* and *Tractatus*.

Critical Analyses and Discussions

Descartes

Cottingham, John, ed. *The Cambridge Companion to Descartes* (Cambridge: Cambridge University Press, 1992). Collection of essays on various topics.

⸻, ed. *Descartes* (New York: Oxford University Press, 1998). Collection of essays on various aspects of Descartes's philosophy.

Leibniz

Jolley, Nicholas, ed. *The Cambridge Companion to Leibniz* (Cambridge: Cambridge University Press, 1995). Collection of essays on various topics.

Mercer, C. *Leibniz's Metaphysics: Its Origins and Development* (Cambridge: Cambridge University Press, 1998). Survey and critical discussion of Leibniz's philosophy.

Malebranche

Nadler, Steven. *The Cambridge Companion to Malebranche* (Cambridge and New York: Cambridge University, Press, 2000). Collection of essays on various topics.

Spinoza

Curley, E. M. *Behind the Geometrical Method, A Reading of Spinoza's Ethics* (Princeton, NJ: Princeton University Press, 1988). The Spinoza Hobbes connection is developed.

Donagan, A. *Spinoza* (Chicago: University of Chicago press, 1989). Survey and critical discussion of Spinoza's philosophy.

CHAPTER 8

BRITISH EMPIRICISM

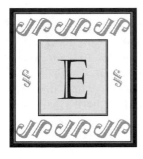

mpiricism" refers to the eighteenth-century philosophical movement, principally in Great Britain, which held that all knowledge comes from experience. Rationalists in Continental Europe maintained that knowledge comes from foundational concepts known intuitively through reason, such as innate ideas. Other concepts are then deductively drawn from these. Empiricists staunchly rejected the theory of innate ideas and argued that knowledge is based on both sense experience and internal mental experiences, such as emotions and self-reflection. Eighteenth-century British Empiricists took their cue from Francis Bacon, who, in the very first aphorism of his *New Organon*, hails the primacy of experience, particularly the observation of nature:

> Man, who is the servant and interpreter of nature, can act and understand no further than he has observed in either the operation or the contemplation of the method and order of nature.

Although Empiricists disavowed innate ideas in favor of ideas from experience, it is important to note that the Empiricists did not reject the notion of instinct or innateness in general. Indeed, they believed that we have inborn propensities that regulate our bodily functions, produce emotions, and even direct our thinking. What Empiricists deny, however, is that we are born with detailed, picturelike concepts of God, causality, and even mathematics.

Like Bacon, British Empiricists also moved away from deductive proofs and used an inductive method of arguing that was more conducive to the data of experience. Despite their advocacy of inductive argumentation, however, Empiricists still made wide use of deductive arguments. Three principal philosophers are associated with British Empiricism: John Locke, George Berkeley, and David Hume.

JOHN LOCKE

John Locke (1632–1704) was born in Wrington, England, just before civil war broke out. He writes, "I no sooner perceived myself in the world than I found myself in a storm." Sporadically, he was a student at Christ Church, Oxford, for more than thirty years until a royal mandate deprived him of his studentship in 1684. His principal area of study was medicine, and he was employed as the house physician and later political advisor to the Earl of Shaftesbury. Shaftesbury's checkered and controversial political career led Locke to flee to Holland for refuge in 1783 because of his association with the earl. Living under an assumed name, Locke used this time for writing. Prior to his return to England in 1689 he completed the manuscript of his greatest philosophical work, *An Essay concerning Human Understanding*. On his return, his previous political services were more favorably recognized and he was offered an ambassadorship at either Berlin or Vienna. He declined this in favor of more minor offices in England. Beginning in 1789, a series of Locke's publications appeared in rapid succession, most of which were composed at earlier dates. Included are his *Letters on Toleration* (1789–1792), *Two Treatises of Government* (1790), and his long-awaited *Essay Concerning Human Understanding* (1790). His final years were spent in residence at the house of Francis and Lady Masham. He died in 1704. Locke's writings had an instant and lasting impact on a variety of disciplines, including political theory, education theory, and theology, as well as philosophy. The following selections are from Locke's *Essay*, which is his longest and most important discussion of metaphysical and epistemological issues. All primary and secondary subdivision titles are from Locke, taken from the *Essay*'s table of contents.

1:2. No Speculative Innate Principles in the Mind

The first book of Locke's *Essay* is devoted to refuting the theory of innate ideas. Although his arguments are often considered to be definitive attacks on Descartes's notion of innate ideas, Locke does not have Descartes specifically in mind. Some Locke commentators question whether Locke has *any* particular philosopher in mind for most of his critique. Nevertheless, defenders of innate ideas suggest that there are both speculative and practical ideas implanted in us at birth. Locke rejects both of these contentions. In the following selections from Book 1, Chapter 2, Locke attacks the view that there are speculative innate ideas. He begins by noting that the theory of innate ideas is an unnatural way of explaining the origin of our ideas.

 From LOCKE: *Essay*, Book 1

1. The Way Shown How We Come by Any Knowledge, Sufficient to Prove It Not Innate. It is an established opinion among some people that there are in the understanding certain innate principles (some primary notions, *koinai ennoiai*, characters) as it were stamped upon the mind of humankind, which the soul receives in its very first being and brings into the world with it. It would be sufficient to convince unprejudiced readers of the falseness of this supposition, if I should only show (as I hope I shall in the following parts of this Discourse) how people, barely by the use of their natural faculties, may attain to all the knowledge they have, without the help of any innate impressions, and may arrive at certainty without any such original notions or principles. For I imagine anyone will easily grant that it would be impertinent to suppose [that] the ideas of colors [are] innate in a creature to whom God has given sight, and a power to receive them by the eyes from external objects. And no less unreasonable would it be to attribute several truths to the impressions of nature, and innate characters, when we may observe in ourselves faculties fit to attain as easy and certain knowledge of them as if they were originally imprinted on the mind.

But because a person is not permitted without censure to follow his own thoughts in the search of truth when they lead him ever so little out of the common road, I shall set down the reasons that made me doubt of the truth of that opinion, as an excuse for my mistake, if I be in one; which I leave to be considered by those who, with me, dispose themselves to embrace truth wherever they find it.

ASK YOURSELF

8.1. What is the reasonable position to take on the origin of our ideas of colors?

The most common argument for innate ideas is that, presumably, people universally agree about the truth of various speculative and practical principles. Locke calls this the argument from "universal consent."

2. General Assent the Great Argument. There is nothing more commonly taken for granted than that there are certain principles, both speculative and practical (for they speak of both), universally agreed upon by all humankind: which therefore, they argue, must needs be the constant impressions which the souls of people receive in their first beings, and which they bring into the world with them, as necessarily and really as they do any of their inherent faculties.

3. Universal Consent Proves Nothing Innate. This argument, drawn from universal consent, has this misfortune in it, that if it were true in matter of fact, that there were certain truths wherein all humankind agreed, it would not prove them innate, if there can be any other way shown how people may come to that universal agreement, in the things they do consent in, which I presume may be done.

 ASK YOURSELF

8.2. For Locke, what will undermine the argument from universal consent?

Locke examines versions of two of Aristotle's famous "laws of thought" that some philosophers believed to be innate: the law of identity (what is, is) and the law of non-contradiction (the same thing cannot be and not be at the same time).

4. "What Is, Is," and "It Is Impossible for the Same Thing to Be and Not to Be," Not Universally Assented To. But, which is worse, this argument of universal consent (which is made use of to prove innate principles) seems to me a demonstration that there are none such. [This is] because there are none to which all humankind give an universal assent. I shall begin with the speculative, and instance in those magnified principles of demonstration, "Whatsoever is, is," and "It is impossible for the same thing to be and not to be"; which, of all others, I think have the most allowed title to innate. These have so settled a reputation of maxims universally received, that it will no doubt be thought strange if any one should seem to question it. But yet I take liberty to say, that these propositions are so far from having an universal assent, that there are a great part of humankind to whom they are not so much as known.

Having presented the two leading candidates for speculative innate ideas, Locke attacks the contention that these principles are innate.

5. Not on the Mind Naturally Imprinted, because Not Known to Children, Idiots, &c. For, first, it is evident, that all children and idiots have not the least apprehension or thought of them. And the want of that is enough to destroy that universal assent which must needs be the necessary concomitant of all innate truths: it seeming to me near a contradiction to say, that there are truths imprinted on the soul, which it perceives or understands not: imprinting, if it signify anything, being nothing else but the making certain truths to be perceived. For to imprint anything on the mind without the mind's perceiving it, seems to me hardly intelligible. If therefore children and idiots have souls, have minds, with those impressions upon them, they must unavoidably perceive them, and necessarily know and assent to these truths. Which since they do not, it is evident that there are no such impressions. For if they are not notions naturally imprinted, how can they be innate? and if they are notions imprinted, how can they be unknown? To say a notion is imprinted on the mind, and yet at the same time to say, that the mind is ignorant of it, and never yet took notice of it, is to make this impression nothing.

 ASK YOURSELF

8.3. What is Locke's argument against the innateness of these ideas based on the knowledge that children and "idiots" (i.e., the retarded) have of them?

The key point of Locke's argument is that if an idea is truly in one's mind, then it must be understood. Since some humans do not understand these ideas, then such ideas are not in their minds, and thus are not innate. He develops this reasoning as follows.

No proposition can be said to be in the mind which it never yet knew, which it was never yet conscious of. For if anyone may [say this], then, by the same reason, all propositions that are true (and the mind is capable ever of assenting to) may be said to be in the mind, and to be imprinted. Since, if any one can be said to be in the mind, which it never yet knew, it must be only because it is capable of knowing it; and so the mind is of all truths it ever shall know. Nay, thus truths may be imprinted on the mind which it never did, nor ever shall know. For a person may live long, and die at last in ignorance of many truths which his mind was capable of knowing, and that with certainty. So that if the capacity of knowing be the natural impression contended for, all the truths a person ever comes to know will, by this account, be every one of them innate; and this great point will amount to no more, but only to a very improper way of speaking; which, whilst it pretends to assert the contrary, says nothing different from those who deny innate principles.

 ASK YOURSELF

8.4. Suppose I claim that I have a proposition in my mind of which I am not conscious. For Locke, what absurd position follows from my contention?

Locke does not dispute the fact that certain human mental faculties are innate. However, Locke argues that the innateness of a faculty does not imply that any ideas are innate.

For nobody, I think, ever denied that the mind was capable of knowing several truths. The capacity, they say, is innate; the knowledge acquired. But then to what end such contest for certain innate maxims? If truths can be imprinted on the understanding without being perceived, I can see no difference there can be between any truths the mind is capable of knowing in respect of their original. They must all be innate or all adventitious. In vain shall a person go about to distinguish them. He therefore that talks of innate notions in the understanding cannot (if he intend thereby any distinct sort of truths) mean such truths to be in the understanding as it never perceived, and is yet wholly ignorant of. For if these words ("to be in the understanding") have any propriety, they signify to be understood. So that to be in the understanding, and not to be understood, [and] to be in the mind and never to be perceived, is all one as to say anything is and is not in the mind or understanding. If therefore these two propositions, "Whatsoever is, is," and "It is impossible for the same thing to be and not to be," are by nature imprinted, children cannot be ignorant of them. Infants, and all that have souls, must necessarily have them in their understandings, know the truth of them, and assent to it.

Defenders of the theory of innate ideas might respond to Locke's reasoning by arguing that even though these ideas are innate, they lie dormant in our minds until we access them through our reason. Thus a child can have such ideas innately implanted in him, yet cannot know them until his rational capacity develops.

6. That People Know Them When They Come to the Use of Reason, Answered. To avoid this, it is usually answered, that all people know and assent to them, when they come to the use of reason; and this is enough to prove them innate. I answer:

7. Doubtful Expressions, That Have Scarce Any Signification, Go for Clear Reasons to Those Who, Being Prepossessed, Take Not the Pains to Examine Even What They Themselves Say. For, to apply this answer with any tolerable sense to our present purpose, it must signify one of these two things: either that as soon as people come to the use of reason these supposed native inscriptions come to be known and observed by them; or else, that the use and exercise of people's reason assists them in the discovery of these principles, and certainly makes them known to them.

 ASK YOURSELF

8.5. What are the two ways reason might uncover innate ideas according to this dormancy theory?

Locke starts by attacking the second of these possible explanations. The function of reason is to deduce one idea from another. Thus, if reason assists in discovering any idea, then that idea is deduced, and cannot be innate.

8. If Reason Discovered Them, That Would Not Prove Them Innate. If they mean that by the use of reason people may discover these principles (and that this is sufficient to prove them innate) their way of arguing will stand thus, viz. that whatever truths reason can certainly discover to us, and make us firmly assent to, those are all naturally imprinted on the mind. Since that universal assent (which is made the mark of them) amounts to no more but this, that by the use of reason we are capable to come to a certain knowledge of and assent to them; and by this means, there will be no difference between the maxims of the mathematicians, and theorems they deduce from them, [then] all must be equally allowed innate (they being all discoveries made by the use of reason, and truths that a rational creature may certainty come to know) if he apply his thoughts rightly that way.

9. It Is False That Reason Discovers Them. But how can these people think [that] the use of reason [is] necessary to discover principles that are supposed innate, when reason (if we may believe them) is nothing else but the faculty of deducing unknown truths from principles or propositions that are already known? That certainly can never be thought innate which we have need of reason to discover; unless, as I have said, we will have all the certain truths that reason ever teaches us to be innate. We may as well think [that] the use of reason [is] necessary to make our eyes discover visible objects, as that there should be need of reason, or the exercise thereof, to make the understanding see what is originally engraven on it, and cannot be in the understanding before it be perceived by it. So that to make reason discover those truths thus imprinted is to say that the use of reason discovers to a person what he knew before. And if people have those innate impressed truths originally, and before the use of reason, and yet are always ignorant of them till they come to the use of reason, it is in effect to say that people know and know them not at the same time.

 ASK YOURSELF

8.6. What is the faculty of reason?

10. No Use Made of Reasoning in the Discovery of These Two Maxims. It will here perhaps be said that mathematical demonstrations, and other truths that are not innate, are not assented to as soon as proposed, wherein they are distinguished from these maxims and other innate truths. I shall have occasion to speak of assent upon the first proposing, more particularly by and by. I shall here only, and that very readily, allow that these maxims and mathematical demonstrations are in this different: that the one have need of reason, using of proofs to make them out and to gain our assent; but the other, as soon as understood, are, without any the least reasoning, embraced and assented to. But I withal beg leave to observe that it lays open the weakness of this subterfuge, which requires the use of reason for the discovery of these general truths: since it must be confessed that in their discovery there is no use made of reasoning at all. And I think those who give this answer will not be forward to affirm that the knowledge of this maxim, "That it is impossible for the same thing to be and not to be," is a deduction of our reason. For this would be to destroy that bounty of nature they seem so fond of, while they make the knowledge of those principles to depend on the labor of our thoughts. For all reasoning is search, and casting about, and requires pains and application. And how can it with any tolerable sense be supposed that what was imprinted by nature, as the foundation and guide of our reason, should need the use of reason to discover it?

 ASK YOURSELF

8.7. What is the main difference between mathematical demonstrations and the two Aristotelian laws of reason given earlier?

---

11. And If There Were, This Would Prove Them Not Innate. Those who will take the pains to reflect with a little attention on the operations of the understanding, will find that this ready assent of the mind to some truths depends not either on native inscription or the use of reason, but on a faculty of the mind quite distinct from both of them, as we shall see hereafter. Reason, therefore, having nothing to do in procuring our assent to these maxims, if by saying, that "people know and assent to them, when they come to the use of reason," be meant, that the use of reason assists us in the knowledge of these maxims, it is utterly false; and were it true, would prove them not to be innate.

Locke continues by attacking the first theory of innateness (described earlier in Section 7), that people know innate ideas once they come to the use of reason. He argues that this theory is false.

12. The Coming to the Use of Reason Not the Time We Come to Know These Maxims. If by knowing and assenting to them "when we come to the use of reason," be meant that this is the time when they come to be taken notice of by the mind; and that as soon as children come to the use of reason, they come also to know and assent to these maxims, this also is false and frivolous. First, it is false because it is evident [that] these maxims are not in the mind so early as the use of reason. And therefore the coming to the use of reason is falsely assigned as the time of their discovery. How many instances of the use of reason may we observe in children, a long time before they have any knowledge of this maxim, "That it is impossible for the same thing to be and not to be?" And a great part of illiterate people and savages pass many years, even of their rational age, without ever thinking on this and the like general propositions.

 ASK YOURSELF

8.8. What examples does Locke give to show that it is false what we have knowledge of Aristotle's laws of thought once we become rational?

Locke claims that we don't gain knowledge of innate ideas until we have gained the appropriate experience and reason about such experience.

I grant, people come not to the knowledge of these general and more abstract truths, which are thought innate, till they come to the use of reason; and I add, nor then neither.

Which is so, because, till after they come to the use of reason, those general abstract ideas are not framed in the mind, about which those general maxims are, which are mistaken for innate principles, but are indeed discoveries made and verities introduced and brought into the mind by the same way, and discovered by the same steps, as several other propositions, which nobody was ever so extravagant as to suppose innate. This I hope to make plain in the sequel of this Discourse. I allow therefore, a necessity that people should come to the use of reason before they get the knowledge of those general truths; but deny that people's coming to the use of reason is the time of their discovery.

After attacking the view that humans have innate knowledge of speculative principles (such as Aristotle's laws of thought), Locke continues in Book 1 by attacking the view that we have innate knowledge of practical principles, such as those of morality and of God. His target here is Lord Herbert of Cherbury (1583–1648), founder of English Deism, who proposed five "common notions" pertaining to the existence of God and our moral obligation. With the theory of innate ideas behind him, Locke turns to Book 2, the longest and most influential of the four books, and explains how our various ideas are based on experience.

2:1. Of Ideas in General and Their Origin

In the first chapter of Book 2, Locke argues that all ideas come from experience. Locke's use of the word "idea" is atypical, as he himself acknowledges in his introduction to the *Essay*:

> I must here in the entrance beg pardon of my reader for the frequent use of the word idea, which he will find in the following treatise. It being that term which, I think, serves best to stand for whatsoever is the object of the understanding when a person thinks, I have used it to express whatever is meant by phantasm, notion, species, or whatever it is which the mind can be employed about in thinking; and I could not avoid frequently using it.

Descartes used the term "idea" in a manner similar to our common use today. Ideas are thoughts that sometimes represent the world, such as the idea I have of my car, and sometimes do not represent the world, such as the idea I have of a unicorn. In either case, however, my "ideas" are different than my initial visual perceptions, such as the visual image I have of my actual car or the visual image I have of a painting of a unicorn. Unlike Descartes, Malebranche used the term "idea" in reference to my initial visual images, such as my immediate perception of my car, and not in reference to my thoughts. Locke combines both Descartes's and Malebranche's use of the term. Thus, for Locke, an idea is any mental event of which we are aware, including both thoughts and our initial visual images.

 From LOCKE: *Essay*, Book 2 _____

1. Idea Is the Object of Thinking. Every man being conscious to himself that he thinks; and that which his mind is applied about whilst thinking being the ideas that are there, it is past doubt that men have in their minds several ideas,—such as are those expressed by the words whiteness, hardness, sweetness, thinking, motion, man, elephant, army, drunkenness, and others: it is in the first place then to be inquired, How he comes by them?

I know it is a received doctrine, that men have native ideas, and original characters, stamped upon their minds in their very first being. This opinion I have at large examined already; and, I suppose what I have said in the foregoing Book will be much more easily admitted, when I have shown whence the understanding may get all the ideas it has; and by what ways and degrees they may come into the mind;—for which I shall appeal to every one's own observation and experience.

2. *All Ideas Come from Sensation or Reflection.* Let us then suppose the mind to be, as we say, white paper, void of all characters, without any ideas:—How comes it to be furnished? Whence comes it by that vast store which the busy and boundless fancy of man has painted on it with an almost endless variety? Whence has it all the materials of reason and knowledge? To this I answer, in one word, from *experience*. In that all our knowledge is founded; and from that it ultimately derives itself. Our observation employed either, about external sensible objects, or about the internal operations of our minds perceived and reflected on by ourselves, is that which supplies our understandings with all the materials of thinking. These two are the fountains of knowledge, from whence all the ideas we have, or can naturally have, do spring.

 ASK YOURSELF

8.9. At birth, what are the contents of our minds?

Locke notes that our various ideas derive from two sources: sensation and reflection. He describes both of these.

3. *The Objects of Sensation, One Source of Ideas.* First, our Senses, conversant about particular sensible objects, do convey into the mind several distinct perceptions of things, according to those various ways wherein those objects do affect them. And thus we come by those ideas we have of yellow, white, heat, cold, soft, hard, bitter, sweet, and all those which we call sensible qualities; which when I say the senses convey into the mind, I mean, they from external objects convey into the mind what produces there those perceptions. This great source of most of the ideas we have, depending wholly upon our senses, and derived by them to the understanding, I call SENSATION.

4. *The Operations of Our Minds, the Other Source of Them.* Secondly, the other fountain from which experience furnisheth the understanding with ideas is,—the perception of the operations of our own mind within us, as it is employed about the ideas it has got;—which operations, when the soul comes to reflect on and consider, do furnish the understanding with another set of ideas, which could not be had from things without. And such are perception, thinking, doubting, believing, reasoning, knowing, willing, and all the different actings of our own minds;—which we being conscious of, and observing in ourselves, do from these receive into our understandings as distinct ideas as we do from bodies affecting our senses.

ASK YOURSELF

8.10. What do ideas of reflection include?

This source of ideas every man has wholly in himself; and though it be not sense, as having nothing to do with external objects, yet it is very like it, and might properly enough be called internal sense. But as I call the other *sensation*, so I call this *reflection*, the ideas it affords being such only as the mind gets by reflecting on its own operations within itself. By reflection then, in the following part of this discourse, I would be understood to mean, that notice which the mind takes of its own operations, and the manner of them, by reason whereof there come to be ideas of these operations in the understanding. These two, I say, viz. external material things, as the objects of *sensation*, and the operations of our own minds within, as the objects of *reflection*, are to me the only originals from whence all our ideas take their beginnings. The term operations here I use in a large sense, as comprehending not barely the actions of the mind about its ideas, but some sort of passions arising sometimes from them, such as is the satisfaction or uneasiness arising from any thought.

Ideas of reflection are based on the operations of our minds. Such operations include reflecting on our various ideas and also reflecting on our emotions. Locke offers an initial proof that all ideas come from only these two sources: For any idea we examine, we will be able to trace it to either sensation or reflection (or a combination of both).

5. All Our Ideas Are of the One or the Other of These. The understanding seems to me not to have the least glimmering of any ideas which it doth not receive from one of these two. External objects furnish the mind with the ideas of sensible qualities, which are all those different perceptions they produce in us; and the mind furnishes the understanding with ideas of its own operations.

These, when we have taken a full survey of them, and their several modes, combinations, and relations, we shall find to contain all our whole stock of ideas; and that we have nothing in our minds which did not come in one of these two ways. Let any one examine his own thoughts, and thoroughly search into his understanding; and then let him tell me, whether all the original ideas he has there, are any other than of the objects of his senses, or of the operations of his mind, considered as objects of his reflection. And how great a mass of knowledge soever he imagines to be lodged there, he will, upon taking a strict view, see that he has not any idea in his mind but what one of these two have imprinted;—though perhaps, with infinite variety compounded and enlarged by the understanding, as we shall see hereafter.

Locke's theory has clear implications for child development. We come into the world with no previous ideas, and as we grow we form our ideas based on experience.

6. Observable in Children. He that attentively considers the state of a child, at his first coming into the world, will have little reason to think him stored with plenty of ideas, that are to be the matter of his future knowledge. It is by degrees he comes to be furnished with them. And though the ideas of obvious and familiar qualities imprint themselves before the memory begins to keep a register of time or order, yet it is often so late before some unusual qualities come in the way, that there are few men that cannot recollect the beginning of their acquaintance with them. And if it were worth while, no doubt a child might be so ordered as to have but a very few, even of the ordinary ideas, till he were grown up to a man. But all that are born into the world, being surrounded with bodies that perpetually and diversely affect them, variety of ideas, whether care be taken of it or not, are imprinted on the minds of children. Light and colors are busy at hand everywhere, when the eye is but open; sounds and some tangible qualities fail not to solicit their proper senses, and force an entrance to the mind;—but yet, I think, it will be granted easily, that if a child were kept in a place where he never saw any other [colors] but black and white till he were a man, he would have no more ideas of scarlet or green, than he that from his childhood never tasted an oyster, or a pine-apple, has of those particular relishes.

 ASK YOURSELF

8.11. Suppose a child was raised in an environment in which he only experienced black and white. What impact would this have on his ideas?

An infant, then, begins with an influx of raw experiences. He becomes familiar with repeated sensory experiences (such as the image of a toy), and thereby acquires his first knowledge about the objects behind the experiences.

22. *The Mind Thinks in Proportion to the Matter It Gets from Experience to Think About.* Follow a child from its birth, and observe the alterations that time makes, and you shall find, as the mind by the senses comes more and more to be furnished with ideas, it comes to be more and more awake; thinks more, the more it has matter to think on. After some time it begins to know the objects which, being most familiar with it, have made lasting impressions. Thus it comes by degrees to know the persons it daily converses with, and distinguishes them from strangers; which are instances and effects of its coming to retain and distinguish the ideas the senses convey to it. And so we may observe how the mind, by degrees, improves in these; and advances to the exercise of those other faculties of enlarging, compounding, and abstracting its ideas, and of reasoning about them, and reflecting upon all these; of which I shall have occasion to speak more hereafter.

 ASK YOURSELF

8.12. By degrees our minds amplify our first distinct ideas. Which faculties "improve" our initial ideas?

23. *A Person Begins to Have Ideas When He First Has Sensation. What Sensation Is.* If it shall be demanded then, when a man begins to have any ideas, I think the true an-

swer is,—when he first has any sensation. For, since there appear not to be any ideas in the mind before the senses have conveyed any in, I conceive that ideas in the understanding are coeval with sensation; which is such an impression or motion made in some part of the body, as produces some perception in the understanding. It is about these impressions made on our senses by outward objects that the mind seems first to employ itself, in such operations as we call perception, remembering, consideration, reasoning, &c.

 ASK YOURSELF

8.13. For Locke, we get our first ideas when we get our first sensations. What kinds of operations do our minds engage in with these elementary ideas?

In short, Locke describes three distinct developments in acquiring our first ideas: (1) We have our first sensory idea, (2) our minds instinctively process these in various ways (such as through one's memory), and (3) we have more ideas when we reflect on these processes (such as the memory process).

24. The Original of All Our Knowledge. In time the mind comes to reflect on its own operations about the ideas got by sensation, and thereby stores itself with a new set of ideas, which I call ideas of reflection. These are the impressions that are made on our senses by outward objects that are extrinsical to the mind; and its own operations, proceeding from powers intrinsical and proper to itself, which, when reflected on by itself, become also objects of its contemplation—are, as I have said, the original of all knowledge. Thus the first capacity of human intellect is,—that the mind is fitted to receive the impressions made on it; either through the senses by outward objects, or by its own operations when it reflects on them. This is the first step a man makes towards the discovery of anything, and the groundwork whereon to build all those notions which ever he shall have naturally in this world. All those sublime thoughts which tower above the clouds, and reach as high as heaven itself, take their rise and footing here: in all that great extent wherein the mind wanders, in those remote speculations it may seem to be elevated with, it stirs not one jot beyond those ideas which sense or reflection have offered for its contemplation.

 ASK YOURSELF

8.14. What is the source of even our most sublime thoughts?

For Locke, this initial process of gaining elementary ideas is a purely instinctive, mechanical procedure and does not involve any willful decisions that we make.

25. In the Reception of Simple Ideas, the Understanding Is for the Most Part Passive. In this part the understanding is merely passive; and whether or no it will have these beginnings, and as it were materials of knowledge, is not in its own power. For the objects of our senses do, many of them, obtrude their particular ideas upon our minds whether we will or not; and the operations of our minds will not let us be without, at least, some obscure notions of them. No man can be wholly ignorant of what he does when he thinks. These simple ideas, when offered to the mind, the understanding can no more refuse to have, nor alter when they are imprinted, nor blot them out and make new ones itself, than a mirror can refuse, alter, or obliterate the images or ideas which the objects set before it do therein produce. As the bodies that surround us do diversely affect our organs, the mind is forced to receive the impressions; and cannot avoid the perception of those ideas that are annexed to them.

2:2. Of Simple Ideas

In the previous section (Book 2, Chapter 1) Locke explained in general how we first arrive at our ideas through sensory and reflective experiences. In this section (Book 2, Chapter 2) Locke explains that these first experiences only give us what he calls *simple ideas*. These simple ideas, in turn, become the building blocks of more *complex ideas*. For example, my unified sense perception of a flower (a complex idea) consists of more elementary perceptions of color, smell, texture, and shape (which are simple ideas).

1. Uncompounded Appearances. The better to understand the nature, manner, and extent of our knowledge, one thing is carefully to be observed concerning the ideas we have; and that is, that some of them are simple and some complex.

Though the qualities that affect our senses are, in the things themselves, so united and blended, that there is no separation, no distance between them; yet it is plain, the ideas they produce in the mind enter by the senses simple and unmixed.

 ASK YOURSELF

8.15. What exactly is "blended" and what is "unblended" in a given sensory event (such as perceiving a flower)?

For, though the sight and touch often take in from the same object, at the same time, different ideas;—as a man sees at once motion and color; the hand feels softness and warmth in the same piece of wax: yet the simple ideas thus united in the same subject, are as perfectly distinct as those that come in by different senses. The coldness and hardness which a man feels in a piece of ice being as distinct ideas in the mind as the smell and whiteness of a lily; or as the taste of sugar, and smell of a rose. And there is nothing can be plainer to a man than the clear and distinct perception he has of those simple ideas; which, being each in itself uncompounded, contains in it nothing but one uniform appearance, or conception in the mind, and is not distinguishable into different ideas.

ASK YOURSELF

8.16. List some of Locke's examples of simple ideas.

Locke continues explaining that our minds can neither create simple idea of their own nor destroy the ones it has formed.

2. The Mind Can Neither Make nor Destroy Them. These simple ideas, the materials of all our knowledge, are suggested and furnished to the mind only by those two ways above mentioned, viz. sensation and reflection. When the understanding is once stored with these simple ideas, it has the power to repeat, compare, and unite them, even to an almost infinite variety, and so can make at pleasure new complex ideas.

ASK YOURSELF

8.17. What processes do our minds use in forming complex ideas out of more simple ones?

But it is not in the power of the most exalted wit, or enlarged understanding, by any quickness or variety of thought, to invent or frame one new simple idea in the mind, not taken in by the ways before mentioned: nor can any force of the understanding destroy those that are there. The dominion of man, in this little world of his own understanding being much what the same as it is in the great world of visible things; wherein his power, however managed by art and skill, reaches no farther than to compound and divide the materials that are made to his hand; but can do nothing towards the making the least particle of new matter, or destroying one atom of what is already in being. The same inability will every one find in himself, who shall go about to fashion in his understanding one simple idea, not received in by his senses from external objects, or by reflection from the operations of his own mind about them. I would have any one try to fancy any taste which had never affected his palate; or frame the idea of a scent he had never smelt: and when he can do this, I will also conclude that a blind man hath ideas of colors, and a deaf man true distinct notions of sounds.

ASK YOURSELF

8.18. What does Locke say about anyone who tries to imagine a taste that never affected one's palate?

For Locke, if we had fewer than five senses or more than five senses, our simple ideas of sensation would be restricted to those.

3. Only the Qualities That Affect the Senses Are Imaginable. This is the reason why—though we cannot believe it impossible to God to make a creature with other organs, and more ways to convey into the understanding the notice of corporeal things than those five, as they are usually counted, which he has given to man—yet I think it is not possible for any man to imagine any other qualities in bodies, howsoever constituted, whereby they can be taken notice of, besides sounds, tastes, smells, visible and tangible qualities. And had mankind been made but with four senses, the qualities then which are the objects of the fifth sense had been as far from our notice, imagination, and conception, as now any belonging to a sixth, seventh, or eighth sense can possibly be;—which, whether yet some other creatures, in some other parts of this vast and stupendous universe, may not have, will be a great presumption to deny. He that will not set himself proudly at the top of all things, but will consider the immensity of this fabric, and the great variety that is to be found in this little and inconsiderable part of it which he has to do with, may be apt to think that, in other mansions of it, there may be other and different intelligent beings, of whose faculties he has as little knowledge or apprehension as a worm shut up in one drawer of a cabinet hath of the senses or understanding of a man; such variety and excellency being suitable to the wisdom and power of the Maker. I have here followed the common opinion of man's having but five senses; though, perhaps, there may be justly counted more;—but either supposition serves equally to my present purpose.

 ASK YOURSELF

8.19. Suppose that a creature in another part of the universe had more than five senses. What would our human knowledge be of that creature's sensory experiences?

2:3. Of Simple Ideas of Sense

In the next few chapters, Locke illustrates the various types of simple ideas we receive. He begins by explaining that simple ideas come from four possible combinations of sensation and reflection.

1. Division of Simple Ideas. The better to conceive the ideas we receive from sensation, it may not be amiss for us to consider them, in reference to the different ways whereby they make their approaches to our minds, and make themselves perceivable by us.

First, then, There are some which come into our minds by one sense only.

Secondly, There are others that convey themselves into the mind by more senses than one.

Thirdly, Others that are had from reflection only.

Fourthly, There are some that make themselves way, and are suggested to the mind by all the ways of sensation and reflection.

We shall consider them apart under these several heads.

Some of our simple ideas, such as the spherical shape of a ball, can be detected by both our visual and tactile senses. Others, however, can only be obtained through a single sense organ, such as the smell of a flower. Locke begins by illustrating the latter of these, which can be experienced only through a single sense organ.

Ideas of One Sense. There are some ideas which have admittance only through one sense, which is peculiarly adapted to receive them. Thus light and colors, as white, red, yellow, blue; with their several degrees or shades and mixtures, as green, scarlet, purple, sea-green, and the rest, come in only by the eyes. All kinds of noises, sounds, and tones, only by the ears. The several tastes and smells, by the nose and palate. And if these organs, or the nerves which are the conduits to convey them from without to their audience in the brain,—the mind's presence-room (as I may so call it)—are any of them so disordered as not to perform their functions, they have no postern to be admitted by; no other way to bring themselves into view, and be perceived by the understanding.

The most considerable of those belonging to the touch, are heat and cold, and solidity: all the rest, consisting almost wholly in the sensible configuration, as smooth and rough; or else, more or less firm adhesion of the parts, as hard and soft, tough and brittle, are obvious enough.

 ASK YOURSELF

8.20. Give some examples of simple ideas that result from single senses.

2. Few Simple Ideas Have Names. I think it will be needless to enumerate all the particular simple ideas belonging to each sense. Nor indeed is it possible if we would; there being a great many more of them belonging to most of the senses than we have names for. The variety of smells, which are as many almost, if not more, than species of bodies in the world, do most of them want names. Sweet and stinking commonly serve our turn for these ideas, which in effect is little more than to call them pleasing or displeasing; though the smell of a rose and violet, both sweet, are certainly very distinct ideas. Nor are the different tastes, that by our palates we receive ideas of, much better provided with names. Sweet, bitter, sour, harsh, and salt are almost all the epithets we have to denominate that numberless variety of relishes, which are to be found distinct, not only in almost every sort of creatures, but in the different parts of the same plant, fruit, or animal. The same may be said of colors and sounds. I shall, therefore, in the account of simple ideas I am here giving, content myself to set down only such as are most material to our present purpose, or are in themselves less apt to be taken notice of though they are very frequently the ingredients of our complex ideas; amongst which, I think, I may well account solidity, which therefore I shall treat of in the next chapter.

 ASK YOURSELF

8.21. According to Locke, a vast number of simple ideas have no names. Describe some of these ideas.

In Book 2, Chapter 4 (not included here) Locke gives an account of the simple idea of solidity that we get from the resistance we feel in a body. The idea of solidity also includes extension in space, which we can see visually.

2:5. Of Simple Ideas of Diverse Senses

Locke briefly lists simple ideas that come from two senses, particularly vision and tactility.

Ideas Received Both by Seeing and Touching. The ideas we get by more than one sense are, of space or extension, figure, rest, and motion. For these make perceivable impressions, both on the eyes and touch; and we can receive and convey into our minds the ideas of the extension, figure, motion, and rest of bodies, both by seeing and feeling. But having occasion to speak more at large of these in another place, I here only enumerate them.

 ASK YOURSELF

8.22. Give some examples of simple ideas that result from both vision and tactile sensation.

In Book 2, Chapter 9 (not included here) Locke amplifies this brief discussion and considers the possible situation in which a person blind from birth formed simple ideas of a globe and cube based on tactile sensation alone. If that person were then made to see, would he visually be able to distinguish a glove from a cube? Locke believes that he could not make the visual distinction.

2:6. Of Simple Ideas of Reflection

Locke turns next to our simple ideas of reflection, that is, the ideas we have when we reflect on the mental operations by which we experience simple ideas of sensation.

1. Simple Ideas Are the Operations of Mind about Its Other Ideas. The mind receiving the ideas mentioned in the foregoing chapters from without, when it turns its view inward upon itself, and observes its own actions about those ideas it has, takes from thence other ideas, which are as capable to be the objects of its contemplation as any of those it received from foreign things.

2. The Idea of Perception, and Idea of Willing, We Have from Reflection. The two great and principal actions of the mind, which are most frequently considered, and which are so frequent that every one that pleases may take notice of them in himself, are these two:—

Perception, or Thinking; and
Volition, or Willing.

The power of thinking is called the Understanding, and the power of volition is called the Will; and these two powers or abilities in the mind are denominated faculties.

Of some of the modes of these simple ideas of reflection, such as are remembrance, discerning, reasoning, judging, knowledge, faith, &c., I shall have occasion to speak hereafter.

ASK YOURSELF

8.23. What are the two key simple ideas of reflection?

In later chapters in Book 2 (not included here) Locke amplifies his discussion of simple ideas of reflection. His list of such ideas includes perception, memory, contemplation, attention, repetition, discernment, comparison, composition, and abstraction. For Locke, these ideas are the result of underlying mental faculties with which we were created.

2:7. Of Simple Ideas of Both Sensation and Reflection

Locke next explores simple ideas that we can obtain either though sensation or through reflecting on our mental processes. He examines five such ideas in the following sections: pleasure/pain, existence, unity, power, and succession.

Locke begins by noting that the ideas of pleasure and pain accompany almost all of our sensory and reflective experiences.

1. Ideas of Pleasure and Pain. There be other simple ideas which convey themselves into the mind by all the ways of sensation and reflection, viz. pleasure or delight, and its opposite, pain, or uneasiness; power; existence; unity.

2. Mix with Almost All Our Other Ideas. Delight or uneasiness, one or other of them, join themselves to almost all our ideas both of sensation and reflection: and there is scarce any affection of our senses from without, any retired thought of our mind within, which is not able to produce in us pleasure or pain. By pleasure and pain, I would be understood to signify, whatsoever delights or molests us; whether it arises from the thoughts of our minds, or anything operating on our bodies. For, whether we call it satisfaction, delight, pleasure, happiness, &c., on the one side, or uneasiness, trouble, pain, torment, anguish, misery, &c., on the other, they are still but different degrees of the same thing, and belong to the ideas of pleasure and pain, delight or uneasiness; which are the names I shall most commonly use for those two sorts of ideas.

ASK YOURSELF

8.24. How does Locke define pleasure and pain?

For Locke, God had a specific purpose in linking pleasure with ideas of sensation and reflection. If an object or thought is pleasing, then we are motivated to pursue it.

3. As Motives of Our Actions. The infinite wise Author of our being, having given us the power over several parts of our bodies, to move or keep them at rest as we think fit; and also, by the motion of them, to move ourselves and other contiguous bodies, in which consist all the actions of our body: having also given a power to our minds, in several instances, to choose, amongst its ideas, which it will think on, and to pursue the inquiry of this or that subject with consideration and attention, to excite us to these actions of thinking and motion that we are capable of,—has been pleased to join to several thoughts, and several sensations a perception of delight. If this were wholly separated from all our outward sensations, and inward thoughts, we should have no reason to prefer one thought or action to another; negligence to attention, or motion to rest. And so we should neither stir our bodies, nor employ our minds, but let our thoughts (if I may so call it) run adrift, without any direction or design, and suffer the ideas of our minds, like unregarded shadows, to make their appearances there, as it happened, without attending to them. In which state man, however furnished with the faculties of understanding and will, would be a very idle, inactive creature, and pass his time only in a lazy, lethargic dream. It has therefore pleased our wise Creator to annex to several objects, and the ideas which we receive from them, as also to several of our thoughts, a concomitant pleasure, and that in several objects, to several degrees, that those faculties which he had endowed us with might not remain wholly idle and unemployed by us.

 ASK YOURSELF

8.25. For Locke, what would happen if pleasures and pains were not linked with our sensations and reflections?

Just as pleasures motivate us to pursue certain objects or thoughts and pains motivate us to avoid other objects and thoughts, Locke notes that some things that cause us pleasure also cause us pain. This prompts us to be cautious about such things since an excess of them might harm us.

4. An End and Use of Pain. Pain has the same efficacy and use to set us on work that pleasure has, we being as ready to employ our faculties to avoid that, as to pursue this: only this is worth our consideration, that pain is often produced by the same objects and ideas that produce pleasure in us. This their near conjunction, which makes us often feel pain in the sensations where we expected pleasure, gives us new occasion of admiring the wisdom and goodness of our Maker, who, designing the preservation of our being, has annexed pain to the application of many things to our bodies, to warn us of the harm that they will do, and as advices to withdraw from them. But he, not designing our preservation barely, but the preservation of every part and organ in its perfection, hath in many cases annexed pain to those very ideas which delight us. Thus heat, that is very agreeable to us in one degree, by a little greater increase of it proves no ordinary torment: and the most pleasant of all sensible objects, light itself, if there be too much of it, if increased beyond a due proportion to our eyes, causes a very painful sensation. Which is wisely and favourably so ordered by nature, that when any object does, by the vehemency of its operation, disorder the instruments of sensation, whose structures cannot but be very nice and delicate, we might, by the pain, be warned to withdraw, before the organ be quite put out of order, and so be unfitted for its proper function for the future. The consideration of those objects that produce it may well persuade us, that this is the end or use of pain. For, though great light be insufferable to our eyes, yet the highest degree of darkness does not at all disease them: because that, causing no disorderly motion in it, leaves that curious organ unharmed in its natural state. But yet excess of cold as well as heat pains us: because it is equally destructive to that temper which is necessary to the preservation of life, and the exercise of the several functions of the body, and which consists in a moderate degree of warmth; or, if you please, a motion of the insensible parts of our bodies, confined within certain bounds.

5. Another End. Beyond all this, we may find another reason why God hath scattered up and down several degrees of pleasure and pain, in all the things that environ and affect us; and blended them together in almost all that our thoughts and senses have to do with;—that we, finding imperfection, dissatisfaction, and want of complete happiness, in all the enjoyments which the creatures can afford us, might be led to seek it in the enjoyment of Him with whom there is fullness of joy, and at whose right hand are pleasures for evermore.

 ASK YOURSELF

8.26. Give one of Locke's examples of something that causes both pain and pleasure.

8.27. What is a second and more spiritual reason why God has us experience both pleasure and pain in the same object?

Just as pleasure and pain accompany our various simple ideas of sensation and reflection, other metaphysical ideas are also present, specifically existence, unity, power, and succession.

7. Ideas of Existence and Unity. Existence and Unity are two other ideas that are suggested to the understanding by every object without, and every idea within. When ideas are in our minds, we consider them as being actually there, as well as we consider things to be actually without us;—which is, that they exist, or have existence. And whatever we can consider as one thing, whether a real being or idea, suggests to the understanding the idea of unity.

8. Idea of Power. Power also is another of those simple ideas which we receive from sensation and reflection. For, observing in ourselves that we do and can think, and that we can at pleasure move several parts of our bodies which were at rest; the effects, also, that natural bodies are able to produce in one another, occurring every moment to our senses,—we both these ways get the idea of power.

9. Idea of Succession. Besides these there is another idea, which, though suggested by our senses, yet is more constantly offered to us by what passes in our minds; and that is the idea of succession. For if we look immediately into ourselves, and reflect on what is observable there, we shall find our ideas always, whilst we are awake, or have any thought, passing in train, one going and another coming, without intermission.

ASK YOURSELF

8.28. How do the ideas of existence and unity emerge along with simple ideas, such as the perception of a round object?

8.29. The term "power" in modern philosophy refers to the causal force present in any cause-and-effect relationship. Explain how the concept of power accompanies a simple idea of bodily motion.

8.30. What is the simple idea of succession?

According to Locke, the simple ideas examined in this and previous chapters are the building blocks of all the more complex ideas.

10. Simple Ideas the Materials of All Our Knowledge. These, if they are not all, are at least (as I think) the most considerable of those simple ideas which the mind has, and out of which is made all its other knowledge; all which it receives only by the two forementioned ways of sensation and reflection.

Nor let any one think these too narrow bounds for the capacious mind of man to expatiate in, which takes its flight further than the stars, and cannot be confined by the limits of the world; that extends its thoughts often even beyond the utmost expansion of Matter, and makes excursions into that incomprehensible Inane. I grant all this, but desire any one to assign any simple idea which is not received from one of those inlets before mentioned, or any complex idea not made out of those simple ones. Nor will it be so strange to think these few simple ideas sufficient to employ the quickest thought, or largest capacity; and to furnish the materials of all that various knowledge, and more various fancies and opinions of all mankind, if we consider how many words may be made out of the various composition of twenty-four letters; or if, going one step further, we will but reflect on the variety of combinations that may be made with barely one of the above-mentioned ideas, viz. number, whose stock is inexhaustible and truly infinite: and what a large and immense field doth extension alone afford the mathematicians?

ASK YOURSELF

8.31. Suppose someone is dissatisfied with Locke's assertion that a few simple ideas are the building blocks of all complex ideas. Give one of Locke's analogies that helps explain his assertion.

2:8. Some Further Considerations Concerning Our Simple Ideas

In this section Locke makes his classic distinction between simple ideas of *primary qualities* and simple ideas of *secondary qualities*. Briefly, a primary quality is a property of an object that resides in the object itself. A secondary quality is a property of an object that is spectator dependent. The conceptual distinction between primary and secondary qualities appears early in the history of philosophy, even though the terms "primary" and "secondary" had not yet been introduced. The origin of the distinction may perhaps be traced to Democritus. In the modern period, however the distinction became more pronounced. In the *Assayer* (1623) Galileo introduces the distinction as follows:

> I say that whenever I conceive any material or corporeal substance, I immediately feel the need to think of it as bounded and as having this or that shape; as being large or small in relation to other things, and in some specific place at any given time; as being in motion or at rest; as touching or not touching some other body; and as being one number, or few, or many. From these conditions I cannot separate such a substance by any stretch of my imagination. But that it must be white or red, bitter or sweet, noisy or silent, and of sweet or foul odor, my mind does not feel compelled to bring in as necessary accompaniments.

For Galileo, then, primary qualities are those that are integral to the notion of material substance, such as shape and motion. Secondary ones, then, are those that do not necessarily belong to the notion of material substance, such as colors and smells. Using Aristotle's terminology, then, primary qualities are essential attributes of all material things. Secondary qualities, by contrast, are accidental attributes of physical things (that is, it would be theoretically possible for such objects to exist without exhibiting those secondary qualities). In the *Meditations* (1641), Descartes echoes this distinction using the terms "objects of mathematics" (primary) and "objects of sense" (secondary). Of the former he writes,

> To such a class of things pertains corporeal nature in general, and its extension, the figure of extended things, their quantity or magnitude and number, as also the place in which they are, the time which measures their duration, and so on. (*Meditation 1*)

Again, for Descartes, the key point of distinction is that primary qualities are essential to an object's extended or physical existence. The words "primary" and "secondary" were occasionally used in this connection by Robery Boyle in his *Origin of Forms and Qualities* (1666; pp. 10, 43, 100, 101), and his *Tracts* (1671; Introduction, p. 18). Using Boyle's terminology, Locke more systematically describes the distinction between primary and secondary qualities. He begins by defining a quality as the power to produce an idea.

8. Our Ideas and the Qualities of Bodies. Whatsoever the mind perceives in itself, or is the immediate object of perception, thought, or understanding, that I call idea; and the power to produce any idea in our mind, I call quality of the subject wherein that power is. Thus a snowball having the power to produce in us the ideas of white, cold, and round,—the power to produce those ideas in us, as they are in the snowball, I call qualities; and as they are sensations or perceptions in our understandings, I call them ideas; which ideas, if I speak of sometimes as in the things themselves, I would be understood to mean those qualities in the objects which produce them in us.

 ASK YOURSELF

8.32. What are the qualities in a snowball?

Like Galileo and Descartes, Locke defines primary qualities as those that are inseparable from any physical body.

9. Primary Qualities of Bodies. Qualities thus considered in bodies are,

First, such as are utterly inseparable from the body, in what state soever it be; and such as in all the alterations and changes it suffers, all the force can be used upon it, it constantly keeps; and such as sense constantly finds in every particle of matter which has bulk enough to be perceived; and the mind finds inseparable from every particle of matter, though less than to make itself singly be perceived by our senses: v.g. Take a grain of wheat, divide it into two parts; each part has still solidity, extension, figure, and mobility: divide it again, and it retains still the same qualities; and so divide it on, till the parts become insensible; they must retain still each of them all those qualities. For division (which is all that a mill, or pestle, or any other body, does upon another, in reducing it to insensible parts) can never take away either solidity, extension, figure, or mobility from any body, but only makes two or more distinct separate masses of matter, of that which was but one before; all which distinct masses, reckoned as so many distinct bodies, after division, make a certain number. These I call original or primary qualities of body, which I think we may observe to produce simple ideas in us, viz. solidity, extension, figure, motion or rest, and number.

 ASK YOURSELF

8.33. For Locke, what are primary qualities?

Locke claims that objects also have the power of producing other ideas (or perceptions) in our minds, although such perceptions do not resemble anything in the objects themselves. These are secondary.

10. Secondary Qualities of Bodies. Secondly, such qualities which in truth are nothing in the objects themselves but power to produce various sensations in us by their primary qualities, i.e. by the bulk, figure, texture, and motion of their insensible parts, as colors, sounds, tastes, &c. These I call secondary qualities. To these might be added a third sort, which are allowed to be barely powers; though they are as much real qualities in the subject as those which I, to comply with the common way of speaking, call qualities, but for distinction, secondary qualities. For the power in fire to produce a new color, or consistency, in wax or clay,—by its primary qualities, is as much a quality in fire, as the power it has to produce in me a new idea or sensation of warmth or burning, which I felt not before,—by the same primary qualities, viz. the bulk, texture, and motion of its insensible parts.

 ASK YOURSELF

8.34. What is the "third sort" of qualities in objects?

In Sections 11–13 (not included here), Locke describes the physiological mechanisms by which objects give us sensations of colors and smells.

14. They Depend on the Primary Qualities. What I have said concerning colors and smells may be understood also of tastes and sounds, and other the like sensible qualities; which, whatever reality we by mistake attribute to them, are in truth nothing in the objects themselves, but powers to produce various sensations in us; and depend on those primary qualities, viz. bulk, figure, texture, and motion of parts as I have said.

15. Ideas of Primary Qualities Are Resemblances; of Secondary, Not. From whence I think it easy to draw this observation,—that the ideas of primary qualities of bodies are resemblances of them, and their patterns do really exist in the bodies themselves, but the ideas produced in us by these secondary qualities have no resemblance of them at all. There is nothing like our ideas, existing in the bodies themselves. They are, in the bodies we denominate from them, only a power to produce those sensations in us: and what is sweet, blue, or warm in idea, is but the certain bulk, figure, and motion of the insensible parts, in the bodies themselves, which we call so.

 ASK YOURSELF

8.35. What other qualities in objects do secondary qualities depend upon?

8.36. What specifically is the power that objects have regarding secondary qualities?

Locke summarizes his points about the three kinds of qualities of objects.

23. Three Sorts of Qualities in Bodies. The qualities, then, that are in bodies, rightly considered, are of three sorts:—

First, The bulk, figure, number, situation, and motion or rest of their solid parts. Those are in them, whether we perceive them or not; and when they are of that size that we can discover them, we have by these an idea of the thing as it is in itself; as is plain in artificial things. These I call primary qualities.

Secondly, The power that is in any body, by reason of its insensible primary qualities, to operate after a peculiar manner on any of our senses, and thereby produce in us the different ideas of several colors, sounds, smells, tastes, &c. These are usually called sensible qualities.

Thirdly, The power that is in any body, by reason of the particular constitution of its primary qualities, to make such a change in the bulk, figure, texture, and motion of another body, as to make it operate on our senses differently from what it did before. Thus the sun has a power to make wax white, and fire to make lead fluid. These are usually called powers.

The first of these, as has been said, I think may be properly called real, original, or primary qualities; because they are in the things themselves, whether they are perceived or not: and upon their different modifications it is that the secondary qualities depend.

The other two are only powers to act differently upon other things: which powers result from the different modifications of those primary qualities.

2:12. Of Complex Ideas

After covering our simple ideas, Locke explains how we build complex ideas from our simple ones. As noted, we receive simple ideas automatically, or, in Locke's terms, "passively." The creation of complex ideas, however, requires an active effort on our part. Complex ideas are created through three distinct mental acts: combining, comparing, and abstracting.

1. Made by the Mind out of Simple Ones. We have hitherto considered those ideas, in the reception whereof the mind is only passive, which are those simple ones received from sensation and reflection before mentioned, whereof the mind cannot make one to itself, nor have any idea which does not wholly consist of them. But as the mind is wholly passive in the reception of all its simple ideas, so it exerts several acts of its own, whereby out of its simple ideas, as the materials and foundations of the rest, the others are framed. The acts of the mind, wherein it exerts its power over its simple ideas, are chiefly these three: (1) Combining several simple ideas into one compound one; and thus all complex ideas are made. (2) The second is bringing two ideas, whether simple or complex, together, and setting them by one another, so as to take a view of them at once, without uniting them into one; by which way it gets all its ideas of relations. (3) The third is separating them from all other ideas that accompany them in their real existence: this is called abstraction: and thus all its general ideas are made. This shows man's power, and its ways of operation, to be much the same in the material and intellectual world. For the materials in both being such as he has no power over, either to make or destroy, all that man can do is either to unite them together, or to set them by one another, or wholly separate them. I shall here begin with the first of these in the consideration of complex ideas, and come to the other two in their due places. As simple ideas are observed to exist in several combinations united together, so the mind has a power to consider several of them united together as one idea; and that not only as they are united in external objects, but as itself has joined them together. Ideas thus made up of several simple ones put together, I call complex;— such as are beauty, gratitude, a man, an army, the universe; which, though complicated of various simple ideas, or complex ideas made up of simple ones, yet are, when the mind pleases, considered each by itself, as one entire thing, and signified by one name.

ASK YOURSELF

8.37. Give some of Locke's examples of complex ideas.

Of the three ways of creating complex ideas, Locke first focuses on the method of combining two or more ideas together.

2. Made Voluntarily. In this faculty of repeating and joining together its ideas, the mind has great power in varying and multiplying the objects of its thoughts, infinitely beyond what sensation or reflection furnished it with: but all this still confined to those simple ideas which it received from those two sources, and which are the ultimate materials of all its compositions. For simple ideas are all from things themselves, and of these the mind can have no more, nor other than what are suggested to it. It can have no other ideas of sensible qualities than what come from without by the senses; nor any ideas of other kind of operations of a thinking substance, than what it finds in itself. But when it has once got these simple ideas, it is not confined barely to observation, and what offers itself from without; it can, by its own power, put together those ideas it has, and make new complex ones, which it never received so united.

 ASK YOURSELF

8.38. To what are our complex ideas confined?

As we create complex ideas, they all fall into one of three categories: modes, substances, or relations. Locke briefly considers each of these. For Locke, modes are complex properties that cannot exist by themselves but must inhere in some substance. For example, the mode "triangularity" is a property of a two-dimensional plane. The mode "gratitude" is a property that a person exhibits.

3. Complex Ideas Are Either of Modes, Substances, or Relations. Complex ideas, however compounded and decompounded, though their number be infinite, and the variety endless, wherewith they fill and entertain the thoughts of men; yet I think they may be all reduced under these three heads:—1. *modes*. 2. *substances*. 3. *relations*.

4. Ideas of Modes. First, Modes I call such complex ideas which, however compounded, contain not in them the supposition of subsisting by themselves, but are considered as dependences on, or affections of substances;—such as are the ideas signified by the words triangle, gratitude, murder, &c. And if in this I use the word mode in somewhat a different sense from its ordinary signification, I beg pardon; it being unavoidable in discourses, differing from the ordinary received notions, either to make new words, or to use old words in somewhat a new signification; the later whereof, in our present case, is perhaps the more tolerable of the two.

5. Simple and Mixed Modes of Simple Ideas. Of these modes, there are two sorts which deserve distinct consideration:

First, there are some which are only variations, or different combinations of the same simple idea, without the mixture of any other;—as a dozen, or score; which are nothing but the ideas of so many distinct units added together, and these I call simple modes as being contained within the bounds of one simple idea.

Secondly, there are others compounded of simple ideas of several kinds, put together to make one complex one;—v.g. beauty, consisting of a certain composition of color and figure, causing delight to the beholder; theft, which being the concealed change of the possession of anything, without the consent of the proprietor, contains, as is visible, a combination of several ideas of several kinds: and these I call mixed modes.

 ASK YOURSELF

8.39. Give some of Locke's examples of both simple and mixed modes.

Later in Book 2 (not included here) Locke discusses how we arrive at complex ideas of several philosophically important modes. Such simple modes include space, duration, number, infinity, motion, various emotions, and the power of one's will. Locke continues describing the second type of complex idea: substance. Unlike modes, substances are complex ideas of things that can exist by themselves, such as a rock or a person. Each substance gets its characteristics from the modes attached to the substance, such as a marbled rock or a grateful person.

6. Ideas of Substances, Single or Collective. Secondly, the ideas of Substances are such combinations of simple ideas as are taken to represent distinct particular things subsisting by themselves; the supposed or confused idea of substance, such as it is, is always the first and chief. Thus if to substance be joined the simple idea of a certain dull whitish color, with certain degrees of weight, hardness, ductility, and fusibility, we have the idea of lead; and a combination of the ideas of a certain sort of figure, with the powers of motion, thought and reasoning, joined to substance, the ordinary idea of a man. Now of substances also, there are two sorts of ideas:—one of single substances, as they exist separately, as of a man or a sheep; the other of several of those put together, as an army of men, or flock of sheep—which collective ideas of several substances thus put together are as much each of them one single idea as that of a man or an unit.

 ASK YOURSELF

8.40. Locke distinguishes between single substances and collective substances. Give one of Locke's examples of each.

Locke turns to the third and final type of complex idea, namely, relations. Later in Book 2 (not included here) Locke discusses several philosophically important relations, including cause and effect, identity and diversity, and moral relations. Locke concludes this chapter by noting that even the most detailed of our complex ideas ultimately reduce to combinations of simple ideas of sensation and reflection.

7. Ideas of Relation. Thirdly, the last sort of complex ideas is that we call Relation, which consists in the consideration and comparing one idea with another.

Of these several kinds we shall treat in their order.

8. The Abstrusest Ideas We Can Have Are All from Two Sources. If we trace the progress of our minds, and with attention observe how it repeats, adds together, and unites its simple ideas received from sensation or reflection, it will lead us further than at first perhaps we should have imagined. And, I believe, we shall find, if we warily observe the originals of our notions, that even the most abstruse ideas, how remote soever they may seem from sense, or from any operations of our own minds, are yet only such as the understanding frames to itself, by repeating and joining together ideas that it had either from objects of sense, or from its own operations about them: so that those even large and abstract ideas are derived from sensation or reflection, being no other than what the mind, by the ordinary use of its own faculties, employed about ideas received from objects of sense, or from the operations it observes in itself about them, may, and does, attain unto. . . .

The remaining two hundred pages of Book 2 analyze the aforementioned complex ideas of modes, substance, and relation. In Book 3 of the *Essay* Locke discusses the nature of words and language and how they denote our various ideas. In Book 4, the final book of the *Essay*, Locke describes the scope of human knowledge, noting the things we are both capable and incapable of knowing.

4:3. Of the Extent of Human Knowledge

At the outset of Book 4 Locke defines knowledge as "the perception of the connection and agreement, or disagreement and repugnancy of any of our ideas." More precisely, we know that a particular proposition is true when our ideas surrounding that proposition agree or disagree with each other. There are four ways ideas can agree or disagree with each other. Most basically, we know that our ideas have identity insofar as each idea agrees with itself. For example, we know that yellow is yellow, or that yellow is not blue. Secondly, we know whether two distinct ideas are similar or different insofar as they agree with each other. For example, we know that "two triangles upon equal basis, between two parallels are equal." Thirdly, we know something about an object X whenever the idea of X is always accompanied by a second idea about a property of X. For example, we know that gold is never consumed by fire. This means that our idea of gold is always accompanied by a second idea that it is never consumed by fire. Finally, we know that an object exists whenever our idea of that object agrees with the object itself. For example, I know that my car exists if my idea of my car agrees with reality. Locke explains that we have varying degrees of knowledge depending on how evident the agreement or disagreement is. In view of his concept of knowledge, Locke argues that knowledge is initially confined to our ideas. Additionally, however, knowledge is restricted by the degree to which the agreement or disagreement is evident.

From LOCKE: *Essay,* Book 4

1. Extent of Our Knowledge. Knowledge, as has been said, lying in the perception of the agreement or disagreement of any of our ideas, it follows from hence That,

It extends no further than we have ideas. First, we can have knowledge no further than we have ideas.

2. It Extends No Further Than We Can Perceive Their Agreement or Disagreement. Secondly, That we can have no knowledge further than we can have perception of that agreement or disagreement. Which perception being: 1. Either by intuition, or the immediate comparing any two ideas; or, 2. By reason, examining the agreement or disagreement of two ideas, by the intervention of some others; or, 3. By sensation, perceiving the existence of particular things: hence it also follows. . . .

 ASK YOURSELF

8.41. What are the three ways in which we can confirm agreement or disagreement of our various ideas?

Each of these three avenues to knowledge involve additional restrictions. That is, intuition, reason, and sensation each applies only to its own special class of ideas.

3. Intuitive Knowledge Extends Itself Not to All the Relations of All Our Ideas. Thirdly, That we cannot have an intuitive knowledge that shall extend itself to all our ideas, and all that we would know about them; because we cannot examine and perceive all the relations they have one to another, by juxta-position, or an immediate comparison one with another. Thus, having the ideas of an obtuse and an acute angled triangle, both drawn from equal bases, and between parallels, I can, by intuitive knowledge, perceive the one not to be the other, but cannot that way know whether they be equal or no; because their agreement or disagreement in equality can never be perceived by an immediate comparing them: the difference of figure makes their parts incapable of an exact immediate application; and therefore there is need of some intervening qualities to measure them by, which is demonstration, or rational knowledge.

4. Nor Does Demonstrative Knowledge. Fourthly, It follows, also, from what is above observed, that our rational knowledge cannot reach to the whole extent of our ideas: because between two different ideas we would examine, we cannot always find such mediums as we can connect one to another with an intuitive knowledge in all the parts of the deduction; and wherever that fails, we come short of knowledge and demonstration.

5. Sensitive Knowledge Narrower Than Either. Fifthly, Sensitive knowledge reaching no further than the existence of things actually present to our senses, is yet much narrower than either of the former.

ASK YOURSELF

8.42. Under what conditions will we fail to have knowledge through intuition?

8.43. Under what conditions will we fail to have knowledge through demonstration?

8.44. Under what conditions will we fail to have knowledge through the senses?

Given the all of these limitations on knowledge, Locke concludes that many of our ideas can never be confirmed. This means that the range of our knowledge is far more narrow than the range of our ideas.

6. Our Knowledge, Therefore, Narrower Than Our Ideas. Sixthly, From all which it is evident, that the extent of our knowledge comes not only short of the reality of things, but even of the extent of our own ideas. Though our knowledge be limited to our ideas, and cannot exceed them either in extent or perfection; and though these be very narrow bounds, in respect of the extent of All-being, and far short of what we may justly imagine to be in some even created understandings, not tied down to the dull and narrow information that is to be received from some few, and not very acute, ways of perception, such as are our senses; yet it would be well with us if our knowledge were but as large as our ideas, and there were not many doubts and inquiries concerning the ideas we have, whereof we are not, nor I believe ever shall be in this world resolved. . . .

4.9. Of Our Threefold Knowledge of Existence

In view of these three general methods of gaining knowledge (intuition, demonstration, and sensation), Locke explores three corresponding areas of knowledge we have of existing things. They are knowledge of oneself (through intuition), knowledge of God (through demonstration), and knowledge of external objects (through sensation).

2. A Threefold Knowledge of Existence. . . . let us proceed now to inquire concerning our knowledge of the existence of things, and how we come by it. I say, then, that we have the knowledge of our own existence by intuition; of the existence of God by demonstration; and of other things by sensation.

3. Our Knowledge of Our Own Existence Is Intuitive. As for our own existence, we perceive it so plainly and so certainly, that it neither needs nor is capable of any proof. For nothing can be more evident to us than our own existence. I think, I reason, I feel pleasure and pain: can any of these be more evident to me than my own existence? If I doubt of all other things, that very doubt makes me perceive my own existence, and will not suffer me to doubt of that. For if I know I feel pain, it is evident I have as certain perception of my own existence, as of the existence of the pain I feel: or if

I know I doubt, I have as certain perception of the existence of the thing doubting, as of that thought which I call doubt. Experience then convinces us, that we have an intuitive knowledge of our own existence, and an internal infallible perception that we are. In every act of sensation, reasoning, or thinking, we are conscious to ourselves of our own being; and, in this matter, come not short of the highest degree of certainty.

 ASK YOURSELF

8.45. List the kinds of internal experiences that immediately inform us as to our own existence.

For Locke, knowledge of God is arrived at through demonstration, in particular, through a cosmological-type argument for God's existence:

    a. The existence we see around us is finite.

    b. Finite existences cannot come from nothing.

    c. Therefore, there exists an eternal being that is responsible for finite existence.

Locke argues further that the power we see in finite objects must also derive from this greater eternal source. God must also be an immaterial mind since (1) human cognition is an immaterial (or spiritual) activity and (2) a material thing cannot create an immaterial thing. Locke turns next to our knowledge of external objects.

4.11. Of Our Knowledge of the Existence of Other Things

For Locke, simply having a mental picture of a thing, such as the idea of my car, doesn't guarantee that the thing actually exists. I am only justified in inferring the existence of my car if I have a sensory perception of it.

1. Knowledge of the Existence of Other Finite Beings Is to Be Had Only by Actual Sensation. The knowledge of our own being we have by intuition. The existence of a God, reason clearly makes known to us, as has been shown.

The knowledge of the existence of any other thing we can have only by sensation: for there being no necessary connection of real existence with any idea a man hath in his memory; nor of any other existence but that of God with the existence of any particular man: no particular man can know the existence of any other being, but only when, by actual operating upon him, it makes itself perceived by him. For, the having the idea of anything in our mind, no more proves the existence of that thing, than the picture of a man evidences his being in the world, or the visions of a dream make thereby a true history.

2. Instance: Whiteness of This Paper. It is therefore the actual receiving of ideas from without that gives us notice of the existence of other things, and makes us know, that something doth exist at that time without us, which causes that idea in us; though perhaps we neither know nor consider how it does it. For it takes not from the certainty of our senses, and the ideas we receive by them, that we know not the manner wherein they are produced: v.g. whilst I write this, I have, by the paper affecting my eyes, that idea produced in my mind, which, whatever object causes, I call white; by which I know that that quality or accident (i.e. whose appearance before my eyes always causes that idea) doth really exist, and hath a being without me. And of this, the greatest assurance I can possibly have, and to which my faculties can attain, is the testimony of my eyes, which are the proper and sole judges of this thing; whose testimony I have reason to rely on as so certain, that I can no more doubt, whilst I write this, that I see white and black, and that something really exists that causes that sensation in me, than that I write or move my hand; which is a certainty as great as human nature is capable of, concerning the existence of anything, but a man's self alone, and of God.

3. *This Notice by Our Senses, though Not So Certain as Demonstration, yet May Be Called Knowledge, and Proves the Existence of Things without Us.* The notice we have by our senses of the existing of things without us, though it be not altogether so certain as our intuitive knowledge, or the deductions of our reason employed about the clear abstract ideas of our own minds; yet it is an assurance that deserves the name of knowledge. If we persuade ourselves that our faculties act and inform us right concerning the existence of those objects that affect them, it cannot pass for an ill-grounded confidence: for I think nobody can, in earnest, be so skeptical as to be uncertain of the existence of those things which he sees and feels. . . .

 ASK YOURSELF

8.46. What proof does Locke have that the white paper that appears before him actually exists?

8.47. What does Locke imply about the possibility of skepticism?

Thus, the testimony of our senses gives us confidence in the existence of external material things. However, this poses a problem for our knowledge of external *spiritual* entities whose existence we do not perceive through our senses.

12. *The Existence of Other Finite Spirits Not Knowable, and Rests on Faith.* What ideas we have of spirits, and how we come by them, I have already shown. But though we have those ideas in our minds, and know we have them there, the having the ideas of spirits does not make us know that any such things do exist without us, or that there are any finite spirits, or any other spiritual beings, but the Eternal God. We have ground from revelation, and several other reasons, to believe with assurance that there are such creatures: but our senses not being able to discover them, we want the means of knowing their particular existences. For we can no more know that there are finite spirits really existing, by the idea we have of such beings in our minds, than by the ideas any one has of fairies or centaurs, he can come to know that things answering those ideas do really exist.

And therefore concerning the existence of finite spirits, as well as several other things, we must content ourselves with the evidence of faith; but universal, certain propositions concerning this matter are beyond our reach. For however true it may be, v.g., that all the intelligent spirits that God ever created do still exist, yet it can never make a part of our certain knowledge. These and the like propositions we may assent to, as highly probable, but are not, I fear, in this state capable of knowing. We are not, then, to put others upon demonstrating, nor ourselves upon search of universal certainty in all those matters; wherein we are not capable of any other knowledge, but what our senses give us in this or that particular.

 ASK YOURSELF

8.48. What is the ground we have in believing in the existence of immaterial beings such as angels?

8.49. What should our attitude be concerning the existence of such immaterial beings?

GEORGE BERKELEY

The second great philosopher in the school of British Empiricism was George Berkeley (1685–1753), an Irish minister and, later in his life, Bishop of Cloyne. Berkeley was born at Dysert Castle, Ireland. He was a student at Trinity College, Dublin, where he later held various teaching and admininstrative offices. Berkeley's most important philosophical writings appeared before he turned thirty. The underlying theme of even his earliest writings is idealism: Nothing, including material objects, exists apart from perception. Berkeley kept a scrapbook of his reflections while in college, and in it he writes that only persons exist: "All other things are not so much existences as manners of the existence of persons." In his first publication, *An Essay towards a New Theory of Vision* (1709), he did not openly announce his idealism. The work addresses a single problem, which is the relation between the ideas we have from vision and those we acquire through touch. A problem was originally proposed by William Molyneux to Locke: Suppose a person who was blind from birth suddenly gained eyesight; from sight alone, would he be able to recognize objects that he previously knew only through touch? Molyneux and Locke thought the person would not be able to recognize the objects. Berkeley agrees, but for a different reason: "The objects of sight and touch make . . . two sets of ideas which are widely different from each other. . . . A person born blind, being made to see, would at first have no idea of distance by sight: the sun and stars, the remotest objects as well as the nearer, would all seem to be in his eye, or rather in his mind."

The next year Berkeley published his *Treatise concerning the Principles of Human Knowledge* (1710); shortly after he produced a more popular account of the same material in *Three Dialogues between Hylas and Philonous* (1713). These works present the theory of idealism for which he is best remembered. According to Berkeley, the only things that exist are minds and the ideas of those minds. Material objects do not exist, and the things we call "external objects" are ultimately collections of ideas and sensations. Thus, to be is to be perceived (*esse is percipi*). Although Berkeley denied the existence of material objects, he is nevertheless an Empiricist. Like Locke, Berkeley denied innate ideas and argued that all ideas derive from sensory impressions.

For Berkeley, however, the ultimate source of external sensory impressions is not material objects (as Locke supposed); instead, our bodiless minds receive external sensory input directly from God. The selections in this section are from the *Dialogues*. In this work, Berkeley presents a three-day discussion in three dialogues between two characters: Philonous and Hylas. Philonous, the mouthpiece of Berkeley, defends idealism, and Hylas initially defends the existence of matter.

Dialogue One

The first Dialogue opens with describing how Hylas could not sleep well the previous night since the evening before he was in a discussion with philosophers about those who deny the existence of matter (particularly Philonous). Hylas believes such a view is dangerous skepticism. He meets with Philonous early in the morning and they discuss this issue. Philonous also believes that skepticism is dangerous, but denies that his rejection of material existence is skeptical. For, by denying matter, one does not necessarily deny sensible things.

Definition of "Sensible Thing."   The key to Berkeley's argument is the definition of a "sensible thing": a thing perceived immediately by the senses, excluding any possible cause of that sensible thing.

 From BERKELEY: *"Dialogue 1"*

PHIL.   This point then is agreed between us—That *sensible things are those only which are immediately perceived by sense*. You will farther inform me, whether we immediately perceive by sight anything beside light, and colors, and figures; or by hearing, anything but sounds; by the palate, anything beside tastes; by the smell, beside odours; or by the touch, more than tangible qualities.

HYL.   We do not.

PHIL.   It seems, therefore, that if you take away all sensible qualities, there remains nothing sensible?

HYL.   I grant it.

PHIL.   Sensible things therefore are nothing else but so many sensible qualities, or combinations of sensible qualities?

HYL.   Nothing else.

PHIL.   *Heat* then is a sensible thing?

HYL.   Certainly.

PHIL.   Doth the *reality* of sensible things consist in being perceived? Or, is it something distinct from their being perceived, and that bears no relation to the mind?

HYL.   To *exist* is one thing, and to be *perceived* is another.

PHIL.   I speak with regard to sensible things only. And of these I ask, whether by their real existence you mean a subsistence exterior to the mind, and distinct from their being perceived?

ASK YOURSELF

8.50. For Philonous, what does the reality of sensible things consist in?

Secondary Qualities of Heat in Sensible Things. Most of the first Dialogue shows that all primary and secondary qualities of sensible things exist only in the mind of the perceiver. Berkeley begins by making his case with secondary qualities: tactile qualities (heat, warmth, coldness), tastes (bitterness, sweetness), smells, sounds, and colors. Even Locke maintained that secondary qualities are spectator dependent. Nevertheless, at this stage of the Dialogue, Hylas resists ascribing secondary qualities to the perceiver.

PHIL.   Is it not an absurdity to think that the same thing should be at the same time both cold and warm?

HYL.   It is.

PHIL.   Suppose now one of your hands hot, and the other cold, and that they are both at once put into the same vessel of water, in an intermediate state; will not the water seem cold to one hand, and warm to the other?

HYL.   It will.

PHIL.   Ought we not therefore, by your principles, to conclude it is really both cold and warm at the same time, that is, according to your own concession, to believe an absurdity?

HYL.   I confess it seems so.

PHIL.   Consequently, the principles themselves are false, since you have granted that no true principle leads to an absurdity.

 ASK YOURSELF

8.51. Suppose we place a hot and cold hand in the same warm water. What does this show about the quality of coldness and warmth?

HYL.   But, after all, can anything be more absurd than to say, *there is no heat in the fire*?

PHIL.   To make the point still clearer; tell me whether, in two cases exactly alike, we ought not to make the same judgment?

HYL.   We ought.

PHIL.   When a pin pricks your finger, doth it not rend and divide the fibres of your flesh?

HYL.   It doth.

PHIL.   And when a coal burns your finger, doth it any more?

HYL.   It doth not.

PHIL.   Since, therefore, you neither judge the sensation itself occasioned by the pin, nor anything like it to be in the pin; you should not, conformably to what you have now granted, judge the sensation occasioned by the fire, or anything like it, to be in the fire.

HYL.   Well, since it must be so, I am content to yield this point, and acknowledge that heat and cold are only sensations existing in our minds. But there still remain qualities enough to secure the reality of external things.

 ASK YOURSELF

8.52. Where does painful feeling produced by a sharp pin reside?

Secondary Qualities of Sound in Sensible Things. As to sounds, Hylas argues that sound qualities in themselves are external air motions, but to us they register differently through our ears.

PHIL.   Then as to *sounds*, what must we think of them: are they accidents really inherent in external bodies, or not?

HYL.   That they inhere not in the sonorous bodies is plain from hence: because a bell struck in the exhausted receiver of an air-pump sends forth no sound. The air, therefore, must be thought the subject of sound.

PHIL.   What reason is there for that, Hylas?

HYL.   Because, when any motion is raised in the air, we perceive a sound greater or lesser, according to the air's motion; but without some motion in the air, we never hear any sound at all.

PHIL.   And granting that we never hear a sound but when some motion is produced in the air, yet I do not see how you can infer from thence, that the sound itself is in the air.

HYL.   It is this very motion in the external air that produces in the mind the sensation of *sound*. For, striking on the drum of the ear, it causeth a vibration, which by the auditory nerves being communicated to the brain, the soul is thereupon affected with the sensation called *sound*.

PHIL.   What! Is sound then a sensation?

HYL.   I tell you, as perceived by us, it is a particular sensation in the mind.

PHIL.   And can any sensation exist without the mind?

HYL.   No, certainly.

PHIL.   How then can sound, being a sensation, exist in the air, if by the *air* you mean a senseless substance existing without the mind?

HYL.   You must distinguish, Philonous, between sound as it is perceived by us, and as it is in itself; or (which is the same thing) between the sound we immediately perceive, and that which exists without us. The former, indeed, is a particular kind of sensation, but the latter is merely a vibrative or undulatory motion the air.

PHIL.   I thought I had already obviated that distinction, by answer I gave when you were applying it in a like case before. But, to say no more of that, are you sure then that sound is really nothing but motion?

HYL.   I am.

PHIL.   Whatever therefore agrees to real sound, may with truth be attributed to motion?

HYL.   It may.

PHIL.   It is then good sense to speak of *motion* as of a thing that is *loud, sweet, acute, or grave.*

 ASK YOURSELF

8.53. For Philonous, why can't we reduce sounds to external motions of the air?

Primary Qualities of Extension in Sensible Things. Having shown that secondary qualities are spectator dependent, Berkeley turns next to primary qualities that, according to Galileo, Descartes, and Locke, reside in the objects themselves. The key primary qualities include extension (the property of occupying space), motion, solidity, and time. As to extension, Philonous argues that the same object appears to have different extension, depending on the size of the perceiver.

PHIL.   But what if the same arguments which are brought against Secondary Qualities will hold good against these also?

HYL.   Why then I shall be obliged to think, they too exist only in the mind.

PHIL.   Is it your opinion the very figure and extension which you perceive by sense exist in the outward object or material substance?

HYL.   It is.

PHIL.   Have all other animals as good grounds to think the same of the figure and extension which they see and feel?

HYL.   Without doubt, if they have any thought at all.

PHIL.   Answer me, Hylas. Think you the senses were bestowed upon all animals for their preservation and well-being in life? Or were they given to men alone for this end?

HYL.   I make no question but they have the same use in all other animals.

PHIL.   If so, is it not necessary they should be enabled by them to perceive their own limbs, and those bodies which are capable of harming them?

HYL.   Certainly.

PHIL.   A mite therefore must be supposed to see his own foot, and things equal or even less than it, as bodies of some considerable dimension; though at the same time they appear to you scarce discernible, or at best as so many visible points?

HYL.   I cannot deny it.

PHIL.   And to creatures less than the mite they will seem yet larger?

HYL.   They will.

PHIL.   Insomuch that what you can hardly discern will to another extremely minute animal appear as some huge mountain?

HYL.   All this I grant.

PHIL.   Can one and the same thing be at the same time in itself of different dimensions?

HYL.   That were absurd to imagine.

PHIL.   But, from what you have laid down it follows that both the extension by you perceived, and that perceived by the mite itself, as likewise all those perceived by lesser animals, are each of them the true extension of the mite's foot; that is to say, by your own principles you are led into an absurdity.

HYL.   There seems to be some difficulty in the point.

PHIL.   Again, have you not acknowledged that no real inherent property of any object can be changed without some change in the thing itself?

HYL.   I have.

PHIL.   But, as we approach to or recede from an object, the visible extension varies, being at one distance ten or a hundred times greater than another. Doth it not therefore follow from hence likewise that it is not really inherent in the object?

HYL.   I own I am at a loss what to think.

PHIL.   Your judgment will soon be determined, if you will venture to think as freely concerning this quality as you have done concerning the rest. Was it not admitted as a good argument, that neither heat nor cold was in the water, because it seemed warm to one hand and cold to the other?

HYL.   It was.

PHIL.   Is it not the very same reasoning to conclude, there is no extension or figure in an object, because to one eye it shall seem little, smooth, and round, when at the same time it appears to the other, great, uneven, and regular?

HYL.   The very same. But does this latter fact ever happen?

PHIL.   You may at any time make the experiment, by looking with one eye bare, and with the other through a microscope.

 ASK YOURSELF

8.54. What examples does Philonous give to show that an object's extension is only a matter of the spectator's perspective?

HYL.   I know not how to maintain it; and yet I am loath to give up *extension*, I see so many odd consequences following upon such a concession.

PHIL.   Odd, say you? After the concessions already made, I hope you will stick at nothing for its oddness. But, on the other hand, should it not seem very odd, if the general reasoning which includes all other sensible qualities did not also include extension? If it be allowed that no idea, nor anything like an idea, can exist in an unperceiving substance, then surely it follows that no figure, or mode of extension, which we can either perceive, or imagine, or have any idea of, can be really inherent in Matter; not to mention the peculiar difficulty there must be in conceiving a material substance, prior to and distinct from extension to be the *substratum* of extension. Be the sensible quality what it will—figure, or sound, or color, it seems alike impossible it should subsist in that which doth not perceive it.

HYL.   I give up the point for the present, reserving still a right to retract my opinion, in case I shall hereafter discover any false step in my progress to it.

 ASK YOURSELF

8.55. For Philonous, where does the mode of extension reside?

Primary Qualities of Motion in Sensible Things. Philonous continues making his case concerning primary qualities of motion. These, too, are spectator dependent. His argument is as follows:

> a. A rapid motion involves the passing of an object through space in a given amount of time.
>
> b. Time is measured by the succession of ideas in our mind, which varies.
>
> c. One motion may be perceived as rapid or slow.
>
> d. Therefore, the quality of motion is not inherent in the object.

PHIL.   That is a right you cannot be denied. Figures and extension being despatched, we proceed next to *motion*. Can a real motion in any external body be at the same time very swift and very slow?

HYL.   It cannot.

PHIL.   Is not the motion of a body swift in a reciprocal proportion to the time it takes up in describing any given space? Thus a body that describes a mile in an hour moves three times faster than it would in case it described only a mile in three hours.

HYL.   I agree with you.

PHIL.   And is not time measured by the succession of ideas in our minds?

HYL.   It is.

PHIL.   And is it not possible ideas should succeed one another twice as fast in your mind as they do in mine, or in that of some spirit of another kind?

HYL.   I own it.

PHIL.   Consequently the same body may to another seem to perform its motion over any space in half the time that it doth to you. And the same reasoning will hold as to any other proportion: that is to say, according to your principles (since the motions perceived are both really in the object) it is possible one and the same body shall be really moved the same way at once, both very swift and very slow. How is this consistent either with common sense, or with what you just now granted?

HYL.   I have nothing to say to it.

 ASK YOURSELF

8.56. A moving object appears to be moving at different speeds by different people. For Philonous, what is wrong (or inconsistent) with saying that the same object moves at different speeds?

Primary Qualities of Solidity in Sensible Things.   The final primary quality considered by Philonous is solidity.

PHIL.   Then as for *solidity*; either you do not mean any sensible quality by that word, and so it is beside our inquiry: or if you do, it must be either hardness or resistance. But both the one and the other are plainly relative to our senses: it being evident that what seems hard to one animal may appear soft to another, who hath greater force and firmness of limbs. Nor is it less plain that the resistance I feel is not in the body.

HYL.   I own the very *sensation* of resistance, which is all you immediately perceive, is not in the body; but the *cause* of that sensation is.

PHIL.   But the causes of our sensations are not things immediately perceived, and therefore are not sensible. This point I thought had been already determined.

HYL.   I own it was; but you will pardon me if I seem a little embarrassed: I know not how to quit my old notions.

PHIL.   To help you out, do but consider that if *extension* be once acknowledged to have no existence without the mind, the same must necessarily be granted of motion, solidity, and gravity; since they all evidently suppose extension. It is therefore superfluous to inquire particularly concerning each of them. In denying extension, you have denied them all to have any real existence.

 ASK YOURSELF

8.57. According to Philonous, what must the notion of solidity mean?

Hylas next questions why is there a distinction made between primary and secondary qualities if both exist only in one's mind.

HYL.   I wonder, Philonous, if what you say be true, why those philosophers who deny the Secondary Qualities any real existence should yet attribute it to the Primary. If there is no difference between them, how can this be accounted for?

PHIL.   It is not my business to account for every opinion of the philosophers. But, among other reasons which may be assigned for this, it seems probable that pleasure and pain being rather annexed to the former than the latter may be one. Heat and cold, tastes and smells, have something more vividly pleasing or disagreeable than the ideas of extension, figure, and motion affect us with. And, it being too visibly absurd to hold that pain or pleasure can be in an unperceiving substance, men are more easily weaned from believing the external existence of the Secondary than the Primary Qualities. You will be satisfied there is something in this, if you recollect the difference you made between an intense and more moderate degree of heat; allowing the one a real existence, while you denied it to the other. But, after all, there is no rational ground for that distinction; for, surely an indifferent sensation is as truly a sensation as one more pleasing or painful; and consequently should not any more than they be supposed to exist in an unthinking subject.

 ASK YOURSELF

8.58. According to Philonous, why do philosophers distinguish between primary and secondary qualities considering that they are both spectator dependent?

Perhaps We Get Sensible Extension through Abstraction. In the final portion of the first Dialogue, Hylas offers several theories attempting to rescue primary qualities from Philonous's idealism. In one argument Hylas says that abstraction is responsible for our notion of extension. Hylas distinguishes between two kinds of extension. Sensible extension is the space an object appears to have to us, and absolute extension is the space an object has in its abstraction.

HYL.   It is just come into my head, Philonous, that I have somewhere heard of a distinction between absolute and sensible extension. Now, though it be acknowledged that *great* and *small*, consisting merely in the relation which other extended beings have to the parts of our own bodies, do not really inhere in the substances themselves; yet nothing obliges us to hold the same with regard to *absolute extension*, which is something abstracted from *great* and *small*, from this or that particular magnitude or figure. So likewise as to motion; *swift* and *slow* are altogether relative to the succession of ideas in our own minds. But, it doth not follow, because those modifications of motion exist not without the mind, that therefore absolute motion abstracted from them doth not.

PHIL.   Pray what is it that distinguishes one motion, or one part of extension, from another? Is it not something sensible, as some degree of swiftness or slowness, some certain magnitude or figure peculiar to each?

HYL.   I think so.

PHIL.   These qualities, therefore, stripped of all sensible properties, are without all specific and numerical differences, as the schools call them.

HYL.   They are.

PHIL.   That is to say, they are extension in general, and motion in general.

HYL.   Let it be so.

PHIL.   But it is a universally received maxim that *Everything which exists is particular*. How then can motion in general, or extension in general, exist in any corporeal substance?

HYL.   I will take time to solve your difficulty.

PHIL.   But I think the point may be speedily decided. Without doubt you can tell whether you are able to frame this or that idea. Now I am content to put our dispute on this issue. If you can frame in your thoughts a distinct *abstract idea* of motion or extension, divested of all those sensible modes, as swift and slow, great and small, round and square, and the like, which are acknowledged to exist only in the mind, I will then yield the point you contend for. But if you cannot, it will be unreasonable on your side to insist any longer upon what you have no notion of.

HYL.   To confess ingenuously, I cannot.

 ASK YOURSELF

8.59. How does Philonous explain the phenomenon of mental abstraction?

Thus, there is no idea of absolute extension apart from sensible extension. Hylas considers other theories that might explain matter.

Perhaps There Is a Material Substratum.   Hylas next tries to rescue the notion of matter by appealing to the Aristotelian concept of *material substratum.*

HYL.   . . . but then, on the other hand, when I look on sensible things in a different view, considering them as so many modes and qualities, I find it necessary to suppose a *material substratum*, without which they cannot be conceived to exist.

PHIL.   *Material substratum* call you it? Pray, by which of your senses came you acquainted with that being?

HYL.   It is not itself sensible; its modes and qualities only being perceived by the senses.

PHIL.   I presume then it was by reflection and reason you obtained the idea of it?

HYL.   I do not pretend to any proper positive *idea* of it. However, I conclude it exists, because qualities cannot be conceived to exist without a support.

PHIL.   It seems then you have only a relative *notion* of it, or that you conceive it not otherwise than by conceiving the relation it bears to sensible qualities?

HYL.   Right.

PHIL.   Be pleased therefore to let me know wherein that relation consists.

HYL.   Is it not sufficiently expressed in the term *substratum*, or *substance*?

 ASK YOURSELF

8.60. How does Hylas initially define "material substratum"?

When pressed, the notion of a material substratum amounts to a substance spread beneath its particular qualities. Philonous attacks this notion with the following argument: If matter is spread beneath all qualities, then such spreading requires extension. And extension is mentally dependent.

PHIL. If so, the word *substratum* should import that it is spread under the sensible qualities or accidents?

HYL. True.

PHIL. And consequently under extension?

HYL. I own it.

PHIL. It is therefore somewhat in its own nature entirely distinct from extension?

HYL. I tell you, extension is only a mode, and Matter is something that supports modes. And is it not evident the thing supported is different from the thing supporting?

PHIL. So that something distinct from, and exclusive of, extension is supposed to be the *substratum* of extension?

HYL. Just so.

PHIL. Answer me, Hylas. Can a thing be spread without extension? Or is not the idea of extension necessarily included in *spreading*?

HYL. It is.

PHIL. Whatsoever therefore you suppose spread under anything must have in itself an extension distinct from the extension of that thing under which it is spread?

HYL. It must.

PHIL. Consequently, every corporeal substance, being the *substratum* of extension, must have in itself another extension, by which it is qualified to be a *substratum*: and so on to infinity. And I ask whether this be not absurd in itself, and repugnant to what you granted just now, to wit, that the *substratum* was something distinct from and exclusive of extension?

 ASK YOURSELF

8.61. What is the infinite regress of substrata that Philonous describes here?

Philonous maintains that similar problems emerge for any metaphor used to describe the function of a substratum, such as spreading, supporting, or standing. After considering more rescue attempts by Hylas, Philonous concludes by briefly noting that matter does not exist, since it would be parasitic on primary qualities, but primary qualities exist only in the mind. This point is further developed in the next Dialogue.

Dialogue Two

The second Dialogue shows that matter, regardless of how it is described, does not exist. The clear implication of the rejection of matter is idealism, where only perceiving minds and perceptions (or ideas) exist.

Proof for God's Existence. Philonous begins the second Dialogue with a causal-type proof for God's existence. When looking out in the world, it is intuitively clear that sensible objects exist apart from us, although they cannot exist apart from mind. It follows that there exists some all-perfect mind that continually perceives all sensible objects. This argument for God's existence is *not* based on the design of the perceived world, but only on the bare existence of the sensible world.

 From BERKELEY: *"Dialogue 2"* ————————

PHIL.   . . . To me it is evident for the reasons you allow of, that sensible things cannot exist otherwise than in a mind or spirit. Whence I conclude, not that they have no real existence, but that, seeing they depend not on my thought, and have all existence distinct from being perceived by me, *there must be some other Mind wherein they exist.* As sure, therefore, as the sensible world really exists, so sure is there an infinite omnipresent Spirit who contains and supports it.

HYL.   What! This is no more than I and all Christians hold; nay, and all others too who believe there is a God, and that He knows and comprehends all things.

PHIL.   Aye, but here lies the difference. Men commonly believe that all things are known or perceived by God, because they believe the being of a God; whereas I, on the other side, immediately and necessarily conclude the being of a God, because all sensible things must be perceived by Him.

HYL.   But, so long as we all believe the same thing, what matter is it how we come by that belief?

PHIL.   But neither do we agree in the same opinion. For philosophers, though they acknowledge all corporeal beings to be perceived by God, yet they attribute to them an absolute subsistence distinct from their being perceived by any mind whatever; which I do not. Besides, is there no difference between saying, *There is a God, therefore He perceives all things*; and saying, *Sensible things do really exist; and, if they really exist, they are necessarily perceived by an infinite Mind: therefore there is an infinite Mind or God*? This furnishes you with a direct and immediate demonstration, from a most evident principle, of the *being of a God*. Divines and philosophers had proved beyond all controversy, from the beauty and usefulness of the several parts of the creation, that it was the workmanship of God. But that—setting aside all help of astronomy and natural philosophy, all contemplation of the contrivance, order, and adjustment of things—an infinite Mind should be necessarily inferred from the bare *existence of the sensible world*, is an advantage to them only who have made this easy reflection: that the sensible world is that which we perceive by our several senses; and that nothing is perceived by the senses beside ideas; and that no idea or archetype of an idea can exist otherwise than in a mind. . . .

   ASK YOURSELF

8.62. According to Philonous, there are important differences between how most philosophers prove God's existence and his own proof. What is one such difference?

Perhaps We See All Things through God. Malebranche argued that God is responsible for providing human souls with ideas. Our immaterial souls cannot directly encounter or perceive material things. God, however, is pure spirit and can encounter both the material and the immaterial. Thus, we see all things through God. Philonous replies by using Ockham's razor: There is no real need for the external material world; hence the material world would be a useless creation.

HYL.   It cannot be denied there is something highly serviceable to religion in what you advance. But do you not think it looks very like a notion entertained by some eminent moderns, of *seeing all things in God*?

PHIL.   I would gladly know that opinion: pray explain it to me.

HYL.   They conceive that the soul, being immaterial, is incapable of being united with material things, so as to perceive them in themselves; but that she perceives them by her union with the substance of God, which, being spiritual, is therefore purely intelligible, or capable of being the immediate object of a spirit's thought. Besides the Divine essence contains in it perfections correspondent to each created being, and which are, for that reason, proper to exhibit or represent them to the mind.

ASK YOURSELF

8.63. According to Hylas, what is Malebranche's position?

PHIL.   I do not understand how our ideas, which are things altogether passive and inert, can be the essence, or any part (or like any part) of the essence or substance of God, who is an impassive, indivisible, pure, active being. Many more difficulties and objections there are which occur at first view against this hypothesis; but I shall only add that it is liable to all the absurdities of the common hypothesis, in making a created world exist otherwise than in the mind of a Spirit. Besides all which it hath this peculiar to itself; that it makes that material world serve to no purpose. And, if it pass for a good argument against other hypotheses in the sciences, that they suppose Nature, or the Divine wisdom, to make something in vain, or do that by tedious roundabout methods which might have been performed in a much more easy and compendious way, what shall we think of that hypothesis which supposes the whole world made in vain?

HYL.   But what say you? Are not you too of opinion that we see all things in God? If I mistake not, what you advance comes near it.

PHIL.   Few men think; yet all have opinions. Hence men's opinions are superficial and confused. It is nothing strange that tenets which in themselves are ever so different, should nevertheless be confounded with each other, by those who do not consider them attentively. I shall not therefore be surprised if some men imagine that I run into the enthusiasm of Malebranche; though in truth I am very remote from it. He builds on the most abstract general ideas, which I entirely disclaim. He asserts an absolute external world, which I deny. He maintains that we are deceived by our senses, and, know not the real natures or the true forms and figures of extended beings; of all which I hold the direct contrary. So that upon the whole there are no Principles more fundamentally opposite than his and mine. It must be owned that I entirely agree with what the holy Scripture saith, "That in God we live and move and have our being." But that we see things in His essence, after the manner above set forth, I am far from believing. Take here in brief my meaning:—It is evident that the things I perceive are my own ideas, and that no idea can exist unless it be in a mind: nor is it less plain that these ideas or things by me perceived, either themselves or their archetypes, exist independently of my mind, since I know myself not to be their author, it being out of my power to determine at pleasure what particular ideas I shall be affected with upon opening my eyes or ears: they must therefore exist in some other Mind, whose Will it is they should be exhibited to me. The things, I say, immediately perceived are ideas or sensations, call them which you will. But how can any idea or sensation exist in, or be produced by, anything but a mind or spirit? This indeed is inconceivable. And to assert that which is inconceivable is to talk nonsense: is it not?

HYL.   Without doubt.

 ASK YOURSELF

8.64. For Philonous, what are the key points of difference between his view and that of Malebranche?

PHIL.   But, on the other hand, it is very conceivable that they should exist in and be produced by a spirit; since this is no more than I daily experience in myself, inasmuch as I perceive numberless ideas; and, by an act of my will, can form a great variety of them, and raise them up in my imagination: though, it must be confessed, these creatures of the fancy are not altogether so distinct, so strong, vivid, and permanent, as those perceived by my senses—which latter are called *red things*. From all which I conclude, *there is a Mind which affects me every moment with all the sensible impressions I perceive. And*, from the variety, order, and manner of these, I conclude *the Author of them to be wise, powerful, and good, beyond comprehension.* Mark it well; I do not say, I see things by perceiving that which represents them in the intelligible Substance of God. This I do not understand; but I say, the things by me perceived are known by the understanding, and produced by the will of an infinite Spirit. And is not all this most plain and evident? Is there any more in it than what a little observation in our own minds, and that which passeth in them, not only enables us to conceive, but also obliges us to acknowledge?

 ASK YOURSELF

8.65. What "daily experiences" does Philonous have that confirm his view that sensations exist in and are produced by a mind or spirit?

Perhaps Matter Is an Instrument.   Hylas next contends that God uses matter as an instrument to cause our ideas. Philonous counters that this kind of instrument would be devoid of all sensible qualities, even extension. Hylas suggests that perhaps matter may be an instrument in a very general sense. Philonous criticizes that instruments are used only when there is a need, but God has no need.

HYL.   I give up the point entirely. But, though Matter may not be a cause, yet what hinders its being an *instrument*, subservient to the supreme Agent in the production of our ideas?

PHIL.   An instrument say you; pray what may be the figure, springs, wheels, and motions, of that instrument?

HYL.   Those I pretend to determine nothing of, both the substance and its qualities being entirely unknown to me.

PHIL.   What? You are then of opinion it is made up of unknown parts, that it hath unknown motions, and an unknown shape?

HYL.   I do not believe that it hath any figure or motion at all, being already convinced, that no sensible qualities can exist in an unperceiving substance.

PHIL.   But what notion is it possible to frame of an instrument void of all sensible qualities, even extension itself?

HYL.   I do not pretend to have any notion of it.

PHIL.   And what reason have you to think this unknown, this inconceivable Somewhat doth exist? Is it that you imagine God cannot act as well without it; or that you find by experience the use of some such thing, when you form ideas in your own mind?

HYL.   You are always teasing me for reasons of my belief. Pray what reasons have you not to believe it?

PHIL.   It is to me a sufficient reason not to believe the existence of anything, if I see no reason for believing it. But, not to insist on reasons for believing, you will not so much as let me know *what it is* you would have me believe; since you say you have no manner of notion of it. After all, let me entreat you to consider whether it be like a philosopher, or even like a man of common sense, to pretend to believe you know not what and you know not why.

HYL.   Hold, Philonous. When I tell you Matter is an *instrument*, I do not mean altogether nothing. It is true I know not the particular kind of instrument; but, however, I have some notion of *instrument in general*, which I apply to it.

PHIL.   But what if it should prove that there is something, even in the most general notion of *instrument*, as taken in a distinct sense from *cause*, which makes the use of it inconsistent with the Divine attributes?

HYL.   Make that appear and I shall give up the point.

PHIL.   What mean you by the general nature or notion of *instrument*?

HYL.   That which is common to all particular instruments composeth the general notion.

PHIL.   Is it not common to all instruments, that they are applied to the doing those things only which cannot be performed by the mere act of our wills? Thus, for instance, I never use an instrument to move my finger, because it is done by a volition.

But I should use one if I were to remove part of a rock, or tear up a tree by the roots. Are you of the same mind? Or, can you shew any example where an instrument is made use of in producing an effect *immediately* depending on the will of the agent?

 ASK YOURSELF

8.66. According to Hylas, what is involved in the notion of an "instrument"?

HYL.   I own I cannot.

PHIL.   How therefore can you suppose that an All-perfect Spirit, on whose Will all things have an absolute and immediate dependence, should need an instrument in his operations, or, not needing it, make use of it? Thus it seems to me that you are obliged to own the use of a lifeless inactive instrument to be incompatible with the infinite perfection of God; that is, by your own confession, to give up the point.

HYL.   It doth not readily occur what I can answer you.

PHIL.   But, methinks you should be ready to own the truth, when it has been fairly proved to you. We indeed, who are beings of finite powers, are forced to make use of instruments. And the use of an instrument sheweth the agent to be limited by rules of another's prescription, and that he cannot obtain his end but in such a way, and by such conditions. Whence it seems a clear consequence, that the supreme unlimited agent useth no tool or instrument at all. The will of an Omnipotent Spirit is no sooner exerted than executed, without the application of means; which, if they are employed by inferior agents, it is not upon account of any real efficacy that is in them, or necessary aptitude to produce any effect, but merely in compliance with the laws of nature, or those conditions prescribed to them by the First Cause, who is Himself above all limitation or prescription whatsoever.

 ASK YOURSELF

8.67. What kind of beings make use of instruments?

Perhaps Matter Is an Occasion for God to Give Us Perceptions.   Hylas considers another theory of Malebranche's, that the presence of matter is the occasion at which God excites ideas in our minds. Philonous responds as earlier by arguing that God's power alone can account for these ideas without the crutch of material things.

HYL.   I will no longer maintain that Matter is an instrument. However, I would not be understood to give up its existence neither; since, notwithstanding what hath been said, it may still be an *occasion*.

PHIL.   How many shapes is your Matter to take? Or, how often must it be proved not to exist, before you are content to part with it? But, to say no more of this (though by all the laws of disputation I may justly blame you for so frequently changing the signification of the principal term)—I would fain know what you mean by affirming that matter is an occasion, having already denied it to be a cause. And, when you have shewn in what sense you understand *occasion*, pray, in the next place, be pleased to shew me what reason induceth you to believe there is such an occasion of our ideas?

HYL.   As to the first point: by *occasion* I mean an inactive unthinking being, at the presence whereof God excites ideas in our minds.

PHIL.   And what may be the nature of that inactive unthinking being?

HYL.   I know nothing of its nature.

PHIL.   Proceed then to the second point, and assign some reason why we should allow an existence to this inactive, unthinking, unknown thing.

HYL.   When we see ideas produced in our minds, after an orderly and constant manner, it is natural to think they have some fixed and regular occasions, at the presence of which they are excited.

 ASK YOURSELF

8.68.   What does Hylas mean by "occasion," and why does he think matter is such an occasion?

PHIL.   You acknowledge then God alone to be the cause of our ideas, and that He causes them at the presence of those occasions.

HYL.   That is my opinion.

PHIL.   Those things which you say are present to God, without doubt He perceives.

HYL.   Certainly; otherwise they could not be to Him an occasion of acting.

PHIL.   Not to insist now on your making sense of this hypothesis, or answering all the puzzling questions and difficulties it is liable to: I only ask whether the order and regularity observable in the series of our ideas, or the course of nature, be not sufficiently accounted for by the wisdom and power of God; and whether it doth not derogate from those attributes, to suppose He is influenced, directed, or put in mind, when and what He is to act, by an unthinking substance? And, lastly, whether, in case I granted all you contend for, it would make anything to your purpose; it not being easy to conceive how the external or absolute existence of an unthinking substance, distinct from its being perceived, can be inferred from my allowing that there are certain things perceived by the mind of God, which are to Him the occasion of producing ideas in us?

HYL.   I am perfectly at a loss what to think, this notion of *occasion* seeming now altogether as groundless as the rest.

PHIL.   Do you not at length perceive that in all these different acceptations of *Matter*, you have been only supposing you know not what, for no manner of reason, and to no kind of use?

 ASK YOURSELF

8.69.   For Philonous, what sufficiently accounts for the order and regularity we observe in the succession of our ideas?

Dialogue Three

In Dialogues One and Two, Berkeley refutes the view that matter is the source of our external sense impressions. He suggests that God, not material objects, feeds us these external sense impressions. In Dialogue Three Berkeley explains why this view is not skepticism, and he further clarifies God's role as the source of external sense impressions.

Hylas's Skepticism. Dialogue Three opens with Hylas conceding to Philonous's arguments against matter. However, Hylas goes a step further and adopts the skeptical position that denies that absolute knowledge of anything, other than our immediate perceptions, is impossible.

 From BERKELEY: *"Dialogue 3"* ——————————

PHIL.   Tell me, Hylas, what are the fruits of yesterday's meditation? Has it confirmed you in the same mind you were in at parting? Or have you since seen cause to change your opinion?

HYL.   Truly my opinion is that all our opinions are alike vain and uncertain. What we approve to-day, we condemn to-morrow. We keep a stir about knowledge, and spend our lives in the pursuit of it, when, alas we know nothing all the while: nor do I think it possible for us ever to know anything in this life. Our faculties are too narrow and too few. Nature certainly never intended us for speculation.

PHIL.   What! Say you we can know nothing, Hylas?

HYL.   There is not that single thing in the world whereof we can know the real nature, or what it is in itself.

PHIL.   Will you tell me I do not really know what fire or water is?

HYL.   You may indeed know that fire appears hot, and water fluid; but this is no more than knowing what sensations are produced in your own mind, upon the application of fire and water to your organs of sense. Their internal constitution, their true and real nature, you are utterly in the dark as to *that*.

PHIL.   Do I not know this to be a real stone that I stand on, and that which I see before my eyes to be a real tree?

HYL.   *Know?* No, it is impossible you or any man alive should know it. All you know is, that you have such a certain idea or appearance in your own mind. But what is this to the real tree or stone? I tell you that color, figure, and hardness, which you perceive, are not the real natures of those things, or in the least like them. The same may be said of all other real things, or corporeal substances, which compose the world. They have none of them anything of themselves, like those sensible qualities by us perceived. We should not therefore pretend to affirm or know anything of them, as they are in their own nature.

 ASK YOURSELF

8.70. According to Hylas, even though we may have an appearance of a rock, what can't we say about the rock itself?

PHIL.   But surely, Hylas, I can distinguish gold, for example, from iron: and how could this be, if I knew not what either truly was?

HYL.   Believe me, Philonous, you can only distinguish between your own ideas. That yellowness, that weight, and other sensible qualities, think you they are really in the gold? They are only relative to the senses, and have no absolute existence in nature. And in pretending to distinguish the species of real things, by the appearances in your mind, you may perhaps act as wisely as he that should conclude two men were of a different species, because their clothes were not of the same color.

PHIL.   It seems, then, we are altogether put off with the appearances of things, and those false ones too. The very meat I eat, and the cloth I wear, have nothing in them like what I see and feel.

HYL.   Even so.

PHIL.   But is it not strange the whole world should be thus imposed on, and so foolish as to believe their senses? And yet I know not how it is, but men eat, and drink, and sleep, and perform all the offices of life, as comfortably and conveniently as if they really knew the things they are conversant about.

HYL.   They do so: but you know ordinary practice does not require a nicety of speculative knowledge. Hence the vulgar retain their mistakes, and for all that make a shift to bustle through the affairs of life. But philosophers know better things.

PHIL.   You mean, they *know* that they *know nothing*.

HYL.   That is the very top and perfection of human knowledge.

PHIL.   But are you all this while in earnest, Hylas; and are you seriously persuaded that you know nothing real in the world? Suppose you are going to write, would you not call for pen, ink, and paper, like another man; and do you not know what it is you call for?

HYL.   How often must I tell you, that I know not the real nature of any one thing in the universe? I may indeed upon occasion make use of pen, ink, and paper. But what any one of them is in its own true nature, I declare positively I know not. And the same is true with regard to every, other corporeal thing. And, what is more, we are not only ignorant of the true and real nature of things, but even of their existence. It cannot be denied that we perceive such certain appearances or ideas; but it cannot be concluded from thence that bodies really exist. Nay, now I think on it, I must, agreeably to my former concessions, farther declare that it is impossible any real corporeal thing should exist in nature.

 ASK YOURSELF

8.71. As a skeptic for the time being, what things does Hylas claim that we cannot know?

Philonous continues by explaining the source of Hylas's skepticism regarding an external reality.

PHIL.   You amaze me. Was ever anything more wild and extravagant than the notions you now maintain: and is it not evident you are led into all these extravagances by the belief of *material substance*? This makes you dream of those unknown natures in everything. It is this occasions your distinguishing between the reality and sensible appearances of things. It is to this you are indebted for being ignorant of what everybody else knows perfectly well. Nor is this all: you are not only ignorant of the true nature of everything, but you know not whether anything really exists, or whether there are any true natures at all; forasmuch as you attribute to your material beings an absolute or external existence, wherein you suppose their reality consists. And, as you are forced in the end to acknowledge such an existence means either a direct repugnancy, or nothing at all, it follows that you are obliged to pull down your own hypothesis of material Substance, and positively to deny the real existence of any part of the universe. And so you are plunged into the deepest and most deplorable skepticism that ever man was. Tell me, Hylas, is it not as I say?

HYL.   I agree with you. *Material substance* was no more than an hypothesis; and a false and groundless one too. I will no longer spend my breath in defense of it. But whatever hypothesis you advance, or whatsoever scheme of things you introduce in its stead, I doubt not it will appear every whit as false: let me but be allowed to question you upon it. That is, suffer me to serve you in your own kind, and I warrant it shall conduct you through as many perplexities and contradictions, to the very same state of skepticism that I myself am in at present.

    ASK YOURSELF

8.72. According to Philonous, why does Hylas fall into skepticism?

Commonsense Notion of External Sense Perceptions.   Philonous argues that we should accept what our common sense tells us about external things as they appear to the senses. And our ordinary experiences tell us that external things are linked to our experiences of them.

PHIL.   I assure you, Hylas, I do not pretend to frame any hypothesis at all. I am of a vulgar cast, simple enough to believe my senses, and leave things as I find them. To be plain, it is my opinion that the real things are those very things I see, and feel, and perceive by my senses. These I know; and, finding they answer all the necessities and purposes of life, have no reason to be solicitous about any other unknown beings. A piece of sensible bread, for instance, would stay my stomach better than ten thousand times as much of that insensible, unintelligible, real bread you speak of. It is likewise my opinion that colors and other sensible qualities are on the objects. I cannot for my life help thinking that snow is white, and fire hot. You indeed, who by snow and fire mean certain external, unperceived, unperceiving substances, are in the right to deny whiteness or heat to be affections inherent in *them*. But I, who understand by those words the things I see and feel, am obliged to think like other folks. And, as I am no skeptic with regard to the nature of things, so neither am I as to their existence. That a thing should be really perceived by my senses, and at the same time not really exist, is to me a plain contradiction; since I cannot prescind or abstract, even in thought, the existence of a sensible thing from its being perceived. Wood, stones, fire, water, flesh, iron, and the like things, which I name and discourse of, are things that I know. And I should not have known them but that I perceived them by my senses; and things perceived by the senses are immediately perceived; and things immediately perceived are ideas; and ideas cannot exist without the mind; their existence therefore consists in being perceived; when, therefore, they are actually perceived there can be no doubt of their existence. Away then with all that skepticism, all those ridiculous philosophical doubts. What a jest is it for a philosopher to question the existence of sensible things, till he hath it proved to him from the veracity of God; or to pretend our knowledge in this point falls short of intuition or demonstration! I might as well doubt of my own being, as of the being of those things I actually see and feel.

HYL.   Not so fast, Philonous: you say you cannot conceive how sensible things should exist without the mind. Do you not?

PHIL.   I do.

 ASK YOURSELF

8.73. Concerning external things, Philonous maintains that "their existence therefore consists in being perceived." What leads him to his conclusion?

God Sustains All Things. Although Hylas (now a skeptic) no longer defends the existence of matter, he still thinks Philonous's idealism has flaws. He contends that it is unreasonable to think that an object disappears once we are through perceiving it. In the *Principles,* Section 23, Berkeley expresses this point as follows: "But, say you, surely there is nothing easier than for me to imagine trees, for instance, in a park, or books existing in a closet, and nobody by to perceive them."

HYL.   Supposing you were annihilated, cannot you conceive it possible that things perceivable by sense may still exist?

PHIL.   I can; but then it must be in another mind. When I deny sensible things an existence out of the mind, I do not mean my mind in particular, but all minds. Now, it is plain they have an existence exterior to my mind; since I find them by experience to be independent of it. There is therefore some other Mind wherein they exist, during the intervals between the times of my perceiving them: as likewise they did before my birth, and would do after my supposed annihilation. And, as the same is true with regard to all other finite created spirits, it necessarily follows there is an *omnipresent eternal Mind*, which knows and comprehends all things, and exhibits them to our view in such a manner, and according to such rules, as He Himself hath ordained, and are by us termed the *laws of nature*.

 ASK YOURSELF

8.74. Why do things continue to exist when we are no longer there to perceive them?

Our Idea of God. Hylas next contends that we have no idea of God; hence we cannot conceive of things existing in his mind. Philonous replies that we have an idea of ourselves; when we strip away the imperfections in this idea, we then have some idea of an active thinking God.

HYL.   Answer me, Philonous. Are all our ideas perfectly inert beings? Or have they any agency included in them?

PHIL.   They are altogether passive and inert.

HYL.   And is not God an agent, a being purely active?

PHIL.   I acknowledge it.

HYL.   No idea therefore can be like unto, or represent the nature of God?

PHIL.   It cannot.

HYL.   Since therefore you have no *idea* of the mind of God, how can you conceive it possible that things should exist in His mind? Or, if you can conceive the mind of God, without having an idea of it, why may not I be allowed to conceive the existence of Matter, notwithstanding I have no idea of it?

PHIL.   As to your first question: I own I have properly no *idea*, either of God or any other spirit; for these being active, cannot be represented by things perfectly inert, as our ideas are. I do nevertheless know that I, who am a spirit or thinking substance, exist as certainly as I know my ideas exist. Farther, I know what I mean by the terms I *and myself*; and I know this immediately or intuitively, though I do not perceive it as I perceive a triangle, a color, or a sound. The Mind, Spirit, or Soul is that indivisible unextended thing which thinks, acts, and perceives. I say *indivisible*, because unextended; and *unextended*, because extended, figured, moveable things are ideas; and that which perceives ideas, which thinks and wills, is plainly itself no idea, nor like an idea. Ideas are things inactive, and perceived. And Spirits a sort of beings altogether different from them. I do not therefore say my soul is an idea, or like an idea.

 ASK YOURSELF

8.75. What are some attributes of mental or spiritual things?

PHIL.   However, taking the word *idea* in a large sense, my soul may be said to furnish me with an idea, that is, an image or likeness of God—though indeed extremely inadequate. For, all the notion I have of God is obtained by reflecting on my own soul, heightening its powers, and removing its imperfections. I have, therefore, though not an inactive idea, yet in *myself* some sort of an active thinking image of the Deity. And, though I perceive Him not by sense, yet I have a notion of Him, or know Him by reflection and reasoning. My own mind and my own ideas I have an immediate knowledge of; and, by the help of these, do mediately apprehend the possibility of the existence of other spirits and ideas. Farther, from my own being, and from the dependency I find in myself and my ideas, I do, by an act of reason, necessarily infer the existence of a God, and of all created things in the mind of God. So much for your first question. For the second: I suppose by this time you can answer it yourself. For you neither perceive Matter objectively, as you do an inactive being or idea; nor know it, as you do yourself, by a reflex act, neither do you mediately apprehend it by similitude of the one or the other; nor yet collect it by reasoning from that which you know immediately. All which makes the case of *Matter* widely different from that of the *Deity*.

 ASK YOURSELF

8.76. Where does our idea of God come from?

Difference between Spiritual and Material Substance. Hylas next asks: If we can conceive of spiritual substances without having a distinct idea of it (e.g., God or ourselves), why can't we conceive of matter in the same way? Philonous replies by noting two differences between asserting the existence of matter and asserting the existence of spirit.

HYL. You say your own soul supplies you with some sort of an idea or image of God. But, at the same time, you acknowledge you have, properly speaking, no *idea* of your own soul. You even affirm that spirits are a sort of beings altogether different from ideas. Consequently that no idea can be like a spirit. We have therefore no idea of any spirit. You admit nevertheless that there is spiritual Substance, although you have no idea of it; while you deny there can be such a thing as material Substance, because you have no notion or idea of it. Is this fair dealing? To act consistently, you must either admit Matter or reject Spirit. What say you to this?

PHIL. I say, in the first place, that I do not deny the existence of material substance, merely because I have no notion of it, but because the notion of it is inconsistent; or, in other words, because it is repugnant that there should be a notion of it. Many things, for aught I know, may exist, whereof neither I nor any other man hath or can have any idea or notion whatsoever. But then those things must be possible, that is, nothing inconsistent must be included in their definition. I say, secondly, that, although we believe things to exist which we do not perceive, yet we may not believe that any particular thing exists, without some reason for such belief: but I have no reason for believing the existence of Matter. I have no immediate intuition thereof: neither can I immediately from my sensations, ideas, notions, actions, or passions, infer an unthinking, unperceiving, inactive Substance—either by probable deduction, or necessary consequence. Whereas the being of my Self, that is, my own soul, mind, or thinking principle, I evidently know by reflection.

 ASK YOURSELF

8.77. The first difference between the concepts of matter and spirit is that the notion of matter is "repugnant," or internally inconsistent. Philonous clarifies this in the following excerpt. The second difference is that there is no basis whatever for the idea of matter. What is the basis of Philonous's idea of spirit?

PHIL.   You will forgive me if I repeat the same things in answer to the same objections. In the very notion or definition of *material Substance*, there is included a manifest repugnance and inconsistency. But this cannot be said of the notion of Spirit. That ideas should exist in what doth not perceive, or be produced by what doth not act, is repugnant. But, it is no repugnancy to say that a perceiving thing should be the subject of ideas, or an active thing the cause of them. It is granted we have neither an immediate evidence nor a demonstrative knowledge of the existence of other finite spirits; but it will not thence follow that such spirits are on a foot with material substances: if to suppose the one be inconsistent, and it be not inconsistent to suppose the other; if the one can be inferred by no argument, and there is a probability for the other; if we see signs and effects indicating distinct finite agents like ourselves, and see no sign or symptom whatever that leads to a rational belief of Matter. I say, lastly, that I have a notion of Spirit, though I have not, strictly speaking, an idea of it. I do not perceive it as an idea, or by means of an idea, but know it by reflection.

 ASK YOURSELF

8.78. What specifically is repugnant or internally inconsistent about the notion of matter?

Unified Self. Anticipating Hume's famous discussion of personal identity, Hylas maintains that the "self" for Philonous reduces to a series of disconnected perceptions.

HYL.   Notwithstanding all you have said, to me it seems that, according to your own way of thinking, and in consequence of your own principles, it should follow that *you* are only a system of floating ideas, without any substance to support them. Words are not to be used without a meaning. And, as there is no more meaning in *spiritual Substance* than in *material Substance*, the one is to be exploded as well as the other.

PHIL.   How often must I repeat, that I know or am conscious of my own being; and that *I myself* am not my ideas, but somewhat else, a thinking, active principle that perceives, knows, wills, and operates about ideas. I know that I, one and the same self, perceive both colors and sounds: that a color cannot perceive a sound, nor a sound a color: that I am therefore one individual principle, distinct from color and sound; and, for the same reason, from all other sensible things and inert ideas. But, I am not in like manner conscious either of the existence or essence of Matter. On the contrary, I know that nothing inconsistent can exist, and that the existence of Matter implies an inconsistency. Farther, I know what I mean when I affirm that there is a spiritual substance or support of ideas, that is, that a spirit knows and perceives ideas. But, I do not know what is meant when it is said that an unperceiving substance hath inherent in it and supports either ideas or the archetypes of ideas. There is therefore upon the whole no parity of case between Spirit and Matter.

ASK YOURSELF

8.79. Why does Philonous believe that he is "one individual principle" distinct from the specific colors and sounds he perceives?

Idealism and Common Sense. Hylas believes that the average person would deny that existence is being perceived. Philonous replies that the average person would say he believes that a tree exists *because* he can see it.

HYL.   I own myself satisfied in this point. But, do you in earnest think the real existence of sensible things consists in their being actually perceived? If so, how comes it that all mankind distinguish between them? Ask the first man you meet, and he shall tell you, *to be perceived* is one thing, and *to exist* is another.

PHIL.   I am content, Hylas, to appeal to the common sense of the world for the truth of my notion. Ask the gardener why he thinks yonder cherry-tree exists in the garden, and he shall tell you, because he sees and feels it; in a word, because he perceives it by his senses. Ask him why he thinks an orange-tree not to be there, and he shall tell you, because he does not perceive it. What he perceives by sense, that he terms a real, being, and saith it *is or exists*; but, that which is not perceivable, the same, he saith, hath no being.

HYL.   Yes, Philonous, I grant the existence of a sensible thing consists in being perceivable, but not in being actually perceived.

PHIL.   And what is perceivable but an idea? And can an idea exist without being actually perceived? These are points long since agreed between us.

HYL.   But, be your opinion never so true, yet surely you will not deny it is shocking, and contrary to the common sense of men. Ask the fellow whether yonder tree hath an existence out of his mind: what answer think you he would make?

PHIL.   The same that I should myself, to wit, that it doth exist out of his mind. But then to a Christian it cannot surely be shocking to say, the real tree, existing without his mind, is truly known and comprehended by (that is, *exists in*) the infinite mind of God. Probably he may not at first glance be aware of the direct and immediate proof there is of this; inasmuch as the very being of a tree, or any other sensible thing, implies a mind wherein it is. But the point itself he cannot deny. The question between the Materialists and me is not, whether things have a *real* existence out of the mind of this or that person, but whether they have an *absolute* existence, distinct from being perceived by God, and exterior to all minds. This indeed some heathens and philosophers have affirmed, but whoever entertains notions of the Deity suitable to the Holy Scriptures will be of another opinion.

 ASK YOURSELF

8.80. According to Philonous, where does the "real" tree exist?

Distinguishing Dreaming from Waking. Hylas contends that dreams and reality are equally dependent upon the mind; thus idealism cannot distinguish between the two. Philonous replies that dreams and products of the imagination are faint and depend on the will. Sense impressions are more lively and do not depend on the will.

HYL.   But, according to your notions, what difference is there between real things, and chimeras formed by the imagination, or the visions of a dream—since they are all equally in the mind?

PHIL.   The ideas formed by the imagination are faint and indistinct; they have, besides, an entire dependence on the will. But the ideas perceived by sense, that is, real things, are more vivid and clear; and, being imprinted on the mind by a spirit distinct from us, have not the like dependence on our will. There is therefore no danger of confounding these with the foregoing: and there is as little of confounding them with the visions of a dream, which are dim, irregular, and confused. And, though they should happen to be never so lively and natural, yet, by their not being connected, and of a piece with the preceding and subsequent transactions of our lives, they might easily be distinguished from realities. In short, by whatever method you distinguish *things from chimeras* on your scheme, the same, it is evident, will hold also upon mine. For, it must be, I presume, by some perceived difference; and I am not for depriving you of any one thing that you perceive.

HYL.   But still, Philonous, you hold, there is nothing in the world but spirits and ideas. And this, you must needs acknowledge, sounds very oddly.

PHIL.   I own the word *idea*, not being commonly used for *thing*, sounds something out of the way. My reason for using it was, because a necessary relation to the mind is understood to be implied by that term; and it is now commonly used by philosophers to denote the immediate objects of the understanding. But, however oddly the proposition may sound in words, yet it includes nothing so very strange or shocking in its sense; which in effect amounts to no more than this, to wit, that there are only things perceiving, and things perceived; or that every unthinking being is necessarily, and from the very nature of its existence, perceived by some mind; if not by a finite created mind, yet certainly by the infinite mind of God, in whom "we live, and move, and have our being." Is this as strange as to say, the sensible qualities are not on the objects: or that we cannot be sure of the existence of things, or know any thing of their real natures—though we both see and feel them, and perceive them by all our senses?

 ASK YOURSELF

8.81. What does Philonous mean by the word "idea"?

Extravagance of Denying Corporeal Causes. Hylas argues that idealism is too extravagant insofar as it denies the reality of external, physical causes. Philonous responds that it is more extravagant to say that an inert thing operates on the mind. Further, the Scriptures represent God as the sole and immediate author of all things.

HYL.   And, in consequence of this, must we not think there are no such things as physical or corporeal causes; but that a Spirit is the immediate cause of all the phenomena in nature? Can there be anything more extravagant than this?

PHIL.   Yes, it is infinitely more extravagant to say—a thing which is inert operates on the mind, and which is unperceiving is the cause of our perceptions, without any regard either to consistency, or the old known axiom, *Nothing can give to another that which it hath not itself.* Besides, that which to you, I know not for what reason, seems so extravagant is no more than the Holy Scriptures assert in a hundred places. In them God is represented as the sole and immediate Author of all those effects which some heathens and philosophers are wont to ascribe to Nature, Matter, Fate, or the like unthinking principle. This is so much the constant language of Scripture that it were needless to confirm it by citations.

God as the Cause of Evil. Hylas implies that if God was the cause of all our perceptions, then God would be the immediate cause of evil conduct—or at least a co-conspirator along with us. Philonous counters that if God was a mediator between matter and mind, then he would be responsible for evil; but God is not a mediator. Further, evil does not consist of outward actions, but inward attitudes; the same action may be good or bad depending on the motive. Evil, then, rests in our human motives, not in God's role as the source of our perceptions

HYL.   You are not aware, Philonous, that in making God the immediate Author of all the motions in nature, you make Him the Author of murder, sacrilege, adultery, and the like heinous sins.

PHIL.   In answer to that, I observe, first, that the imputation of guilt is the same, whether a person commits an action with or without an instrument. In case therefore you suppose God to act by the mediation of an instrument or occasion, called *Matter*, you as truly make Him the author of sin as I, who think Him the immediate agent in all those operations vulgarly ascribed to Nature. I farther observe that sin or moral turpitude doth not consist in the outward physical action or motion, but in the internal deviation of the will from the laws of reason and religion. This is plain, in that the killing an enemy in a battle, or putting a criminal legally to death, is not thought sinful; though the outward act be the very same with that in the case of murder. Since, therefore, sin doth not consist in the physical action, the making God an immediate cause of all such actions is not making Him the Author of sin. Lastly, I have nowhere said that God is the only agent who produces all the motions in bodies. It is true I have denied there are any other agents besides spirits; but this is very consistent with allowing to thinking rational beings, in the production of motions, the use of limited powers, ultimately indeed derived from God, but immediately under the direction of their own wills, which is sufficient to entitle them to all the guilt of their actions.

ASK YOURSELF

8.82. In Philonous's view, only spirits exist, and God interjects perceptions of external things in the minds of human spirits. What type of "motion" (or mental activity) is within the power of humans?

Consensus against Idealism. Hylas suggests that a survey would show that most people affirm material existence. Philonous replies that if the questions were worded impartially, people would deny matter in favor of idealism.

HYL.   But the denying Matter, Philonous, or corporeal Substance; there is the point. You can never persuade me that this is not repugnant to the universal sense of mankind. Were our dispute to be determined by most voices, I am confident you would give up the point, without gathering the votes.

PHIL.   I wish both our opinions were fairly stated and submitted to the judgment of men who had plain common sense, without the prejudices of a learned education. Let me be represented as one who trusts his senses, who thinks he knows the things he sees and feels, and entertains no doubts of their existence; and you fairly set forth with all your doubts, your paradoxes, and your skepticism about you, and I shall willingly acquiesce in the determination of any indifferent person. That there is no substance wherein ideas can exist beside spirit is to me evident. And that the objects immediately perceived are ideas, is on all hands agreed. And that sensible qualities are objects immediately perceived no one can deny. It is therefore evident there can be no substratum of those qualities but spirit; in which they exist, not by way of mode or property, but as a thing perceived in that which perceives it. I deny therefore that there is *any unthinking-substratum* of the objects of sense, and *in that acceptation* that there is any material substance. But if by *material substance* is meant only *sensible body*, that which is seen and felt (and the unphilosophical part of the world, I dare say, mean no more)—then I am more certain of matter's existence than you or any other philosopher pretend to be. If there be anything which makes die generality of mankind averse from the notions I espouse, it is a misapprehension that I deny the reality of sensible things. But, as it is you who are guilty of that, and not I, it follows that in truth their aversion is against your notions and not mine. I do therefore assert that I am as certain as of my own being, that there are bodies or corporeal substances (meaning the things I perceive by my senses); and that, granting this, the bulk of mankind will take no thought about, nor think themselves at all concerned in the fate of those unknown natures, and philosophical quiddities, which some men are so fond of.

ASK YOURSELF

8.83. For the sake of argument, Philonous states that he would agree to the existence of material substance if the term "material substance" were defined according what we actually perceive. What is that definition of "material substance"?

Idealism and Optical Illusions. Hylas argues that idealism cannot explain optical illusions since people judge reality by their senses and we can't be mistaken about our perceptions. Philonous explains that an error in judgment occurs when we connect the ideas we apprehend to those immediately perceived. That is, we err by assuming that all perceptions of the same event (even up close) would be represented in the same way.

HYL. What say you to this? Since, according to you, men judge of the reality of things by their senses, how can a man be mistaken in thinking the moon a plain lucid surface, about a foot in diameter; or a square tower, seen at a distance, round; or an oar, with one end in the water, crooked?

PHIL. He is not mistaken with regard to the ideas he actually perceives, but in the inference he makes from his present perceptions. Thus, in the case of the oar, what he immediately perceives by sight is certainly crooked; and so far he is in the right. But if he thence conclude, that upon taking the oar out of the water he shall perceive the same crookedness; or that it would affect his touch as crooked things are wont to do: in that he is mistaken. In like manner, if he shall conclude from what he perceives in one station, that, in case he advances towards the moon or tower, he should still be affected with the like ideas, he is mistaken. But his mistake lies not in what he perceives immediately, and at present (it being a manifest contradiction to suppose he should err in respect of that), but in the wrong judgment he makes concerning the ideas he apprehends to be connected with those immediately perceived: or, concerning the ideas that, from what he perceives at present, he imagines would be perceived in other circumstances. The case is the same with regard to the Copernican system. We do not here perceive any motion of the earth: but it were erroneous thence to conclude, that, in case we were placed at as great a distance from that as we are now from the other planets, we should not then perceive its motion.

 ASK YOURSELF

8.84. According to the Copernican system, the earth is constantly moving, even though we don't perceive that motion. How does this fact illustrate Philonous's point that perceptions of an object will not be present in differing circumstances?

DAVID HUME

Scottish philosopher David Hume (1711–1776) was born into a moderately wealthy aristocratic family near Edinburgh. Like many other philosophers, Hume was educated in the field of law, but abandoned this in favor of philosophical pursuits. Because of his father's early death—and the fact that he was not the oldest son and principal inheritor—much of Hume's adult life was preoccupied with gaining an independent income. In his brief autobiography *Of My Life*, written just before his death, Hume chronicles the slow but progressive increase of his wealth over the years. Like Berkeley, Hume published his most important philosophical work while he was still in his twenties: *A Treatise of Human Nature* (1739–1740). Despite the *Treatise*'s importance in the history of philosophy, it did poorly when it first came out, selling only a few dozen copies. In Hume's own words, the *Treatise* "fell dead born from the press." The work revealed his affinity with the Pyrrhonian skeptical tradition, and those who did read the *Treatise* accused him of universal skepticism, atheism, and undermining the foundations of morality. Although these attacks are a little strong, they established Hume's reputation as a skeptic. On two occasions he applied for a university teaching post, and in each case he was turned down, as his reputation preceded him. He thus focused on his writing career, occasionally taking administrative posts with the British military. Shortly after the failure of the *Treatise*, he published a collection of light essays. About a decade later—still largely unknown in the literary world—Hume wrote the *Enquiry concerning Human Understanding* (1748) and the *Enquiry concerning the Principles of Morals* (1751) as an attempt to produce a shorter and more popular account of his views. Within three years after the publication of the first *Enquiry*, Hume was famous throughout Europe as a champion of skepticism. Hume continued publishing a collection of political essays, six-volume history of Great Britain, and some controversial works on the subject of religion, most notably his posthumously published *Dialogues concerning Natural Religion* (1779). Paradoxically, Hume's sober skeptical views did not carry over into his active social life. His sharp sense of humor and friendly personality made him desirable company in both British and French intellectual circles. Hume eventually came to reject the *Treatise* as an immature work and wished to have his philosophical views represented by his later writings. Indeed, throughout the eighteenth and most of the nineteenth century, the *Treatise* was ignored in favor of the two *Enquiries*. The selections in this section are from Hume's *Enquiry concerning Human Understanding*.

Section 2: Of the Origin of Ideas

The starting point for Hume's philosophy is his distinction between various mental events. His distinctions assume many of Locke's key notions, such as those between sensation and reflection or simple and complex ideas. Distinctions that took Locke one hundred pages to explain, Hume outlines here in just a few pages. Nevertherless, in this short section Hume lays the foundation for the remaining sections of the *Enquiry*.

Ideas and Impressions.   Hume opens by noting a general distinction between two types of mental events: ideas (thoughts) and impressions (feelings).

 From HUME: *Enquiry*, Section 2

Every one will readily allow, that there is a considerable difference between the perceptions of the mind, when a man feels the pain of excessive heat, or the pleasure of moderate warmth, and when he afterwards recalls to his memory this sensation, or anticipates it by his imagination. These faculties may mimic or copy the perceptions of the senses; but they never can entirely reach the force and vivacity of the original sentiment. The utmost we say of them, even when they operate with greatest vigor, is, that they represent their object in so lively a manner, that we could *almost* say we feel or see it: But, except the mind be disordered by disease or madness, they never can arrive at such a pitch of vivacity, as to render these perceptions altogether undistinguishable. All the colors of poetry, however splendid, can never paint natural objects in such a manner as to make the description be taken for a real landskip. The most lively thought is still inferior to the dullest sensation.

We may observe a like distinction to run through all the other perceptions of the mind. A man in a fit of anger, is actuated in a very different manner from one who only thinks of that emotion. If you tell me, that any person is in love, I easily understand your meaning, and from a just conception of his situation; but never can mistake that conception for the real disorders and agitations of the passion. When we reflect on our past sentiments and affections, our thought is a faithful mirror, and copies its objects truly; but the colors which it employs are faint and dull, in comparison of those in which our original perceptions were clothed. It requires no nice discernment or metaphysical head to mark the distinction between them.

 ASK YOURSELF

8.85. Give some of Hume's examples of thoughts versus feelings.

For Hume, perceptions are of two types: ideas (or thoughts) and impressions (feelings). An initial feature that distinguishes ideas from impressions is that ideas are *less lively* than impressions. This can be referred to as Hume's *liveliness thesis*.

Here therefore we may divide all the perceptions of the mind into two classes or species, which are distinguished by their different degrees of force and vivacity. The less forcible and lively are commonly denominated THOUGHTS or IDEAS. The other species want a name in our language, and in most others; I suppose, because it was not requisite for any, but philosophical purposes, to rank them under a general term or appellation. Let us, therefore, use a little freedom, and call them IMPRESSIONS; employing that word in a sense somewhat different from the usual. By the term impression, then, I mean all our more lively perceptions, when we hear, or see, or feel, or love, or hate, or desire, or will. And impressions are distinguished from ideas, which are the less lively perceptions, of which we are conscious, when we reflect on any of those sensations or movements above mentioned.

 ASK YOURSELF

8.86. What does Hume mean by the term "impression"?

An important difference between Locke and Hume is the use of the term "idea." For Locke, ideas referred to all mental events, including sensations, thoughts, memories, and emotions. In the opening of the *Treatise* Hume writes that "Mr. Locke had perverted it [i.e., the term 'idea'] in making it stand for all our perceptions." Hume prefers the general term "perception" to Locke's term "idea" and initially outlines all mental events as follows:

Copy Thesis. Hume next argues that the content of all ideas is ultimately copied from impressions. This is commonly called Hume's *copy thesis*.

Nothing, at first view, may seem more unbounded than the thought of man, which not only escapes all human power and authority, but is not even restrained within the limits of nature and reality. To form monsters, and join incongruous shapes and appearances, costs the imagination no more trouble than to conceive the most natural and familiar objects. And while the body is confined to one planet, along which it creeps with pain and difficulty; the thought can in an instant transport us into the most distant regions of the universe; or even beyond the universe, into the unbounded chaos, where nature is supposed to lie in total confusion. What never was seen, or heard of, may yet be conceived; nor is any thing beyond the power of thought, except what implies an absolute contradiction.

But though our thought seems to possess this unbounded liberty, we shall find, upon a nearer examination, that it is really confined within very narrow limits, and that all this creative power of the mind amounts to no more than the faculty of compounding, transposing, augmenting, or diminishing the materials afforded us by the senses and experience. When we think of a golden mountain, we only join two consistent ideas, *gold*, and *mountain*, with which we were formerly acquainted. A virtuous horse we can conceive; because, from our own feeling, we can conceive virtue; and this we may unite to the figure and shape of a horse, which is an animal familiar to us. In short, all the materials of thinking are derived either from our outward or inward sentiment: The mixture and composition of these belongs alone to the mind and will. Or, to express myself in philosophical language, all our ideas or more feeble perceptions are copies of our impressions or more lively ones.

  ASK YOURSELF

8.87. At first it appears that our ideas are boundless insofar as they can have anything as their subject. However, what restricts the subject matter of our ideas?

8.88. What is the source of an idea we may have of a golden mountain?

In the previous excerpt, Hume notes that "all the materials of thinking are derived either from our outward or inward sentiment." In the *Treatise* (and later in the *Enquiry*) he describes this as a distinction between impressions of sensation and those of reflection:

This distinction clearly follows Locke, who described ideas of sensation as sense perceptions and those of reflection as ideas we have when reflecting on our own mental operations. In the *Treatise*, Hume reduces impressions of reflection to emotions, such as desire, aversion, hope, and fear. In the *Enquiry*, however, he returns in part to Locke's more general account of "reflection" as impressions we get from reflecting on our mental operations. In the following excerpt, Hume also makes use of Locke's distinction between simple and complex ideas. In the *Treatise* he defines them as follows: "Simple perceptions or impressions and ideas are such as admit of no distinction nor separation. The complex are the contrary to these, and may be distinguished into parts." The simple/complex distinction is less central to Hume's discussion than it is to Locke's. Hume continues by offering two proofs of his copy thesis.

To prove this, the two following arguments will, I hope, be sufficient. First, when we analyze our thoughts or ideas, however compounded or sublime, we always find that they resolve themselves into such simple ideas as were copied from a precedent feeling or sentiment. Even those ideas, which, at first view, seem the most wide of this origin, are found, upon a nearer scrutiny, to be derived from it. The idea of God, as meaning an infinitely intelligent, wise, and good Being, arises from reflecting on the operations of our own mind, and augmenting, without limit, those qualities of goodness and wisdom. We may prosecute this enquiry to what length we please; where we shall always find, that every idea which we examine is copied from a similar impression. Those who would assert that this position is not universally true nor without exception, have only one, and that an easy method of refuting it; by producing that idea, which, in their opinion, is not derived from this source. It will then be incumbent on us, if we would maintain our doctrine, to produce the impression, or lively perception, which corresponds to it.

 ASK YOURSELF

8.89. What is Hume's first argument in defense of the copy thesis?

Secondly. If it happen, from a defect of the organ, that a man is not susceptible of any species of sensation, we always find that he is as little susceptible of the correspondent ideas. A blind man can form no notion of colors; a deaf man of sounds. Restore either of them that sense in which he is deficient; by opening this new inlet for his sensations, you also open an inlet for the ideas; and he finds no difficulty in conceiving these objects. The case is the same, if the object, proper for exciting any sensation, has never been applied to the organ. A LAPLANDER or NEGROE has no notion of the relish of wine. And though there are few or no instances of a like deficiency in the mind, where a person has never felt or is wholly incapable of a sentiment or passion that belongs to his species; yet we find the same observation to take place in a less degree. A man of mild manners can form no idea of inveterate revenge or cruelty; nor can a selfish heart easily conceive the heights of friendship and generosity. It is readily allowed, that other beings may possess many senses of which we can have no conception; because the ideas of them have never been introduced to us in the only manner by which an idea can have access to the mind, to wit, by the actual feeling and sensation.

ASK YOURSELF

8.90. What is Hume's second argument in defense of the copy thesis?

The Missing Shade of Blue. In Book 2, Chapter 2, Section 2 of his *Essay* Locke argues that simple ideas cannot be created by one's mind. Locke then offers the following challenge: "I would have anyone try to fancy any taste which had never affected his palate, or frame the idea of a scent he had never smelt." Although Hume agrees in principle with Locke's position about simple ideas, he accepts Locke's challenge and explains how we might get a simple idea that doesn't come from an immediate experience.

There is, however, one contradictory phenomenon, which may prove that it is not absolutely impossible for ideas to arise, independent of their correspondent impressions. I believe it will readily be allowed, that the several distinct ideas of color, which enter by the eye, or those of sound, which are conveyed by the ear, are really different from each other; though, at the same time, resembling. Now if this be true of different colors, it must be no less so of the different shades of the same color; and each shade produces a distinct idea, independent of the rest. For if this should be denied, it is possible, by the continual gradation of shades, to run a color insensibly into what is most remote from it; and if you will not allow any of the means to be different, you cannot, without absurdity, deny the extremes to be the same. Suppose, therefore, a person to have enjoyed his sight for thirty years, and to have become perfectly acquainted with colors of all kinds except one particular shade of blue, for instance, which it never has been his fortune to meet with. Let all the different shades of that color, except that single one, be placed before him, descending gradually from the deepest to the lightest; it is plain that he will perceive a blank, where that shade is wanting, and will be sensible that there is a greater distance in that place between the contiguous color than in any other. Now I ask, whether it be possible for him, from his own imagination, to supply this deficiency, and raise up to himself the idea of that particular shade, though it had never been conveyed to him by his senses? I believe there are few but will be of opinion that he can: And this may serve as a proof that the simple ideas are not always, in every instance, derived from the correspondent impressions; though this instance is so singular, that it is scarcely worth our observing, and does not merit that for it alone we should alter our general maxim.

 ASK YOURSELF

8.91. Hume finds one exception to his claim that all ideas are ultimately derived from impressions. What is this exception?

Here, therefore, is a proposition, which not only seems, in itself, simple and intelligible; but, if a proper use were made of it, might render every dispute equally intelligible, and banish all that jargon, which has so long taken possession of metaphysical reasonings, and drawn disgrace upon them. All ideas, especially abstract ones, are naturally faint and obscure: The mind has but a slender hold of them: They are apt to be confounded with other resembling ideas; and when we have often employed any term, though without a distinct meaning, we are apt to imagine it has a determinate idea annexed to it. On the contrary, all impressions, that is, all sensations, either outward or inward, are strong and vivid: The limits between them are more exactly determined: Nor is it easy to fall into any error or mistake with regard to them. When we entertain, therefore, any suspicion that a philosophical term is employed without any meaning or idea (as is but too frequent), we need but enquire, *from what impression is that supposed idea derived*? And if it be impossible to assign any, this will serve to confirm our suspicion. By bringing ideas into so clear a light we may reasonably hope to remove all dispute, which may arise, concerning their nature and reality.

 ASK YOURSELF

8.92. On the basis of his copy thesis, Hume formulates a rule by which to determine the meaning of any proposition or idea. What is his rule of meaning?

Section 3: Of the Association of Ideas

Consider the various ideas that float through our minds in a short amount of time. I might visualize my vacation last summer in the Bahamas, then think about my office computer, then the man who cleans my office, then my uncle Pete. It might seem as though my stream of ideas are disconnected. Hume thinks otherwise, and in this section argues that three basic principles of association connect the flow of all ideas. They are resemblance, contiguity (or nearness in space or time), and cause/effect. Hume's theory is part of a larger movement in the history of philosophy and psychology called associationism. Aristotle first suggested that the principles of similarity, contrast, and contiguity connect our thoughts. Locke introduced the phrase "association of ideas" to explain this phenomenon, and over the next 150 years British philosophers quarreled over the exact number of principles.

The Three Principles of Association. Hume argues that there is regularity to our thoughts both with serious and fanciful thinking.

 From HUME: *Enquiry*, Section 3

It is evident that there is a principle of connection between the different thoughts or ideas of the mind, and that in their appearance to the memory or imagination, they introduce each other with a certain degree of method and regularity. In our more serious thinking or discourse this is so observable that any particular thought, which breaks in upon the regular tract or chain of ideas, is immediately remarked and rejected. And even in our wildest and most wandering reveries, nay in our very dreams, we shall find, if we reflect, that the imagination ran not altogether at adventures, but that there was still a connection upheld among the different ideas, which succeeded each other. Were the loosest and freest conversation to be transcribed, there would immediately be observed something which connected it in all its transitions. Or where this is wanting, the person who broke the thread of discourse might still inform you, that there had secretly revolved in his mind a succession of thought, which had gradually led him from the subject of conversation. Among different languages, even where we cannot suspect the least connection or communication, it is found, that the words, expressive of ideas, the most compounded, do yet nearly correspond to each other: A certain proof that the simple ideas, comprehended in the compound ones, were bound together by some universal principle, which had an equal influence on all mankind.

 ASK YOURSELF

8.93. According to Hume, what would we find if we transcribed the loosest and freest conversation?

Hume continues by offering three principles of association of ideas and briefly illustrating each.

Though it be too obvious to escape observation, that different ideas are connected together; I do not find that any philosopher has attempted to enumerate or class all the principles of association; a subject, however, that seems worthy of curiosity. To me, there appear to be only three principles of connection among ideas, namely, *Resemblance*, *Contiguity* in time or place, and *Cause* or *Effect*.

That these principles serve to connect ideas will not, I believe, be much doubted. A picture naturally leads our thoughts to the original [i.e., resemblance]: the mention of one apartment in a building naturally introduces an enquiry or discourse concerning the others [i.e., contiguity]: and if we think of a wound, we can scarcely forbear reflecting on the pain which follows it [i.e., contiguity]. But that this enumeration is complete, and that there are no other principles of association except these, may be difficult to prove to the satisfaction of the reader, or even to a man's own satisfaction. All we can do, in such cases, is to run over several instances, and examine carefully the principle which binds the different thoughts to each other, never stopping till we render the principle as general as possible. The more instances we examine, and the more care we employ, the more assurance shall we acquire, that the enumeration, which we form from the whole, is complete and entire.

 ASK YOURSELF

8.94. Give Hume's illustrations of his three principles of association.

8.95. What is Hume's proof that resemblance, contiguity, and cause and effect are the only three means of associating ideas?

Section 7: Of the Idea of Necessary Connection

Since Aristotle, philosophers believed that the concept of causality was essential to our understanding of the world. The importance of the principle of causality is also evident in theology insofar as it provided an important avenue to our knowledge of God, as formulated in cosmological proofs for God's existence. Descartes believed that the idea of causality was innate, or implanted in us at birth by God. As an Empiricist, Hume did not accept this explanation and argued instead that the idea of causality traces back to experience. In his *Treatise*, Hume explains that causality is a complex idea made up of three more foundational ideas: (1) priority, (2) proximity, and (3) necessary connection. Concerning *priority*, if we say that event A causes event B, one thing we mean is that A is *prior* to B. If B were to occur before A, then it would be absurd to say that A was the cause of B. Concerning the idea of *proximity*, if we say that A causes B, then we mean that B is in *proximity* with (or close to) A. For example, if I throw a rock, and at that moment someone's window in China breaks, I would not conclude that my rock broke a window on the other side of the world since the broken window and the rock must be in *proximity* with each other. Priority and proximity alone, however, do not make up our entire notion of causality. For example, if I sneeze and the lights go out, I would not conclude that my sneeze was the cause, even though the conditions of priority and proximity were fulfilled. We also believe that there is a *necessary connection* between cause A and effect B. During the modern period of philosophy, philosophers thought of necessary connection as a power or force connecting two events. When billiard ball A strikes billiard ball B, there is a power that the one event imparts to the other. In keeping with his Empiricist copy thesis (i.e., all ideas are copied from impressions), Hume tries to uncover the experiences that give rise to our notions of priority, proximity, and necessary connection. The first two are easy to explain. Priority traces back to our various experiences of time. Proximity traces back to our various experiences of space. But what is the experience that gives us the idea of necessary connection? Hume addresses that question in this section of the *Enquiry*.

Hume opens his discussion explaining the general importance of clarifying key philosophical terms, one of which is the idea of necessary connection.

 From HUME: *Enquiry*, Section 7

There are no ideas, which occur in metaphysics, more obscure and uncertain, than those of *power, force, energy* or *necessary connection*, of which it is every moment necessary for us to treat in all our disquisitions. We shall, therefore, endeavor in this section to fix, if possible, the precise meaning of these terms, and thereby remove some part of that obscurity, which is so much complained of in this species of philosophy.

Determining the Meaning of an Idea. As noted in Section 2 of the *Enquiry*, the meaning of any idea is determined by the impressions from which the idea was formed. So, to determine the meaning of the idea of necessary connection, Hume investigates various impressions that may have formed this idea.

It seems a proposition, which will not admit of much dispute, that all our ideas are nothing but copies of our impressions, or, in other words, that it is impossible for us to *think* of any thing, which we have not antecedently *felt*, either by our external or internal senses. I have endeavored to explain and prove this proposition, and have expressed my hopes, that, by a proper application of it, men may reach a greater clearness and precision in philosophical reasonings, than what they have hitherto been able to attain. Complex ideas, may, perhaps, be well known by definition, which is nothing but an enumeration of those parts or simple ideas, that compose them. But when we have pushed up definitions to the most simple ideas, and find still more ambiguity and obscurity; what resource are we then possessed of? By what invention can we throw light upon these ideas, and render them altogether precise and determinate to our intellectual view? Produce the impressions or original sentiments, from which the ideas are copied. These impressions are all strong and sensible. They admit not of ambiguity. They are not only placed in a full light themselves, but may throw light on their correspondent ideas, which lie in obscurity. And by this means, we may, perhaps, attain a new microscope or species of optics, by which, in the moral sciences, the most minute, and most simple ideas may be so enlarged as to fall readily under our apprehension, and be equally known with the grossest and most sensible ideas, that can be the object of our enquiry.

 ASK YOURSELF

8.96. Suppose that we explain a complex idea in terms of the simple ideas that make it up. What should we then do to explain those simple ideas, especially if they are obscure?

Proposed Plan. It was also noted in Section 2 that there are two kinds of impressions: those of sensation (external) and those of reflection (internal). Hume's strategy for defining "necessary connection," then, is to determine if either of these two kinds of impressions produced the idea of a necessary connection. In the second paragraph of the following excerpt, he foreshadows the outcome of his investigation.

To be fully acquainted, therefore, with the idea of power or necessary connection, let us examine its impression; and in order to find the impression with greater certainty, let us search for it in all the sources, from which it may possibly be derived.

When we look about us towards external objects, and consider the operation of causes, we are never able, in a single instance, to discover any power or necessary connection; any quality, which binds the effect to the cause, and renders the one an infallible consequence of the other. We only find, that the one does actually, in fact, follow the other. The impulse of one billiard-ball is attended with motion in the second. This is the whole that appears to the *outward* senses. The mind feels no sentiment or *inward* impression from this succession of objects: Consequently, there is not, in any single, particular instance of cause and effect, any thing which can suggest the idea of power or necessary connection.

ASK YOURSELF

8.97. What does Hume expect to find when he searches for the origin of our idea of necessary connection among impressions of sensation (outward) and impressions of reflection (inward)?

Sense Perceptions. Hume begins the quest for the source of our idea of necessary connection by examining various impressions of sensation (outward). Locke's idea of necessary connection comes from simply observing causal activity in the external world. Hume quickly sees Locke's explanation as a dead end.

From the first appearance of an object, we never can conjecture what effect will result from it. But were the power or energy of any cause discoverable by the mind, we could foresee the effect, even without experience; and might, at first, pronounce with certainty concerning it, by mere dint of thought and reasoning.

ASK YOURSELF

8.98. What is Hume's point about our inability to predict effects without directly experiencing those effects?

In reality, there is no part of matter, that does ever, by its sensible qualities, discover any power or energy, or give us ground to imagine, that it could produce any thing, or be followed by any other object, which we could denominate its effect. Solidity, extension, motion; these qualities are all complete in themselves, and never point out any other event which may result from them. The scenes of the universe are continually shifting, and one object follows another in an uninterrupted succession; but the power of force, which actuates the whole machine, is entirely concealed from us, and never discovers itself in any of the sensible qualities of body. We know that, in fact, heat is a constant attendant of flame; but what is the connection between them, we have no room so much as to conjecture or imagine. It is impossible, therefore, that the idea of power can be derived from the contemplation of bodies, in single instances of their operation; because no bodies ever discover any power, which can be the original of this idea.

ASK YOURSELF

8.99. How does Hume's example of heat and flame show that there is no specific sense perception from which we get the idea of necessary connection?

Various Impressions of Reflection. Since impressions of sensation (outward) fail as a source of our idea of necessary connection, Hume turns next to examine possible impressions of reflection (inward) that might account for the origin of this idea. As noted in Section 2 of the *Enquiry*, Hume follows Locke's account of an impression of reflection, which is an experience we have when reflecting on our own mental operations. For both Locke and Hume, humans have a variety of mental faculties that help us process ideas, such as our memory, imagination, reasoning, and will. We directly experience these mental faculties and get impressions from them. Philosophers before Hume suggested that various impressions of our internal mental operations might be the source of our idea of necessary connection. Hume examines four such impressions, and ultimately rejects them all. The two impressions he proposes to examine involve our wills: We experience a distinct impression when we willfully command parts of our body to move (such as our fingers) or when we willfully conjure up an idea.

Since, therefore, external objects as they appear to the senses, give us no idea of power or necessary connection, by their operation in particular instances, let us see, whether this idea be derived from reflection on the operations of our own minds, and be copied from any internal impression. It may be said, that we are every moment conscious of internal power; while we feel, that, by the simple command of our will, we can move the organs of our body, or direct the faculties of our mind. An act of volition produces motion in our limbs, or raises a new idea in our imagination. This influence of the will we know by consciousness. Hence we acquire the idea of power or energy; and are certain, that we ourselves and all other intelligent beings are possessed of power. This idea, then, is an idea of reflection, since it arises from reflecting on the operations of our own mind, and on the command which is exercised by will, both over the organs of the body and faculties of the soul.

Willful Bodily Motion Hypothesis. Locke believed that the idea of necessary connection could trace back to the impression of reflection we experience when we will a bodily motion. Hume rejects this explanation since we don't have a precise experience of our wills in action. He defends his objection with three arguments. Hume's first argument is based on the fact that we do not know the secret union between the soul and body.

We shall proceed to examine this pretension; and first with regard to the influence of volition over the organs of the body. This influence, we may observe, is a fact, which, like all other natural events, can be known only by experience, and can never be foreseen from any apparent energy or power in the cause, which connects it with the effect, and renders the one an infallible consequence of the other. The motion of our body follows upon the command of our will. Of this we are every moment conscious. But the means, by which this is effected; the energy, by which the will performs so extraordinary an operation; of this we are so far from being immediately conscious, that it must for ever escape our most diligent enquiry.

   For first, is there any principle in all nature more mysterious than the union of soul with body, by which a supposed spiritual substance acquires such an influence over a material one, that the most refined thought is able to actuate the grossest matter? Were we empowered by a secret wish to remove mountains, or control the planets in their orbit, this extensive authority would not be more extraordinary, nor more beyond our comprehension. But if by consciousness we perceived any power or energy in the will, we must know this power. We must know its connection with the effect. We must know the secret union of soul and body, and the nature of both these substances, by which the one is able to operate in so many instances upon the other.

 ASK YOURSELF

8.100. According to Hume, if we were conscious of the precise power of willful bodily motion, what would that enable us to know?

Hume's argument can be summarized as follows:

a. If the experience of willful bodily motion is the source of our idea of necessary connection, then we would know the secret union between mind and body.

b. It is not the case that we know the secret union between mind and body.

c. Therefore, it is not the case that this feeling is the source of our idea of necessary connection.

Hume's remaining arguments follow this model. His second argument is based on the fact that we can't fully explain why we can willfully move some parts of our bodies, such as our arms, and not others, such as our hearts. Hume undoubtedly recognizes that an anatomist could give us the answer by showing us the presence of various nerves. However, if we had a genuine internal experience of willful bodily motion, we could understand this without appealing to the anatomist.

The Resistive Force Hypothesis. Locke argued that our idea of solidity is based on the experience we have when we meet with a resistive physical force, such as pressing one's hand against a wall. As a variation on the willful bodily motion hypothesis, Hume considers that the experience of a resistive force might be a source of our idea of necessary connection. For two reasons Hume does not believe that this experience adequately explains the idea of necessary connection. First, things that don't have physical resistance (such as God and nonphysical minds) are said to have causal power. So, at best, this is an incomplete explanation. Second, the only connection resistance has with power is known by experience. Hume presents the following excerpt as a footnote to his discussion of the willful bodily motion hypothesis.

It may be pretended, that the resistance which we meet with in bodies, obliging us frequently to exert our force, and call up all our power, this gives us the idea of force and power. It is this *nisus*, or strong endeavor, of which we are conscious, that is the original impression from which this idea is copied. But, first, we attribute power to a vast number of objects, where we never can suppose this resistance or exertion of force to take place; to the Supreme Being, who never meets with any resistance; to the mind in its command over its ideas and limbs, in common thinking and motion, where the effect follows immediately upon the will, without any exertion or summoning up of force; to inanimate matter, which is not capable of this sentiment. *Secondly*, This sentiment of an endeavor to overcome resistance has no known connection with any event: What follows it, we know by experience; but could not know it *a priori*. It must, however, be confessed, that the animal *nisus*, which we experience, though it can afford no accurate precise idea of power, enters very much into that vulgar, inaccurate idea, which is formed by it.

 ASK YOURSELF

8.101. What does Hume concede about the "animal *nisus*" (or strong endeavor)?

Thought Control Hypothesis. Malebranche discussed the view that people have the power within themselves to willfully produce ideas. For example, if I wish to think about an idea of an elephant, then the image of an elephant appears in my mind. Malebranche rejected the contention that we have such an ability without God's help. Nevertheless, Hume considers this experience of thought control as a possible source of our idea of necessary connection. Hume rejects this explanation for three reasons, similar to those presented earlier. First, if we had a genuine experience of causal power through thought control, then we would know the precise connection between our minds and the ideas that we conjure up. However, the connection between the two is far from evident to us.

Shall we then assert, that we are conscious of a power or energy in our own minds, when, by an act or command of our will, we raise up a new idea, fix the mind to the contemplation of it, turn it on all sides, and at last dismiss it for some other idea, when we think that we have surveyed it with sufficient accuracy? I believe the same arguments will prove, that even this command of the will gives us no real idea of force or energy.

First, It must be allowed, that, when we know a power, we know that very circumstance in the cause, by which it is enabled to produce the effect: For these are supposed to be synonymous. We must, therefore, know both the cause and effect, and the relation between them. But do we pretend to be acquainted with the nature of the human soul and the nature of an idea, or the aptitude of the one to produce the other? This is a real creation; a production of something out of nothing: Which implies a power so great, that it may seem, at first sight, beyond the reach of any being, less than infinite. At least it must be owned, that such a power is not felt, nor known, nor even conceivable by the mind. We only feel the event, namely, the existence of an idea, consequent to a command of the will: But the manner, in which this operation is performed, the power by which it is produced, is entirely beyond our comprehension.

 ASK YOURSELF

8.102. According to Hume, when we conjure up an idea, what is mere event that we feel?

Hume continues arguing that one's willful power over mental events is limited, and if we actually experienced the power of thought control we would know why.

A Final Explanation. So far Hume has rejected impressions of sensation (outward) as the possible source of our idea of necessary connection and four possible impressions of reflection (inward). Hume repeats his theory of meaning: If we can find no impression that serves as the basis of our idea of necessary connection, then the term "necessary connection" is meaningless. We witness one event following another, but we have no conception of a causal power connecting such events.

But to hasten to a conclusion of this argument, which is already drawn out to too great a length: We have sought in vain for an idea of power or necessary connection in all the sources from which we could suppose it to be derived. It appears that, in single instances of the operation of bodies, we never can, by our utmost scrutiny, discover any thing but one event following another, without being able to comprehend any force or power by which the cause operates, or any connection between it and its supposed effect. The same difficulty occurs in contemplating the operations of mind on body—where we observe the motion of the latter to follow upon the volition of the former, but are not able to observe or conceive the tie which binds together the motion and volition, or the energy by which the mind produces this effect. The authority of the will over its own faculties and ideas is not a whit more comprehensible: So that, upon the whole, there appears not, throughout all nature, any one instance of connection which is conceivable by us. All events seem entirely loose and separate. One event follows another; but we never can observe any tie between them. They seem *conjoined*, but never *connected*. And as we can have no idea of any thing which never appeared to our outward sense or inward sentiment, the necessary conclusion seems to be that we have no idea of connection or power at all, and that these words are absolutely, without any meaning, when employed either in philosophical reasonings or common life.

 ASK YOURSELF

8.103. According to Hume, all we can say is that events are conjoined, but not connected. What is the difference between the two?

Habitual Feeling of Expectation from Observing Constant Conjunction. Before accepting this conclusion, Hume examines one final type of impression of reflection: a feeling of expectation that habitually results from observing two constantly conjoined events. The first step in creating this feeling is the observation of two events, one always following the other.

But there still remains one method of avoiding this conclusion, and one source which we have not yet examined. When any natural object or event is presented, it is impossible for us, by any sagacity or penetration, to discover, or even conjecture, without experience, what event will result from it, or to carry our foresight beyond that object which is immediately present to the memory and senses. Even after one instance or experiment where we have observed a particular event to follow upon another, we are not entitled to form a general rule, or foretell what will happen in like cases; it being justly esteemed an unpardonable temerity to judge of the whole course of nature from one single experiment, however accurate or certain. But when one particular species of event has always, in all instances, been conjoined with another, we make no longer any scruple of foretelling one upon the appearance of the other, and of employing that reasoning, which can alone assure us of any matter of fact or existence. We then call the one object, *Cause*; the other, *Effect*. We suppose that there is some connection between them; some power in the one, by which it infallibly produces the other, and operates with the greatest certainty and strongest necessity.

 ASK YOURSELF

8.104. According to Hume, under what condition do we call one event a cause, and another event an effect?

The second step in creating this feeling is that we instinctively form a habit by which we come to expect the second event every time we see the first.

It appears, then, that this idea of a necessary connection among events arises from a number of similar instances which occur of the constant conjunction of these events; nor can that idea ever be suggested by any one of these instances, surveyed in all possible lights and positions. But there is nothing in a number of instances, different from every single instance, which is supposed to be exactly similar; except only, that after a repetition of similar instances, the mind is carried by habit, upon the appearance of one event, to expect its usual attendant, and to believe that it will exist. This connection, therefore, which we *feel* in the mind, this customary transition of the imagination from one object to its usual attendant, is the sentiment or impression from which we form the idea of power or necessary connection. Nothing farther is in the case. Contemplate the subject on all sides; you will never find any other origin of that idea. This is the sole difference between one instance, from which we can never receive the idea of connection, and a number of similar instances, by which it is suggested. The first time a man saw the communication of motion by impulse, as by the shock of two billiard-balls, he could not pronounce that the one event was *connected*: But only that it was *conjoined* with the other. After he has observed several instances of this nature, he then pronounces them to be *connected*. What alteration has happened to give rise to this new idea of *connection*? Nothing but that he now *feels* these events to be *connected* in his imagination, and can readily foretell the existence of one from the appearance of the other. When we say, therefore, that one object is connected with another, we mean only that they have acquired a connection in our thought, and give rise to this inference, by which they become proofs of each other's existence: A conclusion which is somewhat extraordinary, but which seems founded on sufficient evidence. Nor will its evidence be weakened by any general diffidence of the understanding, or skeptical suspicion concerning every conclusion which is new and extraordinary. No conclusions can be more agreeable to skepticism than such as make discoveries concerning the weakness and narrow limits of human reason and capacity.

ASK YOURSELF

8.105. Hume argues that the first time someone saw billiard ball A move billiard ball B, the most that person could say is that A and B are merely conjoined. What else must happen for that person to say that A and B are causally connected?

Two Definitions of Causality. Hume emphasizes how foundational the notion of causality is to any kind of empirical reasoning and scientific inquiry. Ironically, it is difficult to give any precise definition to the notion of causality. In view of this analysis of the idea of necessary connection, he offers two definitions of causality. The first hinges on the constant conjunction of two events, A and B. The second hinges on the habitual feeling to expect B whenever A arises.

And what stronger instance can be produced of the surprising ignorance and weakness of the understanding than the present. For surely, if there be any relation among objects which it imports to us to know perfectly, it is that of cause and effect. On this are founded all our reasonings concerning matter of fact or existence. By means of it alone we attain any assurance concerning objects which are removed from the present testimony of our memory and senses. The only immediate utility of all sciences, is to teach us, how to control and regulate future events by their causes. Our thoughts and enquiries are, therefore, every moment, employed about this relation: Yet so imperfect are the ideas which we form concerning it, that it is impossible to give any just definition of cause, except what is drawn from something extraneous and foreign to it. Similar objects are always conjoined with similar. Of this we have experience. Suitably to this experience, therefore, we may define a cause to be *an object, followed by another, and where all the objects similar to the first are followed by objects similar to the second.* Or in other words *where, if the first object had not been, the second never had existed.* The appearance of a cause always conveys the mind, by a customary transition, to the idea of the effect. Of this also we have experience. We may, therefore, suitably to this experience, form another definition of cause, and call it, *an object followed by another, and whose appearance always conveys the thought to that other.* But though both these definitions be drawn from circumstances foreign to the cause, we cannot remedy this inconvenience, or attain any more perfect definition, which may point out that circumstances in the cause, which gives it a connection with its effect. We have no idea of this connection, nor even any distant notion what it is we desire to know, when we endeavor at a conception of it. We say, for instance, that the vibration of this string is the cause of this particular sound. But what do we mean by that affirmation? We either mean *that this vibration is followed by this sound, and that all similar vibrations have been followed by similar sounds; or, that this vibration is followed by this sound, and that upon the appearance of one the mind anticipates the senses, and forms immediately an idea of the other.* We may consider the relation of cause and effect in either of these two lights; but beyond these, we have no idea of it.

ASK YOURSELF

8.106. In view of everything that he has argued, what are the two ways Hume defines "causality"?

Section 10: Of Miracles

In this section Hume gives his infamous argument against miracles, which drew more critical reaction during his life than any other aspect of his philosophy. His argument can be summarized in a single sentence: The testimony of uniform natural law outweighs the testimony of any alleged miracle. To explain, imagine a scale with two balancing pans. In the one pan we place the strongest evidence in support of the occurrence of a miracle. In the other we place our lifelong experience of consistent laws of nature. According to Hume, the second pan will always outweigh the first. In a letter to George Campbell, Hume explains the circumstance in which he first formulated this argument:

> I was walking in the cloisters of the Jesuits College of La Fleche, a town in which I passed two years of my youth, and was engaged in a conversation with a Jesuit of some parts and learning, who was relating to me, and urging some nonsensical miracle performed lately in their Convent, when I was tempted to dispute against him; and, as my head was full of the topics of my Treatise of Human Nature, which I was at the time composing, this argument immediately occurred to me, and I thought it very much graveled my companion; but at last he observed to me, that it was impossible for that argument to have any solidity, because it operated equally against the Gospel as the Catholic miracles; which observation I thought proper to admit as a sufficient answer. I believe you will allow that the freedom at least of this reasoning makes it somewhat extraordinary to have been the produce of a Convent of Jesuits, though perhaps you may think that the sophistry of it favors plainly of the place of its birth.

An early draft of Hume's *Treatise* contained a discussion on the subject of miracles, but Hume removed it prior to publication for reasons of "prudence." He waited almost ten years before writing on the subject in his *Enquiry*. To understand Hume's argument, it is important to be clear about what Hume is specifically arguing against. Hume is not arguing that miracles are *impossible*, for there is no logical contradiction in the idea of a miracle. Nor is he arguing that miracles have *never occurred*, since, without the aid of a time machine, we could never establish this absolutely. Instead, he is arguing that it is *never reasonable to believe* that a miracle has occurred. We must also distinguish between a firsthand account of a miracle that we would witness ourselves and a secondhand report of a miracle that we read about in a book or a newspaper. Since few of us claim to witness miracles directly, Hume launches his attack against our belief in *secondhand accounts* of miracles. In short, Hume is arguing that it is never reasonable to believe secondhand reports concerning miracles.

Hume's argument rests on the nature of empirically based belief in general. All empirical judgments ? and not just those involving miracles—are best understood using the metaphor of a weighing scale with two balancing pans, as noted earlier. We place all of our empirical evidence *for* a particular contention in one pan and all of our evidence *against* that contention in the other pan. We then believe whichever view has the weightier evidence.

Levels of Evidence. The evidence we get from our experience is not always accurate, such as when I predict from past experience that the weather will be warmer next June than it will be next December.

 From HUME: *Enquiry*, Section 10 _____

Though experience be our only guide in reasoning concerning matters of fact; it must be acknowledged, that this guide is not altogether infallible, but in some cases is apt to lead us into errors. One, who in our climate, should expect better weather in any week of June than in one of December, would reason justly, and conformably to experience; but it is certain, that he may happen, in the event, to find himself mistaken. However, we may observe, that, in such a case, he would have no cause to complain of experience; because it commonly informs us beforehand of the uncertainty, by that contrariety of events, which we may learn from a diligent observation. All effects follow not with like certainty from their supposed causes. Some events are found, in all countries and all ages, to have been constantly conjoined together: Others are found to have been more variable, and sometimes to disappoint our expectations; so that, in our reasonings concerning matter of fact, there are all imaginable degrees of assurance, from the highest certainty to the lowest species of moral evidence.

 ASK YOURSELF

8.107. What are the possible levels or degrees of assurance when assessing matters of fact?

Given these differing degrees or levels of assurance, Hume argues that the higher the degree of evidence, the stronger our belief should be.

A wise man, therefore, proportions his belief to the evidence. In such conclusions as are founded on an infallible experience, he expects the event with the last degree of assurance, and regards his past experience as a full *proof* of the future existence of that event. In other cases, he proceeds with more caution: He weighs the opposite experiments: He considers which side is supported by the greater number of experiments: To that side he inclines, with doubt and hesitation; and when at last he fixes his judgement, the evidence exceeds not what we properly call *probability*. All probability, then, supposes an opposition of experiments and observations, where the one side is found to overbalance the other, and to produce a degree of evidence, proportioned to the superiority. A hundred instances or experiments on one side, and fifty on another, afford a doubtful expectation of any event; though a hundred uniform experiments, with only one that is contradictory, reasonably beget a pretty strong degree of assurance. In all cases, we must balance the opposite experiments, where they are opposite, and deduct the smaller number from the greater, in order to know the exact force of the superior evidence.

 ## ASK YOURSELF

8.108. How should a wise person proportion his belief in a given claim?

8.109. All judgments about matters of fact (or empirical experience) involve probability. What does probability suppose?

Empirical Evidence from Testimony. There several ways of gaining empirical evidence for a particular contention. We may personally conduct scientific experiments, as Hume notes earlier. We may draw from the ordinary life experiences that we have gained over the years. Perhaps most importantly, we may rely on the testimonies of other people. Testimonies also counts as empirical evidence that we must balance against our other empirical experiences.

To apply these principles to a particular instance; we may observe, that there is no species of reasoning more common, more useful, and even necessary to human life, than that which is derived from the testimony of men, and the reports of eye-witnesses and spectators. This species of reasoning, perhaps, one may deny to be founded on the relation of cause and effect. I shall not dispute about a word. It will be sufficient to observe that our assurance in any argument of this kind is derived from no other principle than our observation of the veracity of human testimony, and of the usual conformity of facts to the reports of witnesses. It being a general maxim, that no objects have any discoverable connection together, and that all the inferences, which we can draw from one to another, are founded merely on our experience of their constant and regular conjunction; it is evident, that we ought not to make an exception to this maxim in favour of human testimony, whose connection with any event seems, in itself, as little necessary as any other. Were not the memory tenacious to a certain degree; had not men commonly an inclination to truth and a principle of probity; were they not sensible to shame, when detected in a falsehood: Were not these, I say, discovered by *experience* to be qualities, inherent in human nature, we should never repose the least confidence in human testimony. A man delirious, or noted for falsehood and villainy, has no manner of authority with us.

 ## ASK YOURSELF

8.110. What other empirical evidence gives or takes away from the confidence we have in a person's testimony?

Other Factors in Evaluating Testimonies. Before discussing testimonies of miracles in particular, Hume continues listing general factors that weigh in favor of or against someone's testimony.

And as the evidence, derived from witnesses and human testimony, is founded on past experience, so it varies with the experience, and is regarded either as a *proof* or a *probability*, according as the conjunction between any particular kind of report and any kind of object has been found to be constant or variable. There are a number of circumstances to be taken into consideration in all judgments of this kind; and the ultimate standard, by which we determine all disputes, that may arise concerning them, is always derived from experience and observation. Where this experience is not entirely uniform on any side, it is attended with an unavoidable contrariety in our judgments, and with the same opposition and mutual destruction of argument as in every other kind of evidence. We frequently hesitate concerning the reports of others. We balance the opposite circumstances, which cause any doubt or uncertainty; and when we discover a superiority on any side, we incline to it; but still with a diminution of assurance, in proportion to the force of its antagonist.

This contrariety of evidence, in the present case, may be derived from several different causes; from the opposition of contrary testimony; from the character or number of the witnesses; from the manner of their delivering their testimony; or from the union of all these circumstances. We entertain a suspicion concerning any matter of fact, when the witnesses contradict each other; when they are but few, or of a doubtful character; when they have an interest in what they affirm; when they deliver their testimony with hesitation, or on the contrary, with too violent asseverations. There are many other particulars of the same kind, which may diminish or destroy the force of any argument, derived from human testimony.

 ASK YOURSELF

8.111. What are some reasons that we are suspicious of some testimonies?

Hume notes that sometimes a reported event seems so improbable that we wouldn't be persuaded of its truth even if told by the most reliable witness. In such cases, the alleged event is incompatible with what we know about the world in general.

Suppose, for instance, that the fact, which the testimony endeavors to establish, partakes of the extraordinary and the marvelous; in that case, the evidence, resulting from the testimony, admits of a diminution, greater or less, in proportion as the fact is more or less unusual. The reason why we place any credit in witnesses and historians, is not derived from any *connection*, which we perceive *a priori*, between testimony and reality, but because we are accustomed to find a conformity between them. But when the fact attested is such a one as has seldom fallen under our observation, here is a contest of two opposite experiences; of which the one destroys the other, as far as its force goes, and the superior can only operate on the mind by the force, which remains. The very same principle of experience, which gives us a certain degree of assurance in the testimony of witnesses, gives us also, in this case, another degree of assurance against the fact, which they endeavor to establish; from which contradiction there necessarily arises a counterpoize, and mutual destruction of belief and authority.

I should not believe such a story were it told me by CATO; was a proverbial saying in Rome, even during the lifetime of that philosophical patriot. The incredibility of a fact, it was allowed, might invalidate so great an authority.

The INDIAN prince, who refused to believe the first relations concerning the effects of frost, reasoned justly; and it naturally required very strong testimony to engage his assent to facts, that arose from a state of nature, with which he was unacquainted, and which bore so little analogy to those events, of which he had had constant and uniform experience. Though they were not contrary to his experience, they were not conformable to it.

 ASK YOURSELF

8.112. Consider a prince from India who never personally witnessed frost. According to Hume, would it be reasonable for him to believe someone's testimony who claimed that water could freeze?

Given these points about evaluating testimonies in general, Hume turns to evaluating testimonies of miracles.

The Evidence of Nature versus the Testimony of Miracles. Just as testimonies of improbable events (such as alien abductions) are counterbalanced by our general life experiences, this is even more so with testimonies of miracles. The testimony itself counts as evidence for the alleged miracle, but this is outweighed by our life experiences that speak against such a possibility.

But in order to increase the probability against the testimony of witnesses, let us suppose, that the fact, which they affirm, instead of being only marvelous, is really miraculous; and suppose also, that the testimony considered apart and in itself, amounts to an entire proof; in that case, there is proof against proof, of which the strongest must prevail, but still with a diminution of its force, in proportion to that of its antagonist.

A miracle is a violation of the laws of nature; and as a firm and unalterable experience has established these laws, the proof against a miracle, from the very nature of the fact, is as entire as any argument from experience can possibly be imagined. Why is it more than probable, that all men must die; that lead cannot, of itself, remain suspended in the air; that fire consumes wood, and is extinguished by water; unless it be, that these events are found agreeable to the laws of nature, and there is required a violation of these laws, or in other words, a miracle to prevent them? Nothing is esteemed a miracle, if it ever happen in the common course of nature. It is no miracle that a man, seemingly in good health, should die on a sudden: Because such a kind of death, though more unusual than any other, has yet been frequently observed to happen. But it is a miracle, that a dead man should come to life; because that has never been observed in any age or country. There must, therefore, be a uniform experience against every miraculous event, otherwise the event would not merit that appellation. And as a uniform experience amounts to a proof, there is here a direct and full *proof*, from the nature of the fact, against the existence of any miracle; nor can such a proof be destroyed, or the miracle rendered credible, but by an opposite proof, which is superior.

ASK YOURSELF

8.113. What is Hume's definition of a miracle?

8.114. Why does uniform experience constitute evidence against the existence of any miracle?

Definition of a Miracle. Hume recognizes that we must be clear about which type of events qualify as miracles. In the previous excerpt he defines a miracle as a violation of a law of nature. This eliminates many events that are commonly called miracles, such as fortunate accidents or improbable medical recoveries. In a footnote he discusses possible events that fit the definition of a miracles.

Sometimes an event may not, *in itself*, seem to be contrary to the laws of nature, and yet, if it were real, it might, by reason of some circumstances, be denominated a miracle; because, in *fact*, it is contrary to these laws. Thus if a person, claiming a divine authority, should command a sick person to be well, a healthful man to fall down dead, the clouds to pour rain, the winds to blow, in short, should order many natural events, which immediately follow upon his command; these might justly be esteemed miracles, because they are really, in this case, contrary to the laws of nature. For if any suspicion remain, that the event and command concurred by accident there is no miracle and no transgression of the laws of nature. If this suspicion be removed, there is evidently a miracle, and a transgression of these laws; because nothing can be more contrary to nature than that the voice or command of a man should have such an influence. A miracle may be accurately defined, *a transgression of a law of nature by a particular volition of the Deity, or by the interposition of some invisible agent*. A miracle may either be discoverable by men or not. This alters not its nature and essence. The raising of a house or ship into the air is a visible miracle. The raising of a feather, when the wind wants ever so little of a force requisite for that purpose, is as real a miracle, though not so sensible with regard to us.

ASK YOURSELF

8.115. Suppose that a divine authority commands some natural event, such as the clouds pouring rain, and that event happens. What aspect of this would involve a violation of a law of nature?

8.116. Suppose that a feather would start to move without any air current. Even though it violated a law of nature, to an observer it would not appear that way. For Hume would this still count as a miracle?

Suppose that a well-respected and rational person reports a miracle. In theory, the evidence in support of his testimony might rise to the level of a proof (given his good reputation). However, Hume argues that most miracle testimonies do not rise to that level of evidence. He describes four factors that reduce the credibility of most miracle testimonies.

In the foregoing reasoning we have supposed, that the testimony, upon which a miracle is founded, may possibly amount to an entire proof, and that the falsehood of that testimony would be a real prodigy: But it is easy to shew, that we have been a great deal too liberal in our concession, and that there never was a miraculous event established on so full an evidence.

Witnesses Lack Integrity. The first factor that reduces the credibility of most miracle testimonies is that the witnesses lack integrity.

For *first*, there is not to be found, in all history, any miracle attested by a sufficient number of men, of such unquestioned good-sense, education, and learning, as to secure us against all delusion in themselves; of such undoubted integrity, as to place them beyond all suspicion of any design to deceive others; of such credit and reputation in the eyes of mankind, as to have a great deal to lose in case of their being detected in any falsehood; and at the same time, attesting facts performed in such a public manner and in so celebrated a part of the world, as to render the detection unavoidable: All which circumstances are requisite to give us a full assurance in the testimony of men.

 ASK YOURSELF

8.117. Which character traits do eyewitnesses of miracles typically lack?

Propensity to Sensationalize. The second factor that reduces the credibility of most miracle testimonies is that people fall prey to a tendency to sensationalize. We enjoy hearing and telling strange stories, and this encourages others to invent strange stories.

Secondly. We may observe in human nature a principle which, if strictly examined, will be found to diminish extremely the assurance which we might, from human testimony, have in any kind of prodigy. The maxim by which we commonly conduct ourselves in our reasonings is that the objects, of which we have no experience, resemble those of which we have; that what we have found to be most usual is always most probable; and that where there is an opposition of arguments, we ought to give the preference to such as are founded on the greatest number of past observations. But though in proceeding by this rule we readily reject any fact which is unusual and incredible in an ordinary degree; yet in advancing farther, the mind observes not always the same rule; but when anything is affirmed utterly absurd and miraculous, it rather the more readily admits of such a fact, upon account of that very circumstance, which ought to destroy all its authority. The passion of surprise and wonder arising from miracles, being an agreeable emotion, gives a sensible tendency towards the belief of those events from which it is derived. And this goes so far, that even those who cannot enjoy this pleasure immediately, nor can believe those miraculous events, of which they are informed, yet love to partake of the satisfaction at second-hand or by rebound, and place a pride and delight in exciting the admiration of others.

ASK YOURSELF

8.118. Which emotions surrounding sensational stories make them so enjoyable?

Hume notes that religious leaders capitalize on this tendency to sensationalize and invent such stories for the greater good of their religious cause.

With what greediness are the miraculous accounts of travelers received, their descriptions of sea and land monsters, their relations of wonderful adventures, strange men, and uncouth manners? But if the spirit of religion join itself to the love of wonder, there is an end of common sense; and human testimony, in these circumstances, loses all pretensions to authority. A religionist may be an enthusiast, and imagine he sees what has no reality: He may know his narrative to be false, and yet persevere in it, with the best intentions in the world, for the sake of promoting so holy a cause: Or even where this delusion has not place, vanity, excited by so strong a temptation, operates on him more powerfully than on the rest of mankind in any other circumstances; and self-interest with equal force. His auditors may not have, and commonly have not, sufficient judgment to canvass his evidence: What judgment they have, they renounce by principle, in these sublime and mysterious subjects: Or if they were ever so willing to employ it, passion and a heated imagination disturb the regularity of its operations. Their credulity increases his impudence: And his impudence overpowers their credulity.

ASK YOURSELF

8.119. What motivates religious leaders to take advantage of our desire to hear sensational stories?

Abound in Barbarous Nations. The third factor that reduces the credibility of most miracle testimonies is that such stories typically originate in ignorant and barbarous countries. This factor is similar to the first factor. However, the first factor targeted the integrity of the *individual eyewitness*, whereas this third factor targets the entire social context from which such stories arise.

Thirdly. It forms a strong presumption against all supernatural and miraculous relations, that they are observed chiefly to abound among ignorant and barbarous nations; or if a civilized people has ever given admission to any of them, that people will be found to have received them from ignorant and barbarous ancestors, who transmitted them with that inviolable sanction and authority, which always attend received opinions. When we peruse the first histories of all nations, we are apt to imagine ourselves transported into some new world; where the whole frame of nature is disjointed, and every element performs its operations in a different manner, from what it does at present. Battles, revolutions, pestilence, famine and death, are never the effect of those natural causes, which we experience. Prodigies, omens, oracles, judgments, quite obscure the few natural events, that are intermingled with them. But as the former grow thinner every page, in proportion as we advance nearer the enlightened ages, we soon learn, that there is nothing mysterious or supernatural in the case, but that all proceeds from the usual propensity of mankind towards the marvelous, and that, though this inclination may at intervals receive a check from sense and learning, it can never be thoroughly extirpated from human nature.

 ASK YOURSELF

8.120. In such countries, what are causes assigned to events such as battles, revolutions, pestilence, famine, and death?

Miracles Support Rival Religious Systems. The fourth factor that reduces the credibility of miracle testimonies is that miracles are done in the context of a given religious system, particularly to defend that religious system. Suppose that there are ten religions, each one doctrinally incompatible with the other nine religions and each one supported by its own miracles. The credibility of a miracle in any single religious system would be outweighed by the miracles of the nine other religious systems.

I may add as a *fourth* reason, which diminishes the authority of prodigies, that there is no testimony for any, even those which have not been expressly detected, that is not opposed by an infinite number of witnesses; so that not only the miracle destroys the credit of testimony, but the testimony destroys itself. To make this the better understood, let us consider, that, in matters of religion, whatever is different is contrary; and that it is impossible the religions of ancient ROME, of TURKEY, of SIAM, and of CHINA should, all of them, be established on any solid foundation. Every miracle, therefore, pretended to have been wrought in any of these religions (and all of them abound in miracles), as its direct scope is to establish the particular system to which it is attributed; so has it the same force, though more indirectly, to overthrow every other system. In destroying a rival system, it likewise destroys the credit of those miracles, on which that system was established; so that all the prodigies of different religions are to be regarded as contrary facts, and the evidences of these prodigies, whether weak or strong, as opposite to each other. According to this method of reasoning, when we believe any miracle of Mahomet or his successors, we have for our warrant the testimony of a few barbarous Arabians: And on the other hand, we are to regard the authority of Titus Livius, Plutarch, Tacitus, and, in short, of all the authors and witnesses, Grecian, Chinese, and Roman Catholic, who have related any miracle in their particular religion; I say, we are to regard their testimony in the same light as if they had mentioned that Mahometan miracle, and had in express terms contradicted it, with the same certainty as they have for the miracle they relate. This argument may appear over subtile and refined; but is not in reality different from the reasoning of a judge, who supposes, that the credit of two witnesses, maintaining a crime against any one, is destroyed by the testimony of two others, who affirm him to have been two hundred leagues distant, at the same instant when the crime is said to have been committed.

 ASK YOURSELF

8.121. Suppose that a miracle in Islam is supported by the testimony of a few Arabic believers. Suppose, also, that the ancient Greeks report their own miracles for their own Greek religion. How should we regard the Greek reports in relation to the initial Muslim report?

Summary. Hume summarizes the key point of his essay. Most testimonies about miracles are unreliable, but even if they were reliable, they should not be believed since they go against the immense evidence we have in favor of constant natural law. His argument can be outlined as follows:

a. The evidence from experience in support of a law of nature is extremely strong.

b. A miracle is a violation of a law of nature.

c. Therefore, the evidence from experience against the occurrence of a miracle is extremely strong.

Upon the whole, then, it appears, that no testimony for any kind of miracle has ever amounted to a probability, much less to a proof; and that, even supposing it amounted to a proof, it would be opposed by another proof; derived from the very nature of the fact, which it would endeavor to establish. It is experience only, which gives authority to human testimony; and it is the same experience, which assures us of the laws of nature. When, therefore, these two kinds of experience are contrary, we have nothing to do but subtract the one from the other, and embrace an opinion, either on one side or the other, with that assurance which arises from the remainder. But according to the principle here explained, this subtraction, with regard to all popular religions, amounts to an entire annihilation; and therefore we may establish it as a maxim, that no human testimony can have such force as to prove a miracle, and make it a just foundation for any such system of religion.

 ASK YOURSELF

8.122. What does Hume believe we should do when comparing two contrary experiences, specifically, miracles versus natural law?

Hume continues by arguing that, even if miracles did occur, it would be unreasonable to make them the foundation of religious systems, as is typically done in the world's religions.

Miracles in Christianity. In conclusion, Hume notes that theologians typically base the truth of Christianity upon the occurrence of miracles (such as the virgin birth and the resurrection). Hume argues instead that Christianity is founded on faith. Thus, he sees his attack on miracles as an aid to true Christian belief since it undermines any attempt to rationally prove Christianity by appealing to Christian miracles. Hume's concluding comments here are among the most problematic for Hume scholars. On the surface, Hume appears to endorse a faith-oriented belief in Christianity, similar to Pascal. However, even Hume's critics in his own day saw his comments as an attempt to conceal his true view, which is that Christianity has no merit whatsoever, whether based on miracles or on faith.

I am the better pleased with the method of reasoning here delivered, as I think it may serve to confound those dangerous friends or disguised enemies to the *Christian Religion*, who have undertaken to defend it by the principles of human reason. Our most holy religion is founded on *Faith*, not on reason; and it is a sure method of exposing it to put it to such a trial as it is, by no means, fitted to endure. To make this more evident, let us examine those miracles, related in scripture; and not to lose ourselves in too wide a field, let us confine ourselves to such as we find in the *Pentateuch*, which we shall examine, according to the principles of these pretended Christians, not as the word or testimony of God himself, but as the production of a mere human writer and historian. Here then we are first to consider a book, presented to us by a barbarous and ignorant people, written in an age when they were still more barbarous, and in all probability long after the facts which it relates, corroborated by no concurring testimony, and resembling those fabulous accounts, which every nation gives of its origin. Upon reading this book, we find it full of prodigies and miracles. It gives an account of a state of the world and of human nature entirely different from the present: Of our fall from that state: Of the age of man, extended to near a thousand years: Of the destruction of the world by a deluge: Of the arbitrary choice of one people, as the favorites of heaven; and that people the countrymen of the author: Of their deliverance from bondage by prodigies the most astonishing imaginable: I desire any one to lay his hand upon his heart, and after a serious consideration declare, whether he thinks that the falsehood of such a book, supported by such a testimony, would be more extraordinary and miraculous than all the miracles it relates; which is, however, necessary to make it be received, according to the measures of probability above established.

     ASK YOURSELF

8.123. How does Hume think that we should evaluate the miracles of the Old Testament (particularly those he describes from Genesis)?

The concluding paragraph is the most controversial part of the whole chapter. Hume argues that Christianity is intimately linked with miracles. Since a reasonable person should not believe reports of miracles, then an act of God is required to make him believe. In Hume's words, it requires a miracle of faith. According to John Briggs, an eighteenth-century critic of Hume, Hume's real point is that belief in Christianity requires "miraculous stupidity."

What we have said of miracles may be applied, without any variation, to prophecies; and indeed, all prophecies are real miracles, and as such only, can be admitted as proofs of any revelation. If it did not exceed the capacity of human nature to foretell future events, it would be absurd to employ any prophecy as an argument for a divine mission or authority from heaven. So that, upon the whole, we may conclude, that the *Christian Religion* not only was at first attended with miracles, but even at this day cannot be believed by any reasonable person without one. Mere reason is insufficient to convince us of its veracity: And whoever is moved by *Faith* to assent to it, is conscious of a continued miracle in his own person, which subverts all the principles of his understanding, and gives him a determination to believe what is most contrary to custom and experience.

 ASK YOURSELF

8.124. Hume concludes that whoever is moved by faith to believe in the miracles of Christianity is "conscious of a continued miracle in his own person." What does this miracle of Christian faith determine us to believe?

Section 12: Of the Academical or Skeptical Philosophy

Hume openly avowed skepticism in his philosophical writings. The term "skepticism" has a variety of philosophical meanings, and Hume's task in this concluding section is to identify and evaluate some of these. In the concluding part of this section Hume endorses a version of skepticism that he calls *mitigated*, which he associates with the ancient Greek Academic school of skepticism (as opposed to the more excessive ancient Greek Pyrrhonian school).

Caution and Modesty. The first type of mitigated skepticism involves resisting dogmatism.

 From HUME: *Enquiry*, Section 12 ⎯⎯⎯⎯⎯⎯⎯

There is, indeed, a more *mitigated* skepticism or *academical* philosophy, which may be both durable and useful, and which may, in part, be the result of this Pyrrhonism, or *excessive* skepticism, when its undistinguished doubts are, in some measure, corrected by common sense and reflection. The greater part of mankind are naturally apt to be affirmative and dogmatical in their opinions; and while they see objects only on one side, and have no idea of any counterpoising argument, they throw themselves precipitately into the principles, to which they are inclined; nor have they any indulgence for those who entertain opposite sentiments. To hesitate or balance perplexes their understanding, checks their passion, and suspends their action. They are, therefore, impatient till they escape from a state, which to them is so uneasy: And they think, that they could never remove themselves far enough from it, by the violence of their affirmations and obstinacy of their belief. But could such dogmatical reasoners become sensible of the strange infirmities of human understanding, even in its most perfect state, and when most accurate and cautious in its determinations; such a reflection would naturally inspire them with more modesty and reserve, and diminish their fond opinion of themselves, and their prejudice against antagonists. The illiterate may reflect on the disposition of the learned, who, amidst all the advantages of study and reflection, are commonly still diffident in their determinations: And if any of the learned be inclined, from their natural temper, to haughtiness and obstinacy, a small tincture of PYRRHONISM might abate their pride, by showing them, that the few advantages, which they may have attained over their fellows, are but inconsiderable, if compared with the universal perplexity and confusion, which is inherent in human nature. In general, there is a degree of doubt, and caution, and modesty, which, in all kinds of scrutiny and decision, ought for ever to accompany a just reasoner.

 ## ASK YOURSELF

8.125. According to this first type of mitigated skepticism, what is the benefit of "a small tincture of Pyrrhonism"?

The Limits of Rational Inquiry. A second form of mitigated skepticism is that all rational inquiry should be confined to very narrow limits.

Another species of *mitigated* skepticism which may be of advantage to mankind, and which may be the natural result of the Pyrrhonian doubts and scruples, is the limitation of our enquiries to such subjects as are best adapted to the narrow capacity of human understanding. The *imagination* of man is naturally sublime, delighted with whatever is remote and extraordinary, and running, without control, into the most distant parts of space and time in order to avoid the objects, which custom has rendered too familiar to it. A correct *Judgment* observes a contrary method, and avoiding all distant and high enquiries, confines itself to common life, and to such subjects as fall under daily practice and experience; leaving the more sublime topics to the embellishment of poets and orators, or to the arts of priests and politicians. To bring us to so salutary a determination, nothing can be more serviceable, than to be once thoroughly convinced of the force of the Pyrrhonian doubt, and of the impossibility, that any thing, but the strong power of natural instinct, could free us from it. Those who have a propensity to philosophy, will still continue their researches; because they reflect, that, besides the immediate pleasure attending such an occupation, philosophical decisions are nothing but the reflections of common life, methodized and corrected. But they will never be tempted to go beyond common life, so long as they consider the imperfection of those faculties which they employ, their narrow reach, and their inaccurate operations. While we cannot give a satisfactory reason, why we believe, after a thousand experiments, that a stone will fall, or fire burn; can we ever satisfy ourselves concerning any determination, which we may form, with regard to the origin of worlds, and the situation of nature, from, and to eternity?

This narrow limitation, indeed, of our enquiries, is, in every respect, so reasonable, that it suffices to make the slightest examination into the natural powers of the human mind and to compare them with their objects, in order to recommend it to us. We shall then find what are the proper subjects of science and enquiry.

It seems to me, that the only objects of the abstract science or of demonstration are quantity and number, and that all attempts to extend this more perfect species of knowledge beyond these bounds are mere sophistry and illusion. As the component parts of quantity and number are entirely similar, their relations become intricate and involved; and nothing can be more curious, as well as useful, than to trace, by a variety of mediums, their equality or inequality, through their different appearances. But as all other ideas are clearly distinct and different from each other, we can never advance farther, by our utmost scrutiny, than to observe this diversity, and, by an obvious reflection, pronounce one thing not to be another. Or if there be any difficulty in these decisions, it proceeds entirely from the undeterminate meaning of words, which is corrected by juster definitions. That *the square of the hypothenuse is equal to the squares of the other two sides*, cannot be known, let the terms be ever so exactly defined, without a train of reasoning and enquiry. But to convince us of this proposition, *that where there is no property, there can be no injustice*, it is only necessary to define the terms, and explain injustice to be a violation of property. This proposition is, indeed, nothing but a more imperfect definition. It is the same case with all those pretended syllogistical reasonings, which may be found in every other branch of learning, except the sciences of quantity and number; and these may safely, I think, be pronounced the only proper objects of knowledge and demonstration.

All other enquiries of men regard only matter of fact and existence; and these are evidently incapable of demonstration. Whatever *is* may *not be*. No negation of a fact can involve a contradiction. The non-existence of any being, without exception, is as clear and distinct an idea as its existence. The proposition, which affirms it not to be, however false, is no less conceivable and intelligible, than that which affirms it to be. The case is different with the sciences, properly so called. Every proposition, which is not true, is there confused and unintelligible. That the cube root of 64 is equal to the half of 10, is a false proposition, and can never be distinctly conceived. But that CAESAR, or the angel GABRIEL, or any being never existed, may be a false proposition, but still is perfectly conceivable, and implies no contradiction.

The existence, therefore, of any being can only be proved by arguments from its cause or its effect; and these arguments are founded entirely on experience. If we reason *a priori*, any thing may appear able to produce any thing. The falling of a pebble may, for aught we know, extinguish the sun; or the wish of a man control the planets in their orbits. It is only experience, which teaches us the nature and bounds of cause and effect, and enables us to infer the existence of one object from that of another. Such is the foundation of moral reasoning, which forms the greater part of human knowledge, and is the source of all human action and behavior.

Moral reasonings are either concerning particular or general facts. All deliberations in life regard the former; as also all disquisitions in history, chronology, geography, and astronomy.

The sciences, which treat of general facts, are politics, natural philosophy, physic, chemistry, &c. where the qualities, causes and effects of a whole species of objects are enquired into.

Divinity or Theology, as it proves the existence of a Deity, and the immortality of souls, is composed partly of reasonings concerning particular, partly concerning general facts. It has a foundation in *reason*, so far as it is supported by experience. But its best and most solid foundation is *faith* and divine revelation.

Morals and criticism are not so properly objects of the understanding as of taste and sentiment. Beauty, whether moral or natural, is felt, more properly than perceived. Or if we reason concerning it, and endeavor to fix its standard, we regard a new fact, to wit, the general tastes of mankind, or some such fact, which may be the object of reasoning and enquiry.

 ASK YOURSELF

8.128. What do all of the preceding areas of experimental reasoning have in common (including history, physics, theology, and morals)?

When we run over libraries, persuaded of these principles, what havoc must we make? If we take in our hand any volume; of divinity or school metaphysics, for instance; let us ask, *Does it contain any abstract reasoning concerning quantity or number?* No. *Does it contain any experimental reasoning concerning matter of fact and existence?* No. Commit it then to the flames: For it can contain nothing but sophistry and illusion.

 ASK YOURSELF

8.129. Hume rejects all remaining areas of study that claim to establish truths about the world but are about neither (1) abstract reasoning concerning quantity and number (relations of ideas) nor (2) experimental reasoning concerning matters of fact. What does he suggest that we do with books that contain such studies?

Personal Identity

Not all of the philosophically important arguments in Hume's *Treatise* made their way into both *Enquiries*. One such argument is Hume's discussion of the personal identity.

Hume's Original Argument in Treatise Book 1. Hume begins his discussion noting how philosophers typically understand the notion of the *self*. One philosopher Hume possibly has in mind is Descartes in Meditation 2. According to Hume, philosophers such as Descartes argue that the *self* (1) is a simple and unified thing/experience and (2) continues over time as a unified thing/experience.

 From HUME: *Treatise*

There are some philosophers who imagine we are every moment intimately conscious of what we call our SELF; that we feel its existence and its continuance in existence; and are certain, beyond the evidence of a demonstration, both of its perfect identity and simplicity. The strongest sensation, the most violent passion, say they, instead of distracting us from this view, only fix it the more intensely, and make us consider their influence on self either by their pain or pleasure. To attempt a farther proof of this were to weaken its evidence; since no proof can be derived from any fact, of which we are so intimately conscious; nor is there any thing, of which we can be certain, if we doubt of this.

 ASK YOURSELF

8.130. What kind of proofs do these philosophers offer for their view?

Keeping with his copy thesis, Hume argues that if we do have an idea of single, continuous self, this idea must have come from some impression. However, it appears that we have no such single, continuous impression of the self.

Unluckily all these positive assertions are contrary to that very experience, which is pleaded for them, nor have we any idea of *self*, after the manner it is here explained. For from what impression could this idea be derived? This question it is impossible to answer without a manifest contradiction and absurdity; and yet 'tis a question, which must necessarily be answered, if we would have the idea of self pass for clear and intelligible. It must be some one impression, that gives rise to every real idea. But self or person is not any one impression, but that to which our several impressions and ideas are supposed to have a reference. If any impression gives rise to the idea of self, that impression must continue invariably the same, thro' the whole course of our lives; since self is supposed to exist after that manner. But there is no impression constant and invariable. Pain and pleasure, grief and joy, passions and sensations succeed each other, and never all exist at the same time. It cannot, therefore, be from any of these impressions, or from any other, that the idea of self is derived; and consequently there is no such idea.

ASK YOURSELF

8.131. Why does Hume think we can form no such idea of a single, continuous self?

But farther, what must become of all our particular perceptions upon this hypothesis? All these are different, and distinguishable, and separable from each other, and may be separately considered, and may exist separately, and have no Deed of tiny thing to support their existence. After what manner, therefore, do they belong to self; and how are they connected with it? For my part, when I enter most intimately into what I call *myself*, I always stumble on some particular perception or other, of heat or cold, light or shade, love or hatred, pain or pleasure. I never can catch *myself* at any time without a perception, and never can observe any thing but the perception. When my perceptions are removed for any time, as by sound sleep; so long am I insensible of *myself*, and may truly be said not to exist. And were all my perceptions removed by death, and could I neither think, nor feel, nor see, nor love, nor hate after the dissolution of my body, I should be entirely annihilated, nor do I conceive what is farther requisite to make me a perfect non-entity.

ASK YOURSELF

8.132. What kind of perceptions do we have of ourselves?

8.133. Why does Hume think that the self must be identical to our varied perceptions?

If any one, upon serious and unprejudiced reflection thinks he has a different notion of *himself*, I must confess I call reason no longer with him. All I can allow him is, that he may be in the right as well as I, and that we are essentially different in this particular. He may, perhaps, perceive something simple and continued, which he calls himself; though I am certain there is no such principle in me.

But setting aside some metaphysicians of this kind, I may venture to affirm of the rest of mankind, that they are nothing but a bundle or collection of different perceptions, which succeed each other with an inconceivable rapidity, and are in a perpetual flux and movement. Our eyes cannot turn in their sockets without varying our perceptions. Our thought is still more variable than our sight; and all our other senses and faculties contribute to this change; nor is there any single power of the soul, which remains unalterably the same, perhaps for one moment.

ASK YOURSELF

8.134. What kind of perceptions are contained in the "bundle"?

The mind is a kind of theatre, where several perceptions successively make their appearance; pass, re-pass, glide away, and mingle in an infinite variety of postures and situations. There is properly no *simplicity* in it at one time, nor identity in different; whatever natural propension we may have to imagine that simplicity and identity. The comparison of the theatre must not mislead us. They are the successive perceptions only, that constitute the mind; nor have we the most distant notion of the place, where these scenes are represented, or of the materials, of which it is composed.

Hume concedes that we have a "natural propensity" or inclination to believe in a simple and continuous self, even though we are *in fact* only a bundle of perceptions. At first he suggests that we instinctively connect our various moments of perception because they resemble each other and are causally related. Thus, we have an artificially constructed idea of a unified self.

Modified View in the Appendix. A year after Hume published Book 1 of the *Treatise*, he abandoned his initial explanation of the artificially constructed idea of the self. His final position on the issue, as appears in the following excerpt from the Appendix to the *Treatise*, is that not only is the self *in fact* merely a bundle of perceptions, but also that he has no explanation of how we arrive at an artificially constructed notion of the self.

But upon a more strict review of the section concerning *personal identity*, I find myself involved in such a labyrinth, that, I must confess I neither know how to correct my former opinions, now how to render them consistent. If this be not a good general reason for skepticism, 'tis at least a sufficient one (if I were not already abundantly supplied) for me to entertain a diffidence and modesty in all my decisions. . . .

In short there are two principles, which I cannot render consistent; nor is it in my power to renounce either of them, viz. *that all our distinct perceptions are distinct existences, and that the mind never perceives any real connection among distinct existences.* Did our perceptions either inhere in something simple and individual, or did the mind perceive some real connection among them, there would be no difficulty in the case. For my part, I must plead the privilege of a skeptic, and confess, that this difficulty is too hard for my Understanding. I pretend not, however, to pronounce it absolutely insuperable. Others, perhaps, or myself, upon more mature reflections, may discover some hypothesis, that will reconcile those contradictions.

 ASK YOURSELF

8.135. What does Hume say about the possibility of solving this problem in the future?

Moral Theory

Hume's discussion of morality appeared first in Book 3 of his *Treatise of Human Nature* (1740). The book did not sell very well, which Hume blamed on its style, rather than its content. A decade later he recast the work in a more popularized form, which was published as *An Enquiry concerning the Principles of Morals* (1751). Hume wrote that of all his writings the moral *Enquiry* "is incomparably the best." There are two principal contributions in Hume's moral writings. The first is his attack on the role of reason in moral judgments and his notion that moral judgments are pleasing feelings experienced by a spectator. The second contribution is that Hume lays the foundations for the utilitarian moral theory. The litmus test for morally proper conduct is that it produces useful or pleasing consequences to the agent himself or the spectator.

Moral Distinctions Not Derived from Reason. Hume opens his moral *Enquiry* arguing that the role of reason in moral decisions is very limited and that moral approval is essentially a feeling. For Hume, the key problem in moral theory is whether a person's moral approval of something is a judgment of reason or only a feeling in the mind of that person.

 From HUME: Moral *Enquiry*, Section 1

There has been a controversy started of late . . . concerning the general foundation of morals: whether they be derived from reason or from sentiment; whether we attain the knowledge of them by a chain of argument and induction, or by an immediate feeling and finer internal sense; whether, like all sound judgment of truth and falsehood, they should be the same to every rational intelligent being; or whether, like the perception of beauty and deformity, they be founded entirely on the particular fabric and constitution of the human species.

The ancient philosophers, though they often affirm that virtue is nothing but conformity to reason, yet, in general, seem to consider morals as deriving their existence from taste and sentiment. On the other hand, our modern inquirers (though they also talk much of the beauty of virtue and deformity of vice, yet) have commonly endeavored to account for these distinctions by metaphysical reasonings, and by deductions from the most abstract principles of the understanding. Such confusion reigned in these subjects, that an opposition of the greatest consequence could prevail between one system and another, and even in the parts of almost each individual system. And yet nobody, till very lately, was ever sensible of it.

 ASK YOURSELF

8.136. What is the controversy concerning the general foundation of morals?

8.137. How do the ancient moral philosophers stand in this controversy?

Reason versus Sentiment. Hume continues by noting that there are arguments on both sides of the dispute between reason and feeling. In the end, however, moral approval appears to be only a pleasing feeling or sentiment. He defends this position arguing that reason can only present us with facts, but reason is incapable of motivating us to action. For example, no matter how many starving people I see, I will not be motivated to help feed these people unless I am driven by emotion, not by reason. Therefore, only emotion can be the source of our moral obligation to act.

It must be acknowledged that both sides of the question are susceptible of specious arguments. Moral distinctions, it may be said, are discernible by pure *reason*. Else, whence the many disputes that reign in common life as well as in philosophy with regard to this subject: the long chain of proofs often produced on both sides, the examples cited, the authorities appealed to, the analogies employed, the fallacies detected, the inferences drawn, and the several conclusions adjusted to their proper principles. Truth is disputable, not taste. What exists in the nature of things is the standard of our judgment, [but] what each man feels within himself is the standard of sentiment. Propositions in geometry may be proved, systems in physics may be controverted. But the harmony of verse, the tenderness of passion, the brilliance of wit must give immediate pleasure. No man reasons concerning another's beauty, but frequently concerning the justice or injustice of his actions. In every criminal trial the first object of the prisoner is to disprove the facts alleged, and deny the actions imputed to him. The second [is] to prove that, even if these actions were real, they might be justified as innocent and lawful. It is confessedly by deductions of the understanding that the first point [of alleged facts] is ascertained. How can we suppose that a different faculty of the mind is employed in fixing the other [point regarding moral justification]?

 ASK YOURSELF

8.138. Hume confesses that there appears to be evidence for both sides of the controversy. How do criminal trials support the claim that morality is based on reason?

On the other hand, those who would resolve all moral determinations into *sentiment* may endeavor to show that it is impossible for reason ever to draw conclusions of this nature. To virtue, say they, it belongs to be *amiable*, and [to] vice *odious*. This forms their very nature or essence. But can reason or argumentation distribute these different epithets to any subjects, and pronounce beforehand that this must produce love, and that hatred? Or what other reason can we ever assign for these affections but the original fabric and formation of the human mind, which is naturally adapted to receive them?

The end of all moral speculations is to teach us our duty, and (by proper representations of the deformity of vice and beauty of virtue) beget correspondent habits, and engage us to avoid the one, and embrace the other. But is this ever to be expected from the inferences and conclusions of the understanding, which, of themselves, have no hold of the affections nor set in motion the active powers of men? They discover truths. But where the truths which they discover are indifferent, and beget no desire or aversion, they can have no influence on conduct and behavior. What is honorable, what is fair, what is becoming, what is noble, what is generous, takes possession of the heart and animates us to embrace and maintain it. What is intelligible, what is evident, what is probable, what is true, procures only the cool assent of the understanding, and gratifying a speculative curiosity, puts an end to our researches.

It is not contrary to reason to prefer the destruction of the whole world to the scratching of my finger. It is not contrary to reason for me to choose my total ruin, to prevent the least uneasiness of an Indian or person wholly unknown to me. It is as little contrary to reason to prefer even my own acknowledged lesser good to my greater, and have a more ardent affection for the former than the latter. A trivial good may, from certain circumstances, produce a desire superior to what arises from the greatest and most valuable enjoyment. Nor is there anything more extraordinary in this than in [the field of] mechanics to see [a] one pound weight raise up a hundred by the advantage of its situation [such as by a lever]. In short, a passion must be accompanied with some false judgment in order to its being unreasonable. [This paragraph is from the *Treatise*, 2.3.3.]

Extinguish all the warm feelings and prepossessions in favor of virtue, and all disgust or aversion to vice; render men totally indifferent towards these distinctions, and morality is no longer a practical study, nor has any tendency to regulate our lives and actions.

 ASK YOURSELF

8.139. In support of the claim that morality is based on sentiment, what would happen if we extinguished our warm feelings of virtue?

These arguments on each side (and many more might be produced) are so plausible, that I am apt to suspect they may, the one as well as the other, be solid and satisfactory, and that *reason* and *sentiment* concur in almost all moral determinations and conclusions. The final sentence, it is probable, which pronounces characters and actions amiable or odious, praise-worthy or blamable; that which stamps on them the mark of honor or infamy, approbation or censure; that which renders morality an active principle and constitutes virtue our happiness, and vice our misery; it is probable, I say, that this final sentence depends on some internal sense or feeling which nature has made universal in the whole species. For what else can have an influence of this nature?

 ASK YOURSELF

8.140. Hume concludes that perhaps reason and sentiment together are involved in moral judgments. What role would sentiment play in this hypothesis?

The Limited Role of Reason. The role of reason in moral decision making is very restrictive. First, reason can inform us of the relevant facts, such as the fact that Jones is starving. Second, reason can help us calculate the consequences of our actions, such as the fact that my feeding Jones would have beneficial consequences for both Jones and myself. In either case, however, that actual moral pronouncement, "I should feed Jones," is a feeling, and not a rational judgment.

But in order to pave the way for such a *sentiment*, and give a proper discernment of its object, it is often necessary, we find, that much *reasoning* should precede,

[so] that nice distinctions be made, just conclusions drawn, distant comparisons formed, complicated relations examined, and general facts fixed and ascertained.

[First,] some species of beauty, especially the natural kinds, on their first appearance, command our affection and approbation. And where they fail of this effect, it is impossible for any reasoning to redress their influence, or adapt them better to our taste and sentiment. But in many orders of beauty, particularly those of the finer arts, it is requisite to employ much reasoning in order to feel the proper sentiment. And a false relish may frequently be corrected by argument and reflection. There are just grounds to conclude that moral beauty partakes much of this latter species, and demands the assistance of our intellectual faculties, in order to give it a suitable influence on the human mind.

[Second,] one principal foundation of moral praise being supposed to lie in the *usefulness* [or beneficial consequences] of any quality or action, it is evident that *reason* must enter for a considerable share in all decisions of this kind. [This follows] since nothing but that faculty can instruct us in the tendency of qualities and actions, and *point out their beneficial consequences* to society and to their possessor. In many cases, this is an affair liable to great controversy. Doubts may arise, opposite interests may occur, and a preference must be given to one side [versus the other side] from very nice views, and a small overbalance of utility [or benefit which is in its favor]. This is particularly remarkable in questions with regard to justice (as is, indeed, natural to suppose from that species of utility, which attends every virtue). Were every single instance of justice, like that of benevolence, useful to society, this would be a more simple state of the case, and seldom liable to great controversy. But as single instances of justice are often pernicious in their first and immediate tendency (and as the advantage to society results only from the observance of the general rule, and from the concurrence and combination of several persons in the same equitable conduct) the case here becomes more intricate and involved. The various circumstances of society, the various *consequences* of any practice, the various interests which may be proposed; these, on many occasions, are doubtful and subject to great discussion and inquiry. The object of municipal laws is to fix all the questions with regard to justice. The debates of civilians, the reflections of politicians, the precedents of history and public records, are all directed to the same purpose. And a very accurate *reason* or *judgment* is often requisite to give the true determination, amidst such intricate doubts arising from obscure or opposite utilities.

But though reason, when fully assisted and improved, be sufficient to instruct us in the pernicious or useful tendency of qualities and actions, it is not alone sufficient to produce any moral blame or approbation. Utility is only a tendency to a certain end. And were the end totally indifferent to us, we should feel the same indifference towards the means. It is requisite [that] a *sentiment* should here display itself, in order to give a preference to the useful above the pernicious tendencies. This sentiment can be no other than a feeling for the happiness of humankind, and a resentment of their misery, since these are the different ends which virtue and vice have a tendency to promote. Here, therefore, *reason* instructs us in the several tendencies of actions, and *humanity* [or sentiment] makes a distinction in favor of those which are useful and beneficial.

ASK YOURSELF

8.141. What roles would reason play in moral judgment?

Thus, the distinct boundaries and offices of *reason* and of *taste* are easily ascertained. The former conveys the knowledge of truth and falsehood. The latter gives the sentiment of beauty and deformity, vice and virtue. The one discovers objects as they really stand in nature, without addition or diminution. The other has a productive faculty and (gilding or staining all natural objects with the colors borrowed from internal sentiment) raises in a manner a new creation. Reason, being cool and disengaged, is no motive to action, and directs only the impulse received from appetite or inclination, by showing us the means of attaining happiness or avoiding misery. Taste, as it gives pleasure or pain (and thereby constitutes happiness or misery) becomes a motive to action, and is the first spring or impulse to desire and volition. From circumstances and relations known or supposed, the former leads us to the discovery of the concealed and unknown. After all circumstances and relations are laid before us, the latter makes us feel from the whole a new sentiment of blame or approbation. The standard of the one, being founded on the nature of things, is eternal and inflexible, even by the will of the Supreme Being. The standard of the other, arising from the internal frame and constitution of animals, is ultimately derived from that Supreme will, which bestowed on each being its peculiar nature, and arranged the several classes and orders of existence.

Deriving Ought from Is. Hume's most influential attack on the role of reason in moral judgment is in Book 3 of his *Treatise.* He argues that Rationalist discussions of morality all begin with statements of fact, such as "Jones is starving," and then conclude with a statement of obligation, such as "We should help feed Jones." According to Hume, it is impossible to rationally deduce statements of obligation from statements of fact. This view of Hume's is encapsulated in the dictum that, "*Ought* cannot be derived from *is.*"

 From HUME: *Treatise* 3.1.1.

I cannot forbear adding to these reasonings an observation, which may, perhaps, be found of some importance. In every system of morality which I have hitherto met with, I have always remarked that the author proceeds for some time in the ordinary way of reasoning, and establishes the being of a God, or makes observations concerning human affairs. When of a sudden, I am surprised to find that, instead of the usual copulations of propositions, *is* and *is not*, I meet with no proposition that is not connected with an *ought* or an *ought not.* The change is imperceptible, but is, however, of the last [and greatest] consequence. For as this *ought* or *ought not* expresses some new relation or affirmation, it is necessary that it should be observed and explained. And at the same time, [it is necessary] that a reason should be given for (what seems altogether inconceivable) how this new relation can be a deduction from others, which are entirely different from it. But as authors do not commonly use this precaution, I shall presume to recommend it to the readers. And [I] am persuaded that this small attention would subvert all the vulgar systems of morality, and let us see that the distinction of vice and virtue is not founded merely on the relations of objects nor is perceived by reason.

The Theory of Utility. In the eighteenth and early nineteenth centuries, Hume was known as the creator of the "theory of utility," especially as described in his *Enquiry concerning the Principles of Morals*. The theory is this: Useful and immediately agreeable actions are the only actions that a spectator will morally approve of. That is, utility and agreeability are the only intrinsic moral goods. Hume's proof of his thesis is straightforward. (1) He lists several actions (and virtues) of a moral agent that produce pleasing sentiments in the mind of the spectator. (2) He observes that all of these actions have the consequence of either utility (i.e., usefulness) or immediate agreeableness. The useful actions include charity, justice, benevolence, and telling the truth. Immediately agreeable actions include wit, eloquence, cleanliness, and pride. The bulk of the moral *Enquiry*—seven of its nine chapters—is devoted to these first two tasks. (3) He then generalizes from this observation and concludes that all morally good actions are either useful or immediately agreeable. Hume notes his intent to use the experimental method of reasoning in discovering the constituents of personal merit (Hume's term for morally applaudable conduct). He says he will begin by listing all those qualities (or virtues) which are traditionally admired. The following selections are from the moral *Enquiry*.

 From HUME: Moral *Enquiry*, Sections 1 and 9

But though this question, concerning the general principles of morals, be curious and important, it is needless for us, at present, to employ farther care in our researches concerning it. For if we can be so happy, in the course of this inquiry, as to discover the true origin of morals, it will then easily appear how far either sentiment or reason enters into all determinations of this nature. In order to attain this purpose, we shall endeavor to follow a very simple method: We shall analyze that complication of mental qualities, which form what, in common life, we call *personal merit*: We shall consider every attribute of the mind, which renders a man an object either of esteem and affection, or of hatred and contempt; every habit or sentiment or faculty, which, if ascribed to any person, implies either praise or blame, and may enter into any panegyric or satire of his character and manners. The quick sensibility, which, on this head, is so universal among humankind, gives a philosopher sufficient assurance, that he can never be considerably mistaken in framing the catalogue, or incur any danger of misplacing the objects of his contemplation: He needs only enter into his own breast for a moment, and consider whether or not he should desire to have this or that quality ascribed to him, and whether such or such an imputation would proceed from a friend or an enemy. The very nature of language guides us almost infallibly in forming a judgment of this nature; and as every tongue possesses one set of words which are taken in a good sense, and another in the opposite, the least acquaintance with the idiom suffices, without any reasoning, to direct us in collecting and arranging the estimable or blamable qualities of men. The only object of reasoning is to discover the circumstances on both sides, which are common to these qualities; to observe that particular in which the estimable qualities agree on the one hand, and the blamable on the other; and thence to reach the foundation of ethics, and find those universal principles, from which all censure or approbation is ultimately derived. As this is a question of fact, not of abstract science, we can only expect success, by following the experimental method, and deducing general maxims from a comparison of particular instances.

 ASK YOURSELF

8.142. Which version of the experimental method does Hume follow in his quest for personal merit?

The other scientifical method, where a general abstract principle is first established, and is afterwards branched out into a variety of inferences and conclusions, may be more perfect in itself, but suits less the imperfection of human nature, and is a common source of illusion and mistake in this as well as in other subjects. Men are now cured of their passion for hypotheses and systems in natural philosophy, and will hearken to no arguments but those which are derived from experience. It is full time they should attempt a like reformation in all moral disquisitions; and reject every system of ethics, however subtle or ingenious, which is not founded on fact and observation.

 ASK YOURSELF

8.143. Which version of the experimental method does Hume *not* follow? Why?

Constituents of Personal Merit. In the concluding section of the moral *Enquiry*, Hume argues that an agent's character trait or action is approved of morally if and only if it is useful or agreeable to oneself or to others.

It may justly appear surprising, that any man, in so late an age, should find it requisite to prove, by elaborate reasoning, that PERSONAL MERIT consists altogether in the possession of mental qualities, *useful* or *agreeable* to the *person himself*, or to *others*. It might be expected, that this principle would have occurred even to the first rude, unpracticed inquirers concerning morals, and been received from its own evidence, without any argument or disputation. Whatever is valuable in any kind, so naturally classes itself under the division of *useful* or *agreeable*, the *utile* or the *dulce*, that it is not easy to imagine, why we should ever seek farther, or consider the question as a matter of nice research or inquiry. And as every thing useful or agreeable must possess these qualities with regard either to the *person himself* or to *others*, the complete delineation or description of merit seems to be performed as naturally as a shadow is cast by the sun, or an image is reflected upon water. If the ground, on which the shadow is cast, be not broken and uneven; nor the surface, from which the image is reflected, disturbed and confused; a just figure is immediately presented, without any art or attention. And it seems a reasonable presumption, that systems and hypotheses have perverted our natural understanding; when a theory, so simple and obvious, could so long have escaped the most elaborate examination.

And as every quality, which is useful or agreeable to ourselves or others, is, in common life, allowed to be a part of personal merit; so no other will ever be received, where men judge of things by their natural, unprejudiced reason, without the delusive glosses of superstition and false religion. Celibacy, fasting, penance, mortification, self-denial, humility, silence, solitude, and the whole train of monkish virtues; for what reason are they every where rejected by men of sense, but because they serve to no manner of purpose; neither advance a man's fortune in the world, nor render him a more valuable member of society; neither qualify him for the entertainment of company, nor increase his power of self-enjoyment? We observe, on the contrary, that they cross all these desirable ends; stupify the understanding and harden the heart, obscure the fancy and sour the temper. We justly, therefore, transfer them to the opposite column, and place them in the catalogue of vices; nor has any superstition force sufficient among men of the world, to pervert entirely these natural sentiments. A gloomy, hair-brained enthusiast, after his death, may have a place in the calendar; but will scarcely ever be admitted, when alive, into intimacy and society, except by those who are as delirious and dismal as himself.

 ASK YOURSELF

8.144. Why does Hume think that the so-called monkish virtues are, in fact, vices?

SUGGESTIONS FOR FURTHER READING

Primary Sources

Berkeley

Berkeley, George. *The Works of George Berkeley, Bishop of Cloyne*, ed. A. A. Luce and T. E. Jessop (Edinburgh: Thomas Nelson, 1948–1957). Standard nine-volume edition of Berkeley's writings; includes his principal philosophical books, the *Principles* and *Dialogues*.

Hume

Hume, David. *An Enquiry concerning Human Understanding*, ed. Tom L. Beauchamp (New York: Oxford Universrity Press, 1999). New standard edition of Hume's *Enquiry*, with introductions geared toward students.

———. *The Philosophical Works of David Hume*, ed. T. H. Green and T. H. Grose (London: Longman, Green, 1875). Four volumes; most complete collection of Hume's writings.

———. *A Treatise of Human Nature*, ed. David Fate Norton and Mary J. Norton (New York: Oxford University Press, 2000). New standard edition of Hume's *Treatise*, with introductions geared toward students.

Locke

Locke, John. *An Essay concerning Human Understanding*, ed. P. H. Nidditch (Oxford: Clarendon Press, 1975). Critical edition of Locke's principal work in metaphysics and epistemology.

———. *Two Treatises of Government*, ed. P. Laslett (Cambridge: Cambridge University Press, 1967). Critical edition of Locke's principal work in political philosophy.

———. *The Works of John Locke* (London: T. Tegg, 1823). Ten-volume standard edition of Locke's works.

Critical Analyses and Discussions

Berkeley

Berman, David, ed. *George Berkeley: Eighteenth-Century Responses* (New York: Garland Publishing, 1989). Two-volume facsimile reprint collection of eighteenth-century critical responses to Berkeley's philosophy.

Grayling, A. C. *Berkeley: The Central Arguments* (London: Duckworth, 1986). Contemporary interpretation of Berkeley.

Winkler, K. P. *Berkeley: An Interpretation* (Oxford: Clarendon Press, 1989). Commentary on Berkeley's philosophy.

Hume

Fieser, James, ed. *Early Responses to Hume's Metaphysical and Epistemological Writings* (Bristol, England: Thoemmes Press, 2000). Two-volume collection of eighteenth- and nineteenth-century critical responses to Hume's philosophy, with editorial introductions.

Norton, David Fate. *The Cambridge Companion to Hume* (Cambridge: Cambridge University Press, 1993). Collection of essays on various topics.

Tweyman, Stanley, ed. *David Hume: Critical Assessments* (London: Routledge, 1991). Four volumes; large collection of critical essays on Hume.

Locke

Ashcraft, R., ed. *John Locke, Critical Assessments* (London: Routledge, 1991). Four volumes; large collection of critical essays on Locke.

Ayers, M. *Locke* (London: Routledge, 1991). Two volumes; detailed account of Locke's philosophy.

Chappell, Vere, ed. *The Cambridge Companion to Locke* (Cambridge: Cambridge University Press, 1994). Collection of essays on various topics.

CHAPTER 9

LATE MODERN AND 19TH–CENTURY PHILOSOPHY

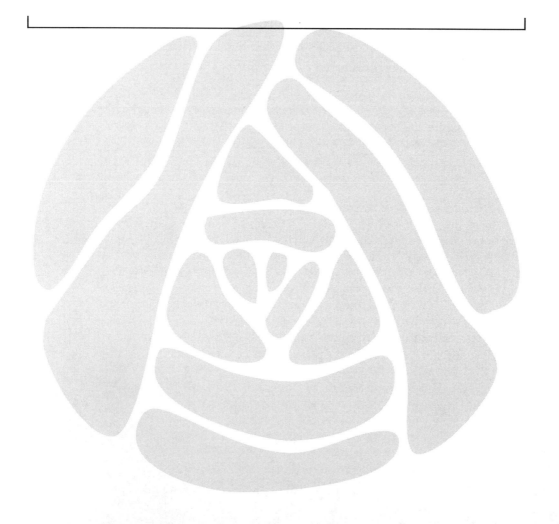

eginning in the late eighteenth century, philosophers attempted to move away from the views of both the Rationalists and Empiricists; two movements in particular emerged in reaction to Hume's skeptical Empiricism. The first was the school of *Scottish commonsense philosophy*, championed by Thomas Reid and adopted by later Scottish philosophers including Dugald Stewart and William Hamilton. Scottish commonsense philosophers believed that we are all naturally implanted with an array of commonsense beliefs and that these beliefs are in fact the foundation of truth. The second movement, influenced by Immanuel Kant, was *German Idealism*, which grounded philosophical truths in mind or spirit, rather than in external physical reality. Kant himself tried to take a middle road between Rationalism and Empiricism by stressing that while the mind plays a constructive role in knowledge, it must limit its activity to possible objects of experience. But Kant's most influential followers, particularly the Idealists Johann Gottlieb Fichte and Georg Wilhelm Friedrich Hegel, were less restrained. They tried to work out universal and comprehensive theories of reality, even though Kant had argued that such endeavors must be useless. Throughout the nineteenth century various versions of Realism, Kantianism, and Idealism had an impact not only on the field of philosophy, but also on the blossoming field of psychology.

The late eighteenth century was a time of political and cultural turmoil. The French Revolution was inspired in part by the Enlightenment notion that reason, emancipated from tradition and authority, could rectify the ills of human life. This belief is evident in work published in the revolutionary era (ca. 1790) by the early feminist Mary Wollstonecraft and in the ethical writings of J. S. Mill, whose ethical and political thought has profoundly influenced democratic and liberal conceptions of community.

New forms of resistance to Rationalism and to speculative thought generally also appeared in the nineteenth century, particularly in the works of Søren Kierkegaard and Friedrich Nietzsche, both of whom are often regarded as forerunners of the twentieth-century movement known as Existentialism. Moreover Nietzsche in particular has also been a source for developments in the later part of the twentieth century often lumped together under the term Postmodernism. The nineteenth century was indeed a time of cultural and intellectual turmoil that produced currents that continue to run deep today. Selections in this chapter are from the writings of Reid, Kant, Hegel, Kierkegaard, Wollstonecraft, Mill, and Nietzsche.

THOMAS REID

Scottish philosopher Thomas Reid (1710–1796) was educated in divinity and for some years was a minister. Later in life he held university teaching positions in Aberdeen and Edinburgh. Reid was disturbed by the increasingly skeptical trend in philosophy, which he believed began with Descartes and culminated with Hume. In 1764 he published his *Inquiry into the Human Mind on the Principles of Common Sense*, in which he attributes the source of this skepticism to a faulty theory of perception. Reid refined his theory in two later works, *Essays on the Intellectual Powers of Man* (1785) and *Essays on the Active Powers of Man* (1788). The selections in this section are from Reid's *Inquiry*; section titles are as they appear in this work.

Introduction

In the introduction to his *Inquiry*, Reid argues that modern philosophers adopted an erroneous philosophical position that he calls the *theory of ideas*. The specific mistake consists of holding that we never perceive real objects themselves, but only mental images (ideas) of those objects. For example, according to this view, when I look at a table in front of me, I do not actually see the real table, but only a mental copy of it. Hume clearly advocates this position in his *Enquiry* when he writes that "nothing can ever be present to the mind but an image or perception, and that the senses are only the inlets, through which these images are conveyed." According to Reid, this view leads to skepticism, since it eliminates the possibility of knowledge of the external world: All that we ever know are our mental images. In contrast to the theory of ideas, Reid offers his own theory of perception, a theory that explains how our senses give us direct knowledge of objects without relying on mental images as middlemen. For Reid, when I perceive the table in front of me, I have some conception of the real table itself, and instinctive principles of common sense convince me that the table indeed exists.

Section 5: Of Bishop Berkeley; the Treatise of Human Nature; and of Skepticism. Reid argues that Descartes, Malebranche, and Locke quietly and unknowingly laid the foundation of philosophical skepticism. With Berkeley and Hume, however, we find blatant and outrageous skeptical assertions, such as the nonexistence of the material world.

 From REID: *Inquiry*

The present age, I apprehend, has not produced two more acute or more practiced in this part of philosophy, than the Bishop of Cloyne, and the author of the *Treatise of Human Nature* [i.e., Hume]. The first [i.e., Berkeley] was no friend to skepticism, but had that warm concern for religious and moral principles which became his order: yet the result of his inquiry was, a serious conviction, that there is no such thing as a material world; nothing in nature but spirits and ideas: and that the belief of material substances, and of abstract ideas, are the chief causes of all our errors in philosophy, and of all infidelity and heresy in religion. His arguments are founded upon the principles which were formerly laid down by Descartes, Malebranche, and Locke, and which have been very generally received.

And the opinion of the ablest judges seems to be, that they neither have been, nor can be confuted; and that he hath proved, by unanswerable arguments, what no man in his senses can believe.

The second [i.e., Hume] proceeds upon the same principles, but carries them to their full length; and as the Bishop undid the whole material world, this author, upon the same grounds, undoes the world of spirits, and leaves nothing in nature but ideas and impressions, without any subject on which they may be impressed.

 ASK YOURSELF

9.1. According to Reid, Berkeley began by denying the material world; following in Berkeley's footsteps, what else did Hume deny?

Reid is referring here to Hume's view of personal identity, namely, that we do not have a unified notion of the self, but instead experience only a bundle of fleeting mental perceptions. Reid points out the absurdity of Hume's view and notes that Hume himself could not act consistently with it. Reid similarly notes that ancient skeptics were incapable of living in accord with their own skeptical philosophy.

It seems to be a peculiar strain of humor in this author [i.e., Hume] to set out in his introduction, by promising, with a grave face, no less than a complete system of the sciences, upon a foundation entirely new, to wit, that of human nature; when the intention of the whole work is to show, that there is neither human nature nor science in the world. It may perhaps be unreasonable to complain of this conduct in an author, who neither believes his own existence, nor that of his reader; and therefore could not mean to disappoint him, or to laugh at his credulity. Yet I cannot imagine, that the author of the *Treatise of Human Nature* is so skeptical as to plead this apology. He believed, against his principles, that he should be read, and that he should retain his personal identity, till he reaped the honor and reputation justly due to his metaphysical *acumen*. Indeed he ingenuously acknowledges, that it was only in solitude and retirement that he could yield any assent to his own philosophy; society, like daylight, dispelled the darkness and fogs of skepticism, and made him yield to the dominion of common sense. Nor did I ever hear him charged with doing any thing, even in solitude, that argued such a degree of skepticism as his principles maintain. Surely if his friends apprehended this, they would have the charity never to leave him alone.

Pyrrho the Elean, the father of this [skeptical] philosophy, seems to have carried it to greater perfection than any of his successors; for if we may believe Antigonus the Carystian, quoted by Diogenes Laertius, his life corresponded to his doctrine. And therefore, if a cart run against him, or a dog attacked him, or if he came upon a precipice, he would not stir a foot to avoid the danger, giving no credit to his senses. But his attendants, who, happily for him, were not so great skeptics, took care to keep him out of harm's way; so that he lived till he was ninety years of age. Nor is it to be doubted, but this author's friends would have been equally careful to keep him from harm, if ever his principles had taken too strong a hold of him.

It is probable the *Treatise of Human Nature* was not written in company; yet it contains manifest indications, that the author every now and then relapsed into the faith of the vulgar, and could hardly, for half a dozen pages, keep up the skeptical character.

In like manner, the great Pyrrho himself forgot his principles on some occasions; and is said once to have been in such a passion with his cook, who probably had not roasted his dinner to his mind, that with the spit in his hand, and the meat upon it, he pursued him even into the market-place.

It is a bold philosophy that rejects, without ceremony, principles which irresistibly govern the belief and the conduct of all mankind in the common concerns of life; and to which the philosopher himself must yield, after he imagines he hath confuted them. Such principles are older, and of more authority, than philosophy: she rests upon them as her basis, not they upon her. If she could overturn them, she must be buried in their ruins; but all the engines of philosophical subtlety are too weak for this purpose, and the attempt is no less ridiculous, than if a mechanic should contrive an *axis in per-itrochio* to remove the earth out of its place; or if a mathematician should pretend to demonstrate, that things equal to the same thing, are not equal to one another.

Zeno endeavored to demonstrate the impossibility of motion; Hobbes, that there was no difference between right and wrong; and this author, that no credit is to be given to our senses, to our memory, or even to demonstration. Such philosophy is justly ridiculous, even to those who cannot detect the fallacy of it. It can have no other tendency, than to show the acuteness of the sophist, at the expense of disgracing reason and human nature, and making mankind Yahoos.

 ASK YOURSELF

9.2. What are some of the absurd views held by skeptics?

Section 6: Of the Treatise of Human Nature. Hume published his *Treatise of Human Nature* anonymously. Even though everyone knew that Hume was the author, out of respect for Hume—whom Reid actually admired—Reid did not attack Hume by name. Reid points out how far Hume's theory falls short of conveying a true account of human nature.

There are other prejudices against this system of human nature, which, even upon a general view, may make one diffident of it.

Descartes, Hobbes, and this author, have each of them given us a system of human nature; an undertaking too vast for any one man, how great soever his genius and abilities may be. There must surely be reason to apprehend, that many parts of human nature never came under their observation; and that others have been stretched and distorted, to fill up blanks, and complete the system. Christopher Columbus, or Sebastian Cabot, might almost as reasonably have undertaken to give us a complete map of America.

There is a certain character and style in nature's works, which is never attained in the most perfect imitation of them. This seems to be wanting in the systems of human nature I have mentioned, and particularly in the last. One may see a puppet make a variety of motions and gesticulations, which strike much at first view; but when it is accurately observed, and taken to pieces, our admiration ceases; we comprehend the whole art of the maker. How unlike is it to that which it represents, what a poor piece of work compared with the body of a man, whose structure the more we know, the more wonders we discover in it, and the more sensible we are of our ignorance! Is the mechanism of the mind so easily comprehended, when that of the body is so difficult? Yet by this system, three laws of association, joined to a few original feelings, explain the whole mechanism of sense, imagination, memory, belief, and of all the actions and passions of the mind. Is this the man that nature made? I suspect it is not so easy to look behind the scenes in nature's work. This is a puppet surely, contrived by too bold an apprentice of nature, to mimic her work. It shows tolerably by candle light, but brought into clear day, and taken to pieces, it will appear to be a man made with mortar and a trowel. The more we know of other parts of nature, the more we like and approve them. The little I know of the planetary system; of the earth which we inhabit; of minerals, vegetables, and animals; of my own body, and of the laws which obtain in these parts of nature; opens to my mind grand and beautiful scenes, and contributes equally to my happiness and power. But when I look within, and consider the mind itself which makes me capable of all these prospects and enjoyments; if it is indeed what the *Treatise of Human Nature* makes it, I find I have been only in an enchanted castle, imposed upon by specters and apparitions. I blush inwardly to think how I have been deluded; I am ashamed of my frame, and can hardly forbear expostulating with my destiny. Is this thy pastime, O Nature, to put such tricks upon a silly creature, and then to take off the mask, and show him how he hath been befooled? If this is the philosophy of human nature, my soul enter thou not into her secrets. It is surely the forbidden tree of knowledge; I no sooner taste of it, than I perceive myself naked, and stripped of all things, yea, even of my very self. I see myself, and the whole frame of nature, shrink into fleeting ideas, which, like Epicurus's atoms, dance about in emptiness.

 ASK YOURSELF

9.3. Reid describes Hume's theory as a "puppet" and an "enchanted castle." What is his point behind these metaphors?

Section 7: The System of All These Authors Is the Same and Leads to Skepticism. Reid argues that no matter how Descartes and others attempted to avoid skepticism, the theory of ideas on which they proceeded is inherently skeptical.

But what if these profound disquisitions into the first principles of human nature, do naturally and necessarily plunge a man into this abyss of skepticism? May we not reasonably judge so from what hath happened? Descartes no sooner began to dig in this mine, than skepticisms was ready to break in upon him. He did what he could to shut it out. Malebranche and Locke, who dug deeper, found the difficulty of keeping out this enemy still to increase; but they labored honestly in the design. Then Berkeley, who carried on the work, despairing of securing all, bethought himself of an expedient: by giving up the material world, which he thought might be spared without loss, and even with advantage, he hoped, by an impregnable partition, to secure the world of spirits. But, alas! the *Treatise of Human Nature* wantonly sapped the foundation of this partition, and drowned all in one universal deluge.

These facts, which are undeniable, do indeed give reason to apprehend, that Descartes's system of the human understanding, which I shall beg leave to call *the ideal system*, and which, with some improvements made by later writers, is now generally received, hath some original defect; that this skepticism is inlaid in it, and reared along with it; and, therefore, that we must lay it open to the foundation, and examine the materials, before we can expect to raise any solid and useful fabric of knowledge on this subject.

 ASK YOURSELF

9.4. According to Reid, how widespread is the "ideal system" (i.e., the theory of ideas)?

Chapter II. Of Smelling

Going through each of our five senses, one by one, Reid attempts to show that we directly perceive external things.

Section 6: Apology for Metaphysical Absurdities. Sensation without a Sentient, a Consequence of the Theory of Ideas. Consequences of This Strange Opinion. Continuing his assault on the theory of ideas, Reid attacks Hume's view that we can have isolated sensations without having a permanent mind to perceive these.

. . . If there are certain principles, as I think there are, which the constitution of our nature leads us to believe, and which we are under a necessity to take for granted in the common concerns of life, without being able to give a reason for them; these are what we call the principles of common sense; and what is manifestly contrary to them, is what we call absurd.

 ASK YOURSELF

9.5. According to Reid, what is the litmus test for determining which philosophical theories we "call absurd"?

Indeed, if it is true, and to be received as a principle of philosophy, that sensation and thought may be without a thinking being; it must be acknowledged to be the most wonderful discovery that this or any other age hath produced. The received doctrine of ideas is the principle from which it is deduced, and of which indeed it seems to be a just and natural consequence. And it is probable, that it would not have been so late a discovery, but that it is so shocking and repugnant to the common apprehensions of mankind, that it required an uncommon degree of philosophical intrepidity to usher it into the world. It is a fundamental principle of the ideal system, that every object of thought must be an impression, or an idea, that is, a faint copy of some preceding impression. This is a principle so commonly received, that the author above mentioned, although his whole system is built upon it, never offers the least proof of it. It is upon this principle, as a fixed point, that he erects his metaphysical engines, to overturn heaven and earth, body and spirit. And indeed, in my apprehension, it is altogether sufficient for the purpose. For if impressions and ideas are the only objects of thought, then heaven and earth, and body and spirit, and every thing you please, must signify only impressions and ideas, or they must be words without any meaning. It seems, therefore, that this notion, however strange, is closely connected with the received doctrine of ideas, and we must either admit the conclusion, or call in question the premises.

 ASK YOURSELF

9.6. What is the "fundamental principle of the ideal system," which Reid ultimately rejects?

Ideas seem to have something in their nature unfriendly to other existences. They were first introduced into philosophy, in the humble character of images or representatives of things; and in this character they seemed not only to be inoffensive, but to serve admirably well for explaining the operations of the human understanding. But since men began to reason clearly and distinctly about them, they have by degrees supplanted their constituents, and undermined the existence of every thing but themselves. First, they discarded all secondary qualities of bodies; and it was found out by their means, that fire is not hot, nor snow cold, nor honey sweet; and, in a word, that heat and cold, sound, color, taste, and smell, are nothing but ideas or impressions. Bishop Berkeley advanced them a step higher, and found out, by just reasoning, from the same principles, that extension, solidity, space, figure, and body, are ideas, and that there is nothing in nature but ideas and spirits. But the triumph of ideas was completed by the *Treatise of Human Nature*, which discards spirits also, and leaves ideas and impressions as the sole existences in the universe. What if at last, having nothing else to contend with, they should fall foul of one another, and leave no existence in nature at all? This would surely bring philosophy into danger; for what should we have left to talk or to dispute about?

 ASK YOURSELF

9.7. What were the main steps by which advocates of the ideal system eliminated all existence?

IMMANUEL KANT

German philosopher Immanuel Kant (1724–1804) was born in Königsberg, the capital of what was then East Prussia. He studied at the University of Königsberg, became a lecturer there in 1755, and finally in 1770 was appointed Professor of Logic and Metaphysics. Although Kant spent virtually all of his life in and around Königsberg, he was an avid reader of philosophical and scientific authors from other countries—especially France and England—which gave his own prolific writings a cosmopolitan feel. In 1781 he published his most influential work, the *Critique of Pure*

Reason. The work is lengthy, technical, and, by his own confession, somewhat dry. To help readers follow its basic themes Kant wrote a summary, which appeared in 1783 under the title *Prolegomena to Any Future Metaphysics* (1783). Shortly after, Kant produced two influential works in moral theory: *The Groundwork of the Metaphysics of Morals* (1785) and the *Critique of Practical Reason* (1788). Kant retired from teaching in 1797 and died in 1804. The selections in this section are from Kant's *Prolegomena* and *Groundwork*.

Introduction

Kant's philosophy in the *Critique of Pure Reason* and the *Prolegomena* is an attempt to resolve the dispute between Rationalists and Empiricists regarding the source of our foundational philosophical concepts. Descartes, for example, believed that causality is an innate idea that we know *a priori*. The term *"a priori"* refers to a type of instinctive or intuitive knowledge that we gain without any appeal to sense perception and experience. By contrast, Empiricists, such as Locke and Hume, believed that our notion of causality is not innate but instead is known *a posteriori*. *A posteriori* knowledge, also called *empirical* knowledge, refers to experiential knowledge that we gain through our external senses or through introspectively experiencing our own feelings and mental operations. Kant opens the *Prolegomena* by discussing the Rationalist/Empiricist dispute over the idea of causality.

Implications of Hume's Problem of Causality. Kant felt that Hume successfully pointed out problems with the standard Rationalist view that our knowledge of cause-and-effect relationships is *a priori*. However, Kant resisted Hume's conclusion that we know causality empirically. Thus, Kant believes that we still need to address the problem that Hume raises with an alleged *a priori* notion of causality.

 From KANT: *Prolegomena*

Since the Essays of Locke and Leibniz, or rather since the origin of metaphysics so far as we know its history, nothing has ever happened which was more decisive to its fate than the attack made upon it by David Hume. He threw no light on this species of knowledge, but he certainly struck a spark from which light might have been obtained, had it caught some inflammable substance and had its smoldering fire been carefully nursed and developed.

Hume started from a single but important concept in Metaphysics, viz., that of Cause and Effect (including its derivatives force and action, etc.). He challenges reason, which pretends to have given birth to this idea from herself, to answer him by what right she thinks anything to be so constituted, that if that thing be posited, something else also must necessarily be posited; for this is the meaning of the concept of cause. He demonstrated irrefutably that it was perfectly impossible for reason to think *a priori* and by means of concepts a combination involving necessity. We cannot at all see why, in consequence of the existence of one thing, another must necessarily exist, or how the concept of such a combination can arise *a priori*. Hence he inferred, that reason was altogether deluded with reference to this concept, which she erroneously considered as one of her children, whereas in reality it was nothing but a bastard of imagination, impregnated by experience, which subsumed certain representations under the Law of Association, and mistook the subjective necessity of habit for an objective necessity arising from insight. Hence he inferred that reason had no power to think such, combinations, even generally, because her concepts would then be purely fictitious, and all her pretended *a priori* cognitions nothing but common experiences marked with a false stamp. In plain language there is not, and cannot be, any such thing as metaphysics at all.

However hasty and mistaken Hume's conclusion may appear, it was at least founded upon investigation, and this investigation deserved the concentrated attention of the brighter spirits of his day as well as determined efforts on their part to discover, if possible, a happier solution of the problem in the sense proposed by him, all of which would have speedily resulted in a complete reform of the science.

 ASK YOURSELF

9.8. According to Kant, what did Hume infer from the problem of causality regarding human reason?

Hume's Critics and the Larger Implication of Hume's Problem. Some of Hume's fellow Scottish philosophers—specifically Thomas Reid, James Oswald, and James Beattie—criticized Hume on the grounds that causality appears to be a dictate of common sense, which we cannot do without. Kant argues that Hume's critics not only misunderstood Hume, but also failed to see that Hume's problem of causality was part of a much larger problem that we find with many other key notions in metaphysics.

But Hume suffered the usual misfortune of metaphysicians, of not being understood. It is positively painful to see how utterly his opponents, Reid, Oswald, Beattie, and lastly Priestley, missed the point of the problem; for while they were ever taking for granted that which he doubted, and demonstrating with zeal and often with impudence that which he never thought of doubting, they so misconstrued his valuable suggestion that everything remained in its old condition, as if nothing had happened.

The question was not whether the concept of cause was right, useful, and even indispensable for our knowledge of nature, for this Hume had never doubted; but whether that concept could be thought by reason *a priori*, and consequently whether it possessed an inner truth, independent of all experience, implying a wider application than merely to the objects of experience. This was Hume's problem. It was a question concerning the *origin*, not concerning *the indispensable need* of the concept. Were the former decided, the conditions of the use and the sphere of its valid application would have been determined as a matter of course.

 ASK YOURSELF

9.9. According to Kant, what is the central question raised by Hume's problem of causality?

Kant's Reaction to Hume.   Kant continues by noting the profound impact that Hume's problem had on Kant personally, and how it forced him to reevaluate the entire subject of metaphysics.

But to satisfy the conditions of the problem, the opponents of the great thinker should have penetrated very deeply into the nature of reason, so far as it is concerned with pure thinking,—a task which did not suit them. They found a more convenient method of being defiant without any insight, viz., the appeal to *common sense*. It is indeed a great gift of God, to possess right, or (as they now call it) plain common sense. But this common sense must be shown practically, by well-considered and reasonable thoughts and words, not by appealing to it as an oracle, when no rational justification can be advanced. To appeal to common sense, when insight and science fail, and no sooner—this is one of the subtle discoveries of modern times, by means of which the most superficial ranter can safely enter the lists with the most thorough thinker, and hold his own. But as long as a particle of insight remains, no one would think of having recourse to this subterfuge. For what is it but an appeal to the opinion of the multitude, of whose applause the philosopher is ashamed, while the popular charlatan glories and confides in it? I should think that Hume might fairly have laid as much claim to common sense as Beattie, and in addition to a critical reason (such as the latter did not possess), which keeps common sense in check and prevents it from speculating, or, if speculations are under discussion restrains the desire to decide because it cannot satisfy itself concerning its own arguments. By this means alone can common sense remain sound. Chisels and hammers may suffice to work a piece of wood, but for steel-engraving we require an engraver's needle. Thus common sense and speculative understanding are each serviceable in their own way, the former in judgments which apply immediately to experience, the latter when we judge universally from mere concepts, as in metaphysics, where sound common sense, so called in spite of the inapplicability of the word, has no right to judge at all.

   I openly confess, the suggestion of David Hume was the very thing, which many years ago first interrupted my dogmatic slumber, and gave my investigations in the field of speculative philosophy quite a new direction. I was far from following him in the conclusions at which he arrived by regarding, not the whole of his problem, but a part, which by itself can give us no information. If we start from a well-founded, but undeveloped, thought, which another has bequeathed to us, we may well hope by continued reflection to advance farther than the acute man, to whom we owe the first spark of light.

   I therefore first tried whether Hume's objection could not be put into a general form, and soon found that the concept of the connection of cause and effect was by no means the only idea by which the understanding thinks the connection of things *a priori*, but rather that metaphysics consists altogether of such connections. I sought to ascertain their number, and when I had satisfactorily succeeded in this by starting from a single principle, I proceeded to the deduction of these concepts, which I was now certain were not deduced from experience, as Hume had apprehended, but sprang from the pure understanding. This deduction (which seemed impossible to my acute predecessor, which had never even occurred to any one else, though no one had hesitated to use the concepts without investigating the basis of their objective validity) was the most difficult task ever undertaken in the service of metaphysics; and the worst was that metaphysics, such as it then existed, could not assist me in the least, because this deduction alone can render metaphysics possible. But as soon as I had succeeded in solving Hume's problem not merely in a particular case, but with respect to the whole faculty of pure reason, I could proceed safely, though slowly, to determine the whole sphere of pure reason completely and from general principles, in its circumference as well as in its contents. This was required for metaphysics in order to construct its system according to a reliable method.

 ASK YOURSELF

9.10. According to Kant, Hume ultimately solved the problem of causality by contending that our experience (and not our *a priori* reason) gives rise to our notion of causality. By contrast, where does Kant think that the notion of causality springs from?

Preamble on the Peculiarities of All Metaphysical Knowledge

In the preamble to the *Prolegomena*, Kant establishes some terminology and conceptual distinctions upon which his whole philosophy depends.

Metaphysics Deals with A Priori *Knowledge.* Unlike Hume, who attempted to ground metaphysical notions such as causality in empirical experience, Kant insists that metaphysics involves *a priori* knowledge. In that sense, he believes, it is similar to our notions of mathematics.

Sect. 1. If it becomes desirable to formulate any cognition as science, it will be necessary first to determine accurately those peculiar features which no other science has in common with it, constituting its characteristics; otherwise the boundaries of all sciences become confused, and none of them can be treated thoroughly according to its nature.

The characteristics of a science may consist of a simple difference of object, or of the sources of cognition, or of the kind of cognition, or perhaps of all three conjointly. On this, therefore, depends the idea of a possible science and its territory.

First, as concerns the sources of metaphysical cognition, its very concept implies that they cannot be empirical. Its principles (including not only its maxims but its basic notions) must never be derived from experience. It must not be physical but metaphysical knowledge, viz., knowledge lying beyond experience. It can therefore have for its basis neither external experience, which is the source of physics proper, nor internal, which is the basis of empirical psychology. It is therefore *a priori* knowledge, coming from pure Understanding and pure Reason.

But so far Metaphysics would not be distinguishable from pure Mathematics; it must therefore be called pure philosophical cognition; and for the meaning of this term I refer to the Critique of the Pure Reason (II. "Method of Transcendentalism," Chap. I., Sec. 1), where the distinction between these two employments of the reason is sufficiently explained. So far concerning the sources of metaphysical cognition.

 ASK YOURSELF

9.11. According to Kant, what are some of the central features of metaphysical knowledge?

Analytical Judgments. Further clarifying the *a priori* nature of metaphysical notions, Kant distinguishes between two types of judgments: analytical and synthetical. Analytical judgments involve statements in which the predicate is contained in the subject, such as "All bachelors are unmarried men" and "Triangles have three angles." These statements are true or false based on the definitions of the words themselves; they also do not provide any new information beyond what is already stated in the subject of the statement. Synthetic statements, by contrast, do not have the predicate contained in the subject, such as "The door is brown." As such, they are not true by definition; for example, the notion of "brown" is not part of the notion of "door." Further, analytical statements provide us with new information—in this case, information that a particular object is brown.

Section 2.a. Of the Distinction between Analytical and Synthetical Judgments in General.—The peculiarity of its sources demands that metaphysical cognition must consist of nothing but *a priori* judgments. But whatever be their origin, or their logical form, there is a distinction in judgments, as to their content, according to which they are either merely explicative, adding nothing to the content of the cognition, or expansive, increasing the given cognition: the former may be called analytical, the latter synthetical, judgments.

Analytical judgments express nothing in the predicate but what has been already actually thought in the concept of the subject, though not so distinctly or with the same (full) consciousness. When I say: All bodies are extended, I have not amplified in the least my concept of body, but have only analyzed it, as extension was really thought to belong to that concept before the judgment was made, though it was not expressed, this judgment is therefore analytical. On the contrary, this judgment, All bodies have weight, contains in its predicate something not actually thought in the general concept of the body; it amplifies my knowledge by adding something to my concept, and must therefore be called synthetical.

b. The Common Principle of All Analytical Judgments Is the Law of Contradiction.—All analytical judgments depend wholly on the law of Contradiction, and are in their nature *a priori* cognitions, whether the concepts that supply them with matter be empirical or not. For the predicate of an affirmative analytical judgment is already contained in the concept of the subject, of which it cannot be denied without contradiction. In the same way its opposite is necessarily denied of the subject in an analytical, but negative, judgment, by the same law of contradiction. Such is the nature of the judgments: all bodies are extended, and no bodies are unextended (i.e., simple).

For this very reason all analytical judgments are *a priori* even when the concepts are empirical, as, for example, Gold is a yellow metal; for to know this

I require no experience beyond my concept of gold as a yellow metal: it is, in fact, the very concept, and I need only analyze it, without looking beyond it elsewhere.

 ASK YOURSELF

9.12. Explain how the law of contradiction applies to analytical judgments.

Synthetical Judgments. Turning to synthetical judgments, Kant notes that the most obvious kind of synthetical judgments are empirical (*a posteriori*), such as "The door is brown," which we know through visual experience. However, in addition to empirical notions, Kant argues that mathematical and metaphysical judgments are also synthetical.

c. Synthetical Judgments Require a Different Principle from the Law of Contradiction.—There are synthetical *a posteriori* judgments of empirical origin; but there are also others which are proved to be certain *a priori*, and which spring from pure Understanding and Reason. Yet they both agree in this, that they cannot possibly spring from the principle of analysis, viz., the law of contradiction, alone; they require a quite different principle, though, from whatever they may be deduced, they must be subject to the law of contradiction, which must never be violated, even though everything cannot be deduced from it. I shall first classify synthetical judgments.

1. *Empirical judgments* are always synthetical. For it would be absurd to base an analytical judgment on experience, as our concept suffices for the purpose without requiring any testimony from experience. That body is extended, is a judgment established *a priori*, and not an empirical judgment. For before appealing to experience, we already have all the conditions of the judgment in the concept, from which we have but to elicit the predicate according to the law of contradiction, and thereby to become conscious of the necessity of the judgment, which experience could not even teach us.

2. *Mathematical judgments* are all synthetical. This fact seems hitherto to have altogether escaped the observation of those who have analyzed human reason; it even seems directly opposed to all their conjectures, though incontestably certain, and most important in its consequences. For as it was found that the conclusions of mathematicians all proceed according to the law of contradiction (as is demanded by all apodictic certainty), men persuaded themselves that the fundamental principles were known from the same law. This was a great mistake, for a synthetical proposition can indeed be comprehended according to the law of contradiction, but only by presupposing another synthetical proposition from which it follows, but never in itself. . . .

It might at first be thought that the proposition $7 + 5 = 12$ is a mere analytical judgment, following from the concept of the sum of seven and five, according to the law of contradiction. But on closer examination it appears that the concept of the sum of $7 + 5$ contains merely their union in a single number, without its being at all thought what the particular number is that unites them. The concept of twelve is by no means thought by merely thinking of the combination of seven and five; and analyze this possible sum as we may, we shall not discover twelve in the concept. We must go beyond these concepts, by calling to our aid some concrete image, i.e., either our five fingers, or five points (as Segner has it in his Arithmetic), and we must add successively the units of the five, given in some concrete image, to the concept of seven. Hence our concept is really amplified by the proposition 7 + 5 = 12, and we add to the first a second, not thought in it. Arithmetical judgments are therefore synthetical, and the more plainly according as we take larger numbers; for in such cases it is clear that, however closely we analyze our concepts without calling visual images to our aid, we can never find the sum by such mere dissection.

 ASK YOURSELF

9.13. Although we might initially think that mathematical propositions are analytical (with the predicate contained in the subject), Kant believes that they are synthetic. Illustrating his point with the proposition "7 + 5 = 12," what does he say about the relation between the predicate "12" and the subject "7 + 5"?

Metaphysical Synthetic A Priori *Judgments.* Like mathematical judgments, Kant believes that metaphysical judgments are also synthetic *a priori*. That is, they are nonempirical yet provide us with new information.

Metaphysical judgments, properly so called, are all synthetical. We must distinguish judgments pertaining to metaphysics from metaphysical judgments properly so called. Many of the former are analytical, but they only afford the means for metaphysical judgments, which are the whole end of the science, and which are always synthetical. For if there be concepts pertaining to metaphysics (as, for example, that of substance), the judgments springing from simple analysis of them also pertain to metaphysics, as, for example, substance is that which only exists as subject; and by means of several such analytical judgments, we seek to approach the definition of the concept. But as the analysis of a pure concept of the understanding pertaining to metaphysics, does not proceed in any different manner from the dissection of any other, even empirical, concepts, not pertaining to metaphysics (such as: air is an elastic fluid, the elasticity of which is not destroyed by any known degree of cold), it follows that the concept indeed, but not the analytical judgment, is properly metaphysical. This science has something peculiar in the production of its *a priori* cognitions, which must therefore be distinguished from the features it has in common with other rational knowledge. Thus the judgment, that all the substance in things is permanent, is a synthetical and properly metaphysical judgment. . . .

The conclusion drawn in this section then is, that metaphysics is properly concerned with synthetical propositions *a priori*, and these alone constitute its end, for which it indeed requires various dissections of its concepts, viz., of its analytical judgments, but wherein the procedure is not different from that in every other kind of knowledge, in which we merely seek to render our concepts distinct by analysis. But the generation of *a priori* cognition by concrete images as well as by concepts, in fine, of synthetical propositions *a priori* in philosophical cognition, constitutes the essential subject of Metaphysics.

ASK YOURSELF

9.14. Although some judgments *pertaining* to metaphysics are analytical, Kant believes that metaphysical judgments *properly speaking* are synthetical. Give one of Kant's examples of a synthetical metaphysical judgment.

Kant argues that the success of metaphysics depends on our ability to show how *synthetic a priori* judgments are even possible. That is, we need to see how the mechanism of human reason provides us with intuitive (nonempirical) knowledge that contains new information.

Section 5. We have above learned the significant distinction between analytical and synthetical judgments. The possibility of analytical propositions was easily comprehended, being entirely founded on the law of Contradiction. The possibility of synthetical *a posteriori* judgments, of those which are gathered from experience, also requires no particular explanation; for experience is nothing but a continual synthesis of perceptions. There remain therefore only synthetical propositions *a priori*, of which the possibility must be sought or investigated, because they must depend upon principles other than the law of contradiction.

But here we need not first establish the possibility of such propositions so as to ask whether they are possible. For there are enough of them which indeed are of undoubted certainty, and as our present method is analytical, we shall start from the fact, that such synthetical but purely rational cognition actually exists; but we must now inquire into the reason of this possibility, and ask, *how* such cognition is possible, in order that we may from the principles of its possibility be enabled to determine the conditions of its use, its sphere and its limits. The proper problem upon which all depends, when expressed with scholastic precision, is therefore: *How are Synthethetic Propositions a priori possible?* . . .

Metaphysics stands or falls with the solution of this problem: its very existence depends upon it. Let any one make metaphysical assertions with ever so much plausibility, let him overwhelm us with conclusions, if he has not previously proved able to answer this question satisfactorily, I have a right to say this is all vain baseless philosophy and false wisdom. You speak through pure reason, and claim, as it were to create cognitions *a priori* by not only dissecting given concepts, but also by asserting connections which do not rest upon the law of contradiction, and which you believe you conceive quite independently of all experience; how do you arrive at this, and how will you justify your pretensions? An appeal to the consent of the common sense of mankind cannot be allowed; for that is a witness whose authority depends merely upon rumor. Says Horace: "To all that which you prove me in this manner, I refuse to give credence."

ASK YOURSELF

9.15. According to Kant, why can't we prove our metaphysical assertions by appealing to the common consent of humankind?

To answer the crucial question of how synthetic *a priori* judgments are possible, Kant divides the question into four separate questions, and address each of these individually: (1) How is pure mathematics possible? (2) How is the science of nature possible? (3) How is metaphysics in general possible? (4) How is metaphysics as a science possible?

How Is Pure Mathematics Possible?

Kant believes that our notions of space and time are intimately connected with all judgments in mathematics. Our purest notions of space and time are instinctive components of our thinking and we do not simply infer them from our sensory experience of the physical world. In fact, to even make sense of our confusing sensory experiences, we must already have the mental concepts of space and time. In Kant's words, our sense experiences provide us with the *material* of our perception, but our underlying intuitions of space and time provide its *form*.

Concepts of Space and Time Underlie Mathematics. Granting that we have these inborn concepts of space and time, Kant believes that these concepts answer the question: "How is pure mathematic possible?" For Kant, when we make synthetic *a priori* mathematical judgments, we draw from our concepts of space and time. This is seen most clearly in the field of geometry, which is the science of our pure concepts of space.

Section 10. Now, the intuitions which pure mathematics lays at the foundation of all its cognitions and judgments which appear at once apodictic and necessary are Space and Time. For mathematics must first have all its concepts in intuition, and pure mathematics in pure intuition, that is, it must construct them. If it proceeded in any other way, it would be impossible to make any headway, for mathematics proceeds, not analytically by dissection of concepts, but synthetically, and if pure intuition be wanting, there is nothing in which the matter for synthetical judgments *a priori* can be given. Geometry is based upon the pure intuition of space. Arithmetic accomplishes its concept of number by the successive addition of units in time; and pure mechanics especially cannot attain its concepts of motion without employing the representation of time. Both representations, however, are only intuitions; for if we omit from the empirical intuitions of bodies and their alterations (motion) everything empirical, or belonging to sensation, space and time still remain, which are therefore pure intuitions that lie *a priori* at the basis of the empirical. Hence they can never be omitted, but at the same time, by their being pure intuitions *a priori*, they prove that they are mere forms of our sensibility, which must precede all empirical intuition, or perception of actual objects, and conformably to which objects can be known *a priori*, but only as they appear to us.

Section 11. The problem of the present section is therefore solved. Pure mathematics, as synthetical cognition *a priori*, is only possible by referring to no other objects than those of the senses. At the basis of their empirical intuition lies a pure intuition (of space and of time) which is *a priori*. This is possible, because the latter intuition is nothing but the mere form of sensibility, which precedes the actual appearance of the objects, insofar as it, in fact, makes them possible. Yet this faculty of intuiting *a priori* affects not the matter of the phenomenon (that is, the sense-element in it, for this constitutes that which is empirical), but its form, viz., space and time. Should any man venture to doubt that these are determinations adhering not to things in themselves, but to their relation to our sensibility, I should be glad to know how it can be possible to know the constitution of things *a priori*, viz., before we have any acquaintance with them and before they are presented to us. Such, however, is the case with space and time. But this is quite comprehensible as soon as both count for nothing more than formal conditions of our sensibility, while the objects count merely as phenomena; for then the form of the phenomenon, i.e., pure intuition, can by all means be represented as proceeding from ourselves, that is, *a priori*.

 ## ASK YOURSELF

9.16. Kant argues that when we make synthetic *a priori* mathematical judgments we refer only to objects of the senses. What, in turn, is at the basis of our empirical sensory experiences?

Transcendental Idealism. In the *Critique of Pure Reason* Kant dubbed his theory of space and time "transcendental idealism," by which he meant that pure notions of space and time are grounded only in our cognitive faculties and are not derived through our experience of the world ("transcendental" being Kant's word for our cognitive faculties). Unfortunately for Kant, the term "idealism" is a loaded word in philosophy, and, in its extreme form, such as we find in Berkeley, it involves a complete denial of the external material world. Kant denies that he is an idealist in this extreme sense.

Remark 3. . . . I have myself given this my theory the name of transcendental idealism, but that cannot authorize any one to confound it either with the empirical idealism of Descartes (indeed, his was only an insoluble problem, owing to which he thought every one at liberty to deny the existence of the corporeal world, because it could never be proved satisfactorily), or with the mystical and visionary idealism of Berkeley, against which and other similar phantasms our Critique contains the proper antidote. My idealism concerns not the existence of things (the doubting of which, however, constitutes idealism in the ordinary sense), since it never came into my head to doubt it, but it concerns the sensuous representation of things, to which space and time especially belong. Of these [viz., space and time], consequently of all appearances in general, I have only shown, that they are neither things (but mere modes of representation), nor determinations belonging to things in themselves. But the word "transcendental," which with me means a reference of our cognition, i.e., not to things, but only to the cognitive faculty, was meant to obviate this misconception. Yet rather than give further occasion to it by this word, I now retract it, and desire this idealism of mine to be called critical. But if it be really an objectionable idealism to convert actual things (not appearances) into mere representations, by what name shall we call him who conversely changes mere representations to things? It may, I think, be called "dreaming idealism," in contradistinction to the former, which may be called "visionary," both of which are to be refuted by my transcendental, or, better, critical idealism.

ASK YOURSELF

9.17. Kant argues that his transcendental idealism does not concern the existence of things; instead, what does it involve?

How Is the Science of Nature Possible?

Solving the first question regarding mathematics, Kant turns to the second question, which concerns how the science of nature is possible. More exactly, Kant investigates the underlying cognitive principles that allow us to make *judgments* about things in the physical world.

Phenomena and Noumena. Throughout his writings, Kant relies on an important distinction between what he calls *phenomena* and *noumena*. Phenomena involve what I actually experience; noumena involve things as they are in themselves apart from how I might experience them. For example, as I look at a desk I can make a list of all of its physical features that appear to my five senses, such as its color and texture. Apart from this list of sensory phenomena, however, there still remain features about the desk that I have no way of investigating or even describing. These hidden features are the noumena of the desk, and I am permanently prevented from knowing them. Kant argues here that our experience of the physical world is in general restricted to the phenomena, and cannot reveal anything about noumenal things in themselves.

Section 14. Nature is the existence of things, so far as it is determined according to universal laws. Should nature signify the existence of things in themselves, we could never know it either *a priori* or *a posteriori*. Not *a priori*, for how can we know what belongs to things in themselves, since this never can be done by the dissection of our concepts (in analytical judgments)? We do not want to know what is contained in our concept of a thing (for the [concept describes what] belongs to its logical being), but what is in the actuality of the thing superadded to our concept, and by what the thing itself is determined in its existence outside the concept. Our understanding, and the conditions on which alone it can connect the determinations of things in their existence, do not prescribe any rule to things themselves; these do not conform to our understanding, but it must conform itself to them; they must therefore be first given us in order to gather these determinations from them, wherefore they would not be known *a priori*.

A cognition of the nature of things in themselves *a posteriori* would be equally impossible. For, if experience is to teach us laws, to which the existence of things is subject, these laws, if they regard things in themselves, must belong to them of necessity even outside our experience. But experience teaches us what exists and how it exists, but never that it must necessarily exist so and not otherwise. Experience therefore can never teach us the nature of things in themselves.

 ASK YOURSELF

9.18. Why can't we investigate things in themselves through *a posteriori* (i.e., empirical) reasoning?

Table of Judgments and the Categories. Kant argued earlier that our instinctive cognitive notions of space and time help organize the confusing influx of raw sensory perceptions that rush in through our senses. Kant argues further that in order to *think about* our various perceptions, we need additional instinctive cognitive notions that organize these experiences. He lays these out in two tables. The first (the logical table of judgments) shows the complete range of judgments that we in fact make about physical things. From this first table he derives the second one (the transcendental table of the pure concepts of the understanding); this lists the complete range of cognitive categories that we need to make all the judgments in the first table. Kant refers to the second table as a list of conceptual *categories*, which he believes supersedes Aristotle's list of categories. Suppose, for example, that I make the judgment "All cows eat grass," which, according to the first table, would be a universal judgment about quantity. For me to make this judgment about *all* cows, however, I need to first have a concept of "unity," which is the first item in the second table. Thus, the twelve items in the two tables parallel each other and are presented in four groups of three items.

Section 21. To prove, then, the possibility of experience so far as it rests upon pure concepts [i.e., categories] of the understanding *a priori*, we must first represent what belongs to judgments in general and the various functions of the understanding, in a complete table. For the pure concepts of the understanding must run parallel to these functions, as such concepts are nothing more than concepts of intuitions in general, so far as these are determined by one or other of these functions of judging, in themselves, that is, necessarily and universally. Hereby also the *a priori* principles of the possibility of all experience, as of an objectively valid empirical cognition, will be precisely determined. For they are nothing but propositions by which all perception is (under certain universal conditions of intuition) subsumed under those pure concepts of the understanding.

LOGICAL TABLE OF JUDGMENTS

1. As to Quantity
Universal
Particular
Singular

2. As to Quality
Affirmative
Negative
Infinite

3. As to Relation
Categorical
Hypothetical
Disjunctive

4. As to Modality
Problematical
Assertorical
Apodictical

TRANSCENDENTAL TABLE OF THE PURE CONCEPTS OF THE
UNDERSTANDING [i.e., THE CATEGORIES]

1. As to Quantity
   Unity (the Measure)
   Plurality (the Quantity)
   Totality (the Whole)

2. As to Quality
   Reality
   Negation
   Limitation

3. As to Relation
   Substance
   Cause
   Community

4. As to Modality
   Possibility
   Existence
   Necessity

 ASK YOURSELF

9.19. The statement "All cows eat grass" is an example of a universal
judgment regarding quantity. Make up a statement that illustrates another
type of judgment on the first table.

The Categories as Universal Rules of Possible Experience. Kant argues that, in order for me to make any kind of judgment, my various experiences must be united
within my own consciousness. They must also be united in a way that would
hold as a rule for *anyone's* experience. Otherwise, each of us would have an entirely different way of judging the world. Thus, the universal nature of the categories—or rules of possible experience—provides the solution to the question
"How is the science of nature possible?" The answer is that universal categories
constitute "universal laws of nature," which allow us to scientifically investigate
nature.

Section 22. The sum of the matter is this: the business of the senses is to intuit—that
of the understanding is to think. But thinking is uniting representations in one consciousness. . . .

   Section 23. Judgments, when considered merely as the condition of the union of
given representations in a consciousness, are rules. These rules, so far as they represent the union as necessary, are rules *a priori*, and so far as they cannot be deduced
from higher rules, are fundamental principles. But in regard to the possibility of all
experience, merely in relation to the form of thinking in it, no conditions of judgments
of experience are higher than those which bring the phenomena, according to the various form of their intuition, under pure concepts of the understanding, and render the

empirical judgment objectively valid. These concepts are therefore the *a priori* principles of possible experience.

The principles of possible experience are then at the same time universal laws of nature, which can be known *a priori*. And thus the problem in our second question, "How is the pure Science of Nature possible?" is solved. For the system which is required for the form of a science is to be met with in perfection here, because, beyond the above-mentioned formal conditions of all judgments in general offered in logic, no others are possible, and these constitute a logical system. The concepts grounded thereupon, which contain the *a priori* conditions of all synthetical and necessary judgments, accordingly constitute a transcendental system. Finally the principles, by means of which all phenomena are subsumed under these concepts, constitute a physical system, that is, a system of nature, which precedes all empirical cognition of nature, makes it even possible, and hence may in strictness be denominated the universal and pure science of nature.

 ASK YOURSELF

9.20. In what sense are the rules of possible experience *a priori*?

The Categories Involve Phenomena, Not Noumena. Kant stresses that the two tables do not apply to things in themselves, but only to our mental arrangement of the phenomena that we experience.

Section 30. . . . This is therefore the result of all our foregoing inquiries: "All synthetical principles *a priori* are nothing more than principles of possible experience, and can never be referred to things in themselves, but to appearances as objects of experience. And hence pure mathematics as well as a pure science of nature can never be referred to anything more than mere appearances, and can only represent either that which makes experience generally possible, or else that which, as it is derived from these principles, must always be capable of being represented in some possible experience."

Section 31. And thus we have at last something definite, upon which to depend in all metaphysical enterprises, which have hitherto, boldly enough but always at random, attempted everything without discrimination. That the aim of their exertions should be so near, struck neither the dogmatical thinkers nor those who, confident in their supposed sound common sense, started with concepts and principles of pure reason (which were legitimate and natural, but destined for mere empirical use) in quest of fields of knowledge, to which they neither knew nor could know any determinate bounds, because they had never reflected nor were able to reflect on the nature or even on the possibility of such a pure understanding.

 ASK YOURSELF

9.21. What must both pure mathematics and the pure science of nature refer to?

How Is Metaphysics in General Possible?

Metaphysics is an investigation into the nature of reality, and it often involves speculations about the existence of God, a spirit realm, and the causes of the universe. The next question that Kant seeks to answer is: "How is metaphysics in general possible?" Kant is highly critical of any dogmatic metaphysics that strays beyond the phenomenal world of appearances into the unknowable noumenal realm of things in themselves. Thus, he aims to dismiss many traditional metaphysical discussions and instead to restrict metaphysics to the domain of possible experience as defined by the categories.

Applying the Categories beyond Experience. For Kant, the categories are required for ordering our experience of the physical world. However, he notes that it is very tempting to apply the categories when thinking about metaphysical issues beyond the realm of experience.

Section 45. We have above shown . . . that the purity of the categories from all admixture of sensuous determinations may mislead reason into extending their use, quite beyond all experience, to things in themselves; though as these categories themselves find no intuition which can give them meaning or sense *in concrete*, they, as mere logical functions, can represent a thing in general, but not give by themselves alone a determinate concept of anything. Such hyperbolical objects are distinguished by the appellation of *Noumena*, or pure beings of the understanding (or better, beings of thought), such as, for example, "substance," but conceived without permanence in time, or "cause," but not acting in time, etc. Here predicates, that only serve to make the conformity-to-law of experience possible, are applied to these concepts, and yet they are deprived of all the conditions of intuition, on which alone experience is possible, and so these concepts lose all significance.

There is no danger, however, of the understanding spontaneously making an excursion so very wantonly beyond its own bounds into the field of the mere creatures of thought, without being impelled by foreign laws. But when reason, which cannot be fully satisfied with any empirical use of the rules of the understanding, as being always conditioned, requires a completion of this chain of conditions, then the understanding is forced out of its sphere. And then it partly represents objects of experience in a series so extended that no experience can grasp, partly even (with a view to complete the series) it seeks entirely beyond it noumena, to which it can attach that chain, and so, having at last escaped from the conditions of experience, make its attitude as it were final. These are then the transcendental ideas, which, though according to the true but hidden ends of the natural determination of our reason, they may aim not at extravagant concepts, but at an unbounded extension of their empirical use, yet seduce the understanding by an unavoidable illusion to a transcendent use, which, though deceitful, cannot be restrained within the bounds of experience by any resolution, but only by scientific instruction and with much difficulty.

 ASK YOURSELF

9.22. What causes the understanding to be "forced out of its sphere"?

The Antinomies. As we apply the categories when thinking about metaphysical issues beyond the realm of experience, we will inevitably be led into conflicting views on four specific issues. Kant argues that these four issues correspond with the four main divisions of the categories.

Section 51. In the first place, the use of a system of categories becomes here so obvious and unmistakable, that even if there were not several other proofs of it, this alone would sufficiently prove it indispensable in the system of pure reason. There are only four such transcendent ideas, as there are so many classes of categories; in each of which, however, they refer only to the absolute completeness of the series of the conditions for a given conditioned. In analogy to these cosmological ideas there are only four kinds of dialectical assertions of pure reason, which, as they are dialectical, thereby prove, that to each of them, on equally specious principles of pure reason, a contradictory assertion stands opposed. As all the metaphysical art of the most subtle distinction cannot prevent this opposition, it compels the philosopher to recur to the first sources of pure reason itself. This Antinomy, not arbitrarily invented, but founded in the nature of human reason, and hence unavoidable and never ceasing, contains the following four theses together with their antitheses:

1.

Thesis: The World has, as to, Time and Space, a Beginning (limit).
Antithesis: The World is, as to Time and Space, infinite.

2.

Thesis: Everything in the World consists of [elements that are] simple.
Antithesis: There is nothing simple, but everything is composite.

3.

Thesis: There are in the World Causes through Freedom.
Antithesis: There is no Liberty, but all is Nature.

4.

Thesis: In the Series of the World-Causes there is some necessary Being.
Antithesis: There is Nothing necessary in the World, but in this Series All is incidental.

 ASK YOURSELF

9.23. According to Kant, these antinomies are "not arbitrarily invented"; instead, on what are they founded?

What is most troubling about the antinomies, according to Kant, is that we might employ rock-solid reasoning in defense of each of the theses and antitheses.

Section 52. Here is the most singular phenomenon of human reason, no other instance of which can be shown in any other use. If we, as is commonly done, represent to ourselves the appearances of the sensible world as things in themselves, if we assume the principles of their combination as principles universally valid of things in themselves and not merely of experience, as is usually, nay without our *Critique*, unavoidably done, there arises an unexpected conflict, which never can be removed in the common dogmatical way; because the thesis, as well as the antithesis, can be shown by equally clear, evident, and irresistible proofs—for I pledge myself as to the correctness of all these proofs—and reason therefore perceives that it is divided with itself, a state at which the skeptic rejoices, but which must make the critical philosopher pause and feel ill at ease. . . .

 ASK YOURSELF

9.24. What reaction might a skeptic have in showing the inherently contradictory nature of human reasoning?

Unlike the skeptic, Kant comes to reason's defense and attempts to explain away the antinomies. Ultimately, he rejects each of the theses and antitheses in the first two antinomies, since they are self-contradictory. However, he accepts each of the theses and antitheses in the final two antinomies since he believes that we can hold these compatibly.

Kant's Ethical Theory

Throughout his writings Kant distinguishes between two general kinds of reasoning, namely, theoretical and practical. Theoretical reasoning—as discussed in the preceding selections from the *Prolegomena*—involve reasoning about mathematics, natural science, and metaphysics. Practical reasoning, by contrast, involves reasoning about moral issues, which dictate how we behave. Just as we have mental categories that regulate our reasoning about the world of experiences, Kant argues that we have a mental conception of *moral duty* that commands us to act morally. He was aware of the moral traditions that went before him, such as virtue theory, which bases morality on good character traits, and consequentialist accounts of morality, which base morality solely on the consequences of actions. Kant rejects these traditional theories of morality and argues instead that moral actions are based on a supreme principle of moral duty, which is objective, rational, and freely chosen; he calls this principle the *categorical imperative*. Kant's clearest account of the categorical imperative is in the *Groundwork of the Metaphysics of Morals*, selections from which are included in this section.

Section 1. In Section 1 of the *Groundwork*, Kant argues against traditional criteria of morality and explains why the categorical imperative can be the only possible standard of moral obligation. He begins with a general account of willful decisions. The function of the human will is to select one course of action from among several possible courses of action. Our specific willful decisions are influenced by several factors, such as laziness, immediate emotional gratification, or what is best in the long run. Kant argues that in moral matters the will is ideally influenced only by rational considerations, and not by subjective considerations such as one's emotions. This is because morality involves what is necessary for us to do (for example, you *must* keep your promises), and only rational considerations can produce necessity.

Morality Not Based on Virtue, Happiness, or Consequences. For Kant, the rational consideration that influences the will must be a single principle of obligation, since only principles can be purely rational considerations. Also, the principle must be a command (or imperative) since morality involves a command for us to perform a particular action. Finally, the principle cannot be one that appeals to the consequences of an action. For example, Kant would reject the view that I should donate to charity merely because it brings happiness to the person receiving the money. The only principle that fulfills these requirements is the categorical imperative; this dictates that we act in a way that we could will to be universal, applying to all people, and thus ruling out any tendency we may have to make an exception of ourselves in order to satisfy our own needs and wants. He argues that it is the principle that would be adopted by a good will.

 From KANT: *Groundwork*

Nothing can possibly be conceived in the world, or even out of it, which can be called good, without qualification, except a good will. Intelligence, wit, judgment, and the other *talents* of the mind, however they may be named, or courage, resolution, perseverance, as qualities of temperament, are undoubtedly good and desirable in many respects; but these gifts of nature may also become extremely bad and mischievous if the will which is to make use of them, and which, therefore, constitutes what is called *character*, is not good. It is the same with the *gifts of fortune*. Power, riches, honor, even health, and the general well-being and contentment with one's condition which is called *happiness*, inspire pride, and often presumption, if there is not a good will to correct the influence of these on the mind, and with this also to rectify the whole principle of acting and adapt it to its end. The sight of a being who is not adorned with a single feature of a pure and good will, enjoying unbroken prosperity, can never give pleasure to an impartial rational spectator. Thus a good will appears to constitute the indispensable condition even of being worthy of happiness.

There are even some qualities which are of service to this good will itself and may facilitate its action, yet which have no intrinsic unconditional value, but always presuppose a good will, and this qualifies the esteem that we justly have for them and does not permit us to regard them as absolutely good. Moderation in the affections and passions, self-control, and calm deliberation are not only good in many respects, but even seem to constitute part of the intrinsic worth of the person; but they are far from deserving to be called good without qualification, although they have been so unconditionally praised by the ancients. For without the principles of a good will, they may become extremely bad, and the coolness of a villain not only makes him far more dangerous, but also directly makes him more abominable in our eyes than he would have been without it.

 ASK YOURSELF

9.25. According to Kant, why is morality not a matter of either (1) having certain character traits, like courage, or (2) producing good results or consequences through our actions?

A good will is good not because of what it performs or effects, not by its aptness for the attainment of some proposed end, but simply by virtue of the volition; that is, it is good in itself, and considered by itself is to be esteemed much higher than all that can be brought about by it in favor of any inclination, nay even of the sum total of all inclinations. Even if it should happen that, owing to special disfavor of fortune, or the niggardly provision of a step-motherly nature, this will should wholly lack power to accomplish its purpose, if with its greatest efforts it should yet achieve nothing, and there should remain only the good will (not, to be sure, a mere wish, but the summoning of all means in our power), then, like a jewel, it would still shine by its own light, as a thing which has its whole value in itself. Its usefulness or fruitfulness can neither add nor take away anything from this value. It would be, as it were, only the setting to enable us to handle it the more conveniently in common commerce, or to attract to it the attention of those who are not yet connoisseurs, but not to recommend it to true connoisseurs, or to determine its value.

 ASK YOURSELF

9.26. For Kant, the will is the only thing that can be called "good" without qualification. What is it about the will that makes it good?

Section 2. In Section 2, Kant explains key terms, presents different formulations of the categorical imperative, and illustrates it with examples of specific immoral acts.

Hypothetical versus Categorical Imperatives. Kant distinguishes between types of imperatives. Imperatives in general are commands that dictate a particular course of action, such as "You shall clean your room." Hypothetical imperatives are commands that depend on my preference for a particular end and are stated in conditional form, such as "If I want to lose weight, then I should eat less." In this case, the command to eat less hinges on my previous preference to lose weight. However, hypothetical imperatives are simply not moral imperatives since the command is based on subjective considerations that are not absolute. A categorical imperative, by contrast, is an absolute command, such as "You shall treat people with respect," which is not based on subjective considerations. Thus, the supreme principle of morality is a categorical imperative since it is not conditional upon one's preferences.

The conception of an objective principle, insofar as it is obligatory for a will, is called a command (of reason), and the formula of the command is called an imperative.

Now all *imperatives* command either *hypothetically* or *categorically*. The former represent the practical necessity of a possible action as means to something else that is willed (or at least which one might possibly will). The categorical imperative would be that which represented an action as necessary of itself without reference to another end, i.e., as objectively necessary.

Since every practical law represents a possible action as good and, on this account, for a subject who is practically determinable by reason, necessary, all imperatives are formulae determining an action which is necessary according to the principle of a will good in some respects. If now the action is good only as a means *to something else*, then the imperative is *hypothetical*; if it is conceived as good *in itself* and consequently as being necessarily the principle of a will which of itself conforms to reason, then it is *categorical*.

Thus the imperative declares what action possible by me would be good and presents the practical rule in relation to a will which does not forthwith perform an action simply because it is good, whether because the subject does not always know that it is good, or because, even if it know this, yet its maxims might be opposed to the objective principles of practical reason.

When I conceive a hypothetical imperative, in general I do not know beforehand what it will contain until I am given the condition. But when I conceive a categorical imperative, I know at once what it contains. For as the imperative contains besides the law only the necessity that the maxims shall conform to this law, while the law contains no conditions restricting it, there remains nothing but the general statement that the maxim of the action should conform to a universal law, and it is this conformity alone that the imperative properly represents as necessary.

 ASK YOURSELF

9.27. For Kant, what kind of imperative is good only as a means to something else?

Kant next presents the single categorical imperative of morality: Act only on that maxim by which you can at the same time will that it should become a universal law.

There is therefore but one categorical imperative, namely, this:

> Act only on that maxim whereby you can at the same time will that it should become a universal law.

Now if all imperatives of duty can be deduced from this one imperative as from their principle, then, although it should remain undecided what is called duty is not merely a vain notion, yet at least we shall be able to show what we understand by it and what this notion means.

Although there is only one categorical imperative, Kant argues that there can be four formulations of this principle:

> The Formula of the Law of Nature: "Act as if the maxim of your action were to become through your will a universal law of nature."
> The Formula of the End Itself: "Act in such a way that you always treat humanity, whether in your own person or in the person of any other, never simply as a means, but always at the same time as an end."
> The Formula of Autonomy: "So act that your will can regard itself at the same time as making universal law through its maxims."
> The Formula of the Kingdom of Ends: "So act as if you were through your maxims a law-making member of a kingdom of ends."

According to Kant, each of these four formulations will produce the same conclusion regarding the morality of any particular action. Thus, each of these formulas offers a step-by-step procedure for determining the morality of any particular action. (Only the first two formulations are covered in the selections provided here.)

The Formula of the Law of Nature. The formula of the law of nature tells us to take a particular action, construe it as a general maxim, then see if it can be willed consistently as a law of nature. If it can be willed consistently, then the action is moral. If not, then it is immoral. To illustrate the categorical imperative, Kant uses four examples that cover the range of morally significant situations that arise. These examples include committing suicide, making false promises, failing to develop one's abilities, and refusing to be charitable. In each case, the action is deemed immoral since a contradiction arises when trying to will the maxim as a law of nature.

Since the universality of the law according to which effects are produced constitutes what is properly called *nature* in the most general sense (as to form), that is the existence of things so far as it is determined by general laws, the imperative of duty may be expressed thus:

> Act as if the maxim of your action were to become by your will a universal law of nature.

We will now enumerate a few duties, adopting the usual division of them into duties to ourselves and ourselves and to others, and into perfect and imperfect duties.

1. A man reduced to despair by a series of misfortunes feels wearied of life, but is still so far in possession of his reason that he can ask himself whether it would not be contrary to his duty to himself to take his own life. Now he inquires whether the maxim of his action could become a universal law of nature. His maxim is: "From self-love I adopt it as a principle to shorten my life when its longer duration is likely to bring more evil than satisfaction." It is asked then simply whether this principle founded on self-love can become a universal law of nature. Now we see at once that a system of nature of which it should be a law to destroy life by means of the very feeling whose special nature it is to impel to the improvement of life would contradict itself and, therefore, could not exist as a system of nature; hence that maxim can-

not possibly exist as a universal law of nature and, consequently, would be wholly inconsistent with the supreme principle of all duty.

 ASK YOURSELF

9.28. With Kant's first formulation of the categorical imperative (i.e., the formula of the law of nature), what is the specific contradiction that arises in the suicide example?

2. Another finds himself forced by necessity to borrow money. He knows that he will not be able to repay it, but sees also that nothing will be lent to him unless he promises stoutly to repay it in a definite time. He desires to make this promise, but he has still so much conscience as to ask himself: "Is it not unlawful and inconsistent with duty to get out of a difficulty in this way?" Suppose however that he resolves to do so: then the maxim of his action would be expressed thus. "When I think myself in want of money, I will borrow money and promise to repay it, although I know that I never can do so." Now this principle of self-love or of one's own advantage may perhaps be consistent with my whole future welfare; but the question now is, "Is it right?" I change then the suggestion of self-love into a universal law, and state the question thus: "How would it be if my maxim were a universal law?" Then I see at once that it could never hold as a universal law of nature, but would necessarily contradict itself. For supposing it to be a universal law that everyone when he thinks himself in a difficulty should be able to promise whatever he pleases, with the purpose of not keeping his promise, the promise itself would become impossible, as well as the end that one might have in view in it, since no one would consider that anything was promised to him, but would ridicule all such statements as vain pretenses.

 ASK YOURSELF

9.29. What contradiction arises in the example of the deceitful borrower?

3. A third finds in himself a talent which with the help of some culture might make him a useful man in many respects. But he finds himself in comfortable circumstances and prefers to indulge in pleasure rather than to take pains in enlarging and improving his happy natural capacities. He asks, however, whether his maxim of neglect of his natural gifts, besides agreeing with his inclination to indulgence, agrees also with what is called duty. He sees then that a system of nature could indeed subsist with such a universal law although men (like the South Sea islanders) should let their talents rest and resolve to devote their lives merely to idleness, amusement, and propagation of their species—in a word, to enjoyment; but he cannot possibly *will* that this should be a universal law of nature, or be implanted in us as such by a natural instinct. For, as a rational being, he necessarily wills that his faculties be developed, since they serve him and have been given him, for all sorts of possible purposes.

ASK YOURSELF

9.30. What contradiction arises from the example of neglecting one's talents?

4. A fourth, who is in prosperity, while he sees that others have to contend with great wretchedness and that he could help them, thinks: "What concern is it of mine? Let everyone be as happy as Heaven pleases, or as he can make himself; I will take nothing from him nor even envy him, only I do not wish to contribute anything to his welfare or to his assistance in distress!" Now no doubt if such a mode of thinking were a universal law, the human race might very well subsist and doubtless even better than in a state in which everyone talks of sympathy and good-will, or even takes care occasionally to put it into practice, but, on the other side, also cheats when he can, betrays the rights of men, or otherwise violates them. But although it is possible that a universal law of nature might exist in accordance with that maxim, it is impossible to *will* that such a principle should have the universal validity of a law of nature. For a will which resolved this would contradict itself, inasmuch as many cases might occur in which one would have need of the love and sympathy of others, and in which, by such a law of nature, sprung from his own will, he would deprive himself of all hope of the aid he desires.

 ASK YOURSELF

9.31. What contradiction arises in the example of failing to be charitable?

The Formula of the End Itself. The formula of the end itself is more straightforward than the previous one: Always treat people as an end and never only as a means. There are two points to this principle. First, when performing an action we should treat people as something that is intrinsically valuable. Second, we should not use people as a means to achieve some further benefit.

Supposing, however, that there were something *whose existence* has *in itself* an absolute worth, something which, being *an end in itself*, could be a source of definite laws; then in this and this alone would lie the source of a possible categorical imperative, i.e., a practical law.

Now I say: man and generally any rational being *exists* as an end in himself, *not merely as a means* to be arbitrarily used by this or that will, but in all his actions, whether they concern himself or other rational beings, must be always regarded at the same time as an end. All objects of the inclinations have only a conditional worth, for if the inclinations and the wants founded on them did not exist, then their object would be without value. But the inclinations, themselves being sources of want, are so far from having an absolute worth for which they should be desired that on the contrary it must be the universal wish of every rational being to be wholly free from them. Thus the worth of any object which is *to be acquired* by our action is always conditional. Beings whose existence depends not on our will but on nature's, have nevertheless, if they are irrational beings, only a relative value as means, and are therefore called *things*; rational beings, on the contrary, are called *persons*, because their very nature points them out as ends in themselves, that is as something which must not be used merely as means, and so far therefore restricts freedom of action (and is an object of respect). These, therefore, are not merely subjective ends whose existence has a worth *for us* as an effect of our action, *but objective ends*, that is, things whose existence is an end in itself; an end moreover for which no other can be substituted, which they should subserve *merely* as means, for otherwise nothing whatever would possess *absolute worth*; but if all worth were conditioned and therefore contingent, then there would be no supreme practical principle of reason whatever.

 ASK YOURSELF

9.32. What is Kant's distinction between *things* and *persons*?

If then there is a supreme practical principle or, in respect of the human will, a categorical imperative, it must be one which, being drawn from the conception of that which is necessarily an end for everyone because it is *an end in itself*, constitutes an *objective* principle of will, and can therefore serve as a universal practical law. The foundation of this principle is: *rational nature exists as an end in itself*. Man necessarily conceives his own existence as being so; so far then this is a *subjective* principle of human actions. But every other rational being regards its existence similarly, just on the same rational principle that holds for me: so that it is at the same time an objective principle, from which as a supreme practical law all laws of the will must be capable of being deduced. Accordingly the practical imperative will be as follows:

So act as to treat humanity, whether in your own person or in that of any other, in every case as an end, never as means only.

We will now inquire whether this can be practically carried out.

Examples. Using the same examples as earlier, Kant continues by showing how this formulation of the categorical imperative also confirms our basic duties.

To abide by the previous examples:

Firstly, under the head of necessary duty to oneself: He who contemplates suicide should ask himself whether his action can be consistent with the idea of humanity *as an end in itself*. If he destroys himself in order to escape from painful circumstances, he uses a person merely as *a means* to maintain a tolerable condition up to the end of life. But a man is not a thing, that is to say, something which can be used merely as means, but must in all his actions be always considered as an end in himself. I cannot, therefore, dispose in any way of a man in my own person so as to mutilate him, to damage or kill him. (It belongs to ethics proper to define this principle more precisely, so as to avoid all misunderstanding, e.g., as to the amputation of the limbs in order to preserve myself, as to exposing my life to danger with a view to preserve it, etc. This question is therefore omitted here.)

ASK YOURSELF

9.33. With Kant's second formulation of the categorical imperative (i.e., the formula of the end itself), why is suicide wrong?

Secondly, as regards necessary duties, or those of strict obligation, towards others: He who is thinking of making a lying promise to others will see at once that he would be using another man *merely as a means*, without the latter containing at the same time the end in himself. For he whom I propose by such a promise to use for my own purposes cannot possibly assent to my mode of acting towards him and, therefore, cannot himself contain the end of this action. This violation of the principle of humanity in other men is more obvious if we take in examples of attacks on the freedom and property of others. For then it is clear that he who transgresses the rights of men intends to use the person of others merely as a means, without considering that as rational beings they ought always to be esteemed also as ends, that is, as beings who must be capable of containing in themselves the end of the very same action.

ASK YOURSELF

9.34. Why would it be wrong to make a deceitful promise?

GEORG WILHELM FRIEDRICH HEGEL

German philosopher Georg Wilhelm Friedrich Hegel (1770–1831) was born in Stuttgart and attended seminary at the University of Tübingen. His intellectual formation was affected by theologians, philosophers, and, notably, the German poet Höderlin. Hegel worked as a tutor and held various short positions for many years but eventually succeeded Fichte as a professor at the University of Berlin. He died of cholera in 1831. Although influenced by Kant, Hegel parted company with his predecessor by arguing that philosophy could establish fundamental truths about ultimate reality and God. In fact, Hegel continues a certain strand of Enlightenment thought in which religion or faith is to be replaced by "science" or systematic thinking able to comprehend all of reality. In this respect he departs from the example of Kant, who thought that philosophy's limitations left some room for faith.

Introduction

Unlike most earlier philosophers, Hegel argued that we find all truth, including even truth about God, *within* history. Hegel did not believe in a God outside the world who created it and sustained it. Instead, he believed that history itself was the unfolding of the divine, and as such was perfectly rational. Hegel was troubled by the "contradictions" that arose in philosophy as well as in common life, between our sense of freedom and the determinism of science, between domination by government and individual liberty, between an eternal God and a mortal and contingent history, and so on. Hegel believed that philosophy could show how everything in history was the result of a completely rational process in which all such apparent contradictions would eventually be resolved. In fact, Hegel thought *his* philosophy showed the resolution of all contradictions in history. Hegel's view seemed to many to sanctify the "status quo" (the way things in fact are). That is to say, in his view it appears that whatever happens in history must happen, and is even in a sense God's will. So, for example, the Nazi regime or the career of a serial killer are both part of the unfolding of the divine! No merely individual human choices could have made things come out differently than they have.

 ASK YOURSELF

9.35. Mention two main characteristics of Hegel's thought.

9.36. Explain how his view seems to "sanctify the status quo."

Philosophy and History

Hegel's ambitions for philosophy as a discipline are extreme. He believes that it is capable of expressing a "concrete universal," that is, a combination of general or universal truths (such as that all effects have a cause, or general laws of science) with all particular, concrete, historical facts. It is thus capable of bringing to light the "absolute," the truth without remainder. This belief comes out strongly in his major work, the *Phenomenology of Mind*, the preface of which is excerpted here.

Philosophy as the Tracing of the Development of Reality. Philosophy arrives at an account of the real by tracing a historical process. That process is both "dialectical," in a sense that will emerge in what follows, and at the same time "organic."

 From HEGEL: *Phenomenology of Mind*

. . . because philosophy has its being essentially in the element of that universality which encloses the particular within it, the end or final result seems, in the case of philosophy more than in that of other sciences, to have absolutely expressed the complete fact itself in its very nature . . .

 ASK YOURSELF

9.37. What is it that Hegel hopes to express?

Hegel contrasts his procedure with that of more conventional historians of philosophy, who present various systems that seem to contradict each other. For example, they explain Descartes's Rationalism and show how it is contradicted by Locke's Empiricism. Hegel, on the contrary, intends to show how these apparently contradictory accounts of philosophy (and also of other domains such as art, religion, and politics) are organically related.

. . . The more the ordinary mind takes the opposition between true and false to be fixed, the more is it accustomed to expect either agreement or contradiction with a given philosophical system, and only to see reason for the one or the other in any explanatory statement concerning such a system. It does not conceive the diversity of philosophical systems as the progressive evolution of truth; rather, it sees only contradiction in that variety.

The bud disappears when the blossom breaks through, and we might say that the former is refuted by the latter; in the same way when the fruit comes, the blossom may be explained to be a false form of the plant's existence, for the fruit appears as its true nature in place of the blossom. These stages are not merely differentiated; they supplant one another as being incompatible with one another. But the ceaseless activity of their own inherent nature makes them at the same time moments of an organic unity, where they not merely do not contradict one another, but where one is as necessary as the other; and this equal necessity of all moments constitutes alone and thereby the life of the whole. But contradiction as between philosophical systems is not wont to be conceived in this way; on the other hand, the mind perceiving the contradiction does not commonly know how to relieve it or keep it free from its one-sidedness, and to recognize in what seems conflicting and inherently antagonistic the presence of mutually necessary moments.

 ASK YOURSELF

9.38. In what way does the "ordinary mind" fail according to Hegel?

9.39. Is Hegel saying that a contradiction between two philosophical systems is not a sure sign that at least one of them must be false and therefore worthless?

The foregoing passage sums up much of Hegel's philosophy in a simple image. It is the image of a plant bud developing into a flower and fruit developing from the flower. The flower arrives only by "negating" the bud. Nonetheless, the bud is essential for the appearance of the flower; it contains the flower potentially or abstractly. Philosophical systems and systems of thought and culture, generally, are like buds that must be "negated" or contradicted in order for higher truth to appear, but the lower form, like the bud, contains the higher implicitly, and negating it does not mean destroying it but surpassing it. The bud, or the "system" (say, for example, the system of Plato), is but a "moment" or stage in the development or "evolution" of something (the plant, or the truth) Each stage is necessary for what follows, and each stage follows from the "contradiction" or "negating" of the previous stage.

Thus we might think of some of Aristotle's thought as arising from the negating of Plato. It too will have to be negated, just as the flower will, but that does not show it to be worthless or merely false. The "inherent nature" of truth is already present in Plato's thought, just as the inherent nature of the flower is in the bud and indeed the inherent nature of the entire plant is in the seed. Each moment or stage of the plant is necessary to the entire thing, the whole. Each moment or stage in the history of thought and culture is also necessary for the whole, which will be absolute truth. And the development of the whole is guided by some ultimate purpose or aim. We can see that Hegel's own thinking is strongly colored by some Aristotelian ideas, not the least of them the stress on development in accordance with some inner "teleology" (striving toward some goal). Hegel's account would thus be the final "system."

We will be returning to this image from time to time, but for now it should enable you to frame some preliminary definitions.

 ASK YOURSELF

9.40. Define: negation; system; moment; contradiction; organic unity.

Be on the lookout in what follows for expressions or turns of phrase that suggest this same "organic" and "developmental" or evolutionary thinking, and also the stress on "concreteness," and make a note of them.

"External" Teleology, and Internal Grasp of Truth. Hegel believes past thinkers were trapped in an external viewpoint.

To trouble oneself in this fashion with the purpose and results, and again with the differences, the positions taken up and judgments passed by one thinker and another, is therefore an easier task than perhaps it seems. For instead of laying hold of the matter in hand, a procedure of that kind is all the while away from the subject altogether. Instead of dwelling within it and becoming absorbed by it, knowledge of that sort is always grasping at something else; such knowledge, instead of keeping to the subject-matter and giving itself up to it, never gets away from itself. The easiest thing of all is to pass judgments on what has a solid substantial content; it is more difficult to grasp it, and most of all difficult to do both together and produce the systematic exposition of it.

The beginning of culture and of the struggle to pass out of the unbroken immediacy of naive psychical life has always to be made by acquiring knowledge of universal principles and points of view, by striving, in the first instance, to work up simply to the *thought* of the subject-matter in general, not forgetting at the same time to give reasons for supporting it or refuting it, to apprehend the concrete riches and fullness contained in its various determinate qualities, and to know how to furnish a coherent, orderly account of it and a responsible judgment upon it.

This beginning of mental cultivation will, however, very soon make way for the earnestness of actual life in all its fullness, which leads to a living experience of the subject-matter itself; and when, in addition, conceptual thought strenuously penetrates to the very depths of its meaning, such knowledge and style of judgment will keep their due place in everyday thought and conversation.

An example of the "unbroken immediacy of naive psychical life" might be the habitual handed-down beliefs, say, about religion or politics, that people inherit from their parents. Those beliefs are in a sense "thoughtless." When we begin to think for ourselves instead of naively accepting what others say, we begin by looking for general principles, for example, the principle "only believe what can be experienced." These principles turn out to be too abstract for the "earnestness of actual life in all its fullness," but their use constitutes a necessary "moment" in the development of thought. They allow us to break with "immediacy."

 ASK YOURSELF

9.41. Give an example of an "immediate" belief in Hegel's sense.

The systematic development of truth in scientific form can alone be the true shape in which truth exists. To help to bring philosophy nearer to the form of science—that goal where it can lay aside the name of love of knowledge and be actual knowledge—that is what I have set before me. The inner necessity that knowledge should be science lies in its very nature; and the adequate and sufficient explanation for this lies simply and solely in the systematic exposition of philosophy itself. The external necessity, however, so far as this is apprehended in a universal way, and apart from the accident of the personal element and the particular occasioning influences affecting the individual, is the same as the internal: it lies in the form and shape in which the process of time presents the existence of its moments.

The external (for example, scientific laws such as the gravitational law, which hold objectively, apart from thought) is the same as the internal. That could only be true if the scientific law was arrived at by a process of thought that conforms perfectly to the way things are. It is an old "Rationalist" idea that reality must conform to thought. Hegel's particular spin on the Rationalist tradition emphasizes development in a new way.

To show that the time process does raise philosophy to the level of scientific system would, therefore, be the only true justification of the attempts which aim at proving that philosophy must assume this character; because the temporal process would thus bring out and lay bare the necessity of it, nay, more, would at the same time be carrying out that very aim itself.

For Hegel, "scientific" refers simply to genuine systematic knowledge. You must keep this use of "scientific" and "science" in mind in all that follows. It does *not* refer to physics, chemistry, and so on.

 ASK YOURSELF

9.42. "The time process does raise philosophy to the level of scientific system." What does this mean? See if you can figure it out in relation to previous discussions and questions.

When we state the true form of truth to be its scientific character—or, what is the same thing, when it is maintained that truth finds the medium of its existence in notions or conceptions alone—I know that this seems to contradict an idea with all its consequences which makes great pretensions and has gained widespread acceptance and conviction at the present time. A word of explanation concerning this contradiction seems, therefore, not out of place, even though at this stage it can amount to no more than a dogmatic assurance exactly like the view we are opposing. If, that is to say, truth exists merely in what, or rather exists merely as what, is called at one time intuition, at another immediate knowledge of the Absolute, Religion, Being—not being in the center of divine love, but the very Being of this center, of the Absolute itself—from that point of view it is rather the opposite of the notional or conceptual form which would be required for systematic philosophical exposition. The Absolute on this view is not to be grasped in conceptual form, but felt, intuited; it is not its conception, but the feeling of it and intuition of it that are to have the say and find expression.

 ASK YOURSELF

9.43. So the "absolute" in Hegel's usage is identical with what (or who)?

Science, Reason, and Feeling. "Intuition" is never enough for a philosopher like Hegel. Nonetheless, thought alone can be cold and can kill our sense for the concreteness and warmth of real life.

[Thought] has not merely lost its essential and concrete life, it is also conscious of this loss and of the transitory finitude characteristic of its content. Turning away from the husks it has to feed on, and confessing that it lies in wickedness and sin, it reviles it self for so doing, and now desires from philosophy not so much to bring it to a knowledge of what it is, as to obtain once again through philosophy the restoration of that sense of solidity and substantiality of existence it has lost. Philosophy is thus expected not so much to meet this want by opening up the compact solidity of substantial existence, and bringing this to the light and level of self-consciousness—is not so much to bring chaotic conscious life back to the orderly ways of thought, and the simplicity of the notion, as to run together what thought has divided asunder, suppress the notion with its distinctions, and restore the feeling of existence.

Thought may literally lead us to "divide asunder," and we may have to kill something, in ourselves or the world, to divide, and thus to think. Wordsworth, the romantic poet and close contemporary of Hegel, complained that "we murder to dissect." That is what we do in biology labs, right? Of course we dissect in order to further our "thinking."

What it [the human mind or soul] wants from philosophy is not so much insight as edification. The beautiful, the holy, the eternal, religion, love—these are the bait required to awaken the desire to bite: not the notion, but ecstasy, not the march of cold necessity in the subject-matter, but ferment and enthusiasm—these are to be the ways by which the wealth of the concrete substance is to be stored and increasingly extended.

We might feel there is a "march of cold necessity" in the way the physical sciences have developed, with each theory developing with necessity out of earlier ones. A clearer example of such a "march" would be the development of theorems out of axioms and postulates in geometry. They follow "with necessity."

A further example has been used elsewhere in this text. A bachelor is necessarily unmarried. That follows from the concept of bachelor. But Hegel thinks that the sort of necessity found in true thought is not at all trivial, in the way "bachelors are unmarried" is trivial.

 ASK YOURSELF

9.44. Hegel uses the word "notion" to refer, roughly, to what is conceptual. Notions are the stock in trade of philosophy. How then does the "notion" connect up with the "march of cold necessity" in his thought? Consult earlier questions.

With this demand there goes the strenuous effort, almost perfervidly zealous in its activity, to rescue mankind from being sunken in what is sensuous, vulgar, and of fleeting importance, and to raise men's eyes to the stars; as if men had quite forgotten the divine, and were on the verge of finding satisfaction, like worms, in mud and water. Time was when man had a heaven, decked and fitted out with endless wealth of thoughts and pictures. The significance of all that is, lay in the thread of light by which it was attached to heaven; instead of dwelling in the present as it is here and now, the eye glanced away over the present to the Divine, away, so to say, to a present that lies beyond. The mind's gaze had to be directed under compulsion to what is earthly, and kept fixed there; and it has needed a long time to introduce that clearness, which only celestial realities had, into the crassness and confusion shrouding the sense of things earthly, and to make attention to the immediate present as such, which was called Experience, of interest and of value. Now we have apparently the need for the opposite of all this; man's mind and interest are so deeply rooted in the earthly that we require a like power to have them raised above that level. His spirit shows such poverty of nature that it seems to long for the mere pitiful feeling of the divine in the abstract, and to get refreshment from that, like a wanderer in the desert craving for the merest mouthful of water. By the little which can thus satisfy the needs of the human spirit we can measure the extent of its loss.

Hegel has just described the transition from a medieval worldview, with its "heavenward glance," to the Enlightenment worldview, with its stress on experiment and reason. Now he goes on to attack the romantic reaction, which is full of longing for a lost divinity but lacks the rigor needed in philosophy ("science" in Hegel's sense).

This easy contentment in receiving, or stinginess in giving, does not suit the character of science. The man who only seeks edification, who wants to envelop in mist the manifold diversity of his earthly existence and thought, and craves after the vague enjoyment of this vague and indeterminate Divinity—he may look where he likes to find this: he will easily find for himself the means to procure something he can rave over and puff himself up withal. But philosophy must beware of wishing to be edifying.

Still less must this kind of contentment, which holds science in contempt, take upon itself to claim that raving obscurantism of this sort is something higher than science. These apocalyptic utterances pretend to occupy the very center and the deepest depths; they look askance at all definiteness and preciseness (*horos*) of meaning; and they deliberately hold back from conceptual thinking and the constraining necessities of thought, as being the sort of reflection which, they say, can only feel at home in the sphere of finitude. But just as there is a breadth which is emptiness, there is a depth which is empty too: as we may have an extension of substance which overflows into finite multiplicity without the power of keeping the manifold together, in the same way we may have an insubstantial intensity which, keeping itself in as mere force without actual expression, is no better than superficiality. The force of mind is only as great as its expression; its depth only as deep as its power to expand and lose itself when spending and giving out its substance. Moreover, when this unreflective emotional knowledge makes a pretence of having immersed its own very self in the depths of the absolute Being, and of philosophizing in all holiness and truth, it hides from itself the fact that instead of devotion to God, it rather, by this contempt for all measurable precision and definiteness, simply attests in its own case the fortuitous character of its content, and in the other endows God with its own caprice. When such minds commit themselves to the unrestrained ferment of sheer emotion, they think that, by putting a veil over self-consciousness, and surrendering all understanding, they are thus God's beloved ones to whom He gives His wisdom in sleep. This is the reason, too, that in point of fact what they do conceive and bring forth in sleep is dreams.

For the rest it is not difficult to see that our epoch is a birth-time, and a period of transition. The spirit of man has broken with the old order of things hitherto prevailing, and with the old ways of thinking, and is in the mind to let them all sink into the depths of the past and to set about its own transformation. It is indeed never at rest, but carried along the stream of progress ever onward. But it is here as in the case of the birth of a child; after a long period of nutrition in silence, the continuity of the gradual growth in size, of quantitative change, is suddenly cut short by the flat breath drawn—there is a break in the process, a qualitative change—and the child is born. In like manner the spirit of the time, growing slowly and quietly ripe for the new form it is to assume, disintegrates one fragment after another of the structure of its previous world. That it is tottering to its fall is indicated only by symptoms here and there. Frivolity and again *ennui* [boredom], which are spreading in the established order of things, the undefined foreboding of something unknown—all these betoken that there is something else approaching. This gradual crumbling to pieces, which did not alter the general look and aspect of the whole, is interrupted by the sunrise, which, in a flash and at a single stroke, brings to view the form and structure of the new world.

But this new world is perfectly realized just as little as the new-born child; and it is essential to bear this in mind. It comes on the stage to begin with in its immediacy, in its bare generality. A building is not finished when its foundation is laid; and just as little, is the attainment of a general notion of a whole the whole itself. When we want to see an oak with all its vigour of trunk, its spreading branches, and mass of foliage, we are not satisfied to be shown an acorn instead. In the same way science, the crowning glory of a spiritual world, is not found complete in its initial stages.

Once again we see Hegel using the imagery of biological development to describe historical changes, in this case, the changes wrought by the Enlightenment and the French Revolution of 1789 in which "the spirit of man" broke with "the old order of things hitherto prevailing, and with the old ways of thinking."

 ASK YOURSELF

9.45. What is Hegel comparing the revolution to, and what is he warning us *not* to do?

The Unity of Subject and Object

We have come to think of knowledge as the grasp of something that exists independently of thought. Hegel denies that there is any such "something," even though he does not equate reality with what any individual thinks.

Absolute Spirit. Reality is what is thought by an absolute Spirit, which is simply Hegel's immanent God. That Spirit must not be thought of as some thing (some being) which stands apart from the object which it thinks.

In my view—a view which the developed exposition of the system itself can alone justify—everything depends on grasping and expressing the ultimate truth not as Substance but as Subject as well. At the same time we must note that concrete substantiality implicates and involves the universal or the immediacy of knowledge itself, as well as that immediacy which is being, or immediacy qua object for knowledge. If the generation which heard God spoken of as the One Substance was shocked and revolted by such a characterization of his nature, the reason lay partly in the instinctive feeling that in such a conception self-consciousness was simply submerged, and not preserved. But partly, again, the opposite position, which maintains thinking to be merely subjective thinking, abstract universality as such, is exactly the same bare uniformity, is undifferentiated, unmoved substantiality. And even if, in the third place, thought combines with itself the being of substance, and conceives immediacy or intuition as thinking, it is still a question whether this intellectual intuition does not fall back into that inert, abstract simplicity, and exhibit and expound reality itself in an unreal manner.

The preceding passage is rich in fundamental Hegelian ideas. Ultimate truth must be expressed as both subject and substance (or object). Spinoza, the seventeenth-century rationalist, seemed to submerge the subject as consciousness or thinking in abstract being. The idea of substance in Spinoza is impersonal, lacking any subjectivity or "personality." God is simply the one being of which all things are aspects. The idea was shocking because people like to believe in a personal God. The other pole consists in construing thinking as merely subjective thinking, that is, my thought conceived as simply or merely mine, without attention to the way in which my capacity for thought is a function of a larger whole.

 ASK YOURSELF

9.46. What larger whole might be necessary in order for me, as an individual, to be able to think and reason?

The living substance, further, is that being which is truly subject, or, what is the same thing, is truly realized and actual solely in the process of positing itself, or in mediating with its own self its transitions from one state or position to the opposite. As subject it is pure and simple negativity, and just on that account a process of splitting up what is simple and undifferentiated, a process of duplicating and setting factors in opposition, which [process] in turn is the negation of this indifferent diversity and of the opposition of factors it entails. True reality is merely this process of reinstating self-identity, of reflecting into its own self in and from its other, and is not an original and primal unity as such, not an immediate unity as such. It is the process of its own becoming, the circle which presupposes its end as its purpose, and has its end for its beginning; it becomes concrete and actual only by being carried out, and by the end it involves.

The life of God and divine intelligence, then, can, if we like, be spoken of as love disporting with itself; but this idea falls into edification, and even sinks into insipidity, if it lacks the seriousness, the suffering, the patience, and the labor of the negative. *Per se* the divine life is no doubt undisturbed identity and oneness with itself, which finds not serious obstacle in otherness and estrangement, and none in the surmounting of this estrangement. But the "per se" is abstract generality, where we abstract from its real nature, which consists in its being objective, to itself, conscious of itself on its own account; and where consequently we neglect altogether the self movement which is the formal character of its activity. If the form is declared to correspond to the essence, it is just for that reason a misunderstanding to suppose that knowledge can be content with the "per se," the essence, but can do without the form, that the absolute principle, or absolute intuition, makes the carrying out of the former, or the development of the latter, needless. Precisely because the form is as necessary to the essence as the essence to itself, absolute reality must not be conceived of and expressed as essence alone, i.e., as immediate substance, or as pure self intuition of the Divine, but as form also, and with the entire wealth of the developed form. Only then is it grasped and expressed as really actual.

The truth is the whole. The whole, however, is merely the essential nature reaching its completeness through the process of its own development. Of the Absolute it must be said that it is essentially a result, that only at the end is it what it is in very truth; and just in that consists its nature, which is to be actual, subject, or self-becoming, self-development.

Think again of the bud–flower–fruit analogy. In a sense we only understand the whole at the end, when we see what it was all headed for. In that sense "only at the end is it what it is in very truth." "The truth is the whole." This is a classic axiom of a certain kind of idealism. Tennyson, for example, writes,

> Flower in the crannied wall
> I pluck you out of the crannies,
> I hold you here, root and all, in my hand,
> Little flower—but if I could understand
> What you are, root and all, and all in all,
> I should know what God and man is.

Should it appear contradictory to say that the Absolute has to be conceived essentially as a result, a little consideration will set this appearance of contradiction in its true light. The beginning, the principle, or the Absolute, as at first or immediately expressed, is merely the universal. If we say "all animals," that does not pass for zoology; for the same reason we see at once that the words absolute, divine, eternal, and so on do not express what is implied in them; and only mere words like these, in point of fact, express intuition as the immediate. Whatever is more than a word like that, even the mere transition to a proposition, is a form of mediation, contains a process towards another state from which we must return once more. It is this process of mediation, however, that is rejected with horror, as if absolute knowledge were being surrendered when more is made of mediation than merely the assertion that it is nothing absolute, and does not exist in the Absolute.

This horrified rejection of mediation, however, arises as a fact from want of acquaintance with its nature, and with the nature of absolute knowledge itself. For mediating is nothing but self-identity working itself out through an active self-directed process; or, in other words, it is reflection into self, the aspect in which the ego is for itself, objective to itself. It is pure negativity, or, reduced to its utmost abstraction, the process of bare and simple becoming. The ego, or becoming in general, this process of mediating, is, because of its being simple, just immediacy coming to be, and is immediacy itself. We misconceive therefore the nature of reason if we exclude reflection or mediation from ultimate truth, and do not take it to be a positive moment of the Absolute. It is reflection which constitutes truth the final result, and yet at the same time does away with the contrast between result and the process of arriving at it. For this process is likewise simple, and therefore not distinct from the form of truth, which consists in appearing as simple in the result; it is indeed just this restoration and return to simplicity. While the embryo is certainly, in itself, implicitly a human being, it is not so explicitly, it is not by itself a human being; man is explicitly man only in the form of developed and cultivated reason, which has made itself to be what it is implicitly. Its actual reality is first found here. But this result arrived at is itself simple immediacy; for it is self-conscious freedom, which is at one with itself, and has not set aside the opposition it involves and left it there, but has made its account with it and become reconciled to it.

What has been said may also be expressed by saying that reason is purposive activity. The exaltation of so-called nature at the expense of thought misconceived, and more especially the rejection of external purposiveness, have brought the idea of purpose in general into disrepute. All the same, in the sense in which Aristotle, too, characterizes nature as purposive activity, purpose is the immediate, the undisturbed, the unmoved which is self-moving; as such it is subject. Its power of moving, taken abstractly, is its existence for itself, or pure negativity. The result is the same as the beginning solely because the beginning is purpose. Stated otherwise, what is actual and concrete is the same as its inner principle or notion simply because the immediate qua purpose contains within it the self or pure actuality. The realized purpose, or concrete actuality, is movement and development unfolded. But this very unrest is the self; and it is one and the same with that immediacy and simplicity characteristic of the beginning just for the reason that it is the result, and has returned upon itself-while this latter again is just the self, and the self is self-referring and self-relating identity and simplicity.

The crucial concepts operative in the preceding paragraphs are "immediacy," "mediation," "negativity," and "purposive activity." The first two are obviously related. We can think of mediation as essentially a kind of articulation, a spelling out. Thus if I simply open my eyes and let the world flood in, the result might be called "immediate" experience, but when I begin to articulate that experience, to say something about it or think about it, I find that I am dividing one thing from another, and that is one way to describe what "mediating" is. Thus if in my visual field there is a tree and a house, to the extent I distinguish them from each other, to that extent I am mediating. In effect I see the tree as a tree, and thus as distinct from, as *not*, a house. "Not" is of course a "negative," so you can see from this example that mediation essentially involves negating activity, or "negativity." To think, in the sense of articulating or distinguishing anything from anything, always involves saying or thinking something as being itself and thus *not* something else.

It is interesting in this connection to recall the Eleatic contention that it is not possible to say or think what is not. From this fundamental premise the Eleatics concluded that being is one, eternal and unchanging. One way to put this would be to say that they conceived (or tried to conceive) being or the real as totally devoid of articulation. Perhaps that explains why the views of Parmenides seem to be unexpressible. One cannot say or think "the one" at all. One must remain mute, with all thought set aside. Now thought conceived in this way seems to break everything apart, and thus to contribute to unintelligibility, but at the same time how could anything be intelligible if not thought about? So thought seems to be at war with itself. For in thinking I seek unity, the "universal," as a condition of intelligibility. I bring a variety under unifying concepts, I try to have oneness (immediate unity) together with manyness (articulation). This is the dialectic (back-and-forth argument) that so preoccupied the ancients, from the Presocratics and Aristotle to their philosophical offspring in the present.

Aristotle's solution to this problem consisted in attempting to show how everything is purposively structured, so that change (which is simply articulation in the most general sense, the disintegrating of what is one in space or time) acquires unity and thus intelligibility by virtue of the *direction* or *goal* of the change. Each stage in the career of a changing thing is achieved by negating, shedding, or shuffling off (the way the flower shuffles off the constricting surface of the bud) something of the previous stage. But the whole process is intelligible by virtue of its direction.

Activity, whether it is the activity of something in nature or the activity of an individual mind thinking about something or the activity of a culture as it develops, thus requires mediation and negation, and the intelligibility of the entire process derives from the goal, the "result" at which the process aims. Hegel takes this Aristotelian solution and gives it a remarkable application, in which everything, that is, the entire history of the universe, is simply a goal-oriented articulation of mind, or Spirit, or God conceived as entirely *immanent*.

 ASK YOURSELF

9.47. Try to give preliminary definitions of the following: mediation; immediacy; negation; purposive activity.

. . . Among the many consequences that follow from what has been said, it is of importance to emphasize this, that knowledge is only real and can only be set forth fully in the form of science, in the form of system; and further, that a so-called fundamental proposition or first principle of philosophy, even if it is true, is yet nonetheless false just because and insofar as it is merely a fundamental proposition, merely a first principle. It is for that reason easily refuted. The refutation consists in bringing out its defective character; and it is defective because it is merely the universal, merely a principle, the beginning. If the refutation is complete and thorough, it is derived and developed from the nature of the principle itself, and not accomplished by bringing in from elsewhere other counterassurances and chance fancies.

An example of a fundamental proposition or first principle of philosophy might be Descartes's "I think, therefore I am" or the Empiricist claim that all knowledge arises from experience. Hegel thinks that such principles are always defective and can be "internally" refuted. Thus these principles are seen to founder when we consider just what the "I" must be, or just what "experience" may be. Yet the process by which these principles are refuted is itself the unfolding of genuine knowledge, unconditioned knowledge that is real science. So these principles are not strictly false; they are a "moment" in the unfolding of the absolute. Thus one should not take account "solely of the negative" aspect, that is, the refutation. The flower "refutes" the bud, but the bud is nonetheless essential to the reality of the flower.

 ASK YOURSELF

9.48. What might lead a person to give up the claim that all knowledge arises from experience? Does it follow that experience is irrelevant to knowledge? Explain.

The Absolute Truth as "Spirit." Hegel is arguing that the truth of real science is nothing less than the truth of "Spirit" developing, flowering into a final form in which subject and object are one. The struggle of the human race to know and understand the world *is* a process, which includes all of culture, in which all the variety and conflict in history are brought together into a "system," a unity that is identical with Spirit or an immanent God. This history of the universe is the unfolding, the blossoming so to speak, of God.

That the truth is only realized in the form of a system, that substance is essentially subject, is expressed in the idea which represents the Absolute as Spirit (Geist)—the grandest conception of all, and one which is due to modern times and its religion. Spirit is alone Reality. It is the inner being of the world, that which essentially is, and is *per se*; it assumes objective, determinate form, and enters into relations with itself—it is externality (otherness), and exists for self; yet, in this determination, and in its otherness, it is still one with itself—it is self-contained and self-complete, in itself and for itself at once. This self-containedness, however, if first something known by us, it is implicit in its nature; it is Substance spiritual. It has to become self-contained *for itself*, on its own account; it must be knowledge of spirit, and must be consciousness of itself as spirit. This means, it must be presented to itself as an object, but at the same time straightway annul and transcend this objective form; it must be its own object in which it finds itself reflected. So far as its spiritual content is produced by its own activity, it is only we [the thinkers] who know spirit to be for itself, to be objective to itself; but insofar as spirit knows itself to be for itself, then this self-production, the pure notion, is the sphere and element in which its objectification takes effect, and where it gets its existential form. In this way it is in its existence aware of itself as an object in which its own self is reflected. Mind, which, when thus developed, knows itself to be mind, is science. Science is its realization, and the kingdom it sets up for itself in its own native element.

 ASK YOURSELF

9.49. What is "Spirit" or God for Hegel?

Kant tried to show that in so-called empirical knowledge one becomes aware of an object in which one's own self is reflected. The "object" is constituted, and is what it is, by virtue of the mind's own activity. Hegel is generalizing this idea to all knowledge and is claiming that ultimately the object encountered in "science" is *entirely* constituted by the subject. Science is this unity of subject and object.

History as Rational

It is natural to think of historical events as contingent, that is, as such that they might not have happened. If, for example, Hitler had not held back but had decided to invade England, history might have gone differently. But contingency is incompatible with complete rationality. What happens cannot just "happen to happen" in Hegel's view. Since history is the unfolding of the divine mind, the perfectly rational mind, it must have a perfect "logic" to it.

The Necessity of Spirits' Development. The unfolding or "budding" of Spirit that constitutes world history is unlike the budding of a flower in this sense: Everything that takes place in history takes place necessarily, in a sense close to "logical" necessity. (If it is true that either Gore or Bush wins, and if it is true that Gore does not win, then it follows with "logical necessity" that Bush wins. Either A or B. Not A. Therefore, B.)

. . . This movement of the spiritual entities constitutes the nature of scientific procedure in general. Looked at as the concatenation [joining together] of their content, this movement is the necessitated development and expansion of that content into an organic systematic whole. By this movement, too, the road, which leads to the notion of knowledge, becomes itself likewise a necessary and complete evolving process. This preparatory stage thus ceases to consist of casual philosophical reflections, referring to objects here and there, to processes and thoughts of the undeveloped mind as chance may direct; and it does not try to establish the truth by miscellaneous ratiocinations, inferences, and consequences drawn from circumscribed thoughts. The road to science, by the very movement of the notion itself, will compass the entire objective world of conscious life in its rational necessity.

The notion of "necessitated development" or of the "rational necessity" of conscious life is of course essential to Hegel's thought. The development of absolute mind or Spirit, its unfolding, is not a merely natural process (thus unlike the way we conceive of the bud turning to a flower) but is driven by rational necessity. So Hegel thinks there is necessity in things and in history. He thus contravenes a principle that was influential in twentieth-century philosophy, to the effect that necessity is a function of meaning (perhaps, of the meaning of logical constants, as given in a truth table). It is as though, for Hegel, each moment in history "follows from" previous moments in somewhat the way that a conclusion "follows from" premises in a deductive argument, as in the Gore/Bush example.

. . . What seems to take place outside it (i.e., mind), to be an activity directed against it, is its own doing, its own activity; and substance shows that it is in reality subject. When it has brought out this completely, mind has made its existence adequate to and one with its essential nature. Mind is object to itself just as it is, and the abstract element of immediacy, of the separation between knowing and the truth, is overcome. Being is entirely mediated; it is a substantial content, that is likewise directly in the possession of the ego, has the character of self, is notion. With the attainment of this the Phenomenology of Mind concludes. What mind prepares for itself in the course of its phenomenology is the element of true knowledge. In this element the moments of mind are now set out in the form of thought pure and simple, which knows its object to be itself. They no longer involve the opposition between being and knowing; they remain within the undivided simplicity of the knowing function; they are the truth in the form of truth, and their diversity is merely diversity of the content of truth. The process by which they are developed into an organically connected whole is Logic or Speculative Philosophy.

There is an obvious sense in which logic, unlike empirical disciplines, is self-contained. You might say that its object is itself. Logic is simply thinking about thinking. In a logic course we discuss the standards for correct thinking. Thus in the Gore/Bush example, it is not the particular subject matter (politicians, elections) that matters, but the abstract form, "A or B," "not A," "therefore B." Logic has no other "subject" matter than "thought" in this very abstract sense. You might even describe it as mind thinking on itself, so that the thinking and the object of the thinking are the same. Hegel is taking this intuitively plausible notion of logic on a very wild ride.

ASK YOURSELF

9.50. Make this a logical argument by filling in the blank:

   a. If Mary is here, Bill will be glad.

   b. Mary is here.

   c. So, _____.

Can you see that (c) follows necessarily from (a) and (b)? But, you might say, "Life isn't like that; it isn't perfectly 'logical.' " Well, Hegel thinks that if you understand fully enough, you will see that life *is* like that in a very fundamental sense. Hegel envisions a world that is dynamic and evolving, according to a perfectly rational plan. Everything that happens makes sense within that plan or system. What appear to be conflicts or "contradictions," say, between democracy and monarchy, between Empiricism and Rationalism, or for that matter between marrying Jane rather than Joan, are really illusory, for when fully understood or "mediated" they all fall into place in the system. Thus, in some peculiar sense there is no room for "choice," since there are no real alternatives to choose between. It only looks as though there are.

SØREN KIERKEGAARD

Much of nineteenth-century philosophy is a reaction against Hegel. That is especially evident in the works of Søren Kierkegaard. Kierkegaard was born in 1813 in Copenhagen, Denmark, the son of a wealthy cloth merchant who was intensely, even morbidly, religious, and who imparted to his son that brooding religiosity. Kierkegaard died a mere forty-two years later, but in the short latter half of his life he produced an enormous literature. The first Danish edition of his collected works, which does not include his journals and papers, comes to twenty volumes, many of them quite lengthy.

Introduction: Kierkegaard's "Existentialism"

In the year Kierkegaard was born the Danish economy was in trouble and the government responded by issuing a lot of worthless paper money. Kierkegaard later remarked, with characteristic wit, that he was born in a year when many false notes (bills) were put into circulation. A sense of irony about oneself, a tendency to ruminate a great deal about one's own life, and a concern for truthfulness in the "inner man" all show up in this clever remark. Kierkegaard's enormous literary output is indeed concerned almost exclusively with deeply personal questions: How should I live? What sort of being is a human being (what makes humans different from other beings)? What is truth, and what sort of truth will really matter to me personally? How can religion be taken seriously? The following early entry from a diary he kept during his entire adult life expresses his concern for his own personal integrity:

> 1 Aug. 1835. . . . What I lack is a single minded determination respecting *what I should do*, not what I should know, except insofar as a certain understanding

is presupposed by every action . . . to see what the Divine uniquely wills that *I* should do; the great thing is to find a Truth which is the Truth *for me*, to find *an idea for which I will live and die.*

Kierkegaard thought that Hegel's attempt to resolve the contradictions in human life through the exercise of philosophical reason made people misunderstand these tensions and contradictions and the way they should be addressed. He thought that Hegel, whose ideas were quite popular in Denmark, denied the importance of choosing between incompatible alternatives, so his ideas also tended to make people spiritually lazy and uncommitted, lacking in the energy needed for serious and responsible choices. Kierkegaard was not an "irrationalist," as has sometimes been claimed, but he certainly denied that reason could do what Hegel thought it could do. There are real contradictions, unresolvable by reason alone, between, for example, good and evil, and people must *choose* one or the other.

Kierkegaard attempted to show that self-knowledge or self-examination is the most essential human activity, much as Socrates had done in ancient Greece. In fact Kierkegaard constantly refers to Socrates, always with great admiration. Kierkegaard is often regarded as the founder or forerunner of a twentieth-century philosophical movement called Existentialism, which stresses choice, individual authenticity, (which itself requires honesty or self-examination), and the limits of reason in the face of the dilemmas of human existence.

 ASK YOURSELF

9.51. How do you suppose Existentialism got its name, and what is Socratic about it?

Kierkegaard portrayed various approaches to life in some of his early works. He does not appear to endorse any particular lifestyle, but simply examines the difficulties that confront various ways of living. Nonetheless, he is working out an answer to the question "How should I live?" The following are excerpts from his first major work, *Either/Or* (volumes 1 and 2), the first volume of which is presented as the work of a young man called simply "A," the second as the work of an older court magistrate, William. They represent two different and contradictory ways of living. The contradiction between them cannot be removed or surpassed by *thought*, as Hegel claimed. What a person knows or *thinks* is only important insofar as it plays a role in what he or she *does*, that is, how he or she *chooses* to live. Thought or reason alone is incapable of grasping what is required for "existing."

The Life of Enjoyment

"A" is a shrewd and sophisticated pleasure seeker. His motto is "Enjoy yourself," and he is clearly very experienced and very thoughtful in his approach to doing just that. The selections in this section are from Kierkegaard, *Either/Or*, Volume 1, "The Rotation Method."

The Problem of Boredom. "A" fully recognizes that there are many difficulties involved in the attempt to live a life of enjoyment. One of the main threats to enjoyment is boredom.

 From KIERKEGAARD: *Either/Or,* Volume 1 ――――――

... Should one wish to attain the maximum momentum, even to the point of almost endangering the driving power, one need only say to oneself: Boredom is the root of all evil. Strange that boredom, in itself so staid and stolid, should have such power to set in motion. The influence it exerts is altogether magical, except that it is not the influence of attraction, but of repulsion. ... In the case of children, the ruinous character of boredom is universally acknowledged. Children are always well-behaved as long as they are enjoying themselves. This is true in the strictest sense; for if they sometimes become unruly in their play, it is because they are already beginning to be bored—boredom is already approaching, though from a different direction. In choosing a governess, one therefore takes into account not only her sobriety, her faithfulness, and her competence, but also her aesthetic qualifications for amusing the children; and there would be no hesitancy in dismissing a governess who was lacking in this respect, even if she had all the other desirable virtues.

Kierkegaard uses the word "aesthetic" to refer to the principles and characteristics involved in the pursuit of enjoyment. Thus "A" is himself an "aesthete" in Kierkegaard's usage.

Here, then, the principle is clearly acknowledged; but so strange is the way of the world, so pervasive the influence of habit and boredom, that this is practically the only case in which the science of aesthetics receives its just dues. If one were to ask for a divorce because his wife was tiresome, or demand the abdication of a king because he was boring to look at, or the banishment of a preacher because he was tiresome to listen to, or the dismissal of a prime minister, or the execution of a journalist, because he was terribly tiresome, one would find it impossible to force it through. What wonder, then, that the world goes from bad to worse, and that its evils increase more and more, as boredom increases, and boredom is the root of all evil.

The history of this can be traced from the very beginning of the world. The gods were bored, and so they created man. Adam was bored because he was alone, and so Eve was created. Thus; boredom entered the world, and increased in proportion to the increase of population.

Now since boredom, as shown above, is the root of all evil, what can be more natural than the effort to overcome it? Here, as everywhere, however, it is necessary to give the problem calm consideration; otherwise one may find oneself driven by the demoniac spirit of boredom deeper and deeper into the mire, in the very effort to escape. Everyone who feels bored cries out for change. With this demand I am in complete sympathy, but it is necessary to act in accordance with some settled principle.

My own dissent from the ordinary view is sufficiently expressed in the use I make of the word "rotation." This word might seem to conceal an ambiguity, and if I wished to use it so as to find room in it for the ordinary method, I should have to define it as a change of field. But the farmer does not use the word in this sense. I shall, however, adopt this meaning for a moment, in order to speak of the rotation which depends on change in its boundless infinity, its extensive dimension, so to speak.

This [change in the extensive dimension] is the vulgar and inartistic method, and needs to be supported by illusion. One tires of living in the country, and moves to the city; one tires of one's native land, and travels abroad; one is tired of Europe and goes to America, and so on; finally one indulges in a sentimental hope of endless journeyings from star to star. Or the movement is different but still extensive. One tires of porcelain dishes and eats on silver; one tires of silver and turns to gold; one burns half of Rome to get an idea of the burning of Troy. This method defeats itself; it is plain endlessness. And what did Nero gain by it?

 ASK YOURSELF

9.52. The farmer rotates his crops and leaves some fields fallow in order to avoid exhaustion of the soil. What analogous action must a pleasure seeker perform in order to avoid boredom?

There are better and worse methods of rotation, however. The method just described is "extensive" but is crude and bound to fail. A better method is "intensive" and is described in what follows. As you study the next section, think about how to answer the Question 9.53.

 ASK YOURSELF

9.53. According to "A" the best kind of "rotation" is the intensive kind, which does not require "new things and places" but rather requires something of *me*, namely _____.

Antonine was wiser; he says: "It is in your power to review your life, to look at things you saw before, but from another point of view." . . . Here we have at once the principle of limitation, the only saving principle in the world. The more you limit yourself, the more fertile you become in invention. A prisoner in solitary confinement for life becomes very inventive, and a spider may furnish him with much entertainment. . . . How close an observer does not one become under such circumstances, when not the least noise nor movement escapes one's attention! Here we have the extreme application of the method which seeks to achieve results intensively, not extensively.

Extensive rotation can go on forever, but experience will not necessarily become more pleasurable or boredom avoided. (Is a butterscotch sundae likely to give more pleasure than the hot fudge variety that now bores me, and will I not get bored with it even more quickly?) Intensive rotation, on the other hand, requires imagination.

Boredom and Time. It is becoming clear that the difficulty of living for enjoyment is connected with the fact that humans live in *time*, for boredom is the result of the passage of time. But time itself is closely connected with memory and anticipation.

The more resourceful in changing the mode of cultivation one can be, the better; but every particular change will always come under the general categories of *remembering and forgetting*. Life in its entirety moves in these two currents, and hence it is essential to have them under control. It is impossible to live artistically before one has made up one's mind to abandon hope; for hope precludes self-limitation. It is a very beautiful sight to see a man put out to sea with the fair wind of hope, and one may even use the opportunity to be taken in tow; but one should never permit hope to be taken aboard one's own ship, least of all as a pilot; for hope is a faithless shipmaster. Hope was one of the dubious gifts of Prometheus; instead of giving men the foreknowledge of the immortals, he gave them hope.

To forget—all men wish to forget, and when something unpleasant happens, they always say: Oh, that one might forget! But forgetting is an art that must be practiced beforehand. The ability to forget is conditioned upon the method of remembering, but this again depends upon the mode of experiencing. Whoever plunges into his experiences with the momentum of hope, will remember so that he cannot forget. *Nil admirari* is therefore the real philosophy.

 ASK YOURSELF

9.54. Complete the argument:

    a. If you want to have a pleasant life, you need to avoid disappointment.

    b. If you do a lot of hoping, you will probably be disappointed.

    c. Therefore, if you want a pleasant life, you need to _____ .

We could translate *nil admirari* as "keep cool," "don't be too attached to anything," "don't admire anything too much." Living a pleasant life requires careful manipulation of one's own experience. For example, one must not enjoy anything too much, for remembrance of it will interfere with the present in various ways. We express this dilemma with the proverb "You cannot have you cake and eat it too."

In a poetic memory the experience has undergone a transformation, by which it has lost all its painful aspects. To remember in this manner, one must be careful how one lives, how one enjoys. Enjoying an experience to its full intensity to the last minute will make it impossible either to remember or to forget.

For there is then nothing to remember except a certain satiety, which one desires to forget, but which now comes back to plague the mind with an involuntary remembrance. Hence, when you begin to notice that a certain pleasure or experience is acquiring too strong a hold upon the mind, you stop a moment for the purpose of remembering. No other method can better create a distaste for continuing the experience too long. From the beginning one should keep the enjoyment under control, never spreading every sail to the wind in any resolve; one ought to devote oneself to pleasure with a certain suspicion, a certain wariness, if one wants to give the lie to the proverb which says that one cannot have ones cake and eat it too. The carrying of concealed weapons is usually forbidden, but no weapon is so dangerous as the art of remembering. It gives one a very peculiar feeling in the midst of enjoyment to look back on it for the purpose of remembering it. One who has perfected himself in the twin arts of remembering and forgetting is in a position to play at battledore and shut-tlecock with the whole of existence.

The extent of one's power to forget is the final measure of one's elasticity of spirit. If a man cannot forget he will never amount to much. Whether there be somewhere a Lethe [a river in Greek mythology associated with forgetfulness] gushing forth, I do not know; but this I know, that the art of forgetting can be developed. However, this art does not consist in permitting the impressions to vanish completely; forget-fulness is one thing, and the art of forgetting is something quite different. It is easy to see that most people have a very meager understanding of this art, for they or-dinarily wish to forget only what is unpleasant, not what is pleasant. This betrays a complete one-sidedness. . . . As a result of attempting to forget only what is un-pleasant, most people have a conception of oblivion as an untameable force which drowns out the past. But forgetting is really a tranquil and quiet occupation, and one which should be exercised quite as much in connection with the pleasant as with the unpleasant.

A pleasant experience has as past something unpleasant about it, by which it stirs a sense of privation; this unpleasantness is taken away by an act of forgetfulness. The unpleasant has a sting, as all admit. This, too, can be removed by the art of forgetting. But if one attempts to dismiss the unpleasant absolutely from mind, as many do who dabble in the art of forgetting, one soon learns how little that helps. In an unguarded moment it pays a surprise visit, and it is then invested with all the forcibleness of the unexpected. This is absolutely contrary to every orderly arrangement in a reasonable mind. No misfortune or difficulty is so devoid of affability, so deaf to all appeals, but that it may be flattered a little; even Cerberus accepted bribes of honey-cakes, and it is not only the lassies who are beguiled. The art in dealing with such experiences con-sists in talking them over, thereby depriving them of their bitterness; not forgetting them absolutely, but forgetting them for the sake of remembering them. Even in the case of memories such that one might suppose an eternal oblivion to be the only safe-guard, one need permit oneself only a little trickery, and the deception will succeed for the skillful. Forgetting is the shears with which you cut away what you can-not use, doing it under the supreme direction of memory. Forgetting and remem-bering are thus identical arts, and the artistic achievement of this identity is the Archimedean point from which one lifts the whole world. When we say that we *con-sign something* to oblivion, we suggest simultaneously that it is to be forgotten and yet also remembered.

Even in the midst of very pleasurable moments we may start thinking about what it will be like to look back on them. Does this fact have any bearing on the use of cam-eras and video cameras?

If you want a pleasant life you might think you should try to remember only what is pleasant and forget everything unpleasant. Otherwise you will be haunted with un-pleasant memories. But "A" contests this reasoning.

☞ ASK YOURSELF

9.55. "A" asserts that if you try to forget everything unpleasant the suppressed memory may take you by _____. On the other hand, if you try to remember all that is pleasant you may begin to feel deprived because the pleasant experiences are _____.

The solution, then, is a carefully controlled mixture of remembering and forgetting and controlled modes of experience (for example, experience without attachment or hope).

Pleasure Seeking versus Commitments. "A" tries to show that any kind of commitment will get in the way of enjoyment.

The art of remembering and forgetting will also insure against sticking fast in some relationship of life, and make possible the realization of a complete freedom.

One must guard against *friendship*. How is a friend defined? He is not what philosophy calls the necessary other, but the superfluous third. What are friendship's ceremonies? You drink each other's health, you open an artery and mingle your blood with that of the friend. It is difficult to say when the proper moment for this arrives, but it announces itself mysteriously; you feel some way that you can no longer address one another formally. When once you have had this feeling, then it can never appear that you have made a mistake, like Geert Westphaler, who discovered that he had been drinking to friendship with the public hangman. What are the infallible marks of friendship? Let antiquity answer: *idem velle, idem none, ea demum firma amicitia* [agreement in likes and dislikes, that alone makes lasting friendship] and is also extremely tiresome. What are the infallible marks of friendship? Mutual assistance in word and deed. Two friends form a close association in order to be everything to one another, and they try to do that even though it is impossible for one human being to be anything to another human being except to be in his way.

But because you abstain from friendship it does not follow that you abstain from social contacts. On the contrary, these social relationships may at times be permitted to take on a deeper character, provided you always have so much more momentum in yourself that you can sheer off at will, in spite of sharing for a time in the momentum of the common movement. It is believed that such conduct leaves unpleasant memories, the unpleasantness being due to the fact that a relationship which has meant something now vanishes and becomes as nothing. But this is a misunderstanding. The unpleasant is merely a piquant ingredient in the dullness of life. Besides, it is possible for the same relationship again to play a significant role, though in another manner. The essential thing is never to stick fast, and for this it is necessary to have oblivion back of one. The experienced farmer lets his land lie fallow now and then, and the theory of social prudence recommends the same. Everything will doubtless return, though in a different form; that which has once been present in the rotation will remain in it, but the mode of cultivation will be varied. You therefore quite consistently hope to meet your friends and acquaintances in a better world, but you do not share the fear of the crowd that they will be altered so that you cannot recognize them; your fear is rather lest they be wholly unaltered. It is remarkable how much significance even the most insignificant person can gain from a rational mode of cultivation.

One must never enter into the relation of *marriage*. Husband and wife promise to love one another for eternity. This is all very fine, but it does not mean very much; for if their love comes to an end in time, it will surely be ended in eternity. If, instead of promising forever, the parties would say until Easter, or until May-day comes, there might be some meaning in what they say; for then they would have said something definite, and also something that they might be able to keep. And how does a marriage usually work out? In a little while one party begins to perceive that there is something wrong, then the other party complains and cries to heaven: faithless! faithless! A little later the second party reaches the same standpoint, and a neutrality is established in which the mutual faithlessness is mutually cancelled, to the satisfaction and contentment of both parties. But it is now too late, for there are great difficulties connected with divorces.

 ASK YOURSELF

9.56. Probably many people think that having friends is necessary for a pleasant life. Why does "A" disagree?

9.57. Is boredom a problem in many marriages? If so, why?

As you read what follows, be looking for an answer to Question 9.58.

 ASK YOURSELF

9.58. What are two ways having a family might interfere with living a pleasant and enjoyable life?

Such being the case with marriage, it is not surprising that the attempt should be made in so many ways to bolster it up with moral supports. When a man seeks separation from his wife, the cry is at once raised that he is depraved, a scoundrel, etc. How silly, and what an indirect attack upon marriage! If marriage has reality, then he is sufficiently punished by forfeiting this happiness; if it has no reality, it is absurd to abuse him because he is wiser than the rest. When a man grows tired of his money and throws it out the window, we do not call him a scoundrel; for either money has reality, and so he is sufficiently punished by depriving himself of it, or it has none, and then he is, of course, a wise man.

One must always take care not to enter into any relationship in which there is a possibility of many members. For this reason friendship is dangerous, to say nothing of marriage. Husband and wife are indeed said to become one, but this is a very dark and mystic saying. When you are one of several, then you have lost your freedom;

you cannot send for your traveling boots whenever you wish, you cannot move aimlessly about in the world. If you have a wife and perhaps a child, it is troublesome; if you have a wife and children, it is impossible. True, it has happened that a gypsy woman has carried her husband through life on her back, but for one thing this is very rare, and for another, it is likely to be tiresome in the long run—for the husband. Marriage brings one into fatal connection with custom and tradition, and traditions and customs are like the wind and weather, altogether incalculable. In Japan, I have been told, it is the custom for husbands to lie in childbed. Who knows but the time will come when the customs of foreign countries will obtain a foothold in Europe?

But because a man does not marry, it does not follow that his life need be wholly deprived of the erotic element. And the erotic ought also to have infinitude; but poetic infinitude, which can just as well be limited to an hour as to a month. When two beings fall in love with one another and begin to suspect that they were made for each other, it is time to have the courage to break it off; for by going on they have everything to lose and nothing to gain. This seems a paradox, and it is so for the feeling, but not for the understanding. In this sphere it is particularly necessary that one should make use of one's moods; through them one may realize an inexhaustible variety of combinations.

One should never undertake any *business*. If you do, you will become a mere *Peter Flere*, a tiny little cog in the machinery of the body politic; you even cease to be master of your own conduct, and in that case your theories are of little help. You receive a title, and this brings in its train every sin and evil. The law under which you have become a slave is equally tiresome, whether your advancement is fast or slow. A title can never be got rid of except by the commission of some crime which draws down on you a public whipping; even then you are not certain, for you may have it restored to you by royal pardon.

Even if one does not engage in business, one ought not to be inactive, but should pursue such occupations as are compatible with a sort of leisure, one should engage in all sorts of breadless arts. In this connection the self-development should be intensive rather than extensive, and one should, in spite of mature years, be able to prove the truth of the proverb that children are pleased with a rattle and tickled with a straw.

If one now, according to the theory of social prudence, varies the soil—for if he had contact with one person only, the rotation method would fail as badly as if a farmer had only one acre of land, which would make it impossible for him to fallow, something which is of extreme importance—then one must also constantly vary himself, and this is the essential secret. For this purpose one must necessarily have control over one's moods. To control them in the sense of producing them at will is impossible, but prudence teaches how to utilize the moment. As an experienced sailor always looks out over the water and sees a squall coming from far away, so one ought always to see the mood a little in advance. One should know how the mood affects one's own mind and the mind of others, before putting it on. You first strike a note or two before evoking the pure tones, and see what there is in a man, the middle tones follow later. The more experience you have, the more readily you will be convinced that there is often much in a man which is not suspected. When sentimental people, who as such are extremely tiresome, become angry, they are often very entertaining. Badgering a man is a particularly effective method of exploration.

ASK YOURSELF

9.59. In order to lead a pleasant life, a person must not _____ and also must control _____.

"A" is deeply involved in trying to control the content of his own life, including both his actions and his moods. He is a poet of life, trying to fashion the most beautiful life possible. He is very skilled, but his pessimism, cynicism, and disappointment keep showing through. It is no easy matter to devote a life to enjoyment, even when one has plenty of money and free time. Boredom and related difficulties constantly threaten the attempt to live for pleasure. But "A" obviously does have some enjoyments.

The pseudonymous author of Volume 2 of *Either/Or* is Judge William, an older friend of "A." He tries to persuade "A" to give up his life of pleasure seeking and find happiness in a different kind of life. The book is in the form of two long letters written to "A," who is simply referred to as "you" in the excerpts that follow.

The Ethical Life

Judge William argues that commitments are exactly what is needed in order to achieve happiness.

Marriage and the Romantic. Judge William tries to show that the deep commitment involved in marriage is not incompatible with the "aesthetic" (the concern for beauty, pleasure, romance, and so on) when properly understood. Unfortunately, proper understanding is not the most common thing in this domain. The following selections are from Kierkegaard, *Either/Or*, Volume 2, "The Aesthetic Validity of Marriage."

 From KIERKEGAARD: *Either/Or*, Volume 2

. . . [T]hrough many centuries have not knights and adventurers undergone incredible pains and trouble in order to come to harbor in the quiet peace of a happy marriage? Have not novelists and novel readers worked their way through one volume after another in order to stop with a happy marriage? And has not one generation after another endured the troubles and complications of four acts if only there was some likelihood of a happy marriage in the fifth? However, by these prodigious efforts very little has been accomplished for the glorification of marriage, and I doubt very much if by the reading of such works any man has been made capable of performing the task he set himself, or has felt oriented in life. For this precisely is the pernicious, the unwholesome feature of such works, that they end where they ought to begin. After the many fates they have overcome, the lovers finally sink into one another's arms. The curtain falls, the book ends; but the reader is none the wiser. For truly (assuming that the first flame of love is present) it requires no great art to have courage and shrewdness enough to fight with all one's might for the good which one regards as the only good; but on the other hand it surely requires discretion, wisdom, and patience to overcome the lassitude which often is wont to follow upon a wish fulfilled.

ASK YOURSELF

9.60. "Lassitude" might be another word for what? (Think back to "A's" main problem, and look it up in a dictionary if necessary.)

It is still the case that novels and films present lovers as struggling against all sorts of external obstacles in order to be together. Consider, for example, the film *A Room with a View* (based on a novel by E. M. Forster). At the end the lovers are finally united, after overcoming many misunderstandings and other troubles. They are shown on their honeymoon in the last frame. And then what? William is saying, *that* is where the struggles really begin.

As you read the following look for the answer to Question 9.61.

ASK YOURSELF

9.61. What is true in the romantic or dramatic view of love, and what is false in it?

It is natural that to love in its first outflaming it seems as if it could not suffer enough hardships in acquiring possession of the beloved object, yea, that in case there are no dangers present it is disposed to provide them in order to overcome them. Upon this the whole attention is directed in plays of this sort, and as soon as the dangers are overcome the scenery shifter knows well what he has to do. Hence it is rather rare to see a wedding on the stage or to read of one, except in case the opera or the ballet holds in reserve this factor, which may well furnish an occasion for some sort of dramatic galimatias, for a gorgeous procession, for the significant gesticulations and the heavenly glance of a ballet dancer, for the exchange of rings, etc. The *truth* in this whole exposition, the real aesthetic element consists in the fact that love is striving, that this feeling is seen fighting its way through opposition. The fault is that this struggle, this dialectic, is entirely external, and that love comes out of this fight quite as abstract as when it entered into it. When once there awakens an apprehension of love's proper dialectic, an apprehension of its pathological struggle, of its relation to the ethical, to the religious, verily one will not have need of hard-hearted fathers or ladies' bowers or enchanted princesses or ogres and monsters in order to give love plenty to do. In our age one rarely encounters such cruel fathers or such frightful monsters, and insofar as modern literature has fashioned itself in conformity with the antique, money has become essentially the opposition medium through which love moves, and again we sit patiently through the four acts if there is a reasonable prospect of a rich uncle dying in the fifth.

Romantic Love and Immediacy. William shows how immediate feelings (feelings that come over me or overwhelm me) are determinative for romantic love.

First, however, I will indicate the mark by which romantic love may be known. One might say in one word that it is *immediate:* to see her was to love her; or, though she saw him only once through a slit in the shuttered window of her chamber, nevertheless from this instant she loved him, him alone in the whole world. Here I ought properly, according to agreement, leave place for a few polemical outbursts in order to promote in you the secretion of bile which is an indispensable condition for the wholesome and profitable appropriation of what I have to say. But for all that I cannot make up my mind to do so, and for two reasons: partly because this is a rather hackneyed theme in our time (and honestly it is incomprehensible to me that in this instance you want to go with the current, whereas ordinarily you go against it); and partly because I really have conserved a certain faith in the reality of romantic love, a sort of reverence for it, accompanied by some feeling of sadness. . . . After all, is it not beautiful to imagine that two beings are meant for one another? How often one has felt the need of reaching out beyond the historical consciousness, a longing, a nostalgia for the primeval forest which lies behind us. And does not this longing acquire a double significance when with it there is associated the conception of another being which also has its home in these regions? Hence every marriage, even one which was entered upon after reflective deliberation, feels the need, at least in certain moments, of such a foreground. And how beautiful it is that the God who is spirit loves also the love which is earthly. The fact that among married people there is a great deal of lying in this respect I am very ready to concede to you, and also that your observations in this field have amused me; but one ought never to forget the truth that is in it. Perhaps one or another man may think that it is better to exercise his own sovereign discretion in the choice of "his life's companion," but such an opinion discloses a high degree of narrow-mindedness and a foolish self-importance on the part of the understanding, with no inkling of the fact that romantic love is by its very nature free, and that its greatness consists precisely in this quality.

   ASK YOURSELF

9.62. What is legitimate in the romantic idea that two people were destined for each other?

Romantic Love and the Eternal.   There is a certain kind of relation to the eternal in romantic love, which, however, is ultimately illusory.

Romantic love shows that it is immediate by the fact that it follows a natural necessity. It is based upon beauty, in part upon sensuous beauty, in part upon the beauty which can be conceived through and with and in the sensuous. . . . In spite of the fact that this love is essentially based upon the sensuous, it is ennobled by reason of the consciousness of eternity which it embodies, the fact that it bears an impress of eternity. The lovers are sincerely convinced that their relationship is in itself a complete whole which never can be altered. But since this assurance is founded only upon a natural determinant, the eternal is thus based upon the temporal and thereby cancels itself. Since this assurance has undergone no test, has found no higher attestation, it shows itself to be an illusion, and for this reason it is easy to make it ridiculous.

ASK YOURSELF

9.63. Many love songs speak of love being forever or of the lover as being everything. What is true in these expressions, and what false, according to William?

People should not, however, be so ready to do this, and it is truly disgusting to see in modern comedy these experienced, intriguing, dissolute women who know that love is an illusion. I know of no creature so abominable as such a woman. No debauchery is so loathsome to me and nothing is so revolting as to see a lovable young girl in the hands of such a woman. Truly this is more terrible than to imagine her in the hands of a club of seducers. It is sad to see a man who has learned to discount every substantial value of life, but to see a woman on this false path is horrible. Romantic love, however, as I have said, presents an analogy to morality by reason of the presumptive eternity which ennobles it and saves it from being mere sensuality. For the sensual is the momentary. The sensual seeks instant satisfaction, and the more refined it is, the better it knows how to make the instant of enjoyment a little eternity.

The true eternity in love, as true morality, delivers it, therefore, first of all from the sensual. But in order to produce this true eternity a determination of the will is called for. Of this I shall say more later.

Our age has perceived very clearly the weak points of romantic love, and its ironical polemic against it has sometimes been thoroughly amusing. . . . [T]he eternity [romantic love] claims was built upon the temporal, and . . . although the knight of romantic love was sincerely convinced of its absolute durability, there nevertheless was no certainty of this, inasmuch as its trials and temptations have hitherto been in a medium which was entirely external. Such being the case, it was able with a pretty piety to accept marriage along with love, although, after all, this acquired no very deep significance. We have seen how this immediate and beautiful but also very naive love, being embodied in the consciousness of a reflective age, must become the object of its mockery and of its irony; and we have seen too what such an age was capable of substituting for it.

 ASK YOURSELF

9.64. According to William, what is the "age" (the time in which he is living) like in its attitudes toward romance?

9.65. What, do you suppose, does "such an age" substitute for romantic love?

9.66. Is that age anything like ours, and if so, how?

The Relations of Romantic and Married Love to Time. William offers further reasons for thinking that marriage and romance are not simply two different things. It is significant that, like "A," he recognizes that a person must come to grips with time in order to live well.

. . . However many painful confusions life may still have in store, I fight for two things: for the prodigious task of showing that marriage is the transfiguration of first love, that it is its friend, not its enemy; and for the task (which to others is very trivial but to me is all the more important) of showing that my humble marriage has had such a meaning for me, so that from it I derive strength and courage to fulfill constantly this task. . . .

Let us now glance at the relation between romantic and conjugal love. Romantic love remains constantly abstract in itself, and if it is able to acquire no external history, death already is lying in wait for it, because its eternity is illusory. Conjugal love begins with possession and acquires inward history. It is faithful. So is romantic love— but now note the difference. The faithful romantic lover waits, let us say, for fifteen years—then comes the instant which rewards him. Here poetry rightly sees that the fifteen years can very well be concentrated. It hastens on, then, to the moment. A married man is faithful for fifteen years, yet during those fifteen years he has had possession, so in the long succession of time he has acquired faithfulness. But such an ideal marriage cannot be represented, for the very point is time in its extension. At the end of the fifteen years he apparently got no further than he was at the beginning, yet he has lived in a high degree aesthetically. His possession has not been like dead property, but he has constantly been acquiring his possession. He has not fought with lions and ogres, but with the most dangerous enemy, with time.

Kierkegaard is suggesting that the kind of life an ethical married person lives cannot be "represented" by a poet, who appeals to our "immediate" reactions, our taste for beauty, excitement, and so on. But could it be represented by a novelist?

 ASK YOURSELF

9.67. The aesthete ("A") fights with time. As time passes he is threatened with _____. The ethical person also fights with time. He wins by bringing what is permanent, the _____ , into time, through his commitments.

For him eternity does not come afterwards as in the case of the knight, but he has had eternity in time. He alone, therefore, has triumphed over time; for one can say of the knight that he has killed time, as indeed a man constantly wishes to kill time when it has no reality for him. But this is never the perfect victory. The married man, being a true conqueror, has not killed time but has saved it and preserved it in eternity. The married man who does this truly lives poetically. He solves the great riddle of living in eternity and yet hearing the hall clock strike, and hearing it in such a way that the stroke of the hour does not shorten but prolongs his eternity—a contradiction as profound but far more glorious than the situation described in a well known tale of the Middle Ages which tells of an unhappy man who awoke in hell and cried out, "What time is it?" and the devil answered, "An eternity." And now even if this is something which cannot be represented in art, let it be your comfort as it is mine that the highest and most beautiful things in life are not to be heard about, nor read about, nor seen but, if one will, are to be *lived*.

Compare this last remark and what follows to the excerpt from Kierkegaard's diary in the introduction to this section.

When, then, I willingly admit that romantic love lends itself more aptly to artistic representation than does conjugal love, this is not by any means to say that the latter is less aesthetic than the former; on the contrary, it is more aesthetic. In one of the tales of the Romantic School which evinces the greatest genius, there is one character who has no desire to write poetry like the others among whom he lives, because it is a waste of time and deprives him of the true enjoyment; he prefers to live. Now if he had had the right conception of what it is to live, he would have been the man for me.

Conjugal love has its foe in time, its triumph in time, its eternity in time, and so it would have its problems, even if I were to imagine it free from all the so-called external and internal trials. Generally, it has these too; but if one were to interpret them rightly, one must observe two things: that these trials are constantly inward determinants; and that they constantly have in them the determinant of time.

An "inward determinant" is something that determines and is determined by a person's own "inwardness," that is, their passion, seriousness, and ability to will.

 ASK YOURSELF

9.68. Suppose a married couple runs low on money. Sometimes that can lead to a deterioration in their relationship, even to a divorce. How would ethical persons face such a problem?

9.69. How would the couple's solution involve "inward determinants"? (Try to imagine what kinds of thoughts, feelings, and effort would be found in an ethical person in such a situation.)

It is easy to see that for this reason, too, conjugal love cannot be represented. It constantly drags itself back inwardly, and (to use the expression in a good sense) it constantly drags along in time; but what is to be represented by reproduction must let itself be lured out, and its time must be capable of abbreviation. You may convince yourself of this more thoroughly by considering the predicates commonly applied to conjugal love. It is faithful, constant, humble, patient, long-suffering, indulgent, sincere, contented, vigilant, willing, joyful.

The Importance of Choosing. In William's first letter he focuses on the importance of choice and commitment in terms of the marriage relationship. In his second letter to "A," William reflects on the importance of choice and commitment in general. The remaining selections from Kierkegaard are from *Either/Or*, Volume 2, "The Balance between the Aesthetic and the Ethical."

. . . If you will understand me aright, I should like to say that in making a choice it is not so much a question of choosing the right as of the energy, the earnestness, the pathos with which one chooses. Thereby the personality announces its inner infinity, and thereby, in turn, the personality is consolidated. Therefore, even if a man were to choose the wrong, he will nevertheless discover, precisely by reason of the energy with which he chose, that he has chosen the wrong. For, the choice being made with the whole inwardness of his personality, his nature is purified and he himself brought into immediate relation to the eternal Power whose omnipresence interpenetrates the whole of existence. This transfiguration, this higher consecration, is never attained by that man who chooses merely aesthetically.

To choose aesthetically is to choose with a view to enjoyment. An example would be choosing the tastiest dishes from a buffet. This hardly counts as "choosing" at all, in William's terms.

 ASK YOURSELF

9.70. What then is it to choose ethically, do you suppose?

The rhythm in that man's soul (the aesthete), in spite of all its passion, is a *spiritus levis* [light breathing, i.e. something essentially "lightweight"]. So, like a Cato, I shout at you my either/or, and yet not like a Cato, for my soul has not yet acquired the resigned coldness which he possessed. But I know that only this incantation, if I have the strength for it, will be capable of rousing you, not to an activity of thought, for of that you have no lack, but to earnestness of spirit. Perhaps you will succeed without that in accomplishing much, perhaps even in astonishing the world (for I am not niggardly), and yet you will miss the highest thing, the only thing which truly has significance—perhaps you will gain the whole world and lose your own self. What is it, then, that I distinguish in my either/or? Is it good and evil? No, I would only bring you up to the point where the choice between the evil and the good acquires significance for you. Everything hinges upon this. As soon as one can get a man to stand at the crossways in such a position that there is no recourse but to choose, he will choose the right. Hence if it should chance that, while you are in the course of reading this somewhat lengthy dissertation, you were to feel that the instant for choice had come, then throw the rest of this away, never concern yourself about it, you have lost nothing—but choose,— and you shall see what validity there is in this act, yea, no young girl can be so happy in the choice of her heart as is a man who knows how to choose. So then, one either has to live aesthetically, or one has to live ethically. In this alternative as I have said, there is not yet in the strictest sense any question of a choice; for he who lives aesthetically does not choose, and he who after the ethical has manifested itself to him chooses the aesthetical is not living aesthetically, for he is sinning and is subject to ethical determinants even though his life may be described as unethical. Lo, this is, as it were, a *character indelebis* [an indelible mark] impressed upon the ethical, that though it modestly places itself on a level with the aesthetical, it is nevertheless that which makes the choice a choice. And this is the pitiful thing to one who contemplates human life, that so many live on in a quiet state of perdition; they outlive themselves, not in the sense that the content of life is successively unfolding and now is possessed in this expanded state, but live their lives, as it were, outside of themselves, they vanish—like shadows, their immortal soul is blown away, and they are not alarmed by the problem of its immortality, for they are already in a state of dissolution before they die. They do not live aesthetically, but neither has the ethical manifested itself in its entirety, so they have not exactly rejected it either; they therefore are not sinning, except insofar as it is sin not to be either one thing or the other; neither are they ever in doubt about their immortality, for he who deeply and sincerely is in doubt of it on his own behalf will surely find the right, and surely it is high time to utter a warning against the great-hearted, heroic objectivity with which many thinkers think on behalf of others and not on their own behalf. If one would call this which I here require selfishness, I would reply that this comes from the fact that people have no conception of what this "self" is, and that it would be of very little use to a man if he were to gain the whole world and lose himself, and that it must necessarily be a poor proof which does not first of all convince the man who presents it.

The remarks about "objectivity" in the preceding passage should be compared to the quote from Kierkegaard's diary, keeping in mind Hegel's stress on objective knowledge.

 ASK YOURSELF

9.71. Only when I choose seriously do I acquire a _____. It follows that "A" lacks a _____, doesn't it?

My either/or does not in the first instance denote the choice between good and evil, it denotes the choice whereby one chooses good *and* evil/or excludes them. Here the question is under what determinants one would contemplate the whole of existence and would himself live. That the man who chooses good and evil chooses the good is indeed true, but this becomes evident only afterwards; for the aesthetical is not the evil but neutrality, and that is the reason why I affirmed that it is the ethical which constitutes the choice. It is therefore not so much a question of choosing between willing the good or the evil, as of choosing to *Will*, but by this in turn the good and the evil are posited.

Judge William has argued that what makes a person ethical is that he or she takes his or her choices seriously and lives decisively. He doesn't waffle; she sticks with her choices (the spouse chosen, for instance). Only in this way can a person acquire a kind of substance, a definiteness and reliableness.

 ASK YOURSELF

9.72. Could an evil person also be decisive, serious, and reliable? Why or why not?

MARY WOLLSTONECRAFT

The influence of enlightenment ideas can be seen in a contemporary of Kant's who wrote the work excerpted in this section at the end of the eighteenth century. Her life ended before the nineteenth century, but her work is included here since her work and that of J. S. Mill are mutually illuminating.

Up until the twentieth century few women were involved in philosophical discussion, although there are notable exceptions, as well as exceptional periods. For example, eighteenth-century French women of the aristocracy presided over soirees in which conversations between the leading intellectuals of the day were the main ingredient. Mary Wollstonecraft would have been a worthy participant in those conversations. She lived at the right time, but not in the right place or social class. She was born in London in 1759, the second of seven children of an abusive father, and she had to educate herself and take responsibilities in her family at an early age. With the encouragement of friends she began writing and published her first work in 1786. The last four years of her life were tumultuous. She conceived a child out of wedlock, married twice, and attempted suicide twice. Her second husband was the noted English writer William Godwin, who wrote a memoir in tribute to her. She died in 1797 after giving birth to a second child, also named Mary, who married poet Percy Bysshe Shelley and became famous as the author of the novel *Frankenstein*.

The confidence in reason that marks the selections here from *A Vindication of the Rights of Women* (1792) is characteristic of the Enlightenment, as is the distrust of hereditary kingship and the established church.

The Rights of Women; True Virtue and True Social Flourishing

Wollstonecraft argues that everyone will profit from the liberation of women from the various forms of social oppression she describes.

Both the Elevation of Men to Kingship and the Exaggerated "Worship" of Women Is Inconsistent with the Development of True Virtue in Either. Women may have power of a sort, but it is corrupt and corrupting power.

 From WOLLSTONECRAFT: *A Vindication of the Rights of Women*

It is impossible for any man, when the most favorable circumstances concur, to acquire sufficient knowledge and strength of mind to discharge the duties of a king, entrusted with uncontrolled power; how then must they be violated when his very elevation is an insuperable bar to the attainment of either wisdom or virtue; when all the feelings of a man are stifled by flattery, and reflection shut out by pleasure! Surely it is madness to make the fate of thousands depend on the caprice of a weak fellow creature, whose very station sinks him necessarily below the meanest of his subjects! But one power should not be thrown down to exalt another—for all power inebriates weak men; and its abuse proves that the more equality there is established among men, the more virtue and happiness will reign in society. But this and any similar maxim deduced from simple reason, raises an outcry—the church or the state is in danger, if faith in the wisdom of antiquity is not implicit; and they who, roused by the sight of human calamity, dare to attack human authority, are reviled as despisers of God, and enemies of man.

 ASK YOURSELF

9.73. What is it that makes a king deficient both in feeling and in thought (reflection)?

To account for, and excuse the tyranny of man, many ingenious arguments have been brought forward to prove, that the two sexes, in the acquirement of virtue, ought to aim at attaining a very different character: or, to speak explicitly, women are not allowed to have sufficient strength of mind to acquire what really deserves the name of virtue. Yet it should seem, allowing them to have souls, that there is but one way appointed by Providence to lead mankind to either virtue or happiness. If then women are not a swarm of ephemeron triflers, why should they be kept in ignorance under the specious name of innocence? Men complain, and with reason, of the follies and caprices of our sex, when they do not keenly satirize our headstrong passions and groveling vices.—Behold, I should answer, the natural effect of ignorance! The mind will ever be unstable that has only prejudices to rest on, and the current will run with destructive fury when there are no barriers to break its force. Women are told from their infancy, and taught by the example of their mothers, that a little knowledge of human weakness, justly termed cunning, softness of temper, outward obedience, and a scrupulous attention to a puerile kind of propriety, will obtain for them the protection of man; and should they be beautiful, every thing else is needless, for, at least, twenty years of their lives.

 ASK YOURSELF

9.74. What are some of the bad qualities the author claims are common among women, and what produced them?

The Educating Force of Society. Wollstonecraft argues that society must be transformed with respect to attitudes toward women in order for there to be any worthwhile education for them, since the social order itself educates (and miseducates).

To prevent any misconstruction, I must add, that I do not believe that a private education can work the wonders which some sanguine writers have attributed to it. Men and women must be educated, in a great degree, by the opinions and manners of the society they live in. In every age there has been a stream of popular opinion that has carried all before it, and given a family character, as it were, to the century. It may then fairly be inferred, that, till society be differently constituted, much cannot be expected from education. It is, however, sufficient for my present purpose to assert, that, what ever effect circumstances have on the abilities, every being may become virtuous by the exercise of its own reason; . . . Consequently, the most perfect education, in my opinion, is such an exercise of the understanding as is best calculated to strengthen the body and form the heart. Or, in other words, to enable the individual to attain such habits of virtue as will render it independent. In fact, it is a farce to call any being virtuous whose virtues do not result from the exercise of its own reason. This was Rousseau's opinion respecting men: I extend it to women, and confidently assert that they have been drawn out of their sphere by false refinement, and not by an endeavor to acquire masculine qualities. Still the regal homage which they receive is so intoxicating, that till the manners of the times are changed, and formed on more reasonable principles, it may be impossible to convince them that the illegitimate power, which they obtain, by degrading themselves, is a curse, and that they must return to nature and equality, if they wish to secure the placid satisfaction that unsophisticated affections impart. But for this epoch we must wait—wait, perhaps, till kings and nobles, enlightened by reason, and, preferring the real dignity of man to childish state, throw off their gaudy hereditary trappings: and if then women do not resign the arbitrary power of beauty—they will prove that they have less mind than man.

 ASK YOURSELF

9.75. The problem, in Wollstonecraft's view, is not that women lack power in the present social order, but that the power they do have is, like the power of _____, disconnected from true virtue and self-worth.

According to some, the kind of thinking or reasoning typical of women lacks systematic character and is defective for that reason. Wollstonecraft thinks that the characteristic ways in which women think are not the result of their being women but of their being miseducated by a corrupt social order. Her views here contrast with those of some modern feminists who insist that women have different ways of thinking than men, in fact different in some of the ways Wollstonecraft mentions, and furthermore that these ways of thinking are superior in some or all ways to "male" ways, or at least as good.

To do every thing in an orderly manner, is a most important precept, which women, who, generally speaking, receive only a disorderly kind of education, seldom attend to with that degree of exactness that men, who from their infancy are broken into method, observe. This negligent kind of guesswork, for what other epithet can be used to point out the random exertions of a sort of instinctive common sense, never brought to the test of reason? prevents their generalizing matters of fact—so they do to-day, what they did yesterday, merely because they did it yesterday. This contempt of the understanding in early life has more baneful consequences than is commonly supposed; for the little knowledge which women of strong minds attain, is, from various circumstances, of a more desultory kind than the knowledge of men, and it is acquired more by sheer observations on real life, than from comparing what has been individually observed with the results of experience generalized by speculation. Led by their dependent situation and domestic employments more into society, what they learn is rather by snatches; and as learning is with them, in general, only a secondary thing, they do not pursue any one branch with that persevering ardor necessary to give vigor to the faculties, and clearness to the judgment.

ASK YOURSELF

9.76. What sort of knowledge is it that women of strong minds attain?

Some Men Are Miseducated in Much the Same Way Women Are. In fact, claims Wollstonecraft, a preoccupation with manners, with artificial social graces, and with trivial social "niceness," all of which are supposedly common among women, can be found among a most "masculine" group of men, too.

. . . As a proof that education gives this appearance of weakness to females, we may instance the example of military men, who are, like them, sent into the world before their minds have been stored with knowledge or fortified by principles. The consequences are similar; soldiers acquire a little superficial knowledge, snatched from the muddy current of conversation, and, from continually mixing with society, they gain, what is termed a knowledge of the world; and this acquaintance with manners and customs has frequently been confounded with a knowledge of the human heart. But can the crude fruit of casual observation, never brought to the test of judgment, formed by comparing speculation and experience, deserve such a distinction? Soldiers, as well as women, practice the minor virtues with punctilious politeness. Where is then the sexual difference, when the education has been the same? All the difference that I can discern, arises from the superior advantage of liberty, which enables the former to see more of life. It is wandering from my present subject, perhaps, to make a political remark; but, as it was produced naturally by the train of my reflections, I shall not pass it silently over. Standing armies can never consist of resolute, robust men; they may be well disciplined machines, but they will seldom contain men under the influence of strong passions, or with very vigorous faculties. And as for any depth of understanding, I will venture to affirm, that it is as rarely to be found in the army as amongst women; and the cause, I maintain, is the same. It may be further observed, that officers are also particularly attentive to their persons, fond of dancing, crowded rooms, adventures, and ridicule. Like the fair sex, the business of their lives is gallantry.— They were taught to please, and they only live to please. Yet they do not lose their rank in the distinction of sexes, for they are still reckoned superior to women, though in what their superiority consists, beyond what I have just mentioned, it is difficult to discover.

There is, of course, a particular motive for keeping women ignorant and obedient.

Strengthen the female mind by enlarging it, and there will be an end to blind obedience; but, as blind obedience is ever sought for by power, tyrants and sensualists are in the right when they endeavor to keep women in the dark, because the former only want slaves, and the latter a plaything.

Wollstonecraft, like many modern feminists, sees romantic love as an obstacle as much as a means to happiness.

To speak disrespectfully of love is, I know, high treason against sentiment and fine feelings; but I wish to speak the simple language of truth, and rather to address the head than the heart. To endeavor to reason love out of the world, would be to out Quixote Cervantes, and equally offend against common sense; but an endeavor to restrain this tumultuous passion, and to prove that it should not be allowed to dethrone superior powers, or to usurp the scepter which the understanding should ever coolly wield, appears less wild. . . . Love, from its very nature, must be transitory. To seek for a secret that would render it constant, would be as wild a search as for the philosopher's stone, or the grand panacea: and the discovery would be equally useless, or rather pernicious to mankind. The most holy band of society is friendship. . . . Why must the female mind be tainted by coquettish arts to gratify the sensualist, and prevent love from subsiding into friendship, or compassionate tenderness, when there are not qualities on which friendship can be built? Let the honest heart shew itself, and reason teach passion to submit to necessity; or, let the dignified pursuit of virtue and knowledge raise the mind above those emotions which rather embitter than sweeten the cup of life, when they are not restrained within due bounds.

        ASK YOURSELF

9.77. Why should friendship be encouraged rather than love? Do you agree with Wollstonecraft? Why or why not?

Feminine "Gentleness" and Other Traits Are Not the Real, Worthwhile Thing. Supposedly feminine traits are the result of fear and repression.

The Gentleness of manners, forbearance and long-suffering, are such amiable Godlike qualities, that in sublime poetic strains the Deity has been invested with them; and, perhaps, no representation of his goodness so strongly fastens on the human affections as those that represent him abundant in mercy and willing to pardon. Gentleness, considered in this point of view, bears on its front all the characteristics of grandeur, combined with the winning graces of condescension; but what a different aspect it assumes when it is the submissive demeanor of dependence [i.e., when it is feminine genteelness], the support of weakness that loves, because it wants protection; and is forbearing, because it must silently endure injuries; smiling under the lash at which it dare not snarl. Abject as this picture appears, it is the portrait of an accomplished woman, according to the received opinion of female excellence, separated by specious reasoners from human excellence. Or, they (Rousseau and Swedenborg) kindly restore the rib, and make one moral being of a man and woman; not forgetting to give her all the "submissive charms."

        ASK YOURSELF

9.78. Why is the "gentleness" of women not worth keeping?

Proper Relations between the Sexes. Neither sex should dominate. Rather, "reason" should rule.

I love man as my fellow; but his scepter, real, or usurped, extends not to me, unless the reason of an individual demands my homage; and even then the submission is to reason, and not to man. In fact, the conduct of an accountable being must be regulated by the operations of its own reason; or on what foundation rests the throne of God? It appears to me necessary to dwell on these obvious truths, because females have been insulated, as it were; and, while they have been stripped of the virtues that should clothe humanity, they have been decked with artificial graces that enable them to exercise a short-lived tyranny. Love, in their bosoms, taking place of every nobler passion, their sole ambition is to be fair, to raise emotion instead of inspiring respect; and this ignoble desire, like the servility in absolute monarchies, destroys all strength of character. Liberty is the mother of virtue, and if women be, by their very constitution, slaves, and not allowed to breathe the sharp invigorating air of freedom, they must ever languish like exotics, and be reckoned beautiful flaws in nature. As to the argument respecting the subjection in which the sex has ever been held, it retorts on man. The many have always been enthralled by the few; and monsters, who scarcely have shewn any discernment of human excellence, have tyrannized over thousands of their fellow-creatures. Why have men of superior endowments submitted to such degradation? For, is it not universally acknowledged that kings, viewed collectively, have ever been inferior, in abilities and virtue, to the same number of men taken from the common mass of mankind—yet, have they not, and are they not still treated with a degree of reverence that is an insult to reason? China is not the only country where a living man has been made a God. Men have submitted to superior strength to enjoy with impunity the pleasure of the moment—women have only done the same, and therefore till it is proved that the courtier, who servilely resigns the birthright of a man, is not a moral agent, it cannot be demonstrated that woman is essentially inferior to man because she has always been subjugated. Brutal force has hitherto governed the world. . . . The divine right of husbands, like the divine right of kings, may, it is to be hoped, in this enlightened age, be contested without danger, and, though conviction may not silence many boisterous disputants, yet, when any prevailing prejudice is attacked, the wise will consider, and leave the narrow-minded to rail with thoughtless vehemence at innovation.

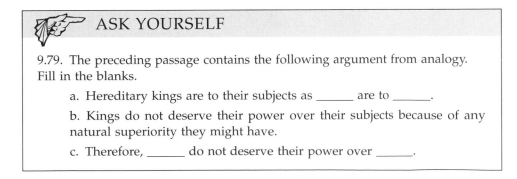

☞ ASK YOURSELF

9.79. The preceding passage contains the following argument from analogy. Fill in the blanks.

    a. Hereditary kings are to their subjects as _____ are to _____.

    b. Kings do not deserve their power over their subjects because of any natural superiority they might have.

    c. Therefore, _____ do not deserve their power over _____.

Education, Virtue, and the Need for a Revolution in Manners

The evil effects of unequal treatment of women can only be overcome by a complete overhaul of current customs.

The Miseducation of Women. The miseducation of women through social custom needs to be replaced by a real education, equal to male education, and even coeducational.

As for Rousseau's remarks, which have since been echoed by several writers, that they have naturally, that is from their birth, independent of education, a fondness for dolls, dressing, and talking—they are so puerile as not to merit a serious refutation. That a girl, condemned to sit for hours together listening to the idle chat of weak nurses, or to attend at her mother's toilet, will endeavor to join the conversation, is, indeed, very natural; and that she will imitate her mother or aunts, and amuse herself by adorning her lifeless doll, as they do in dressing her, poor innocent babe! is undoubtedly a most natural consequence. For men of the greatest abilities have seldom had sufficient strength to rise above the surrounding atmosphere; and, if the page of genius have always been blurred by the prejudices of the age, some allowance should be made for a sex, who, like kings, always see things through a false medium. . . . It is time to effect a revolution in female manners—time to restore to them their lost dignity—and make them, as a part of the human species, labor by reforming themselves to reform the world. It is time to separate unchangeable morals from local manners.—If men be demi-gods—why let us serve them! And if the dignity of the female soul be as disputable as that of animals—if their reason does not afford sufficient light to direct their conduct whilst unerring instinct is denied—they are surely of all creatures the most miserable! and, bent beneath the iron hand of destiny, must submit to be a fair defect in creation. But to justify the ways of Providence respecting them, by pointing out some irrefragable reason for thus making such a large portion of mankind accountable and not accountable, would puzzle the subtlest casuist. I have already animadverted on the bad habits which females acquire when they are shut up together; and, I think, that the observation may fairly be extended to the other sex, till the natural inference is drawn which I have had in view throughout—that to improve both sexes they ought, not only in private families, but in public schools, to be educated together.

 ASK YOURSELF

9.80. There is disagreement among contemporary feminists as to the value of sex segregation in education. What is Wollstonecraft's view?

9.81. Argue either for or against Wollstonecraft's view.

Equality for Women, Marriage, Love, and Virtue. Marriage would improve and sexual relations would be elevated to a more satisfactory level when women escape oppression, become occupied with something more than romance, and acquire real virtues.

If marriage be the cement of society, mankind should all be educated after the same model, or the intercourse of the sexes will never deserve the name of fellowship, nor will women ever fulfill the peculiar duties of their sex, till they become enlightened citizens, till they become free by being enabled to earn their own subsistence, independent of men; in the same manner, I mean, to prevent misconstruction, as one man is independent of another. Nay, marriage will never be held sacred till women, by being brought up with men, are prepared to be their companions rather than their mistresses; for the mean doublings of cunning will ever render them contemptible, whilst oppression renders them timid. So convinced am I of this truth, that I will venture to predict that virtue will never prevail in society till the virtues of both sexes are founded on reason; and, till the affections common to both are allowed to gain their due strength by the discharge of mutual. The best method, I believe, that can be adopted to correct a fondness for novels is to ridicule them: not indiscriminately, for then it would have little effect; but, if a judicious person, with some turn for humor, would read several to a young girl, and point out both by tones, and apt comparisons with pathetic incidents and heroic characters in history, how foolishly and ridiculously they caricatured human nature, just opinions might be substituted instead of romantic sentiments. In one respect, however, the majority of both sexes resemble, and equally shew a want of taste and modesty. Ignorant women, forced to be chaste to preserve their reputation, allow their imagination to revel in the unnatural and meretricious scenes sketched by the novel writers of the day, slighting as insipid the sober dignity and matron graces of history, whilst men carry the same vitiated taste into life, and fly for amusement to the wanton, from the unsophisticated charms.

 ### ASK YOURSELF

9.82. It would appear that Wollstonecraft does *not* have in mind such novelists as her contemporary Jane Austen. To what contemporary (to you) forms of entertainment might the bad novels of her day be compared?

9.83. Austen renders the life of women in the late eighteenth and early nineteenth centuries as the *individual* struggle for, and achievement of, genuine virtues, such as practical wisdom, self-control, courage, and constancy. Has Wollstonecraft proved that what Austen thought possible is not possible? Give reasons for your answer.

Women are supposed to possess more sensibility, and even humanity, than men, and their strong attachments and instantaneous emotions of compassion are given as proofs; but the clinging affection of ignorance has seldom any thing noble in it, and may mostly be resolved into selfishness, as well as the affection of children and brutes. I have known many weak women whose sensibility was entirely engrossed by their husbands; and as for their humanity, it was very faint indeed, or rather it was only a transient emotion of compassion. Humanity does not consist "in a squeamish ear," says an eminent orator. "It belongs to the mind as well as the nerves." But this kind of exclusive affection, though it degrades the individual, should not be brought forward as a proof of the inferiority of the sex, because it is the natural consequence of confined views: for even women of superior sense, having their attention turned to little employments, and private plans, rarely rise to heroism, unless when spurred on by love! and love, as an heroic passion, like genius, appears but once in an age. I therefore agree with the moralist who asserts, "that women have seldom so much generosity as men;" and that their narrow affections, to which justice and humanity are often sacrificed, render the sex apparently inferior, especially, as they are commonly inspired by men; but I contend that the heart would expand as the understanding gained strength, if women will lie fallow.

 ## ASK YOURSELF

9.84. Wollstonecraft debunks the supposed feminine virtues ("sensibility," instantaneous compassion, strong attachments). Some contemporary feminists regard these as the *real* virtues of women. Who is right, and why, in your judgment?

Yet, true voluptuousness must proceed from the mind—for what can equal the sensations produced by mutual affection, supported by mutual respect? What are the cold, or feverish caresses of appetite, but sin embracing death, compared with the modest overflowings of a pure heart and exalted imagination? Yes, let me tell the libertine of fancy when he despises understanding in woman—that the mind, which he disregards, gives life to the enthusiastic affection from which rapture, short-lived as it is, alone can flow! And, that, without virtue, a sexual attachment must expire, like a tallow candle in the socket, creating intolerable disgust. To prove this, I need only observe, that men who have wasted great parts of their lives with women, and with whom they have sought for pleasure with eager thirst, entertain the meanest opinion of the sex.—Virtue, true refiner of joy!—if foolish men were to fright thee from earth, in order to give loose to all their appetites without a check—some sensual wight of taste would scale the heavens to invite thee back, to give a zest to pleasure! That women at present are by ignorance rendered foolish or vicious, is, I think, not to be disputed; and, that the most salutary effects tending to improve mankind might be expected from a *revolution* in female manners, appears, at least, with a face of probability, to rise out of the observation.

 ## ASK YOURSELF

9.85. The theme of revolution is very much in the spirit of the age in which Wollstonecraft lived. What great political and cultural revolution was taking place as she wrote this book?

9.86. Wollstonecraft and many modern feminists agree on one fundamental point: Mere legal and public policy changes (such as extending the vote to women, opening the labor market to them, and so on) will not suffice to bring about the true liberation of women. (1) What then *is* required? (2) Do you agree? Explain.

JOHN STUART MILL

John Stuart Mill (1806–1873) was a precocious child whose father started him in the study of Greek at three and Latin at eight. He was a member of parliament from 1865–1868. He wrote on epistemology and science, very much in the British Empiricist manner, but he is perhaps best know for his work on ethics and on political philosophy. Mill's moral theory is *utilitarianism*, which is a subset of a larger theoretical approach to ethics called *consequentialism*. Consequentialism is the view that right actions are those that produce the greatest benefit. Utilitarianism specifies that right actions are those which produce the greatest benefit for everyone affected by the action (as opposed to merely the agent, or people other than the agent). Mill argued that the ultimate criterion of morality is the amount of pleasure that is produced for everyone. There are several versions of the utilitarian theory, but the one endorsed by Mill focuses exclusively on the pleasure that results from an action. This version is called *hedonistic* utilitarianism, since "hedonism" means a devotion to pleasure as a way of life. Mill does not claim originality, noting that utilitarianism was defended as far back as ancient Greece by Epicurus and more recently by Jeremy Bentham. Mill's brief essay *Utilitarianism* (1861) is a popular defense of the utilitarian doctrine and was originally published in three installments in *Fraser's Magazine*. The essay was quickly received as the definitive statement of the utilitarian theory and has become one of the most influential writings in ethics. The essay has five chapters; key selections from each are reprinted here.

1: General Remarks

In the first chapter, Mill laments the lack of progress regarding the basis of morality and evaluates the two principal schools on the subject.

 From MILL: *Utilitarianism*

From the dawn of philosophy, the question concerning the *summum bonum*, or, what is the same thing, concerning the foundation of morality, has been accounted the main problem in speculative thought, has occupied the most gifted intellects, and divided them into sects and schools, carrying on a vigorous warfare against one another. And, after more than two thousand years, the same discussions continue, philosophers are still ranged under the same contending banners, and neither thinkers nor mankind at large seem nearer to being unanimous on the subject than when the youth Socrates listened to the old Protagoras, and asserted (if Plato's dialogue be grounded on a real conversation) the theory of utilitarianism against the popular morality of the so-called sophist.

Inductive versus Intuitive School of Ethics. Mill argues that moral theories are divided between two distinct approaches: the intuitive and inductive schools. Although both schools agree that there is a single and highest normative principle, they disagree about whether we have knowledge of that principle intuitively (without appeal to experience) or inductively (through experience and observation).

The intuitive, no less than what may be termed the inductive, school of ethics, insists on the necessity of general laws. They both agree that the morality of an individual action is not a question of direct perception, but of the application of a law to an individual case. They recognize also, to a great extent, the same moral laws, but differ as to their evidence, and the source from which they derive their authority. According to the one opinion, the principles of morals are evident *a priori*; requiring nothing to command assent, except that the meaning of the terms be understood. According to the other doctrine, right and wrong, as well as truth and falsehood, are questions of observation and experience. But both hold equally, that morality must be deduced from principles; and the intuitive school affirm, as strongly as the inductive, that there is a science of morals. Yet they seldom attempt to make out a list of the *a priori* principles which are to serve as the premises of the science; still more rarely do they make any effort to reduce those various principles to one first principle, or common ground of obligation. They either assume the ordinary precepts of morals as of *a priori* authority, or they lay down as the common groundwork of those maxims some generality much less obviously authoritative than the maxims themselves, and which has never succeeded in gaining popular acceptance. Yet, to support their pretensions, there ought either to be some one fundamental principle or law at the root of all morality; or, if there be several, there should be a determinate order of precedence among them; and the one principle, or the rule for deciding between the various principles when they conflict, ought to be self-evident.

Kant represents the best of the intuitive school, and Mill himself defends the inductive school. Mill criticizes Kant's categorical imperative, noting that it is essentially the same as utilitarianism since it involves calculating the good or bad consequences of an action to determine the morality of that action. Mill argues that his task is to demonstrate this highest principle inductively.

It is not my present purpose to criticize these thinkers; but I cannot help referring, for illustration, to a systematic treatise by one of the most illustrious of them— the "Metaphysics of Ethics," by Kant. This remarkable man, whose system of thought will long remain one of the landmarks in the history of philosophical speculation, does in the treatise in question, lay down an universal first principle as the origin and ground of moral obligation. It is this: "So act, that the rule on which thou actest would admit of being adopted as a law by all rational beings." But, when he begins to deduce from this precept any of the actual duties of morality, he fails, almost grotesquely, to show that there would be any contradiction, any logical (not to say physical) impossibility, in the adoption by all rational beings of the most outrageously immoral rules of conduct. All he shows is that the *consequences* of their universal adoption would be such as no one would choose to incur.

On the present occasion, I shall, without further discussion of the other theories, attempt to contribute something towards the understanding and appreciation of the Utilitarian or Happiness theory, and towards such proof as it is susceptible of.

ASK YOURSELF

9.87. According to Kant's categorical imperative, wrong actions are those that cannot be willed universally without contradiction. Contrary to Kant, what, for Mill, is the only thing that the categorical imperative shows about wrong actions?

2: What Utilitarianism Is

In this chapter Mill gives a precise formulation of the highest principle and defends the principle against attacks. The highest normative principle is that, "Actions are right in proportion as they tend to promote happiness; wrong as they tend to produce the reverse of happiness." Following his predecessors, such as Hume and Bentham, he refers to this as the principle of utility.

Mill argues that the principle of utility should be seen as a tool for generating secondary moral principles, such as "Don't steal," which promote general happiness. Most of our actions, then, will be judged according to these secondary principles.

The creed which accepts, as the foundation of morals, Utility, or the Greatest Happiness Principle, holds that actions are right in proportion as they tend to promote happiness, wrong as they tend to produce the reverse of happiness. By happiness is intended pleasure and the absence of pain; by unhappiness, pain and the privation of pleasure. To give a clear view of the moral standard set up by the theory, much more requires to be said; in particular, what things it includes in the ideas of pain and pleasure, and to what extent this is left an open question. But these supplementary explanations do not affect the theory of life on which this theory of morality is grounded—namely, that pleasure, and freedom from pain, are the only things desirable as ends; and that all desirable things (which are as numerous in the utilitarian as in any other scheme) are desirable either for the pleasure inherent in themselves, or as means to the promotion of pleasure and the prevention of pain.

Higher and Lower Pleasures. Mill argues that by "happiness" he means pleasure—both intellectual and sensual. However, we have a sense of dignity that has us prefer intellectual pleasures over sensual ones.

Now, such a theory of life excites in many minds, and among them in some of the most estimable in feeling and purpose, inveterate dislike. To suppose that life has (as they express it) no higher end than pleasure—no better and nobler object of desire and pursuit—they designate as utterly mean and groveling; as a doctrine worthy only of swine, to whom the followers of Epicurus were, at a very early period, contemptuously likened: and modern holders of the doctrine are occasionally made the subject of equally polite comparisons by its German, French, and English assailants.

When thus attacked, the Epicureans have always answered, that it is not they, but their accusers, who represent human nature in a degrading light, since the accusation supposes human beings to be capable of no pleasures except those of which swine are capable. If this supposition were true, the charge could not be gainsaid, but would then be no longer an imputation; for, if the sources of pleasure were precisely the same to human beings and to swine, the rule of life which is good enough for the one would be good enough for the other. The comparison of the Epicurean life to that of beasts is felt as degrading, precisely because a beast's pleasures do not satisfy a human being's conceptions of happiness. Human beings have faculties more elevated than the animal appetites; and, when once made conscious of them, do not regard any thing as happiness which does not include their gratification. I do not, indeed, consider the Epicureans to have been by any means faultless in drawing out their scheme of consequences from the utilitarian principle. To do this in any sufficient manner, many Stoic as well as Christian elements require to be included.

 ASK YOURSELF

9.88. How have Epicureans responded to the accusation that they propose a doctrine worthy only of swine?

But there is no known Epicurean theory of life which does not assign to the pleasures of the intellect, of the feelings and imagination, and of the moral sentiments, a much higher value as pleasures than to those of mere sensation. It must be admitted, however, that utilitarian writers in general have placed the superiority of mental over bodily pleasures chiefly in the greater permanency, safety, uncostliness, &c., of the former—that is, in their circumstantial advantages rather than in their intrinsic nature. And, on all these points, utilitarians have fully proved their case; but they might have taken the other, and, as it may be called, higher ground, with entire consistency. It is quite compatible with the principle of utility to recognize the fact, that some *kinds* of pleasure are more desirable and more valuable than others. It would be absurd, that while, in estimating all other things, quality is considered as well as quantity, the estimation of pleasures should be supposed to depend on quantity alone.

 ASK YOURSELF

9.89. What does the Epicurean theory of life include?

If I am asked what I mean by difference of quality in pleasures, or what makes one pleasure more valuable than another, merely as a pleasure, except its being greater in amount, there is but one possible answer. Of two pleasures, if there be one to which all or almost all who have experience of both give a decided preference, irrespective of any feeling of moral obligation to prefer it, that is the more desirable pleasure. If one of the two is, by those who are competently acquainted with both, placed so far above the other that they prefer it, even though knowing it to be attended with a greater amount of discontent, and would not resign it for any quantity of the other pleasure which their nature is capable of, we are justified in ascribing to the preferred enjoyment a superiority in quality, so far outweighing quantity, as to render it, in comparison, of small account.

ASK YOURSELF

9.90. What is Mill's test for determining the qualitative difference between a higher and a lower pleasure?

9.91. Give some examples of higher and lower pleasures.

Higher Pleasures and the Sense of Dignity. According to Mill, people choose higher pleasures over the lower ones because they have a sense of dignity.

Now, it is an unquestionable fact, that those who are equally acquainted with and equally capable of appreciating and enjoying both do give a most marked preference to the manner of existence which employs their higher faculties. Few human creatures would consent to be changed into any of the lower animals, for a promise of the fullest allowance of a beast's pleasures: no intelligent human being would consent to be a fool, no instructed person would be an ignoramus, no person of feeling and conscience would be selfish and base, even though they should be persuaded that the fool, the dunce, or the rascal is better satisfied with his lot than they are with theirs. They would not resign what they possess more than he for the most complete satisfaction of the desires which they have in common with him. If they ever fancy they would, it is only in cases of unhappiness so extreme, that, to escape from it, they would exchange their lot for almost any other, however undesirable in their own eyes. A being of higher faculties requires more to make him happy, is capable probably of more acute suffering, and certainly accessible to it at more points, than one of an inferior type; but, in spite of these liabilities, he can never really wish to sink into what he feels to be a lower grade of existence. We may give what explanation we please of this unwillingness; we may attribute it to pride, a name which is given indiscriminately to some of the most and to some of the least estimable feelings of which mankind are capable; we may refer it to the love of liberty and personal independence—an appeal to which was with the Stoics one of the most effective means for the inculcation of it; to the love of power, or to the love of excitement, both of which do really enter into and contribute to it: but its most appropriate appellation is a sense of dignity, which all human beings possess in one form or other, and in some, though by no means in exact, proportion to their higher faculties, and which is so essential a part of the happiness of those in whom it is strong, that nothing which conflicts with it could be, otherwise than momentarily, an object of desire to them.

ASK YOURSELF

9.92. What are come of the common explanations for why we chose higher pleasures?

Whoever supposes that this preference takes place at a sacrifice of happiness; that the superior being, in any thing like equal circumstances, is not happier than the inferior—confounds the two very different ideas of happiness and content. It is indisputable, that the being whose capacities of enjoyment are low has the greatest chance of having them fully satisfied; and a highly endowed being will always feel that any happiness which he can look for, as the world is constituted, is imperfect. But he can learn to bear its imperfections, if they are at all bearable; and they will not make him envy the being who is indeed unconscious of the imperfections, but only because he feels not at all the good which those imperfections qualify. It is better to be a human being dissatisfied, than a pig satisfied; better to be Socrates dissatisfied, than a fool satisfied. And if the fool or the pig are of a different opinion, it is because they only know their own side of the question. The other party to the comparison knows both sides.

 ASK YOURSELF

9.93. Mill states that it is better to be Socrates dissatisfied than a fool satisfied. What does he mean?

Why People Reject Higher Pleasures.   Mill continues explaining why many people reject higher pleasures for lower ones.

It may be objected, that many who are capable of the higher pleasures, occasionally, under the influence of temptation, postpone them to the lower. But this is quite compatible with a full appreciation of the intrinsic superiority of the higher. Men often, from infirmity of character, make their election for the nearer good, though they know it to be the less valuable, and this no less when the choice is between two bodily pleasures than when it is between bodily and mental. They pursue sensual indulgences to the injury of health, though perfectly aware that health is the greater good. It may be further objected, that many who begin with youthful enthusiasm for every thing noble, as they advance in years sink into indolence and selfishness. But I do not believe that those who undergo this very common change voluntarily choose the lower description of pleasures in preference to the higher. I believe, that, before they devote themselves exclusively to the one, they have already become incapable of the other. Capacity for the nobler feelings is in most natures a very tender plant, easily killed, not only by hostile influences, but by mere want of sustenance; and, in the majority of young persons, it speedily dies away if the occupations to which their position in life has devoted them, and the society into which it has thrown them, are not favorable to keeping that higher capacity in exercise. Men lose their high aspirations as they lose their intellectual tastes, because they have not time or opportunity for indulging them; and they addict themselves to inferior pleasures, not because they deliberately prefer them, but because they are either the only ones to which they have access, or the only ones which they are any longer capable of enjoying. It may be questioned, whether any one, who has remained equally susceptible to both classes of pleasures, ever knowingly and calmly preferred the lower; though many in all ages have broken down in an ineffectual attempt to combine both.

ASK YOURSELF

9.94. What are some of the reasons people often choose lower pleasures over higher ones?

From this verdict of the only competent judges, I apprehend there can be no appeal. On a question, which is the best worth having of two pleasures, or which of two modes of existence is the most grateful to the feelings, apart from its moral attributes and from its consequences, the judgment of those who are qualified by knowledge of both, or, if they differ, that of the majority among them, must be admitted as final. And there needs be the less hesitation to accept this judgment respecting the quality of pleasures, since there is no other tribunal to be referred to even on the question of quantity. What means are there of determining which is the acutest of two pains, or the intensest of two pleasurable sensations, except the general suffrage of those who are familiar with both? Neither pains nor pleasures are homogeneous, and pain is always heterogeneous with pleasure. What is there to decide whether a particular pleasure is worth purchasing at the cost of a particular pain, except the feelings and judgment of the experienced? When, therefore, those feelings and judgment declare the pleasures derived from the higher faculties to be preferable *in kind*, apart from the question of intensity, to those of which the animal nature, disjoined from the higher faculties, is susceptible, they are entitled on this subject to the same regard.

An essential feature of utilitarianism is the fact that we judge an action according to the general happiness it produces, rather than merely the agent's private happiness.

I have dwelt on this point, as being a necessary part of a perfectly just conception of Utility or Happiness, considered as the directive rule of human conduct. But it is by no means an indispensable condition to the acceptance of the utilitarian standard; for that standard is not the agent's own greatest happiness, but the greatest amount of happiness altogether: and, if it may possibly be doubted whether a noble character is always the happier for its nobleness, there can be no doubt that it makes other people happier, and that the world in general is immensely a gainer by it. Utilitarianism, therefore, could only attain its end by the general cultivation of nobleness of character, even if each individual were only benefited by the nobleness of others, and his own, so far as happiness is concerned, were a sheer deduction from the benefit. But the bare enunciation of such an absurdity as this last renders refutation superfluous.

ASK YOURSELF

9.95. What is the only way that utilitarianism could achieve its aim of advancing general happiness over private happiness?

According to the Greatest Happiness Principle, as above explained, the ultimate end, with reference to and for the sake of which all other things are desirable (whether we are considering our own good or that of other people), is an existence exempt as far as possible from pain, and as rich as possible in enjoyments, both in point of quantity and quality; the test of quality, and the rule for measuring it against quantity, being the preference felt by those, who in their opportunities of experience, to which must be added their habits of self-consciousness and self-observation, are best furnished with the means of comparison. This, being, according to the utilitarian opinion, the end of human action, is necessarily also the standard of morality: which may accordingly be defined, the rules and precepts for human conduct, by the observance of which an existence such as has been described might be, to the greatest extent possible, secured to all mankind; and not to them only, but, so far as the nature of things admits, to the whole sentient creation.

 ASK YOURSELF

9.96. Mill again notes that there is a test for determining the qualitative value of a pleasure (as opposed to its quantitative value). What is that test?

Whether Happiness Is Unattainable. Mill continues addressing objections to his theory. One objection is that happiness is simply unattainable. If that is so, then the utilitarian goal of general happiness is misguided. Mill concedes that a life of continuous excitement is impossible. However, he offers an alternative notion of happiness.

Against this doctrine, however, arises another class of objectors, who say that happiness, in any form, cannot be the rational purpose of human life and action; because, in the first place, it is unattainable: and they contemptuously ask, What right hast thou to be happy? a question which Mr. Carlyle clinches by the addition, What right, a short time ago, hadst thou even *to be*? Next, they say that men can do *without* happiness; that all noble human beings have felt this, and could not have become noble but by learning the lesson of Entsagen, or renunciation; which lesson, thoroughly learnt and submitted to, they affirm to be the beginning and necessary condition of all virtue.

The first of these objections would go to the root of the matter, were it well founded; for, if no happiness is to be had at all by human beings, the attainment of it cannot be the end of morality, or of any rational conduct. Though, even in that case, something might still be said for the utilitarian theory; since utility includes not solely the pursuit of happiness, but the prevention or mitigation of unhappiness: and, if the former aim be chimerical, there will be all the greater scope and more imperative need for the latter, so long at least as mankind think fit to live, and do not take refuge in the simultaneous act of suicide recommended under certain conditions by Novalis. When, however, it is thus positively asserted to be impossible that human life should be happy, the assertion, if not something like a verbal quibble, is at least an exaggeration. If by happiness be meant a continuity of highly pleasurable excitement, it is evident enough that this is impossible. A state of exalted pleasure lasts only moments, or in some cases, and with some intermissions, hours or days; and is the occasional brilliant flash of enjoyment, not its permanent and steady flame. Of this the philosophers who have taught that happiness is the end of life were as fully aware as those who taunt them. The happiness which they meant was not a life of rapture, but moments of such, in an existence made up of few and transitory pains, many and various pleasures, with a decided predominance of the active over the passive, and having, as the foundation of the whole, not to expect more from life than it is capable of bestowing. A life thus composed, to those who have been fortunate enough to obtain it, has always appeared worthy of the name of "happiness." And such an existence is even now the lot of many, during some considerable portion of their lives. The present wretched education and wretched social arrangements are the only real hindrance to its being attainable by almost all.

 ASK YOURSELF

9.97. When Mill speaks of a life of happiness, what kind of life does he have in mind?

Rejection of Virtue Theory. Mill continues that the principle of utility involves an assessment of only an action's consequences, and not the motives or character traits of the agent performing the action. In this regard, he rejects classical virtue theory.

It is often affirmed, that utilitarianism renders men cold and unsympathizing; that it chills their moral feelings towards individuals; that it makes them regard only the dry and hard consideration of the consequences of actions, not taking into their moral estimate the qualities from which those actions emanate. If the assertion means that they do not allow their judgment respecting the rightness or wrongness of an action to be influenced by their opinion of the qualities of the person who does it, this is a complaint, not against utilitarianism, but against having any standard of morality at all: for certainly no known ethical standard decides an action to be good or bad because it is done by a good or a bad man; still less because done by an amiable, a brave, or a benevolent man, or the contrary. These considerations are relevant, not to the estimation of actions, but of persons; and there is nothing in the utilitarian theory inconsistent with the fact, that there are other things which interest us in persons besides the rightness and wrongness of their actions. The Stoics indeed, with the paradoxical misuse of language which was part of their system, and by which they strove to raise themselves above all concern about any thing but virtue, were fond of saying, that he who has that, has every thing; that he, and only he, is rich, is beautiful, is a king. But no claim of this description is made for the virtuous man by the utilitarian doctrine. Utilitarians are quite aware that there are other desirable possessions and qualities besides virtue, and are perfectly willing to allow to all of them their full worth. They are also aware that a right action does not necessarily indicate a virtuous character; and that actions which are blamable often proceed from qualities entitled to praise. When this is apparent in any particular case, it modifies their estimation, not certainly of the act, but of the agent. I grant that they are, notwithstanding, of opinion, that, in the long run, the best proof of a good character is good actions; and resolutely refuse to consider any mental disposition as good, of which the predominant tendency is to produce bad conduct. This makes them unpopular with many people: but it is an un-

popularity which they must share with every one who regards the distinction between right and wrong in a serious light; and the reproach is not one which a conscientious utilitarian need be anxious to repel.

ASK YOURSELF

9.98. For Mill, one way of understanding the virtue theorist's criticism is that
moral judgments are made impartially of the agent's character. What is Mill's
response to this?

If no more be meant by the objection than that many utilitarians look on the morality of actions, as measured by the utilitarian standards, with too exclusive a regard, and do not lay sufficient stress upon the other beauties of character which
go towards making a human being lovable or admirable, this may be admitted.
Utilitarians who have cultivated their moral feelings, but not their sympathies nor
their artistic perceptions, do fall into this mistake; and so do all other moralists
under the same conditions. What can be said in excuse for other moralists is equally
available for them; namely, that, if there is to be any error, it is better that it should
be on that side. As a matter of fact, we may affirm that among utilitarians, as among
adherents of other systems, there is every imaginable degree of rigidity and of lax-
ity in the application of their standard: some are even puritanically rigorous, while
others are as indulgent as can possibly be desired by sinner or by sentimentalist.
But, on the whole, a doctrine which brings prominently forward the interest that
mankind have in the repression and prevention of conduct which violates the moral
law, is likely to be inferior to no other in turning the sanctions of opinion against
such violations. It is true, the question, What does violate the moral law? is one
on which those who recognize different standards of morality are likely now and
then to differ. But difference of opinion on moral questions was not first introduced into the world by utilitarianism; while that doctrine does supply, if not
always an easy, at all events a tangible and intelligible, mode of deciding such
differences.

ASK YOURSELF

9.99. A second way of interpreting the virtue theorist's criticism is that
utilitarianism takes no regard of any motive. What is Mill's response to this?

Whether There Is Time to Calculate Consequences. Another criticism of utilitarianism
is that we simply don't have time to calculate all the relevant consequences of an action, so utilitarianism is a useless guideline. In response, Mill argues that we don't
need to weigh the consequences of each action we perform.

Again: defenders of Utility often find themselves called upon to reply to such objections as this—that there is not time, previous to action, for calculating and weighing
the effects of any line of conduct on the general happiness. This is exactly as if any

one were to say that it is impossible to guide our conduct by Christianity, because there is not time, on every occasion on which any thing has to be done, to read through the Old and New Testaments. The answer to the objection is, that there has been ample time; namely, the whole past duration of the human species. During all that time, mankind have been learning by experience the tendencies of actions, on which experience all the prudence as well as all the morality of life are dependent. People talk as if the commencement of this course of experience had hitherto been put off, and as if, at the moment when some man feels tempted to meddle with the property or life of another, he had to begin considering for the first time whether murder and theft are injurious to human happiness. Even then, I do not think that he would find the question very puzzling; but, at all events, the matter is now done to his hand. It is truly a whimsical supposition, that, if mankind were agreed in considering utility to be the test of morality, they would remain without any agreement as to what *is* useful, and would take no measures for having their notions on the subject taught to the young, and enforced by law and opinion.

 ASK YOURSELF

9.100. Mill contends that we shouldn't calculate the consequences of each of our actions, but consult a type of record showing results of our actions. Where do we find that record?

There is no difficulty in proving any ethical standard whatever to work ill, if we suppose universal idiocy to be conjoined with it: but, on any hypothesis short of that, mankind must by this time have acquired positive beliefs as to the effects of some actions on their happiness; and the beliefs which have thus come down are the rules of morality for the multitude, and for the philosopher, until he has succeeded in finding better. That philosophers might easily do this, even now, on many subjects; that the received code of ethics is by no means of divine right; and that mankind have still much to learn as to the effects of actions on the general happiness—I admit, or, rather, earnestly maintain. The corollaries from the principle of utility, like the precepts of every practical art, admit of indefinite improvement; and, in a progressive state of the human mind, their improvement is perpetually going on. But to consider the rules of morality as improvable is one thing; to pass over the intermediate generalizations entirely, and endeavor to test each individual action directly by the first principle, is another. It is a strange notion, that the acknowledgment of a first principle is inconsistent with the admission of secondary ones. To inform a traveler respecting the place of his ultimate destination is not to forbid the use of landmarks and direction posts on the way. The proposition that happiness is the end and aim of morality does not mean that no road ought to be laid down to that goal, or that persons going thither should not be advised to take one direction rather than another. Men really ought to leave off talking a kind of nonsense on this subject which they would neither talk nor listen to on other matters of practical concernment. Nobody argues that the art of navigation is not founded on astronomy, because sailors cannot wait to calculate the "Nautical Almanac." Being rational creatures, they go to sea with it ready calculated;

and all rational creatures go out upon the sea of life with their minds made up on the common questions of right and wrong, as well as on many of the far more difficult questions of wise and foolish. And this, as long as foresight is a human quality, it is to be presumed they will continue to do. Whatever we adopt as the fundamental principle of morality, we require subordinate principles to apply it by: the impossibility of doing without them, being common to all systems, can afford no argument against any one in particular; but gravely to argue as if no such secondary principles could be had, and as if mankind had remained till now, and always must remain, without drawing any general conclusions from the experience of human life, is as high a pitch, I think, as absurdity has ever reached in philosophical controversy.

Bending Moral Rules. Finally, a critic might object that the utilitarian theory fails since it is easy to make exceptions in particular cases and thereby bend the moral rules a little bit. For example, if I am late to work I might justify speeding with the following reasoning: There is little harm done by my speeding, the risks of getting caught are small, and the benefit I get from showing up to work on time are substantial. Thus, on balance, speeding will create more happiness than unhappiness. Mill responds to this rationale by saying that all moral theories allow for some similar measure of rule bending, so this isn't a criticism unique to utilitarianism.

The remainder of the stock arguments against utilitarianism mostly consist in laying to its charge the common infirmities of human nature, and the general difficulties which embarrass conscientious persons in shaping their course through life. We are told that a utilitarian will be apt to make his own particular case an exception to moral rules; and, when under temptation, will see an utility in the breach of a rule greater than he will see in its observance. But is utility the only creed which is able to furnish us with excuses for evil doing, and means of cheating our own conscience? They are afforded in abundance by all doctrines which recognize as a fact in morals the existence of conflicting considerations; which all doctrines do that have been believed by sane persons. It is not the fault of any creed, but of the complicated nature of human affairs, that rules of conduct cannot be so framed as to require no exceptions, and that hardly any kind of action can safely be laid down as either always obligatory or always condemnable. There is no ethical creed which does not temper the rigidity of its laws by giving a certain latitude, under the moral responsibility of the agent, for accommodation to peculiarities of circumstances; and under every creed, at the opening thus made, self-deception and dishonest casuistry get in. There exists no moral system under which there do not arise unequivocal cases of conflicting obligation. These are the real difficulties; the knotty points both in the theory of ethics, and in the conscientious guidance of personal conduct. They are overcome practically with greater or with less success according to the intellect and virtue of the individual; but it can hardly be pretended that any one will be the less qualified for dealing with them, from possessing an ultimate standard to which conflicting rights and duties can be referred.

Mill continues arguing that we should appeal directly to the principle of utility itself only when we face a moral dilemma between two secondary principles. Suppose, for example, that a moral principle of charity dictates that I should feed a starving neighbor, and a moral principle of self-preservation dictates that I should feed myself. If I do not have enough food to do both, then I should determine whether general happiness would be better served by feeding my neighbor or feeding myself.

If utility is the ultimate source of moral obligations, utility may be invoked to decide between them when their demands are incompatible. Though the application of the standard may be difficult, it is better than none at all: while in other systems, the moral laws all claiming independent authority, there is no common umpire entitled to interfere between them; their claims to precedence one over another rest on little better than sophistry; and unless determined, as they generally are, by the unacknowledged influence of considerations of utility, afford a free scope for the action of personal desires and partialities. We must remember that only in these cases of conflict between secondary principles is it requisite that first principles should be appealed to. There is no case of moral obligation in which some secondary principle is not involved; and, if only one, there can seldom be any real doubt which one it is, in the mind of any person by whom the principle itself is recognized.

 ASK YOURSELF

9.101. According to Mill, what are the only circumstances under which we should directly evaluate the morality of an action by the principle of utility?

FRIEDRICH NIETZSCHE

Friedrich Nietzsche was born in 1844 in Lutzen, now in Germany. His father, a Lutheran pastor, died while Friedrich was a child, leaving him in the care of his mother (the daughter of a Lutheran pastor) and two aunts. Friedrich claimed that the low point in his own physical health came in his thirty-sixth year, a fact he considered significant, since his "incomparable father" had died at the age of thirty-six. He did not have any similar sense of connection to his mother, and he never married, although he did make a proposal to the remarkable Russian princess Lou Andreas Salome, which she rejected. Despite the sense of a close connection to his father, Nietzsche came to completely reject Christianity. His intellectual brilliance was early recognized by his teacher Ritschl, who saw to it that Nietzsche was appointed to a professorship even before he had completed his doctoral dissertation. Nietzsche was afflicted with migraines and stomach problems for much of his life, and he retired from teaching when only thirty-five years old partly because of these physical ills. Toward the end of his life he went quite mad and had to be cared for by relatives and in institutional settings until his death in 1900.

Art, Morality, and Religion

Nietzsche was deeply concerned with suffering and cruelty. He was convinced that no explanation of tragic suffering was possible and that there is no way of ensuring ourselves against such suffering. People often try to explain tragic events in terms of morality (the sufferer was bad and deserved it), religion (it is all part of God's plan), or a combination of the two, and they are often surprised and inconsolable when tragic suffering (e.g., the violent death of their own innocent child) overtakes them. According to Nietzsche, religion and morality amount to ways of denying what is actually happening; they amount to saying "no" to life in all of its tragic complexity and absurdity. Religion and morality are expressions of a deep dissatisfaction with life as it actually is and are dishonest attempts to escape it or interpret it in a way that makes it less terrible. Nietzsche wanted to be able to affirm life even in the midst of absurd suffering. In his first book, *The Birth of Tragedy*, he argued that the Greek tragedians, Sophocles for example, managed to do just that. Only in art (for example, Greek drama) is life faced as it truly is. Art represents life without distortion and at the same time enables us to accept it and even to celebrate it, as the Greeks did in their dramatic festivals, which were dedicated to Dionysios, the God of revelry, celebration, and intoxication. Logic and science, on the other hand, gain the upper hand when people are afraid to face the absurdity of life and are becoming superficial and weak.

Madness and Reason. Nietzsche sees strength in the "Dionysian" attitudes of the Greek tragedies, but only weakness in philosophical reason.

 ASK YOURSELF

9.102. Nietzsche mentions several symptoms of decline and weakness in the following passage from the Preface to *The Birth of Tragedy*. Note five of them here.

 From NIETZSCHE: Preface to *The Birth of Tragedy* —

What if the Greeks in the very wealth of their youth had the will to be tragic and were pessimists? What if it was madness itself, to use a word of Plato's, which brought the greatest blessings upon Hellas? And what if, on the other hand and conversely, at the very time of their dissolution and weakness, the Greeks became always more optimistic, more superficial, more histrionic, also more ardent for logic and the logicizing of the world—consequently at the same time more "cheerful" and more "scientific"? Ay, despite all "modern ideas" and prejudices of the democratic taste, may not the triumph of optimism, the common sense that has gained the upper hand, the practical and theoretical utilitarianism, like democracy itself, with which it is synchronous, be symptomatic of declining vigor, of approaching age, of physiological weariness? And not at all—pessiniism? Was Epicurus an optimist—because a sufferer? . . . We see it is a whole bundle of weighty questions which this book has taken upon itself—let us not fail to add its weightiest question. Viewed through the optics of life, what is the meaning of morality? . . .

Nietzsche hoped that something like the Greek tragic and Dionysian conception of art would be recovered in the musical dramas of his contemporary Richard Wagner.

Later in life Nietzsche came to reject parts of his first book and to give up his hopes in Wagner, but the basic ideas just mentioned persist throughout his authorship. This can be seen in the following selection, from the Preface to *The Birth of Tragedy*, written late in his life.

Art Is Closer to Reality Than Morality.   Metaphysics is the attempt to say what is really real. Nietzsche denied that metaphysics is possible, but the impulse that makes people ask what is real can be satisfied in art.

Already in the foreword to Richard Wagner, art—and not morality—is set down as the properly metaphysical activity of man; in the book itself the piquant proposition recurs time and again, that the existence of the world is justified only as an aesthetic phenomenon. Indeed, the entire book recognizes only an artist—thought and artist—afterthought behind all occurrences—a "God," if you will, but certainly only an altogether thoughtless and unmoral artist—God, who, in construction as in destruction, in good as in evil, desires to become conscious of his own equable joy and sovereign glory; who, in creating worlds, frees himself from the anguish of fullness and overfullness, from the suffering of the contradictions concentrated within him. The world, that is, the redemption of God attained at every moment, as the perpetually changing, perpetually new vision of the most suffering, most antithetical, most contradictory being, who contrives to redeem himself only in appearance: this entire artist metaphysics, call it arbitrary, idle, fantastic, if you will—the point is, that it already betrays a spirit, which is determined some day, at all hazards, to make a stand against the moral interpretation and significance of life. Here, perhaps for the first time, a pessimism "Beyond Good and Evil" announces itself, here that "perverseness of disposition" obtains expression and formulation, against which Schopenhauer never grew tired of hurling beforehand his angriest imprecations and thunderbolts—a philosophy which dares to put, derogatorily put, morality itself in the world of phenomena, and not only among "Phenomena" (in the sense of the idealistic *terminus technicus* [technical term]), but among the "illusions," as appearance, semblance, error, interpretation, accommodation, art. Perhaps the depth of this anti-moral tendency may be best estimated from the guarded and hostile silence with which Christianity is treated throughout this book—Christianity, as being the most extravagant burlesque of the moral theme to which mankind has hitherto been obliged to listen. In fact, to the purely aesthetic world—interpretation and justification taught in this book, there is no greater antithesis than the Christian dogma, which is only and will be only moral, and which, with its absolute standards, for instance, its truthfulness of God, relegates—that is, disowns, convicts, condemns—art, all art, to the realm of falsehood. Behind such a mode of thought and valuation, which, if at all genuine, must be hostile to art, I always experienced what was hostile to life, the wrathful, vindictive counterwill to life itself; for all life rests on appearance, art, illusion, optics, necessity of perspective and error. From the very first Christianity was, essentially and thoroughly, the nausea and surfeit of Life for Life, which only disguised, concealed, and decked itself out under the belief in "another" or "better" life. The hatred of the "world," the curse on the affections, the fear of beauty and sensuality, another world, invented for the purpose of slandering this world the more, at bottom a longing for Nothingness, for the end, for rest, for the "Sabbath of Sabbaths"—all this, as also the unconditional will of Christianity to recognize only moral values, has always appeared to me as the most dangerous and ominous of all possible forms of a "will to perish"; at the least, as the symptom of a most fatal disease, of profoundest weariness, despondency, exhaustion, impoverishment of life—for before the tribunal of morality (especially Christian, that is, unconditional morality) life must constantly and inevitably be the loser, because life is something essentially unmoral—indeed, oppressed with the weight of contempt and the everlasting. No, life must finally be regarded as unworthy of desire, as in itself unworthy.

 ASK YOURSELF

9.103. State three reasons why, in Nietzsche's view, morality, especially Christian morality, involves saying "no" to life?

The Critique of Morality

Nietzsche attacks conventional, and especially Christian morality, from several sides. It is part of a herd mentality, and it is rooted in the resentments and fears of the weak.

Morality, Custom, and the Individual. Nietzsche argues that morality annihilates the individual because of its close connection to custom.

 From NIETZSCHE: *The Dawn of Day*

In comparison with the mode of life which prevailed among men for thousands of years, we men of the present day are living in a very immoral age: the power of custom has been weakened to a remarkable degree, and the sense of morality is so refined and elevated that we might almost describe it as volatilized. That is why we latecomers experience such difficulty in obtaining a fundamental conception of the origin of morality: and even if we do obtain it, our words of explanation stick in our throats, so coarse would they sound if we uttered them! or to so great an extent would they seem to be a slander upon morality! Thus, for example, the fundamental clause: morality is nothing else (and, above all, nothing more) than obedience to customs, of whatsoever nature they may be. But customs are simply the traditional way of acting and valuing. Where there is no tradition there is no morality; and the less life is governed by tradition, the narrower the circle of morality. The free man is immoral, because it is his will to depend upon himself and not upon tradition: in all the primitive states of humanity "evil" is equivalent to "individual," "free," "arbitrary," "unaccustomed," "unforeseen," "incalculable." In such primitive conditions, always measured by this standard, any action performed—not because tradition commands it, but for other reasons (e.g., on account of its individual utility), even for the same reasons as had been formerly established by custom—is termed immoral, and is felt to be so even by the very man who performs it, for it has not been done out of obedience to the tradition.

What is tradition? A higher authority, which is obeyed, not because it commands what is useful to us, but merely because it commands. And in what way can this feeling for tradition be distinguished from a general feeling of fear? It is the fear of a higher intelligence which commands, the fear of an incomprehensible power, of something that is more than personal—there is superstition in this fear. In primitive times the domain of morality included education and hygienics, marriage, medicine, agriculture, war, speech, and silence, the relationship between man and man, and between man and the gods—morality required that a man should observe her prescriptions without thinking of himself as individual. Everything, therefore, was originally custom, and whoever wished to raise himself above it had first of all to make himself a kind of lawgiver and medicine man, a sort of demigod—in other words, he had to create customs, a dangerous and fearful thing to do! Who is the most moral man? On the one hand, he who most frequently obeys the law, e.g., he who, like the Brahmins [Hindu priests], carries a consciousness of the law about with him wherever he may go, and introduces it into the smallest divisions of time, continually exercising his mind in finding opportunities for obeying the law. On the other hand, he who obeys the law in the most difficult cases. The most moral man is he who makes the greatest sacrifices to morality, but what are the greatest sacrifices? In answering this question several different kinds of morality will be developed, but the distinction between the morality of the most frequent obedience and the morality of the most difficult obedience is of the greatest importance. Let us not be deceived as to the motives of that moral law which requires, as an indication of morality, obedience to custom in the most difficult cases. Self conquest is required, not by reason of its useful consequences for the individual, but that custom and tradition may appear to be dominant, in spite of all individual counter desires and advantages. The individual shall sacrifice himself—so demands the morality of custom.

 ASK YOURSELF

9.104. Why can a person not be both free and moral? Because being moral requires following _____, whereas being free requires being willing to

_____.

9.105. Do you think that a person can be an "individualist" and still follow the customs and traditions of his or her community? Explain.

On the other hand, those moralists who, like the followers of Socrates, recommend self-control and sobriety to the individual as his greatest possible advantage and the key to his greatest personal happiness are exceptions—and if we ourselves do not think so, this is simply due to our having been brought up under their influence. They all take a new path, and thereby bring down upon themselves the utmost disapproval of all the representatives of the morality of custom. They sever their connection with the community, as immoralists, and are, in the fullest sense of the word, evil ones. In the same way, every Christian who "sought, above all things, his own salvation" must have seemed evil to a virtuous Roman of the old school. Wherever a community exists, and consequently also a morality of custom, the feeling prevails that any punishment for the violation of a custom is inflicted, above all, on the community: this punishment is a supernatural punishment, the manifestations and limits of which are so difficult to understand, and are investigated with such superstitious fear. The community can compel any one member of it to make good, either to an individual or to the community itself, any ill consequences which may have followed upon such a member's action. It can also call down a sort of vengeance upon the head of the individual by endeavoring to show that, as the result of his action, a storm of divine anger has burst over the community—but, above all, it regards the guilt of the individual more particularly as its own guilt, and bears the punishment of the isolated individual as its own punishment. "Morals," they bewail in their innermost heart, "morals have grown lax, if such deeds as these are possible." And every individual action, every individual mode of thinking, causes dread. It is impossible to determine how much the more select, rare, and original minds must have suffered in the course of time by being considered as evil and dangerous, yea, because they even looked upon themselves as such. Under the dominating influence of the morality of custom, originality of every kind came to acquire a bad conscience, and even now the sky of the best minds seems to be more overcast by this thought than it need be.

 ASK YOURSELF

9.106. Some "individualists," Socrates for instance, have also been moralists. Why does this fact seem to contradict Nietzsche's view of morality?

9.107. How does Nietzsche deal with this apparent contradiction?

Suspicion of Morality and Selflessness. Nietzsche questions the whole notion of morality and suspects that it is connected with weakness. What is needed is a study that uncovers the roots of morality, rather than mere surveys of its history and problems.

 From NIETZSCHE: *Joyful Wisdom*

"Selflessness" has no value either in heaven or on earth; the great problems all demand great love, and it is only the strong, well-rounded, secure spirits, those who have a solid basis, that are qualified for them. It makes the most material difference whether a thinker stands personally related to his problems, having his fate, his need, and even his highest happiness therein; or merely impersonally, that is to say, if he can only feel and grasp them with the tentacles of cold, prying thought. . . .

If you have studied the section on Kierkegaard you should be able to recognize this last sentence as one that could easily have been uttered by that anti-Hegelian Dane.

How is it that I have not yet met with anyone, not even in books, who seems to have stood to morality in this position, as one who knew morality as a problem, and this problem as his own personal need, affliction, pleasure, and passion? It is obvious that up to the present morality has not been a problem at all; it has rather been the very ground on which people have met, after all distrust, dissension, and contradiction, the hallowed place of peace, where thinkers could obtain rest even from themselves, could recover breath and revive. I see no one who has ventured to criticize the estimates of moral worth. I miss in this connection even the attempts of scientific curiosity, and the fastidious, groping imagination of psychologists and historians, which easily anticipates a problem and catches it on the wing, without rightly knowing what it catches. With difficulty I have discovered some scanty data for the purpose of furnishing a history of the origin of these feelings and estimates of value (which is something different from a criticism of them, and also something different from a history of ethical systems). In an individual case, I have done everything to encourage the inclination and talent for this kind of history—in vain, as it would seem to me at present. There is little to be learned from those historians of morality (especially Englishmen); they themselves are usually, quite unsuspiciously, under the influence of a definite morality, and act unwittingly as its armor-bearers and followers—perhaps still repeating sincerely the popular superstition of Christian Europe, that the characteristic of moral action consists in abnegation, self-denial, self-sacrifice, or in fellow feeling and fellow suffering. The usual error in their premises is their insistence on a certain consensus among human beings, at least among civilized human beings, with regard to certain propositions of morality, and from thence they conclude that these propositions are absolutely binding even upon you and me; or reversely, they come to the conclusion that no morality at all is binding, after the truth has dawned upon them that to different peoples moral valuations are necessarily different: both of which conclusions are equally childish follies. The error of the more subtle amongst them is that they discover and criticize the probably foolish opinions of a people about its own morality, or the opinions of mankind about human morality generally; they treat accordingly of its origin, its religious sanctions, the superstition of free will, and such matters; and they think that just by so doing they have criticized the morality itself.

But the worth of a precept, "Thou shalt," is still fundamentally different from and independent of such opinions about it, and must be distinguished from the weeds of error with which it has perhaps been overgrown: just as the worth of a medicine to a sick person is altogether independent of the question whether he has a scientific opinion about medicine, or merely thinks about it as an old wife would do. A morality could even have grown out of an error, but with this knowledge the problem of its worth would not even be touched. Thus, no one has hitherto tested the value of that most celebrated of all medicines, called morality: for which purpose it is first of all necessary for one to call it in question. Well, that is just our work.

 ASK YOURSELF

9.108. Nietzsche has mentioned three main kinds of mistakes people make when attempting to understand morality. What are they?

Slave Morality versus Aristocratic Morality. Nietzsche claims to find slavish values and resentments at the base of moral beliefs and standards.

From NIETZSCHE: *Genealogy of Morals*

The revolt of the slaves in morals begins in the very principle of resentment becoming creative and giving birth to values—a resentment experienced by creatures who, deprived as they are of the proper outlet of action, are forced to find their compensation in an imaginary revenge. While every aristocratic morality springs from a triumphant affirmation of its own demands, the slave morality says "no" from the very outset to what is "outside itself," "different from itself," and "not itself": and this "no" is its creative deed. This turn about [*volte-face*] of the valuing standpoint—this inevitable gravitation to the objective instead of back to the subjective is typical of "resentment": the slave morality requires as the condition of its existence an external and objective world, to employ physiological terminology, it requires objective stimuli to be capable of action at all—its action is fundamentally a reaction. The contrary is the case when we come to the aristocrat's system of values: it acts and grows spontaneously, it merely seeks its antithesis in order to pronounce a more grateful and exultant "yes" to its own self; its negative conception, "low," 'vulgar," "bad," is merely a pale late born foil in comparison with its positive and fundamental conception (saturated as it is with life and passion) of "we aristocrats, we good ones, we beautiful ones, we happy ones."

 ASK YOURSELF

9.109. Does it sound as though an aristocrat is a kind of "positive" thinker, a slave a "negative" thinker? Explain.

The Greeks and Aristocratic Morality. Nietzsche thinks that in the ancient Greek writers we can find a conception of the "good" person as the proud person who is too far above ordinary folk to care what they think or do. Only the aristocrat is really honest in his morality.

. . . [D]ue weight should be given to the consideration that in any case the mood of contempt, or disdain, or superciliousness, even on the supposition that it falsely portrays the object of its contempt, will always be far removed from that degree of falsity which will always characterize the attacks—in effigy, of course, of the vindictive hatred and revengefulness of the weak in onslaughts on their enemies. In point of fact, there is in contempt too strong an admixture of nonchalance, of casualness, of boredom, of impatience, even of personal exultation, for it to be capable of distorting its victim into a real caricature or a real monstrosity. Attention again should be paid to the almost benevolent nuances which, for instance, the Greek nobility imports into all the words by which it distinguishes the common people from itself; note how continuously a kind of pity, care, and consideration imparts its honeyed flavor, until at last almost all the words which are applied to the vulgar man survive finally as expressions for "unhappy," "worthy of pity" . . . and how, conversely, "bad," "low," "unhappy" have never ceased to ring in the Greek ear with a tone in which "unhappy" is the predominant note: this is a heritage of the old noble aristocratic morality, which remains true to itself even in contempt. . . . The "well-born" simply felt themselves the "happy"; they did not have to manufacture their happiness artificially through looking at their enemies, or in cases to talk and lie themselves into happiness (as is the custom with all resentful men); and similarly, complete men as they were, exuberant with strength, and consequently necessarily energetic, they were too wise to dissociate happiness from action—activity becomes in their minds necessarily counted as happiness . . . all in sharp contrast to the "happiness" of the weak and the oppressed, with their festering venom and malignity, among whom happiness appears essentially as a narcotic, a deadening, a quietude, a peace, a "Sabbath," an enervation of the mind and relaxation of the limbs—in short, a purely passive phenomenon. While the aristocratic man lived in confidence and openness with himself (the term for "noble-born," emphasizes the nuance "sincere," and perhaps also "naive"), the resentful man, on the other hand, is neither sincere nor naive, nor honest and candid with himself.

 ASK YOURSELF

9.110. Mention four traits of the noble person.

9.111. Mention four traits of the slavish person.

The Difference between the Aristocrat and the Slave with Regard to Revenge. Nietzsche argues that the differences between the noble person and the slave show up in different attitudes toward revenge.

 From NIETZSCHE: *Human, All Too Human*, Book 1

Hence they [aristocrats] practice the duel, although the law also offers them aid in obtaining satisfaction for what they have suffered. They are not satisfied with a safe means of recovering their honor, because this would not prove their fearlessness. In the first-named variety of revenge [the slavish] it is just fear that strikes the counterblow; in the second case it is the absence of fear, which, as has been said, wishes to manifest itself in the counterblow. Thus nothing appears more different than the motives of the two courses of action which are designated by the one word "revenge." Yet it often happens that the avenger is not precisely certain as to what really prompted his deed: perhaps he struck the counterblow from fear and the instinct of self-preservation, but in the background, when he has time to reflect upon the standpoint of wounded honor, he imagines that he has avenged himself for the sake of his honor—this motive is in any case more reputable than the other. An essential point is whether he sees his honor injured in the eyes of others (the world) or only in the eyes of his offenders: in the latter case he will prefer secret, in the former open revenge. Accordingly, as he enters strongly or feebly into the soul of the doer and the spectator, his revenge will be more bitter or more tame. If he is entirely lacking in this sort of imagination, he will not think at all of revenge, as the feeling of "honor" is not present in him, and accordingly cannot be wounded. In the same way, he will not think of revenge if he despises the offender and the spectator; because as objects of his contempt they cannot give him honor, and accordingly cannot rob him of honor.

 ASK YOURSELF

9.112. According to Nietzsche, if a noble person was insulted by a slavish person in the presence of other slavish persons, would he take revenge? Why or why not?

Finally, he will forego revenge in the not uncommon case of his loving the offender. It is true that he then suffers loss of honor in the other's eyes, and will perhaps become less worthy of having his love returned. But even to renounce all requital of love is a sacrifice that love is ready to make when its only object is to avoid hurting the beloved object: this would mean hurting oneself more than one is hurt by the sacrifice. Accordingly, everyone will avenge himself, unless he be bereft of honor or inspired by contempt or by love for the offender. Even if he turns to the law courts, he desires revenge as a private individual; but also, as a thoughtful, prudent man of society, he desires the revenge of society upon one who does not respect it. Thus by legal punishment private honor as well as that of society is restored—that is to say, punishment is revenge. Punishment undoubtedly contains the first-mentioned element of revenge, in as far as by its means society helps to preserve itself, and strikes a counterblow in self-defense. Punishment desires to prevent further injury, to scare other offenders. In this way the two elements of revenge, different as they are, are united in punishment, and this may perhaps tend most of all to maintain the abovementioned confusion of ideas, thanks to which the individual avenger generally does not know what he really wants.

 ASK YOURSELF

9.113. Would Nietzsche think that most people who want capital punishment want it for revenge, for deterrence, or for both?

 From NIETZSCHE: *Human, All Too Human*, Book II

The Word "Vanity." It is annoying that certain words, with which we moralists positively cannot dispense, involve in themselves a kind of censorship of morals, dating from the times when the most ordinary and natural impulses were denounced. Thus that fundamental conviction that on the waves of society we either find navigable waters or suffer shipwreck far more through what we appear than through what we are (a conviction that must act as guiding principle of all action in relation to society) is branded with the general word "vanity." In other words, one of the most weighty and significant of qualities is branded with an expression which denotes it as essentially empty and negative: a great thing is designated by a diminutive, ay, even slandered by the strokes of caricature. There is no help for it; we must use such words, but then we must shut our ears to the insinuations of ancient habits.

ASK YOURSELF

9.114. Why do you suppose Nietzsche would think vanity a *good* thing?

The Real Reason for Hanging on to Morality. Morality, as already indicated, is an expression of weakness. It is also a disguise, or clothing to conceal our shame over the fact that we are willful, immoral animals.

 From NIETZSCHE: *Joyful Wisdom*

Why We Can Hardly Dispense with Morality. The naked man is generally an ignominious spectacle—I speak of us European males (and by no means of European females!). If the most joyous company at table suddenly found themselves stripped and divested of their garments through the trick of an enchanter, I believe that not only would the joyousness be gone and the strongest appetite lost—it seems that we Europeans cannot at all dispense with the masquerade that is called clothing. But should not the disguise of "moral men," the screening under moral formulas and notions of decency, the whole kindly concealment of our conduct under conceptions of duty, virtue, public sentiment, honorableness, and disinterestedness, have just as good reasons in support of it? Not that I mean hereby that human wickedness and baseness, in short, the evil wild beast in us, should be disguised; on the contrary, my idea is that it is precisely as tame animals that we are an ignominious spectacle and require moral disguising—that the "inner man" in Europe is far from having enough of intrinsic evil "to let himself be seen" with it (to be beautiful with it). The European disguises himself in morality because he has become a sick, sickly, crippled animal, who has good reasons for being "tame," because he is almost an abortion, an imperfect, weak, and clumsy thing. . . . [I]t is not the fierceness of the beast of prey that finds moral disguise necessary, but the gregarious animal, with its profound mediocrity, anxiety, and ennui. Morality dresses up the European—let us acknowledge it!—in more distinguished, more important, more conspicuous guise—in "divine" guise.

If we were strong, says Nietzsche we would not have to disguise our "evil" behavior. And the disguise consists not only of our lip service to morality, but also of our lip service to religion, the "divine" disguise.

The Death of God

It should already be clear how Nietzsche combines his critique of morality with a critique of religion. In his book *The Joyful Wisdom* (quoted in this section) he makes this critique of religion explicit in a famous parable.

The Significance of the End of Religious Belief. Nietzsche was not a casual atheist who thought that giving up belief in God would make no difference. But he thinks that people are giving up that belief without fully realizing the consequences. The following parable expresses these ideas.

The Madman.—Have you ever heard of the madman who on a bright morning lighted a lantern and ran to the market place calling out unceasingly: "I seek God! I seek God!"—As there were many people standing about who did not believe in God, he caused a great deal of amusement. Why? is he lost? said one. Has he strayed away like a child? said another. Or does he keep himself hidden? Is he afraid of us? Has he taken a sea voyage? Has he emigrated?—the people cried out laughingly, all in a hubbub. The insane man jumped into their midst and transfixed them with his glances. "Where is God gone?" he called out. "I mean to tell you. We have killed him—you and I. We are all his murderers. But how have we done it? How were we able to drink up the sea? Who gave us the sponge to wipe away the whole horizon? What did we do when we loosened this earth from its sun? Whither does it now move? Whither do we move? Away from all suns? Do we not dash on unceasingly? Backward, sideways, forward, in all directions? Is there still an above and below? Do we not stray, as through infinite nothingness? Does not empty space breathe upon us?"

 ASK YOURSELF

9.115. In this passage Nietzsche refers to certain modern beliefs that all of us hold. What are they?

A "horizon" is a limit. In the most literal sense, it is the limit of our vision; it is "as far as we can see." But there are also moral, religious, and other cultural "horizions," that is, limits on our vision or understanding, beyond which we feel unable to see anything, or which hem us in in various ways. Keep this in mind in evaluating the claim made in the previous passage about "wiping away" the horizon.

"Has it not become colder? Does not night come on continually, darker and darker? Shall we not have to light lanterns in the morning? Do we not hear the noise of the gravediggers who are burying God? Do we not smell the divine putrefaction? For even Gods putrefy. God is dead. God remains dead. And we have killed him. How shall we console ourselves, the most murderous of all murderers? The holiest and the mightiest that the world has hitherto possessed has bled to death under our knife—who will wipe the blood from us? With what water could we cleanse ourselves? What lustrums, what sacred games shall we have to devise? Is not the magnitude of this deed too great for us? Shall we not ourselves have to become Gods, merely to seem worthy of it? There never was a greater event, and on account of it, all who are born after us belong to a higher history than any history hitherto"—Here the madman was silent and looked again at his hearers; they also were silent and looked at him in surprise. At last he threw his lantern on the ground, so that it broke in pieces and was extinguished. "I come too early," he then said, "I am not yet at the right time. This prodigious event is still on its way, and is traveling—it has not yet reached men's ears. Lightning and thunder need time, the light of the stars needs time, deeds need time, even after they are done, to be seen and heard. This deed is as yet further from them than the furthest star and yet they have done it!"—It is further stated that the madman made his way into different churches on the same day, and there intoned his Requiem aeternam deo. When led out and called to account, he always gave the reply: "What are these churches now, if they are not the tombs and monuments of God?"

 ## ASK YOURSELF

9.116. What does the madman mean when he says he has "come too early"?

9.117. Do you think your belief in God is as strong as your grandparents' belief in God? It is as strong as the belief of someone who lived a thousand years ago?

9.118. In Europe today the great cathedrals are largely empty on Sunday mornings. Does that fact tend to confirm the madman's claims?

Scientific and Religious Dogmatism. Nietzsche argues that the belief in science that has come to replace religious belief for many people is really itself a hangover from religious and "metaphysical" attitudes.

. . . [I]t is always a metaphysical belief on which our belief in science rests—and that even we knowing ones of today, the godless and anti-metaphysical, still take our fire from the conflagration kindled by a belief a millennium old, the Christian belief, which was also the belief of Plato, that God is truth, that the truth is divine. . . . But what if this itself always becomes more untrustworthy, what if nothing any longer proves itself divine, except it be error, blindness, and falsehood; what if God himself turns out to be our most persistent lie?

Nietzsche seems to be suggesting that the belief in "truth" is itself outmoded. There is no fixed truth, not even in science. The belief that there is truth is a leftover from belief in God. The two go together.

 ## ASK YOURSELF

9.119. If there is no truth, what might we have to say (or avoid saying) about Nietzsche's own writings?

The Consequences of the End of Religious Belief. Nietzsche believes that the consequences of the loss of religion are so radical that it is difficult to imagine them.

The most important of more recent events—that "God is dead," that the belief in the Christian God has become unworthy of belief—already begins to cast its first shadows over Europe. To the few at least whose eye, whose suspecting glance, is strong enough and subtle enough for this drama, some sun seems to have set, some old, profound confidence seems to have changed into doubt: our old world must seem to them daily more darksome, distrustful, strange, and "old." In the main, however, one may say that the event itself is far too great, too remote, too much beyond most people's power of apprehension for one to suppose that so much as the report of it could have reached them; not to speak of many who already knew what had really taken place, and what must all collapse now that this belief had been undermined—because so much was built upon it, so much rested on it, and had become one with it: for example, our entire European morality. This lengthy, vast, and uninterrupted process of crumbling, destruction, ruin, and overthrow which is now imminent: who has realized it sufficiently today to have to stand up as the teacher and herald of such a tremendous logic of terror, as the prophet of a period of gloom and eclipse, the like of which has probably never taken place on earth before? . . . Even we, the born riddle-readers, who wait as it were on the mountains posted 'twixt today and tomorrow, and engirt by their contradiction, we, the firstlings and premature children of the coming century, into whose sight especially the shadows which must forthwith envelop Europe should already have come—how is it that even we, without genuine sympathy for this period of gloom, contemplate its advent without any personal solicitude or fear?

Religion, Science, Pessimism, and So On and Need. People are reluctant to give up religion because of a certain need to believe, to rely on something. But that same need shows itself in many other forms.

347. *Believers and Their Need of Belief.* How much faith a person requires in order to flourish, how much "fixed opinion" he requires which he does not wish to have shaken, because he holds himself thereby—is a measure of his power (or more plainly speaking, of his weakness). Most people in old Europe, as it seems to me, still need Christianity at present, and on that account it still finds belief. For such is man: a theological dogma might be refuted to him a thousand times—provided, however, that he had need of it, he would again and again accept it as "true" according to the famous "proof of power" of which the Bible speaks. Some have still need of metaphysics; but also the impatient longing for certainty which at present discharges itself in scientific, positivist fashion among large numbers of the people, the longing by all means to get at something stable (while on account of the warmth of the longing the establishing of the certainty is more leisurely and negligently undertaken): even this is still the longing for a hold, a support; in short, the instinct of weakness, which, while not actually creating religions, metaphysics, and convictions of all kinds, nevertheless, preserves them. In fact, around all these positivist systems there fume the vapors of a certain pessimistic gloom, something of weariness, fatalism, disulusionment, and fear of new disillusionment—or else manifest animosity, ill-humor, anarchic exasperation, and whatever there is of symptom or masquerade of the feeling of weakness. Even the readiness with which our cleverest contemporaries get lost in wretched corners and alleys, for example,

in Vaterliinderei (so I designate Jingoism, called chauvinisme in France, and deutsch in Germany) [i.e., extreme patriotism], or in petty aesthetic creeds in the manner of Parisian nature (which only brings into prominence and uncovers that aspect of nature which excites simultaneously disgust and astonishment, they like at present to call this aspect la verite vraie), or in Nihilism in the St. Petersburg style (that is to say, in the belief in unbelief, even to martyrdom for it): this shows always and above all the need of belief, support, backbone, and buttress. . . .

 ## ASK YOURSELF

9.120. The need (for certainty, and so on) that fuels religious belief also fuels at least six other movements or tendencies. List them.

9.121. Nietzsche was attractive to some Nazis, for reasons that might be obvious. Given what Nietzsche has just said about patriotism and false certainties, do you think *he* would have been attracted to *them*?

The Need Mentioned Above Is the Result of a Lack of Will. A central theme in Nietzsche is "the will to power." The healthy person, the aristocrat, does as he wills, not as religion or morality or science or anything else dictates.

Belief is always most desired, most pressingly needed where there is a lack of will, for the will, as emotion of command, is the distinguishing characteristic of sovereignty and power. That is to say, the less a person knows how to command, the more urgent is his desire for one who commands, who commands sternly—a God, a prince, a caste, a physician, a confessor, a dogma, a party conscience. From whence perhaps it could be inferred that the two world religions, Buddhism and Christianity, might well have had the cause of their rise, and especially of their rapid extension, in an extraordinary malady of the will. And in truth it has been so: both religions lighted upon a longing, monstrously exaggerated by malady of the will, for an imperative, a "Thou shalt," a longing going the length of despair; both religions were teachers of fanaticism in times of slackness of will power, and thereby offered to innumerable persons a support, a new possibility of exercising will, an enjoyment in willing. For in fact fanaticism is the sole "volitional strength" to which the weak and irresolute can be excited, as a sort of hypnotizing of the entire sensory-intellectual system, in favor of the over-abundant nutrition (hypertrophy) of a particular point of view and a particular sentiment, which then dominates—the Christian calls it his faith. When a man arrives at the fundamental conviction that he requires to be commanded, he becomes "a believer." Reversely, one could imagine a delight and a power of self determining, and a freedom of will whereby a spirit could bid farewell to every belief, to every wish for certainty, accustomed as it would be to support itself on slender cords and possibilities, and to dance even on the verge of abysses. Such a spirit would be the free spirit par excellence.

Nietzsche wants to affirm that the person who frees herself of religion, morality, and so on will not fall into pessimism, despair, or nihilism, but will be affirming of life, joyous, dancing "even on the verge of abysses." But he has a question.

Is This Nihilism? Nietzsche wonders if his own exhortations might lead to nihilism, the denial that anything is of any worth.

Our Note of Interrogation. But you don't understand it? As a matter of fact, an effort will be necessary in order to understand us. We seek for words; we seek perhaps also for ears. Who are we after all? If we wanted simply to call ourselves in older phraseology, atheists, unbelievers, or even immoralists, we should still be far from thinking ourselves designated thereby: we are all three in too late a phase for people generally to conceive, for you, my inquisitive friends, to be able to conceive, what is our state of mind under the circumstances. No, we have no longer the bitterness and passion of him who has broken loose, who has to make for himself a belief, a goal, and even a martyrdom out of his unbelief! We have become saturated with the conviction (and have grown cold and hard in it) that things are not at all divinely ordered in this world, nor even according to human standards do they go on rationally, mercifully, or justly: we know the fact that the world in which we live is ungodly, immoral, and "inhuman"; we have far too long interpreted it to ourselves falsely and mendaciously, according to the wish and will of our veneration, that is to say, according to our need.

 ASK YOURSELF

9.122. See the section that discusses Nietzsche's first book, and explain its connection to the remarks just made.

For man is a venerating animal. But he is also a distrustful animal: and that the world is not worth what we have believed it to be worth is about the surest thing our distrust has at last managed to grasp. So much distrust, so much philosophy! We take good care not to say that the world is of less value; it seems to us at present absolutely ridiculous when man claims to devise values to surpass the values of the actual world; it is precisely from that point that we have retraced our steps; as from an extravagant error of human conceit and irrationality, which for a long period has not been recognized as such. This error had its last expression in modern Pessimism; an older and stronger manifestation in the teaching of Buddha; but Christianity also contains it, more dubiously, to be sure, and more ambiguously, but nonetheless seductive on that account. The whole attitude of "man versus the world," man as world-denying principle, man as the standard of the value of things, as judge of the world, who in the end puts existence itself on his scales and finds it too light—the monstrous impertinence of this attitude has dawned upon us as such, and has disgusted us—we now laugh when we find, "Man and World" placed beside one another, separated by the sub-lime presumption of the little word "and." But how is it? Have we not in our very laughing just made a further step in despising mankind? And consequently also in Pessimism, in despising the existence cognizable by us? Have we not just thereby become liable to a suspicion of an opposition between the world in which we have hitherto been at home with our venerations—for the sake of which we perhaps endure life—and another world which we ourselves are: an inexorable, radical, most profound suspicion concerning ourselves, which is continually getting us Europeans more annoyingly into its power, and could easily face the coming generation with the terrible alternative: Either do away with your venerations, or with yourselves! The latter would be Nihilism; but would not the former also be Nihilism? This is our note of interrogation.

 ASK YOURSELF

9.123. What sort of thing does Nietzsche have in mind when he speaks of "venerations"?

Nietzsche advocates living life willfully, with self-confidence, pride, honest contempt for weakness, and respect only for those who respect themselves and are one's equals. He speaks of a coming "superman" who would embody these ideals. The superman would live "beyond good and evil."

 ASK YOURSELF

9.124. Discuss in some detail why this ideal of life seems to be inconsistent with both Christianity and morality. Then give your personal opinion of Nietzsche's ideal.

In his book *Thus Spake Zarathustra*, Nietzsche imagines the Persian prophet Zarathustra proposing a new morality appropriate to a "superman."

 From NIETZSCHE: *Thus Spake Zarathustra*

. . . 3. When Zarathustra arrived at the nearest town which adjoins the forest, he found many people assembled in the market-place; for it had been announced that a rope-dancer would give a performance. And Zarathustra spoke so to the people:

I teach you the Superman. Man is something that is to be surpassed. What have you done to surpass man?

All beings formerly have created something beyond themselves: and you want to be the ebb of that great tide, and would rather go back to the beast than surpass man?

What is the ape to man? A laughing-stock, a thing of shame. And just the same shall man be to the Superman: a laughing-stock, a thing of shame.

You have made your way from the worm to man, and much within you is still worm. Once were you apes, and even yet man is more of an ape than any of the apes.

ASK YOURSELF

9.125. Nietzsche was very interested in Darwin. What is "Darwinian" in the preceding passage?

Even the wisest among you is only a disharmony and hybrid of plant and phantom. But do I bid you become phantoms or plants?

Observe, I teach you the Superman!

The Superman is the meaning of the earth. Let your will say: The Superman shall be the meaning of the earth!

I summon you, my brothers, remain true to the earth, and believe not those who speak to you of super-earthly hopes! They are Poisoners, whether they know it or not.

 ASK YOURSELF

9.126. What sort of people, most typically, are inclined to speak of super-earthly hopes?

They are Despisers of life, decaying ones and poisoned ones themselves, of whom the earth is weary: so away with them!

Once blasphemy against God was the greatest blasphemy; but God died, and then also those blasphemers. To blaspheme the earth is now the dreadfulest sin, and to rate the heart of the unknowable higher than the meaning of the earth!

Once the soul looked contemptuously on the body, and then that contempt was the supreme thing:—the soul wished the body meager, ghastly, and famished. So it thought to escape from the body and the earth.

Oh, that soul was itself meager, ghastly, and famished; and cruelty was the delight of that soul!

But you, also, my brothers, tell me: What does your body say about your soul? Is your soul not poverty and pollution and wretched self-complacency?

To be sure, a polluted stream is man. One must be a sea, to receive a polluted stream without becoming impure.

So you see, I teach you the Superman: he is that sea; in him can your great contempt be submerged.

What is the greatest thing you can experience? It is the hour of great contempt. The hour in which even your happiness becomes loathsome to you, and so also your reason and virtue.

The hour when you say: "What good is my happiness! It is poverty and pollution and wretched self-complacency. But my happiness should justify existence itself!"

The hour when you say: "What good is my reason! Does it long for knowledge as the lion for his food? It is poverty and pollution and wretched self-complacency!"

The hour when you say: "What good is my virtue! As yet it has not made me passionate. How weary I am of my good and my bad! It is all poverty and pollution and wretched self-complacency!"

The hour when you say: "What good is my justice! I do not see that I am fervor and fuel. The just, however, are fervor and fuel!"

The hour when you say: "What good is my pity! Is not pity the cross on which he is nailed who loves man? But my pity is not a crucifixion."

Have you ever spoken so? Have you ever cried so? Ah! would that I had heard you crying so!

It is not your sin—it is your self-satisfaction that cries to heaven; your very sparingness in sin cries to heaven!

Where is the lightning to lick you with its tongue? Where is the frenzy with which you should be inoculated?

So you see, I teach you the Superman: he is that lightning, he is that frenzy!

When Zarathustra had so spoken, one of the people called out: "We have now heard enough of the rope-dancer; it is time now for us to see him!" And all the people laughed at Zarathustra. But the rope-dancer, who thought the words applied to him, began his performance.

4. Zarathustra, however, looked at the people and wondered. Then he spoke so:

Man is a rope stretched between the animal and the Superman—a rope over an abyss.

A dangerous crossing, a dangerous wayfaring, a dangerous looking-back, a dangerous trembling and halting.

What is great in man is that he is a bridge and not a goal: what is lovable in man is that he is an over-going and a down-going.

I love those that know not how to live except as down-goers, for they are the over-goers.

I love the great despisers, because they are the great adorers, and arrows of longing for the other shore.

I love those who do not first seek a reason beyond the stars for going down and being sacrifices, but sacrifice themselves to the earth, that the earth of the Superman may hereafter arrive.

I love him who lives in order to know, and seeks to know in order that the Superman may hereafter live. So seeks he his own down-going.

Much of the preceding passages can be related to the "Dionysian" theme in Nietzsche (see pp. 594–95) and can also be compared to the character Ivan Karamozov in Dostoyevsky's novel *The Karamozov Brothers*. Like Zarathustra, Ivan does not "seek a reason . . . for going down" (for his experience of meaningless sufferings, for instance).

I love him who labors and invents, that he may build the house for the Superman, and prepare for him earth, animal, and plant: for so seeks he his own down-going.

I love him who loves his virtue: for virtue is the will to down-going, and an arrow of longing.

I love him who reserves no share of spirit for himself, but wants to be wholly the spirit of his virtue: so walks he as spirit over the bridge.

I love him who makes his virtue his inclination and destiny: so, for the sake of his virtue, he is willing to live on, or live no more.

I love him who desires not too many virtues. One virtue is more of a virtue than two, because it is more of a knot for one's destiny to cling to.

I love him whose soul is lavish, who wants no thanks and does not give back: for he always bestows, and does not desire to keep for himself.

I love him who is ashamed when the dice fall in his favor, and who then asks: "Am I a dishonest player?"—for he is willing to succumb.

I love him who scatters golden words in advance of his deeds, and always does more than he promises: for he seeks his own down-going.

I love him who justifies the future ones, and redeems the past ones: for he is willing to succumb through the present ones.

I love him who chastens his God, because he loves his God: for he must succumb through the wrath of his God.

I love him whose soul is deep even in the wounding, and may succumb through a small matter: so goes he willingly over the bridge.

I love him whose soul is so overfull that he forgets himself, and all things are in him: so all things become his down-going.

I love him who is of a free spirit and a free heart: so is his head only the bowels of his heart; his heart, however, causes his down-going.

I love all who are like heavy drops falling one by one out of the dark cloud that lowers over man: they herald the coming of the lightning, and succumb as heralds.

So you see, I am a herald of the lightning, and a heavy drop out of the cloud: the lightning, however, is the Superman.

5. When Zarathustra had spoken these words, he again looked at the people, and was silent. "There they stand," he said to his heart; "there they laugh: they understand me not; I am not the mouth for these ears.

Must one first batter their ears, that they may learn to hear with their eyes? Must one clatter like kettledrums and penitential preachers? Or do they only believe the stammerer?

They have something whereof they are proud. What do they call it, that which makes them proud? Culture, they call it; it distinguishes them from the goatherds.

They dislike, therefore, to hear of 'contempt' of themselves. So I will appeal to their pride.

I will speak to them of the most contemptible thing: that, however, is the last man!"

And so spoke Zarathustra to the people:

It is time for man to fix his goal. It is time for man to plant the germ of his highest hope.

Still is his soil rich enough for it. But that soil will one day be poor and exhausted, and no lofty tree will any longer be able to grow thereon.

Alas! there comes the time when man will no longer launch the arrow of his longing beyond man—and the string of his bow will have unlearned to whizz!

I tell you: one must still have chaos in one, to give birth to a dancing star. I tell you: you have still chaos in you.

Alas! There comes the time when man will no longer give birth to any star. Alas! There comes the time of the most despicable man, who can no longer despise himself.

Notice: I show you the last man.

"What is love? What is creation? What is longing? What is a star?"—so asks the last man and blinks.

The earth has then become small, and on it there hops the last man who makes everything small. His species is ineradicable like that of the ground-flea; the last man lives longest.

"We have discovered happiness"—say the last men, and blink thereby.

 ASK YOURSELF

9.127. What philosophers have made maximizing happiness the crucial criterion for action?

They have left the regions where it is hard to live; for they need warmth. One still loves one's neighbor and rubs against him; for one needs warmth.

Turning ill and being distrustful, they consider sinful: they walk warily. He is a fool who still stumbles over stones or men!

A little poison now and then: that makes pleasant dreams. And much poison at last for a pleasant death.

One still works, for work is a pastime. But one is careful unless the pastime should hurt one.

One no longer becomes poor or rich; both are too burdensome. Who still wants to rule? Who still wants to obey? Both are too burdensome.

No shepherd, and one herd! Everyone wants the same; everyone is equal: those who have other sentiments go voluntarily into the madhouse.

"Formerly all the world was insane,"—say the subtlest of them, and blink thereby.

They are clever and know all that has happened: so there is no end to their raillery. People still fall out, but are soon reconciled—otherwise it spoils their stomachs.

They have their little pleasures for the day, and their little pleasures for the night, but they have a regard for health.

"We have discovered happiness,"—say the last men, and blink thereby.—

And here ended the first discourse of Zarathustra, which is also called "The Prologue," for at this point the shouting and mirth of the multitude interrupted him. "Give us this last man, O Zarathustra,"—they called out—"make us into these last men! Then will we make you a present of the Superman!" And all the people exulted and smacked their lips. Zarathustra, however, turned sad, and said to his heart:

"They didn't understand me: I am not the mouth for these ears.

Too long, perhaps, have I lived in the mountains; too much have I listened to the brooks and trees: now do I speak to them as to the goatherds.

My soul is calm and clear, like the mountains in the morning. But they think I am cold, and a mocker with terrible jests.

And now they look at me and laugh: and while they laugh they hate me too. There is ice in their laughter."

SUGGESTIONS FOR FURTHER READING

Primary Sources

Hegel

Hegel, G. W. F. *Elements of the Philosophy of Right*, trans. H. B. Nisbet, ed. A. Wood (Cambridge: Cambridge University Press, 1991). One variety of conservative political thought.

———. *Introduction to the Philosophy of History*, trans. L. Rauch (Indianapolis: Hackett Publishing Company, 1988). History is fundamental to Hegel's thinking about all topics.

———. *Lectures on the Philosophy of Religion*, trans. C. P. Hodgson and R. F. Brown (Los Angeles. University of California Press, 1984–1987) Three volumes; religion turned into philosophy.

———. *Phenomenology of Spirit*, trans. A. V. Miller (Oxford: Clarendon Press, 1970). A more recent translation of this major work than the one used in this text.

———. *Philosophy of Nature*, trans. and ed. M. J. Petry (London: Allen & Unwin, 1970). Three volumes; informative introduction and excellent explanatory notes.

Kant

Kant, Immanuel. *Critique of Pure Reason*, trans. Werner S. Pluhar and patricia Kitcher (Indianapolis: Hackett Publishing Company, 1996). Recent translation of Kant's principal work in metaphysics and epistemology.

———. *Grounding for the Metaphysics of Morals*, trans. James W. Ellington (Indianapolis: Hackett Publishing Company, 1985). Translation of Kant's most accessible discussion of his moral theory.

———. *Prolegomena to Any Future Metaphysics That Will Be Able to Come Forward as Science*, trans. Paul Carus and James W. Ellington (Indianapolis: Hackett Publishing Company, 1977). Kant's simplified account of his *Critique of Pure Reason*.

Kierkegaard

Kierkegaard, Søren. *Kierkegaard's Writings*, ed. and trans. Howard Hong (Princeton, NJ: Princeton University Press). The complete works of Kierkegaard in relatively recent English translations; from Princeton University Press, Howard Hong, General editor and Principal translator *Either/Or* is contained in Volumes III and IV.

Mill

Mill, John Stuart. *Essays on Ethics, Religion and Society*, ed. J. M. Robson (Toronto: University of Toronto Press, 1969). Critical edition of various essays, which includes *Utilitarianism*.

———. *A System of Logic*, ed. J. M. Robson (Toronto: University of Toronto Press, 1973). Critical edition of Mill's principal work in epistemology.

Nietzsche

Nietzsche, F. W. *Basic Writings of Nietzsche*, ed. Walter Kaufmann (New York: Modern Library, 1968.) A large selection.

———. *The Complete Works of Nietzsche*, ed. Oscar Levy (London: Foulis, 1910). A variety of older translations.

———. *The Portable Nietzsche*, ed. Walter Kaufmann (New York: Viking Press, 1954). A good collection of selections from major works.

Reid

Reid, Thomas. *An Inquiry into the Human Mind on the Principles of Common Sense: A Critical Edition* (Edinburgh: Edinburgh University Press, 1997). Critical edition of Reid's first philosophical work.

———. *The Works of Thomas Reid*, ed. William Hamilton (Bristol, England: Thoemmes Press, 1994). Facsimile reprint of the standard two-volume collection of Reid's published philosophical works with extensive introductions by William Hamilton.

Wollstonecraft

Wollstonecraft, Mary. *The Works of Mary Wollstonecraft*, ed. J. Todd and M. Butler (London: William Pickering, 1989). Seven-volume collection of Wollstonecraft's complete writings, including *A Vindication of the Rights of Woman*.

Critical Analyses and Discussions

Hegel

Beiser, Frederick C., ed. *The Cambridge Companion to Hegel* (Cambridge University Press, 1993). Collection of essays on various topics in Hegel's philosophy.

Hardimon, M. *The Project of Reconciliation: Hegel's Social Philosophy* (Cambridge: Cambridge University Press. 1994). Hegel's views on the relation between the individual and the modern social world.

Harris, H. S. *Hegel's Development*. Vol. 1, *Toward the Sunlight 1770–1801*; vol. 2, *Night Thoughts. Jena 1801–1806* (Oxford: Oxford University Press). Hegel's intellectual development in the light of his early writings.

Inwood, M. *Hegel* (London: Routledge & Kegan Paul, 1983). Critical discussion of central topics.

Pippin, R. B. *Hegel's Idealism: The Satisfactions of Self-Consciousness* (Cambridge: Cambridge University Press, 1989). Focus on Hegel's epistemology and its Kantian sources.

Stern, R., ed. *G. W. F. Hegel: Critical Assessments* (London: Routledge & Kegan Paul, 1993). Four volumes; a large collection of essays on Hegel.

Taylor, C. *Hegel* (Cambridge: Cambridge University Press, 1975). A fine and comprehensive introduction to Hegel for the English-speaking reader.

Kant

Chadwick, R., ed. *Immanuel Kant: Critical Assessments* (London: Routledge, 1992). Four volumes; large collection of essays on Kant.

———, ed. *Kant's Groundwork of the Metaphysics of Morals: Critical Essays* (New York: Rowman & Littlefield, 1998). Recent collection of essays on Kant's moral theory.

Guyer, Paul, ed. *The Cambridge Companion to Kant* (Cambridge: Cambridge University Press, 1992). Collection of essays on various topics.

Höffe, O. *Immanuel Kant* (Albany: State University of New York Press, 1994). Overview of Kant's theory.

Walker, R. C. S. *Kant* (London: Routledge & Kegan Paul, 1978). Overview of Kant's theory.

Wolff, R. P., ed. *Kant: A Collection of Critical Essays* (Garden City: Doubleday Anchor, 1967).

Kierkegaard

Gardiner, Patrick. *Kierkegaard* (Oxford: Oxford University Press, 1988). A brief general introduction.

Hannay, Alastair, and Marino, Gordon, eds. *The Cambridge Companion to Kierkegaard* (Cambridge: Cambridge University Press, 1998). Essays on the major pseudonymous works, but with copious references to other parts of Kierkegaard's works.

Krimse, Bruce. *Kierkegaard in Golden Age Denmark* (Bloomington: Univeristy of Indiana Press, 1990). In-depth study of the historical setting for Kierkegaard's work and a discussion of each major work.

Lowrie, Walter. *A Short Life of Kierkegaard* Princeton; NJ:) Princeton University Press, 1942). A well-known biography of a remarkable personality.

Malantschuk, G. *Kierkegaard's Thought*, ed. and trans. H. V. and E. H. Hong (Princeton, NJ: Princeton University Press, 1971). Exploration of the interrelations of Kierkegaard's leading ideas.

Rudd, A. *Kierkegaard and the Limits of the Ethical* (Oxford: Oxford University Press, 1993). Relates Kierkegaard to modern analytical philosophy.

Weston, M. *Kierkegaard and Modern Continental Philosophy* (London and New York: Routledge, 1994). Relates Kierkegaard's critique of traditional forms of philosophy to the radical tradition represented by such later thinkers as Nietzsche, Heidegger, and Derrida.

Mill

Skorupski, John, ed. *The Cambridge Companion to Mill* (Cambridge: Cambridge University Press, 1998). Collection of essays on various topics.

Berger, F. R. *Happiness, Justice and Freedom: The Moral and Political Philosophy of John Stuart Mill* (London: University of California Press, 1984). Very informative study of Mill's moral and political philosophy.

Crisp, R. *Mill on Utilitarianism* (London: Routledge. 1997). Very recent up-to-date study of utilitarianism.

Nietzsche

Kaufmann, W. *Nietzsche: Philosopher, Psychologist Antichrist* (Princeton, NJ: Princeton University Press, 1974). Critiques the picture of Nietzsche as a Nazi sympathizer and an anti-Socratic irrationalist.

Magnus, Bernd, ed. *The Cambridge Companion to Nietzsche* (Cambridge: Cambridge University Press, 1996). Collection of recent essays on various topics.

Morgen, G., *What Nietzsche Means* (New York: Harper & Row, 1941). Accessible introduction to the main themes of Nietzsche's philosophy.

Nehamas, A. *Nietzsche: Life as Literature* (Cambridge, MA: Harvard University Press, 1985). Relates Nietzsche's philosophical views to his literary styles.

Schacht, R. *Nietzsche* (London: Routledge & Kegan Paul, 1983). Survey of the main themes of Nietzsche's philosophy.

Reid

Dalgarno, M., and Matthews, E., eds. *The Philosophy of Thomas Reid* (London: Kluwer, 1989).

Fieser, James, ed. *Early Responses to Reid, Oswald, Beattie and Stewart* (Briston, England: Thoemmes Press, 2000). Two-volume collection of eighteenth- and nineteenth-century critical responses to Reid and other Scottish commonsense philosophers.

Wollstonecraft

Sapiro, V. *A Vindication of Political Virtue: The Political Theory of Mary Wollstonecraft* (Chicago: University of Chicago Press, 1992). Survey and critical discussion of Wollstonecraft's philosophy.

CHAPTER 10

20TH–CENTURY AND CONTEMPORARY PHILOSOPHY

wentieth-century philosophy carried forward the preoccupations and arguments of the nineteenth century. The quest for a certain basis for knowledge, particularly of an empirical kind, is evident in the selection from Bertrand Russell included in this chapter. The influence of Kant, Kierkegaard, and Nietzsche is detectable in the reading from Sartre. But something relatively new in several of the authors in this chapter makes them representative of their time, namely, an intense concern with language. New developments in logic early in the twentieth century were part of the stimulus for this linguistic turn. The works of Russell and Quine both exemplify some of the ways in which the new logic, which is considerably more powerful than the Aristotelian logic that dominated logic courses through the nineteenth century, can be brought to bear on puzzles about meaning, reference, and related troublesome notions.

New and often anti-Cartesian ways of thinking about mind and the self also surfaced in the twentieth century and are very evident in the works of Quine and Wittgenstein included here. It is also perhaps worth mentioning that more or less "pragmatist" styles of reasoning appealed to many twentieth-century thinkers. Although pragmatism is particularly associated with such American thinkers of the late nineteenth and early twentieth century as C. S. Pierce and William James, the emphasis on the "practical" in some sense is very evident in much of twentieth-century philosophy, including most of the works cited here. That is not to claim that these thinkers deserve to be called "pragmatists," but it does highlight some interesting similarities between positions that in other respects are quite diverse.

Finally, the last third of the twentieth century saw developments in ethics that departed from the focus on the Kantian, utilitarian, and emotivist theories that characterized much of nineteenth- and twentieth-century thought. The essay by Anscombe, from 1958, has proved to be one of the main sources for that departure and for a return to an interest in the "classical tradition" (as found in Aristotle), a tradition in which questions about moral psychology and the virtues are prominent.

This chapter begins with Russell, because of his importance for both Wittgenstein and Quine. It continues with Sartre and concludes with Anscombe's essay.

BERTRAND RUSSELL

Knowledge by Acquaintance and Knowledge by Description

British philosopher Bertrand Russell (1872–1970) was one of the leading figures in early twentieth-century philosophy. Throughout his long life he made a mark both as a prolific writer on a variety of philosophical subjects and also as a political activist. Following in the Empiricist tradition set by David Hume, Russell was a philosophical and religious skeptic. His most memorable philosophical contributions are in the area of philosophical logic. Espousing a position called *logicism*, he argued that all of pure mathematics can be deduced from logical principles. He also believed that embedded in our vague verbal utterances is a more precise logical structure to our meaning, and it is the job of philosophy to develop this more perfect logical language. One application of this idea is mentioned in what follows. Russell's "theory of descriptions" tried to remove the mystery that seems to result from the use of names or descriptions of nonexistent things. What are we to say, for instance, of "the present king of France is bald"? If we deny that this is true we seem to have to assume the existence of the present king of France in order to do so. Russell tried to show that the referential work done by the definite description "the present king of France" could be taken over by variables and quantifiers (x, y, all, at least one) in such a way that we could escape having to assume or presuppose the existence of that king while using that form of words. The details of that theory, and its representation in the notation of symbolic logic, are not discussed here, but the theory was considered by many, notably Quine, to be a model of how logic could be applied to philosophical problems.

Many of Russell's writings on logic and language are highly technical and dominated by symbolic notation. But in 1912 he published a short book titled *The Problems of Philosophy*, in which he presents many of his views in a nontechnical fashion. In Chapter 5 of that work—titled "Knowledge by Acquaintance and Knowledge by Description"—he explores two key ways of discovering knowledge about existing things.

Knowledge by Acquaintance. According to Russell, if I say, "I know that the President of the United States exists," I may mean one of two things. First, I may mean that I know of his existence by experiencing him directly; this Russell calls knowledge by acquaintance. Or, I may mean that I know of his existence only indirectly, such as by reading about him in the paper; this Russell calls knowledge by description. Russell thinks that this is an obvious distinction, but one that philosophers often ignore when they place too much emphasis on knowledge acquired through immediate experience.

 From RUSSELL: *Problems of Philosophy*

In the preceding chapter we saw that there are two sorts of knowledge: knowledge of things, and knowledge of truths. In this chapter we shall be concerned exclusively with knowledge of things, of which in turn we shall have to distinguish two kinds. Knowledge of things, when it is of the kind we call knowledge by *acquaintance*, is essentially simpler than any knowledge of truths, and logically independent of knowledge of truths, though it would be rash to assume that human beings ever, in fact, have acquaintance with things without at the same time knowing some truth about them. Knowledge of things by *description*, on the contrary, always involves, as we shall find in the course of the present chapter, some knowledge of truths as its source and ground. But first of all we must make clear what we mean by "acquaintance" and what we mean by "description."

We shall say that we have *acquaintance* with anything of which we are directly aware, without the intermediary of any process of inference or any knowledge of truths. Thus in the presence of my table I am acquainted with the sense-data that make up the appearance of my table—its color, shape, hardness, smoothness, etc.; all these are things of which I am immediately conscious when I am seeing and touching my table. The particular shade of color that I am seeing may have many things said about it—I may say that it is brown, that it is rather dark, and so on. But such statements, though they make me know truths *about* the color, do not make me know the color itself any better than I did before: so far as concerns knowledge of the color itself, as opposed to knowledge of truths about it, I know the color perfectly and completely when I see it, and no further knowledge of it itself is even theoretically possible. Thus the sense-data which make up the appearance of my table are things with which I have acquaintance, things immediately known to me just as they are.

 ## ASK YOURSELF

10.1. What does Russell mean by "acquaintance"?

10.2. What things about the table can we know by acquaintance?

My knowledge of the table as a physical object, on the contrary, is not direct knowledge. Such as it is, it is obtained through acquaintance with the sense-data that make up the appearance of the table. We have seen that it is possible, without absurdity, to doubt whether there is a table at all, whereas it is not possible to doubt the sense-data. My knowledge of the table is of the kind which we shall call "knowledge by description." The table is "the physical object which causes such-and-such sense-data." This *describes* the table by means of the sense-data. In order to know anything at all about the table, we must know truths connecting it with things with which we have acquaintance: we must know that "such-and-such sense-data are caused by a physical object." There is no state of mind in which we are directly aware of the table; all our knowledge of the table is really knowledge *of truths*, and the actual thing which is the table is not, strictly speaking, known to us at all. We know a description, and we know that there is just one object to which this description applies, though the object itself is not directly known to us. In such a case, we say that our knowledge of the object is knowledge by description.

 ## ASK YOURSELF

10.3. What things do we not know about the table by acquaintance?

Sense Data, Memory, and Introspection. Russell argues that we can have direct acquaintance of only a few types of things. One type is sense data, that is, information that is directly presented to our senses. Another is memory. Here our ideas of past events are perceived directly before our mind's eye. We are also directly acquainted with our bodily feelings, such as hunger, and our emotions, such as anger. Additionally, we are directly acquainted with our awareness of our hunger, or, more generally, with our own introspection.

All our knowledge, both knowledge of things and knowledge of truths, rests upon acquaintance as its foundation. It is therefore important to consider what kinds of things there are with which we have acquaintance.

Sense-data, as we have already seen, are among the things with which we are acquainted; in fact, they supply the most obvious and striking example of knowledge by acquaintance. But if they were the sole example, our knowledge would be very much more restricted than it is. We should only know what is now present to our senses: we could not know anything about the past—not even that there was a past— nor could we know any truths about our sense-data, for all knowledge of truths, as we shall show, demands acquaintance with things which are of an essentially different character from sense-data, the things which are sometimes called "abstract ideas," but which we shall call "universals." We have therefore to consider acquaintance with other things besides sense-data if we are to obtain any tolerably adequate analysis of our knowledge.

The first extension beyond sense-data to be considered is acquaintance by *memory*. It is obvious that we often remember what we have seen or heard or had otherwise present to our senses, and that in such cases we are still immediately aware of what we remember, in spite of the fact that it appears as past and not as present. This immediate knowledge by memory is the source of all our knowledge concerning the past: without it, there could be no knowledge of the past by inference, since we should never know that there was anything past to be inferred.

The next extension to be considered is acquaintance by *introspection*. We are not only aware of things, but we are often aware of being aware of them. When I see the sun, I am often aware of my seeing the sun; thus "my seeing the sun" is an object with which I have acquaintance. When I desire food, I may be aware of my desire for food; thus "my desiring food" is an object with which I am acquainted. Similarly we may be aware of our feeling pleasure or pain, and generally of the events which happen in our minds. This kind of acquaintance, which may be called self-consciousness, is the source of all our knowledge of mental things. It is obvious that it is only what goes on in our own minds that can be thus known immediately. What goes on in the minds of others is known to us through our perception of their bodies, that is, through the sense-data in us which are associated with their bodies. But for our acquaintance with the contents of our own minds, we should be unable to imagine the minds of others, and therefore we could never arrive at the knowledge that they have minds. It seems natural to suppose that self-consciousness is one of the things that distinguish men from animals: animals, we may suppose, though they have acquaintance with sense-data, never become aware of this acquaintance. I do not mean that they *doubt* whether they exist, but that they have never become conscious of the fact that they have sensations and feelings, nor therefore of the fact that they, the subjects of their sensations and feelings, exist.

 ASK YOURSELF

10.4. What, for Russell, is one of the differences between humans and animals?

Knowledge of the Self. Russell next raises the question of whether we are directly acquainted with one's *self*. Hume argued in his *Treatise of Human Nature* that we have no direct experience of the self: "For my part, when I enter most intimately into what I call myself, I always stumble on some particular perception or other, of heat or cold, light or shade, love or hatred, pain or pleasure. I never can catch myself at any time without a perception, and never can observe anything but the perception." Russell attempts to avoid Hume's conclusion.

We have spoken of acquaintance with the contents of our minds as *self*-consciousness, but it is not, of course, consciousness of our *self*: it is consciousness of particular thoughts and feelings. The question whether we are also acquainted with our bare selves, as opposed to particular thoughts and feelings, is a very difficult one, upon which it would be rash to speak positively. When we try to look into ourselves we always seem to come upon some particular thought or feeling, and not upon the "I" which has the thought or feeling. Nevertheless there are some reasons for thinking that we are acquainted with the "I," though the acquaintance is hard to disentangle from other things. To make clear what sort of reason there is, let us consider for a moment what our acquaintance with particular thoughts really involves.

When I am acquainted with "my seeing the sun," it seems plain that I am acquainted with two different things in relation to each other. On the one hand there is the sense-datum which represents the sun to me, on the other hand there is that which sees this sense-datum. All acquaintance, such as my acquaintance with the sense-datum which represents the sun, seems obviously a relation between the person acquainted and the object with which the person is acquainted. When a case of acquaintance is one with which I can be acquainted (as I am acquainted with my acquaintance with the sense-datum representing the sun), it is plain that the person acquainted is myself. Thus, when I am acquainted with my seeing the sun, the whole fact with which I am acquainted is "Self-acquainted-with-sense-datum."

 ASK YOURSELF

10.5. What is one reason why we might believe that we are directly acquainted with the self?

Further, we know the truth "I am acquainted with this sense-datum." It is hard to see how we could know this truth, or even understand what is meant by it, unless we were acquainted with something which we call "I." It does not seem necessary to suppose that we are acquainted with a more or less permanent person, the same to-day as yesterday, but it does seem as though we must be acquainted with that thing, whatever its nature, which sees the sun and has acquaintance with sense-data. Thus, in some sense it would seem we must be acquainted with our Selves as opposed to our particular experiences. But the question is difficult, and complicated arguments can be adduced on either side. Hence, although acquaintance with ourselves seems *probably* to occur, it is not wise to assert that it undoubtedly does occur.

We may therefore sum up as follows what has been said concerning acquaintance with things that exist. We have acquaintance in sensation with the data of the outer senses, and in introspection with the data of what may be called the inner sense—thoughts, feelings, desires, etc.; we have acquaintance in memory with things which have been data either of the outer senses or of the inner sense. Further, it is probable, though not certain, that we have acquaintance with Self, as that which is aware of things or has desires towards things.

 ASK YOURSELF

10.6. What does Russell finally conclude about knowledge of the self?

Knowledge by Description. For Russell, we can be directly acquainted with sense-data, memory, bodily sensations, emotions, introspection, and possibly the self. Along with these he adds that we may be directly acquainted with universals. He then turns to an examination of knowledge by description, that is, knowledge we have by reading or hearing about something, but not directly perceiving it. The list of things about which we have knowledge by description is endless. Anything that we know from reading in print, seeing on television, or hearing reports of by other people is knowledge by description. Russell is not interested in listing all the things about which we can have this sort of knowledge. Instead, he is interested in explaining what linguistically takes place when we say, "I know X" by description. He begins his investigation by distinguishing between ambiguous and definite descriptions.

In addition to our acquaintance with particular existing things, we also have acquaintance with what we shall call *universals*, that is to say, general ideas, such as *whiteness*, *diversity*, *brotherhood*, and so on. Every complete sentence must contain at least one word which stands for a universal, since all verbs have a meaning which is universal. We shall return to universals later on, in Chapter IX; for the present, it is only necessary to guard against the supposition that whatever we can be acquainted with must be something particular and existent. Awareness of universals is called *conceiving*, and a universal of which we are aware is called a *concept*.

It will be seen that among the objects with which we are acquainted are not included physical objects (as opposed to sense-data), nor other people's minds. These things are known to us by what I call "knowledge by description," which we must now consider.

By a "description" I mean any phrase of the form "a so-and-so" or "the so-and-so." A phrase of the form "a so-and-so" I shall call an "ambiguous" description; a phrase of the form "the so-and-so" (in the singular) I shall call a "definite" description. Thus "a man" is an ambiguous description, and "the man with the iron mask" is a definite description. There are various problems connected with ambiguous descriptions, but I pass them by, since they do not directly concern the matter we are discussing, which is the nature of our knowledge concerning objects in cases where we know that there is an object answering to a definite description, though we are not *acquainted* with any such object. This is a matter which is concerned exclusively with definite descriptions. I shall therefore, in the sequel, speak simply of "descriptions" when I mean "definite descriptions." Thus a description will mean any phrase of the form "the so-and-so" in the singular.

ASK YOURSELF

10.7. What is the difference between ambiguous and definite descriptions?

Definite Descriptions Regarding Existence. Russell focuses next on definite descriptions. One type of definite description involves a simple existence claim about someone, such as, "I know that the current President of the United States exists." Russell argues that the description of the object in question (e.g., "the current President of the United States") must be unique and apply to only one person. Another type of definite description involves a piece of information about someone, such as "I know that the current President of the United States lives in the White House."

We shall say that an object is "known by description" when we know that it is "the so-and-so," i.e. when we know that there is one object, and no more, having a certain property; and it will generally be implied that we do not have knowledge of the same object by acquaintance. We know that the man with the iron mask existed, and many propositions are known about him; but we do not know who he was. We know that the candidate who gets the most votes will be elected, and in this case we are very likely also acquainted (in the only sense in which one can be acquainted with someone else) with the man who is, in fact, the candidate who will get most votes; but we do not know which of the candidates he is, i.e. we do not know any proposition of the form "A is the candidate who will get most votes" where A is one of the candidates by name. We shall say that we have "merely descriptive knowledge" of the so-and-so when, although we know that the so-and-so exists, and although we may possibly be acquainted with the object which is, in fact, the so-and-so, yet we do not know any proposition "*a* is the so-and-so," where *a* is something with which we are acquainted.

When we say "the so-and-so exists," we mean that there is just one object which is the so-and-so. The proposition "*a* is the so-and-so" means that *a* has the property so-and-so, and nothing else has. "Mr. A. is the Unionist candidate for this constituency" means "Mr. A. is a Unionist candidate for this constituency, and no one else is." "The Unionist candidate for this constituency exists" means "someone is a Unionist candidate for this constituency, and no one else is." Thus, when we are acquainted with an object which is the so-and-so, we know that the so-and-so exists; but we may know that the so-and-so exists when we are not acquainted with any object which we know to be the so-and-so, and even when we are not acquainted with any object which, in fact, is the so-and-so.

ASK YOURSELF

10.8. With an existence claim, when we say an object is known by description, what do we mean?

Names Are Disguised Definite Descriptions. Russell argues that proper names and pronouns are in fact disguised definite descriptions. For example, if I look at a picture in a history book and say, "He is the current President of the United States," the word "he" here stands for a definite description such as "the person who posed for this particular photo," since only one unique person posed for that picture. Written out more precisely, then, when I look at that photo and say, "He is the so-and-so," my utterance really means, "I know that the person who posed for this particular photo is the current President of the United States." Thus, this statement involves two definite descriptions. Russell illustrates this point with reference to Otto von Bismarck, the first Chancellor of the German Empire.

Common words, even proper names, are usually really descriptions. That is to say, the thought in the mind of a person using a proper name correctly can generally only be expressed explicitly if we replace the proper name by a description. Moreover, the description required to express the thought will vary for different people, or for the same person at different times. The only thing constant (so long as the name is rightly used) is the object to which the name applies. But so long as this remains constant, the particular description involved usually makes no difference to the truth or falsehood of the proposition in which the name appears.

Let us take some illustrations. Suppose some statement made about Bismarck. Assuming that there is such a thing as direct acquaintance with oneself, Bismarck himself might have used his name directly to designate the particular person with whom he was acquainted. In this case, if he made a judgment about himself, he himself might be a constituent of the judgment. Here the proper name has the direct use which it always wishes to have, as simply standing for a certain object, and not for a description of the object. But if a person who knew Bismarck made a judgment about him, the case is different. What this person was acquainted with were certain sense-data which he connected (rightly, we will suppose) with Bismarck's body. His body, as a physical object, and still more his mind, were only known as the body and the mind connected with these sense-data. That is, they were known by description. It is, of course, very much a matter of chance which characteristics of a man's appearance will come into a friend's mind when he thinks of him; thus the description actually in the friend's mind is accidental. The essential point is that he knows that the various descriptions all apply to the same entity, in spite of not being acquainted with the entity in question.

When we, who did not know Bismarck, make a judgment about him, the description in our minds will probably be some more or less vague mass of historical knowledge—far more, in most cases, than is required to identify him. But, for the sake of illustration, let us assume that we think of him as "the first Chancellor of the German Empire." Here all the words are abstract except "German." The word "German" will, again, have different meanings for different people. To some it will recall travels in Germany, to some the look of Germany on the map, and so on. But if we are to obtain a description which we know to be applicable, we shall be compelled, at some point, to bring in a reference to a particular with which we are acquainted. Such reference is involved in any mention of past, present, and future (as opposed to definite dates), or of here and there, or of what others have told us. Thus it would seem that, in some way or other, a description known to be applicable to a particular must involve some reference to a particular with which we are acquainted, if our knowledge about the thing described is not to be merely what follows *logically* from the description. For example, "the most long-lived of men" is a description involving only universals, which must apply to some man, but we can make no judgments concerning this man which involve knowledge about him beyond what the description gives. If, however, we say, "The first Chancellor of the German Empire was an astute diplomatist," we can only be assured of the truth of our judgment in virtue of something with which we are acquainted—usually a testimony heard or read. Apart from the information we convey to others, apart from the fact about the actual Bismarck, which gives importance to our judgment, the thought we really have contains the one or more particulars involved, and otherwise consists wholly of concepts.

 ASK YOURSELF

10.9. When we use the name "Bismarck," what definite description are we likely to have in mind?

All names of places—London, England, Europe, the Earth, the Solar System—similarly involve, when used, descriptions which start from some one or more particulars with which we are acquainted. I suspect that even the Universe, as considered by metaphysics, involves such a connection with particulars. In logic, on the contrary, where we are concerned not merely with what does exist, but with whatever might or could exist or be, no reference to actual particulars is involved.

It would seem that, when we make a statement about something only known by description, we often *intend* to make our statement, not in the form involving the description, but about the actual thing described. That is to say, when we say anything about Bismarck, we should like, if we could, to make the judgment which Bismarck alone can make, namely, the judgment of which he himself is a constituent. In this we are necessarily defeated, since the actual Bismarck is unknown to us. But we know that there is an object B, called Bismarck, and that B was an astute diplomatist. We can thus *describe* the proposition we should like to affirm, namely, "B was an astute diplomatist," where B is the object which was Bismarck. If we are describing Bismarck as "the first Chancellor of the German Empire," the proposition we should like to affirm may be described as "the proposition asserting, concerning the actual object which was the first Chancellor of the German Empire, that this object was an astute diplomatist." What enables us to communicate in spite of the varying descriptions we employ is that we know there is a true proposition concerning the actual Bismarck, and that however we may vary the description (so long as the description is correct) the proposition described is still the same. This proposition, which is described and is known to be true, is what interests us; but we are not acquainted with the proposition itself, and do not know it, though we know it is true.

Description Rests on Acquaintance. Russell notes that definite descriptions must ultimately reduce to knowledge by acquaintance. For example, my knowledge that "the current President of the United States lives in the White House" is based on my reading this fact, which involves direct acquaintance with visual sense data.

It will be seen that there are various stages in the removal from acquaintance with particulars: there is Bismarck to people who knew him; Bismarck to those who only know of him through history; the man with the iron mask; the longest-lived of men. These are progressively further removed from acquaintance with particulars; the first comes as near to acquaintance as impossible in regard to another person; in the second, we shall still be said to know "who Bismarck was"; in the third, we do not know who was the man with the iron mask, though we can know many propositions about him which are not logically deducible from the fact that he wore an iron mask; in the fourth, finally, we know nothing beyond what is logically deducible from the definition of the man. There is a similar hierarchy in the region of universals. Many universals, like many particulars, are only known to us by description. But here, as in the case of particulars, knowledge concerning what is known by description is ultimately reducible to knowledge concerning what is known by acquaintance.

The fundamental principle in the analysis of propositions containing descriptions is this: *Every proposition which we can understand must be composed wholly of constituents with which we are acquainted.*

 ASK YOURSELF

10.10. What is the fundamental principle in the analysis of propositions containing descriptions?

We shall not at this stage attempt to answer all the objections which may be urged against this fundamental principle. For the present, we shall merely point out that, in some way or other, it must be possible to meet these objections, for it is scarcely conceivable that we can make a judgment or entertain a supposition without knowing what it is that we are judging or supposing about. We must attach *some* meaning to the words we use, if we are to speak significantly and not utter mere noise; and the meaning we attach to our words must be something with which we are acquainted. Thus when, for example, we make a statement about Julius Caesar, it is plain that Julius Caesar himself is not before our minds, since we are not acquainted with him. We have in mind some *description* of Julius Caesar: "the man who was assassinated on the Ides of March," "the founder of the Roman Empire," or, perhaps, merely "the man whose name was *Julius Caesar.*" (In this last description, *Julius Caesar* is a noise or shape with which we are acquainted.) Thus our statement does not mean quite what it seems to mean, but means something involving, instead of Julius Caesar, some description of him which is composed wholly of particulars and universals with which we are acquainted.

The chief importance of knowledge by description is that it enables us to pass beyond the limits of our private experience. In spite of the fact that we can only know truths which are wholly composed of terms which we have experienced in acquaintance, we can yet have knowledge by description of things which we have never experienced. In view of the very narrow range of our immediate experience, this result is vital, and until it is understood, much of our knowledge must remain mysterious and therefore doubtful.

LUDWIG WITTGENSTEIN

Introduction

Wittgenstein (1889–1951) was born and raised in Vienna but spent much of his adult life at the University of Cambridge in England. He studied with Russell at Cambridge and later taught there himself. Russell's search for an exact language underlying ordinary languages appealed to him at first, but he later rejected it emphatically. He published only a few works, most notably an early book titled *Tractatus Logico Philosophicus*, which made a deep impression on Russell and the logical positivists of the Vienna Circle. Toward the end of his life he was working on the *Philosophical Investigations*, which is excerpted in this section. He never completed another book, but the impression he made as a teacher and thinker was so powerful that every effort was made to preserve a record of his thought; his students kept notes, some of which have been published, and his literary executors collected together various of his notes (including the manuscript for the *Investigations*) and published them after his death.

As the selections here will show, his style is epigrammatic and seemingly unsystematic. Partly for that reason, and because of the original and unusual character of his thinking, the correct interpretation of his works continues to be a matter of controversy. The editorial comments and questions interspersed in the following selections try to steer clear of interpretative bias, but that is a particularly difficult task in this case and no claim to success is made here. Wittgenstein was constantly preoccupied with language and with mind, and he was highly critical of much of the philosophical discussion of both. This is evident in the following selections from Part I of *Philosophical Investigations*, which is in the form of 691 numbered paragraphs.

Language and Use

What is it that makes marks on paper, or utterances, meaningful? Wittgenstein begins his *Philosophical Investigations* by examining this question.

Meaning and Reference. Many philosophers from Plato to the present have supposed that reference is a key to meaning. The meaning of a word or symbol is what it refers to. A variant of that view is present in the quotation from Augustine with which Wittgenstein opens his *Philosophical Investigations*. In the *Tractatus* Wittgenstein himself developed a complex version of such a view, but here he criticizes it. What such a view requires is an account of *how* words refer. It is natural to suppose that something "in the mind" makes the connection between the word and the thing for which it stands. Thus, if an ant crawling around in the sand should spell out the word "book" we would not suppose that the ant "meant" a book or referred to a book, since it was not "thinking" or "meaning" anything (obviously it has no "mind" capable of "meaning" things). But when a human being utters or writes that word, we usually take it to mean something, and we may suppose that what makes the marks "mean" has something to do with the "thought" behind their utterance.

From WITTGENSTEIN: *Philosophical Investigations*, _
Part 1

1. "When they (my elders) named some object, and accordingly moved towards something, I saw this and I grasped that the thing was called by the sound they uttered when they meant to point it out. Their intention was shown by their bodily movements, as it were the natural language of all peoples: the expression of the face, the play of the eyes, the movement of other parts of the body, and the tone of voice which expresses our state of mind in seeking, having, rejecting, or avoiding something. Thus, as I heard words repeatedly used in their proper places in various sentences, I gradually learned to understand what objects they signified; and after I had trained my mouth to form these signs, I used them to express my own desires" (Augustine, *Confessions*, I.8).

These words, it seems to me, give us a particular picture of the essence of human language. It is this: the individual words in language name objects—sentences are combinations of such names.—In this picture of language we find the roots of the following idea: Every word has a meaning. This meaning is correlated with the word. It is the object for which the word stands.

Augustine does not speak of there being any difference between kinds of word. If you describe the learning of language in this way you are, I believe, thinking primarily of nouns like "table," "chair," "bread," and of people's names, and only secondarily of the names of certain actions and properties; and of the remaining kinds of word as something that will take care of itself.

Now think of the following use of language: I send someone shopping. I give him a slip marked "five red apples." He takes the slip to the shopkeeper, who opens the drawer marked "apples"; then he looks up the word "red" in a table and finds a color sample opposite it; then he says the series of cardinal numbers—I assume that he knows them by heart—up to the word "five" and for each number he takes an apple of the same color as the sample out of the drawer.—It is in this and similar ways that one operates with words.—"But how does he know where and how he is to look up the word 'red' and what he is to do with the word 'five'?"—Well, I assume that he *acts* as I have described. Explanations come to an end somewhere.—But what is the meaning of the word "five"?—No such thing was in question here, only how the word "five" is used.

We may suppose that meaning something by a word is a matter of having some sort of mental image. For example, I am able to mean something by "red" because I have a kind of image in my mind of redness, and when something comes along that matches that image I may call it red.

 ASK YOURSELF

10.11. In Wittgenstein's discussion so far, is there any need to postulate such an image in order to explain how the shopkeeper manages to pick apples of the right color?

2. That philosophical concept of meaning has its place in a primitive idea of the way language functions. But one can also say that it is the idea of a language more primitive than ours.

Let us imagine a language for which the description given by Augustine is right.

That is, "right" in the sense that each word in the language seems to label some object.

The language is meant to serve for communication between a builder A and an assistant B. A is building with building-stones: there are blocks, pillars, slabs and beams. B has to pass the stones, and that in the order in which A needs them. For this purpose they use a language consisting of the words "block," "pillar," "slab," "beam." A calls them out;—B brings the stone which he has learnt to bring at such-and-such a call.—Conceive this as a complete primitive language.

3. Augustine, we might say, does describe a system of communication; only not everything that we call language is this system. And one has to say this in many cases where the question arises "Is this an appropriate description or not?" The answer is: "Yes, it is appropriate, but only for this narrowly circumscribed region, not for the whole of what you were claiming to describe."

It is as if someone were to say: "A game consists in moving objects about on a surface according to certain rules . . ."—and we replied: You seem to be thinking of board games, but there are others. You can make your definition correct by expressly restricting it to those games.

4. Imagine a script in which the letters were used to stand for sounds, and also as signs of emphasis and punctuation. (A script can be conceived as a language for describing sound-patterns.) Now imagine someone interpreting that script as if there were simply a correspondence of letters to sounds and as if the letters had not also completely different functions. Augustine's conception of language is like such an over-simple conception of the script.

5. If we look at the example in §1, we may perhaps get an inkling how much this general notion of the meaning of a word surrounds the working of language with a haze which makes clear vision impossible. It disperses the fog to study the phenomena of language in primitive kinds of application in which one can command a clear view of the aim and functioning of the words.

A child uses such primitive forms of language when it learns to talk. Here the teaching of language is not explanation, but training.

6. We could imagine that the language of §2 was the *whole* language of A and B; even the whole language of a tribe. The children are brought up to perform *these* actions, to use *these* words as they do so, and to react in *this* way to the words of others.

An important part of the training will consist in the teacher's pointing to the objects, directing the child's attention to them, and at the same time uttering a word; for instance, the word "slab" as he points to that shape. (I do not want to call this "ostensive definition," because the child cannot as yet *ask* what the name is. I will call it "ostensive teaching of words."—I say that it will form an important part of the training, because it is so with human beings; not because it could not be imagined otherwise.) This ostensive teaching of words can be said to establish an association between the word and the thing. But what does this mean? Well, it can mean various things; but one very likely thinks first of all that a picture of the object comes before the child's mind when it hears the word. But now, if this does happen—is it the purpose of the word?—Yes, it *can* be the purpose.—I can imagine such a use of words (of series of sounds). (Uttering a word is like striking a note on the keyboard of the imagination.) But in the language of §2 it is *not* the purpose of the words to evoke images. (It may, of course, be discovered that that helps to attain the actual purpose.)

 ASK YOURSELF

10.12. What then *is* the purpose of the words as described in Section 2?

But if the ostensive teaching has this effect,—am I to say that it effects an understanding of the word? Don't you understand the call "Slab!" if you act upon it in such-and-such a way?—Doubtless the ostensive teaching helped to bring this about; but only together with a particular training. With different training the same ostensive teaching of these words would have effected a quite different understanding.

"I set the brake up by connecting up rod and lever."—Yes, given the whole of the rest of the mechanism. Only in conjunction with that is it a brake-lever, and separated from its support it is not even a lever; it may be anything, or nothing.

Something is a brake handle only by virtue of its connection with other parts of a mechanism. Otherwise it may be just a nice handlelike thing or a good club. By analogy, a mark or utterance has meaning (is the meaning-bearing sort of thing) only by virtue of its connection to other utterances, to actions and ways of getting things done, and so forth.

7. In the practice of the use of language (2) one party calls out the words, the other acts on them. In instruction in the language the following process will occur: the learner *names* the objects; that is, he utters the word when the teacher points to the stone.— And there will be this still simpler exercise: the pupil repeats the words after the teacher—both of these being processes resembling language.

We can also think of the whole process of using words in (2) as one of those games by means of which children learn their native language. I will call these games "language-games" and will sometimes speak of a primitive language as a language-game.

And the processes of naming the stones and of repeating words after someone might also be called language-games. Think of much of the use of words in games like ring-a-ring-a-roses.

I shall also call the whole, consisting of language and the actions into which it is woven, the "language-game."

8. Let us now look at an expansion of language (2). Besides the four words "block," "pillar," etc., let it contain a series of words used as the shopkeeper in (1) used the numerals (it can be the series of letters of the alphabet); further, let there be two words, which may as well be "there" and "this" (because this roughly indicates their purpose), that are used in connection with a pointing gesture; and finally a number of

color samples. A gives an order like: "d–slab—there." At the same time he shows the assistant a color sample, and when he says "there" he points to a place on the building site. From the stock of slabs B takes one for each letter of the alphabet up to "d," of the same color as the sample, and brings them to the place indicated by A.—On other occasions A gives the order "this—there." At crisis he points to a building stone. And so on.

9. When a child learns this language, it has to learn the series of numerals a, b, c, . . . by heart. And it has to learn their use.—Will this training include ostensive teaching of the words?—Well, people will, for example, point to slabs and count: "a, b, c slabs." Something more like the ostensive teaching of the words "block," "pillar," etc. would be the ostensive teaching of numerals that serve not to count but to refer to groups of objects that can be taken in at a glance. Children do learn the use of the first five or six cardinal numerals in this way.

Are "there" and "this" also taught ostensively?—Imagine how one might perhaps teach their use. One will point to places and things—but in this case the pointing occurs in the *use* of the words too and not merely in learning the use.—

It often seems natural to suppose that we learn words by "ostension" (i.e., by pointing to an object and saying its name). Someone points to an object and says "slab" or "cow" and in that way we come to learn what those words mean (i.e., refer to). But that is too simple an account. Ostension itself (pointing to something) is just part of an activity that includes actions and the use of words that could not possibly have been learned by ostension, such words as "this" and "there." (What would you point to to teach them?)

10. Now what do the words of this language *signify*?—*What is* supposed to show what they signify, if not the kind of use they have? And we have already described that. So we are asking for the expression "This word signifies *this*" to be made a part of the description. In other words the description ought to take the form: "The word . . . signifies . . .

Of course, one can reduce the description of the use of the word "slab" to the statement that this word signifies this object. This will be done when, for example, it is merely a matter of removing the mistaken idea that the word "slab" refers to the shape of building-stone that we in fact call a "block"—but the kind of *referring* this is, that is to say the use of these words for the rest, is already known.

Equally one can say that the signs "a," "b," etc. signify numbers; when for example this removes the mistaken idea that "a," "b," "c" play the part actually played in language by "block," "slab," "Pillar." And one can also say that "c" means this number and not that one; when for example this serves to explain that the letters are to be used in the order a, b, c, d, etc. and not in the order a, b, d, C.

But assimilating the descriptions of the uses of words in this way cannot make the uses themselves any more like one another. For, as we see, they are absolutely unlike.

The notion of reference, Wittgenstein shows, and of teaching the reference of a word by ostension, is not the notion of one thing or activity. Thus we can say that "slab" refers to the shape of a stone provided we have some contrast in mind, such as the difference in shape between a slab and a block. Getting someone to understand that difference involves training them into activities in which these words play a role. Merely pointing to a slab will not somehow enable someone to understand that what is "meant" is the shape, rather than, say, the color.

 ASK YOURSELF

10.13. Why not?

11. Think of the tools in a tool-box: there is a hammer, pliers, a saw, a screw-driver, a rule, a glue-pot, glue, nails and screws.—The functions of words are as diverse as the functions of these objects. (And in both cases there are similarities.)

Of course, what confuses us is the uniform appearance of words when we hear them spoken or meet them in script and print. For their *application* is not presented to us so clearly. Especially when we are doing philosophy!

12. It is like looking into the cabin of a locomotive. We see handles all looking more or less alike. (Naturally, since they are all supposed to be handled.) But one is the handle of a crank which can be moved continuously (it regulates the opening of a valve); another is the handle of a switch, which has only two effective positions, it is either off or on; a third is the handle of a brake-lever, the harder one pulls on it, the harder it brakes; a fourth, the handle of a pump: it has an effect only so long as it is moved to and fro.

13. When we say: "Every word in language signifies something" we have so far said *nothing whatever*; unless we have explained *exactly what* distinction we wish to make. (It might be, of course, that we wanted to distinguish the words of language (8) from words "without meaning" such as occur in Lewis Carroll's poems, or words like "Lilliburlero" in songs.)

14. Imagine someone's saying: "All tools serve to modify something. Thus the hammer modifies the position of the nail, the saw the shape of the board, and so on."— And what is modified by the rule, the glue-pot, the nails?—"Our knowledge of a thing's length, the temperature of the glue, and the solidity of the box." Would anything be gained by this assimilation of expressions?—

Again, Wittgenstein provides an analogy. There is no one thing that "referring" or "meaning something by a word" comes to, just as there is not one thing that all tools are used for, although we can artificially try to assimilate all the differences to one thing.

15. The word "to signify" is perhaps used in the most straightforward way when the object signified is marked with the sign. Suppose that the tools A uses in building bear certain marks. When A shows his assistant such a mark, he brings the tool that has that mark on it.

It is in this and more or less similar ways that a name means and is given to a thing.—It will often prove useful in philosophy to say to ourselves: naming something is like attaching a label to a thing.

16. What about the color samples that A shows to B: are they part of the *language*? Well, it is as you please. They do not belong among the words; yet when I say to someone: "Pronounce the word "the," you will count the second "the" as part of the sen-

tence. Yet it has a role just like that of a color-sample in language-game (8); that is, it is a sample of what the other is meant to say.

It is most natural, and causes least confusion, to reckon the samples among the instruments of the language.

((Remark on the reflexive pronoun "*this* sentence".))

17. It will be possible to say: In language (8) we have different *kinds of word*. For the functions of the word "slab" and the word "block" are more alike than those of "slab" and "d." But how we group words into kinds will depend on the aim of the classification,—and on our own inclination.

Think of the different points of view from which one can classify tools or chess-men.

18. Do not be troubled by the fact that languages (2) and (8) consist only of orders. If you want to say that this shows them to be incomplete, ask yourself whether our language is complete;—whether it was so before the symbolism of chemistry and the notation of the infinitesimal calculus were incorporated in it; for these are, so to speak, suburbs of our language. (And how many houses or streets does it take before a town begins to be a town?) Our language can be seen as an ancient city: a maze of little streets and squares, of old and new houses, and of houses with additions from various periods; and this surrounded by a multitude of new boroughs with straight regular streets and uniform houses.

19. It is easy to imagine a language consisting only of orders and reports in battle.—Or a language consisting only of questions and expressions for answering yes and no. And innumerable others. And to imagine a language means to imagine a form of life.

 ASK YOURSELF

10.14. What is misleading in saying that the language of Section 2 is "incomplete?"

The expression "form of life" does not occur frequently in this work, but there are reasons for thinking it very important. Wittgenstein is trying to show that what makes words and utterances meaningful, what separates my written "slab" from the ant's "slab" traced in the sand, is a "way of living" distinctive to humans in which words are interwoven with all sorts of nonverbal activities. To know the meaning of a word is to be initiated into such forms of life.

But what about this: is the call "Slab!" in example (1) a sentence or a word?—If a word, surely it has not the same meaning as the like sounding word of our ordinary language, for in §2 it is a call. But if a sentence, it is surely not the elliptical sentence: "Slab!" of our language.—As far as the first question goes you can call "Slab!" a word and also a sentence; perhaps it could be appropriately called a "degenerate sentence" (as one speaks of a degenerate hyperbola); in fact it *is* our "elliptical" sentence.—But that is surely only a shortened form of the sentence "Bring me a slab," and there is no such sentence in example (2).—But why should I not on the contrary have called the sentence "Bring me a slab" a *lengthening* of the sentence "Slab"? Because if you shout "Slab!" you really mean: "Bring me a slab." But how do you do this: how do you *mean that* while you *say "Slab!"*? Do you say the unshortened sentence to yourself? And why should I translate the call "Slab" into a different expression in order to say what someone means by it? And if they mean the same thing—why should I not say: "When he says 'Slab!' he means 'Slab!'"? Again, if you can mean "Bring me the slab," why should you not be able to mean "Slab!"?—But when I call "Slab!", then what I want is, *that he should bring me a slab!*—Certainly, but does "wanting this" consist in thinking in some form or other a different sentence from the one you utter?—

 ## ASK YOURSELF

10.15. Again, what is involved in "meaning something" by a word? Is it having certain "thoughts"?

10.16. What is one reason Wittgenstein gives for denying that when the builder in Section 2 shouts "Slab!" he must *mean* "Bring me a slab"?

---

20. But now it looks as if when someone says "Bring me a slab" he could mean this expression as *one* long word corresponding to the single word "Slab!' Then can one mean it sometimes as one word and sometimes as four? And how does one usually mean it?—I think we shall be inclined to say: we mean the sentence *as four* words when we use it in contrast with other sentences such as "*Hand* me a slab," "Bring *him* a slab," "Bring *two* slabs," etc.; that is, in contrast with sentences containing the separate words of our command in other combinations.—But what does using one sentence in contrast with others consist in? Do the others, perhaps, hover before one's mind? *All* of them? And *while* one is saying the one sentence, or before, or afterwards?—No. Even if such an explanation rather tempts us, we need only think for a moment of what actually happens in order to see that we are going astray here. We say that we use the command in contrast with other sentences because *our language* contains the possibility of those other sentences. Someone who did not understand our language, a foreigner, who had fairly often heard someone giving the order: "Bring me a slab!", might believe that this whole series of sounds was one word corresponding perhaps to the word for "building-stone" in his language. If he himself had then given this order perhaps he would have pronounced it differently, and we should say: he pronounces it so oddly because he takes it for a *single* word.

But then, is there not also something different going on in him when he pronounces it,—something corresponding to the fact that he conceives the sentence as a *single* word?—Either the same thing may go on in him, or something different. For what goes on in you when you give such an order? Are you conscious of its consisting of four words *while* you are uttering it? Of course you have a *mastery* of this language—which contains those other sentences as well—but is this having a mastery something that *happens* while you are uttering the sentence? And I have admitted that the foreigner will probably pronounce a sentence differently if he conceives it differently; but what we call his wrong conception *need* not lie in anything that accompanies the utterance of the command.

ASK YOURSELF

10.17. Here are two of many reasons for doubting that what makes an utterance meaningful is that it is accompanied by particular thoughts or by something "hovering before one's mind."

(1) What makes the builder's use of "slab" amount to the same as "bring me a slab" is not that the builder _____ those four words when he utters "slab," but rather the fact that the single word "slab" can enter into _____ with other words, such as in "hand me a slab" or "bring two slabs."

(2) If thought were what gave meaning to an expression such as "slab," and if what it means in Paragraph 2 is "bring me a slab," then someone using it as it is used in Paragraph 2 should be thinking _____ while they speak it, but that is obviously not so.

The sentence is "elliptical," not because it leaves out something that we think when we utter it, but because it is shortened—in comparison with a particular paradigm of our grammar.—Of course one might object here: "You grant that the shortened and the unshortened sentence have the same sense.—What is this sense, then? Isn't there a verbal expression for this sense?"!—But doesn't the fact that sentences have the same sense consist in their having the same *use*? (In Russian one says "stone red" instead of "the stone is red"; do they feel the copula to be missing in the sense, or attach it in *thought*?)

 ASK YOURSELF

10.18. What is the obvious answer to the question just asked?

21. Imagine a language-game in which A asks and B reports the number of slabs or blocks in a pile, or the colors and shapes of the building-stones that are stacked in such-and-such a place.—Such a report might run: "Five slabs." Now what is the difference between the report or statement "Five slabs" and the order "Five Slabs!"? Well, it is the part which uttering these words plays in the language game. No doubt the tone of voice and the look with which they are uttered, and much else besides, will also be different. But we could also imagine the tone's being the same—for an order and a report can be spoken in a *variety* of tones of voice and with various expressions of face—the difference being only in the application. (Of course, we might use the words "statement" and "command" to stand for grammatical forms of sentence and intonations; we do in fact call "Isn't the weather glorious today?" a question, although it is used as a statement.) We could imagine a language in which all statements had the form and tone of rhetorical questions; or every command the form of the question "Would you like to . . . ?" Perhaps it would then be said: "What he says has the form of a question but is really a command" that is, has the function of a command in the technique of using the language. (Similarly one says "You

will do this" not as a prophecy but as a command. What makes it the one or the other?)

22. Frege's idea that every assertion contains an assumption, which is the thing that is asserted, really rests on the possibility found in our language of writing every statement in the form: "It is asserted that such-and-such is the case."—But "that such-and-such is the case" is not a sentence in our language—so far it is not a *move* in the language game. And if I write, not "It is asserted that . . . ," but "It is asserted: such-and-such is the case," the words "It is asserted" simply become superfluous.

We might very well also write every statement in the form of a question followed by a "Yes"; for instance: "Is it raining? Yes!" Would this show that every statement contained a question?

 ASK YOURSELF

10.19. Again, the answer is obviously _____.

Of course we have the right to use an assertion sign in contrast with a question mark, for example, or if we want to distinguish an assertion from a fiction or a supposition. It is only a mistake if one thinks that the assertion consists of two actions, entertaining and asserting (assigning the truth-value, or something of the kind), and that in performing these actions we follow the propositional sign roughly as we sing from the musical score. Reading the written sentence loud or soft is indeed comparable with singing from a musical score, but *meaning* (thinking) the sentence that is read is not.

Frege's ideas can be and are often connected to the notion that the most important thing we do with language is to make assertions, and that these assertions are important because they alone are the bearers of truth values. In what follows Wittgenstein stresses, in contrast, that there are many different things we do with words, and no particular priority among them. All of them enter into the activities that are our lives.

Many Types of Language Games.   Instead of thinking of language as something that refers to or somehow attaches to the world via a mysterious mental act in which words are *made* to refer, think of it as part of a multitude of different sorts of activities that are not reducible to one another. "Logicians," on the other hand, have often tried to reduce the variety of uses to just a few types, for example, fact-stating or describing, expressing feelings, and giving orders, with the latter two somehow parasitic upon the former.

23. But how many kinds of sentence are there? Say assertion, question, and command?—There are *countless* kinds: countless different kinds of uses of what we call "symbols," "words," and "sentences." And this multiplicity is not something fixed, given once for all; but new types of language, new language-games, as we may say, come into existence, and others become obsolete and get forgotten. (We can get a *rough picture* of this from the changes in mathematics.)

Here the term "language-game" is meant to bring into prominence the fact that the *speaking* of language is part of an activity, or of a form of life.

Review the multiplicity of language-games in the following examples, and in others:

Giving orders, and obeying them—
Describing the appearance of an object, or giving its measurements—
Constructing an object from a description (a drawing)—
Reporting an event—
Speculating about an event—
Forming and testing a hypothesis presenting the results of an experiment in tables
and diagrams—
Making up a story; and reading it—
Play-acting—
Singing catches—
Guessing riddles—
Making a joke; telling it—
Solving a problem in practical arithmetic—
Translating from one language into another—
Asking, thanking, cursing, greeting, praying.

—It is interesting to compare the multiplicity of the tools in language and of the ways they are used, the multiplicity of kinds of word and sentence, with what logicians have said about the structure of language. (Including the author of the *Tractatus Logico-Philosophicus.*) [i.e., Wittgenstein himself].

 ASK YOURSELF

10.20. Might it be that animals do not talk because they lack the thoughts necessary to give words meaning?

25. It is sometimes said that animals do not talk because they lack the mental capacity. And this means: "they do not think, and that is why they do not talk." But—they simply do not talk. Or to put it better: they do not use language—if we except the most primitive forms of language.—Commanding, questioning, recounting, chatting, are as much a part of our natural history as walking, eating, drinking, playing.

26. One thinks that learning language consists in giving names to objects. Viz, to human beings, to shapes, to colors, to pains, to moods, to numbers, etc. To repeat—naming is something like attaching a label to a thing. One can say that this is preparatory to the use of a word. But *what* is it a preparation for?

27. "We name things and then we can talk about them: can refer to them in talk."—As if what we did next were given with the mere act of naming. As if there were only one thing called "talking about a thing." Whereas in fact we do the most various things with our sentences. Think of exclamations alone, with their completely different functions.

Water!
Away!

Ow!
Help!
Fine!
No!

Are you inclined still to call these words "names of objects"?

In languages (2) and (8) there was no such thing as asking something's name. This, with its correlate, ostensive definition, is, we might say, a language-game on its own. That is really to say: we are brought up, trained, to ask: "What is that called?"—upon which the name is given. And there is also a language-game of inventing a name for something, and hence of saying, "This is . . . ." and then using the new name. (Thus, for example, children give names to their dolls and then talk about them and to them. Think in this connection how singular is the use of a person's name to *call him*!)

28. Now one can ostensively define a proper name, the name of a color, the name of a material, a numeral, the name of a point of the compass and so on. The definition of the number two, "That is called 'two' "—pointing to two nuts—is perfectly exact.—But how can two be defined like that? The person one gives the definition to doesn't know what one wants to call "two"; he will suppose that "two" is the name given to *this* group of nuts—He *may* suppose this; but perhaps he does not. He might make the opposite mistake; when I want to assign a name to this group of nuts, he might understand it as a numeral. And he might equally well take the name of a person, of which I give an ostensive definition, as that of a color, of a race, or even of a point of the compass. That is to say: an ostensive definition can be variously interpreted in *every case*.

 ASK YOURSELF

10.21. Once again, ostensive definition will not tie language to the world. Give some reasons why.

. . . [O]ne has already to know (or be able to do) something in order to be capable of asking a thing's name. But what does one have to know?

31. When one shows someone the king in chess and says: "This is the king," this does not tell him the use of this piece—unless he already knows the rules of the game up to this last point: the shape of the king. You could imagine his having learnt the rules of the game without ever having been shown an actual piece. The shape of the chessman corresponds here to the sound or shape of a word.

One can also imagine someone's having learnt the game without ever learning or formulating rules. He might have learnt quite simple board-games first, by watching, and have progressed to more and more complicated ones. He too might be given the explanation "This is the king,"—if, for instance, he were being shown chessmen of a shape he was not used to. This explanation again only tells him the use of the piece because, as we might say, the place for it was already prepared. Or even: we shall only say that it tells him the use, if the place is already prepared. And in this case it is so, not because the person to whom we give the explanation already knows rules, but because in another sense he is already master of a game.

Consider this further case: I am explaining chess to someone; and I begin by pointing to a chessman and saying: "This is the king; it can move like this . . . and so on."— In this case we shall say: the words "This is the king" (or "This is called the 'king'") are a definition only if the learner already "knows what a piece in a game is." That is, if he has already played other games, or has watched other people playing "and understood"—and *similar things*. Further, only under these conditions will he be able to ask relevantly in the course of learning the game: "What do you call this?"—that is, this piece in a game.

We may say: only someone who already knows how to do something with it can significantly ask a name. . . .

32. Someone coming into a strange country will sometimes learn the language of the inhabitants from ostensive definitions that they give him; and he will often have to *guess* the meaning of these definitions; and will guess sometimes right, sometimes wrong.

And now, I think, we can say: Augustine describes the learning of human language as if the child came into a strange country and did not understand the language of the country; that is, as if it already had a language, only not this one. Or again: as if the child could already *think*, only not yet speak. And "think" would here mean something like "talk to itself."

33. Suppose, however, someone were to object: "It is not true that you must already be master of a language in order to understand an ostensive definition: all you need— of course!—is to know or guess what the person giving the explanation is pointing to. That is, whether for example to the shape of the object, or to its color, or to its number, and so on." And what does "pointing to the shape," "pointing to the color" consist in? Point to a piece of paper.—And now point to its shape—now to its color— now to its number (that sounds queer).—How did you do it?—You will say that you "meant" a different thing each time you pointed. And if I ask how that is done, you will say you concentrated your attention on the color, the shape, etc.

But I ask again: how is *that* done?

 ASK YOURSELF

10.22. Could you point to the number of a thing? Explain.

Wittgenstein goes on to adduce a host of considerations that undermine the idea that words get attached to the world either through some mental act or through "ostension" (or both together). We are left with the notion of language as an activity interwoven with nonlinguistic activities, woven into forms of life that are distinctively human and too complex to come under any philosophical formula. At the same time simplistic pictures of a "world" waiting to be named or described are upset.

Rules, Practices, and Privacy. Later in this work Wittgenstein continues to argue that the notion of a practice (a game, for instance), or a more or less rule-governed custom, is essential to a good account of language and meaning. The very notion of a practice is the notion of something public, he argues. One consequence is that there cannot be "private" languages, languages separated logically from public practices.

199. Is what we call "obeying a rule" something that it would be possible for only *one* man to do, and to do only *once* in his life? This is of course a note on the grammar of the expression "to obey a rule."

It is not possible that there should have been only one occasion on which someone obeyed a rule. It is not possible that there should have been only one occasion on which a report was made, an order given or understood; and so on.—To obey a rule, to make a report, to give an order, to play a game of chess, are *customs* (uses, institutions).

To understand a sentence means to understand a language. To understand a language means to be master of a technique.

. . .

201. This was our paradox: no course of action could be determined by a rule, because every course of action can be made out to accord with the rule. The answer was: if everything can be made out to accord with the rule, then it can also be made out to conflict with it. And so there would be neither accord nor conflict here.

 ASK YOURSELF

10.23. Why not?

One of the mentalistic notions that often figures in discussions of language and meaning is "interpretation." We suppose that we understand someone's speech or writing, we understand a rule, a recommendation, a command, a claim, by "interpreting" it, and interpreting may seem like an "inner" activity.

It can be seen that there is a misunderstanding here from the mere fact that in the course of our argument we give one interpretation after another; as if each one contented us at least for a moment, until we thought of yet another standing behind it. What this shows is that there is a way of grasping a rule which is *not an interpretation*, but which is exhibited in what we call "obeying the rule" and "going against it" in actual cases.

Hence there is an inclination to say: every action according to the rule is an interpretation. But we ought to restrict the term "interpretation" to the substitution of one expression of the rule for another.

202. And hence also "obeying a rule" is a practice. And to *think one* is obeying a rule is not to obey a rule. Hence it is not possible to obey a rule "privately": otherwise thinking one was obeying a rule would be the same thing as obeying it.

 ASK YOURSELF

10.24. Suppose I think I am obeying the rule for the movement of the king in chess. Would that show that I *am* obeying it? If not, why not?

10.25. What I "think" cannot provide the standard for correctness implied in the idea of following a rule. What then can?

204. As things are I can, for example, invent a game that is never played by anyone.— But would the following be possible too: mankind has never played any games; once, however, someone invented a game—which no one ever played?

205. "But it is just the queer thing about *intention*, about the mental process, that the existence of a custom, of a technique, is not necessary to it. That, for example, it is imaginable that two people should play chess in a world in which otherwise no games existed; and even that they should begin a game of chess—and then be interrupted."

But isn't chess defined by its rules? And how are these rules present in the mind of the person who is intending to play chess?

206. Following a rule is analogous to obeying an order. We are trained to do so; we react to an order in a particular way. But what if one person reacts in one way and another in another to the order and the training? Which one is right?

Suppose you came as an explorer into an unknown country with a language quite strange to you. In what circumstances would you say that the people there gave orders, understood them, obeyed them, rebelled against them, and so on?

The common behavior of mankind is the system of reference by means of which we interpret an unknown language.

Just what is the "common behavior of mankind"? Wittgenstein does not say, but we can infer that he is referring to such facts as that we do share a great deal in terms of the ways we act and respond. There is, for example, order-giving behavior universally as well as agreement on what counts as obeying an order. Although Wittgenstein has given examples of many different kinds of language games, his examples are still quite general, since, for example, the particular contexts in which utterances can be understood as orders, the particular practices in which ordering is a move, can be quite various. Thus you cannot extract a general account of ordering from the description in Paragraph 206.

If private languages are impossible, then a central idea of Descartes, namely, that we have identifiable mental content, directly accessible to ourselves but completely inaccessible to anyone else, is untenable. Suppose I feel a pain in my toe. I tell you I have a pain. How can you know what "pain" refers to, since my pain, which is what I am referring to, is now and always has been and always will be inaccessible to you? In Descartes's view (and in the view of the British Empiricists, too), Wittgenstein points outs, the individual words of this language are to refer to what can only be known to the person speaking; to his immediate private sensations. So another person cannot understand the language.

244. How do words *refer* to sensations?—There doesn't seem to be any problem here; don't we talk about sensations every day, and give them names? But how is the connection between the name and the thing named set up? This question is the same as: how does a human being learn the meaning of the names of sensations?—of the word "pain" for example. Here is one possibility: words are connected with the primitive, the natural, expressions of the sensation and used in their place. A child has hurt himself and he cries; and then adults talk to him and teach him exclamations and, later, sentences. They teach the child new pain-behavior.

"So you are saying that the word 'pain' really means crying?" On the contrary: the verbal expression of pain replaces crying and does not describe it.

245. For how can I go so far as to try to use language to get between pain and its expression?

246. In what sense are my sensations *private*?—Well, only I can know whether I am really in pain; another person can only surmise it.—In one way this is wrong, and in another nonsense. If we are using the word "to know" as it is normally used (and how else are we to use it?), then other people very often know when I am in pain. Yes, but all the same not with the certainty with which I know it myself.—It can't be said of me at all (except perhaps as a joke) that I know I am in pain. What is it supposed to mean—except perhaps that *I am* in pain?

 ASK YOURSELF

10.26. Is there indeed something funny in the idea that someone knows they are in pain? Ask yourself whether a claim to knowledge normally implies that I might *not* have known the thing in question. And then ask whether it makes sense to say that you might be in pain but not know it.

Other people cannot be said to learn of my sensations *only* from my behavior,—for I cannot be said to learn of them. I *have them*.

The truth is: it makes sense to say about other people that they doubt whether I am in pain; but not to say it about myself. . . .

249. Are we perhaps over-hasty in our assumption that the smile of an unweaned infant is not a pretense?—And on what experience is our assumption based?

(Lying is a language-game that needs to be learned like any other one.)

250. Why can't a dog simulate pain? Is he too honest? Could one teach a dog to simulate pain? Perhaps it is possible to teach him to howl on particular occasions as if he were in pain, even when he is not. But the surroundings which are necessary for this behavior to be real simulation are missing.

 ASK YOURSELF

10.27. What might some of those "surroundings" be? Might they include the possibility of being honest? Could a dog be honest? Are some honest and others not?

If lying or deception are "language games," then, like any game, they are complex activities that need to be learned. Part of their complexity consists in their requiring a background, such as that mentioned in Paragraph 31 or Paragraph 199.

256. Now, what about the language which describes my inner experiences and which only I myself can understand? *How* do I use words to stand for my sensations?—As we ordinarily do? Then are my words for sensations tied up with my natural expressions of sensation? In that case my language is not a "private" one. Someone else might understand it as well as I.—But suppose I didn't have any natural expression

for the sensation, but only had the sensation? And now I *simply associate* names with sensations and use these names in descriptions.—

257. "What would it be like if human beings showed no outward signs of pain (did not groan, grimace, etc.)? Then it would be impossible to teach a child the use of the word "tooth-ache."—Well, let's assume the child is a genius and itself invents a name for the sensation. But then, of course, he couldn't make himself understood when he used the word.—So does he understand the name, without being able to explain its meaning to anyone?—But what does it mean to say that he has "named his pain"?— How has he done this naming of pain? And whatever he did, what was its purpose?— When one says "He gave a name to his sensation" one forgets that a great deal of stage-setting in the language is presupposed if the mere act of naming is to make sense. And when we speak of someone's having given a name to pain, what is presupposed is the existence of the grammar of the word "pain"; it shows the post where the new word is stationed.

"Grammar" has been mentioned several times so far. The grammar of a word, it appears, is that context which gives it sense. In the ordinary sense of "ungrammatical," ungrammatical constructions (for example, where words are put in the wrong place [wrong context], such as adjectives where only a noun could go), render sentences unintelligible or nonsensical. But we have seen that the way in which context determines sense for Wittgenstein is much broader. The context includes whole activities in which words play a role, for instance.

258. Let us imagine the following case. I want to keep a diary about the recurrence of a certain sensation. To this end I associate it with the sign "S" and write this sign in a calendar for every day on which I have the sensation. I will remark first of all that a definition of the sign cannot be formulated.—But still I can give myself a kind of ostensive definition.—How? Can I point to the sensation? Not in the ordinary sense. But I speak, or write the sign down, and at the same time I concentrate my attention on the sensation—and so, as it were, point to it inwardly.—But what is this ceremony for? For that is all it seems to be! A definition surely serves to establish the meaning of a sign.—Well, that is done precisely by the concentrating of my attention; for in this way I impress on myself the connection between the sign and the sensation.—But "I impress it on myself" can only mean: this process brings it about that I remember the connection *right* in the future. But in the present case I have no criterion of correctness. One would like to say: whatever is going to seem right to me is right. And that only means that here we can't talk about "right."

 ASK YOURSELF

10.28. Again, why can't we?

260. . . . Then did the man who made the entry in the calendar make a note of *nothing whatever?*—Don't consider it a matter of course that a person is making a note of something when he makes a mark—say in a calendar. For a note has a function, and this "S" so far has none. . . .

261. What reason have we for calling "S" the sign for a *sensation*? For "sensation" is a word of our common language, not of one intelligible to me alone. So the use of this word stands in need of a justification which everybody understands.—And it would not help either to say that it need not be a *sensation*; that when he writes "S," he has *something*—and that is all that can be said. "Has" and "something" also belong to our common language.—So in the end when one is doing philosophy one gets to the point where one would like just to emit an inarticulate sound.—But such a sound is an expression only as it occurs in a particular language-game, which should now be described.

Wittgenstein gives many more illustrations and examples to show the incoherence of the idea of a private language. He imagines someone objecting along the following lines: When I refer to a sensation of mine I must be doing something more than referring to something that all people understand. My pain is mine, is unique. Wittgenstein, it is objected, seems to remove the actual experience, with all its concreteness, from his account. It would be a mistake, however, to suppose that he wishes to revert to a behaviorism in which "inner" experiences are reduced to outward manifestations. Rather, he wishes to get this very public language about our sensations correctly described. Part of the task is to remember such things as this: Sensations only belong to living things.

281. "But doesn't what you say come to this: that there is no pain, for example, without *pain-behavior*?" It comes to this: only of a living human being and what resembles (behaves like) a living human being can one say: it has sensations; it sees; is blind; hears; is deaf; is conscious or unconscious.

282. "But in a fairy tale the pot too can see and hear!" (Certainly; but it *can* also talk.)

"But the fairy tale only invents what is not the case: it does not talk *nonsense*."—It is not as simple as that. Is it false or nonsensical to say that a pot talks? Have we a clear picture of the circumstances in which we should say of a pot that it talked? (Even a nonsense-poem is not nonsense in the same way as the babbling of a child.)

We do indeed say of an inanimate thing that it is in pain: when playing with dolls for example. But this use of the concept of pain is a secondary one. Imagine a case in which people ascribed pain *only* to inanimate things; pitied *only* dolls. (When children play at trains their game is connected with their knowledge of trains. It would nevertheless be possible for the children of a tribe unacquainted with trains to learn this game from others, and to play it without knowing that it was copied from anything. One might say that the game did not make the same *sense* to them as to us.)

283. What gives us *so much as the idea* that living beings, things, can feel?

Is it that my education has led me to it by drawing my attention to feelings in myself, and now I transfer the idea to objects outside myself? That I recognize that there is something there (in me) which I can call "pain" without getting into conflict with the way other people use this word?—I do not transfer my idea to stones, plants, etc.

Couldn't I imagine having frightful pains and turning to stone while they lasted? Well, how do I know, if I shut my eyes, whether I have not turned into a stone? And if that has happened, in what sense will *the stone* have the pains? In what sense will they be ascribable to the stone? . . .

284. Look at a stone and imagine it having sensations.—One says to oneself.—How

could one so much as get the idea of ascribing a *sensation* to a *thing*? One might as well ascribe it to a number!—And now look at a wriggling fly and at once these difficulties vanish and pain seems able to get a foothold here. . . .

 ASK YOURSELF

10.29. Exactly why could a stone, or the number 1, not feel pain?

A common philosophical problem in the modern era has been how to come to knowledge that other people have feelings when the only direct knowledge I have of such things is purportedly the knowledge I have of my own feelings. Wittgenstein tried to dismantle this "problem," at least as usually formulated. But doing so does not involve erecting a theory, such as behaviorism, which eliminates references to what is inner and private. What is eliminated is the idea that I can, on my own, contrive to think about and talk about those inner experiences simply by attending to them and labeling them. Rather, I learn how to talk about them together with living others, those in whose lives I share. Language-games are uses of words intertwined with activities, including such activities as comforting those in pain. I could not know what "pain" means or what pain is apart from such activities.

Wittgenstein's attack on the confusion expressed by "private language" is part of a general posture in which attention to how we actually speak and think (as opposed to how we theorize about language and thought in philosophy or psychology) plays a central role. Likewise, his account of meaning relies upon careful attention to how we actually live with words. For this reason he became a source for what was called "ordinary language philosophy." But there does not appear to be any such thing. There are countless different kinds of use of what we call "symbols," "words," and "sentences." And this multiplicity is not something fixed, given once for all; but new types of language, new language-games, as we may say, come into existence, and others become obsolete. Some uses might be quite technical, or nonordinary in many other ways. What is crucial is that we attend to the ways in which language is actually "engaged" with our lives (in somewhat the way gears can be engaged to power a mechanism). A disengaged engine does not work. In philosophy, Wittgenstein warns, theories about mind and language are often disengaged from their usual work and become like idling engines. These sorts of points suggest what is "pragmatist" in Wittgenstein's thinking. But his thought can also be seen as somewhat Kantian or Idealist, and in fact invites a variety of characterizations. The selections here can only give a hint of his originality and the vividness of his thinking. His impact on others has been pervasive and often goes unacknowledged, and despite the changes of philosophical fashion he continues, after fifty years, to evoke fresh debate and discussion about the nature of language, mind, morality, religion, indeed the entire whirl of organisms that he calls "forms of life."

WILLARD VAN ORMAN QUINE

W. V. O. Quine was born in 1908. As a graduate student at Harvard he wrote a dissertation dealing with Russell and Whitehead's *Principia Mathematica*. His thought was deeply influenced by Russell, both positively and negatively. Russell came to lecture at Harvard and gave Quine his "most dazzling exposure to greatness" (Quine's own words). But Quine became critical of some of the main features of the Empiricist tradition that Russell represented. Quine was particularly anxious to avoid any philosophical "dogmas" that depend upon the notion of meaning (such as the analytic/synthetic distinction) and upon a reductionism that gives indubitable status to empirical claims. Thus he rejected Russell's notion that we have direct and indubitable knowledge by acquaintance with sense-data. For Quine, epistemology must be "naturalized," which implies, among other things, that no claims are indubitable. We must settle for the best truths we can find, using the principle of parsimony and other principles operative in the sciences, but even our best theories and most secure beliefs are subject to correction. This rejection of certainty and with it any particular species of "philosophical truth," and an emphasis upon whatever is "working" in current science, makes Quine a pragmatist of sorts. His "naturalism" is radical; notions of mentality and all the philosophical baggage that go with them are eschewed. For example, the dependence of the British Empiricist tradition upon mental "impressions" (sense-data in Russell) is rejected. The following quote gives some of the flavor of Quine's naturalism: (from *The Way of Paradox and Other Essays*, p. 215)

> I am a physical object sitting in a physical world. Some of the forces of this physical world impinge on my surface. Light rays strike my retinas; molecules bombard my eardrums and fingertips. I strike back, emanating concentric air waves. These waves take the form of a torrent of discourse about tables, people, molecules, light rays, retinas, air waves, prime numbers, infinite classes, joy and sorrow, good and evil.

Quine's "Two Dogmas of Empiricism" presents central themes of his thought, which he continued to refine over the next fifty years. The following is from the first edition of his essay, initially published in 1951.

The Nature of Modern Empiricism

 From QUINE: *Two Dogmas of Empiricism*

Modern empiricism has been conditioned in large part by two dogmas. One is a belief in some fundamental cleavage between truths which are analytic, or grounded in meanings independently of matters of fact and truths which are synthetic, or grounded in fact. The other dogma is reductionism: the belief that each meaningful statement is equivalent to some logical construct upon terms which refer to immediate experience. Both dogmas, I shall argue, are ill founded. One effect of abandoning them is, as we shall see, a blurring of the supposed boundary between speculative metaphysics and natural science. Another effect is a shift toward pragmatism.

Background for Analyticity (Section 1 of Original Paper)

The Analytic/Synthetic Distinction. Quine intends to dismantle this distinction, which played a crucial role in both Rationalist and Empiricist philosophy.

Kant's cleavage between analytic and synthetic truths was foreshadowed in Hume's distinction between relations of ideas and matters of fact, and in Leibniz's distinction between truths of reason and truths of fact. Leibniz spoke of the truths of reason as true in all possible worlds. Picturesqueness aside, this is to say that the truths of reason are those which could not possibly be false. In the same vein we hear analytic statements defined as statements whose denials are self-contradictory. But this definition has small explanatory value; for the notion of self-contradictoriness, in the quite broad sense needed for this definition of analyticity, stands in exactly the same need of clarification as does the notion of analyticity itself. The two notions are the two sides of a single dubious coin.

Kant conceived of an analytic statement as one that attributes to its subject no more than is already conceptually contained in the subject. This formulation has two shortcomings: it limits itself to statements of subject-predicate form, and it appeals to a notion of containment which is left at a metaphorical level. But Kant's intent, evident more from the use he makes of the notion of analyticity than from his definition of it, can be restated thus: a statement is analytic when it is true by virtue of meanings and independently of fact. Pursuing this line, let us examine the concept of meaning which is presupposed.

Meaning and Naming. They Must Be Distinguished

We must observe to begin with that meaning is not to be identified with naming or reference. Consider Frege's example of "Evening Star" and "Morning Star." Understood not merely as a recurrent evening apparition but as a body, the Evening Star is the planet Venus, and the Morning Star is the same. The two singular terms name the same thing. But the meanings must be treated as distinct, since the identity "Evening Star = Morning Star" is a statement of fact established by astronomical observation. If "Evening Star" and "Morning Star" were alike in meaning, the identity "Evening Star = Morning Star" would be analytic.

. . . The distinction between meaning and naming is no less important at the level of abstract terms. The terms "9" and "the number of planets" name one and the same abstract entity but presumably must be regarded as unlike in meaning; for astronomical observation was needed, and not mere reflection on meanings, to determine the sameness of the entity in question.

"Bachelors are unmarried" is often proposed as an analytic statement, that is, a statement true by virtue of the meanings of "bachelor" and "unmarried." One can know such statements to be true just by thinking about the meanings of their terms. "It is raining," on the other hand, if it is true at all, is so not because of meanings but because of how the weather is as a matter of empirical fact. But Quine thinks the relevant notion of "meaning" is unexplained. Could the meanings of words be their references, for example, so that some analytic statements are true because their terms have the same reference?

ASK YOURSELF

10.30. Meaning, Quine argues, is not a matter of reference, since what "evening star" and "morning star" refer to is the same, but obviously "the morning is identical with the evening star" (both terms refer to Venus), although true, is not true by virtue of _____ and is thus obviously not analytic. In fact, it was only discovered to be true long after people knew the "meaning" of its key expressions.

With general terms, or predicates [e.g., "brown," "dog"], the situation is somewhat different but parallel. Whereas a singular term purports to name an entity, abstract or concrete, a general term does not; but a general term is true of an entity, or of each of many, or of none. The class of all entities of which a general term is true is called the extension of the term. Now paralleling the contrast between the meaning of a singular term and the entity named, we must distinguish equally between the meaning of a general term and its extension. The general terms "creature with a heart" and "creature with a kidney," e.g., are perhaps alike in extension but unlike in meaning.

 ASK YOURSELF

10.31. To say that these two terms are alike in "extension" is to say that they are _____ of all and only the same _____.

It follows that meaning the same cannot be reduced to having the same extension, otherwise, "All creatures with a heart are creatures with a kidney" would be analytic, which it obviously is not.

Confusion of meaning with extension, in the case of general terms, is less common than confusion of meaning with naming in the case of singular terms. It is indeed a commonplace in philosophy to oppose intention (or meaning) to extension, or, in a variant vocabulary, connotation to denotation.

. . . For the theory of meaning the most conspicuous question is as to the nature of its objects: what sort of things are meanings? They are evidently intended to be ideas, somehow—mental ideas for some semanticists, Platonic ideas for others. Objects of either sort are so elusive, not to say debatable, that there seems little hope of erecting a fruitful science about them. It is not even clear, granted meanings, when we have two and when we have one; it is not clear when linguistic forms should be regarded as synonymous, or alike in meaning, and when they should not. If a standard of synonymy should be arrived at, we may reasonably expect that the appeal to meanings as entities will not have played a very useful part in the enterprise.

A felt need for meant entities may derive from an earlier failure to appreciate that meaning and reference are distinct. Once the theory of meaning is sharply separated from the theory of reference, it is a short step to recognizing as the business of the theory of meaning simply the synonymy of linguistic forms and the analyticity of statements; meanings themselves, as obscure intermediate entities, may well be abandoned. The description of analyticity as truth by virtue of meanings started us off in pursuit of a concept of meaning. But now we have abandoned the thought of any special realm of entities called meanings. So the problem of analyticity confronts us anew. . . .

Statements which are analytic by general philosophical acclaim are not, indeed, far to seek. They fall into two classes. Those of the first class, which may be called logically true, are typified by:

1. No unmarried man is married.

The relevant feature of this example is that it is not merely true as it stands, but remains true under any and all reinterpretations of "man" and "married." If we suppose a prior inventory of logical particles, comprising "no," "un-," "if," "then," "and," etc., then in general a logical truth is a statement which is true and remains true under all reinterpretations of its components other than the logical particles.

 ASK YOURSELF

10.32. A "reinterpretation" of the components of (1) might be "No brown duck is _____ ."

But there is also a second class of analytic statements, typified by:

2. No bachelor is married.

The characteristic of such a statement is that it can be turned into a logical truth by putting synonyms for synonyms; thus (2) can be turned into (1) by putting "unmarried man" for its synonym "bachelor." We still lack a proper characterization of this second class of analytic statements, and therewith of analyticity generally, inasmuch as we have had in the above description to lean on a notion of "synonymy" which is no less in need of clarification than analyticity itself.

Definition (Section 2 of Original Paper)

Analytic statements are said to be true by definition. Does that explain anything? Only if we can make sense of the notion of synonymy.

The Notion of Synonomy. This notion is as obscure as the notion of meaning.

There are those who find it soothing to say that the analytic statements of the second class reduce to those of the first class, the logical truths, by definition; "bachelor," for example, is defined as "unmarried man." But how do we find that "bachelor" is defined as "unmarried man"? Who defined it thus, and when? Are we to appeal to the nearest dictionary, and accept the lexicographer's formulation as law? Clearly this would be to put the cart before the horse. The lexicographer is an empirical scientist, whose business is the recording of antecedent facts; and if he glosses "bachelor" as "unmarried man" it is because of his belief that there is a relation of synonymy between these forms, implicit in general or preferred usage prior to his own work. The notion of synonymy presupposed here has still to be clarified, presumably in terms relating to linguistic behavior. Certainly the "definition" which is the lexicographer's report of an observed synonymy cannot be taken as the ground of the synonymy.

Definition is not, indeed, an activity exclusively of philologists. Philosophers and scientists frequently have occasions to "define" a recondite term by paraphrasing it into terms of a more familiar vocabulary. But ordinarily such a definition, like the philologist's, is pure lexicography, affirming a relationship of synonymy antecedent to the exposition in hand.

Just what it means to affirm synonymy, just what the interconnections may be which are necessary and sufficient in order that two linguistic forms be properly describable as synonymous, is far from clear; but, whatever these interconnections may be, ordinarily they are grounded in usage. Definitions reporting selected instances of synonymy come then as reports upon usage.

     ASK YOURSELF

10.33. Quine objects to attempts to define "analytic truths" as those that are true by definition. Why?

Quine goes on to consider variations on the idea that analytic truths are true by definition. All of them depend upon an unexplained notion of synonymy.

. . . In formal and informal work alike, thus, we find that definition—except in the extreme case of the explicitly conventional introduction of new notation—hinges on prior relationships of synonymy. Recognizing then that the notation of definition does not hold the key to synonymy and analyticity, let us look further into synonymy and say no more of definition.

Interchangeability (Section 3 of Original Paper)

Perhaps to say that "All bachelors are unmarried male adults" is analytic is simply to say that its terms ("bachelor" and "unmarried male adult") are interchangeable.

Interchangeability Depends upon the Notion of Synonymy. This maneuver does not help, since we only know what terms are interchangeable if we know they are synonymous. And synonymy continues to be obscure.

A natural suggestion, deserving close examination, is that the synonymy of two linguistic forms consists simply in their interchangeability in all contexts without change of truth value; interchangeability, in Leibniz's phrase, salva veritate. Note that synonyms so conceived need not even be free from vagueness, as long as the vaguenesses match. . . .

The question remains whether interchangeability salva veritate (apart from occurrences within words) is a strong enough condition for synonymy, or whether, on the contrary, some non-synonymous expressions might be thus interchangeable. Now let us be clear that we are not concerned here with synonymy in the sense of complete identity in psychological associations or poetic quality; indeed no two expressions are synonymous in such a sense. We are concerned only with what may be called cognitive synonymy. Just what this is cannot be said without successfully finishing the present study . . .

 ASK YOURSELF

10.34. Is "9" interchangeable with "the number of the planets" *salva veritate?* Explain.

Quine goes on to consider various explanations of interchangeability. The following seems to be the most promising.

Interchangeability salva veritate is meaningless until relativized to a language whose extent is specified in relevant respects. Suppose now we consider a language containing just the following materials. There is an indefinitely large stock of one- and many-place predicates mostly having to do with extralogical subject matter. The rest of the language is logical. The atomic sentences consist each of a predicate followed by one or more variables "x," "y," etc.; and the complex sentences are built up of atomic ones by truth functions ("not," "and," "or," etc.) and quantification. In effect such a language enjoys the benefits also of descriptions and class names and indeed singular terms generally, these being contextually definable in known ways.

The following would be an example of the sort of language Quine is describing: "There is at least one x such that x is brown, and x is clever." The truth of this sentence is a *function* of its parts, namely, "there is at least one x (this is called a quantifier) such that x is brown" and "x is clever." ("Brown" is a "one place predicate.") The "logical term" "and" is such that in this sentence both parts would have to be true for the whole sentence to be true (which is obvious).

Such a language can be adequate to classical mathematics and indeed to scientific discourse generally, except insofar as the latter involves debatable devices such as modal adverbs and contrary-to-fact conditionals.

Now a language of this type is extensional, in this sense: any two predicates which agree extensionally (i.e., are true of the same objects) are interchangeable salva veritate. In an extensional language, therefore, interchangeability salva veritate is no assurance of cognitive synonymy of the desired type. That "bachelor" and "unmarried man" are interchangeable salva veritate in an extensional language assures us of no more than that (3) ("All and only bachelors are unmarried men") is true. There is no assurance here that the extensional agreement of "bachelor" and "unmarried man" rests on meaning rather than merely on accidental matters of fact, as does extensional agreement of "creature with a heart" and "creature with a kidney."

ASK YOURSELF

10.35. Quine is claiming that since "creature with a heart" and "creature with a kidney" refer to all and only the same entities, and thus are "extensionally equivalent," that we cannot explain synonymy in terms of extensional _____ . For it is obvious that these two expressions are not _____ .

For most purposes extensional agreement is the nearest approximation to synonymy we need care about. But the fact remains that extensional agreement falls far short of cognitive synonymy of the type required for explaining analyticity in the manner of Section 1. The type of cognitive synonymy required there is such as to equate the synonymy of "bachelor" and "unmarried man" with the analyticity of (3), not merely with the truth of (3).

So we must recognize that interchangeability salva veritate, if construed in relation to an extensional language, is not a sufficient condition of cognitive synonymy in the sense needed for deriving analyticity in the manner of Section 1.

In Section 4 of his paper Quine goes on to consider whether an adequate account of "analytic" might be given for artificial or precisely defined languages. He concludes that such attempts to salvage analyticity also fail.

So—and this is the point—the famous distinction between analytic and synthetic, between an important class of truths supposedly known by simply grasping meanings, and truth known only through experience, has collapsed. This idea was a "dogma of Empiricism" since it allowed people like Hume to account for the fact that some statements (e.g., "2 + 2 = 4" or "All bachelors are unmarried") are supposedly known independently of experience, without falling back into Rationalist accounts of such knowledge. But a distinction between what is known on the basis of experience and what is not cannot be maintained in this way, Quine has argued.

The Verification Theory and Reductionism (Section 5 of Original Paper)

In the course of these somber reflections we have taken a dim view first of the notion of meaning, then of the notion of cognitive synonymy: and finally of the notion of analyticity. But what, it may be asked, of the verification theory of meaning? This phrase has established itself so firmly as a catchword of empiricism that we should be very unscientific indeed not to look beneath it for a possible key to the problem of meaning and the associated problems.

The verification theory of meaning, which has been conspicuous in the literature from Peirce onward, is that the meaning of a statement is the method of empirically confirming or infirming it. An analytic statement is that limiting case which is confirmed no matter what.

As urged in Section 1, we can as well pass over the question of meanings as entities and move straight to sameness of meaning, or synonymy. Then what the verification theory says is that statements are synonymous if and only if they are alike in point of method of empirical confirmation or infirmation.

So, if the verification theory can be accepted as an adequate account of statement synonymy, the notion of analyticity is saved after all. However, let us reflect. Statement synonymy is said to be likeness of method of empirical confirmation or infirmation. Just what are these methods which are to be compared for likeness? What, in other words, is the nature of the relationship between a statement and the experiences which contribute to or detract from its confirmation?

The most naive view of the relationship is that it is one of direct report. This is radical reductionism. Every meaningful statement is held to be translatable into a statement (true or false) about immediate experience. Radical reductionism, in one form or another, well antedates the verification theory of meaning explicitly so called. Thus Locke and Hume held that every idea must either originate directly in sense experience or else be compounded of ideas thus originating; and taking a hint from Tooke we might rephrase this doctrine in semantical jargon by saying that a term, to be significant at all, must be either a name of a sense datum or a compound of such names or an abbreviation of such a compound. So stated, the doctrine remains ambiguous as between sense data as sensory events and sense data as sensory qualities; and it remains vague as to the admissible ways of compounding. Moreover, the doctrine is unnecessarily and intolerably restrictive in the term-by-term critique which it imposes. More reasonably, and without yet exceeding the limits of what I have called radical reductionism, we may take full statements as our significant units—thus demanding that our statements as wholes be translatable into sense-datum language, but not that they be translatable term by term.

This emendation would unquestionably have been welcome to Locke and Hume and Tooke, but historically it had to await two intermediate developments. One of these developments was the increasing emphasis on verification or confirmation, which came with the explicitly so-called verification theory of meaning. The objects of verification/confirmation being statements, this emphasis gave statement an ascendancy over the word or term as unit of significant discourse. The other development, consequent upon the first, was Russell's discovery of the concept of incomplete symbols defined in use.

Radical reductionism, conceived now with statements as units, sets itself the task of specifying a sense-datum language and showing how to translate the rest of significant discourse, statement by statement, into it. Carnap embarked on this project in the *Aufbau*.

 ASK YOURSELF

10.36. In the view now being considered, a term, or statement, would have the same "meaning" as another term or statement if their method of _____ were the same.

Quine goes on to consider and criticize Carnap's version of reductionism. He concludes that is it a failure. But reductionism of the Empiricist sort seems to live on.

. . . But the dogma of reductionism has, in a subtler and more tenuous form, continued to influence the thought of empiricists. The notion lingers that to each statement, or each synthetic statement, there is associated a unique range of possible sensory events such that the occurrence of any of them would add to the likelihood of truth of the statement, and that there is associated also another unique range of possible sensory events whose occurrence would detract from that likelihood. This notion is of course implicit in the verification theory of meaning.

The dogma of reductionism survives in the supposition that each statement, taken in isolation from its fellows, can admit of confirmation or infirmation at all. My counter-suggestion, issuing essentially from Carnap's doctrine of the physical world in the *Aufbau*, is that our statements about the external world face the tribunal of sense experience not individually but only as a corporate body.

Take "the earth is flat." Until recently no one had direct empirical evidence against this claim. But an Empiricist might argue that it was known to be false empirically by, for example, our observations of sailing ships on the sea. As the ship sails away, we see that the hull goes out of sight before the masts. How could that be so unless the earth was round? Yet it turns out that we might have this visual experience even on a flat earth provided that certain other things we believe, such as that light travels in straight lines, that it travels in straight lines over water, or that our telescope (supposing we are using one to track the ship) is working properly should turn out to be false. We could keep our belief that the world is flat if we rejected some or all of these other beliefs. It turns out that even more direct empirical beliefs also stand together with other beliefs. These empirical beliefs are thus judged innocent by the "tribunal of sense experience" only because we accept other beliefs along with them. Our beliefs (for example, about the shape of the earth) change not because of some infallible perception of fact, but because we choose to reject certain members of the "corporate body" of beliefs and keep others for reasons that have, it turns out, nothing to do with direct experience in the sense postulated by the Empiricist criterion of meaning.

 ASK YOURSELF

10.37. How might giving up the belief that light travels in straight lines enable us to maintain the belief that the earth is flat even when we see with our own eyes that the hull disappears first, the masts later?

The dogma of reductionism, even in its attenuated form, is intimately connected with the other dogma: that there is a cleavage between the analytic and the synthetic. We have found ourselves led, indeed, from the latter problem to the former through the verification theory of meaning. More directly, the one dogma clearly supports the other in this way: as long as it is taken to be significant in general to speak of the confirmation and infirmation of a statement, it seems significant to speak also of a limiting kind of statement which is vacuously confirmed, ipso facto, come what may; and such a statement is analytic.

The two dogmas are, indeed, at root identical. We lately reflected that in general the truth of statements does obviously depend both upon extra-linguistic fact; and we noted that this obvious circumstance carries in its train, not logically but all too naturally, a feeling that the truth of a statement is somehow analyzable into a linguistic component and a factual component. The factual component must, if we are empiricists, boil down to a range of confirmatory experiences. In the extreme case where the linguistic component is all that matters, a true statement is analytic. But I hope we are impressed with how stubbornly the distinction between analytic and synthetic has resisted any straightforward drawing. I am impressed also, apart from prefabricated examples of black and white balls in an urn, with how baffling the problem has always been of arriving at any explicit theory of the empirical confirmation of a synthetic statement. My present suggestion is that it is nonsense, and the root of much nonsense, to speak of a linguistic component and a factual component in the truth of any individual statement. Taken collectively, science has its double dependence upon language and experience; but this duality is not significantly traceable into the statements of science taken one by one.

If analytic statements are true come what may, independently of experience, then people who persist in believing the world is flat by using the strategies mentioned here (rejecting the truth of other related claims) might claim that "the world is flat" is analytic, since no experience counts against the claim that it is flat. "The world is flat" will be true "come what may."

 ASK YOURSELF

10.38. In fact, Quine is arguing that science is empirical only in the sense that groups of scientific statements are supported by _____.

. . . But what I am now urging is that even in taking the statement as unit we have drawn our grid too finely. The unit of empirical significance is the whole of science.

Empiricism without the Dogmas (Section 6 of Original Paper)

The Web of Knowledge. Science and common sense grasp the world not through direct bits of experience but through a "fabric" of interrelated beliefs.

The totality of our so-called knowledge or beliefs, from the most casual matters of geography and history to the profoundest laws of atomic physics or even of pure mathematics and logic, is a man-made fabric which impinges on experience only along the edges. Or, to change the figure, total science is like a field of force whose boundary conditions are experience. A conflict with experience at the periphery occasions readjustments in the interior of the field. Truth values have to be redistributed over some of our statements. Re-evaluation of some statements entails re-evaluation of others, because of their logical interconnections—the logical laws being in turn simply certain further statements of the system, certain further elements of the field. Having re-evaluated one statement we must re-evaluate some others, whether they be statements logically connected with the first or whether they be the statements of logical connections themselves. But the total field is so undetermined by its boundary conditions, experience, that there is much latitude of choice as to what statements to re-evaluate in the light of any single contrary experience.

When we first notice that the hull disappears before the mast, what shall we reject? Our belief that the world is flat? Or that light travels in straight lines? Or some other related belief? "Experience" does not determining what to reject. There is "latitude of choice."

No particular experiences are linked with any particular statements in the interior of the field, except indirectly through considerations of equilibrium affecting the field as a whole.

If this view is right, it is misleading to speak of the empirical content of an individual statement—especially if it be a statement at all remote from the experiential periphery of the field. Furthermore it becomes folly to seek a boundary between synthetic statements, which hold contingently on experience, and analytic statements which hold come what may. Any statement can be held true come what may, if we make drastic enough adjustments elsewhere in the system. Even a statement very close to the periphery can be held true in the face of recalcitrant experience by pleading hallucination or by amending certain statements of the kind called logical laws. Conversely, by the same token, no statement is immune to revision. Revision even of the logical law of the excluded middle has been proposed as a means of simplifying quantum mechanics; and what difference is there in principle between such a shift and the shift whereby Kepler superseded Ptolemy, or Einstein Newton, or Darwin Aristotle?

For vividness I have been speaking in terms of varying distances from a sensory periphery. Let me try now to clarify this notion without metaphor. Certain statements, though about physical objects and not sense experience, seem peculiarly germane to sense experience—and in a selective way some statements to some experiences, others to others. Such statements, especially germane to particular experiences, I picture as near the periphery. But in this relation of "germaneness" I envisage nothing more than a loose association reflecting the relative likelihood, in practice, of our choosing one statement rather than another for revision in the event of recalcitrant experience. For example, we can imagine recalcitrant experiences to which we would surely be inclined to accommodate our system by re-evaluating just the statement that there are brick houses on Elm Street, together with related statements on the same topic.

 ASK YOURSELF

10.39. Mention some experiences that might lead you to give up the belief that there are brick buildings on the campus of your college (assuming there are some).

We can imagine other recalcitrant experiences to which we would be inclined to accommodate our system by re-evaluating just the statement that there are no centaurs, along with kindred statements. A recalcitrant experience can, I have already urged, be accommodated by any of various alternative re-evaluations in various alternative quarters of the total system; but, in the cases which we are now imagining, our natural tendency to disturb the total system as little as possible would lead us to focus our revisions upon these specific statements concerning brick houses or centaurs. These statements are felt, therefore, to have a sharper empirical reference than highly theoretical statements of physics or logic or ontology. The latter statements may be thought of as relatively centrally located within the total network, meaning merely that little preferential connection with any particular sense data obtrudes itself.

If I could only hang on to the belief that the earth is flat by rejecting such a principle of logic as "For any statement S, either S is true or it is not the case that S is true," I would probably not want to hang on to my flat-earth belief, since the logical principle just mentioned figures so centrally in my thinking about nearly everything.

 ASK YOURSELF

10.40. Give an example of a belief I would have to give up if I gave up the logical principle just mentioned.

As an empiricist I continue to think of the conceptual scheme of science as a tool, ultimately, for predicting future experience in the light of past experience. Physical objects are conceptually imported into the situation as convenient intermediaries—not by definition in terms of experience, but simply as irreducible posits comparable, epistemologically, to the gods of Homer. Let me interject that for my part I do, qua lay physicist, believe in physical objects and not in Homer's gods; and I consider it a scientific error to believe otherwise. But in point of epistemological footing the physical objects and the gods differ only in degree and not in kind. Both sorts of entities enter our conception only as cultural posits. The myth of physical objects is epistemologically superior to most in that it has proved more efficacious than other myths as a device for working a manageable structure into the flux of experience.

By way of analogy, Quine goes on to compare the "positing" of physical objects to the positing of irrational numbers. Both posits are justified by what they allow us to do. In the case of irrational numbers certain operations are made easier, for example. This stress on "what works best" is typical of pragmatism.

. . . Positing does not stop with macroscopic physical objects. Objects at the atomic level and beyond are posited to make the laws of macroscopic objects, and ultimately the laws of experience, simpler and more manageable; and we need not expect or demand full definition of atomic and subatomic entities in terms of macroscopic ones, any more than definition of macroscopic things in terms of sense data. Science is a continuation of common sense, and it continues the common-sense expedient of swelling ontology to simplify theory.

Physical objects, small and large, are not the only posits. Forces are another example; and indeed we are told nowadays that the boundary between energy and matter is obsolete. Moreover, the abstract entities which are the substance of mathematics— ultimately classes and classes of classes and so on up—are another posit in the same spirit. Epistemologically these are myths on the same footing with physical objects and gods, neither better nor worse except for differences in the degree to which they expedite our dealings with sense experiences.

The over-all algebra of rational and irrational numbers is underdetermined by the algebra of rational numbers, but is smoother and more convenient; and it includes the algebra of rational numbers as a jagged or gerrymandered part. Total science, mathematical and natural and human, is similarly but more extremely underdetermined by experience. The edge of the system must be kept squared with experience; the rest, with all its elaborate myths or fictions, has as its objective the simplicity of laws.

Ontological questions, under this view, are on a par with questions of natural science. Consider the question whether to countenance classes as entities. This, as I have argued elsewhere, is the question whether to quantify with respect to variables which take classes as values. Now Carnap [In "Empiricism, Semantics, and Ontology," Revue internationale de philosophie 4 (1950), 20–40] has maintained that this is a question not of matters of fact but of choosing a convenient language form, a convenient conceptual scheme or framework for science. With this I agree, but only on the proviso that the same be conceded regarding scientific hypotheses generally. Carnap has recognized that he is able to preserve a double standard for ontological questions and scientific hypotheses only by assuming an absolute distinction between the analytic and the synthetic; and I need not say again that this is a distinction which I reject.

Some issues do, I grant, seem more a question of convenient conceptual scheme and others more a question of brute fact. The issue over there being classes seems more a question of convenient conceptual scheme; the issue over there being centaurs, or brick houses on Elm Street, seems more a question of fact. But I have been urging that this difference is only one of degree, and that it turns upon our vaguely pragmatic inclination to adjust one strand of the fabric of science rather than another in accommodating some particular recalcitrant experience. Conservatism figures in such choices, and so does the quest for simplicity.

Carnap, Lewis, and others take a pragmatic stand on the question of choosing between language forms, scientific frameworks; but their pragmatism leaves off at the imagined boundary between the analytic and the synthetic. In repudiating such a boundary I espouse a more thorough pragmatism. Each man is given a scientific heritage plus a continuing barrage of sensory stimulation; and the considerations which guide him in warping his scientific heritage to fit his continuing sensory promptings are, where rational, pragmatic.

Quine's Empiricism may not seem very Empiricist considering that it treats physical objects merely as "posits" (but consider Berkeley's view of such objects!) or denies that I can know with certainty the color of an object directly in front of me in normal light. But how do we (how does an "Empiricist") determine what light is "normal"? Reflection on that question may lead to Quinean views on the "web of belief." Over many years Quine has worked out further details of the views expressed here. These views have provoked a great deal of discussion, thus making Quine's ideas central to many developments in twentieth century thought.

JEAN-PAUL SARTRE

Sartre (1905–1980) was a leader of French existentialism, which reached a peak of popularity in the 1940s. Existentialists focus upon lived human "existence," in which free choices made within complex and unpredictable circumstances plays a fundamental role. They concluded that human existence is not capable of being fully understood by the methods of science or captured in a purely rational scheme. Thus many of them have turned to literature, which is imaginative rather than scientific, for insight into human life. Sartre produced both philosophical and literary works (plays, novels) that have been widely translated and discussed. The following is from *Existentialism and Humanism* (1946).

Freedom in a Godless World

The Sartrean version of existentialism proceeds from the assumption that there is no God, and infers from that assumption certain facts about humans.

The Distinctive Feature of Human Life. Sartre argues that human nature, or "essence," is not determined by a God or anything else. That lack of an essence is exactly what distinguishes humans from other things.

 From SARTRE: *Existentialism and Humanism*

What they [the various versions of Existentialism] have in common is that they think that existence precedes essence, or, if you prefer, that subjectivity must be the starting point.

Just what does that mean? Let us consider some object that is manufactured, for example, a book or a paper-cutter: here is an object which has been made by an artisan whose inspiration came from a concept. He referred to the concept of what a paper-cutter is and likewise to a known method of production. . . .

When we conceive God as the Creator, He is generally thought of as a superior sort of artisan. . . . [W]hen God creates He knows exactly what He is creating. Thus, the concept of man in the mind of God is comparable to the concept of a paper-cutter in the mind of the manufacturer, and, following certain techniques and a conception, God produces man, just as the artisan, following a definition and a technique, makes a paper-cutter. Thus, the individual man is the realization of a certain concept in the divine intelligence.

In the eighteenth century, the atheism of the philosophers discarded the idea of God, but not so much for the notion that essence precedes existence. To a certain extent, this idea is found everywhere; we find it in Diderot, in Voltaire, and even in Kant. Man has a human nature; this human nature, which is the concept of the human, is found in all men, which means that each man is a particular example of a universal concept, man. In Kant, the result of this universality is that the wild-man, the natural man, as well as the bourgeois, are circumscribed by the same definition and have the same basic qualities. Thus, here too the essence of man precedes the historical existence that we find in nature.

Atheistic existentialism, which I represent, is more coherent. It states that if God does not exist, there is at least one being in whom existence precedes essence, a being who exists before he can be defined by any concept, and that this being is man, or, as Heidegger says, human reality. What is meant here by saying that existence precedes essence? It means that, first of all, man exists, turns up, appears on the scene, and, only afterwards, defines himself. If man, as the existentialist conceives him, is indefinable, it is because at first he is nothing. Only afterward will he be something, and he himself will have made what he will be. Thus, there is no human nature, since there is no God to conceive it. Not only is man what he conceives himself to be, but he is also only what he wills himself to be after this thrust toward existence.

Man is nothing else but what he makes of himself. Such is the first principle of existentialism.

 ASK YOURSELF

10.41. What does Sartre mean when he says that in humans "existence precedes essence"?

In what follows Sartre explains subjectivity (a notion that was fundamental for Kierkegaard) in terms of willing or conscious decision. Unlike artifacts, vegetables, or nonhuman animals, humans can will into being many different life-possibilities. This is not, however, to be confused with the idea that I can be whatever I "wish." My wishes reflect deeper choices I have already made about what I think human life should be like.

It is also what is called subjectivity, the name we are labeled with when charges are brought against us. But what do we mean by this, if not that man has a greater dignity than a stone or table? For we mean that man first exists, that is, that man first of all is the being who hurls himself toward a future and who is conscious of imagining himself as being in the future. Man is at the start a plan which is aware of itself, rather than a patch of moss, a piece of garbage, or a cauliflower; nothing exists prior to this plan; there is nothing in heaven; man will be what he will have planned to be. Not what he will want to be. Because by the word "will" we generally mean a conscious decision, which is subsequent to what we have already made of ourselves. I may want to belong to a political party, write a book, get married; but all that is only a manifestation of an earlier, more spontaneous choice that is called "will." But if existence really does precede essence, man is responsible for what he is. Thus, existentialism's first move is to make every man aware of what he is and to make the full responsibility of his existence rest on him. And when we say that a man is responsible for himself, we do not only mean that he is responsible for his own individuality, but that he is responsible for all men.

The word subjectivism has two meanings, and our opponents play on the two. Subjectivism means, on the one hand, that an individual chooses and makes himself; and, on the other, that it is impossible for man to transcend human subjectivity. The second of these is the essential meaning of existentialism. When we say that man chooses his own self, we mean that every one of us does likewise; but we also mean by that that in making his choice he also chooses all men. In fact, in creating the man that we want to be, there is not a single one of our acts which does not at the same time create an image of man as we think he ought to be. To choose to be this or that is to affirm at the same time the value of what we choose, because we can never choose evil.

We always choose the good, and nothing can be good for us without being good for all.

If, on the other hand, existence precedes essence, and if we grant that we exist and fashion our image at one and the same time, the image is valid for everybody and for our whole age. Thus, our responsibility is much greater than we might have supposed, because it involves all mankind. If I am a workingman and choose to join a Christian trade-union rather than be a communist, and if by being a member I want to show that the best thing for man is resignation, that the kingdom of man is not of this world, I am not only involving my own case—I want to be resigned for everyone. As a result, my action has involved all humanity. To take a more individual matter, if I want to marry, to have children; even if this marriage depends solely on my own circumstances or passion or wish, I am involving all humanity in monogamy and not merely myself. Therefore, I am responsible for myself and for everyone else. I am creating a certain image of man of my own choosing. In choosing myself, I choose man.

Sartre's claim that in choosing what I should be I indicate what I think all people should be is unsupported by argument here. It may be true that the person who chooses a monogamous marriage, for instance, normally thinks that that would be the right life for all people. But don't some people actually say, "I choose monogamy, but if someone else chooses polygamy, celibacy, and so on, that is fine with me"? Would they be contradicting themselves?

 ASK YOURSELF

10.42. Sartre's remarks in the previous passage are reminiscent of Kant, who argued that a rational being must consistently choose in a way that he or she could will all others to choose (see the next section for more "Kantian" comments). There is also a remark in the preceding passage that is reminiscent of an ancient Greek philosopher. Which one, and what is the remark?

The Vocabulary of Existentialism. Sartre now undertakes to define certain typical "existentialist" terms.

This helps us understand what the actual content is of such rather grandiloquent words as anguish, forlornness, despair. As you will see, it's all quite simple.

First, what is meant by anguish? The existentialists say at once that man is anguish. What that means is this: the man who involves himself and who realizes that he is not only the person he chooses to be, but also a lawmaker who is, at the same time, choosing all mankind as well as himself, can not help escape the feeling of his total and deep responsibility. Of course, there are many people who are not anxious; but we claim that they are hiding their anxiety, that they are fleeing from it. Certainly, many people believe that when they do something, they themselves are the only ones involved, and when someone says to them, "What if everyone acted that way?" they shrug their shoulders and answer, "Everyone doesn't act that way." But really, one should always ask himself, "What would happen if everybody looked at things that way?" There is no escaping this disturbing thought except by a kind of double-dealing. A man who lies and makes excuses for himself by saying "Not everybody does that," is someone with an uneasy conscience, because the act of lying implies that a universal value is conferred upon the lie.

Anguish is evident even when it conceals itself. This is the anguish that Kierkegaard called the anguish of Abraham. You know the story: an angel has ordered Abraham to sacrifice his son; if it really were an angel who has come and said, "You are Abraham, you shall sacrifice your son," everything would be all right. But everyone might first wonder, "Is it really an angel, and am I really Abraham? What proof do I have?"

There was a madwoman who had hallucinations; someone used to speak to her on the telephone and give her orders. Her doctors asked her, "Who is it who talks to you?" She answered, "He says it's God." What proof did she really have that it was God? If an angel comes to me, what proof is there that it's an angel? And if I hear voices, what proof is there that they come from heaven and not from hell, or from the subconscious, or a pathological condition? What proves that they are addressed to me? What proof is there that I have been appointed to impose my choice and my conception of man on humanity? I'll never find any proof or sign to convince me of that. If a voice addresses me, it is always for me to decide that this is the angel's voice; if I consider that such an act is a good one, it is I who will choose to say that it is good rather than bad.

 ASK YOURSELF

10.43. What does Sartre mean by "anguish"?

Sartre's unsupported claims about choice as "universal" determine his account of anguish. Clearly part of Sartre's aim here is to stress individual responsibility. You will find the same stress in Kierkegaard's Judge William. But Sartre claims that my choice is what itself creates value. William claimed no such thing.

. . . [W]hen a military officer takes the responsibility for an attack and sends a certain number of men to death, he chooses to do so, and in the main he alone makes the choice. Doubtless, orders come from above, but they are too broad; he interprets them, and on this interpretation depend the lives of ten or fourteen or twenty men. In making a decision he can not help having a certain anguish. All leaders know this anguish. That doesn't keep them from acting; on the contrary, it is the very condition of their action. For it implies that they envisage a number of possibilities, and when they choose one, they realize that it has value only because it is chosen. We shall see that this kind of anguish, which is the kind that existentialism describes, is explained, in addition, by a direct responsibility to the other men whom it involves. It is not a curtain separating us from action, but is part of action itself.

 ASK YOURSELF

10.44. Argue for and against Sartre's claim about the creation of value by choice made in the immediately preceding sentence. Use the case of the military commander to illustrate your arguments.

When we speak of forlornness, a term Heidegger was fond of, we mean only that God does not exist and that we have to face all the consequences of this. The existentialist is strongly opposed to a certain kind of secular ethics which would like to abolish God with the least possible expense. About 1880, some French teachers tried to set up a secular ethics which went something like this: God is a useless and costly hypothesis; we are discarding it; but, meanwhile, in order for there to be an ethics, a society, a civilization, it is essential that certain values be taken seriously and that they be considered as having an a priori existence. It must be obligatory, a priori, to be honest, not to lie, not to beat your wife, to have children, etc., etc. So we're going to try a little device which will make it possible to show that values exist all the same, inscribed in a heaven of ideas, though otherwise God does not exist. In other words—and this, I believe, is the tendency of everything called reformism in France—nothing will be changed if God does not exist. We shall find ourselves with the same norms of honesty, progress, and humanism, and we shall have made of God an outdated hypothesis which will peacefully die off by itself.

The existentialist, on the contrary, thinks it very distressing that God does not exist, because all possibility of finding values in a heaven of ideas disappears along with Him; there can no longer be an a prior Good, since there is no infinite and perfect consciousness to think it. Nowhere is it written that the Good exists, that we must be honest, that we must not lie; because the fact is we are on a plane where there are only men. Dostoievsky said, "If God didn't exist, everything would be possible." That is the very starting point of existentialism. Indeed, everything is permissible if God does not exist, and as a result man is forlorn, because neither within him nor without does he find anything to cling to. He can't start making excuses for himself.

 ASK YOURSELF

10.45. What does Sartre mean by the claim that we are all "forlorn"?

If existence really does precede essence, there is no explaining things away by reference to a fixed and given human nature. In other words, there is no determinism, man is free, man is freedom. On the other hand, if God does not exist, we find no values or commands to turn to which legitimize our conduct. So, in the bright realm of values, we have no excuse behind us, nor justification before us. We are alone, with no excuses.

That is the idea I shall try to convey when I say that man is condemned to be free. Condemned, because he did not create himself, yet, in other respects is free; because, once thrown into the world, he is responsible for everything he does. The existentialist does not believe in the power of passion. He will never agree that a sweeping passion is a ravaging torrent which fatally leads a man to certain acts and is therefore an excuse. He thinks that man is responsible for his passion.

 ASK YOURSELF

10.46. Since we normally think freedom a good thing, it may seem very strange to claim that "we are condemned to be free." Yet this claim is perfectly consistent with what Sartre is arguing. Show how it is consistent and why someone might think of freedom in such a manner.

The Rejection of Competing Ethical Views. Sartre attempts to show the superiority of existentialist ethics to some of its main competitors.

To give you an example which will enable you to understand forlornness better, I shall cite the case of one of my students who came to see me under the following circumstances: his father was on bad terms with his mother, and, moreover, was inclined to be a collaborationist; his older brother had been killed in the German offensive of 1940, and the young man, with somewhat immature but generous feelings, wanted to avenge him. His mother lived alone with him, very much upset by the half-treason of her husband and the death of her older son; the boy was her only consolation.

The boy was faced with the choice of leaving for England and joining the Free French Forces—that is, leaving his mother behind—or remaining with his mother and helping her to carry on. He was fully aware that the woman lived only for him and that his going-off—and perhaps his death—would plunge her into despair. He was also aware that every act that he did for his mother's sake was a sure thing, in the sense that it was helping her to carry on, whereas every effort he made toward going off and fighting was an uncertain move which might run aground and prove completely useless; for example, on his way to England he might, while passing through Spain, be detained indefinitely in a Spanish camp; he might reach England or Algiers and be stuck in an office at a desk job. As a result, he was faced with two very different kinds of action: one, concrete, immediate, but concerning only one individual; the other concerned an incomparably vaster group, a national collectivity, but for that very reason was dubious, and might be interrupted en route. And, at the same time, he was wavering between two kinds of ethics. On the one hand, an ethics of sympathy, of personal devotion; on the other, a broader ethics, but one whose efficacy was more dubious. He had to choose between the two.

Who could help him choose? Christian doctrine? No. Christian doctrine says, "Be charitable, love your neighbor, take the more rugged path, etc., etc." But which is the more rugged path? Whom should he love as a brother? The fighting man or his mother? Which does the greater good, the vague act of fighting in a group, or the concrete one of helping a particular human being to go on living? Who can decide a priori? Nobody. No book of ethics can tell him. The Kantian ethics says, "Never treat any person as a means, but as an end." Very well, if I stay with mother, I'll treat her as an end and not as a means; but by virtue of this very fact, I'm running the risk of treating the people around me who are fighting, as means; and, conversely, if I go to join those who are fighting, I'll be treating them as an end, and, by doing that, I run the risk of treating my mother as a means.

If values are vague, and if they are always too broad for the concrete and specific case that we are considering, the only thing left for us is to trust our instincts. That's what this young man tried to do; and when I saw him, he said, "In the end, feeling is what counts. I ought to choose whichever pushes me in one direction. If I feel that I love my mother enough to sacrifice everything else for her—my desire for vengeance, for action, for adventure—then I'll stay with her. If, on the contrary, I feel that my love for my mother isn't enough, I'll leave."

But how is the value of a feeling determined? What gives his feeling for his mother value? Precisely the fact that he remained with her. I may say that I like so-and-so well enough to sacrifice a certain amount of money for him, but I may say so only if

I've done it. I may say "I love my mother well enough to remain with her" if I have remained with her. The only way to determine the value of this affection is, precisely, to perform an act which confirms and defines it. But, since I require this affection to justify my act, I find myself caught in a vicious circle.

Sartre has just alluded to two ways in which people often try to legitimate their ethical choices. The Kantian way stresses reason as it expresses itself in consistency and, since it presupposes freedom and is found in all humans, requires respect for all humans. Various "sentimentalists" such as Hutcheson or Hume have stressed the centrality of "feelings," for example, feelings of benevolence.

 ASK YOURSELF

10.47. State here why Sartre rejects both of the approaches to ethics just mentioned.

Bad Faith. Sartre goes on to develop an idea central to his thought, the idea of "bad faith," which is something like what we might call "phoniness," but, in his view, a very deep phoniness, which is shown in the way we always try to appeal to something beyond our own choice in defending our actions and projects.

On the other hand, Gide has well said that a mock feeling and a true feeling are almost indistinguishable; to decide that I love my mother and will remain with her, or to remain with her by putting on an act, amount somewhat to the same thing. In other words, the feeling is formed by the acts one performs; so, I can not refer to it in order to act upon it. Which means that I can neither seek within myself the true condition which will impel me to act, nor apply to a system of ethics for concepts which will permit me to act. You will say, "At least, he did go to a teacher for advice." But if you seek advice from a priest, for example, you have chosen this priest; you already knew, more or less, just about what advice he was going to give you. In other words, choosing your adviser is involving yourself. The proof of this is that if you are a Christian, you will say, "Consult a priest." But some priests are collaborating, some are just marking time, some are resisting. Which to choose? If the young man chooses a priest who is resisting or collaborating, he has already decided on the kind of advice he's going to get. Therefore, in coming to see me he knew the answer I was going to give him, and I had only one answer to give: "You're free, choose, that is, invent." No general ethics can show you what is to be done; there are no omens in the world. The Catholics will reply. "But there are." Granted—but, in any case, I myself choose the meaning they have.

When I was a prisoner, I knew a rather remarkable young man who was a Jesuit. He had entered the Jesuit order in the following way: he had had a number of very bad breaks; in childhood, his father died, leaving him in poverty, and he was a scholarship student at a religious institution where he was constantly made to feel that he was being kept out of charity; then, he failed to get any of the honors and distinctions that children like; later on, at about eighteen, he bungled a love affair; finally, at twenty-two, he failed in military training, a childish enough matter, but it was the last straw.

This young fellow might well have felt that he had botched everything. It was a sign of something, but of what? He might have taken refuge in bitterness or despair. But he very wisely looked upon all this as a sign that he was not made for secular triumphs, and that only the triumphs of religion, holiness, and faith were open to him. He saw the hand of God in all this, and so he entered the order. Who can help seeing that he alone decided what the sign meant?

Some other interpretation might have been drawn from this series of setbacks; for example, that he might have done better to turn carpenter or revolutionist. Therefore, he is fully responsible for the interpretation. Forlornness implies that we ourselves choose our being. Forlornness and anguish go together.

In each of the examples given a person excuses himself or tries to account for his actions and choices in terms of factors bearing on him from the outside, when in fact it is quite clear that it is his own decision that has put him where he is. Thus he is not being honest about himself. Sartre see a kind of pervasive dishonesty or self-deception in human life.

 ASK YOURSELF

10.48. As you read what follows work out an answer to this question: What does "despair" mean in Sartre (the word "despair" is rooted in the phrase "without hope")?

As for despair, the term has a very simple meaning. It means that we shall confine ourselves to reckoning only with what depends upon our will, or on the ensemble of probabilities which make our action possible. When we want something, we always have to reckon with probabilities. I may be counting on the arrival of a friend. The friend is coming by rail or street-car; this supposes that the train will arrive on schedule, or that the street-car will not jump the track. I am left in the realm of possibility; but possibilities are to be reckoned with only to the point where my action comports with the ensemble of these possibilities, and no further. The moment the possibilities I am considering are not rigorously involved by my action, I ought to disengage myself from them, because no God, no scheme, can adapt the world and its possibilities to my will. When Descartes said, "Conquer yourself rather than the world," he meant essentially the same thing.

. . . According to this, we can understand why our doctrine horrifies certain people. Because often the only way they can bear their wretchedness is to think, "Circumstances have been against me. What I've been and done doesn't show my true worth. To be sure, I've had no great love, no great friendship, but that's because I haven't met a man or woman who was worthy. The books I've written haven't been very good because I haven't had the proper leisure. I haven't had children to devote myself to because I didn't find a man with whom I could have spent my life. So there remains within me, unused and quite viable, a host of propensities, inclinations, possibilities, that one wouldn't guess from the mere series of things I've done."

Now, for the existentialist there is really no love other than one which manifests itself in a person's being in love. There is no genius other than one which is expressed in works of art; the genius of Proust is the sum of Proust's works; the genius of Racine is his series of tragedies. Outside of that, there is nothing. Why say that Racine could have written another tragedy, when he didn't write it? A man is involved in life, leaves his impress on it, and outside of that there is nothing. To be sure, this may seem a harsh thought to someone whose life hasn't been a success. But, on the other hand, it prompts people to understand that reality alone is what counts, that dreams, expectations, and hopes warrant no more than to define a man as a disappointed dream, as miscarried hopes, as vain expectations. In other words, to define him negatively and not positively. However, when we say, "You are nothing else than your life," that does not imply that the artist will be judged solely on the basis of his works of art; a thousand other things will contribute toward summing him up. What we mean is that a man is nothing else than a series of undertakings, that he is the sum, the organization, the ensemble of the relationships which make up these undertakings.

 ## ASK YOURSELF

10.49. A famous poem by Thomas Gray titled "Elegy Written in a Country Churchyard" contains the lines: "full many a flower has bloomed to blush unseen,/and waste its sweetness on the desert air." The idea is, evidently, that there have been many great people who have not been recognized because they never had the chance to perform the great deeds (for example, a chance to write the great poetry) that they had it within them to perform. What would Sartre say about this idea?

10.50. In studying what follows, work out an answer to this question: What would Sartre say about the claim often made that people are a product of heredity and environment, and why would he say it?

When all is said and done, what we are accused of, at bottom, is not our pessimism, but an optimistic toughness. If people throw up to us our works of fiction in which we write about people who are soft, weak, cowardly, and sometimes even downright bad, it's not because these people are soft, weak, cowardly, or bad; because if we were to say, as Zola did, that they are that way because of heredity, the workings of environment, society, because of biological or psychological determinism, people would be reassured. They would say, "Well, that's what we're like, no one can do anything about it." But when the existentialist writes about a coward, he says that this coward is responsible for his cowardice. He's not like that because he has a cowardly heart or lung or brain; he's not like that on account of his physiological make-up; but he's like that because he has made himself a coward by his acts. There's no such thing as a cowardly constitution; there are nervous constitutions; there is poor blood, as the common people say, or there are strong constitutions. But the man whose blood is poor is not a coward on that account, for what makes cowardice is the act of renouncing or yielding. A constitution is not an act; the coward is defined on the basis of the acts he performs. People feel, in a vague sort of way, that this coward we're talking about is guilty of being a coward, and the thought frightens them. What people would like is that a coward or a hero be born that way.

Further Explanation and Defense of the Idea of "Subjectivity." Does existentialist doctrine imply that "everything is subjective" in the sense that choices are all completely arbitrary and equally valuable or worthless?

. . . [I]f it is impossible to find in every man some universal essence which would be human nature, yet there does exist a universal human condition. It's not by chance that today's thinkers speak more readily of man's condition than of his nature. By condition they mean, more or less definitely, the a priori limits which outline man's fundamental situation in the universe. Historical situations vary; a man may be born a slave in a pagan society or a feudal lord or a proletarian. What does not vary is the necessity for him to exist in the world, to be at work there, to be there in the midst of other people, and to be mortal there. The limits are neither subjective nor objective, or, rather, they have an objective and a subjective side. Objective because they are to be found everywhere and are recognizable everywhere; subjective because they are lived and are nothing if man does not live them, that is, freely determine his existence with reference to them. And though the configurations may differ, at least none of them are completely strange to me, because they all appear as attempts either to pass beyond these limits or recede from them or deny them or adapt to them. Consequently, every configuration, however individual it may be, has a universal value.

 ASK YOURSELF

10.51. Is it true that every purpose of a person from China can be understood by a person from Europe? Argue pro and con, indicating why Sartre would reply affirmatively.

. . . This does not completely settle the objection to subjectivism. In fact, the objection still takes several forms. First, there is the following: we are told, "So you're able to do anything, no matter what!" This is expressed in various ways. First we are accused of anarchy; then they say, "You're unable to pass judgment on others, because there's no reason to prefer one configuration to another"; finally they tell us, "Everything is arbitrary in this choosing of yours. You take something from one pocket and pretend you're putting it into the other."

These three objections aren't very serious. Take the first objection. "You're able to do anything, no matter what" is not to the point. In one sense choice is possible, but what is not possible is not to choose. I can always choose, but I ought to know that if I do not choose, I am still choosing. Though this may seem purely formal, it is highly important for keeping fantasy and caprice within bounds. If it is true that in facing a situation, for example, one in which, as a person capable of having sexual relations, of having children, I am obliged to choose an attitude, and if I in any way assume responsibility for a choice which, in involving myself, also involves all mankind, this has nothing to do with caprice, even if no a prior value determines my choice.

. . . [M]an is in an organized situation in which he himself is involved. Through his choice, he involves all mankind, and he can not avoid making a choice: either he will remain chaste, or he will marry without having children, or he will marry and have children; anyhow, whatever he may do, it is impossible for him not to take full responsibility for the way he handles this problem. Doubtless, he chooses without referring to pre-established values, but it is unfair to accuse him of caprice. Instead, let us say that moral choice is to be compared to the making of a work of art.

 ASK YOURSELF

10.52 What is it, in Sartre's view, that prevents existentialist "choice" from being mere "caprice"? Criticize Sartre's argument here.

Sartre goes on to compare the creative freedom of the artist to the freedom required for morality.

. . . Nobody can tell what the painting of tomorrow will be like. Painting can be judged only after it has once been made. What connection does that have with ethics? We are in the same creative situation. We never say that a work of art is arbitrary. When we speak of a canvas of Picasso, we never say that it is arbitrary; we understand quite well that he was making himself what he is at the very time he was painting, that the ensemble of his work is embodied in his life.

The same holds on the ethical plane. What art and ethics have in common is that we have creation and invention in both cases. We can not decide *a priori* what there is to be done. I think that I pointed that out quite sufficiently when I mentioned the case of the student who came to see me, and who might have applied to all the ethical systems, Kantian or otherwise, without getting any sort of guidance. He was obliged to devise his law himself. Never let it be said by us that this man—who, taking affection, individual action, and kindheartedness toward a specific person as his ethical first principle, chooses to remain with his mother, or who, preferring to make a sacrifice, chooses to go to England—has made an arbitrary choice. Man makes himself. He isn't ready made at the start. In choosing his ethics, he makes himself, and force of circumstances is such that he can not abstain from choosing one. We define man only in relationship to involvement. It is therefore absurd to charge us with arbitrariness of choice.

In the second place, it is said that we are unable to pass judgment on others. In a way this is true, and in another way, false. It is true in this sense, that, whenever a man sanely and sincerely involves himself and chooses his configuration, it is impossible for him to prefer another configuration, regardless of what his own may be in other respects. It is true in this sense, that we do not believe in progress. Progress is betterment. Man is always the same. The situation confronting him varies. Choice always remains a choice in a situation. The problem has not changed since the time one could choose between those for and those against slavery, for example, at the time of the Civil War, and the present time, when one can side with the Maquis Resistance Party, or with the Communists.

But, nevertheless, one can still pass judgment, for, as I have said, one makes a choice in relationship to others. First, one can judge (and this is perhaps not a judgment of value, but a logical judgment) that certain choices are based on error and others on truth. If we have defined man's situation as a free choice, with no excuses and no recourse, every many who takes refuge behind the excuse of his passions, every man who sets up a determinism, is a dishonest man.

The objection may be raised, "But why mayn't he choose himself dishonestly?" I reply that I am not obliged to pass moral judgment on him, but that I do define his dishonesty as an error. One can not help considering the truth of the matter. Dishonesty is obviously a falsehood because it belies the complete freedom of involvement. On the same grounds, I maintain that there is also dishonesty if I choose to state that certain values exist prior to me; it is self-contradictory for me to want them and at the same time state that they are imposed on me. Suppose someone says to me, "What if I want to be dishonest?" I'll answer, "There's no reason for you not to be, but I'm saying that that's what you are, and that the strictly coherent attitude is that of honesty."

   ASK YOURSELF

10.53. There is one way in which we can "judge" another person, according to Sartre. What is it?

10.54. If someone chose to be a serial killer, or a "fascist," and they made it completely clear that they alone were responsible for that choice and all that followed from it, would we be able to "judge" them (claim they were "wrong" or in any way "immoral") in Sartre's view? Explain.

Further Examples of the Centrality of Free Involvement. Apparently opposed moralities are all rooted in the same freedom, freedom as Sartre has construed it.

. . . Once again, take the case of the student. In the name of what, in the name of what great moral maxim do you think he could have decided, in perfect peace of mind, to abandon his mother or to stay with her? There is no way of judging. The content is always concrete and thereby unforeseeable; there is always the element of invention. The one thing that counts is knowing whether the inventing that has been done, has been done in the name of freedom.

For example, let us look at the following two cases. You will see to what extent they correspond, yet differ. Take *The Mill on the Floss.* We find a certain young girl, Maggie Tulliver, who is an embodiment of the value of passion and who is aware of it. She is in love with a young man. Stephen, who is engaged to an insignificant young girl. This Maggie Tulliver, instead of heedlessly preferring her own happiness, chooses, in the name of human solidarity, to sacrifice herself and give up the man she loves. On the other hand, Sanseverina, in *The Charterhouse of Parma,* believing that passion is man's true value, would say that a great love deserves sacrifices; that it is to be preferred to the banality of the conjugal love that would tie Stephen to the young ninny he had to marry. She would choose to sacrifice the girl and fulfill her happiness; and, as Stendhal shows, she is even ready to sacrifice herself for the sake of passion, if this life demands it. Here we are in the presence of two strictly opposed moralities. I claim that they are much the same thing; in both cases what has been set up as the goal is freedom.

You can imagine two highly similar attitudes: one girl prefers to renounce her love out of resignation; another prefers to disregard the prior attachment of the man she loves out of sexual desire. On the surface these two actions resemble those we've just described. However, they are completely different. Sanseverina's attitude is much nearer that of Maggie Tulliver, one of heedless rapacity.

Thus, you seen that the second charge is true and, at the same time, false. One may choose anything if it is on the grounds of free involvement.

The third objection is the following: "You take something from one pocket and put it into the other. That is, fundamentally, values aren't serious, since you choose them." My answer to this is that I'm quite vexed that that's the way it is; but if I've discarded God the Father, there has to be someone to invent values. You've got to take things as they are. Moreover, to say that we invent values means nothing else but this: life has no meaning *a priori*. Before you come alive, life is nothing; it's up to you to give it a meaning, and value is nothing else but the meaning that you choose.

What It Means to Say "Existentialism Is a Humanism." Sartre sums up his views in the course of explaining what is meant by "existentialist humanism," which is to be distinguished from any "humanism" that depends upon a specific concept of human nature or essence.

. . . But there is another meaning of humanism. Fundamentally it is this: man is constantly outside of himself; in projecting himself, in losing himself outside of himself, he makes for man's existing; and, on the other hand, it is by pursuing transcendent goals that he is able to exist; man, being this state of passing-beyond, and seizing upon things only as they bear upon this passing-beyond, is at the heart, at the center of this passing-beyond. There is no universe other than a human universe, the universe of human subjectivity. This connection between transcendency, as a constituent element of man—not in the sense that God is transcendent, but in the sense of passing beyond—and subjectivity, in the sense that man is not closed in on himself but is always present in a human universe, is what we call existentialist humanism. Humanism, because we remind man that there is no lawmaker other than himself, and that in his forlornness he will decide by himself; because we point out that man will fulfill himself as man, not in turning toward himself, but in seeking outside of himself a goal which is just this liberation, just this particular fulfillment.

    ASK YOURSELF

10.55. Sartre speaks of a "goal of liberation." Does he help us to understand what the content of liberation would be? Argue pro and con.

G. E. M. ANSCOMBE
Modern Moral Philosophy

British philosopher Gertrude Elizabeth Margaret Anscombe (1919–2001) made important contributions to many areas of philosophy, but she is particularly noted for her work in the philosophy of mind and ethics. The following essay, "Modern Moral Philosophy" (1958), shows something of the relation between the two and contains brief critiques of the major traditions in ethics through the twentieth century. This essay helped to provoke a new interest in virtue ethics (cf. Aristotle) and influenced one of the most widely discussed works of moral philosophy in the last few decades, MacIntyre's *After Virtue* (1981).

The Inadequacies of the Dominant Approaches. Anscombe states the main theses of her paper and goes on to reject Butler, Hume, Kant, and Mill as viable sources of moral philosophy.

 From ANSCOMBE: *Modern Moral Philosophy*

I will begin by stating three theses which I present in this paper. The first is that it is not profitable for us at present to do moral philosophy; that should be laid aside at any rate until we have an adequate philosophy of psychology, in which we are conspicuously lacking. The second is that the concepts of obligation, and duty—moral obligation and moral duty, that is to say—and of what is morally right and wrong, and of the moral sense of "ought," ought to be jettisoned if this is psychologically possible; because they are survivals, or derivatives from survivals, from an earlier conception of ethics which no longer generally survives, and are only harmful without it. My third thesis is that the differences between the well-known English writers on moral philosophy from Sidgwick to the present day are of little importance.

Anyone who has read Aristotle's *Ethics* and has also read modern moral philosophy must have been struck by the great contrasts between them. The concepts which are prominent among the moderns seem to be lacking, or at any rate buried or far in the background, in Aristotle. Most noticeably, the term "moral" itself, which we have by direct inheritance from Aristotle, just doesn't seem to fit, in its modern sense, into an account of Aristotelian ethics. Aristotle distinguishes virtues as moral and intellectual. Have some of what he calls "intellectual" virtues what we should call a "moral" aspect? It would seem so; the criterion is presumably that a failure in an "intellectual" virtue—like that of having good judgment in calculating how to bring about something useful, say in municipal government—may be blameworthy. But—it may reasonably be asked—cannot any failure be made a matter of blame or reproach? Any derogatory criticism, say of the workmanship of a product or the design of a machine can be called blame or reproach. So we want to put in the word "morally" again: sometimes such a failure may be morally blameworthy, sometimes not. Now has Aristotle got this idea of moral blame, as opposed to any other? If he has, why isn't it more central? There are some mistakes, he says, which are causes, not of involuntariness in actions, but of scoundrelism, and for which a man is blamed. Does this mean that there is a moral obligation not to make certain intellectual mistakes? Why doesn't he discuss obligation in general, and this obligation in particular? If someone professes to be expounding Aristotle and talks in a modern fashion about "moral" such-and-such, he must be very imperceptive if he does not constantly feel like someone whose jaws have somehow got out of alignment: the teeth don't come together in a proper bite.

We cannot, then, look to Aristotle for any elucidation of the modern way of talking about "moral" goodness, obligation, etc. And all the best-known writers on ethics in modern times, from Butler to Mill, appear to me to have faults as thinkers on the subject which make it impossible to hope for any direct light on it from them. I will state these objections with the brevity which their character makes possible.

Butler exalts conscience, but appears ignorant that a man's conscience may tell him to do the vilest things.

Hume defines "truth" in such a way as to exclude ethical judgments from it, and professes that he has proved that they are so excluded. He also implicitly defines "passion" in such a way that aiming at anything is having a passion. His objection to passing from "is" ' to "ought" would apply equally to passing from "is" to "owes" or from "is" to "needs." (However, because of the historical situation, he has a point here, which I shall return to.)

Kant introduces the idea of "legislating for oneself," which is as absurd as if in these days, when majority votes command great respect, one were to call each reflective decision a man made a vote resulting in a majority, which as a matter of proportion is overwhelming, for it is always 1–0. The concept of legislation requires superior power in the legislator. His own rigoristic convictions on the subject of lying were so intense that it never occurred to him that a lie could be relevantly described as anything but just a lie (e.g. as "a lie in such-and-such circumstances"). His rule about universalizable maxims is useless without stipulations as to what shall count as a relevant description of an action with a view to constructing a maxim about it.

Bentham and Mill do not notice the difficulty of the concept of "pleasure." They are often said to have gone wrong through committing the "naturalistic fallacy"; but this charge does not impress me, because I do not find accounts of it coherent. But the other point—about pleasure—seems to me a fatal objection from the very outset. The ancients found this concept pretty baffling. It reduced Aristotle to sheer babble about "the bloom on the cheek of youth" because, for good reasons, he wanted to make it out both identical with and different from the pleasurable activity. Generations of modern philosophers found this concept quite unperplexing, and it reappeared in the literature as a problematic one only a year or two ago when Ryle wrote about it. The reason is simple: since Locke, pleasure was taken to be some sort of internal impression. But it was superficial, if that was the right account of it, to make it the point of actions.

One might adapt something Wittgenstein said about "meaning" and say "Pleasure cannot be an internal impression, for no internal impression could have the consequences of pleasure."

Mill also, like Kant, fails to realize the necessity for stipulation as to relevant descriptions, if his theory is to have content. It did not occur to him that acts of murder and theft could be otherwise described. He holds that where a proposed action is of such a kind as to fall under some one principle established on grounds of utility, one must go by that; where it falls under none or several, the several suggesting contrary views of the action, the thing to do is to calculate particular consequences. But pretty well any action can be so described as to make it fall under a variety of principles of utility (as I shall say for short) if it falls under any.

Kant claimed that telling a lying promise in order to secure needed funds cannot consistently be willed to be a universal law (see p. 537). It thus violates the categorical imperative (which in his view provides the definitive test for rightness/wrongness) and thus is always wrong. But that very same action, given certain circumstances, might also be described as "telling a lying promise to a tyrant in order to secure funds to save a life."(Suppose, for example, that I need the funds to arrange for the escape of a Jew from a death camp and can only get them from a Nazi official.) And it might fall under many other descriptions. It seems possible that under some of these descriptions the action would be universalizable after all. But Kant never tells us how to determine which description to use. So how can we apply his test? Likewise, Mill argued that a rule such as "Do not lie" has a high utility and should usually be followed, but again, a single action of lying can be described in many ways; under some of those descriptions it might seem to have a very high utility, under others a low or zero utility. So how do we know when to switch from following useful rules to calculating particular circumstances (and, for that matter, how can we even do the latter without "relevant act descriptions")?

 ASK YOURSELF

10.56. Add something to the description of a single case of lying to a friend (i.e., simply add something to the description "lying to a friend") so that telling the lie would have a high utility.

Anscombe also criticizes the notion of pleasure as it is used (for very fundamental purposes) in Mill. If pleasure were merely a more or less passive mental state, like a sensation, it would be much less important to us than it is. We take pleasure in doing certain things (playing tennis, for instance), and it is nonsense to suppose that the pleasure involved in such an activity is reducible to a set of internal states.

Problems with Hume. Hume had claimed (see the selection from Hume's *Treatise* on p. 502) that you cannot derive "ought" statements (such as "You *ought* to help George") from any mere "is" statements (statements of fact, such as "George *is* in dire need of help, and you *are* in a position to supply it"). The "ought" statement always requires something more than the facts in the "is" statements; for example, it may require a desire that George be helped.

 ASK YOURSELF

10.57. Give a further example to illustrate Hume's claim.

I will now return to Hume. The features of Hume's philosophy which I have mentioned, like many other features of it, would incline me to think that Hume was a mere brilliant sophist; and his procedures are certainly sophistical. But I am forced, not to reverse, but to add to, this judgement by a peculiarity of Hume's philosophizing: namely that although he reaches his conclusions—with which he is in love—by sophistical methods, his considerations constantly open up very deep and important problems. It is often the case that in the act of exhibiting the sophistry one finds oneself noticing matters which deserve a lot of exploring: the obvious stands in need of investigation as a result of the points that Hume pretends to have made. In this, he is unlike, say, Butler. It was already well known that conscience could dictate vile actions; for Butler to have written disregarding this does not open up any new topics for us. But with Hume it is otherwise: hence he is a very profound and great philosopher, in spite of his sophistry. For example:

Suppose that I say to my grocer "Truth consists in *either* relations of ideas, as that 20 shillings = 1 pound, or matters of fact, as that I ordered potatoes, you supplied them, and you sent me a bill. So it doesn't apply to such a proposition as that I *owe* you such-and-such a sum."

Now if one makes this comparison, it comes to light that the relation of the facts mentioned to the description "X owes Y so much money" is an interesting one, which I will call that of being "brute relative to" that description. Further, the "brute" facts mentioned here themselves have descriptions relatively to which *other* facts are "brute"—as, e.g., *he had potatoes carted to my house and they were left there* are brute facts relative to "he supplied me with potatoes." And the fact X *owes Y money* is in turn "brute" relative to other descriptions e.g. "X is solvent." Now the relation of "relative bruteness" is a complicated one. To mention a few points; if xyz is a set of facts brute relative to a description A, then xyz is set out of a range some set among which holds if A holds; but the holding of some set among these does not necessarily entail A, because exceptional circumstances can always make a difference; and what are exceptional circumstances relatively to A can generally only be explained by giving a few diverse examples, and no theoretically adequate provision can be made for exceptional circumstances, since a further special context can theoretically always be imagined that would reinterpret any special context. Further, though in normal circumstances, xyz would be a justification for A, that is not to say that A just comes to the same as "xyz"; and also there is apt to be an institutional context which gives its point to the description A, of which institution A is of course not itself a description. (E.g. the statement that I give someone a shilling is not a description of the institution of money or of the currency of this country.) Thus, though it would be ludicrous to pretend that there can be no such thing as a transition from, e.g., "is" to "owes," the character of the transition is in fact rather interesting and comes to light as a result of reflecting on Hume's arguments.

If the fact that you delivered potatoes to my door would be "brute" relative to (provide factual support for the claim that) "you supplied me with potatoes" and the latter fact brute relative to "you owe me x amount of money," then we seem on the way to saying that this last fact is brute relative to "you ought to pay me x amount of money." This last fact would "follow from" or be supported by the previous facts, contrary to Hume's claim that no "ought" statement follows from mere "is" (factual) statements. But Anscombe believes that the notion of a special "moral" sense of "ought" is the unrecognized source of Hume's claim. Unfortunately for Hume, there is no such special sense. The belief is that there is, is a "hangover" from a historical period in which "ought" got its force from a connection to divine commands, as she further explains below.

That I owe the grocer such-and-such a sum would be one of a set of facts which would be "brute" in relation to the description "I am a bilker." "Bilking," is of course a species of "dishonesty" or "injustice." (Naturally the consideration will not have any effect on my actions unless I want to commit or avoid acts of injustice.)

So far, in spite of their strong associations, I conceive "bilking," "injustice" and "dishonesty" in a merely "factual" way. That I can do this for "bilking" is obvious enough; "justice" ' I have no idea how to define, except that its sphere is that of actions which relate to someone else, but "injustice," its defect, can for the moment be offered as a generic name covering various species. E.g.: "bilking," "theft" (which is relative to whatever property institutions exist) "slander," "adultery," "punishment of the innocent."

In present-day philosophy an explanation is required how an unjust man is a bad man, or an unjust action a bad one; to give such an explanation belongs to ethics; but it cannot even be begun until we are equipped with a sound philosophy of psychology. For the proof that an unjust man is a bad man would require a positive account of justice as a "virtue." This part of the subject-matter of ethics is, however, completely closed to us until we have an account of what *type of characteristic* a virtue is—a problem, not of ethics, but of conceptual analysis—and how it relates to the actions in which it is instanced: a matter which I think Aristotle did not succeed in really making clear. For this we certainly need an account at least of what a human action is at all, and how its description as "doing such-and-such" is affected by its motive and by the intention or intentions in it; and for this an account of such concepts is required.

The terms "should" or "ought" or "needs" relate to good and bad: e.g. machinery needs oil, or should or ought to be oiled, in that running without oil is bad for it, or it runs badly without oil. According to this conception, of course, "should" and "ought" are not used in a special "moral" sense when one says that a man should not bilk. (In Aristotle's sense of the term "moral" (*ethikos*) they are being used in connection with a moral subject-matter: namely that of human passions and [nontechnical] actions.) But they have now acquired a special so-called "moral" sense—i.e. a sense in which they imply some absolute verdict (like one of guilty/not guilty on a man) on what is described in the "ought" sentences used in certain types of context: not merely the contexts that *Aristotle* would call "moral"—passions and actions—but also some of the contexts that he would call "intellectual."

The ordinary (and quite indispensable) terms—"should," "needs," "ought," "must"—acquired this special sense by being equated in the relevant contexts with "is obliged," or "is bound," or "is required to," in the sense in which one can be obliged or bound by law or something can be required by law.

The "ought" in "You ought to push the clutch in sooner" sounds quite different to many people from the "ought" in "You ought to tell the truth." The second sounds "moral"; the first does not. A principal thesis of this essay is that the so-called "moral sense" of "ought" and related terms is a hangover from a time in which people considered that what we now call "moral obligations" were rooted in the commands of God.

ASK YOURSELF

10.58. Give your own examples of moral and nonmoral uses of "ought." Does it seem to you as though the "moral" case is in some sense *commanded*?

How did this come about? The answer is in history: between Aristotle and us came Christianity, with its law conception of ethics. For Christianity derived its ethical notions from the Torah. (One might be inclined to think that a law conception of ethics could arise only among people who accepted an allegedly divine positive law; that this is not so is shown by the example of the Stoics, who also thought that whatever was involved in conformity to human virtues was required by divine law.)

In consequence of the dominance of Christianity for many centuries, the concepts of being bound, permitted, or excused became deeply embedded in our language and thought. The Greek word *"harmatanein,"* the aptest to be turned to that use, acquired the sense "sin," from having meant "mistake," "missing the mark," "going wrong." The Latin *peccatum* which roughly corresponded to *harmatema* was even apter for the sense "sin," because it was already associated with "culpa"—"guilt"—a juridical notion. The blanket term "illicit," "unlawful," meaning much the same as our blanket term "wrong," explains itself. It is interesting that Aristotle did not have such a blanket term. He has blanket terms for wickedness—"villain," "scoundrel"; but of course a man is not a villain or a scoundrel by the performance of one bad action, or a few bad actions. And he has terms like "disgraceful," "impious"; and specific terms signifying defect of the relevant virtue, like "unjust"; but no term corresponding to "illicit." The extension of this term (i.e. the range of its application) could be indicated in his terminology only by a quite lengthy sentence: that is "illicit" which, whether it is a thought or a consented-to passion or an action or an omission in thought or action, is something contrary to one of the virtues the lack of which shows a man to be bad qua man. That formulation would yield a concept coextensive with the concept "illicit."

Aristotle does not suppose that (apart from the particular laws of a community) there is some "law" applicable to all, a single violation of which deserves punishment or makes a person a "sinner." Rather, he thinks of a bad or evil or vicious person as one who has developed certain patterns of action and feeling, such as are indicated by a term like "lazy." Such patterns of action and feeling are "bad" because they stand in the way of *eudaimonia*, happiness or "flourishing," not because they involve the violation of some divine law. It would be possible to believe that any action or trait that hinders flourishing also involves a violation of divine law, but that is not how Aristotle thinks of it.

ASK YOURSELF

10.59. If you believe that adultery is wrong because God has forbidden it, then you will think of yourself as _____ by that "divine command" in a manner similar to your obligation to keep a _____ law.

To have a law conception of ethics is to hold that what is needed for conformity with the virtues failure in which is the mark of being bad qua man (and not merely, say, qua craftsman or logician)—that what is needed for *this*, is required by divine law. Naturally it is not possible to have such a conception unless you believe in God as a law-giver; like Jews, Stoics, and Christians. But if such a conception is dominant for many centuries, and then is given up, it is a natural result that the concepts of "obligation," of being bound or required as by a law, should remain though they had lost their root; and if the word "ought" has become invested in certain contexts with the sense of "obligation," it too will remain to be spoken with a special emphasis and a special feeling in these contexts.

It is as if the notion "criminal" were to remain when criminal law and criminal courts had been abolished and forgotten. A Hume discovering this situation might conclude that there was a special sentiment, expressed by "criminal," which alone gave the word its sense. So Hume discovered the situation in which the notion "obligation" survived, and the notion "ought" was invested with that peculiar force having which it is said to be used in a "moral" sense, but in which the belief in divine law had long since been abandoned: for it was substantially given up among Protestants at the time of the Reformation. The situation, if I am right, was the interesting one of the survival of a concept outside the framework of thought that made it a really intelligible one.

When Hume produced his famous remarks about the transition from "is" to "ought," he was, then, bringing together several quite different points. One I have tried to bring out by my remarks on the transition from "is" to "owes" and on the relative "bruteness" of facts. It would be possible to bring out a different point by inquiring about the transition from "is" to "needs"; from the characteristics of an organism to the environment that it needs, for example. To say that it needs that environment is not to say, e.g., that you want it to have that environment, but that it won't flourish unless it has it. Certainly, it all depends whether you want it to flourish! as Hume would say. But what "all depends" on whether you want it to flourish is whether the fact that it needs that environment, or won't flourish without it, has the slightest influence on your actions. Now that such-and-such "ought" to be or "is needed" is supposed to have an influence on your actions: from which it seemed natural to infer that to judge that it "ought to be" was in fact to grant what you judged "ought to be" influence on your actions. And no amount of truth as to what is the case could possibly have a logical claim to have influence on your actions. (It is not judgement as such that sets us in motion; but our judgement on how to get or do something we *want*.) Hence it *must* be impossible to infer "needs" or "ought to be" from "is." But in the case of a plant, let us say, the inference from "is" to "needs" is certainly not in the least dubious. It is interesting and worth examining; but not at all fishy. Its interest is similar to the interest of the relation between brute and less brute facts: these relations have been very little considered. And while you can contrast "what it needs" with "what it's got"—like contrasting *de facto* and *de jure*—that does not make its needing this environment less of a "truth."

Certainly in the case of what the plant needs, the thought of a need will only affect action if you want the plant to flourish. Here, then, there is no necessary connection between what you can judge the plant "needs" and what you want. But there is some sort of necessary connection between what you think you need, and what you want. The connection is a complicated one; it is possible not to want something that you judge you need. But, e.g., it is not possible never to want *anything* that you judge you need. This, however, is not a fact about the meaning of the word "to need," but about the phenomenon of *wanting*. Hume's reasoning, we might say, in effect, leads one to think it must be about the word "to need," or "to be good for."

What something (a plant, or a person) needs is obviously a factual matter. It is a fact that my houseplant needs light, for instance. Whether it gets it depends upon whether I care what happens to it, that is, upon what I want, so there is no necessary connection between "My plant needs light" and "I ought to put it in the light." But, Anscombe claims, there is a (complicated) necessary connection between what *I* need and what *I* want.

 ASK YOURSELF

10.60. Is Anscombe working toward the view that a fact, one about what I need, might imply something about what I ought to do, so that an "ought" statement could be derived from a factual or "is" statement, despite what Hume claimed?

Anscombe goes on to argue that Hume is, in a way, right to think that no ought statement follows from a statement of fact. He is right insofar as he simply is reflecting the fact that the sense of obligation expressed by "ought" under a divine command conception becomes mysterious when one no longer believes in divine commands. But he, and his modern followers, do not realize that that is the reason why "is" does not seem to imply "ought." So they claim that there is *no* connection, or go looking for a "fishy" one.

Thus we find two problems already wrapped up in the remark about a transition from "is" to "ought"; now supposing that we had clarified the "relative bruteness" of facts on the one hand, and the notions involved in "needing," and "flourishing" on the other—there would still remain a third point. For, following Hume, someone might say: Perhaps you have made out your point about a transition from "is" to "owes" and from "is" to "needs": but only at the cost of showing "owes" and "needs" sentences to express a *kind* of truths, a *kind* of facts. And it remains impossible to infer "*morally ought*" from "is" sentences.

This comment, it seems to me, would be correct. This word "ought," having become a word of mere mesmeric force, could not, in the character of having that force, be inferred from anything whatever. . . . [It is] a word retaining the suggestion of force, and apt to have a strong psychological effect, but which no longer signifies a real concept at all.

For its suggestion is one of a *verdict* on my action, according as it agrees or disagrees with the description in the "ought" sentence. And where one does not think there is a judge or a law, the notion of a verdict may retain its psychological effect, but not its meaning. Now imagine that just this word "verdict" were so used—with a characteristically solemn emphasis—as to retain its atmosphere but not its meaning, and someone were to say: "For a *verdict*, after all, you need a law and a judge." The reply might be made: "Not at all, for if there were a law and a judge who gave a verdict, the question for us would be whether accepting that verdict is something that there is a *verdict on*." This is an analogue of an argument which is so frequently referred to as decisive: If someone does have a divine law conception of ethics, all the same, he has to agree that he has to have a judgment that he *ought* (morally ought) to obey the divine law; so his ethic is in exactly the same position as any other: he merely has a "Practical major premise"*: "Divine law ought to be obeyed" where someone else has, e.g., "The greatest happiness principle ought to be employed in all decisions."

I should judge that Hume and our present-day ethicists had done a considerable service by showing that no content could be found in the notion "morally ought"; if it were not that the latter philosophers try to find an alternative (very fishy) content and to retain the psychological force of the term. It would be most reasonable to drop it. It has no reasonable sense outside a law conception of ethics; they are not going to maintain such a conception; and you can do ethics without it, as is shown by the example of Aristotle. It would be a great improvement if, instead of "morally wrong," one always named a genus such as "untruthful," "unchaste," "unjust." We should no longer ask whether doing something was "wrong," passing directly from some description of an action to this notion; we should ask whether, e.g., it was unjust; and the answer would sometimes be clear at once.

 ASK YOURSELF

10.61. What would be the problem with supposing that we might need a verdict on whether to accept a verdict issued by a judge?

10.62. How does the answer to the previous question bear on the claim made by some modern moral philosophers, that it is not clear that one should obey a divine command, even if we knew there were such things?

We now come to the epoch in modern English moral philosophy marked by Sidgwick. There is a startling change that seems to have taken place between Mill and Moore. Mill assumes, as we saw, that there is no question of calculating the particular consequences of an action such as murder or theft; and we saw too that his position was stupid, because it is not at all clear how an action can fall under just one principle of utility. In Moore and in subsequent academic moralists of England we find it taken to be pretty obvious that "the right action" is the action which produces the best possible consequences. . . . Now it follows from this that a man does well, subjectively speaking, if he acts for the best in the particular circumstances according to his judgement of the total consequences of this particular action. . . . [E]very one of the best known English academic moral philosophers has put out a philosophy according to

---

*As it is absurdly called. Since major premise = premise containing the term which is predicate in the conclusion, it is a solecism to speak of it in the connection with practical reasoning.

which, e.g., it is not possible to hold that it cannot be right to kill the innocent as a means to any end whatsoever and that someone who thinks otherwise is in error. (I have to mention both points; because Mr. Hare, for example, while teaching a philosophy which would encourage a person to judge that killing the innocent would be what he "ought" to choose for over-riding purposes, would also teach, I think, that if a man chooses to make avoiding killing the innocent for any purpose his "supreme practical principle," he cannot be impugned for error: that just is his "Principle." But with that qualification, I think it can be seen that the point I have mentioned holds good of every single English academic moral philosopher since Sidgwick.) Now this is a significant thing: for it means that all these philosophies are quite incompatible with the Hebrew-Christian ethic. For it has been characteristic of that ethic to teach that there are certain things forbidden whatever *consequences* threaten, such as: choosing to kill the innocent for any purpose, however good; vicarious punishment; treachery (by which I mean obtaining a man's confidence in a grave matter by promises of trustworthy friendship and then betraying him to his enemies); idolatry; sodomy; adultery; making a false profession of faith. The prohibition of certain things simply in virtue of their description as such-and-such identifiable kinds of action, regardless of any further consequences, is certainly not the whole of the Hebrew-Christian ethic; but it is a noteworthy feature of it; and if every academic philosopher since Sidgwick has written in such a way as to exclude this ethic, it would argue a certain provinciality of mind not to see this incompatibility as the most important fact about these philosophers, and the differences between them as somewhat trifling by comparison.

It is noticeable that none of these philosophers displays any consciousness that there is such an ethic, which he is contradicting: it is pretty well taken for obvious among them all that a prohibition such as that on murder does not operate in face of some consequences. But of course the strictness of the prohibition has as its point *that you are not to be tempted by fear or hope of consequences*.

If you notice the transition from Mill to Moore, you will suspect that it was made somewhere by someone; Sidgwick will come to mind as a likely name; and you will in fact find it going on, almost casually, in him. . . .

Consequentialism and Intention. Consequentialism is sometimes defined as the view that the goodness of actions is a function of their foreseeable consequences—good (foreseeable) consequences, good actions (and I ought to do them); bad consequences, bad actions (and I ought to avoid them). But what about the case of foreseeable consequences that are not intended? How, if at all, should those consequences be included when calculating the best course of action?

From the point of view of the present enquiry, the most important thing about Sidgwick was his definition of intention. He defines intention in such a way that one must be said to intend any foreseen consequences of one's voluntary action. This definition is obviously incorrect, and I dare say that no one would be found to defend it now. He uses it to put forward an ethical thesis which would now be accepted by many people: the thesis that it does not make any difference to a man's responsibility for something that he foresaw, that he felt no desire for it, either as an end or as a means to an end. Using the language of intention more correctly, and avoiding Sidgwick's faulty conception, we may state the thesis thus: it does not make any difference to a man's responsibility for an effect of his action which he can foresee, that he does not intend it. Now this sounds rather edifying; it is I think quite characteristic of very bad degenerations of thought on such questions that they sound edifying. We can see what it amounts to by considering an example. Let us suppose that a man has a responsibility for the maintenance of some child. Therefore deliberately to withdraw support from it is a bad sort of thing for him to do. It would be bad for him to withdraw its maintenance because he didn't want to maintain it any longer; and also bad for him to withdraw it because by doing so he would, let us say, compel someone else to do something. (We may suppose for the sake of argument that compelling that person to do that thing is in itself quite admirable.) But now he has to choose between doing something disgraceful and going to prison; if he goes to prison, it will follow that he withdraws support from the child. By Sidgwick's doctrine, there is no difference in his responsibility for ceasing to maintain the child, between the case where he does it for its own sake or as a means to some other purpose, and when it happens as a foreseen and unavoidable consequence of his going to prison rather than do something disgraceful. It follows that he must weigh up the relative badness of withdrawing support from the child and of doing the disgraceful thing; and it may easily be that the disgraceful thing is in fact a less vicious action than intentionally withdrawing support from the child would be; if then the fact that withdrawing support from the child is a side effect of his going to prison does not make any difference to his responsibility, this consideration will incline him to do the disgraceful thing; which can still be pretty bad. And of course, once he has started to look at the matter in this light, the only reasonable thing for him to consider will be the consequences and not the intrinsic badness of this or that action. So that, given that he judges reasonably that no *great* harm will come of it, he can do a much more disgraceful thing than deliberately withdrawing support from the child. And if his calculations turn out in fact wrong, it will appear that he was not responsible for the consequences, because he did not foresee them. For in fact Sidgwick's thesis leads to its being quite impossible to estimate the badness of an action except in the light of *expected* consequences. But if so, then you must estimate the badness in the light of the consequences you expect; and so it will follow that you can exculpate yourself from the *actual* consequences of the most disgraceful actions, so long as you can make out a case for not having foreseen them. Whereas I should contend that a man is responsible for the bad consequences of his bad actions, but gets no credit for the good ones; and contrariwise is not responsible for the bad consequences of good actions.

We often act in ways that we know will produce bad consequences, even though we do not intend those consequences. For instance, a surgeon knows that a certain procedure will produce a lot of pain in his patient, but his intention is not to produce pain but to, say, remove a tumor.

  ASK YOURSELF

10.63. Is the surgeon *responsible* for producing the pain? *Blamable*? Why or why not?

The denial of any distinction between foreseen and intended consequences, as far as responsibility is concerned, was not made by Sidgwick in developing any one "method of ethics"; he made this important move on behalf of everybody and just on its own account; and I think it plausible to suggest that *this* move on the part of Sidgwick explains the difference between old-fashioned Utilitarianism and the *consequentialism*, as I name it, which marks him and every English academic moral philosopher since him. By it, the kind of consideration which would formerly have been regarded as a temptation, the kind of consideration urged upon men by wives and flattering friends, was given a status by moral philosophers in their theories.

It is a necessary feature of consequentialism that it is a shallow philosophy. For there are always borderline cases in ethics. Now if you are either an Aristotelian, or a believer in divine law, you will deal with a borderline case by considering whether doing such-and-such in such-and-such circumstances is, say, murder, or is an act of injustice. . . . Now the consequentialist has no footing on which to say "This would be permissible, this not"; because by his own hypothesis, it is the consequences that are to decide, and he has no business to pretend that he can lay it down what possible twists a man could give doing this or that; the most he can say is: a man must not *bring about* this or that; he has no right to say he will, in an actual case, bring about such-and-such unless he does so-and-so. Further, the consequentialist, in order to be imagining borderline cases at all, has of course to assume some sort of law or standard according to which this is a borderline case. Where then does he get the standard from? In practice the answer invariably is: from the standards current in his society or his circle. And it has in fact been the mark of all these philosophers that they have been extremely conventional; they have nothing in them by which to revolt against the conventional standards of their sort of people; it is impossible that they should be profound. But the chance that a whole range of conventional standards will be decent is small. Finally, the point of considering hypothetical situations, perhaps very improbable ones, *seems* to be to elicit from yourself or someone else a hypothetical decision to do something of a bad kind. I don't doubt this has the effect of predisposing people—who will never get into the situations for which they have made hypothetical choices—to consent to similar bad actions, or to praise and flatter those who do them, so long as their crowd does so too, when the desperate circumstances imagined don't hold at all.

Here is an actual case that might seem "borderline." During World War II a Nazi code was deciphered. It was learned as a result that certain spies on "furlough" who were about to be sent back to Germany had been identified by the Nazis. It was argued that if they were not sent back, the Nazis would infer that the code had been broken and cease using it. And that would make it impossible to decode the messages the knowledge of which might save thousands of lives. It was feared that if the spies were informed of the situation, they might refuse to go back. So they were sent back without being told that they would surely be apprehended and executed.

ASK YOURSELF

10.64. How would Anscombe probably treat this case?

10.65. How would what she calls a "consequentialist" probably handle this case? Would that way of handling it probably reflect communal norms of the time? Would it show those norms to be corrupt? Explain and defend your answers.

Those who recognize the origins of the notions of "obligation" and of the emphatic, "moral," *ought*, in the divine law conception of ethics, but who reject the notion of a divine legislator, sometimes look about for the possibility of retaining a law conception without a divine legislator. This search, I think, has some interest in it. Perhaps the first thing that suggests itself is the "norms" of a society. But just as one cannot be impressed by Butler when one reflects what conscience can tell people to do, so, I think, one cannot be impressed by this idea if one reflects what the "norms" of a society can be like. That legislation can be "for oneself" I reject as absurd; whatever you do "for yourself" may be admirable; but is not legislating. Once one sees this, one may say: I have to frame my own rules, and these are the best I can frame, and I shall go by them until I know something better: as a man might say "I shall go by the customs of my ancestors." Whether this leads to good or evil will depend on the *content* of the rules or of the customs of one's ancestors. If one is lucky it will lead to good. Such an attitude would be hopeful in this at any rate: it seems to have in it some Socratic doubt where, from having to fall back on such expedients, it should be clear that Socratic doubt is good; in fact rather generally it must be good for anyone to think "Perhaps in some way I can't see, I may be on a bad path, perhaps I am hopelessly wrong in some essential way." The search for "norms" might lead someone to look for laws of nature, as if the universe were a legislator; but in the present day this is not likely to lead to good results: it might lead one to eat the weaker according to the laws of nature, but would hardly lead anyone nowadays to notions of justice; the pre-Socratic feeling about justice as comparable to the balance or harmony which kept things going is very remote to us.

Anscombe goes on to consider another possible source of obligation, namely, a contract. If I have made a promise to you, or have entered into a "contract" with society, then, it might be argued, I ought to do certain things just for that reason. Anscombe argues that there is little hope of getting a full-fledged notion of obligation out of such considerations, partly because a contract requires knowing that you entered into it, which is not the case with a "social contract." Such ignorance is destructive of the contract, in a way that ignorance of the law is not destructive of my obligations under it.

Virtues, Justice, and What Is Required Regardless of the Consequences. Anscombe now argues for another central thesis of this essay, namely, that we need to revive the notion of a "virtue" in order to do ethics at all in the modern era. But doing so would require a better grasp of some "psychological" concepts, such as the concept of intention. Although a consideration of consequences sometimes plays a role in a "virtues" conception of ethics such as that found in Aristotle, the nature of the various virtues, for example, justice, is not determined simply by considering what consequences their exercise might involve. For some things are intrinsically unjust, and thus should not be done no matter what the consequences, and knowing that and acting accordingly belong to the virtue of justice.

. . . It might remain to look for "norms" in human virtues: just as man has so many teeth, which is certainly not the average number of teeth men have, but is the number of teeth for the species, so perhaps the species man, regarded not just biologically, but from the point of view of the activity of thought and choice in regard to the various departments of life powers and faculties and use of things needed—"has" such-and-such virtues: and this "man" with the complete set of virtues is the "norm" as "man" with, e.g., a complete set of teeth is a norm. But in *this* sense "norm" has ceased to be roughly equivalent to "law." In *this* sense the notion of a "norm" brings us nearer to an Aristotelian than a law conception of ethics. There is, I think, no harm in that; but if someone looked in this direction to give "norm" a sense, then he ought to recognize what has happened to the notion "norm," which he wanted to mean "law—without bringing God in"—it has ceased to mean "law" at all; and so the notions of "moral obligation," "the moral ought," and "duty" are best put on the Index [a list of forbidden books, or in this case, terms], if he can manage it.

But meanwhile—is it not clear that there are several concepts that need investigating simply as part of the philosophy of psychology and,—as I should recommend—banishing *ethics* totally from our minds? Namely—to begin with: "action," "intention," "pleasure," "wanting." More will probably turn up if we start with these. Eventually it might be possible to advance to considering the concept "virtue"; with which, I suppose, we should be beginning some sort of a study of ethics.

I will end by describing the advantages of using the word "ought" in a non-emphatic fashion, and not in a special "moral" sense; of discarding the term "wrong" in a "moral" sense, and using such terms as "unjust."

It is possible, if one is allowed to proceed just by giving examples, to distinguish between the intrinsically unjust, and what is unjust given the circumstances. To arrange to get a man judicially punished for something which it can be clearly seen he has not done is intrinsically unjust. This might be done, of course, and often has been done, in all sorts of ways; by suborning false witnesses, by a rule of law by which something is "deemed" to be the case which is admittedly not the case as a matter of fact, and by open insolence on the part of the judges and powerful people when they more or less openly say: "A fig for the fact that you did not do it; we mean to sentence you for it all the same." What is unjust given, e.g., normal circumstances is to deprive people of their ostensible property without legal procedure, not to pay debts, not to keep contracts, and a host of other things of the kind. Now, the circumstances can clearly make a great deal of difference in estimating the justice or injustice of such procedures as these; and these circumstances may *sometimes* include expected consequences; for example, a man's claim to a bit of property can become a nullity when its seizure and use can avert some obvious disaster: as, e.g., if you could use a machine of his to produce an explosion in which it would be destroyed, but by means of which you could divert a flood or make a gap which a fire could not jump. Now this certainly does not mean that what would ordinarily be an act of injustice, but is not intrinsically unjust, can always be rendered just by a reasonable calculation of better consequences; far from it; but the problems that would be raised in an attempt to draw a boundary line (or boundary area) here are obviously complicated. And while there are certainly some general remarks which ought to be made here, and some boundaries that can be drawn, the decision on particular cases would for the most part be determined *kata ton orthon logon* "according to what's reasonable."—E.g. that *such-and-such* a delay of payment of a *such-and-such* debt to a person so circumstanced, on the part of a person so circumstanced, would or would not be unjust, is really only to be decided "according to what's reasonable"; and for this there can *in principle* be no canon other than giving a few examples. That is to say, while it is because of a big gap in philosophy that we can give no general account of the concept of virtue and of the concept of justice, but have to proceed, using the concepts, only by giving examples; still there is an area where it is not because of any gap, but is in principle the case, that there is no account except by way of examples: and that is where the canon is "what's reasonable"; which of course is *not* a canon.

That is all I wish to say about what is just in some circumstances, unjust in others; and about the way in which expected consequences can play a part in determining what is just. Returning to my example of the intrinsically unjust: if a procedure *is* one of judicially punishing a man for what he is clearly understood not to have done, there can be absolutely no argument about the description of this as unjust. No circumstances, and no expected consequences, which do not modify the description of the procedure as one of judicially punishing a man for what be is known not to have done can modify the description of it as unjust. Someone who attempted to dispute this would only be pretending not to know what "unjust" means: for this is a paradigm case of injustice.

And here we see the superiority of the term "unjust" over the terms "morally right" and "morally wrong." For in the context of English moral philosophy since Sidgwick it appears legitimate to discuss whether it might be "morally right" in some circumstances to adopt that procedure; but it cannot be argued that the procedure would in any circumstances be just.

Now I am not able to do the philosophy involved—and I think that no one in the present situation of English philosophy can do the philosophy involved—but it is clear that a good man is a just man; and a just man is a man who habitually refuses to commit or participate in any unjust actions for fear of any consequences, or to obtain any advantage, for himself or anyone else. Perhaps no one will disagree. But, it will be said, what is unjust is sometimes determined by expected consequences; and certainly that is true. But there are cases where it is not: now if someone says, "I agree, but all this wants a lot of explaining," then he is right, and, what is more, the situation at present is that we can't do the explaining; we lack the philosophic equipment. But if someone really thinks, in *advance*, that it is open to question whether such an action as procuring the judicial execution of the innocent should be quite excluded from consideration—I do not want to argue with him; he shows a corrupt mind.

In such cases our moral philosophers seek to impose a dilemma upon us. "If we have a case where the term 'unjust' applies purely in virtue of a factual description, can't one raise the question whether one sometimes conceivably ought to do injustice? If 'what is unjust' is determined by consideration of whether it is *right* to do so-and-so in such-and-such circumstances, then the question whether it is 'right' to commit injustice can't arise, just because 'wrong' has been built into the definition of injustice. But if we have a case where the description 'unjust' applies purely in virtue of the facts, without bringing 'wrong' in, then the question can arise whether one 'ought' perhaps to commit an injustice, whether it might not be 'right' to? And of course 'ought' and 'right' are being used in their *moral* senses here. Now either you must decide what is 'morally right' in the light of certain *other* 'principles,' or you make a 'principle' about *this* and decide that an injustice is never 'right'; but even if you do the latter you are going beyond the facts; you are making a decision that you will not, or that it is wrong to, commit injustice. But in either case, if the term 'unjust' is determined simply by the facts, it is not the term 'unjust' that determines that the term 'wrong' applies, but a decision that injustice is *wrong*, together with the diagnosis of the 'factual' description as entailing injustice. But the man who makes an absolute decision that injustice is 'wrong' has no footing on which to criticize someone who does not make that decision as judging falsely."

We have returned to what we might call "Hume's dilemma." Although it seems odd to say that it might sometimes be right to do what is unjust, if we suppose that certain facts, say the fact that Mr. X is innocent, is known to be so, and so forth, show that executing him would be "unjust," then according to "modern moral philosophers" we can always wonder whether we "ought" perhaps to do what is unjust. Thus even where we agree that some act's being unjust is indeed a matter of "fact," it will no longer have definite implications for what we "ought" to do. "Is" will still not imply "ought."

 ASK YOURSELF

10.66. Describe a case where someone might claim that we "ought" to execute an innocent person (for help in thinking about this, consider the "spy" example given earlier).

In a footnote Anscombe herself mentions as an example a case where executing an innocent person would be the only way of avoiding a nuclear war. She remarks that "the most important thing about the way in which cases like this are invented in discussions, is the assumption that only two courses are open: here, compliance and open defiance. No one can say in advance of such a situation what the possibilities are going to be e.g. that there is none of stalling by a feigned willingness to comply, accompanied by a skillfully arranged 'escape' of the victim." Thus she appears to be claiming that such examples are faulty, that is, do not convincingly establish the conclusion that it would be sometimes right to do what is unjust.

 ASK YOURSELF

10.67. If they were not faulty in some such ways as she suggests, would that show that she has not made a case against sometimes executing the innocent? Explain.

In this argument "wrong" of course is explained as meaning "morally wrong," and all the atmosphere of the term is retained while its substance is guaranteed quite null. Now let us remember that "morally wrong" is the term which is the heir of the notion "illicit," or "what there is an obligation not to do"; which belongs in a divine law theory or ethics. Here it really does add something to the description "unjust" to say there is an obligation not to do it; for what obliges is the divine law as rules oblige in a game. So if the divine law obliges not to commit injustice by forbidding injustice, it really does add something to the description "unjust" to say there is an obligation not to do it, And it is because "morally wrong" is the heir of this concept, but an heir that is cut off from the family of concepts from which it sprang, that "morally wrong" both goes beyond the mere factual description "unjust" and seems to have no discernible content except a certain compelling force, which I should call purely psychological. And such is the force of the term that philosophers actually suppose that the divine law notion can be dismissed as making no essential difference even if it is *held*—*because* they think that a "practical principle" running "I *ought* (i.e. am morally obliged) to obey divine laws" is required for the man who believes in divine laws. But actually this notion of obligation is a notion which only operates in the context of law. And I should be inclined to congratulate the present-day moral philosophers on depriving "morally ought" of its now delusive appearance of content, if only they did not manifest a detestable desire to retain the atmosphere of the term.

It may be possible, if we are resolute, to discard the notion "morally ought," and simply return to the ordinary "ought" which, we ought to notice, is such an extremely frequent term of human language that it is difficult to imagine getting on without it. Now if we do return to it, can't it reasonably be asked whether one might ever need to commit injustice, or whether it won't be the best thing to do? Of course it can. And the answers will be various. One man—a philosopher—may say that since justice is a virtue, and injustice a vice, and virtues and vices are built up by the performances of the action in which they are instanced, an act of injustice will tend to make a man bad; and essentially the flourishing of a man qua man consists in his being good (e.g. in virtues); but for any X to which such terms apply, X needs what makes it flourish, so a man needs, or ought to perform, only virtuous actions; and even if, as it must be admitted may happen, he flourishes less, or not at all, in inessentials, by avoiding injustice, his life is spoiled in essentials by not avoiding injustice—so he still needs to perform only just actions. That is roughly how Plato and Aristotle talk; but it can be seen that philosophically there is a huge gap, at present unfillable as far as we are concerned, which needs to be filled by an account of human nature, human action, the type of characteristic a virtue is, and above all of human "flourishing." And it is the last concept that appears the most doubtful. For it is a bit much to swallow that a man in pain and hunger and poor and friendless is "flourishing" as Aristotle himself admitted. Further, someone might say that one at least needed to stay alive to "flourish." Another man unimpressed by all that will say in a hard case "What we need is such-and-such, which we won't get without doing this (which is unjust)—so this is what we ought to do." Another man, who does not follow the rather elaborate reasoning of the philosophers, simply says "I know it is in any case a disgraceful thing to say that one had better commit this unjust action." The man who believes in divine laws will say perhaps "It is forbidden, and however it looks, it cannot be to anyone's profit to commit injustice"; he like the Greek philosophers can think in terms of "flour-

ishing." If he is a Stoic, he is apt to have a decidedly strained notion of what "flourishing" consists in; if he is a Jew or Christian, he need not have any very distinct notion: the way it will profit him to abstain from injustice is something that he leaves it
to God to determine, himself only saying "It can't do me any good to go against his
law." (But he also hopes for a great reward in a new life later on, e.g. at the coming
of Messiah; but in this he is relying on special promises.)

   ## ASK YOURSELF

10.68. If the person who believes in divine law does so because he thinks that
only in that way he will truly flourish, is there not something self-serving or
even servile in such "obedience"?

10.69. Might it be possible to hold that what one understands by "flourishing" is
determined by one's prior commitment to divine commands, so that no matter
what happens to me I will be, by definition as it were, "flourishing" as long as I
follow those commands? Say whether your answer would be compatible with
Anscombe's approach here.

It is left to modern moral philosophy—the moral philosophy of all the well-known
English ethicists since Sidgwick—to construct systems according to which the man
who says "We need such-and-such, and will only get it this way" may be a virtuous
character: that is to say, it is left open to debate whether such a procedure as the judicial punishment of the innocent may not in some circumstances be the "right" one
to adopt; and though the present Oxford moral philosophers would accord a man *per-
mission* to "make it his principle" not to do such a thing, they teach a philosophy according to which the particular consequences of such an action could "morally" be
taken into account by a man who was debating what to do; and if they were such as
to conflict with his "ends," it might be a step in his moral education to frame a moral
principle under which he "managed" (to use Mr. Nowell-Smith's phrase) to bring the
action; or it might be a new "decision of principle," making which was an advance in
the formation of his moral thinking (to adopt Mr. Hare's conception), to decide: in
such-and-such circumstances one ought to procure the judicial condemnation of the
innocent. And that is my complaint.

SUGGESTIONS FOR FURTHER READING

Primary Sources

Anscombe

Anscombe, G. E. M. *Three Philosophers* (Ithaca, NY: Cornell University Press, 1961). Au-
    thored together with her husband, Peter Geach, the first essay, an interpretation
    of Aristotle's doctrine of substance, is by Anscombe.

———. *Intention*, (Oxford: Blackwell; 2nd ed., 1963.) Described by one prominent
    American philosopher as "the best essay on human action since Aristotle."

———. *Collected Philosophical Papers*, (Minneapolis, MN: University of Minnesota Press,

1981) 3 vols. The definitive edition of Anscombe' works. Important papers on action, ethics, mind.

———. "Action, Intention and Double Effect." *Proceedings of the American Catholic Philosophical Association* 56: 12–25.

———. "Murder and the Morality of Euthanasia," reprinted in L. Gormally, ed. *Euthanasia, Clinical Practice and the Law* (Indianapolis, IN: Hackett, 1994), 37–50. Accessible attempt at a definition of murder as a moral category.

———. "Von Wright on Practical Reason," reprinted in R. Hursthouse, G. Lawrence, and W. Quinn, eds., *Virtues and Reasons* (Oxford: Oxford University Press, 1995), 1–34. A revision of Anscombe's earlier accounts of intention and practical reason.

Quine

Quine, W. V. A. "Truth by Convention," in O. H. Lee, ed, *Philosophical Essays for A. N. Whitehead* (New York: Longmans, 1936) Critique of attempts to justify logical truths in a nonempirical way.

———. *Mathematical Logic* (Cambridge, MA: Harvard University Press, 1940) A systematic logic text with alternative account of the foundation of mathematics.

———. *From a Logical Point of View* (Cambridge, MA: Harvard University Press, 1953; revised, 1961). An early collection of essays, including "New Foundations for Mathematical Logic," "On What There Is" and "Two Dogmas of Empiricism," (the essay excerpted in this anthology). The 1961 edition incorporates many important revisions.

———. *Word and Object* (New York: Wiley & Sons, 1960) A major work on meaning, translation, reference, and modality.

———. *The Ways of Paradox and Other Essays* (New York: Random House, 1966) Includes such important essays as "Truth by Convention" and "Three Grades of Modal Involvement."

———. *Ontological Relativity and Other Essays* (New York: Columbia University Press, 1969). Includes an essay titled "Epistemology Naturalized."

———. *From Stimulus to Science* (Cambridge, MA: Harvard University Press, 1995) Brief history of philosophy, followed by an exploration of typical Quinean topics.

Quine, W. V. A. and Ullian, J. S. *The Web of Belief* (New York: Random House, 1970). A fairly accessible introduction to the scientific method from a Quinian perspective.

Russell

Russell, B. A. W. *The Collected Papers of Bertrand Russell*, London: Routledge, in press). The McMaster University edition, various editors, 30 vols. Russell's shorter writings and unpublished works, many of crucial importance. His philosophical papers are to be found in volumes 1–11.

———. *A Critical Exposition of the Philosophy of Leibniz* (London: Routledge, 1992). Originally published in 1900, long an influential work on Leibniz, it also foreshadows aspects of Russell's own realist philosophy.

———. *Human Knowledge: Its Scope and Limits* (London: Routledge, 1992). Russell's last major statement, from 1948, on epistemology.

———. *An Introduction to Mathematical Philosophy* (London: Routledge, 1993). Relativity accessible introduction to the logic of *Principia*.

———. "On Denoting," *Mind* 14: 479–493, 1905; reprinted in Russell in collected papers (1983–), vol. 4: 415–727. First published statement of Russell's theory of definite descriptions, widely discussed.

———. *Our Knowledge of the External World* (London: Routledge, 1993). A work from 1913 which attempts to "construct" the phenomenal world out of sense-data.

———. *The Problems of Philosophy* (Oxford: Oxford University Press, 1974). Popular introduction to philosophy, especially epistemology.

Whitehead, A. N., and Russell, B. A. W. *Principia Mathematica*, 2nd ed. (Cambridge: Cambridge University Press, 1925–1927). Three volumes; The definitive and highly technical statement of Russell's attempt to reduce mathematics to logic.

Sartre

Sartre, J. P. *Being and Nothingness*, trans. H. Barnes (Philosophical Library, 1956). Sartre's major philosophical opus.

———. *Nausea, or The Diary of Antoine Roquentin*, trans. R. Baldick (Middlesex: Penguin, 1965). Novel in diary form describing Roquentin's realization of the contingency of existence.

———. *No Exit and Three Other Plays* (New York: Vintage Books, 1949). Contains best-known examples of Sartre's writings for theater.

———. *Sketch for a Theory of the Emotions*, trans. P. Mairet (London: Methuen, 1962). Examination of the psychology of the emotions.

Wittgenstein

Wittgenstein, L. *The Blue and Brown Books* (Oxford: Blackwell, 1958). Good preparation for studying the *Investigations*.

———. *Culture and Value*, ed. G. H. von Wright and H. Nyman; trans. P. Winch (Oxford: Blackwell, 1980). Intriguing collection of remarks on music, religion, literature, and so forth.

———. *On Certainty*, ed. G. E. M. Anscombe and G. H. von Wright; trans. D. Paul and G. E. M. Anscombe (Oxford: Blackwell, 1969). Material on knowledge and certainty from the last year and a half of Wittgenstein's life.

———. *Philosophical Grammar*, ed. R. Rhees; trans. A. Kenny (Oxford: Blackwell, 1974). Deals with logic and mathematics, as well as language and meaning.

———. *Philosophical Investigations*, ed. G. E. M. Anscombe and R. Rhees; trans. G. E. M. Anscombe (Oxford: Blackwell, 1953). The most discussed of Wittgenstein's works, presenting those versions of his thought with which he was most satisfied.

———. *Philosophical Occasions*, ed. J. C. Klagge and A. Nordmann (Indianapolis: Hackett, 1980). Includes the "Lecture on Ethics" (1929) and the striking "Remarks on Frazer's Golden Bough" (1931).

———. *Philosophical Remarks*, ed. R. Rhees; trans. R. Hargreaves and R. White (Oxford: Blackwell, 1975). Shows some of the considerations that took Wittgenstein from his earlier to his later outlook.

———. *Remarks on the Foundations of Mathematics*, ed. G. H. von Wright, R. Rhees, and G. E. M. Anscombe; trans. G. E. M. Anscombe, 3rd ed. (Oxford: Blackwell, 1978).

Selections from Wittgenstein's notebooks. A wider range of topics than the title suggests.

————. *Tractatus Logico-Philosophicus*, trans. D. F. Pears and B. F. McGuiness (London: Routledge, 1961). The major early work of Wittgenstein and his only book published during his lifetime.

————. *Zettel*, ed. G. E. M. Anscombe and G. H. von Wright; trans. G. E. M. Anscombe (Oxford: Blackwell, 1967). Wittgenstein's own selection of remarks from 1945–1948.

Critical Discussions

Anscombe

Bennett, J. "Whatever the Consequences." *Analysis* 26: 83–102 (1966). An attack on the 'absolutism' of Anscombe's moral philosophy.

Davidson, D. *Essays on Actions and Events* (Oxford: Oxford University Press, 1980) The first six essays present an important critique of Anscombe's philosophy of action.

Diamond, C., and Teichmann, J. *Intention and Intentionality*, (Ithaca, NY: Cornell University Press, 1979). A volume dedicated to Anscombe and containing many important discussions of her work.

Foot, P. "Abortion and the Doctrine of Double Effect" reprinted in P. Foot, *Virtues and Vices* (Berkeley, CA: University of California Press, 1978). A critique, friendlier than that of Bennett (1966), of Anscombe's 'absolutism.'

Quine

Barrett, R. B., and Gibson, R., eds. *Perspectives on Quine* (Oxford: Blackwell, 1990). Papers from a conference for Quine's eightieth birthday with his replies.

Davidson, D., and Hintikka, J., eds. *Words and Objections* (Dordrecht: Reidel, 1975). Collection of essays on *Word and Object* followed by Quine's comments.

Gibson, R. *The Philosophy of W. V. Quine* (Gainesville, FL: University Presses of Florida, 1982). Good secondary source on Quine.

Hahn, L. E., and Schilpp, P. A., eds. *The Philosophy of W. V. Quine* (La Salle, IL: Open Court, 1986) Includes an intellectual autobiography by Quine, essays on his work and his replies. Good bibliography of Quine's works.

Orenstein, A. *Williard Van Orman Quine* (Boston: G. K. Hall, 1977). An introduction to Quine's thought and its place in twentieth-century philosophy.

Russell

Clark, R. W. *The Life of Bertrand Russell* (London: Cape and Weidenfeld & Nicolson, 1975). The standard biography.

Grayling, A. C. *Russell*, Past Masters series (Oxford: Oxford University Press, 1996). Popular introduction to Russell's thought, including his politics.

Savage, C. W., and Andeson, C. A., eds. *Rereading Russell: Essays in Bertrand Russell's Metaphysics and Epistemology* (Minneapolis, MN: University of Minnesota Press, 1989). Papers on Russell's early logic and later epistemology.

Watling, J. *Bertrand Russell* (Edinburgh: Olivier & Boyd, 1970) Clear introduction to Russell's less technical work to 1914.

Sartre

Caws, P. *Sartre* (London: Routledge & Kegan Paul, 1979). Accessible and comprehensive exposition.

Cohen-Solal, A. *Sartre: A Life* (New York: Pantheon; London: Heinemann, 1987). Excellent biography of Sartre.

Danto, A. *Sartre*, Modern Masters (London: Fontana, 1975) Short account by well-known American philosopher.

Howells, C. Sartre: *The Necessity of Freedom* (Cambridge: Cambridge University Press, 1988). A study of both literature and philosophy.

Howells, C., ed. *The Cambridge Companion to Sartre* (Cambridge: Cambridge University Press, 1992). Essays by American and European specialists on Sartre.

Wilcocks, R., ed. *Critical Essays on Jean-Paul Sartre* (Boston: G. K. Hall, 1988). Excellent collection of relatively recent essays.

Wittgenstein

Baker, G. P., and Hacker, P. M. S. *An Analytical Commentary on the Philosophical Investigations* (Oxford: Blackwell, 1980, 1988, 1990) (The third volume is by P. M. S. Hacker alone.) A very detailed commentary on a complex work.

Canfield, J. V., ed. *The Philosophy of Wittgenstein* (New York and London: Garland Publishing Company, 1986–88) 15 volumes. Articles on all aspects of Wittgenstein's thought.

Cavell, S. *The Claim of Reason* (Oxford: Oxford University Press, 1979). Attempts to show how seriously Wittgenstein took skepticism, and the significance of his way of facing it. Interesting discussions of relevant literature (Shakespeare, etc.).

Hacker, P. M. S. *Insight and Illusion*, 2nd ed. (Oxford: Oxford University Press, 1986). Particularly good on Wittgenstein's treatment of the self.

Johnston, P. *Wittgenstein: Rethinking the Inner* (London: Routledge 1993). Discusses Wittgenstein's later views on mind.

Kenny, A. *Wittgenstein* (London: Allen Lane, 1973). Perhaps the best general introduction.

Kripke, S. *Wittgenstein on Rules and Private Language*, (Oxford: Blackwell, 1982). A tightly argued but controversial exploration of the skeptical implications of Wittgenstein's ideas about rule following. Of considerable independent interest.

Malcolm, Norm. *Ludwig Wittgenstein: A Memoir*. (Oxford: Oxford University Press, 1958). Interesting description of Wittgenstein's character by one of his American students.

McGinn, M. *Sense and Certainty: A Dissolution of Scepticism* (Oxford: Blackwell, 1989) Clear discussion of Wittgenstein's views on knowledge and certainty.

a posteriori: known on the basis of, or after ("posterior"), experience.

a priori: known to be true independently of, or "prior" to, experience.

Academy: ancient Greek school founded by Plato, which became skeptical a few generations after Plato's death.

aesthetic life: notion in Kierkegaard's philosophy regarding a life lived for enjoyment.

aesthetics: study of the principles of art; the concepts of beauty, style, and genre; the principles of evaluation of artworks; and the ontological status of artworks.

Anaxagoras (500–428 BCE): ancient Greek philosopher who held that the world is comprised of infinitely divisible elements or seeds that are organized by mind (*nous*).

Anaximander (ca. 610–546 BCE): ancient Greek philosopher from Meletus who held that the boundless is the source of everything.

Anaximenes (*fl.* sixth century BCE): ancient Greek philosopher from Meletus who held that the condensed and rarefied air is the source of everything.

Anselm (1033–1109): medieval Christian philosopher who developed what is now called the ontological argument for God's existence.

antilogic: technique advocated by sophists that involves learning to argue both sides of a case as strongly as possible.

Aquinas, Thomas (1225–1274): medieval philosopher who proposed five proofs for God's existence and developed the definitive medieval account of natural law theory.

Aristotle (384–322 BCE): ancient Greek philosopher who emphasized the notion of a thing's purpose (*telos*) and argued that morality involves the development of virtues.

Atomism: ancient Greek view championed by Leucippus and Democritus that the world is composed of indivisible particles.

Augustine (354–430): medieval Christian philosopher, influenced by neo-Platonism, who offered the free will defense in response to the problem of evil.

Bacon, Francis (1561–1626): British philosopher who argued in favor of inductive reasoning in science, as opposed to deductive reasoning.

Bayle, Pierre (1647–1706): French historian and Pyrrhonian philosopher who argued that skepticism can assist religious faith.

Berkeley, George (1685–1753): Irish philosopher of the empiricist tradition who argued for the Idealist position that there is no material world and that all reality exists in the minds of spirits.

Butler, Joseph (1692–1752): British philosopher who opposed Hobbes's theory of selfishness and argued instead that human actions are sometimes motivated by benevolent concerns.

Calvin, John (1509–1564): French Protestant reformer who emphasized human depravity and predestination.

Cartesians: followers of Descartes's philosophical and scientific theories.

categorical imperative: a central principle in Kant's moral theory, namely, "Act only on that maxim by which you can at the same time will that it should become a universal law."

Cicero (106–43 BCE): eclectic Roman philosopher.

cogito ergo sum: "I think, therefore I am"; a central philosophical claim associated with Descartes's philosophy.

Copernicus, Nicholas (1473–1543): Renaissance astronomer from Poland who proposed the Sun-centered theory of the heavens.

Cynicism: ancient Greek school founded by Diogenes of Sinope, which emphasized denying established conventions.

Deism: eighteenth-century theory that God created a self-sustaining world and does not intervene in its operation.

Democritus (fifth century. BCE): ancient Greek philosopher who held that the world is composed of indivisible particles.

Descartes, René (1596–1650): Rationalist philosopher who developed a method of scientific investigation and argued that all knowledge is derived from the truth of one's existence.

determinism: the theory that everything that happens, including human actions, is determined by prior conditions; determinism is incompatible with free will.

dialectic: a process of argument in which contradictory or opposing views are pitted against one another.

Diogenes of Sinope (fourth century BCE): founder of the ancient Greek school of Cynicism, which emphasized denying established conventions.

dualism: the metaphysical position, opposed to monism, that there are two main types of ultimate reality, namely, matter and spirit.

Eclecticism: philosophical tradition in ancient Greece and Rome that blended the views of the major philosophical schools.

Empedocles (ca. 495–435 BCE): ancient Greek philosopher who emphasized that the two forces of love and strife organize the four elements or roots of the world—namely, earth, air, fire, and water.

Empiricism: the view that knowledge is gained primarily or entirely through the five senses.

Empiricism, British: seventeenth- and eighteenth-century philosophical movement associated with Locke, Berkeley, and Hume that denies innate ideas and emphasizes knowledge through experience and inductive reasoning.

Enlightenment: eighteenth-century intellectual movement that emphasized that true knowledge is attained through reason, independent of tradition and religion.

Epictetus (ca. 50–120 CE): ancient Greek Stoic philosopher who emphasized resigning oneself to fate.

Epicureanism: ancient Greek school founded by Epicurus, which emphasizes achieving happiness by minimizing pain and pursuing pleasure.

Epicurus (341–270 BCE): ancient Greek philosopher and founder of the Epicurean school, which emphasized achieving happiness by minimizing pain and pursuing pleasure.

epistemology: the part of philosophical inquiry that focuses on the nature and sources of knowledge.

Erasmus, Desiderius (1466–1563): Renaissance Humanist who satirized medieval intellectual traditions.

Existentialism: twentieth-century philosophical movement with roots in Kierkegaard and Nietzsche that stressed the freedom for self-creation and the anxiety that characterize human existence.

fideism: the view that religious knowledge is obtained through faith alone, not through reason.

forms, theory of: Plato's theory that the most real and knowable objects exist in a realm "apart" from the physical world that contains archetypes of ordinary objects.

formula of the end itself: a version of the categorical imperative in Kant's theory maintaining that we should treat persons as an ends in themselves, and never as means to an end.

formula of the law of nature: a version of the categorical imperative in Kant's theory, namely, "Act as if the maxim of your action were to become through your will a universal law of nature."

Galileo Galilei (1564–1642): Renaissance Italian scientist who developed the telescope for astronomical use.

Gorgias (late fifth century BCE): ancient Greek sophist.

hedonism: a moral theory associated with Epicurus and utilitarians based on the idea that humans are pleasure seeking and pleasure is the criterion of moral goodness.

Hegel, Georg Wilhelm Friedrich (1770–1831): German Idealist philosopher who argued that the universe is the dialectical development of God or "absolute Spirit."

Heraclitus (ca. 540–480 BCE): ancient Greek philosopher from Ionia who emphasized that an ever-changing world is sustained and given a kind of permanence through the *logos*.

Hesiod (*fl.* ca. 700 BCE): ancient Greek poet and author of the *Theogony* and *Works and Days*; a precursor to the first Greek philosophers.

Hobbes, Thomas (1588–1679): British philosopher who argued the egoistic position that human actions are largely motivated by self-interest.

Homer (*fl.* ca. 750 BCE): ancient Greek poet and author of the *Iliad* and the *Odyssey*; a precursor to the first Greek philosophers.

Humanism: philosophical movement of the Renaissance emphasizing human worth and secular studies; key figures were Pico della Mirandola, Thomas More, and Erasmus.

Hume, David (1711–1776): Scottish skeptical philosopher and British Empiricist who argued that causal connections are grounded in mental habits.

hypothetical imperatives: in Kant's theory, hypothetical imperatives are obligations that are of the form "If you want *some thing*, then you must do *some act*"; this is in contrast with the categorical imperative.

Idealism: the metaphysical theory (opposed to materialism) that reality exists in the minds of spirits or is mindlike.

Idealism, German: eighteenth- and nineteenth-century philosophical movement in Germany associated with Kant and Hegel that postulates the creative powers of mind or spirit as the source of the form and (in Hegel) even the matter of all that is real.

idols, the four: Bacon's term for the four sources of bias in science, namely, from human nature, individual constitution, words, and accepted philosophers.

immediacy: experiences that are unmediated by thought or reasoning.

Ionian philosophers: ancient Greek philosophers from Ionia, the coastal area of Asia Minor, which include Thales, Anaximander, Anaximines, Xenophanes, Pythagoras, and Heraclitus.

James, William (1842–1910): American philosopher of the school of pragmatism who emphasized belief in God on pragmatic grounds.

Kant, Immanuel (1724–1804): German philosopher who argued that human knowledge is grounded in mental categories and that morality consists in following the categorical imperative.

Kepler, Johannes (1571–1603): Renaissance German astronomer who argued that planets travel in elliptical orbits around the Sun.

Kierkegaard, Søren (1813–1855): Danish philosopher who poetically portrayed various ways of living (aesthetic, ethical, religious) in order to stimulate genuine decisions about life.

Leibniz, Gottfried Wilhelm (1646–1716): German philosopher of the rationalist tradition who developed the theory of monads and argued that this is the best possible world that God could create.

Leucippus (fifth century BCE): ancient Greek philosopher who held that the world is composed of indivisible particles.

Locke, John (1632–1704): British philosopher of the Empiricist tradition who denied innate ideas and argued that knowledge come from experience.

Luther, Martin (1483–1546): German Protestant reformer who criticized the use of Aristotle in theology.

Malebranche, Nicolas de (1638–1715): French Rationalist philosopher who developed the theory of occasionalism and argued that we see all things through God.

materialism: the monistic metaphysical theory, opposed to idealism, that all reality is physical in nature.

mean, doctrine of the: Aristotle's view that virtues lie at a mean between two more extreme vices; for example, courage is a mean between cowardice and rashness.

metaphysics: the part of philosophical inquiry that attempts to answer such questions as "What is real?" and "What are the ultimate, irreducible constituents of reality?"

Miletus: a Greek city-state on the coast of Asia Minor and home to the ancient Greek philosophers Thales, Anaximander, and Anaximines.

Mill, John Stuart (1806–1873): British philosopher in the Empiricist tradition who advocated utilitarianism and emphasized the difference between higher and lower pleasures.

monads: in Leibniz, monads are the true atoms of which all physical things are composed.

monism: the metaphysical position that there is only one reality or one kind of underlying reality.

Montaigne, Michel Eyquem de (1533–1592): French philosopher influenced by the Pyrrhonian skeptical tradition.

More, Thomas (1478–1535): Renaissance Humanist who emphasized Epicureanism.

Mothe le Vayer, François de la (1588–1669): French Pyrrhonian philosopher who argued that skepticism can assist religious faith.

Natural Law Theory: the theory that God endorses specific moral standards and fixes them in human nature, which we discover through rational intuition.

neo-Platonism: ancient Greek school of mystical philosophy indebted to Plato; founded by Plotinus, who taught that the universe consists of levels of reality emanating from the One.

Newton, Isaac (1642–1727): British scientist who developed calculus and the theory of gravitation.

Nietzsche, Friedrich (1844–1900): German philosopher who argued that we should replace traditional values with new values of the new ideal Superhuman (*Übermensch*).

nomos **("law" or "custom"):** notion in ancient Greek thought that conceptions such as justice are simply human conventions rather a matter of nature (*physis*).

Ockham, William of (1285–1349): English medieval philosopher who advocated nominalism in opposition to realist theories of universals.

occasionalism: the view that God is the principal force behind all causal events.

pantheism: the view that God is identical to nature as a whole; this theory is commonly associated with Xenophanes, Parmenides, Plotinus, Spinoza, and Hegel.

Parmenides (*fl.* ca. 450 BCE): ancient Greek philosopher from Elea who argued that all reality is the *One*—a single, undifferentiated, and unchanging thing.

Pascal, Blaise (1623–1662): French religious philosopher of the fideist tradition who proposed that we wager in favor of belief in God when reason is neutral.

peripatetics: followers of the Aristotelian tradition of philosophy.

physis **("nature"):** notion in ancient Greek thought that conceptions such as justice are matters of nature rather than simply human conventions.

Pico della Mirandola (1463–1494): renaissance Humanist who emphasized human uniqueness.

Plato (428–348 BCE): ancient Greek philosopher who argued for the theory of the forms, the immortality of the soul, and the grounding of justice in eternal invariant norms.

Plotinus (204–270 CE): taught that the universe consists of levels of reality emanating from the One.

pluralism: metaphysical position, opposed to monism, that ultimate reality is constituted by more than one thing or kind of thing.

pluralism, ancient Greek: the view associated with Empedocles and Anaxagoras that more than one thing exists.

practical wisdom: in Aristotle's ethics, the indispensable master virtue that is required for the right use of any other virtue, such as courage or patience.

Presocratic philosophy: ancient Greek philosophy before Socrates; examples are Thales, Anaximander, Pythagoras, Heraclitus, Parmenides, Zeno of Elea, Empedocles, Anaxagoras, and Democritus.

Protagoras (ca. 490–ca. 420 BCE): ancient Greek sophist who is remembered for the statement, "Man is the measure of all things."

psychological egoism: the theory sometimes attributed to Hobbes that humans are motivated exclusively by selfish inclinations.

Pyrrho (ca. 365–275 BCE): ancient Greek moral philosopher of the skeptical tradition who advocated avoiding dogmatism and suspending judgment.

Pyrrhonism: ancient Greece skeptical school founded by Pyrrho.

Pythagoras (ca. 570–497 BCE): ancient Greek philosopher from Samos who emphasized the mathematical relations that underlie reality.

Quine, Willard Van Orman (1908–2000): American philosopher and logician who insisted that the natural sciences give us the best knowledge we can hope for and that scientific knowledge itself is always subject to revision.

Rationalism: the philosophical view that knowledge is acquired through reason, without the aid of the senses.

Rationalism, Continental: seventeenth-century philosophical movement begun by Descartes that emphasizes innate ideas and the use of deductive reasoning.

Reformation, Protestant: sixteenth-century religious movement sparked by Martin Luther that opposed some Roman Catholic doctrines and led to the breakup of the medieval church in Europe.

Reid, Thomas (1710–1796): Scottish philosopher of the commonsense tradition who criticized philosophers from Descartes through Hume for holding the theory of mental images.

relativism: the view that there is no absolute truth that is independent of particular people at particular times and places.

Renaissance: European intellectual movement from the fourteenth through sixteenth centuries, which emphasized the rebirth of classical Greek culture.

Russell, Bertrand (1872–1970): British philosopher in the linguistic and analytical tradition who sought to develop the precise logical language that underlies our vague verbal utterances.

scientific method: formalized procedures by which we gain scientific knowledge, such as proposed by Bacon and Descartes.

scientific revolution: intellectual movement started in the Renaissance, which emphasized scientific discoveries and theories of scientific method.

Sextus Empiricus (fl. 200 CE): Greek philosopher of the Pyrrhonian skeptical tradition who offered ten modes of skepticism.

skepticism: philosophical position that questions the ability to attain various kinds of knowledge.

Skepticism, ancient Greek: school of thought in ancient Greece founded by Pyrrho.

Socrates (469–399 BCE): ancient Greek moral philosopher and teacher of Plato, famous for his professions of ignorance, his irony, his moral earnestness, and his dialectical method of questioning people.

sophists ancient Greek philosophers and freelance teachers, the most famous of whom were Protagoras, Gorgias, and Hippias.

Spinoza, Benedict (1632–1677): Jewish philosopher of the Rationalist tradition who argued that God (in a nonpersonal sense) is the single substance of the universe.

Stoicism: ancient Greek school founded by Zeno of Citium, which emphasizes resigning oneself to fate.

teleology: an explanation of some event or thing in terms of goals or purposes or aims or functions.

Thales (*fl.* ca. 585 BCE): ancient Greek philosopher from Meletus who held that water is the basic stuff.

universals: general terms that apply to more than one thing, such as "dog" or "black."

utilitarianism: the ethical theory associated with J. S. Mill that morally right actions are those that promote or tend to produce the best overall consequences.

virtue theory: the theory that the foundation of morality is the development of good character traits or virtues.

Wittgenstein, Ludwig (1889–1951): Austrian philosopher who argued that meaning is grounded in language games or social practice, rather than in some kind of mental state.

Xenophanes (ca. 570–478 BCE): ancient Greek philosopher from Ionia who satirized anthropomorphic conceptions of the gods.

Zeno (*fl.* ca. 450 BCE): ancient Greek philosopher from Elea who defended Parmenides' notion of the eternal unchanging *One* by presenting paradoxes designed to show the impossibility of motion or any other change.

Zeno of Citium (334–262 BCE): ancient Greek philosopher and founder of the Stoic school, which emphasized resigning oneself to fate.

CREDITS

INDEX